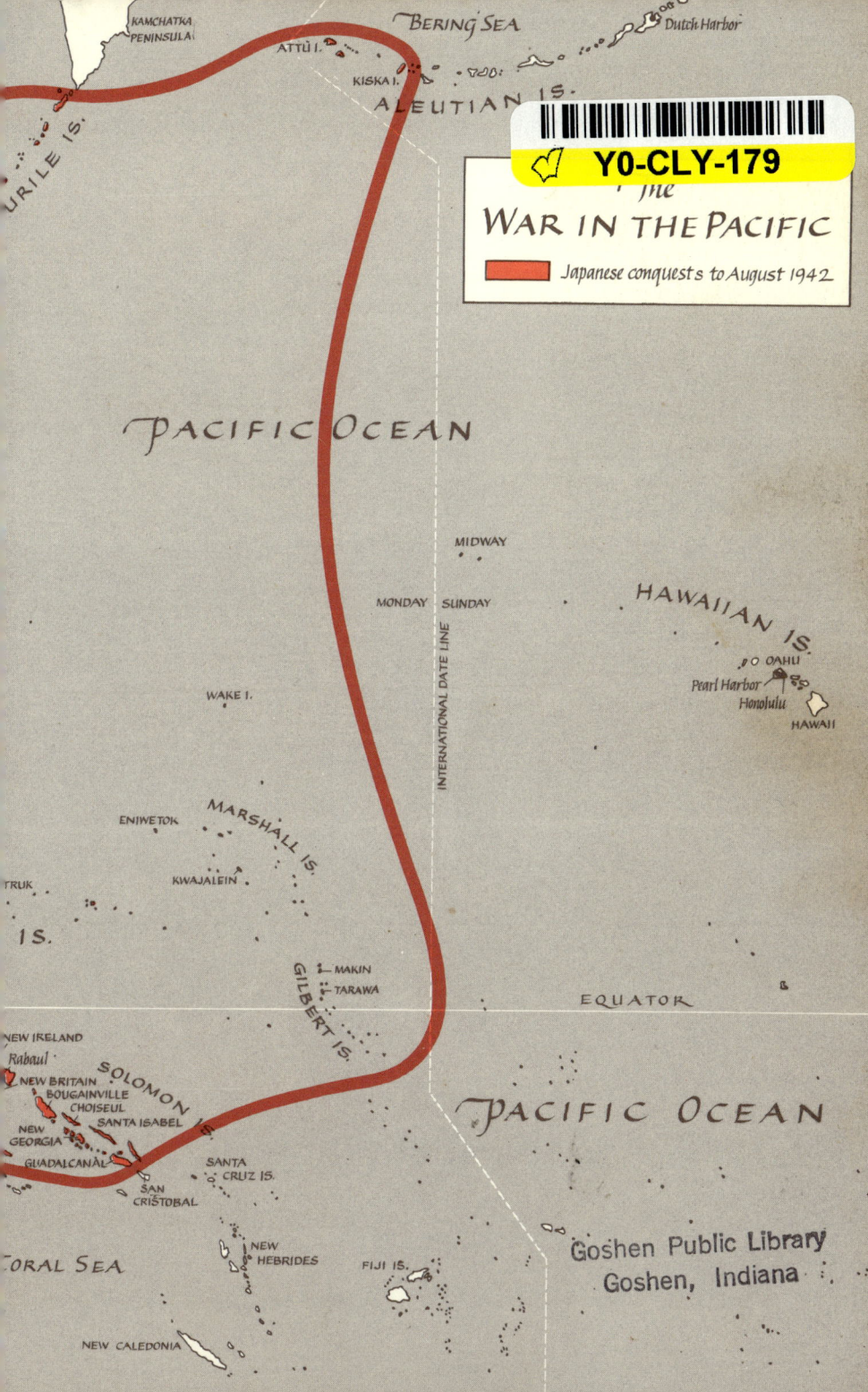

The Rising Sun

VOLUME 1

VOLUME 1

The Rising Sun

The Decline and Fall of the Japanese Empire

1936-1945

JOHN TOLAND

RANDOM HOUSE / NEW YORK

940.53
TOL
Copy B
Vol. 1

Copyright © 1970 by John Toland

All rights reserved under International and Pan-American Copyright Conventions. Published in the United States by Random House, Inc., New York, and simultaneousy in Canada by Random House of Canada Limited, Toronto.

Manufactured in the United States of America

Pictorial Layout: Wladisaw Finne

To Orie and Tokiji Matsumura
and
Paul R. Reynolds

Contents

VOLUME 1

Foreword   xxxiii

Part One—The Roots of War
1. Gekokujo   3
2. To the Marco Polo Bridge   42
3. "Then the War Will Be a Desperate One"   68

Part Two—The Lowering Clouds
4. "Go Back to Blank Paper"   113
5. The Fatal Note   154
6. Operation Z   189
7. "This War May Come Quicker Than Anyone Dreams"   219

Part Three—*Banzai!*
8. "I Shall Never Look Back"   265
9. "The Formidable Years That Lie Before Us"   297
10. "For a Wasted Hope and Sure Defeat"   323
11. "To Show Them Mercy Is to Prolong the War"   355
12. "But Not in Shame"   377
13. The Tide Turns   401

Part Four—Isle of Death
14. Operation Shoestring   431
15. Green Hell   454
16. "I Deserve Ten Thousand Deaths"   484
17. The End   513

VOLUME 2

Part Five—The Gathering Forces

18	Of Mice and Men	547
19	To the Marianas	587
20	"Seven Lives to Repay Our Country!"	624

Part Six—The Decisive Battle

21	"Let No Heart Be Faint"	653
22	The Battle of Leyte Gulf	682
23	The Battle of Breakneck Ridge	715
24	Debacle	740

Part Seven—Beyond the Bitter End

25	"Our Golden Opportunity"	759
26	"Like Hell with the Fire Out"	794
27	The Flowers of Edo	831
28	The Last Sortie	845
29	The Iron Typhoon	872
30	The Stragglers	899

Part Eight—"One Hundred Million Die Together"

31	In Quest of Peace	915
32	"That Was Not Any Decision That You Had to Worry About"	939
33	Hiroshima	963
34	. . . and Nagasaki	981
35	"To Bear the Unbearable"	1002
36	The Palace Revolt	1026
37	The Voice of the Crane	1054
	Epilogue	1079
	Acknowledgments	1088
	Sources	1093
	Notes	1120
	Index	1151

The Road to Pearl Harbor

Young officers, opposed to expansion into China take over Tokyo in 1936. The failure of their revolt led to war with America.

Japan joins the Axis—1940. In Germany, Foreign Minister Matsuoka announces Tripartite Pact. To his left, wearing glasses, is General Eugen Ott, Hitler's envoy in Tokyo.

In Washington, Ambassador Nomura greets three unofficial peace emissaries—Colonel Hideo Iwakuro (far left) and two Maryknoll priests, Father Drought and Bishop Walsh.

Prime Minister Konoye's persistent efforts to keep peace with the United States, including a proposed summit meeting with Roosevelt, ended in the fall of his cabinet.

General Hideki Tojo, who succeeded Prince Konoye as prime minister weeks before Pearl Harbor.

Ambassador Grew, with Foreign Minister Togo, repeatedly warned that war would come "with dangerous and dramatic suddenness" unless Washington relaxed its rigid policy.

December 7, 1941. Ambassador Nomura and Special Envoy Kurusu wait in Secretary of State Hull's office to deliver Japan's last note. They were unaware at that moment that bombs were falling on Pearl Harbor.

Pearl Harbor

Admiral Nagumo, commander of Pearl Harbor Striking Force.

Admiral Kusaka, Nagumo's chief of staff and de facto commander of Striking Force.

Commander Fuchida, leader of the first assault wave.

Map of entrance to Pearl Harbor hastily drawn by Suguru Suzuki when espionage material he was bringing back from Hawaii was mislaid.

Japanese photographer catches first attack on Battleship Row. Bomb from circled plane sent geyser of water towering over ships.

Fall of Singapore and the Philippines

General Yamashita—"the Tiger of Malaya"—who led the successful assault on the "impregnable" fortress of Singapore.

Bataan Death March—the end of a tragic ordeal.

"God of Operations"—Colonel Masanobu Tsuji, one of the most influential and controversial officers in the Japanese Army.

General Manuel Roxas, who became first President of the liberated Philippines, and Colonel Nobuhiko Jimbo, who saved him from execution.

Guadalcanal

Correspondent Gen Nishino, who covered much of Guadalcanal campaign. Nishino took this photograph of General Kawaguchi briefing his officers before the attack on Henderson Field.

Twenty-five thousand Japanese lost their lives on Guadalcanal, but 13,000 were saved in a secret withdrawal.

Admiral Yamamoto, a few days before he was shot down by American fliers, addressing Japanese pilots about to bomb enemy bases on Guadalcanal.

Conferences—1943

The first Big Three conference at Teheran—Stalin, Roosevelt, and Churchill.

The Greater East Asia Conference in Tokyo, presided over by Tojo with seven countries represented.

The Supreme Command holds a conference at the Imperial Palace in the presence of the Emperor, April 1943.

Unpublished photograph of private sushi *party in 1944. Many of the men standing here were later involved in efforts to seek an early peace. Left to right: Chikuhei Nakajima (former railways minister. Leader of the* Seiyu *Kai); Mamoru Shigemitsu (Foreign Minister); General Jiro Minami (former governor of Korea); Tsuneo Matsudaira (Imperial Household Minister); Admiral Keisuke Okada (former prime minister); Koki Hirota (former prime minister); Gisuke Ayukawa (financier); Prince Fumimaro Konoye (former prime minister); Marquis Koichi Kido (the Lord Keeper of the Privy Seal); General Kuniaki Koiso (Prime Minister); Admiral Kantaro Suzuki (President of the Privy Council); Baron Bunkichi Ito (grandson of Meiji Restoration leader); Admiral Mitsumasa Yonai (former prime minister and last navy minister).*

Saipan

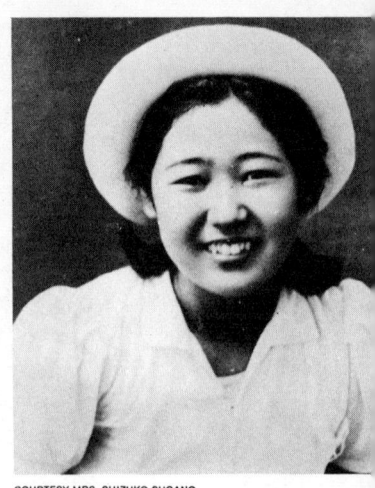

Shizuko Miura, the only army nurse on Saipan, watched Marine landings (below) from the inland heights.

COURTESY MRS. SHIZUKO SUGANO

Leyte

General Sosaku Suzuki, commander of all Japanese troops on Leyte and the southern Philippines, who after defeat had a dream of establishing an independent colony on Mindanao.

"I shall return." MacArthur lands on Leyte. On his left, wearing pith helmet, is President Sergio Osmeña; just behind him, in helmet, is General Carlos Romulo.

The end of Japanese carriers. Rare picture shows Zuikaku *moments before sinking. Her crew stands at attention singing traditional naval song.*

Iwo Jima

Americans swarm toward Iwo's beaches under heavy fire from Mount Suribachi.

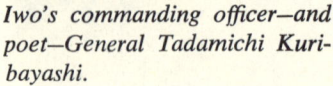

Ensign Toshihiko Ohno, one of the few survivors of the battle.

Iwo's commanding officer—and poet—General Tadamichi Kuribayashi.

This Japanese soldier lay buried in sand for thirty-six hours, live grenade in hand, before Marines disarmed him.

Okinawa

General Mitsuru Ushijima, commander at Okinawa.

General Isamu Cho, Ushijima's aggressive chief of staff.

Flamethrowers approach Shuri Castle.

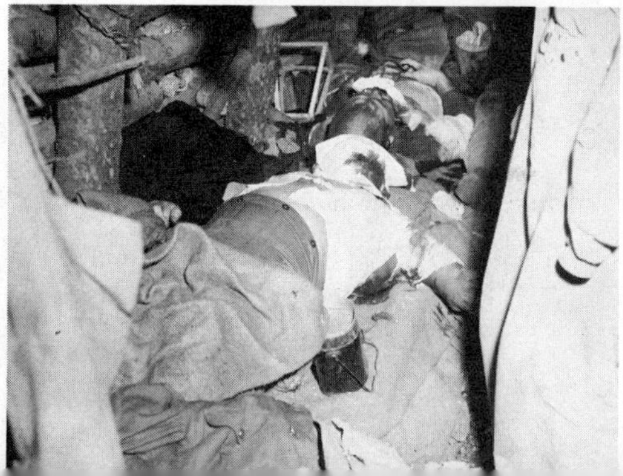

Hara-kiri. Ushijima and Cho meet death in their last headquarters cave.

Kamikaze

Kamikaze *pilots on eve of their mission.*

Determined to die, Yasunori Aoki missed his target by yards, crashed into the sea. His bombs failed to detonate and he was rescued against his will.

"After I die you'll have to do everything," Aoki wrote to his younger brother just before his mission.

Admiral Matome Ugaki, head of all naval kamikaze units and Yamamoto's former chief of staff, disappeared on the day of surrender in the last suicide mission of the war.

COURTESY ENSIGN AOKI

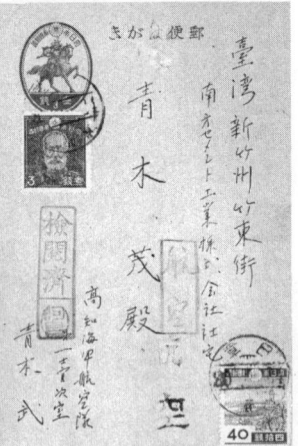

COURTESY ENSIGN AOKI

COURTESY CAPTAIN YASUJI WATANABE

Home Front

Women of Tokyo prepare for air raids.

Defenseless Tokyo. B-29 flies unmolested over Diet Building.

Results of the first fire bombing of Tokyo—March 10, 1945. 140,000 died.

The Bomb

Crew of Enola Gay *just before leaving Tinian Island with the first atom bomb. In foreground: Major Ferebee, Colonel Tibbets and Captain Van Kirk.*

News photographer Gonichi Kimura snapped this unique picture two miles from ground zero at Hiroshima.

One hundred thousand died the first day at Hiroshima, and another 100,000 were doomed.

The center of Hiroshima.

Nagasaki. Survivors look for relatives among charred bodies. Stacks of Mitsubishi Steel and Arms Works loom in background.

The Palace Revolt

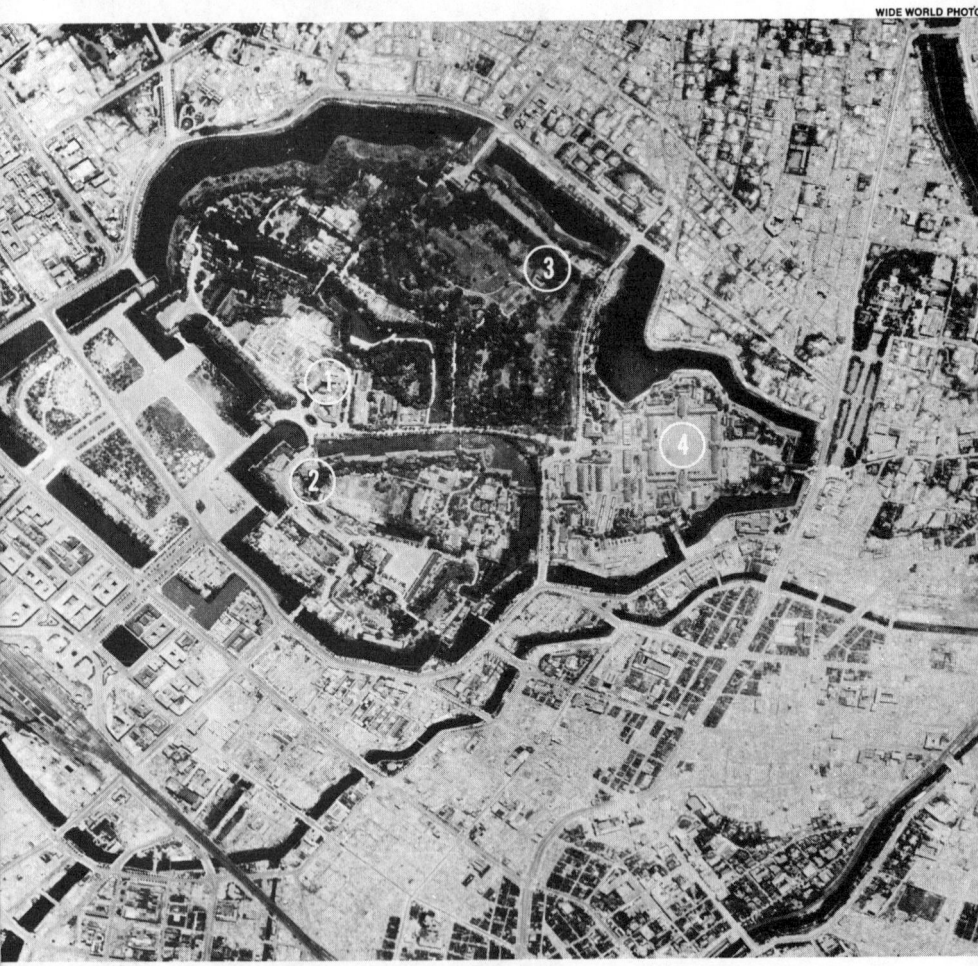

The Palace grounds. (1) Ruins of Palace, (2) Imperial Household Ministry, (3) the obunko, *temporary house of royal family. Adjacent to Palace grounds (4) command post of rebels, Konoye Division barracks.*

WIDE WORLD PHOTOS—COURTESY COLONEL MASAHIKO TAKESHITA

Army Chief of Staff General Yoshijiro Umezu (left) and War Minister General Korechika Anami sympathized with the dissidents but refused to join them.

Major Kenji Hatanaka, idealistic leader of the revolt.

Colonel Masahiko Takeshita, the ranking officer in the revolt and brother-in-law of the War Minister.

Colonel Masataka Ida, who gave his reluctant support to Hatanaka.

The End

Admiral Takijiro Onishi, originator of kamikaze corps. A few hours after this picture was taken, he committed hara-kiri.

All Japan, silent and weeping, listens to the Emperor announce surrender on August 15, 1945.

Surrender on Missouri. *Foreign Minister Shigemitsu and Army Chief of Staff Umezu head Japanese delegation.*

The suicide that failed. Former Prime Minister Hideki Tojo shot himself in the chest, barely missing his heart, just before he was to be arrested.

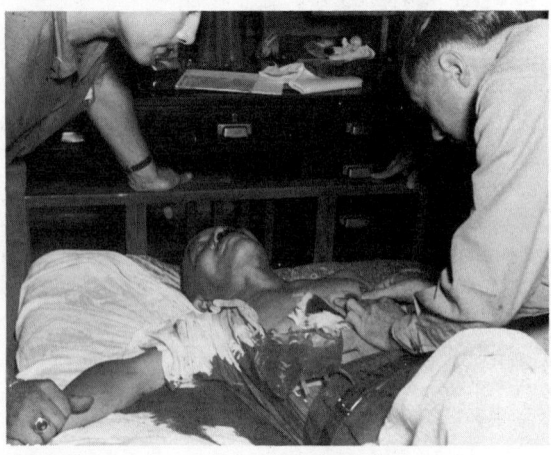

Foreword

After World War II most Westerners felt that General Tojo and other Japanese leaders—indeed the mass of Japanese—were no better than Hitler and his Nazi cohorts, and deserved whatever punishment and misfortune that befell them.

Twenty-five years have passed and Japan has recovered from almost total moral and economic disaster to resume a respected place among nations of the world. Still, the question remains: How could we have come to admire and respect a people who often acted like barbarians during the war?

This book, which is largely seen from the Japanese point of view, is an attempt to answer that question as well as others about the war that changed the face of Asia. Why did a country the size of California launch the suicidal attack on Pearl Harbor which involved it in a death struggle with an enemy ten times stronger? Was war between the two nations, which today find so much in common, inevitable and essential? Did the winning of that war perpetuate American involvement in Asian affairs?

I would not have attempted to write this book—even with the assistance of a Japanese wife and her family—but for two things: a drastic change in Japanese attitudes toward their own immediate past and the appearance of significant new documents. In addition to the mountain of material already available in the Japanese Ministry of Foreign Affairs and the Military History Archives of the Japan Defense Agency, valuable documents that had been hidden or lost were recently discovered, such as records of the imperial and liaison conferences, the supposedly burned portions of the Konoye Diary, and the thousand-page "Notes" of Field Marshal Gen Sugiyama, Chief of the Army General Staff from 1940 to February 21, 1944.

Even more important has been the willingness of Japan's former military and civilian leaders—including Marquis Koichi Kido, the Emperor's chief adviser; Prince Mikasa, the Emperor's youngest brother; Admiral Ryunosuke Kusaka, de facto commander at Pearl Harbor and Midway; and General Kenryo Sato, perhaps Tojo's most trusted confidant—to talk freely and at length about the unhappy past. Gone is the reluctance, apparent only a few years ago during research for *But Not in Shame,* to discuss certain sensitive subjects. Moreover, they are convinced that Westerners, after their postwar experiences in Asia, will have more understanding of the blunders they made in Manchuria and China. Those who fought the war, from generals to privates, have also been more willing to talk of their mistakes, and speak of the unspeakable: cowardice, murder, cannibalism, surrender—and desertion.

In the interest of accuracy these men, as well as everyone else interviewed whose story is included in the book, read the passages about themselves and often added illuminating comments. The dialogue in the book is not fictional. It comes from transcripts, records and stenographic notes, and the memory of the participants. The extensive debates during the various imperial and liaison conferences, for example, are based on the Sugiyama "Notes"; the recently assembled official records; diaries; and interviews with Marquis Kido, who was given an immediate report of each conference the Emperor attended, and participants including General Teiichi Suzuki, Naoki Hoshino and Okinori Kaya. The *Notes* (at the end of the book) list sources for all material used, chapter by chapter.

America's greatest mistake in World War II, I believe, was in failing to recognize that she was fighting two different kinds of war simultaneously: one in Europe against another Western people and philosophy, Nazism, and one in Asia which was not only a struggle against an aggressive nation fighting for survival as a modern power but an ideological contest against an entire continent. Millions of Orientals saw Japan's battle as their own, as a confrontation of race and color; they also saw in Japan's victories their own liberation from Western domination.

"Each nation, the United States not excepted, has made its contribution to the welter of evil which now comprises the Far East question." Tyler Dennett, an authority on the Far East, wrote in 1922: "We shall all do well to drop for all time the pose of self-righteousness and injured innocence and penitently face the facts."

If we had done so, it is very probable that our negotiations with Japan in 1941 would have ended in peace, not war, and America would not have been forced to become the moral policeman of Asia for many years. And a moral policeman's lot is not a happy one, particularly when his own morality is in question.

What follows is a factual saga of people caught up in the flood of the most overwhelming war of mankind, told as it happened—muddled, ennobling, disgraceful, frustrating, full of contradiction and paradox. I have done my utmost to let the events speak for themselves, and if any conclusion was reached, it was that there are no simple lessons in history, that it is human nature that repeats itself, not history. We often learn more about the past from the present, in fact, than the reverse. The lessons of our own brutalities in postwar Asia, for example, have undoubtedly given Americans insight into the actions of the Japanese a generation ago.

J. T.

PART ONE

The Roots of War

1

Gekokujo

1.

The sky over Tokyo on the afternoon of February 25, 1936, was dark and foreboding. A thick blanket of snow already covered the city and there was threat of more to come. Three nights earlier more than a foot had fallen, breaking a record of fifty-four years, and causing such a traffic snarl that some theaters had to be turned into temporary hotels for audiences unable to get home.

Even under its white cloak of snow, Tokyo looked almost as Western as Oriental. Japan had left much of its feudal past behind to become by far the most progressive, westernized nation of Asia. A few hundred yards from the Imperial Palace with its traditional tile roof was a modern four-story concrete building, the Imperial Household Ministry, where all court business was conducted and the Emperor's offices were located. Just outside the ancient stone walls and moat surrounding the spacious Palace grounds was the same mélange of East and West: a long line of modern structures, including the Imperial Theater and the Dai Ichi Building, as Occidental as the skyline of Chicago, while a few blocks away, in narrow cobblestone streets, were row upon row of geisha houses, *sushi* stands and kimono stores, and assorted little ramshackle shops, gay even on that cloudy day with their flapping doorway curtains and colorful lanterns.

Next to the Palace on a small hill was the not quite completed Diet Building, constructed mainly of stone from Okinawa and looking quasi-Egyptian. Behind this commanding edifice was a cluster of spacious houses, the official residence of government leaders. The largest was that of the Prime Minister. It was two buildings in one, the business part Western in the early Frank Lloyd Wright style, the living quarters Japanese with paper-thin walls, tatami floors and sliding doors.

But beneath the peaceful exterior of Tokyo seethed an unrest which would soon spill violently into the snow-covered streets. At one end of the Palace grounds were the barracks of the 1st (Gem) Division. Here authorities were already prepared for trouble after a tip about a military insurrection from a major in the War Ministry: he had learned from a young officer that a group of radicals planned to assassinate several advisers to the Emperor that day. Suspects had been put under surveillance, and important public figures were given emergency bodyguards. The doors of the Prime Minister's official residence were reinforced with steel, iron bars installed in the windows, and a warning system connected directly to police headquarters. But the *kempeitai* (military police organization)* and the regular police felt they could easily handle the situation. After all, what real damage could a handful of rebels do, however strongly motivated? And by now they were wondering how reliable the information was that the uprising was at hand. The day was almost over.

It seems strange that they were so complacent, since the spirit of rebellion was high among elite troops charged with defense of the Palace grounds. Their defiance was so apparent that they were on orders to be shipped out to Manchuria in a few days, and their contempt for authority so open that one unit, ostensibly on maneuvers, had urinated in cadence at metropolitan police headquarters. Fourteen hundred of these unruly officers and men were preparing to revolt. Just before dawn the next morning, attack groups would strike simultaneously at six Tokyo targets: the homes

---

* *Kempei* were soldiers acting as armed policemen, with some authority over civilians. (In Japanese, one form serves for both singular and plural; there is no suffix to indicate number.)

of several government leaders, as well as metropolitan police headquarters.

While intricate preparations for these attacks were proceeding, pleasure seekers roamed the darkening streets in search of entertainment. Already the Ginza, Tokyo's Broadway–Fifth Avenue, was teeming. To young Japanese it had long been a romantic symbol of the outside world, a fairyland of neon lights, boutiques, coffee shops, American and European movies, Western-style dance halls and restaurants. A few blocks away, in the Akasaka section, where the kimono was common for both men and women, the old Japan also anticipated a night of pleasure. Geishas looking like something out of antiquity in their theatrical make-up and resplendent costumes were pulled in rickshaws through the winding, willow-lined streets. Here the lights were more muted, and the traditional red lanterns carried by the police gave off a soft, nostalgic glow. It was a charming woodcut come alive.

These insurrectionists were not motivated by personal ambition. Like half a dozen groups before them—all of which had failed—they were about to try once again to redress the social injustices in Japan through force and assassination. Tradition had legitimized such criminal action, and the Japanese had given it a special name, *gekokujo* (insubordination), a term first used in the fifteenth century when rebellion was rampant on every level, with provincial lords refusing to obey the shogun,* who in turn ignored the orders of the emperor.

The crumbling of autocracy in Europe after World War I, followed by the tide of democracy, socialism and Communism, had had dramatic impact on the young people of Japan, and they too set up a cry for change. Political parties emerged and a universal manhood suffrage bill was enacted in 1924. But it all happened too fast. Too many Japanese looked upon politics as a game or a source of easy money and there was a series of exposés—the Matsushima Red-Light District Scandal, the Railway Scandal, the Korean Scandal. Charges of bribery and corruption resulted in mob brawls on the floor of the Diet.

---

* De facto ruler in feudal Japan; a sort of generalissimo. Until the reign of Meiji, the present ruler's grandfather, the emperor had for centuries been little more than a figurehead, a puppet of the shogun.

The population explosion which accompanied Japan's westernization added to the confusion. Hokkaido, Honshu, Kyushu and Shikoku (her four main islands, comprising an area scarcely the size of California) already burst with eighty million people. The national economy could not absorb a population increase of almost one million a year; farmers who were close to starvation following the plunge of produce prices began to organize in protest for the first time in Japanese history; hundreds of thousands of city workers were thrown out of work. Out of all this came a wave of left-wing parties and unions.

These movements were counteracted by nationalist organizations, whose most popular leader was Ikki Kita,* a nationalist as well as a fiery revolutionary who managed to combine a program of socialism with imperialism. His tract on reform, "A General Outline of Measures for the Reconstruction of Japan," was devoured by radicals and worshipers of the Emperor alike. His words appealed to all who yearned for reform. "The Japanese are following the destructive examples of the Western nations," he wrote. "The possessors of financial, political and military power are striving to maintain their unjust interests under cover of the imperial power. . . .

"Seven hundred million brethren in India and China cannot gain their independence without our protection and leadership.

"The history of East and West is a record of the unification of feudal states after an era of civil wars. The only possible international peace, which will come after the present age of international wars, must be a feudal peace. This will be achieved through the emergence of the strongest country, which will dominate all other nations of the world."

He called for the "removal of the barriers between nation and Emperor"—that is, the Diet and the Cabinet. Voting should be restricted to heads of families and no one would be allowed to accumulate more than 1,000,000 yen (about $500,000 at the time). Important industries should be nationalized, a dictatorship established, and women restricted to activities in the home "cultivating the ancient Japanese arts of flower arrangement and the tea ceremony."

* In Japan the family name comes first but is reversed in this book for easier reading.

It was no wonder that millions of impressionable, idealistic young men, already disgusted by corruption in government and business and poverty at home, were enthralled.* They could battle all these wicked forces as well as Communism, free the Orient of Occidental domination and make Japan the leading country in the world.

In the West these young men could have found an outlet for action as unionists or political agitators, but in Japan many, particularly those from small landowning and shopkeeping families, found they could serve best as Army and Navy officers. Once in the service, they gained an even more profound understanding of poverty from their men, who would be weeping over letters from home—with their sons away, the families were on the verge of starvation. The young officers blamed their own superiors, politicians, court officials. They joined secret organizations of which some, like Tenkento, called for direct action and assassination, while others, like Sakurakai (the Cherry Society), demanded territorial expansion as well as internal reforms.

By 1928 this ferment came to a head, but it took two extraordinary men operating within the military framework to put it into action. One was a lieutenant colonel, Kanji Ishihara, and the other a colonel, Seishiro Itagaki. The first was brilliant, inspired, flamboyant, a fountain of ideas; the second was cool, thoughtful, a master organizer. They made a perfect team. What Ishihara envisioned, Itagaki could bring to pass. Both were staff officers in the Kwantung Army, which had originally, in 1905, been sent to Manchuria to guard Japanese interests in a wild territory larger than California, Oregon and Washington combined.

The two officers felt that Manchuria was the only answer to poverty in Japan. It could be transformed from a wilderness into a civilized, prosperous area, alleviating unemployment at home and providing an outlet for the overpopulated homeland, where more

---

* The song of Nikkyo (the All-Japan Council for the Joint Struggle of Patriots) indicated the peculiarly Japanese spirit of such young rebels:

> Daily we submit to hypocrisy and lies,
> While national honor lingering dies.
> Arise ye! O patriots, arise!
> Onward we march, defying death!
> Come prison bars! Come gory death!

than two thirds of all farms were smaller than two and a quarter acres. Manchuria could also supply Japan with what she so desperately needed to remain an industrial state—a guaranteed source of raw materials and a market for finished goods. But all this could not come about, Ishihara and Itagaki reasoned, until the Japanese gained complete control of Manchuria, which was loosely governed by a Chinese war lord, Marshal Chang Tso-lin. At the time, Japan had only the right to station troops along railroads and to engage in mining, farming and business activities.

There had been a struggle over the vast territory north of China for several hundred years, with the Chinese occupying Manchuria and Korea, and the Russians taking over Maritime Province, the coastal region of Siberia from Bering Strait to Vladivostok. For centuries Japan had cut herself off from the outside world and did not join this scramble for territory until 1853. In that year an American commodore, Matthew C. Perry, sailed into Edo (Tokyo) Bay and, at cannon point, opened up a medieval Japan to modern life. The Japanese took to it with a will. They assiduously copied the latest techniques of mass production and even added original procedures—girls in textile factories, for example, worked on roller skates to handle more spindles. They built a strong army and navy and began imitating the European game of forceful diplomacy, by sending out punitive expeditions. Within a few decades Japan controlled most of Korea and in 1894 fought a war with China for this country. Japan won easily, and also gained possession of Formosa, the southern tip of Manchuria and the Liaotung Peninsula with the important seaports of Port Arthur and Dairen.

Alarmed that an interloper was taking a piece of their "Chinese Melon," Russia, Germany and France joined forces and compelled Japan to give up the peninsula she had just won in battle. Russia then appropriated Liaotung for herself but could keep it less than ten years. In 1904 the Japanese, their national pride stung, struck back at the Czar, whose empire covered one sixth of the earth's land surface, and astonished the world by winning overwhelming victories. Once more Japan had Port Arthur and Dairen.

She also had all the railways built by Russia in southern Manchuria. Japan could have seized the rest of the country but wanted to be recognized by the Europeans as a respected member of the imperialist community. Accordingly, she poured a billion dollars into the bandit-infested, sparsely populated territory, and maintained such law and order along the railroads that hundreds of thousands of Japanese, Chinese and Korean traders and settlers flooded into the area.

It was this mass influx that had inspired Ishihara and Itagaki to envision a Manchuria free of its Chinese war-lord ruler. Ishihara dreamed of making it an autonomous state, a haven for all of its ethnic groups—Japanese, Chinese, Manchurians, Koreans and White Russians. Here genuine democracy and eventual socialism would be practiced and a buffer set up against Soviet Russia.*

All this was to be effected by the Kwantung Army, with the blessing of Tokyo. But the Emperor and the War Ministry refused to sanction a plan that appeared to be masked aggression. Undeterred, Ishihara, Itagaki and their followers decided to act on their own—to commit *gekokujo*. The first step was to eliminate Marshal Chang, the aging Chinese war lord. On June 4, 1928, a Kwantung Army staff officer commanding men from an Engineer regiment dynamited Chang's special train and he was fatally injured. From then on, and despite numerous warnings from Tokyo, Ishihara and Itagaki used the Kwantung Army as if it were their private legion. At last, in the summer of 1931, they were ready for the final step and secretly massed troops to take Manchuria from the Chinese by force. Hearing rumors of this, the Foreign Minister persuaded the War Minister to send an officer from Tokyo to bring the Kwantung Army under control. The man selected, a major general, arrived in Mukden on the evening of September 18. A few miles away a charge of dynamite was being planted on the tracks of the South Manchurian Railway near the barracks of the 7th Chinese Brigade. The explosion would be the excuse "to bring order" by sending in troops and seizing Mukden.

The general was easily diverted by Colonel Itagaki to the Kikubumi, a Japanese inn, for an evening with the geishas.

---

* Itagaki wrote: "Manchuria is, of course, important from the point of view of Japanese capitalism. From the standpoint of the proletariat, which finds it necessary to demand equalization of national wealth, no fundamental solution can be found within the boundaries of naturally poor Japan that will ensure a livelihood for the people at large."

About ten o'clock there was a detonation, but the damage to the tracks was so slight that a southbound train passed by safely a few minutes later. A Japanese consular officer wanted to adjust the matter with the Chinese, but a Kwantung Army staff major drew his sword and threatened to run him through. At ten-thirty Japanese troops fired on the Chinese barracks while other detachments converged on the walls of Mukden. At the Kikubumi, the general was too drunk to notice the fusillade. If he had, it would have made no difference. He had known about the plot from the beginning—and approved of it.

By morning Mukden was in Japanese hands, to the dismay of not only the world but Tokyo itself. At the request of the Cabinet, the Army General Staff ordered the Kwantung Army to limit the expanse of hostilities. This group of individualists simply ignored the command and continued to sweep over the rest of Manchuria. It was *gekokujo* on a grand scale.

In Tokyo, members of the Cherry Society were already secretly conspiring to support the rebel action in Manchuria with a coup d'état of their own. Their primary purpose was to impose radical internal reforms. These reforms, together with the conquest of Manchuria, would lead to the new Japan. The plot (the Brocade Flag Revolution) involved 120 officers and their troops, augmented by followers of the firebrand Ikki Kita. The rebels planned to assassinate government and court officials, then assemble in front of the Palace, and by way of apologizing to the Emperor, commit hara-kiri.

But so many groups with so many differing opinions were involved in the coup that someone turned informer, in pique or for pay, and the plotters were arrested on October 17, 1931. The leader of the conspiracy was sentenced to twenty days' confinement and his assistant got half that. Their accomplices were merely reprimanded. It was the old story: amnesty for any actual or planned violence if it was done for the glory of the nation.

That evening the War Minister radioed the Kwantung Army a limp reproach:

1. THE KWANTUNG ARMY IS TO REFRAIN FROM ANY NEW PROJECT SUCH AS BECOMING INDEPENDENT FROM THE IM-

PERIAL ARMY AND SEIZING CONTROL OF MANCHURIA AND MONGOLIA.

2. THE GENERAL SITUATION IS DEVELOPING ACCORDING TO THE INTENTIONS OF THE ARMY, SO YOU MAY BE COMPLETELY REASSURED.

As if this wasn't enough, the War Vice Minister added these conciliatory words:

WE HAVE BEEN UNITED IN MAKING DESPERATE EFFORTS TO SOLVE THE EXISTING DIFFICULTY . . . TRUST OUR ZEAL, ACT WITH GREAT PRUDENCE. . . . GUARD AGAINST IMPETUOUS ACTS, SUCH AS DECLARING THE INDEPENDENCE OF THE KWANTUNG ARMY, AND WAIT FOR A FAVORABLE TURN OF EVENTS ON OUR SIDE.

Rather than being appeased, the Kwantung commander indignantly denied that his army was seeking independence, and though admitting it had "tended to act overpositively and arbitrarily," claimed it had done so "for the country."

The abortive Brocade Flag Revolution did achieve one of its purposes: in the next few years it assured the success of the Manchurian adventure. It also convinced many Japanese that politics and business were so corrupt that a military-led reform had to be supported. At the same time it engendered such bitterness that the two wings of the reform movement began to split. One, nicknamed "the Control" clique by newsmen, believed it was not enough to take Manchuria, since security against a possible attack by the Soviet Union could be forestalled only by control of China itself. The Kita followers, known as "the Imperial Way" clique, were convinced this new expansion would be folly; an industrialized Manchuria would be a sturdy enough fortress against Communism.

The younger, more idealistic officers belonged to the latter faction, while field-grade officers as well as key men in the War Ministry supported the Control clique. The more radical nationalists turned immediately to assassination. Each member of the Blood Brotherhood, for example, was pledged to kill at least one "corrupt" political or financial leader on or about February 11, 1932, the 2,592nd celebration of the ascension to the throne of Jinmu, the first human emperor of Japan, the fifth in line of descent from the Sun Goddess, according to legend. Those marked for death included Finance Minister Junnosuke Inoue, a forthright man who often opposed the mounting Army appropriation. The conspirator assigned to kill Inoue practiced shooting on a deserted beach, and four days ahead of schedule put three bullets into Inoue right on the sidewalk. Less than a month later, the second murder took place under similar circumstances. As Baron Takuma Dan, president of Mitsui, stepped out of his car, a young assassin jabbed a pistol in his back and pulled the trigger.

Once again the trials provided the citizens of Japan with melodrama and propaganda. The assassin in Japanese history had often been a more sympathetic figure than the victim. Wasn't there some lack of virtue in a man who let himself be killed, and wasn't an assassin who murdered for lofty purposes merely defending the common people against tyranny? Overwhelming evidence of guilt notwithstanding, the two killers were not executed but given life imprisonment, from which it was obvious they would be paroled in a few years.

On Sunday, May 15, only two months after the death of Dan, a pair of taxis pulled up at the side entrance to the Yasukuni Shrine in Tokyo, a Shinto temple dedicated to all who have died in Japan's wars. Nine Navy and Army officers alighted from the cabs and bowed toward the Sun Goddess; then, armed with charms bought from a priest, returned to the taxis and headed for the Prime Minister's official residence. Here they forced their way past a police sergeant and into the room of Prime Minister Tsuyoshi Inukai, a diminutive man of seventy-five with a goatee. The old man calmly led the would-be assassins to a Japanese-style room, where they politely removed their shoes and sat down. At that moment a comrade who had got lost in the corridors entered, dagger in hand, and cried out, "No use talking! Fire!" Everyone began shooting at the courageous little man who had opposed the conquest of Manchuria and steadfastly refused to recognize the puppet government of the province now going under the manufactured name of Manchukuo ("State of Manchu"). The assassins left by taxi for police headquarters to launch an attack, but it was

Sunday, and except for a few duty officers there was no one to fight. Before surrendering they heaved a grenade at the Bank of Japan. Other conspirators scattered handbills in the streets, and threw bombs which shattered a few windows.

The coup itself—named the 5/15 (May 15) Incident—had fizzled out, but it brought forth even more sensational trials. There were three in all—one for civilians, one each for Army and Navy personnel. As usual a large segment of the public sympathized with the assassins, and there was general applause when one defendant declared that he and his comrades only wanted to sound an alarm to awaken the nation. The people had heard so much about "corruption" that little sympathy was shown the memory of gallant little Inukai. His death was a warning to politicians.

Feeling ran so high that 110,000 petitions for clemency, signed or written entirely in blood, inundated officials of the trial. Nine young men from Niigata asked to take the place of those on trial, and to show their good faith enclosed their own nine little fingers pickled in a jar of alcohol.

One of Inukai's assassins did express regret but said that the Prime Minister had to be "sacrificed on the altar of national reformation." Another declared, "Life or death does not count with me. I say to those who bemoan my death, 'Do not shed tears for me but sacrifice yourselves on the altars of reform.'"

The results of the trials could have been predicted. No one was sentenced to death, and of the forty to receive sentences almost all were free in a few years. To the people they were martyrs, their own champions. Who else called for such drastic methods to end the crippling depression?* Who else would lead the farmers and workers out of poverty? Who else dared publicly assail leading politicians, court officials and financial barons for corruption? And since so many people believed in this so implicitly, the power of the militarists and rightists continued to grow.

For three years the idealistic young officers, chafed by the corruption surrounding them, bided their time. Only their reverence for the Emperor prevented them from supporting a Communist revolution. But one of them, driven by "an impulse from on high,"

---

* Poverty in Japan had increased in the wake of America's depression. The price of raw silk, Japan's main export, had dropped more than 50 percent.

took matters into his own hands. It was a bloody and bizarre action even for a country with one foot planted in feudalism. One morning in August 1935, Lieutenant Colonel Saburo Aizawa, after visiting the Meiji Shrine for advice, entered the back door of Army General Staff headquarters, a decrepit two-story wooden building just outside the Palace grounds. Like so many other idealistic, radical officers of the day, he had become incensed when their idol, General Jinsaburo Mazaki, was dismissed from his post as Inspector General of Military Education.*

Aizawa strode unannounced into the office of another general, Tetsuzan Nagata, chief of the Military Affairs Bureau and one of Mazaki's most outspoken foes. "I feel an impulse to assassinate Nagata," Aizawa had recently told the Sun Goddess at the Ise Shrine. "If I am right, please help me succeed. If I am wrong, please make me fail." Nagata, at his desk, did not even look up as Aizawa pulled his sword, lunged and missed. Slightly wounded on the second thrust, the general lurched for an exit but Aizawa stabbed him through the back, pinning him momentarily to the door. Aizawa slashed his neck twice, then walked to the office of a friend to say he had just carried out Heaven's judgment and went off to buy a cap—he'd lost his in the fracas. When a military policeman arrested him, Aizawa thought he'd be examined briefly and allowed to return to duty. Instead he found himself the star of a sensational trial that was shaking the foundations of the Army and became the rallying point of all the young superpatriots who wanted to reform the nation overnight.

At his trial Aizawa was treated gingerly by the five judges and was allowed to use the witness stand to attack statesmen, politicians and the *zaibatsu* (family business combines such as Mitsui and Mitsubishi) for corruption. Pleading guilty to the charge of murder, he claimed he had only done his duty as an honorable soldier of the Emperor. "The country was in a deplorable state: the farmers were impoverished, officials were involved in scandals, diplomacy was weak, and the prerogative of the Supreme Com-

---

* The three most important posts in the Japanese Army were the Chief of the General Staff, the War Minister and the Inspector General of Military Education (referred to as "the Big Three"). This triangular system dating from 1878 had been recommended by a Prussian major, Jacob Meckel, on loan to Japan from the Kaiser.

Gekokujo

mand had been violated by the naval-limitation agreements," he declared in the stilted prose of reform.* "I came to realize that the senior statesmen, those close to the Throne, powerful financiers and bureaucrats, were attempting gradually to corrupt the government and the Army for their own selfish interests." These conditions had inspired him to murder—to commit *gekokujo*.

"If the court fails to understand the spirit which guided Colonel Aizawa," his defense counsel said ominously, "a second Aizawa, and even a third, will appear."

2.

These prophetic words were uttered on February 25, 1936, in snowbound Tokyo, even as the leaders of the most ambitious coup in the history of modern Japan were ready to strike. Their principal target the following morning would be Prime Minister Keisuke Okada, a retired admiral. Okada was hosting a banquet at his official residence on the evening of the twenty-fifth, in celebration of the victory of the government party (Minseito) in the general election for the House of Representatives five days earlier. He was a politician by request, not choice. The previous fall the Emperor had asked him to form a new cabinet after a scandal involving Finance Ministry officials forced the resignation of his predecessor, Viscount Makoto Saito, also a retired admiral.

While Okada's guests toasted the election results as a resounding triumph for the admiral's policies and a blow to fascism and militarism, his private wish was that he could resign. He was weary from the struggle, and it seemed to him that despite the victory at the polls, the militarists and chauvinists were as strong as ever.

Two other men marked for assassination were at a party several blocks away at the American embassy, where Ambassador Joseph C. Grew was giving a dinner for thirty-six in honor of the recently cashiered prime minister, who had been made Lord Keeper of the Privy Seal. Among the guests was still another re-

---

* His last charge referred to the naval disarmament conference held in Washington (1922), which adopted a 5–5–3 ratio as to capital ships belonging to America, Britain and Japan. The Japanese (particularly the young radicals) were still incensed at the big-power curtailment of their naval strength. The lower ratio for Japan implied a stigma of national inferiority.

tired admiral, Kantaro Suzuki, Grand Chamberlain to the Emperor.

Grew was a tall, courtly man with black bushy eyebrows, mustache and gray-white hair. Born in Boston's Back Bay, as was his great-grandfather, he had attended Groton and Harvard with Franklin D. Roosevelt. An aristocrat with democratic instincts, he had already distinguished himself as a diplomat in Europe. He was particularly qualified to serve in Tokyo, since he had a rare understanding and affection for Japan and all things Japanese, as well as a wife who had previously lived in the country, spoke the language and was a descendant of Commodore Perry.

That evening Grew had gone to the trouble of providing special entertainment for his guest of honor: a private showing of *Naughty Marietta,* starring Jeanette MacDonald and Nelson Eddy. He had chosen the film because "it was full of lovely old Victor Herbert music, beautiful scenes, a pretty, romantic story and no vulgarity whatever. . . ." After dinner he escorted former Prime Minister Saito to a comfortable armchair in the salon. Grew knew the old gentleman had never attended a sound movie and if he was bored he could take a nap. But Viscount Saito was too enraptured to sleep; and though it was his custom to leave parties promptly at ten o'clock, not only did he stay for refreshments at the end of the first half of the film but remained until the end. The other guests must also have been moved by the romantic story, for when the lights went on, the eyes of all the Japanese ladies "were distinctly red."

It was half past eleven when the Privy Seal and his wife got up to leave. The Grews saw them to the door, pleased that the admiral had enjoyed himself so much. Scattered flakes of snow drifted down gently as the Saito car drove off.

At four o'clock in the morning on February 26, Captain Kiyosada Koda and the other rebel leaders routed out their enlisted men, who still knew nothing of the plot; they thought they were going out on another night maneuver. A few were told there would be killing that night.

"I want you to die with me," Lieutenant Kurihara told Pfc. Kuratomo.

Completely taken by surprise, Kuratomo nevertheless answered immediately, "Yes, sir. I'll die." A superior officer's order was absolute, never to be disobeyed. "This," Kuratomo later recalled, "was the first time I realized something very serious was taking place."

Snow was now falling steadily in huge flakes, and it reminded several of the insurgent officers of the incident of "the forty-seven *ronin*." In the seventeenth century a provincial lord was so disgraced by Kira, the chief minister of the shogun, that he committed suicide. Oishi, a samurai warrior serving the dishonored man, vowed to avenge his death, and for the next seven years he pretended, in the tradition of samurai sacrifice, to be a dissolute drunk while secretly planning revenge. Early one morning in a snowstorm, the forty-seven *ronin* (samurai who had lost their master and were forced to become wanderers; they might be compared to America's drifting cowboy heroes) raided the Kira home, not far from the Imperial Palace. They assassinated the chief minister, cut off his head and brought it to the temple where their master's ashes were enshrined. Then, in true *bushido* style, all forty-seven committed hara-kiri. A factual story, it represented an ideal of samurai behavior and was a favorite theme in Japanese movies and the kabuki theater.

The groups headed for their various destinations: one, led by Koda himself, would seize the War Minister's official residence and force high-ranking officers to support them; another would occupy police headquarters; four other groups would assassinate the Prime Minister, the Finance Minister, the Lord Keeper of the Privy Seal and the Grand Chamberlain. The killers of the Privy Seal would then proceed to the suburban home of the Inspector General of Military Education and murder him while two other units raced out of town as well, to kill Count Nobuaki Makino, former Privy Seal and counselor to the Emperor, and eighty-seven-year-old Prince Kinmochi Saionji, the Emperor's closest adviser, the nation's most honored elder statesman, the last *genro*.*

Lieutenant Kurihara and a military police officer approached the

---

* The *genro* were important statesmen who had helped Emperor Meiji draw up the Imperial Constitution in 1889 and afterward became advisers to the Emperor. In 1916 Saionji had been added to the group, and by 1936 he was the only surviving *genro*.

front gate to the Prime Minister's official residence. A police officer on guard inside the gate asked what was going on. The *kempei* said, "Open the gate quick." The guard didn't think anything of it because they were a colleague and an Army officer. As they came closer to the gate Lieutenant Kurihara's hand grabbed the police guard, and poking his pistol at him with the other hand, ordered, "Open up!"

Kurihara and other officers broke in ahead of their men and disarmed the sleeping policemen in the guardhouse by the gate. Kurihara pushed past them into the residence, which was in total darkness. He turned on the hall light, got his bearings and snapped it off. Suddenly the corridors reverberated with deafening gunfire. This was the signal the rebels outside had been waiting for; they opened up with heavy machine guns. The chandelier in the hall shattered and plummeted to the floor.

Just before five o'clock young Hisatsune Sakomizu, one of Prime Minister Okada's secretaries, had been wakened by a muffled commotion outside his house, which was across the street from the rear gate of the official residence. They have finally come! he thought, for he had long anticipated an attack on his employer, and jumped out of bed. His ties to the old man were close; he was married to Okada's daughter, and his father's younger sister was Okada's wife.

Sakomizu softly opened the window and in the whirling snow saw the policemen who were guarding the rear gate mill around in confusion. He phoned police headquarters.

"We just heard the minister's alarm bell ring," replied a voice. "One platoon is already on the way. Reinforcement units are just leaving." Reassured, Sakomizu started to go back upstairs, when he heard the clop of boots in the street. He looked out expecting to see either the police reinforcements or the special Army troops detailed to protect the Prime Minister, but a rifle shot cracked and he saw one policeman fall and others retreat before a group of soldiers with glittering bayonets. There was a shattering burst of fire—it sounded like rifles and machine guns—and the secretary finally realized that Army troops were attacking the residence. He hastily dressed so he could help the admiral. As he rushed into the street he could hear shots inside the Japanese section of the ministry. Soldiers at the gate came forward brandishing their rifles. They forced Sakomizu back into his own house and followed him without taking off their wet boots. Frustrated, Sakomizu paced up and down. What had happened to the special Army troops or the police reinforcements? The police had already come and been driven off; the troops were among the rebels.

Sakomizu again called police headquarters. "This is the insurgent unit," said a voice. About five hundred rebels were occupying the building. Sakomizu hung up and called the Kojimachi *kempeitai* station nearby. "The situation is out of control" was the sheepish answer. "What can we do?"

A few blocks from the Prime Minister's official residence 170 men, commanded by a first cousin of Sakomizu's, stormed into the official residence of War Minister Yoshiyuki Kawashima. With them was Captain Koda. He routed out Kawashima and began to read off a list of demands: political and social reforms; the arrest of leaders of the Control clique; the assignment of Imperial Way clique officers to key positions (the insurgents were against expansion into China); the assignment of General Araki* as commander of the Kwantung Army "for the purpose of coercing Red Russia." Koda also insisted that martial law be proclaimed and that the War Minister visit the Palace at once to convey the rebels' intentions to the Emperor.

While the argument was going on, Captain Teruzo Ando and 150 men were bursting into the official residence of Grand Chamberlain Kantaro Suzuki, who, like Viscount Saito, had so enjoyed the private showing of *Naughty Marietta* a few hours earlier. The elderly admiral, wakened by a maid, rushed to a storage room for a sword. He couldn't find it. Hearing footsteps in the corridor, he stepped into the next room—it would have been a disgrace to die in a closet. In moments he was hemmed in by a score of bayonets. One soldier stepped forward and asked politely, "Are you His Excellency?"

Suzuki said he was and raised his hands for quiet. "You must have some reason for doing this. Tell me what it is." Nobody answered and Suzuki repeated the question. Silence. The third

---

* General Sadao Araki had long been the idol of the reformists and had figured prominently in the 1932 insurrection, when he was war minister. He was known throughout the world for his outspoken remarks and ferocious handlebar mustache.

time he asked, a man with a pistol (he looked to the Grand Chamberlain like a noncom) said impatiently, "There's no more time. We're going to shoot."

Suzuki supposed they were acting under orders from a superior and didn't know why. "Then it can't be helped," he said stoically. "Go ahead and shoot." He drew himself erect as if facing a firing squad. Just behind him hung the pictures of his parents. Three pistols erupted. One bullet missed, one hit him in the crotch, and the third went through his heart. As he fell, still conscious, bullets struck him in the head and shoulder.

"*Todome* [*Coup de grâce*]!" someone shouted repeatedly. Suzuki felt the muzzle of a pistol pressed against his throat, then heard his wife say, "Don't do it!" At that moment Captain Ando entered. "*Todome?*" asked the man with the pistol.

Two years earlier Captain Ando had come to Suzuki with a program for reform; the admiral had refuted his arguments so forthrightly that Ando still secretly admired him. Now he said that *todome* would be "too cruel," and ordered the men to salute His Excellency. They all knelt by the fallen admiral and presented arms.

"Get up! Leave!" Captain Ando told his men. He turned to Mrs. Suzuki. "Are you *okusan* [madam]?" She nodded. "I have heard about you. I am particularly sorry about this." He said they had no ill feeling toward the admiral. "But our views on how to bring about reformation in Japan differ from His Excellency's, and so we had to come to this."

The captain left, burdened by a sense of guilt and certain Suzuki was dying (one of the maids heard him say that he was going to commit suicide). But miraculously Suzuki would survive to play a leading role in Japan's last days as an empire.

A lieutenant led his men to the large sprawling home of Finance Minister Korekiyo Takahashi. They broke down the door of the inner entrance, and while one group seized half a dozen police guards and servants, the rest roamed through the house, kicking down the doors of room after room looking for their victim.

Minister Takahashi was alone in a spacious ten-mat bedroom. He was a remarkable man who had started as a footman, turned Christian and become president of the Bank of Japan and a member of the House of Peers. The young officers loathed him for having fought the previous year's huge military budget.

Finally the lieutenant entered the minister's room brandishing a pistol. He kicked the quilt off Takahashi, crying *"Tenchu!"* (Punishment of Heaven!). Takahashi looked up unafraid and shouted "Idiot!" at the lieutenant, who hesitated before emptying his pistol into the old man. Another rebel officer leaped forward and with a shout swung his sword with such force that it cut through the padded coat Takahashi was wearing for extra warmth and severed his right arm; he then stabbed the minister through the belly and slashed him viciously right and left.

Mrs. Takahashi burst from her room in the attached Western-style section, and at the sight of her disemboweled husband, cried out in anguish. As the lieutenant shouldered through the crowd of servants gathered horrified in the corridors, he said, "Excuse me for the annoyance I have caused."

Prime Minister Okada had been awakened by the sound of the alarm bell just before five o'clock and moments later his brother-in-law, Denzo Matsuo, a retired colonel, pushed into the bedroom with two police officers.

"They've finally come," said Okada, adding fatalistically that there was nothing anyone could do about it.

"It's no time to talk like that!" shouted the sixty-one-year-old Matsuo. An energetic, dogmatic man, he had insisted on serving his brother-in-law, whether Okada liked it or not, as unofficial factotum without pay. He pulled the reluctant Okada, clad in a thin nightgown, across the corridor toward a secret exit, but on hearing the rebels break down doors, one of the policemen shoved Okada and Matsuo into a bathroom which was used primarily as a storeroom, and closed the door. A moment later they heard shouts from the corridor, several shots, a scuffle, then silence.

"Stay here," said the impetuous Matsuo and left. The Prime Minister tried to follow but in the darkness bumped into a shelf, knocking down several *sake* bottles. He stiffened with fear. Silence. Okada moved again, this time stumbling noisily over the *sake* bottles.

"Don't come out yet!" one of the policemen called weakly from the corridor, so Okada quickly returned to the bathroom. When he heard a voice shouting, "There's someone in the courtyard!" he looked through the window and saw his brother-in-law standing pressed against the building and half a dozen soldiers watching him from inside.

"Shoot him!" yelled their leader, but the soldiers hesitated. "You men will be in Manchuria soon! What are you going to do, if you can't kill a man or two now?"

Reluctantly the men stuck their rifles through the windows and fired into the courtyard.

"*Tenno Heika banzai* [Long live His Majesty the Emperor]!" cried Matsuo and slumped down on a doorstep, bleeding profusely. Painfully he straightened his shoulders, as if on parade, but could not keep from groaning.

Lieutenant Kurihara, followed by Pfc. Kuratomo, pushed their way through a wall of soldiers, rigid with shock. They told Kurihara that it was Prime Minister Okada. The lieutenant hesitated, then turned to Kuratomo and ordered, "*Todome!*"

Kuratomo was reluctant; all he had was a pistol. "Use it!" said Kurihara impatiently.

Against his will Kuratomo leveled the weapon and fired one bullet into Matsuo's chest, another between his eyes. The colonel toppled forward, dyeing the snow red.

Kurihara, who had taken the Prime Minister's photograph from his bedroom, knelt beside the body and compared it with Matsuo's face. "Okada!" he said without hesitation. "*Banzai!*" shouted the soldiers and carried the body to the Prime Minister's bedroom, laying it on a thin mattress.

To find out what had happened, Okada crept out of the bathroom into the corridor. One of the police guards was lying there unconscious, his left arm slashed off; a few yards away the other was jackknifed over a chair, dead. Okada bowed his head in tribute and continued on to his bedroom. Seeing Matsuo's body on the mattress, he sobbed and flung himself down. Finally he rose and began putting on a kimono. As he was tying the strings on an outer garment he heard footsteps and went out to the corridor.

"What's that?" a soldier called out and Okada lurched to a dark corner.

"I just saw something strange," the soldier told several comrades. "It was an old man. But he disappeared like a ghost."

Death seemed to be everywhere and yet by a miracle Okada was alive. Until that moment he had been sure he would die. For the first time he began to think of the future. Had the rebels seized the Palace? Were the *jushin** assassinated? He decided it was his responsibility to stay alive, and once the uprising was suppressed, enforce discipline on the Army. But where could he hide in a house overrun with rebels? The answer was solved for him when he suddenly came upon two maids in the corridor. They hustled him to their room, pushed him into a large closet and covered him with a pile of soiled laundry.

By now two of the attack groups assigned to out-of-town missions had reached their destinations. Lieutenant Taro Takahashi and thirty men broke into the suburban home of Mazaki's successor, Inspector General Jotaro Watanabe. Mrs. Watanabe and a maid tried to stop Takahashi, but he pulled free and broke into the bedroom where the general lay on a *futon* with his young daughter. Takahashi fired a pistol at Watanabe, then drew his sword and slashed at his head.

The other group was ranging through a resort in the mountains in search of Count Nobuaki Makino, whom Saito had succeeded as Privy Seal and who still was one of the Emperor's closest advisers. Unable to find him, the rebels set fire to the hotel to drive him into the open. The old man was led out through the rear of the hotel by his twenty-year-old granddaughter, Kazuko. They struggled up a steep hill, but the soldiers were at their heels and loosed a fusillade. Ignoring the bullets, Kazuko stepped in front of her grandfather and spread out her kimono sleeves. One of the rebels, perhaps moved by the girl's heroism, shouted "Success!" and persuaded his mates to leave.

The third group, the one assigned to kill Prince Saionji, never left Tokyo. At the last moment the officer in charge refused to go; he could not bring himself to do any violence to the last *genro*.

At his home in Okitsu, the aged prince had just wakened from a

---

* Former prime ministers were referred to as *jushin* (senior statesmen); their main duty was to recommend prime ministers to His Majesty.

horrifying dream—he was surrounded by decapitated heads and a heap of bloody bodies. Once news of the uprising was received from the capital, the local police arrived in force and took Saionji to a nearby cottage. Then came a telegram announcing that a large automobile filled with young men in khaki uniform was heading for Okitsu. The prince was wrapped up like a mummy and transferred from place to place to fool the assassins—who turned out to be patent-medicine salesmen.

At the War Minister's official residence, Captain Koda found continued vacillation among the hierarchy. The generals were still reluctant to either join the uprising or confront the rebels. Major Tadashi Katakura, a brilliant, impetuous career officer, was one of the few showing any resolve. The rebels infuriated him. He was not so much against their aims as against disorder and insubordination. The Army, he believed, could only exist through stern discipline and absolute loyalty to the Emperor.

Katakura was in the courtyard of War Minister Kawashima's residence assailing a group of rebels for misusing the power of His Majesty's Army. The Emperor alone had the right to mobilize troops, he shouted, and demanded to see the minister, General Kawashima.

"The Showa Restoration* is what we are all thinking of," he told a crowd that gathered around him. "I feel as you do about the reforms. But we must continue to revere the Emperor and honor the Supreme Command. Don't make private use of the troops."

A rebel commander emerged from the building. "We cannot let you in to see the minister," he said.

"Did the minister himself tell you that?"

"No, Captain Koda gave the order. The minister is just getting

---

* The present ruler, Hirohito, had named his reign Showa (Enlightened Peace). On Japanese calendars the current year, 1936, was Showa 11, the eleventh year of his reign. Only after his death, however, will he be referred to as Emperor Showa. His father, Yoshihito, took the name of Taisho (Great Righteousness). His grandfather, Mutsuhito, chose Meiji (Enlightened Rule); his era saw the greatest reforms and development in Japanese history and was known as the Meiji Restoration. The young reformers of the moment wanted to emulate the achievements of their fathers with the Showa Restoration.

ready to go to the Imperial Palace. Please wait awhile. The situation will soon clear up."

Katakura assumed the rebels were using violence to force the War Minister to help them set up a military government. He started toward the entrance, where General Mazaki was standing aggressively with his legs apart, like one of the *deva* kings that guard Buddhist temples. Katakura had an impulse to rush at Mazaki and stab him—Mazaki must be behind all this; he probably wanted to be prime minister. Katakura controlled himself; first he would find out more what was going on. Just then the Vice Minister came out of the building. Katakura accosted him and asked to have a few words. As the other put him off, the War Minister himself came out of the door buckling on his sword.

Something crashed against Katakura's head and he noticed a peculiar odor. He instantly put his left hand to his head. "You don't have to shoot," he yelled. A pale-faced captain (it was Senichi Isobe, another of the leaders of the uprising) advanced with drawn sword.

"We can talk! Sheathe your sword!" Katakura cried out. Isobe slid it back in its scabbard, then changed his mind and pulled it out again.

"You must be Captain Koda," Katakura continued. "You can't mobilize troops unless you get an imperial order." Faintly he heard someone, perhaps Mazaki, say, "We must not shed blood like this."

He staggered, and several officers helped him to the War Minister's car. As it was passing through the main gate, he dimly saw several *kempei*. "Get the *kempei* in the car," he exclaimed. They did. Someone suggested they take him to the Army Hospital or the Army Medical College, and again he forced himself to speak: "No . . . some private hospital in the city." He didn't want to be assassinated in bed.

3.

William Henry Chamberlin, chief Far Eastern correspondent for the *Christian Science Monitor,* first heard of the rebellion from a Japanese news agency. In town he encountered a rash of conflicting rumors. The Ministry of Foreign Affairs was open and unoccupied by rebels, but no one was there to tell the foreign correspondents what was going on. Troops were posted at the main crossings in the center of Tokyo. Chamberlin didn't know whose side they were on. Was any government in existence?

The office workers throughout the city had no idea this was anything but an ordinary day until police detoured their buses around the Imperial Palace and government offices. By now the violence was over. The rebels occupied a square mile of central Tokyo—the Diet Building and the entire area around the Prime Minister's residence—and were using the Sanno Hotel as a temporary headquarters. They commandeered tablecloths from the Peers Club dining room, paid for them, and made them into banners reading in black ink, "Revere the Emperor—Restoration Army," and hoisted them over the Prime Minister's residence.

When General Rokuro Iwasa, head of the *kempeitai,* learned of the revolt he got out of bed, half paralyzed from palsy, and drove to the rebel area. Here he was stopped by guards. "Is this the Emperor's Army?" he asked and wept in mortification.

The rebels were distributing their "manifesto" to all newspapers and news agencies. The police impounded almost every copy, but correspondent Chamberlin managed to get one. To most Westerners it seemed further proof of the inscrutability of the Orient, but to Chamberlin, a student of Japanese history, it made frightening sense.

The national essence [*kokutai*] of Japan, as a land of the gods, exists in the fact that the Emperor reigns with undiminished power from time immemorial into the farthest future in order that the natural beauty of the country may be propagated throughout the universe, so that all men under the sun may be able to enjoy their lives to the fullest extent. . . .

In recent years, however, there have appeared many persons whose chief aim and purpose have been to amass personal material wealth, disregarding the general welfare and prosperity of the Japanese people, with the result that the sovereignty of the Emperor has been greatly impaired. The people of Japan have suffered deeply as a result of this tendency and many vexing issues now confronting Japan are attributable to this fact.

The *genro,* the senior statesmen, military cliques, plutocrats, bureaucrats and political parties are all traitors who are destroying the national essence. . . .

It is our duty to remove the evil retainers from around the Throne and to smash the group of senior statesmen. It is our duty as subjects of His Majesty the Emperor.

May the gods bless and help us in our endeavor to save the land of our ancestors from the worst that confronts it.

Near the edge of the rebel zone at the American Embassy, Ambassador Grew cabled the first news of the revolt to the State Department:

THE MILITARY TOOK PARTIAL POSSESSION OF THE GOVERNMENT AND CITY EARLY THIS MORNING AND IT IS REPORTED HAVE ASSASSINATED SEVERAL PROMINENT MEN. IT IS IMPOSSIBLE AS YET TO CONFIRM ANYTHING. THE NEWS CORRESPONDENTS ARE NOT PERMITTED TO SEND TELEGRAMS OR TO TELEPHONE ABROAD. THIS TELEGRAM IS BEING SENT PRIMARILY AS A TEST MESSAGE, TO ASCERTAIN IF OUR CODE TELEGRAMS WILL BE TRANSMITTED. CODE ROOM PLEASE ACKNOWLEDGE IMMEDIATELY UPON RECEIPT.

The German embassy was also in range of rebel fire. Here the unofficial correspondent for the *Frankfurter Zeitung* and secretary to the military attaché was writing his preliminary report on the revolt—one copy for the German Foreign Ministry and a duplicate for the Red Army's Fourth Bureau, Intelligence. This was Dr. Richard Sorge, born in Russia of a German father and Russian mother and raised in Germany. Sorge was flamboyant and resourceful. He had managed to gain the complete confidence of the German ambassador, General Eugen Ott (who unwittingly supplied Sorge with some of the most devastating intelligence material which he sent to Moscow), and their business relationship had grown into a warm personal friendship. He was irresistible to women and was at the time writing love letters to his first wife in Russia, living with a second in Tokyo and carrying on several love affairs. He could not resist alcohol in any form and often shocked his fellow countrymen by drunken bouts which were sometimes staged. He was a Communist of bohemian bent (his great-uncle had been friends with Marx and Engels) who had joined the Nazi party as a cover for his role as head of the Red Army spy ring in the Far East. It had taken him almost two years to set up his organization in Japan, and this rebellion was his first genuine test.

The coup, he later wrote, had "a very typical Japanese character and hence its motivations required particular study. A discerning study of it, and, in particular, a study of the social strains and internal crisis it revealed, was of much greater value to an understanding of Japan's internal structure than mere records of troop strength or secret documents." Once the report was dispatched to Moscow, Sorge ordered his ring to find out all possible details of the uprising. Then he induced the German ambassador and the military and naval attachés to make independent investigations and share their findings with him.

At the Palace the War Minister had just informed the Emperor about the rebellion. Ordinarily, if His Majesty spoke at all, it would be in vague terms, but today he was so distressed that he replied directly. "This event is extremely regrettable regardless of the question of spirit. In my judgment this action mars the glory of our national essence." Later he confided to his chief aide-de-camp that he felt the Army was going "to tie its own neck with floss silk"— that is, no more than gently admonish the rebels.

The role the Emperor played was difficult if not impossible for foreigners to understand. His powers and duties were unlike those of any other monarch in the world. His grandfather, Meiji, a man of strong will and conviction, had led the nation from semifeudalism to modern times under the slogans "Rich Country, Strong Army" and "Civilization and Enlightenment"; in his reign the welfare of the nation took precedence over that of the individual. Meiji's heir, Taisho, was an eccentric who once rolled up a speech he was to make to the Diet and used it as a telescope; his antics and tantrums became so exaggerated that his heir, the crown prince, was named regent in 1921. Five years later, on Christmas Day, Taisho died and his twenty-five-year-old son became emperor.

Since childhood Hirohito had been trained for this role principally by Prince Saionji, who himself had been influenced by the French Revolution and English liberalism. Time and again the last *genro* would tell the young man that Japan needed a father figure, not a despot, and that he should therefore assume a position of responsibility in all affairs of state, yet never issue any positive order on his own volition. He should be objective and selfless.

Theoretically the Emperor had plenary power; all state decisions needed his sanction. But according to tradition, once the Cabinet and military leaders had agreed on a policy, he could not withhold his approval. He was to remain above politics and transcend party considerations and feuds, for he represented the entire nation.

All these restrictions notwithstanding, he exercised prodigious influence since he was in the unique position of being able to warn or approve without getting involved. More important, every Japanese was pledged to serve him unto death. This moral power was so potent that he used it sparingly and then only in vague terms. Those reporting to the Throne had to divine his wishes, since he almost always spoke cryptically without expression.

A more positive emperor, like his grandfather, might have consolidated his power; by the Meiji Constitution he was Commander in Chief of the Armed Forces. But Hirohito was a studious man who would rather be a scientist than a monarch. His happiest days were Monday and Saturday when he could retire to his modest laboratory and study marine biology. Neither did he have the slightest wish to be a despot. From his trip to Europe as crown prince he had brought back a taste for whiskey, Occidental music and golf, along with an abiding respect for the English version of constitutional monarchy. He could also defy tradition and court pressure when principle was involved. After the Empress Nagako had given birth to four daughters he refused to take a concubine or two so he could sire a male heir—and within a few years was rewarded with two sons by Nagako.

He was an unlikely-looking emperor, slouching around the Palace in frayed, baggy trousers and crooked tie, dreamily peering through glasses as thick as portholes, so oblivious of his appearance that occasionally his jacket would be fastened with the wrong button. He disliked buying new clothes, on the grounds that he couldn't "afford" them. He was so frugal that he even refrained from buying books he wanted, and he wore down every pencil to a stub. He was completely without vanity, a natural and unaffected individual who looked and acted like a village mayor. Yet this small round-shouldered man had some of the qualifications of a great one: he was pure, free of pride, ambition and selfishness. He wanted what was best for the nation.

His subjects regarded him as a god, and children were warned that they would be struck blind if they dared look at his face. If a public speaker mentioned the word "Emperor" the entire audience would sit at attention. If a reporter had the temerity to ask a personal question about the Emperor, he was icily told one should not pose such queries about a deity.

But "god" did not mean in Japan what it meant in the West. To a Japanese the emperor was a god, just as his own mother, father and teacher were lesser gods. His reverence for the monarch was not only a feeling of awe but also of affection and obligation, and no matter how low his station, each subject felt a family kinship to the emperor, who was the father of them all. As Meiji lay on his deathbed, all Japan prayed for his recovery and multitudes remained in the Palace plaza day and night; the entire nation grieved his death as a single family. For Japan *was* one great family, a modernized clan which had evolved from a number of warring tribes.

Every child was taught *kodo,* the Imperial Way: that the basis for Japanese morality was *on* (obligation) to the emperor and one's parents. Without the emperor one would be without country; without parents, homeless. For centuries the Japanese ruler had been benevolent, never attempting to exert his authority. Just as a parent loved and guided his children, he loved and guided his people with compassion. The imperial line had once gone 346 years without sanctioning a single execution throughout the land.

Out of the present Emperor's vague status evolved an almost autocratic power for the Army and Navy Chiefs of Staff. They had become, in essence, responsible to themselves alone. Only once had the Emperor challenged the military and that was in 1928 upon learning of the assassination of old Marshal Chang Tso-lin by the Ishihara-Itagaki group. His fury was such that he forgot his rigid training and sharply criticized the Prime Minister. Prince Saionji, who was the influence behind the Emperor's distrust of the military, was just as angry—but his target was the Emperor. He spoke out as a teacher, not as a subject, and accused Hirohito of acting like a tyrant. The old man's rebuke so shook the Emperor that with three exceptions, he would never again fail to follow the last *genro's* primary rule: "Reign, not rule."*

4.

Okada's secretary, Hisatsune Sakomizu, had returned to the Prime Minister's official residence with the rebels' permission, and when he found his father-in-law safe in the closet he whispered, "I'll come back; keep up your spirits," and returned to his own home to plan a rescue. Shortly before ten o'clock an official of the Imperial Household Ministry phoned, with polite condolences on the Prime Minister's demise. He said the Emperor wished to send an imperial messenger to the family; should the messenger go to the ministry or to Okada's home?

Fearing the phone was tapped, Sakomizu put him off; the truth had to be reported in person to the Emperor, and Sakomizu changed into a morning suit, with a bulletproof vest underneath. Armed with an umbrella, he walked across the street to the official residence, and after an argument got authorization from the rebels to pass through their lines. He took a taxi to the Hirakawa Gate of the Imperial Palace grounds, and struggled on foot through the deep snow to the concrete headquarters of the Imperial Household Ministry.

Household Minister Kurahei Yuasa began to express his condolences, but Sakomizu interrupted to tell him Okada was still alive. Startled, Yuasa dropped something, said he must relay the good news to His Majesty and disappeared. He must have run all the way to the Emperor's wing of the rambling building and back, for he returned in minutes to tell Sakomizu in a solemn voice, "When I reported that Prime Minister Okada was alive, His Majesty was most pleased. He said, 'That is excellent,' and told me to bring Okada to safety as soon as possible."

Sakomizu suggested that they get help from the commander of

---

* Prince Mikasa, the Emperor's youngest brother, was convinced that the assassination of Chang was the basic cause of war with America. It not only actuated the Manchurian Incident but was the turning point in his brother's role as emperor. Prince Mikasa revealed this in an interview on December 27, 1966.

the 1st Division, who could send troops to rescue Okada. Yuasa disagreed; it would be too risky because the commander would have to get clearance from his superiors. "And you never know which way *they* are looking."

This made sense and Sakomizu decided to seek help from a more independent source. He went into a room filled with high-ranking officers. They all looked worried, as if they were about to be reprimanded. Many expressed regrets at Okada's death, but a few rudely remarked that something like this was bound to happen, since the Prime Minister ignored the Army's suggestions.

The rebels' manifesto was being passed around and hotly debated but nobody seemed to be in charge. War Minister Kawashima appeared to be completely perplexed; he certainly couldn't be depended on. Sakomizu surveyed the gathering in dismay. This was the hierarchy of the Army and it was a mob—vacillating, undependable, opportunistic. There was not one he felt he could trust with his secret, so he elbowed his way out of the crowd. He went into another room where the Cabinet was convening and found just as chaotic a scene. The ministers were apprehensive and truculent and doing nothing until the arrival of their senior member, Minister of the Interior Fumio Goto. They descended on Sakomizu, deluging him with questions about the Prime Minister. How had he died? Where was the body? Who killed him? While Sakomizu gave evasive answers, he caught sight of someone he could trust—the Navy Minister, who was an old friend of Okada's and a fellow admiral. Picking his words carefully in case someone was eavesdropping, Sakomizu said, "Mr. Minister, we'd like to claim the body of a senior member of the Navy. Will you send a landing force unit to the Prime Minister's residence to give us protection?"

The admiral failed to see through this charade and said, "Impossible. What if it ends in a skirmish between the Army and Navy?"

Sakomizu lowered his voice. "I'm going to tell you something important. Now, if you don't accept my proposal, I would like you to forget everything I say." Sakomizu informed the puzzled minister that Okada was still alive and should be rescued by naval troops.

"I haven't heard a thing," said the embarrassed admiral and drifted away.

There didn't seem to be anyone else to turn to and Sakomizu

began to dream up wild schemes. He thought of imitating the dramatic balloon escape from Paris of French President Gambetta during the Franco-Prussian War, until he realized there were only advertising balloons in Tokyo. What about spiriting Okada and Matsuo's body out of the residence in one coffin? No, that would take a suspiciously large coffin. It was already past noon and every moment counted. Desperate, he wandered restlessly from room to room, at a loss as to what to do.

By midafternoon there was a semblance of normalcy in the streets outside the square mile held by the rebels. Boys on bicycles pedaled through the snow with groceries. Shopkeepers near the edge of the action came out in their aprons and quizzed the young soldiers manning the barricades. Nobody seemed to know much about anything.

The Army leaders still vacillated. Though they were all repelled by the seditious actions of the rebels, so many agreed in principle with their aims that no decision could be reached. They couldn't even agree on an appeal to Captain Koda and his comrades, not until it was watered down and hopelessly vague. Labeled an "admonition," it failed to call them what they were—rebels:

1. The purpose of the uprising has reached the Emperor's ears.
2. Your action has been recognized as motivated by your sincere feelings to seek manifestation of the national essence.
3. The present state of manifestation of *kokutai* is such that we feel unbearably awed.
4. The War Councilors unanimously agree to endeavor to attain the above purposes.
5. Anything else will be subject to the Emperor's wishes.

This was published at three o'clock in the afternoon, along with a ridiculous emergency defense order placing the center of Tokyo under the jurisdiction of the 1st Division, the unit that had revolted. It was an attempt at expediency; with orders to guard the area they had seized, the rebels supposedly would regard themselves as loyal government troops.

Neither the conciliatory "admonition" nor the emergency order had the desired effect; they merely convinced Koda's group that a large segment of the military hierarchy was on their side. Koda's answer was: "If our original demands are granted, we will obey your orders. Otherwise we cannot evacuate the territory we have occupied."

That night reinforcements arrived from Kofu and Sakura to take up positions opposite the barricades. At the American embassy, observers on the roof could see the rebel banner waving from the Prime Minister's residence and the Sanno Hotel. Mrs. Grew was so nervous that she insisted on sleeping in a different room, even though the ambassador assured her that the last thing the insurgents wanted was trouble with the United States.

A few blocks away a car drove up to *kempeitai* headquarters and three spruce military figures stepped out—Captain Koda and two other rebel leaders. As they marched through the entrance to continue negotiations with the Army, two sentries smartly presented arms.

"*Bakayaro* [Idiot]!" shouted a noncom leaning out of a window. "Saluting rebel officers! They aren't the Imperial Army!"

The three spent the next thirty minutes listening to Generals Mazaki and Araki urge them to end the rebellion, but again conciliation only made them more steadfast.

At the Imperial Household Ministry, Interior Minister Goto had finally arrived after a curious six-hour delay to get himself appointed "temporary and concurrent prime minister." A few minutes later he was listening to demands for martial law by War Minister Kawashima. Goto and the other civilians in the Cabinet feared this might degenerate into a military dictatorship and argued that since this was strictly an Army insurrection which had nothing to do with the public, it should be settled within the Army itself.

Kawashima replied that there must have been instigators from the outside and it was therefore necessary to take extraordinary measures to ensure the nation's safety. Feeble as this retort was, it swayed the undecided members and at a meeting held at midnight in the presence of the Emperor it was agreed that martial law should be declared at once.

By this time a *kempei* sergeant had been told of Okada's whereabouts: one of his men, permitted to bring out the dead and wounded police officers, had chanced to open the closet where the Prime Minister was sitting resigned like a Buddha. The startling news about Okada was reported to their commander, who decided not to relay the information to his own superiors—if it was a mistake, he'd be ridiculed, and if true, some *kempei* sympathetic to the rebels would tell them and Okada would be killed. But to the sergeant, Keisuke Kosaka, this was dereliction of duty. On his own initiative he and two volunteers stole through the rebel lines late that night and just before dawn of February 27 boldly marched into the Prime Minister's residence. Kosaka went directly to the maid's room, opened the closet, assured Okada he would soon be rescued, and crossed the street to get help from a secretary of the Prime Minister's named Ko Fukuda who lived next door to Sakomizu.

The secretary and the sergeant cautiously sounded each other out as they sipped black tea until Kosaka finally revealed that Okada was alive. Only then did Fukuda admit that he and Sakomizu also knew and hoped to smuggle Okada out of the ministry in a crowd of mourners that would soon arrive to pay their respects.

In the next half-hour the resourceful sergeant and his two men spirited a suit of Western clothes for Okada from the bedroom and commandeered a car in the courtyard. They were just in time. Two black sedans pulled up and a dozen condolence callers filed into the ministry. Fukuda led them to the bedroom, where one of the sergeant's men was waiting to make sure they wouldn't get close enough to the corpse to realize it wasn't the Prime Minister.

While the callers burned incense and honored the dead, Fukuda and Kosaka practically carried the cramped Okada, his face half hidden behind a germ mask, to the rear. A group of rebels stood at the door and Kosaka called out authoritatively, "Emergency patient! He shouldn't have taken a look at the corpse."

The rebels stepped aside and the trio was in the courtyard. But there was no car waiting, and curious to see what was going on, the commander of the guard approached. Suddenly the commandeered car drew up. Fukuda opened the door, pushed the exhausted Okada into the 1935 Ford and climbed in after him. Kosaka watched with pounding heart as the car drove slowly through the gates and disappeared. Tears flowed down his face and he remained standing there as if in a trance.

So Okada had escaped, but there was still the problem of getting rid of Matsuo's body before someone discovered the deception. This was Sakomizu's task but he felt it would be best to do nothing until Okada was in a secure hiding place. Hour after hour he sat in lonely vigil next to the corpse. At last the phone rang. His wife reported that her father was safe in a Buddhist temple. Now Sakomizu could act. First he phoned the Imperial Household Ministry to tell of Okada's escape, then called the Okada home to ask that a coffin be sent to the official residence as soon as possible. The answer was that a ready-made coffin wasn't proper for a Prime Minister, and it would take several hours to make one.

The delay began to unnerve Sakomizu: he'd be found out and murdered. As his terror grew he recalled that in his father's day boys used to hold a contest of courage called *shibedate* (standing a rice stalk on end). One boy would put some object on a grave; the next would retrieve it; a third would stick a rice stalk on the grave. This went on and on until someone lost his nerve. The boys believed that fear came only if their testicles shrank, so when they walked toward the grave they would pluck at them to stretch them out. Sakomizu discovered that, sure enough, his testicles had contracted to almost nothing. He managed to stretch them and to his amazement found his own fear disappearing. People in the old days were clever.

It was dark by the time the coffin finally arrived. Sakomizu dismissed the pallbearers, wrapped Matsuo's body completely in a blanket and got it in the coffin. As the cortege slowly left the ministry, the rebel in charge saluted and said a few courteous words of farewell. The funeral carriage moved quietly through the gate, and after a harrowing trip, safely reached the home of the Prime Minister. A crowd had already collected for services. A tombstone was placed on the coffin along with a large photograph of Okada, framed in black ribbon.

Sakomizu gave strict orders not to open the coffin and was off for the Imperial Household Ministry, where Cabinet members had again gathered. Now he told them that Okada was still alive, and while they were recovering from the shock, proposed that the Prime Minister see the Emperor as soon as possible. To Sakomizu's amazement, Acting Prime Minister Goto protested: Okada was responsible for the rebellion and should resign on the spot. Goto refused to listen to any explanations—apparently he liked being prime minister—and Sakomizu was compelled to phone influential men for support.

He found none. The consensus was that if the rebel troops learned that Okada was on the Palace grounds they might fire toward the Palace. And that would be "too appalling." In resignation Sakomizu phoned Fukuda not to bring Okada there and returned to the Okada home to see that the prefuneral ceremonies went off without discovery of the deception—otherwise the rebels would start a manhunt.

Mrs. Matsuo sat silently in front of the coffin. As the hours passed and she asked no questions about her husband, Sakomizu felt such pity that he could no longer hold back the truth. He gathered the Prime Minister's close relatives, including three of his four children and three of Matsuo's four children, and controlling his emotions, told how Colonel Matsuo had sacrificed his life so that the Prime Minister could escape.

"I am very pleased if my husband could be of service," said the widow softly. She was the daughter of a samurai.

5.

By now the mutiny had a name, the 2/26 (February 26) Incident, and though the attitude of the military leaders was beginning to harden, it took the Emperor himself to get them into action. Exasperated by their dallying, he stepped out of his role for the first time since the murder of Marshal Chang and spoke out clearly: "If the Army cannot subdue the rebels, I will go out and dissuade them myself."

This forced the Army to issue an edict at 5:06 A.M., February 28. It ordered the rebels, in the Emperor's name, to "speedily withdraw" from their present positions and return to their respective units. Inhabitants in the danger zones would be evacuated; if the rebels had not withdrawn by 8 A.M. the following day, they would be fired on.

This order split the rebels into two camps: one wanted to obey the Emperor; the other insisted it was not truly the wish of the Emperor but the result of pressure from the Control clique.

During the day Sakomizu met with more disappointment. Goto still opposed Okada's visit to the Emperor, and in any case, the police refused to provide an escort for the Prime Minister to the Palace—it was "too grave a responsibility." Fearing that Okada might commit hara-kiri, Sakomizu ignored Goto and the police and brought the Prime Minister to the Imperial Household Ministry.

Shortly before seven o'clock in the evening the old man was escorted to the Emperor's wing of the building. In the corridors they passed Household officials who stared in terror at the grim-faced Okada, imagining they were seeing a ghost. A few ran off as the rest crouched in fright.

Once in the imperial presence, the Prime Minister humbly apologized for the mutiny, as if it had been his fault, and offered his resignation. "Carry on your duty for as long as you live," the Emperor replied and added that he was very pleased.

Okada was too awed to speak or stop the flow of tears but finally managed to say, "I am going to behave myself from now on." This time the Emperor did not reply.

Okada slept that night in the Household Ministry but Sakomizu returned to the Prime Minister's home, which was still crowded with mourners. A group of irate admirals hemmed him in. "As a samurai, how dared you surrender the castle?" one shouted. "Even with the Prime Minister dead, you should have stayed to protect his body and defend the official residence to the death. How can you be so irresponsible as to run off to the Imperial Household Ministry for what business I don't know!"

They were disgusted with the way Sakomizu was handling the funeral arrangements and said they were taking the body to the Navy Officers Club the next day for a proper service. Sakomizu begged them to be patient, but was immediately set upon by yet another admiral: "Your father was a fine military man. I arranged your marriage for you because, since you are his son, I thought you'd be a reliable man. But you've proven by this case to be a miserable fellow, a weak-kneed man unable even to manage a funeral. Okada must be weeping for having given his daughter to such a fellow. Your father is weeping too. Pull yourself together!"

Despite the Emperor's edict, all but a few of the rebels refused to withdraw. As more Army reinforcements invested Tokyo from outlying cities, the Combined Fleet steamed into Tokyo Bay and landing forces took positions outside the Navy Ministry and other naval installations. The younger men were itching for action and revenge: three of their senior officers—Admirals Saito, Suzuki and Okada—had been assassinated or gravely wounded by the Army. One young officer, whose ship's main guns were trained on the Diet Building, was "tempted by an impulse" to blow off the tower but controlled himself.

At six o'clock in the morning on February 29—it was leap year— the Army announced: "We are positively going to suppress the rebels who caused disturbances in the neighborhood of Kojimachi in the imperial capital." For the first time the word "rebels" was officially used. It was a cloudy day with a threat of more snow. Except for soldiers, it was a dead city. Schools were closed; there were no streetcars or trains. It was impossible to make a phone call or send a telegram. Tokyo was isolated. All civilian traffic in the city was suspended while the Army marshaled its forces for the attack, but even as tanks were brought to assault positions, other tanks clanked up to rebel barricades, their sides placarded with messages invoking the insurgents to "respectfully follow the Emperor's order" and withdraw at once. Fully loaded bombers droned overhead while other planes dropped leaflets addressed to noncommissioned officers:

1. Return to your units. It is not yet too late.
2. All those who resist are rebels; therefore, we will shoot them.
3. Your parents and brothers are weeping to see you become traitors.

An advertising balloon was raised above the Aviation Building, its long trailer in large characters reading: IMPERIAL ORDER ISSUED. DON'T RESIST THE ARMY FLAG. Loudspeakers were brought up to strategic places, and Chokugen Wada, the noted announcer of radio station NHK, began reading a plea to the rebel enlisted men in a choked voice: "You faithfully and sincerely obeyed your officers, trusting their orders to be just. But the Emperor now orders you to return to your units. If you continue to resist, you will be traitors for disobeying the Emperor's order. You believed you were doing the right thing but now that you realize you were wrong, you must not continue to revolt against His Majesty and inflict upon yourselves eternal disgrace as traitors. It is not too late. Your past crime will be forgiven. Your fathers and brothers, as well as the entire nation, sincerely pray that you do this. Immediately leave your present positions and come back."

The rebellious soldiers began to look at one another questioningly. Still each waited for the other to act first. By midmorning the solidarity of the ranks began to crack. Thirty noncoms and soldiers walked away from their positions with rifles and machine guns. By noon almost all enlisted men had returned to their units except for small detachments at the Prime Minister's official residence and the Sanno Hotel. At two o'clock the banner flying over the Prime Minister's residence came down and an hour later Army headquarters announced by radio that the rebels had surrendered without a shot being fired.

The leaders of the insurrection were still at the War Ministry and the Sanno Hotel, but the loyal troops made no attempt to capture them; they were giving the rebels a chance to act like samurai. General Araki, who admired their spirit and sympathized with their motives, asked them to commit hara-kiri, since they had performed an outrageous, reckless act that grieved the Emperor. The young officers considered mass suicide, but finally decided to submit to a court-martial where, like Aizawa, they could alert the nation to the corruption besetting Japan.

One officer, however, refused to surrender. Captain Shiro Nonaka went off by himself and wrote a final statement regretting that his division hadn't seen action for over thirty years while other units were shedding their blood in glory. "In recent years the sins of the traitors at home have been redeemed by the blood of our comrades in Manchuria and Shanghai. What answer can I give to the souls of these men if I spend the rest of my days in vain here in the capital? Am I insane or am I a fool? There is but one road for me to take." He signed the declaration, then took the road: hara-kiri.

At four-thirty that afternoon the weary Sakomizu assembled the mourners at Okada's home to read a prepared statement revealing the details of Matsuo's death and Okada's escape. The listeners

Gekokujo

were stunned to silence. Finally someone shouted *"Banzai!"* All the others joined and the news was spread throughout the neighborhood.

The 2/26 Incident was over. What violence there was had been incredibly bloody; yet only seven people had been killed and the mutineers had surrendered peacefully. The most outstanding feats of courage had been performed by women, and the vacillation by generals. To most foreigners the mutiny was no more than another ultranationalist bloodbath, and few realized its significance. The Soviets did, largely because of Richard Sorge, who correctly guessed that this would lead to expansion into China.*

It was over, but like a stone tossed in a millpond, its ripples were already spreading across the Pacific.

---

* Dr. Sorge's detailed report to Moscow included an analysis of the deep social unrest that had inspired the rebellion. Sorge also sent photographs of the cream of the material gathered by the German military attachés, including a secret pamphlet written the previous year by two of the rebel leaders, entitled "Views on the Housecleaning of the Army." The Fourth Bureau was pleased with its new secret agent and requested additional information: Would it affect Japanese foreign policy? Would it make Japan more anti-Soviet or less?

With the help of a highly connected journalist and an artist turned Communist, Sorge answered all these questions, as well as observing that the 2/26 Incident would result in either social reforms or a policy of permanent expansion. And expansion would go in the direction of China. He was careful to be circumspect and objective, since he was aware that unlike Berlin and Washington, "Moscow knew China and Japan too well to be fooled easily."

To this day a number of informed Japanese believe the meeting was inspired by Communist agents. They claim that General Mazaki secretly conferred with left-wing leaders prior to the rebellion, and point out that not only the young officers but Ikki Kita and other civilian nationalists were unwitting tools of the Communists, whose plan it was to communize Japan through the action of idealists who preached socialism and the Imperial Way simultaneously. Realizing the power of emperor worship, the Communists intended to utilize the imperial system, not do away with it. This theory was somewhat shared by Sorge himself, who later told a friend that Japanese Communists may have had some connection with the uprising and that it was possible to have a Communist Japan ruled by an emperor.

2

To the Marco Polo Bridge

1.

Uneasy relief hung over the five million people of Tokyo, as it had after the great earthquake of 1923. During the mutiny they had shown little sympathy for the young rebels. For the first time public condemnation of mutineers was almost unanimous and there was criticism of the unruly streak running throughout the Army.

At the time of the 5/15 Incident the people had been confident that the militarists and nationalists would smash corrupt party politics and right social wrongs by direct acts of force. But corruption and social injustice had persisted and now, after the past four wild days, the public had lost its blind faith in force and wanted a return to orderly ways—at almost any cost.

And although every performance at the Kabuki Theater of that paean to revenge, violence and bloody self-sacrifice, *The Forty-seven Ronin,* was still packed, there was increasing support for the group in the Army that seemed the answer to chaos—the Control clique. Its very name stood for the need of the hour, discipline, even though what it really advocated was control of China. Civilian leaders, swayed by this same desire for law and order, began a move to crush the Imperial Way clique; and inadvertently jarred open the door to the gradual weakening of their own power by the military.

On the surface it looked as if the civilians had won new power when a new cabinet was formed by Foreign Minister Koki Hirota. Ambassador Grew informed the State Department that Hirota would "curb the dangerous tendencies of the Army in China and Manchuria," and wrote in his diary that he was pleased at the choice "because I believe that Hirota is a strong, safe man and that while he will have to play ball with the Army to a certain extent, I think that he will handle foreign affairs as wisely as they can be handled . . ."

Hirota made a promising start by selecting the openly pro-American diplomat Shigeru Yoshida as his foreign minister, but the Army's protest was so violent that Hirota dropped him. This was only the first of a series of conciliatory moves, climaxed by the new Prime Minister's acceptance of a demand that all future war ministers be approved by the Big Three of the Army. Apparently an innocent move, this return to the old system meant that the policies of the country were now at the mercy of the Army. If the military disapproved of a cabinet, the war minister could resign and the Big Three would simply refuse to approve anyone else, thereby bringing about the fall of the cabinet. The Army could then refuse to provide a minister until a cabinet to their liking was selected. It meant the voluntary abandonment of one of the last civilian controls over the affairs of state.

Although the Army leaders were gaining political control, this was not their primary goal. They were striving above all to prevent another "2/26." They realized that no amount of discipline could control idealistic young officers passionately dedicated to wiping out poverty and corruption. The solution was to eradicate the causes of discontent, which could only be done by correcting what the insurgents considered to be the evils of free economy. Already the settlers of Manchuria were demanding that their planned economy, which had brought such rapid material progress, be applied to the homeland. But who would carry out such a sweeping economic reform? The capitalists were busy defending their interests, and their servants—the politicians—were not only unsuited for the job but had lost the confidence of the public. And since the Army could not openly enter into politics without being corrupted itself, there was but one course left: to "propel reform" without too much involvement.

To forestall public hostility, the Army leaders placed Araki, Mazaki and a dozen other generals sympathetic to the Imperial Way clique on the inactive list and transferred many of the younger officers to unimportant posts.*

Martial law, invoked during the rebellion, continued month after month, with the press rigidly controlled and voices of dissent silenced. The mutineers were tried swiftly and in private. Thirteen officers and four civilians, including Ikki Kita, were sentenced to death. On July 12 they were bound to racks, blindfolded, and their foreheads marked with bull's-eyes. Lieutenant Takahashi, who had helped assassinate General Watanabe, sang a song before remarking, "Indeed, indeed, I hope the privileged classes will reflect upon their conduct and be more prudent." One embittered young officer cried out, "O, people of Japan, don't trust the Imperial Army!" Another shouted, "The people trust the Army! Don't let the Russians beat us!" Almost all gave three *banzai* for His Majesty just before the shots rang out.

Even with the purge of Imperial Way officers, there was a small but influential group in Tokyo dedicated to their main principle— the end of expansion. Their leader was the man who had engineered the seizure of Manchuria, Kanji Ishihara. Now on the General Staff, he had become appalled by the results of his own deed. He had dreamed of a democratic Manchuria comprised of five nationalities, all living in harmony as well as providing a bulwark against Russian aggression. But this idealistic goal had degenerated into a determination by the Army leadership to use Manchuria as a base for a takeover of North China.

Soon after the execution of the mutineers, Ishihara secretly met with eleven other key officers from the War Ministry and Army General Staff at the Takara-tei restaurant in Tokyo. These men shared his fear of expansion into China and had convened to discuss what should be done.

---

* In an interview a few weeks before his death in 1966 General Araki said, "We [Imperial Way] were idealists, they [Control] were pragmatists. We thought force was necessary at times but it was more important to set the nation in a proper course according to Meiji's five principles. Therefore it was not right simply to crush China." He then added wryly, "But those who speak of ideals lose. The realists always get their own way in the end."

Ishihara opened with a question: Why risk war with China when the most dangerous enemy was their traditional foe, Russia? Two wars at once would be suicidal to a Japan weak in heavy industries, he continued. Instead the nation should concentrate all its energies on expanding its productive power until it could compete with that of the Soviet Union. To attain self-sufficiency in heavy industry, Japan would have to develop the resources of Manchuria in a series of five-year programs, avoiding all conflicts with Russia and China. When Japanese industry reached its peak in 1952, then an all-out war could be waged with Russia—and won. This alone could save Japan, not the expansion policy of the Control clique which called for a push into China and perhaps Southeast Asia that had to result in war with Britain and America. If this happened, the only one to profit would be the real enemy, Russia. Ishihara added that the greatest danger to the nation lay not in Tokyo, with the hierarchy comprised of men open to reason and persuasion, but in Manchuria.

In that country, influential radicals in the Kwantung Army were already organizing unauthorized forays into North China. Their leader was Major General Kenji Doihara, much like Ishihara with the same brilliance, flamboyance and talent for intrigue. He had already been nicknamed "The Lawrence of Manchuria" by Western newsmen. The previous year he had gone alone into North China inveigling the war lords and officials of the northernmost five provinces to break away from China and form an autonomous government under the wing of the Imperial Japanese Army. Once Prime Minister Okada learned this, he had sent out word to check the impetuous Doihara. But he ignored Tokyo—as had Ishihara—and continued to plot so successfully that an autonomous government of sorts was set up. Opportunistic Japanese merchants flooded into North China under their slogan "Follow the Japanese Flag," irritating Chinese merchants and stirring up anti-Japanese feeling all over China. Doihara claimed he had established the puppet regime merely as a buffer between Manchuria and China, but a few weeks later he brought in five thousand Japanese troops on the grounds that Japanese merchants needed protection from bandits.

Now Ishihara charged that this influx of troops was but the beginning of a mass raid into China and that Doihara's buffer area was "a poisonous flower" which should be destroyed before it involved Japan in total war with Nationalist forces under Chiang Kai-shek. Both the Russians and the Chinese Communists were plotting to this end so they could step in once both sides were exhausted and establish a Red China.

Ishihara concluded that the best way to curb Doihara was to get back to their offices and advise their chiefs to remove Japanese troops from trouble spots in North China. One such was the ancient Marco Polo Bridge fifteen miles southwest of Peking.

Japanese troops had been stationed in the Peking area ever since an international expeditionary force—including European, American and Japanese troops—suppressed the bloody, xenophobic Boxer Rebellion in 1900. The next year the chastened Chinese signed the so-called Boxer Protocol allowing certain foreign powers to occupy key points near Peking "for the maintenance of open communications between the capital and the sea."

With the Boxers crushed, China became even more of a plundering ground for Western imperialism, but the continued depredation of her resources at last stirred her people to revolt. Long ago Napoleon had sounded the warning that China was but a sleeping giant: "Let him sleep! For when he wakes he will move the world."

In 1911 the collapse of the decadent Manchu Empire under the attacks of Dr. Sun Yat-sen, China's first genuine nationalist, finally wakened the sleeping giant. At once the fledgling republic was besieged on all sides by local war lords hungry for spoils, and although Dr. Sun's Kuomintang (National People's Party) continued to gain support throughout the country, China was torn to pieces. Finally, after a dozen frustrating years of bloody conflict, Dr. Sun called for help from a country which was glad to oblige —the Soviet Union. Soon Canton was swarming with Communists offering advice on everything from mass propaganda to military tactics. The moving spirit behind the Kuomintang armies called himself Galen but was in truth a Soviet general named Bluecher; and the chief political adviser was a colorful man who had taught in a Chicago business college and was one of the Kremlin's top political agitators, Michael Borodin. With their help the republic grew in power, and its armies, under an able young general, Chiang Kai-shek, crushed its war-lord foes and pushed north, capturing

Shanghai and Nanking. But success brought a much greater problem, the rising power of Communism within the ranks of the Kuomintang itself. In 1927 Chiang, now Sun's successor, concluded that continued help from Russia would lead to a Red China; he outlawed the Communists.* From that day until the 2/26 Incident a triple war raged through China. On Monday, Kuomintang troops fought war lords; on Tuesday, the two would unite to fight one of the growing Red armies; and on Wednesday, war lords and Communists would jointly fall upon Chiang Kai-shek.

This constant turmoil, along with the relentless surge of international Communism, alarmed Japanese military leaders. They were threatened from the north by Stalin's bombers in Vladivostok, less than seven hundred miles from Tokyo, and from the west by the bourgeoning legions of the Chinese Communists under a determined peasant named Mao Tse-tung.**

To the militarists, there was no choice but to consolidate Manchuria, which lay between the two threats, as a breakwater against Communism. Those in the Control clique further argued that Manchuria was not enough and North China should also be

---

* After he had been forced to leave China, Borodin reportedly said, "When the next Chinese general comes to Moscow and shouts, 'Hail to the world revolution!,' better send at once for the OGPU. All that any of them want is rifles."

** On their part, the Soviets accused America and Britain of plotting against them in Asia. *A Short History of the U.S.S.R.*, Part II, put out by the Academy of Sciences of the U.S.S.R. Institute of History, states: "In April 1927, political circles in Britain and the U.S.A. tried to provoke a military conflict between the Soviet Union and China. Police and troops broke into the Soviet Embassy in Peking, arrested members of the staff and searched and ransacked the premises. This provocation was instigated by representatives of the Western powers, a fact which was confirmed by the Chinese chargé d'affaires in the U.S.S.R. in his reply to the Soviet protest note. He stated quite clearly that the action of the Chinese military authorities and police had been prearranged with Western diplomats." This same work further declares: "In the summer of 1929 . . . ruling circles in the U.S.A., Japan, Britain and France made another attempt to provoke a Sino-Soviet clash and involve the U.S.S.R. in war in the Far East. On May 27, 1929, bandits attacked the Soviet consulate in Harbin, and on July 10, Chinese militarists tried to seize the Chinese Eastern Railway, which was administered jointly by the U.S.S.R. and China . . . In September and October 1929, detachments of Chinese militarists and Russian whiteguards invaded Soviet territory." No corroborating evidence could be found to these accusations.

seized. A state of anarchy existed throughout that area, and the considerable Japanese interests there needed protection. The claim of anarchy was somewhat justified. According to the *Survey by the Royal Institute of International Affairs,* banditry was rampant but Communism itself had become "an organized and effective political power exercising exclusive administrative authority over large stretches of territory." There were also indications that the Chinese Communists were in league with the Soviets. "The possibility that Chinese and Russian Communism might join hands was thus to be reckoned with if Chinese Communism were Communism in the Russian sense."

Most of the world lived in terror of Communism, and it was not remarkable that the Control clique regarded its spread in China as Japan's principal danger. For the Chinese Communists, unlike those in America and Europe, were not merely members of a party but actual rivals of the national government, with their own laws and sphere of action. Already large sections of China had been Sovietized, and Shanghai itself was a fount of Communist propaganda.

At this time Mao was declaring that his Red troops alone were fighting the Japanese, while Chiang was simply waging a "war of extermination" against Communism. "I solemnly declare here, in the name of the Chinese Soviet government," he told Western newsmen, "that if Chiang Kai-shek's army or any other army ceases hostilities against the Red Army, then the Chinese Soviet government will immediately order the Red Army to stop military action against them. . . . If Chiang Kai-shek really means to take up the struggle against Japan, then obviously the Chinese Soviet government will extend to him the hand of friendship on the field of battle against Japan."

This call for a united front, which had originated in Moscow, failed to move Chiang, but one of his most important field commanders, Chang Hsueh-liang, was not so adamant and Mao decided to work through him. Chang was known as "the Young Marshal," since his father was Old Marshal Chang Tso-lin, whose assassination had led to the Japanese occupation of Manchuria. Though the Young Marshal commanded the Northeastern Army, which had been ordered by the Kuomintang to wipe out all Red forces in North China, he had serious reservations about Chiang's course; he had come to believe that those he was fighting were also patriots and perhaps both sides should unite against the Japanese.

In the fall of 1936 Mao sent his most able negotiator, Chou En-lai, to work out a truce with the Young Marshal. Chou was mild-mannered, soft-spoken, almost effeminate-looking, but it was he who had directed the gory massacres of anti-Communists in Shanghai in 1927. Like all good diplomats, he was blessed with endless patience. "No matter how angry I get," said an old school friend named Han, "he always smiles and goes back over the same ground covered in our argument, only in a different way—different enough to make you feel as though he were presenting a new point."

He met with Chang in a Catholic mission in Sian, a remote city in North China, and after admitting that Chiang Kai-shek was the logical leader against the Japanese, promised that the Red generals would serve under him. In return Chang would have to assure him that the Red troops get equal treatment with the Nationalists. In addition, Communists held in Nationalist prisons would be released, and the Communist party allowed to operate legally once Japan was defeated.

They signed a document listing these conditions and shook hands to seal the bargain. "Young Marshal, now that it is all settled," said Chou, "I am ready to take orders from you this very moment."

Chang replied coldly that they would both have to wait and take orders from Chiang Kai-shek.

"If you still have any doubt about the determination of my party to join in a united front against Japan," said Chou, "I will gladly stay here in Sian with you as a hostage."

Chang said this wouldn't be necessary and that he was as determined as anyone to fight the Japanese—after all, he had a personal account to settle with them. Nevertheless, he was a soldier and must first attempt to persuade his superior, the Generalissimo, to accept the terms of the truce just signed.

But before such a meeting could take place, another of Chiang's field commanders, General Yang Hu-cheng, an ex-bandit chief, convinced the Young Marshal that the Generalissimo could only be made to co-operate with the Reds if he were kidnapped. Chiang was already on his way to Sian to confront Chang with evidence that the Young Marshal was being influenced by leftists and to warn him that "unless timely measures were taken, the situation could lead to rebellion."

Although he had agreed to the kidnapping, the presence of Chiang Kai-shek in Sian weakened Chang's resolve; he continued to vacillate until General Yang took matters in his own hands on the morning of December 12. He seized the Generalissimo and all troops in the area loyal to him. Chiang had been badly injured in a fall while trying to escape, but he was more composed than the Young Marshal when they came face to face. "Both for your own sake and for the sake of the nation, the only thing for you to do is to repent at once and send me back to Nanking," he said. "You must not fall into the trap set by the Communists. Repent before it is too late."

It took the sheepish Chang two days to get up his nerve to show his superior a proposed eight-point agreement similar to the one made with Chou. Once it was signed, Chang promised, the Generalissimo would be escorted back to the Nationalist capital.

"So long as I am a captive, there can be no discussion," said Chiang. He dared the other to shoot him and went back to the Bible.

The distressed Chang turned to the Reds for help. When Chou arrived he praised Chang for his courage, scolded him for bungling the kidnapping and went in to see the prisoner. They knew each other well. Chou had once served under the Generalissimo at the Whampoa Military Academy, China's West Point; here, with Chiang's approval, he had set up a political-commissar system. What Chiang didn't realize until too late was that most of the commissars selected were Communists.

Chiang had since offered $80,000 for Chou's head and was understandably pale and apprehensive. But Chou was all affability. He swore that the Communists would not exploit the situation if Chiang joined them. All they wanted was an end to civil war, and a joint effort against the Japanese.

Hostile at first, Chiang listened with growing interest but still refused to commit himself. Within a week, however—according to the Communist version—Chou persuaded him to lead the fight against the Japanese on his own terms. In any case, he was flown back to Nanking on Christmas Day. Surprisingly, the Young Marshal went along with him and once there the two went through a typically Oriental face-saving game. It was like a stylized duel in Chinese opera. First Chang abased himself, confessing that he was "surly and unpolished" and had acted impudently and illegally: "Blushing with shame, I have followed you to the capital in order to receive from you appropriate punishment. Whatever is best for the state I will not evade, if I have to die ten thousand deaths." Then it was Chiang's turn: "Due to my lack of virtue and defects in my training of subordinates, an unprecedented revolt broke out." Chang was tried, sentenced to ten years' imprisonment, and pardoned within twenty-four hours.

At the same time Chiang was publicly proclaiming that despite stories from Sian, he had been freed "without having to accept any conditions." It was undoubtedly a version contrived to appease those in Nanking much more violently opposed to any dealing with the Reds than he, because within weeks he was dickering with Mao. The negotiations went so well that early in 1937 the Chinese Communist Party Central Committee wired the Kuomintang that they would abandon their policy of armed uprising against the Nationalist government and place the Red Army under Chiang's full control. The terms were informally accepted and once more, as in the honeymoon days of Borodin, the Kuomintang and Communists were united.

This brought China her first semblance of tranquillity in more than ten years. "Peace is achieved," declared Chou En-lai in an interview. "There is now no fighting between us. We have the opportunity to participate in the actual preparations for the defensive war against Japan. As to the problem of achieving democracy, this aim has only begun to be realized. . . . One must consider the anti-Japanese war preparations and democracy like the two wheels of a rickshaw, for example. That is to say, the preparation for the anti-Japanese war comes first, and following it, the movement for democracy—which can push the former forward."

A few months later, on July 5, 1937, a formal Kuomintang-Communist agreement was signed and both sides made preparations to drive the Japanese out of Peking and the rest of North China.

2.

In Japan, the increasing influence of the military over the government had become an issue. In the name of law and order, Prime Minister Hirota was now so obviously subservient to the generals that liberal members of the Diet denounced them. One aroused deputy told the War Minister he should commit harakiri. This was greeted by such enthusiastic shouts and applause that the minister resigned in anger. And of course, with his resignation, in February 1937, came the end of the Hirota Cabinet.

Without hesitation Prince Saionji advised the Emperor to name another general, Kazushige Ugaki, to succeed Hirota. This choice infuriated almost everyone in the Army, since Ugaki was a moderate who had once reduced their number by four divisions. Consequently the Big Three said they simply couldn't find anyone who would serve with Ugaki. He was compelled to report to the Emperor that he was unable to form a cabinet and gave vent to his indignation in a statement to the newspapers: "What I see is that only a few men in authoritative positions in the Army have formed a group [the Control clique] and are forcing their views on the authorities, propagandizing as if their action represents the general will of the Army. The Army belongs to the Emperor. Whether their action during the last few days represents the general will of the Army of the Emperor or not is not too clear. The selection of a war minister by the Big Three of the Army is too formal and lacks sincerity. . . . I believe that Japan stands at the crossroads between fascism and parliamentary politics. I am partly responsible for the present condition in the Army, which has become a political organization. I feel sorry for the Emperor because of this state of affairs. Moreover, I greatly regret that the Army, which I have loved so long, has been brought to such a pass. . . ."

A general named Senjuro Hayashi who was sympathetic to the

Control clique was selected as prime minister, but he ran into such opposition from the Diet that his government, nicknamed the "eat-and-run cabinet," lasted just four months. Hayashi was succeeded by a civilian, Prince Fumimaro Konoye, a descendant of the Fujiwara family, which had ruled the land for several centuries. A disciple of Saionji's, he had long resisted the last *genro*'s efforts to get him involved in politics. In the harrowing days following the 2/26 Incident, the old prince had concluded that Konoye alone could lead the new government and recommended him formally to the Emperor. Konoye had refused—he preferred to remain as President of the House of Peers and besides was in poor health—causing Saionji's "most embarrassing moment."

But Konoye considered the present crisis so critical that he was persuaded to accept the position hitherto reserved for old men. At forty-six years of age he was a popular choice to lead the country, since the people had little confidence in politicians and feared a continuance of military rule. For their part, most military men trusted him because he was above political greed. The *zaibatsu* counted on him to bring stability, the intellectuals to stem the tide of fascism. Ordinary people were impressed by his comparative youth and good looks and his very reluctance to be prime minister. Any man with such an utter lack of ambition had to be sincere.

"Evolutionary reforms and progress within the Constitution must be our watchdogs," he promised upon assuming the premiership in June, "but the country demands national reform, and the government, while neither socialist nor fascist, must listen to its call. The impetus of the great [Meiji] Restoration has carried us thus far with honor and success; but now it is for the young men to take up the task and carry the country forward into a new age."

The new age came sooner than he expected and was not at all what he had envisaged. It was ushered in on the night of July 7 at the ancient stone bridge named after Marco Polo. A Japanese company stationed near this historic landmark was holding night maneuvers about a mile from a large Chinese unit. Just as a bugle signaled the end of the operation, bullets came whistling from the Chinese lines. The Japanese returned fire, but within minutes the skirmish was over. There was a single Japanese casualty—one man was missing. The company commander reported the incident to his battalion commander, who phoned regimental headquarters in nearby Peking. A second company was sent to the bridge, as well as a staff officer who began arranging a truce with the Chinese. Both sides had just agreed it was an unfortunate mistake when a second fusillade poured into the two Japanese companies.

The first shots had probably been accidental. The second volley was suspicious, particularly since relations between the Chinese and Japanese troops in the area were so good. This had come about through a close friendship between General Sung Chi-yuen, commander of all Chinese troops in North China, and General Gun Hashimoto, chief of staff of the North China Garrison. The question was who had fired the second volley, if not the Chinese troops. Cohorts of Doihara trying to aggravate the incident into an excuse to invade China in force? Or Communists hoping to start a full-scale war between Chiang Kai-shek and the Japanese that would probably end in the communization of China?*

Whoever it was, the Japanese counterattacked, and it wasn't until the next morning that the negotiators agreed that both sides should peacefully withdraw. While the Japanese were pulling out, they again drew fire, retaliated and the fight was resumed.

Though it should have seemed obvious by now that a third party was trying to keep the skirmish going, each side accused the other of breaking the truce and the negotiations floundered. When

* It was not until after the war that the Japanese officers involved in the Marco Polo Bridge incident generally concluded that Mao's agents had sparked the incident. "We were then too simple to realize this was all a Communist plot," General Akio Doi, a Russian expert, said in 1967. General Ho Ying-chin, Chiang's minister of war at the time, still believes, like most Chinese, that the incident was plotted by Japanese radical militarists, although he did admit in a recent interview that after Chou En-lai read Chiang's diary in Sian and realized the Generalissimo was strongly anti-Japanese, he began conspiring to get the Kuomintang involved in an all-out war with Japan.

Without doubt, both the Russians and the Chinese Communists were doing their best to foster a long, enervating conflict between Chiang and the Japanese. That fall Mao Tse-tung told his troops in Yenan, "The Sino-Japanese conflict gives us, the Chinese Communists, an excellent opportunity for expansion. Our policy is to devote seventy percent of our effort to this end, twenty percent to coping with the Government, and ten percent to fighting the Japanese. This policy is to be carried out in three stages. During the first stage, we are to work with the Kuomintang in order to ensure our existence and growth. During the second stage, we are to achieve parity in strength with the Kuomintang. During the third stage, we are to penetrate deep into parts of Central China to establish bases for counterattacks against the Kuomintang."

the news arrived in Tokyo, the Army Chief of Staff cabled a routine order to settle the trouble locally. Later in the day representatives of the War, Navy and Foreign ministries agreed on a policy of "nonexpansion" and "local settlement." This was approved by Prince Konoye and his cabinet, but at a special meeting of the Army General Staff, the expansionists argued that more troops should be sent into China to teach Chiang a lesson, otherwise he might use this incident as an excuse to retake Manchuria; this would endanger Japanese-controlled Korea and eventually put Japan at the mercy of Russian and Chinese Communists. They promised to make the military action brief and come to a quick agreement with Chiang. Then all Japanese troops would be withdrawn into North China, which would be used purely as a buffer against Russia.

The greatest opposition came from Kanji Ishihara, now a general and head of Operations. He argued for hours but finally had to admit that the poorly disciplined Chinese troops in North China were bound to start massacring the Japanese traders and settlers in the area. This would arouse the Japanese public and bring about what he feared and abhorred the most, an endless war of retribution.

That was why the man who once said, "The first soldier marching into China will only do so over my dead body," approved the reinforcement of North China with two brigades from the Kwantung Army, one division from Korea and three from the homeland. And on July 11 Prince Konoye, who had so recently pledged international integrity, gave his consent to the flood of troops into another country. But there was little else he could have done, according to his private secretary, Tomohiko Ushiba, "in the face of the War Minister's assurance that it was merely a troop movement to stop local fighting."

At the Marco Polo Bridge, after hours of wrangling, the negotiators had just arranged another truce. But as both sides pulled back, a loud crackling like machine-gun fire broke out (it turned out to be firecrackers) and the battle was on again. This time the two friendly generals, Sung Chi-yuen and Gen Hashimoto, personally stepped in and before the day was over a firm local agreement had been signed. In it Sung apologized for the entire incident. He promised to punish the officers responsible, rigidly control any Red elements in his forces and withdraw troops from the bridge area. On his part Hashimoto, acting for his dying commander, agreed to bring no more reinforcements into North China.

Chiang Kai-shek ignored the truce and sent Sung orders to concentrate more forces in the troubled area. Instead Sung kept his promise and began withdrawing troops. It looked as if the crisis was over, but unfortunately communications were so bad that Tokyo had no idea the problem was being solved, and on July 17 peremptorily demanded that the Chinese stop sending troops into North China and recognize the puppet government Doihara had helped set up. This so incensed Chiang that he issued a defiant proclamation from Nanking: "If we allow one more inch of our territory to be lost or sovereign rights to be encroached upon, then we shall be guilty of committing an unpardonable crime against our Chinese race. . . . China's sovereign rights cannot be sacrificed, even at the expense of war, and once war has begun there is no looking back."

The Japanese military attaché in Nanking, General Seiichi Kita, told his old friend, Chinese War Minister General Ho Ying-chin, himself a graduate of the Japanese Military Academy, that if Chinese troops were not withdrawn at once from North China, the "situation might get out of hand." Ho was not averse to some co-operation with the Japanese but said, "If war breaks out, both Japan and the Chinese Republic will be defeated and only the Russian and Chinese Communists will benefit. If you don't believe it now, you will in ten years." He asked Kita to pass this warning on to his government with a promise that the Chinese would "fight to the last man."

Already concerned by exaggerated reports of the large number of Chinese troops flowing up into North China, the Japanese public was indignant at Chiang's proclamation; and one paper, the *Nichi Nichi*, declared editorially that the Chinese reply left Japan no choice but "to cross the Rubicon."

Only then did the long-delayed information from Hashimoto reach Tokyo that all was quiet at the Marco Polo Bridge and that it was not necessary to send any reinforcements to North China. The transfer orders were canceled and even the expansionists in the Army high command were relieved that a crisis had been averted. It was assumed that Chiang would agree to the terms signed by Sung, and peace return to China.

Sung continued to do his part by removing all sandbag barricades from the streets of Peking and relaxing martial law. Passenger trains from the south at last began entering the ancient capital. But there was still no word of reconciliation from Chiang Kai-shek, and what the negotiators on both sides feared came about: Japanese and Chinese troops, at trigger's edge for almost three weeks, began firing at one another in earnest. It happened on the night of July 25 at the railroad station of Langfang, some fifty miles below Peking. Within an hour a skirmish turned into a major conflict. Heavy Japanese reinforcements were dispatched to Langfang and at dawn seventeen planes bombed a Chinese barracks. A few hours later the city was occupied.

The friendship between Sung and Hashimoto was now of little avail. The latter's commander had died and a new one, Lieutenant General Kiyoshi Katsuki, had arrived. He was strictly a military man who felt he had been sent "to chastise the outrageous Chinese." He cabled Tokyo that he had done everything to bring about a peaceful settlement and asked for permission to "use force" wherever necessary to protect Japanese lives and property. The Army leaders approved and one division was ordered to Shanghai and another to Tsingtao.

Again Prime Minister Konoye, assured by the military that the Chinese problem could be "solved in three months," felt constrained to go along lest his cabinet fall. The following day, July 27, he announced in the Diet that the government must now achieve a "new order" in East Asia. To patriotic Japanese it seemed proper and equitable. Japanese lives and property had to be protected and Communism contained; it was time for firmness, not weakness. Nobody realized that it was a declaration of total war with China. The Army leaders were truly convinced they could force Chiang to negotiate before fall.*

---

*James B. Crowley, assistant professor of history at Amherst College, wrote in the May 1963 issue of *Journal of Asian Studies* that "it would be safe to conclude that this incident was not caused by any 'conspiracy' of Japanese army officers and that the Japanese military was not primarily responsible for the steady drift towards war." More likely, he believes, it was the Chinese—and they had plenty of provocation—who raised Marco Polo into a major crisis. "The tragedy is that the interaction of conflicting national policies and aspirations transformed an incident into a war from which neither government was to derive substantial benefit."

It bore no resemblance to the Manchurian coup. In 1931 the Kwantung Army had deliberately provoked the incident at Mukden, but in 1937 the North China Army neither sought nor organized the confrontation at the Marco Polo Bridge. In 1931 the Army General Staff sanctioned the seizure of Manchuria; in 1937 they did their utmost to forestall operations in North China. In 1931 Prime Minister Reijiro Wakatsuki's failure to execute a diplomatic settlement satisfactory to the Control clique brought about the fall of his government; in 1937 there would be no change of cabinet.

With approval from Tokyo in hand, General Katsuki issued a proclamation that he was going to "launch a punitive expedition against the Chinese troops, who have been taking acts derogatory to the prestige of the Empire of Japan." Copies of this proclamation were dropped from planes at dawn on July 28. Bombers struck at three cities and shelled others as ground troops attacked Chinese forces all over the Peking area except in the city itself.

The Rubicon had, in truth, been crossed. The rhetoric of the China conflict had evolved into action without benefit of credible strategic calculations, and Japan had taken the first giant step to war with America.

3.

"Crush the Chinese in three months and they will sue for peace," War Minister Sugiyama predicted. As city after city fell, patriotic fervor swept through Japan, but almost the entire Western world condemned Japan's aggression, and even Germany (because she feared for her interests in China) was critical. China appealed to the League of Nations, and while the world awaited its report, a bold attack came from another quarter. On October 5, 1937, President Franklin D. Roosevelt made a forceful speech in Chicago condemning all aggressors and equating the Japanese, by inference, with the Nazis and Fascists.* "When an epidemic of physical

---

* Ever since his school days at Groton, Roosevelt had been convinced of Japan's long-range plans of conquest. He pored over Admiral Alfred Mahan's *The Influence of Sea Power Upon History* until, according to his mother, he had "practically memorized the book." Later he corresponded

disease starts to spread, the community approves and joins in a quarantine of the patients in order to protect the health of the community," he said and explained that war was a contagion, whether declared or undeclared. "We are adopting such measures as will minimize our risk of involvement, but we cannot have complete protection in a world of disorder in which confidence and security have broken down." There was no mistaking Roosevelt's meaning when on the following day, after the League of Nations had censured Japan, the United States, although not a member, quickly concurred.

At home, Roosevelt's action was largely applauded but Secretary of State Cordell Hull was unhappy about the "quarantine" clause, feeling that it set back "for at least six months our constant educational campaign intended to create and strengthen public opinion towards international co-operation." Ambassador Joseph Grew also felt it was a grievous mistake. No American interest in China justified risking a war with Japan and it was futile to hurl "moral thunderbolts" at a country which respected force above all; it would create bitterness between the two countries and destroy the good will he had been building. Aware that his staff members shared his shock and resentment, he warned them two days later not to express their opinions outside the embassy. That night he wrote in his diary:

This was the day that I felt my carefully built castle tumbling about my ears and we all wandered about the chancery, depressed, gloomy, and with not a smile in sight. That afternoon Alice, Elsie and I went to the cinema to see *Captains Courageous* . . . And then I sunk myself in *Gone with the Wind*—which is precisely the way I felt.

Japanese reaction, of course, was quick and bitter. "Japan is expanding," retorted Yosuke Matsuoka, a diplomat whose sharp

---

with Mahan and learned that the admiral shared with him a strong concern over Japan as a major threat in the Pacific.

At Harvard, in 1920, a Japanese student told Roosevelt in confidence about his nation's hundred-year plan for conquest, drafted in 1889. It allegedly covered the annexation of Manchuria, the establishment of a protectorate in North China, the acquisition of American and British possessions in the Pacific, including Hawaii, as well as bases in Mexico and Peru. In 1934 Roosevelt informed his Secretary of State, Henry L. Stimson, of this "plot," pointing out to him that many of its particulars had already been verified.

tongue and ready wit was winning him many followers. "And what country in its expansion era has ever failed to be trying to its neighbors? Ask the American Indian or the Mexican how excruciatingly trying the young United States used to be once upon a time." Japan's expansion, like that of America's, was as natural as the growth of a child. "Only one thing stops a child from growing—death." He declared that Japan was fighting for two goals: to prevent Asia from falling completely under the white man's domination, as in Africa, and to save China from Communism. "No treasure trove is in her eyes—only sacrifices upon sacrifices. No one realizes this more than she does. But her very life depends on it, as do those of her neighbors as well. The all-absorbing question before Japan today . . . is: Can she bear the cross?"*

A few weeks later, on November 16, Koki Hirota, now foreign minister, officially accused America of initiating an anti-Japanese front. An economic boycott against Japan, he told Grew, would not stop the fighting in China, but encouraged the Chinese to prolong the hostilities. Hirota said that until now the Japanese had felt America was the only country with genuine impartiality and would help bring about peace, as Theodore Roosevelt had done in the Russo-Japanese War.

Three days later Japan took Soochow, and the roads to Nanking and Shanghai were open. On December 12, the eve of the fall of Nanking, relations with America and Great Britain were almost shattered when Japanese naval aviators sank the gunboat *Panay* on the Yangtze River, though its American flag was clearly visible. A week earlier an artillery regiment commanded by Colonel Kingoro Hashimoto (founder of the Cherry Society) had fired on the British gunboat *Ladybird,* then seized it.

These incidents revived President Roosevelt's hope of quarantining the aggressor. He summoned the British ambassador in Washington, Sir Ronald Lindsay, and suggested their two nations join in a naval blockade which would cut Japan off from raw materials. Lindsay protested that such a quarantine would lead to war. He

* In interviews in 1966–67 a number of former Japanese leaders, including Generals Teiichi Suzuki, Sadao Araki and Kenryo Sato, pointed to this and similar speeches regarding Japan's increasing involvement in China as parallels to America's accelerating war in Vietnam. Both countries, they agreed, were fighting a sacrificial war despite the world's censure—and both had gone about wiping out Communism the wrong way.

cabled London that his "horrified criticisms" had "made little impression upon the President." The next day, December 17, Roosevelt sketched out his quarantine plan to the Cabinet. His resolve was strengthened by a report from the Navy's official Court of Inquiry in Shanghai that the attack on *Panay* had been wanton and ruthless; more important, a message to Combined Fleet had been intercepted and decoded by the U.S. naval intelligence indicating that the raid had been deliberately planned by an officer on the carrier *Kaga*.

In Tokyo the Konoye government was as aggrieved by the destruction of *Panay* and *Ladybird* as the Americans and the British. Foreign Minister Hirota brought a note to Ambassador Grew expressing regrets and offering full restitution for the sinking of the *Panay*. Abjectly apologetic, Hirota said, "I am having a very difficult time. Things happen unexpectedly." The Japanese Navy high command also showed its disapproval by dismissing the *Kaga* commander, who was responsible for the *Panay* bombing. "We have done this to suggest that the Army do likewise and remove Hashimoto from his command," said Admiral Isoroku Yamamoto, the Navy Vice Minister, who had no relish for doing battle with the U.S. fleet, since he had spent considerable time in America and was cognizant of her potentialities.

The Japanese apology was officially accepted in Washington on Christmas Day (Grew observed that its arrival on Christmas Eve was a "masterly" arrangement) and the incident was apparently closed.* Great Britain also gracefully accepted an apology for the

---

* Roosevelt was still intent on his quarantine. He sent Captain Royal Ingersoll, chief of the Navy's War Plans Division, to London with instructions to explore the implementation of a long-range naval blockade of Japan. The proposal that had "horrified" Ambassador Lindsay found approval in the British Admiralty. They told Ingersoll that they were "prepared to stop all Japanese traffic crossing a line roughly from Singapore through the Dutch East Indies, New Guinea, New Hebrides and around to the east of Australia and New Zealand." They considered "that the United States could prevent all westbound trade to Japan by controlling by embargo or ships the entire Pacific coast from Alaska to Cape Horn." But eight days later, on January 13, 1938, Prime Minister Neville Chamberlain abruptly rejected another proposal of Roosevelt's calling for Britain to join an international conference to discuss essential principles of international law that would, incidentally, awaken American public opinion to the true nature of the "bandit nations," as Roosevelt was privately calling them. At first the President did not grasp the full implication of Chamberlain's un-

attack on the *Ladybird,* despite the refusal of the Japanese Army to follow Yamamoto's advice. Hashimoto was not even reprimanded. He had been allowed to proceed to Nanking with his troops.

By the time the Japanese entered the city in December, all resistance had ended, and their commander, General Iwane Matsui —who had left Japan with the announcement: "I am going to the front not to fight an enemy, but in the state of mind of one who sets out to pacify his brother"—ordered them "to exhibit the honor and glory of Japan and augment the trust of the Chinese people" and to "protect and patronize Chinese officials and people, as far as possible."

Instead they roamed the city, looting, burning, raping, murdering. According to one witness, men, women and children were "hunted like rabbits; everyone seen to move was shot." Even the friendly Germans in an official report condemned the Japanese Army as "bestial machinery."

It was not until General Matsui triumphantly entered the city that he learned there had been "breaches of military discipline and morality." He ordered strict compliance with his former orders to "insure that no act whatsoever, which tends to disgrace honor, be perpetrated." He declared: "Now the flag of the Rising Sun is floating over Nanking, and the Imperial Way is shining forth in the area south of the Yangtze. The dawn of the renaissance is about to take place. On this occasion, it is my earnest hope that the four hundred million people of China will reconsider." Matsui returned to Shanghai, only to hear rumors a week later that "illegal acts"

---

anticipated rejection, but within a week it was clear that the Prime Minister's refusal to join an international conference meant that his government would take no part in a quarantine of the aggressor, either in the Orient or in Europe.

The above information (much of it based on notes of the Ingersoll talks recently uncovered in the archives of the United States Navy) indicates beyond argument that as early as 1938, President Roosevelt was prepared to do more than assail the "bandit nations" by words. If Chamberlain had joined him in the naval quarantine, further aggression in both Asia and Europe might have been stemmed. But Chamberlain's rebuff forced Roosevelt to abandon his vigorous foreign policy and allow his country to revert to isolation. Within two months it was too late. On March 12 Hitler's seizure of Austria started the world on the road to its most devastating war.

were still being committed. "Anyone guilty of misconduct must be severely punished," he wrote the Nanking commander.

But the atrocities continued for another month. About one third of the city was gutted by fire; more than 20,000 Chinese male civilians of military age were marched out of the city and massacred by bayoneting or machine-gun fire. As many women and young girls were raped, murdered and then mutilated. Numerous older civilians were robbed and shot. By the end of the month at least 200,000, perhaps as many as 300,000 civilians had been slaughtered.

Why was such savagery inflicted on a nation the Japanese regarded as their main source of cultural inspiration, their Rome and Greece? It is axiomatic that soldiers of any army get out of hand in a foreign land and act with a brutality they would never dare exhibit at home, but this could hardly account for the extent and intensity of the atrocities. They could only have been incited by some of the more radical officers, in the belief that the Chinese should be taught a lesson.

Back home, Prime Minister Konoye knew less about the atrocities in Nanking than the Germans. He was aware, however, that with all the conquest of vast areas, the Japanese were no nearer to victory but were sinking more deeply into a quagmire. Konoye was a unique individual—a prince by birth and a socialist at heart. He seemed soft, shy and effete, if not weak. To those who knew him best, he was a man of almost painfully discriminating taste, of such wide interests and objectivity that he could listen with sympathy to those of all political beliefs. In fact, he listened with such sympathy that each in turn thought the prince agreed with him. It always took him an interminable time to make up his mind, since he first wanted to know all sides of a question, but once decision was made, almost nothing could make him change it. "He was simply impregnable," his private secretary, Tomohiko Ushiba, recalled. Konoye had few idols and one was Lord Balfour, considered not quite qualified for the job of prime minister but decisive and effective once he took office. Undoubtedly Konoye hoped to be the Japanese Balfour.

Prince Konoye was the eldest son of Prince Atsumaro Konoye and the first heir in 250 years in the Konoye family to be born of a lawful wife—an occasion which prompted his great-grandfather to write numerous poems expressing his joy. Eight days after his birth, his mother died of puerperal fever, but until he was an adolescent he believed that his father's second wife, his mother's sister, was his real mother. "When I learned that she wasn't," he later said, "I began to think that life was a tissue of lies."

When he was still a young man he was stricken with tuberculosis and spent two years doing little but staring at a ceiling and thinking. From this time he had a feeling for the underdog. He disliked money, millionaires and politicians and wrote many radical essays. Some of these socialistic convictions clung to him as he matured and even now he was against the privileged classes. To outsiders he gave the appearance of being democratic and treated all alike with courtesy. "Even beggars are guests," he once told Ushiba. But his innermost self remained aristocratic—"far more so," Ushiba recently recalled, "than you can possibly imagine."

Almost everything about him seemed contradictory but made sense. He felt ill at ease with Americans, yet sent his eldest son, Fumitaka, to Lawrenceville and Princeton. He was fond of kimonos and wore them with fastidious care, yet he was equally at ease in Western clothes. His marriage was a love match but he treated his mistress, a geisha, with great affection. He had upset family tradition twice: first, by abolishing the system of having rooms in the main house for second, third and fourth "wives" ("It's pardonable to have just one mistress, don't you agree?"); and second, by discontinuing the family diary ("How could I possibly write the truth if it were unfavorable to me?").

Only once did he seriously scold any of his five children, this in a stern letter to Fumitaka at Princeton chastising him for drinking and neglecting his studies. Fumitaka replied that he was just following the American way of life and the subject was closed.

His own father, who died when Konoye was thirteen, was so overprotective that Konoye spent his childhood with a leash around his waist to keep him from falling. Konoye showed affection to all his children, including the youngest, a daughter by his mistress. He would eat with them, singing and cavorting for their amusement more like an American father than a Japanese.

Product of an elegant society, with one foot in the past and one in the future, Prince Konoye's considerable personal charm and polish hid to all but the discerning his profound sense of obligation to his country and a cynicism so deep that he trusted no man, including himself. He seemed to be what he was not, and even his family rarely saw the man behind the façade. Ushiba, probably as close to him as anyone, did see beyond the overly fond father, the loving husband, the charming dilettante, the considerate employer, to a strange, cold man; he was self-restrained and refined, and sophisticated to such a degree "that it was sometimes quite difficult to make out his real thinking."

Once Ushiba asked him which Japanese historical figures he respected. "None," was the answer. "Not even General Nogi or Admiral Togo [heroes of the Russo-Japanese War]?" "Certainly not!"

He treated the Emperor, for whom he had a warm personal feeling, rather intimately. While others sat on the edge of their chairs like ramrods in His Majesty's presence, Konoye would sprawl comfortably. He didn't do this as an insult, but because he felt so close to Hirohito. When he told someone on his way to an audience, "Oh, do remember me to the Emperor," he was not being facetious, merely natural. He felt he came from just as good a family.

As hope of a solution in China had faded with every month, Prince Konoye looked desperately in another direction—a negotiated peace. He preferred England as mediator but the Army persuaded him to use the good offices of Germany, which was friendly with both parties. Hitler had sent Chiang Kai-shek arms and military advisers and was bound, if tenuously, to Japan by the year-old Anti-Comintern Pact. The terms were so reasonable that when the strongly pro-Chinese German ambassador to China, Oskar Trautmann, presented them, Chiang Kai-shek seemed about to accept them.

But those two banes of stability in Japan—*gekokujo* and opportunism—again appeared. First, news came of another great triumph in China, and War Minister Sugiyama raised the price of negotiation; then the commander of the North China Garrison unexpectedly set up a puppet regime in Peking, against the specific orders of Konoye and the General Staff. Though the latter, under the urging of Ishihara, still called for negotiations with Chiang Kai-shek, Trautmann labored in vain. After conversations in Washington between their ambassador and President Roosevelt, China insisted that the Japanese terms were too broad. The Japanese saw this as evasion, and being inflexible negotiators themselves, lost their patience. Concluding that Chiang Kai-shek really didn't want to negotiate, Konoye decided to take a shortcut to peace and deal with those Chinese who "shared Japan's ideals." On January 16, 1938, he announced that "the Imperial Government shall cease to deal with the National Government of China, and shall rely upon the establishment and growth of a new Chinese regime for co-operation."

This brought sharp rebukes from intellectuals and a number of liberal Diet members. Ishihara also warned Konoye that it was a policy which would inevitably lead to endless trouble. Such criticism forced the Prime Minister to review his position and he began to realize that his hasty act might have committed Japan to a rigid, do-or-die policy—a settlement by full-scale war, the last thing he wanted. Assailed by self-doubts, he wondered if he should resign. But court officials persuaded him to remain in office, otherwise the Chinese would quite properly assume that failure to settle the China question had caused his resignation and it would be more difficult than ever to achieve the solution they wanted.

It was at last apparent to Konoye that the Army itself didn't have a fixed policy on China and was drifting with the tide of events, but unable to get reliable information about Supreme Command matters, he could only watch in frustration as the situation in China worsened.

In the name of national defense the Army proposed a national mobilization law, designed to take away the Diet's last vestiges of control over war measures and direct every aspect of national life toward an efficient war economy. Army spokesmen argued persuasively and not unreasonably that Japan was a small, overpopulated country with almost no natural resources; surrounded as it was by enemies—Russians, Chinese, Americans and British—total mobilization of the nation's strength was the sole solution. The law was passed in March 1938—the Diet, in effect, voting for its own capitulation to the Army. "Liberties lost to the Japanese Army," commented Sir Robert Craigie, the British ambassador in Tokyo, "were lost for good."

The people were also being prepared psychologically for the

crusade in East Asia with two slogans borrowed from the past. One was *"kokutai,"* the national essence, and the other was *"kodo,"* connected, ironically, with the recently crushed clique. The original meaning of *kodo,* the Imperial Way, was twisted now into signifying world order and peace to be achieved by Japanese control of East Asia.

Both *kokutai* and *kodo* underlined the father relationship of the Emperor to the people as well as his divinity and were already rousing millions with ardor for a holy war to free Asia from both colonialism and Communism.

3

"Then the War Will Be a Desperate One"

1.

The Japanese continued to win. They took Hankow and Canton, forcing Chiang Kai-shek to move his government far inland to Chungking. But they were conquering territory, not people, and by the beginning of 1939 were still far from final victory. They had lost thousands of men, millions of yen and incurred the wrath of the Western world, and Americans in particular.

The relations between the two countries had begun precariously the day Commodore Perry's ships steamed into Tokyo Bay with a letter from President Millard Fillmore inviting Japan to open doors long closed to the outside world. The Americans were inspired by three motives: a desire to trade, spread the Gospel to the yellow pagans and export the ideals of 1776. The Japanese reluctantly, resentfully complied, but the ensuing years brought improved relations as American officials and private citizens materially helped Japan make the transition from feudalism to modern times in the fields of education, science, medicine and production. American obtrusion into the Pacific late in the nineteenth century with acquisitions of Hawaii, Guam, Wake Island and the Philippines perturbed the Japanese, but in 1900 the Boxer

"Then the War Will Be a Desperate One" 69

Rebellion brought the two nations together again in a common cause.

These fraternal bonds were strengthened four years later by Japan's war with Czarist Russia. American sympathies were overwhelmingly for the underdog. The New York *Journal of Commerce* declared that Japan stood as "the champion of commercial rights," and cartoonists pictured the Japanese soldier as a heroic figure—a noble samurai confronting the Russian Bear. Jacob Schiff, president of Kuhn, Loeb & Company, distressed by reports of Russian anti-Semitism, felt that the effort of Japan was "not only her own cause, but the cause of the entire civilized world." Practicing what he preached, he made the resources of his company available to the Japanese war effort. Despite spectacular victories, Japan could not terminate the war and turned to President Theodore Roosevelt for help. He accomplished this with the Treaty of Portsmouth, New Hampshire, in 1905, achieving for Japan the best possible terms. In one of the perverse twists of history, this act of friendship ended the good will between the two nations: the Japanese, who were unaware that their country was close to bankruptcy, were incensed at a treaty which gave them no indemnity. Anti-American riots erupted throughout the land, and martial law had to be established in Tokyo. Still not a word came from the Japanese government explaining that Roosevelt had saved the empire from embarrassment, perhaps disaster.

The next year the situation deteriorated. This time America was to blame. An unreasonable fear that a resurgent Asia under Japanese leadership would engulf Western civilization gained force in the United States, particularly on the Pacific coast. The San Francisco *Chronicle* averred that it was "a pressing world-wide issue as to whether the high-standard Caucasian races or the low-standard Oriental races would dominate the world." Caught up in the "yellow peril"* hysteria, the San Francisco school board ordered all Nisei children to attend a school in Chinatown.

The Japanese government responded hotly that this was "an act

---

* The phrase originated with Kaiser Wilhelm in 1895. He had a revelation of Oriental hordes overwhelming Europe and made a sketch of his vision: a Buddha riding upon a dragon above ruined cities. The caption read: *"Die gelbe Gefahr!"*—"The Yellow Peril." Several copies were made and presented to royal relatives all over Europe as well as every embassy in Berlin.

of discrimination carrying with it a stigma and odium which is impossible to overlook." There was talk of war, and Roosevelt secretly warned his commander in the Philippines to prepare for a Japanese attack.

The crisis passed, but not the resentment, and antagonism reached a climax during World War I, even though the two countries were allies. Already President Woodrow Wilson was calling for "territorial integrity and political independence throughout the world" and a return to China of land and rights lost to conquerors. This idealistic stance was a direct threat to the empire Japan had won in the past few decades and it seemed inevitable to her military leaders that they were destined to fight America for supremacy of the western Pacific and Asia. They gained popular support in 1924 when Congress passed the Exclusion Act barring Japanese from immigration to the United States. It seemed like a deliberate challenge to the proud, sensitive Japanese, and even those with pro-American sympathies were discomposed. "Japan felt as if her best friend had, of a sudden and without provocation, slapped her on the cheek," wrote a well-known Japanese scholar. "Each year that passes without amendment or abrogation only strengthens our sense of injury, which is destined to show itself, in one form or another, in personal and public intercourse."

With the seizure of Manchuria and the invasion of North China, the gulf widened as America denounced Japanese aggression with increasingly forceful words. This moral denunciation only hardened the resolve of the average Japanese. Why should there be a Monroe Doctrine in the Americas and an Open Door principle in Asia? The Japanese takeover in bandit-infested Manchuria was no different from American armed intervention in the Caribbean.* Moreover, how could a vast country like the United States even begin to understand the problems that had beset Japan since World War I? Why was it perfectly acceptable for England and Holland to occupy India, Hong Kong, Singapore and the East

---

* Arnold Toynbee saw some logic in their point of view. He later wrote that Japan's "economic interests in Manchuria were not superfluities but vital necessities of her international life. . . . The international position of Japan—with Nationalist China, Soviet Russia, and the race-conscious English-speaking peoples of the Pacific closing in upon her—had suddenly become precarious again."

Indies, but a crime for Japan to follow their example? Why should America, which had grabbed its lands from Indians by trickery, liquor and massacre, be so outraged when Japan did the same in China?*

Superpatriots plotted to assassinate pro-Western leaders and blow up the American and British embassies. Mass meetings were held denouncing both countries for giving help to China, and calling for acceptance of Hitler's invitation to join Germany and Italy in a tripartite pact. Westerners were refused rooms in some hotels, insulted publicly and occasionally beaten in sight of police.

All this emotional turmoil was worsened by marked differences between East and West in morality, religion and even patterns of thinking. Western logic was precise, with axioms, definitions, and proofs leading to a logical conclusion. Born dialecticians, the Japanese held that any existence was a contradiction. In everyday life they instinctively practiced the concept of the contradiction of opposites, and the means of harmonizing them. Right and wrong, spirit and matter, God and man—all these opposing elements were harmoniously united. That was why a thing could be good and bad at the same time.

Unlike Westerners, who tended to think in terms of black and white, the Japanese had vaguer distinctions, which in international relations often resulted in "policies" and not "principles," and seemed to Westerners to be conscienceless. Western logic was like a suitcase, defined and limited. Eastern logic was like the *furoshiki,* the cloth Japanese carry for wrapping objects. It could be large or small according to circumstances and could be folded and put in the pocket when not needed.

To Westerners, the Japanese were an incomprehensible contradiction: polite and barbarous, honest and treacherous, brave and cowardly, industrious and lazy—all at the same time. To the Japanese, these were not anomalies at all but one united whole,

---

* In this connection, Ambassador Grew once told the State Department: "We should not lose sight of the fact, deplorable but true, that no practical and effective code of international morality upon which the world can rely has yet been discovered, and that the standards of morality of one nation in given circumstances have little or no relation to the standards of the individuals of the nations in question. To shape our foreign policy on the unsound theory that other nations are guided and bound by our present standards of international ethics would be to court sure disaster."

and they could not understand why Westerners didn't comprehend it. To the Japanese, a man without contradictions could not be respected; he was just a simple person. The more numerous the contradictions in a man, the deeper he was. His existence was richer the more acutely he struggled with himself.

This philosophy was derived mainly from Buddhism, a doctrine wherein all is absorbed in the spaceless, timeless abyss of nondifference.* All is vanity and nothing can be differentiated because nothing has entity or identity. "I" has no entity and is an illusion appearing transitorily and momentarily on constantly floating relations of fallacious phenomena which come and go as the Almighty Wheel of Causality moves on. Nobody knows or is responsible for the movements of change, since there is no Creator or Heavenly Father or Fate.

Among the reasons for Japan's plunge into military adventures in Manchuria and China, this Wheel of Causality loomed significantly. Out of cowardice, or in some cases out of self-interest or simple indecision, a number of military and political leaders failed to curb the fanatic group of young officers who engineered these aggressions. But many on all levels just moved along with the tide, caught up in the Wheel of Causality. They lay down obediently and quietly, as it were, on the road of Blind Change, following the Buddhist belief that the Wheel of Causality went on externally and absolutely nonteleologically. With characteristic flexibility, some sects believed that everyone could become a Buddha, or "blessed one," after death; others that the individual was nothing and salvation lay only in the negation of self, that man was a bubble on the Ocean of Nothingness who would eventually vanish in the boundless water where there was no birth, no death, no beginning, no end. Buddha himself was nothing more than a finger pointing at the moon.

This was all expressed in the word *sayonara* (*sayo*—so, *nara*—if), that is, "So be it." The Japanese said *sayonara* every moment

---

* Almost every Japanese household had two shrines—one Buddhist, one Shinto. Shinto ("the way of the gods") was the national religion. It was based on awe inspired by any phenomenon of nature. More of a cult of ancestor worship and communion with the past than a religion per se, it had been revived in the nineteenth century and transformed into a nationalistic ideology.

to everything, for he felt each moment was a dream. Life was *sayonara*. Empires could rise or fall, the greatest heroes and philosophers crumble to dust, planets come and go, but Change never changed, including Change itself.

This strong recognition of death gave the Japanese not only the strength to face disaster stoically but an intense appreciation of each moment, which could be the last. This was not pessimism but a calm determination to let nothing discourage or disappoint or elate, to accept the inevitable. The most admirable fish was the carp. He swam gallantly upstream, leaping the sheerest falls, but once caught and put on the cutting board, lay quiet, accepting serenely what must be. So be it. *Sayonara*.

Understanding little or nothing of either the Wheel of Causality or the power wielded by the dedicated young rebels, informed Americans mistakenly assumed that the takeover in Manchuria and the foray into China were steps plotted by military leaders who, like Hitler, wished to seize the world for themselves.

Within the Japanese, metaphysical intuition and animalistic, instinctive urges lay side by side. Thus philosophy was brutalized and brutality was philosophized. The assassinations and other bloody acts committed by the rebels were inspired by idealism; and the soldiers who sailed to China to save the Orient for the Orient ended by slaughtering thousands of fellow Orientals in Nanking.

There was no buffer zone in their thinking between the transcendental and the empirical—between the chrysanthemum and the sword. They were religious but had no God in the Western sense—that is, a single Divine Being. They were sincere but had no concept of sin; they had sympathy but little humanity; they had clans but no society; they had a rigid family system which gave security but took away individuality. They were, in short, a great and energetic people often driven by opposing forces and often trying to go in opposite directions at the same time.

There were also numerous petty differences between East and West that needlessly aggravated matters. If a Westerner asked, "This isn't the road to Tokyo, is it?" the Japanese would reply yes, meaning, "What you say is correct; it is *not* the road to Tokyo." Confusion also resulted when the Japanese agreed with the Westerner just to be agreeable or to avoid embarrassment, or gave wrong information rather than admit his ignorance.

To most Westerners, the Japanese was utterly inscrutable. The way he handled his tools was all wrong: he squatted at an anvil; he pulled rather than pushed a saw or plane; he built his house from the roof down. To open a lock, he turned a key to the left, the wrong direction. Everything the Japanese did was backwards. He spoke backwards, read backwards, wrote backwards. He sat on the floor instead of in chairs; ate raw fish and live, wriggling shrimp. He would tell of the most tragic personal events and then laugh; fall in the mud in his best suit and come up with a grin; convey ideas by misdirection; discuss matters in a devious, tortuous manner; treat you with exaggerated politeness in his home and rudely shove you aside in a train; even assassinate a man and apologize to the servants for messing up the house.

What Westerners did not realize was that underneath the veneer of modernity and westernization, Japan was still Oriental and that her plunge from feudalism to imperialism had come so precipitously that her leaders, who were interested solely in Western methods, not Western values, had neither the time nor inclination to develop liberalism and humanitarianism.

2.

Hostility between the Russians and the Japanese also continued, but this was less a misunderstanding of cultures than a struggle for territory. In the summer of 1938 their troops battled for possession of a barren hill on the Manchurian-Soviet border, and the Red Army and air force gave the Japanese such a drubbing that within two weeks they agreed to a settlement. Some ten months later another squabble started near Nomonhan on the Manchurian-outer Mongolian border, relatively close to Peking. In a few weeks it turned into full-fledged warfare, with the first large-scale tank battles in history. Once again the Russians crushed the Japanese, who suffered more than fifty thousand casualties. This embarrassing rehearsal for war not only caused a revolution in Japanese weaponry and military tactics but drove Japan closer to an alliance with Germany and Italy, since she felt that the Soviet

Union, England, China and America might combine against her at any moment.*

Before this border war could be settled, Stalin threw both the Chinese and the Japanese into turmoil by signing, on August 23, 1939, a pact with his bitterest enemy, Hitler. Prime Minister Kiichiro Hiranuma, who had succeeded Prince Konoye in January, and whose cabinet had held more than seventy meetings in a futile effort to reach agreement on a Tripartite Pact, was so embarrassed and dismayed that he announced, "The Cabinet herewith resigns because of complicated and inscrutable situations recently arising in Europe."

Both Hitler and Stalin trumpeted to the world the clauses of their historic treaty—except for a secret protocol dividing up eastern Europe—and nine days later, on September 1, one and a half million German troops invaded Poland. World War II had begun. Though Poland, crushed between two massive forces, disintegrated in a few weeks, the western front remained so quiet that newsmen sardonically labeled the conflict "the phony war."

As the fighting in China dragged on into 1940, the Japanese Army General Staff decided in secret that unless total victory was achieved within the year, forces would be gradually withdrawn, leaving only troops in the northern part of China as defense against Communism. However, six weeks later, on May 10, Hitler again changed the course of Japan by launching a blitzkrieg against the western front. At dusk, four days later, the Dutch commander surrendered. The next morning at seven-thirty Britain's brand-new Prime Minister, Winston Churchill, was wakened by a phone call from Paris. "We have been defeated!"

* This was not mere paranoia. Shortly before, Stalin had written to Chiang Kai-shek: "If our negotiations with the European countries should produce satisfactory results—which is not impossible—this may be an important step toward the creation of a bloc of peace-loving nations in the Far East as well. Time is working favorably toward the formation of such a bloc.

"As a result of the now two-year-old war with China, Japan has lost her balance, begun to get nervous, and is hurling herself recklessly, now against Britain, and now against Soviet Russia and the Republic of Outer Mongolia. This is a sign of Japanese weakness and her conduct may unite all others against her. From Soviet Russia, Japan has already received the counterblows she deserves. Britain and the United States are waiting for an opportune moment to harm Japan. And we have no doubt that before long she will receive another counterblow from China, one that will be a hundred times mightier."

exclaimed Premier Paul Reynaud. "We are beaten!" Two weeks later King Leopold III surrendered, ignoring the advice of his government, and refused to seek refuge in England. "I have decided to stay," he said. "The cause of the Allies is lost." Within a month France capitulated and England herself appeared doomed.

The Japanese military leaders, intoxicated by Hitler's easy victories, changed their minds about the war in China and adopted the slogan "Don't miss the bus!" With France defeated and Britain fighting for survival, the time had come to strike into Southeast Asia for oil and other sorely needed resources. On the morning of June 22 the Army General Staff and the War Ministry held a joint meeting, and those who had recently advocated a withdrawal from China recommended an immediate surprise attack on Singapore. Conservatives squashed this scheme, but the spirit of chance lingered in the air and the virus of opportunism spread with each passing day. Reconciled to defeat in China a few months earlier, the Japanese were tempted by Hitler's sudden fortune in Europe to make a bid for the resources of Southeast Asia.

Before the end of July, Prince Konoye was persuaded to re-enter politics and form his second cabinet. Two of the key posts were filled by rising men—one a diplomat, the talkative, brilliant, quixotic Yosuke Matsuoka, who became foreign minister, and the other a soldier, Lieutenant General Hideki Tojo, who became war minister. Hard-working, hard-headed and dedicated, Tojo had already earned the nickname "the Razor." As simple as Konoye was complicated, he enjoyed great prestige within the Army, having ably executed a number of difficult assignments, including command of the *kempeitai* in the Kwantung Army. He was incorruptible, a rigid disciplinarian who demanded and got absolute discipline, and he selected subordinates for their ability and experience alone. Unlike other generals who wavered during the 2/26 Incident, he had acted with dispatch proclaiming a state of emergency in Manchuria, thus crushing any sympathetic revolt. To his legalistic mind, *gekokujo* was "absolutely unpardonable," not to be tolerated. This brought him respect from conservative military circles as well as from civilians who dreaded another bloody revolt, and it was undoubtedly the main reason Konoye selected him.

Foreign Minister Matsuoka, president of the South Manchurian

Railway and a close associate of Tojo's while the general was in the Kwantung Army, was almost his opposite. He was equally strong-minded but far more flamboyant, venturesome and intuitive. Whereas Tojo was a man of few words, Matsuoka was an orator of extraordinary eloquence who deserved his nicknames "Mr. 50,000 Words" and "the Talking Machine." He good-naturedly denied he was loquacious. "Being verbose means trying to cancel out or excuse what one has just said. I'd never do that. Therefore I'm not verbose." "I have never known anyone talk so much to say so little," observed Ambassador Craigie, who judged him also to be a stubborn and determined man with an acute mind.

Matsuoka was small and swarthy, and his clipped bullethead, mustache, big tortoise-shell glasses and flare for the dramatic had brought him world attention when he precipitously stalked out of the League of Nations Assembly during the debate on Manchuria. At the age of thirteen he had gone to sea, and was dumped ashore in America by the captain, his uncle, and told to fend for himself. An American family in Portland, Oregon, gave him refuge and he spent the next formative years working diligently as a laborer, in a law office, and even as a substitute minister while getting himself an education. After graduation from the University of Oregon he worked for three more years before returning to Japan, where he rose to fame by brilliance and energy alone.

Prince Konoye listened to practically everybody, Matsuoka to practically nobody. He was too busy expounding the ideas that kept leaping to his agile mind. His mystifying statements confused many, and some thought he was insane, but subordinates in the Foreign Ministry, like Dr. Yoshie Saito and Toshikazu Kase, felt it was merely his paradoxical nature in action. An intellectual gymnast, he would often say something contrary to what he believed and propose something he opposed in order to get his own way by default. A man of broad visions, he seldom explained these visions, or if he did, talked at such cross-purposes that it was no wonder he left a wake of confusion behind him; even those who thought him one of the most brilliant men in Japan watched anxiously as he nimbly played his dangerous diplomatic games. He assured his associates over and over again that he was pro-American, yet talked insultingly about America; he distrusted

Germany, yet courted Hitler; he was against the rise of militarism, yet spouted his arguments for war.

In his home he also played the paradox. He shouted at his seven children, and let them ride on his back; he was autocratic, yet gave unstintingly of his love and attention. Kiwamu Ogiwara, who worked for Matsuoka as *shosei* (a combination secretary and personal servant) became so terrified at his temper tantrums that he could never look directly at him. One day after taking a bath, Matsuoka shouted *"Oi!"* (Hey!) from his room, and when Ogiwara peered in, gestured impatiently at his middle. The *shosei* brought in an *obi* and this set Matsuoka off on a furious pantomime. Ogiwara had to find out from the maid that this particular gesture meant the master wanted his loincloth. On days when he was "not at home," a visitor would sometimes insist on seeing the master and the *shosei* would announce him to Matsuoka. "How can a man who isn't here see anyone!" he would yell. Almost constantly in a nervous state, Ogiwara left Matsuoka's employ detesting him. Yet a few years later, when he wrote asking for a job on the South Manchurian Railway, Matsuoka saw to it that he got a position. Under the fierce, arrogant, impatient exterior was a different person which few ever glimpsed.

The Cabinet was just four days old when it unanimously approved a new national policy to cope with "a great ordeal without precedence" in Japan's past. The basic aim of this policy was world peace, and to bring it about, a "new order in Greater East Asia" would have to be established by uniting Japan with Manchukuo and China—under the leadership, of course, of Japan. The entire nation was to be mobilized, with every citizen devoting himself to the state. Planned economy would be established, the Diet reformed and the China Incident brought to a satisfactory conclusion.

Moreover, a tripartite pact would be signed with Germany and Italy, and a nonaggression treaty arranged with the Soviet Union. Although America had placed an embargo on strategic materials to Japan, attempts would be made to placate her as long as she went along with Japan's "just claims." In addition, Japan would move into Indochina and perhaps farther, seizing an empire by force of arms if necessary while Europe was involved in its own war.

This policy was the brainchild of the military leaders, but they had convinced Prime Minister Konoye and the civilians in the Cabinet that it was Japan's last hope for survival in the chaotic modern world. What it meant was that the "Don't miss the bus" fever had become national policy, escalating the China Incident into war and pushing Japan to further aggressions. While the supremacy of civilian leaders over the military was a fundamental aspect of American democracy, the reverse was true in Japan. The Meiji Constitution had divided the power of decision between the Cabinet and the Supreme Command, but the military leaders, who had little understanding of political and diplomatic affairs, could almost always override the civilians in the Cabinet; their resignation would bring down the government. Their influence, however, went beyond the threat of resignation. Military monopoly had become a tradition and was rarely questioned. Consequently, it was the policies of well-meaning but ill-equipped generals and admirals, based on narrow military thinking, which dominated Japan.

The militarists who had formed this "Don't miss the bus" policy did not want or foresee the possibility of war. With France defeated, and England battling for its own existence, Indochina with its rubber, tin, tungsten, coal and rice was to them "a treasure lying in the street just waiting to be picked up." Within two months Japan forced the impotent Vichy government to sign a convention in Hanoi allowing Japan to set up air bases in northern Indochina* and use that area as a jumping-off place for attacks on China.

All this was not done without protests from Matsuoka and more thoughtful men in the Supreme Command who foresaw a collision course with the Anglo-Saxons in the making. The Army Chief of Staff, Prince Kanin, resigned in tears.

The United States reacted violently to the Japanese move; it meant a potential threat to the Burma Road, through which America was sending supplies into China. Prime Minister Churchill, however, felt quite sanguine about the Japanese garrisons in northern Indochina and suggested that two Indian brigades be removed from Singapore. Foreign Secretary Anthony Eden disagreed. "It

---

* Now North Vietnam.

seems to me difficult to maintain now that the Japanese threat to Malaya is not serious," he wrote in a minute to the Prime Minister. "There is every indication that Germany has made some deal with Japan within these last few days, and it seems, therefore, wise to make some provision for the land defense of Singapore."

Eden had guessed right. The long-discussed Tripartite Pact with Germany and Italy was near conclusion even though the Navy still objected, fearing that such an agreement would require Japan's automatic entry into war under certain circumstances. Matsuoka countered this with persuasive and interminable rebuttals. The pact, he declared, "would force the United States to act more prudently in carrying out her plans against Japan" and would prevent war between the two countries. Furthermore, if Germany did get into a fight with America, Japan would not be automatically obliged to come to her aid.

Unable to withstand the onslaught of Matsuoka's arguments —and, incidentally, vociferous popular support for the alliance— the dissidents were won over. Konoye gave his grudging approval because he well knew he would again be forced to resign if he opposed the Army. "My idea is to ride on the military *away* from war," he told his son-in-law. Like the Navy, the Emperor opposed the pact, and before affixing the official seal, he warned Konoye that he feared it would eventually lead to war with America and Britain. "You must, therefore," he added ominously, "share with me the joys and sorrows that will follow." On September 27, 1940, the pact was signed in Berlin.* To British and Americans this was further evidence that Japan was no better than Nazi Germany and Fascist Italy, and that the three "gangster" nations had joined forces to conquer the world. The United States retaliated immediately by adding scrap metal of every kind to the list

* At this time Hitler did not want war with Japan *and* the Anglo-Saxons and felt, like Matsuoka, that the pact obviated such a conflict. He wrote Mussolini that "a close co-operation with Japan is the best way either to keep America entirely out of the picture or to render her entry into the war ineffective." Almost as soon as the pact was signed the Führer changed his mind about keeping peace in the Far East. He decided that Japan had to become involved in the war as soon as possible, and the German ambassador in Tokyo was ordered to inveigle Japan into attacking Singapore at the risk of provoking the United States.

of embargoes, such as strategic materials and aviation fuel, which had been announced in July.

Not only the Anglo-Saxons were dismayed by the treaty. *Pravda* called it a "further aggravation of the war and an expansion of its realm." German Foreign Minister Joachim von Ribbentrop assured Vyacheslav Molotov, his Russian counterpart, that it was directed exclusively against the American warmongers. "The treaty, of course, does not pursue any aggressive aims against America. Its exclusive purpose is rather to bring the elements pressing for America's entry into the war to their senses, by conclusively demonstrating to them that if they enter the present struggle, they will automatically have to deal with the three great powers as adversaries." Why not join the pact, he suggested, and wrote a long letter to Stalin saying that it was

the historical mission of the four powers—the Soviet Union, Italy, Japan, and Germany—to adopt a long-range policy and to direct the future developments of their people into the right channel by delimitation of their interests on a world-wide scale. . . .

Matsuoka was positive he had engineered a plan for world peace. To confused intimates who considered him friendly toward America, he said it was the best way to prevent war with the United States. "If you stand firm and start hitting back," he told his eldest son, "the American will know he's talking to a man, and you two can then talk man to man." He thought he, and he alone, knew the real America. "It is my America and my American people that really exist," he once said. "There is no other America; there are no other American people."

"I admit people will call all this a tricky business," he told Dr. Saito; but he had allied with Hitler "to check the Army's aggressive policy . . . and to keep American warmongers from joining the war in Europe. And after that we can shake hands with the United States. This would keep peace in the Pacific while forming a great combine of capitalistic nations around the world against Communism."

The Tripartite Pact was also a means of settling the China Incident, he said. "The solution of the incident should rest on mutual assistance and prosperity, not on the hope of getting outside help to threaten China. To do this we should use the good offices of a third nation. I think the United States would do admirably for this purpose. But here the question is, What concessions will Japan (or rather, the Army) make? Japan should agree to a complete withdrawal of her troops from China."

The devious Matsuoka concluded that his aims could best be accomplished by supporting Ribbentrop's plan for a grand quadruple alliance uniting Germany, Italy and Japan with their common enemy, Russia, and requested permission to go to Europe so he could personally bring this to pass. After lengthy debate the military chiefs approved the trip but rejected his request to bring along a gift for Hitler—promise of a Japanese attack on Singapore.

On March 12, 1941, a large crowd gathered at Tokyo Station to bid Matsuoka farewell. As the bell rang announcing the train's departure, he rushed up to General Sugiyama and pestered him once more about Singapore. When was he going to take the city?

"I cannot tell you now," the general replied stiffly, thinking to himself, What a troublesome fellow this Matsuoka is!

That he was became evident when, on the long trip across Siberia, he said privately to Colonel Yatsuji Nagai, sent along by the Army to see that he would make no rash promises about Singapore, "Nagai-*san,* you try to stir up some trouble along the border; I'm going to try to close a Japanese-Soviet neutrality pact."

In Berlin he first saw Hitler and even in these discussions it was Matsuoka who, as usual, dominated the conversation. In fact, Hitler rarely talked, and when he did he usually railed against England, exclaiming, "She must be beaten!"

Both Ribbentrop and Hitler, as well as high officials of the Reich, did their best to convince Matsuoka that seizure of Singapore would be advantageous to Japan. Ribbentrop argued that it would "perhaps be most likely to keep America out of war," because then Roosevelt couldn't risk sending his fleet into Japanese waters, while Hitler assured him that if Japan *did* get into war, Germany would come to her aid and "would be more than a match for America, entirely apart from the fact that the German soldiers were, obviously, far superior to the Americans."

But Matsuoka became evasive at every mention of Singapore. For example, when Hermann Göring, after accepting a scroll of

Mount Fuji, jokingly promised to come and see the real thing only "if Japan takes Singapore," Matsuoka nodded toward the edgy Nagai and said, "You'll have to ask him."

Matsuoka was not at all reticent about the treaty he hoped to make with Stalin and was surprised to hear Ribbentrop, who had given him the idea of a grand quadruple pact, say, "How can you conclude such a pact at this time? Just remember, the U.S.S.R. never gives anything for nothing." Nagai took this to be a warning, but Matsuoka's enthusiasm could not be damped even when the ambassador to Germany, General Hiroshi Oshima, told him in confidence that there was a good likelihood Germany and Russia would soon go to war.

On April 6 the party left Berlin. At the Soviet border they learned that Germany had invaded Yugoslavia. Nagai and the other advisers were disturbed—just the previous day Russia had signed a neutrality pact with Yugoslavia—but Matsuoka himself was effervescent. "Now I have the agreement with Stalin in my pocket!" he told his private secretary, Toshikazu Kase.

He was right. A week after arriving in Moscow, he signed a neutrality pact in the Kremlin. At the extravagant celebration party, Stalin was so obviously delighted at the turn of events that he personally brought plates of food to the Japanese, embraced them, kissed them, and danced around like a performing bear. The treaty was a coup for his diplomacy, convincing proof that he could disregard rumors about a German attack on Russia. After all, if Hitler had any such plans, would he have allowed Japan to conclude this agreement? *"Banzai* for His Majesty the Emperor!" was his opening toast. He averred that diplomatic pledges should never be broken, even if ideologies differed.

Matsuoka toasted him in turn and then added something no other Japanese diplomat would have said. "The treaty has been made," he blurted out. "I do not lie. If I lie, my head shall be yours. If you lie, be sure I will come for your head."

"My head is important to my country," Stalin retorted coldly. "So is yours to your country. Let's take care to keep both our heads on our shoulders." It was an embarrassing moment made worse when Matsuoka, in an attempt to be funny, remarked that Nagai and his naval counterpart "were always talking of how to beat the devil out of you."

Stalin wasn't joking when he replied that while Japan was very strong, the Soviet Union was not the Czarist Russia of 1904. But an instant later he had regained his good humor. "You are an Asiatic," he said. "And so am I."

"We're all Asiatics. Let us drink to the Asiatics!"

The innumerable toasts made it necessary to delay the eastbound train for an hour. At the station platform the Japanese were taken aback to see Stalin and Molotov tipsily converging on them from a side door for a final good-bye. Stalin kissed Nagai. "The reason England's in trouble today," he bellowed, "is because she has a low opinion of soldiers." Beaming, Stalin then encompassed the diminutive Matsuoka in a bear hug and gave him several affectionate smacks. "There is nothing to fear in Europe," he said, "now that there is a Japan-Soviet neutrality pact!"

Matsuoka should have heeded Corneille's character who said, "I embrace my rival, but only to choke him." Instead, he blithely exclaimed, "There is nothing to fear in the whole world!" and like a conqueror, climbed aboard the train. (Stalin was already embracing another ambassador—Hitler's envoy, Count Friedrich Werner von der Schulenburg—and telling him, "We must remain friends, and you must do everything to that end.") As the train carrying Matsuoka traversed Siberia, he told Kase that just before leaving Moscow he had talked freely with his old friend Laurence Steinhardt, the American ambassador, and they had agreed to try to restore good relations between their two countries. "Now the stage is set," he said. "Next I will go to Washington."

3.

On the other side of the world Matsuoka's ambassador in Washington, the good-natured, one-eyed Kichisaburo Nomura, a retired admiral, was already endeavoring to patch up the differences between Japan and America with Secretary of State Cordell Hull. Their talks had been inspired by two energetic Catholic priests, Bishop James E. Walsh, Superior General of the Maryknoll Society, and his assistant, Father James M. Drought. Some six months earlier, armed with an introductory letter from Lewis L. Strauss of Kuhn, Loeb & Company, the two priests had gone to Tokyo, where they visited Tadao Ikawa, a director of the Central Agricultural and Forestry Bank. They persuaded him that men of good will in both Japan and America could help bring about a peaceful settlement, and showed Ikawa a memorandum calling for a Japanese "Far Eastern Monroe Doctrine" and a stand against Communism, "which is not a political form of government but a corroding social disease that becomes epidemic." Ikawa was impressed by the memorandum and felt sure any reasonable Japanese would agree to its terms. During several years' service in the United States as an official of the Finance Ministry, he had made numerous friends in New York banking circles and acquired an American wife. He assumed that the proposal had the backing of President Roosevelt, since Father Drought had mentioned he was acting with the approval of "top personnel" in the U. S. government and, fired with enthusiasm, introduced the clergymen to Prime Minister Konoye and Matsuoka. The former suggested that Ikawa sound out the Army in the person of an influential colonel in the War Ministry named Hideo Iwakuro. He was a unique combination of idealism and intrigue and was just the man to put the priests' project into action: he ardently believed that peace with America was Japan's salvation, and plotting was a way of life with him. Behind his impish smile was one of the most agile brains in the Army. An espionage and intelligence expert, he had founded the prestigious Nakano School for spies, which was at the time sending out groups of well-trained agents throughout Asia imbued with his own idealistic views of a free amalgamation of Asian nations. It was he, too, who had dreamed up the idea for wrecking the Chinese economy by flooding that country with a billion and a half dollars' worth of counterfeit yen. He had also succeeded in getting refuge in Manchuria for some five thousand wandering Jews who had fled Hitler, by persuading the Kwantung Army leaders on grounds that no true Japanese could deny: a debt was owed the Jews; the Jewish firm of Kuhn, Loeb & Company had helped finance the Russo-Japanese War.

Colonel Iwakuro arranged an interview for the two Americans with General Akira Muto, chief of the Military Affairs Bureau, and the latter was equally impressed by their proposal; he gave it his blessing. Around New Year's the two priests returned to America, where they made an ally out of Postmaster General Frank C.

Walker, a prominent Catholic. He set up an interview with President Roosevelt. The President met Bishop Walsh, read his long, enthusiastic memorandum and passed it on to Hull with the notation: ". . . What do you think we should do? FDR."

"In general, I am skeptical whether the plan offered is a practical one at this time," Hull replied in a note drafted largely by Dr. Stanley Hornbeck, his senior adviser on Far Eastern affairs, well known for his sympathy toward China and hostility toward Japan.* It seems to me that there is little or no likelihood that the Japanese Government and the Japanese people would in good faith accept any such arrangement at this stage."

But the President was so intrigued by the idea that he asked Postmaster General Walker to turn over his duties to an assistant and give Bishop Walsh whatever assistance he could. As a "presidential agent," Walker was empowered to set up secret headquarters on the eighteenth floor of the Berkshire Hotel in New York City, and was given a code name, "John Doe."

Late in January, Bishop Walsh cabled Ikawa: AS A RESULT OF MEETING WITH THE PRESIDENT, HOPEFUL OF PROGRESS, AWAITING DEVELOPMENTS. Ikawa wondered if he should go to Washington

---

* Hornbeck's views on China were shared by an America which had made Pearl Buck's novel *The Good Earth* a best seller. For three decades Americans had held a highly idealized picture of the Chinese, looking upon them as childlike innocents who needed protection against the imperialism of Britain and Japan. China was a helpless, deserving nation whose virtues America alone understood.

"In this highly subjective picture of the Chinese," wrote George F. Kennan, "there was no room for a whole series of historical and psychological realities. There was no room for the physical ruthlessness that had characterized Chinese political life generally in recent decades; for the formidable psychological and political powers of the Chinese people themselves; for the strong streak of xenophobia in their nature; for the lessons of the Boxer Rebellion; for the extraordinary exploitative talent shown by Chinese factions, of all times, in turning outside aid to domestic political advantage."

The so-called China Lobby did much to further China's cause in America. It was created by T. V. Soong, a clever and charming member of China's most omnipotent family. One sister had married Sun Yat-sen; another, a descendant of Confucius, H. H. Kung; and a third, Chiang Kai-shek. Educated at Harvard and Columbia, Soong became close friends with influential Americans such as Henry Morgenthau, Harry Hopkins, Roy Howard, Henry Luce, Joseph Alsop and Thomas Corcoran. With their help, and that of a Pole, Ludwig Rajchman, Soong set up the lobby in 1940 and found he now had direct access to President Roosevelt without having to go through Hull.

as well, to help the priests and Ambassador Nomura, who was about to sail for the United States, find a formula for coexistence. The admiral was a straightforward, honest man of good will and good nature, with many American friends, including President Roosevelt, but unfortunately had no foreign office experience and little aptitude for diplomacy.

Ikawa went to Colonel Iwakuro for advice. The colonel encouraged him to go and, moreover, wangled a commercial passport for him, as well as money for the trip from two industrialists who were willing to make a contribution toward peace. Ikawa would assist Nomura on the pretext of negotiating with American businessmen. When word of the trip leaked out, Matsuoka (just before his trip to Europe) accused the Army of "taking upon itself negotiations with America" and of "putting up the money." War Minister Hideki Tojo knew nothing of the arrangement and summoned Iwakuro to his office. Iwakuro was so persuasive that Tojo categorically, and in good faith, informed the Foreign Ministry that the Army had no knowledge whatsoever of the Ikawa mission.

It was a dangerous game but Iwakuro felt that friendly relations with America were well worth it, and playing dangerous games was his hobby. He thought this ended his part in the matter but it had just begun, for Tojo had become so impressed with Iwakuro's grasp of the situation that he was ordered to proceed to America to help Nomura in his mission.

To prepare himself for the assignment, Iwakuro consulted with those who called for war as well as those who wanted peace. One night at a party in the Ginza, Nissho Inoue, leader of the Blood Brotherhood, urged him to become a spy: "We are going to fight against Britain and the United States, since they are blockading us, and your duty in America is to find out when we should start the war." But these saber rattlers were far outnumbered by those who urged Iwakuro to arrange any kind of honorable settlement.

Exuding an air of conspiracy, he arrived in New York City on March 30 to find an America widely split on the issue of war or peace. The interventionists, convinced their country's future and ultimate safety depended on helping the democracies crush the aggressor nations, had just pushed through Congress the Lend-Lease Act committing America to unlimited aid, "short of war," to the enemies of the Axis. She was to be the Arsenal of Democracy.

Supporting this measure, and war itself, were such groups as "Bundles for Britain," as well as national minorities whose European relatives had suffered at the hands of Hitler and Mussolini. Their antiwar opponents included strange bedfellows: the right-wing "America Firsters" of Charles Lindbergh, Senator Borah and the German-American Bund; the "American Peace Mobilization" of the American Communist and Labor parties; and the traditionally isolationist Midwest which, though sympathetic to Britain and China, wanted no part of a shooting war.

Iwakuro was taken from the airport to St. Patrick's Cathedral to confer with Bishop Walsh and Father Drought. "Because of the Tripartite Pact, Japan cannot do anything to betray its co-signers," he said. "The thirteenth disciple, Judas, betrayed Christ, and every Christian despises him. It is the same with us Japanese. So if you insist that we withdraw from the pact, it will be hopeless to go on." The priests said they understood, and Iwakuro proceeded to Washington. He got a room at the Wardman Park Hotel, where Cordell Hull had recently taken an apartment. The next morning he reported to Admiral Nomura and found him affable and eager to utilize the unofficial channel opened up by the two priests and Ikawa. Most of the professional diplomats at the embassy, however, were hostile to this approach and were already treating Ikawa with open contempt. To them the new arrival was even more of an enigma. Iwakuro appeared to be "engagingly frank" but they felt he had come to camouflage the aggressive intents of the Army, and were wary.

On April 2 Father Drought began helping the two unofficial Japanese diplomats draw up a Draft Understanding between Japan and the United States. In three days it was completed. It was a broad agreement, conciliatory in tone, touching on problems ranging from the Tripartite Pact to economic activity in the southwest Pacific. Its most significant points concerned China, with Japan promising to withdraw troops and renounce all claims to any Chinese territory, provided China recognized Manchukuo and provided the government of Chiang Kai-shek was merged with that of a rival regime in Nanking under a former premier of the Republic of China, Wang Ching-wei.*

---

* Several months earlier, on November 30, 1940, Japan had signed a treaty with the Wang government. The son of a scholar, Wang had studied political science in Tokyo and became Sun Yat-sen's chief disciple. It was

Drought took one copy to Postmaster General Walker, who called it "a revolution in Japanese 'ideology' and policy, as well as a proof of the complete success of American statesmanship," and passed it along to Roosevelt, with the recommendation that he sign it immediately before "the Japanese leaders [were] assassinated." At the Japanese embassy Nomura, Minister Kaname Wakasugi, the military and naval attachés and a man from the Treaties Section, after some changes in wording, unanimously approved it.

The Draft Understanding was carefully examined at the State Department by the Far Eastern experts. They concluded that "most of its provisions were all that the ardent Japanese imperialists could want." Hull concurred but felt that "however objectionable some of the points might be, there were others that could be accepted as they stood and still others that could be agreed to if modified." On April 14 Ikawa told Nomura that he had arranged a private meeting with Hull at the Wardman Park Hotel that evening. Nomura was to go to Hull's apartment by a rear corridor and knock on the door at eight o'clock. Nomura did this, but he was afraid it was a practical joke. To his surprise, Hull opened the door. His was a sad, thoughtful face and he spoke slowly and gently except—as Nomura was to learn—when aroused. He came from Tennessee, land of mountain feuds, and was himself a man of implacable hatreds.

Nomura announced cryptically that he knew all about a certain "Draft Understanding," and though he hadn't yet forwarded it to Tokyo, thought his government "would be favorably disposed

---

he who wrote down Sun's last wishes at his deathbed. He served twice as premier of the Republic of China before becoming vice president of the Nationalist party. From the beginning he had been a rival of Chiang Kai-shek's, and their relations became so strained that at a private luncheon late in 1938 he suggested they both resign their offices and "redeem the sins they had committed against China." This infuriated Chiang and a few days later Wang thought it best to escape by plane to Hanoi. On March 30, 1940, he established his own splinter government in Nanking, although he had little popular support and not much money.

What he wanted primarily was peace with Japan for the good of the Chinese people, and if he had succeeded he would have become a national hero. But the treaty, which, by recognizing Wang's government, purportedly gave Japan a legal basis for fighting in China, was turning out badly for both Wang and the Japanese. It ruined any chance there was for Japan to make peace with Chiang Kai-shek and made the Nanking government a puppet of Japan. As a result, Wang had already become the symbol of treachery in China.

toward it." Hull raised objections to some of the points in the agreement but said that once these had been worked out, Nomura could send the revised document to Tokyo to ascertain whether the imperial government would take it as a "basis for negotiations." The inexperienced Nomura inferred from this that a revised Draft Understanding would be acceptable to the United States.

But the admiral was seriously mistaken. Hull had unwittingly misled Nomura, since he did *not* regard the proposals as a solid basis for negotiations. Perhaps the misunderstanding was a result of Nomura's faulty English. Or perhaps Nomura's great desire for a settlement had influenced his interpretation of Hull's vague phraseology. Nevertheless, it was largely Hull's fault. He should have known he was giving some encouragement to Nomura, when he had no such intentions. He had committed a tactical error.

The two diplomats met again two days later at Hull's apartment. "The one paramount preliminary question about which my Government is concerned," Hull began in his slow, circuitous manner, "is a definite assurance in advance that the Japanese Government has the willingness and ability to go forward with a plan . . . in relation to the problems of a settlement; to abandon its present doctrine of military conquest by force and . . . adopt the principles which this Government has been proclaiming and practicing as embodying the foundation on which all relations between nations should properly rest." He handed over a piece of paper listing these four principles:

1. Respect for the territorial integrity and the sovereignty of each and all nations.
2. Support of the principle of noninterference in the internal affairs of other countries.
3. Support of the principle of equality, including equality of commercial opportunity.
4. Nondisturbance of the status quo in the Pacific except as the status quo may be altered by peaceful means.

Wondering if his earlier optimism had been well founded, Nomura asked if Hull "would to a fairly full extent approve the proposals contained" in the Draft Understanding. Some would be readily approved, Hull replied, while others would have to be changed or eliminated. ". . . But if [your] Government is in real earnest about changing its course," he continued, "I [can] see no good reason why ways could not be found to reach a fairly mutually satisfactory settlement of all the essential questions and problems presented." This reassured Nomura and he remained optimistic even when Hull pointed out that they had "in no sense reached the stage of negotiations" and were "only exploring in a purely preliminary and unofficial way what action might pave the way for negotiations later."

Nomura transmitted Hull's suggestions and objections to the unofficial diplomats and most of his comments were incorporated in a revised Draft Understanding. The document was enciphered and dispatched to Tokyo, accompanied by a strong recommendation from Nomura for a favorable response. He added that Hull had "on the whole no objections" to the Draft Understanding (which Hull had said, in so many words) and was willing to use it as a basis for negotiations (which he had no intention of doing).

It was now Nomura's turn to commit a diplomatic blunder—as serious as Hull's. He failed to relay the Secretary of State's four basic principles to Tokyo. Certainly this information would have cooled some of Prime Minister Konoye's enthusiasm for the Draft Understanding. As it was, the Prime Minister was so encouraged by the way things seemed to be working out that he convened an emergency meeting of government and military leaders. They were just as enthused, including the military, and agreed that the American proposal—for that is what they thought the Draft Understanding was—should be promptly accepted in principle.*

Matsuoka's deputy protested. They should wait for a few days, until the Foreign Minister returned from Moscow. Konoye wanted no collision with the troublesome Matsuoka and acquiesced. On April 21 he learned that Matsuoka had at last arrived at Dairen,

* The Army General Staff had already received an optimistic report from the military attaché in Washington: IMPROVEMENT OF DIPLOMATIC RELATIONS BETWEEN JAPAN AND THE UNITED STATES CAN BE ESTABLISHED. PLEASE EXERT ALL EFFORTS TO SEND INSTRUCTIONS IMMEDIATELY.

One of War Minister Tojo's most trusted advisers, Colonel Kenryo Sato, was astounded that America would make such concessions. It was all "too good to be true," he felt, and passed along his suspicions to Tojo. But the War Minister was willing to do almost anything to settle the war in China honorably and went along with the rest of the Cabinet.

not far from the battlefields of the Russo-Japanese War, and told him over the phone to come home at once to consider an important proposal from Washington. Matsuoka assumed this was a result of his talk in Moscow with U. S. Ambassador Laurence Steinhardt and triumphantly told his secretary that he would soon be heading for America to complete his plan for world peace.

The next afternoon Matsuoka's plane landed at Tachikawa Air Base and he stepped out warmed by the cheers of the waiting crowd. Prime Minister Konoye was on hand, even though he was suffering so intensely from piles that he had to sit on an inflated circular tube. He offered to take Matsuoka to the Prime Minister's official residence, where other Cabinet ministers were waiting; he would brief the Foreign Minister on the negotiations with America en route. Matsuoka mentioned that he wanted to stop briefly at the plaza outside the Palace moat to pay his respects to the Emperor. To Konoye it was pretentious and in bad taste to bow deeply while newsmen took pictures, and he could not stand to the side while Matsuoka went through the ceremony or he'd be accused of insolence to the Emperor.

Since Matsuoka insisted on having his own way and Konoye was too proud to join him, the two left the airport in separate cars.* On the drive to the Palace, Matsuoka learned from his Vice Minister that the proposal for a peaceful settlement was not his own doing but the work of a couple of amateur diplomats. He was mortified, and that night was late for a conference at the Prime Minister's official residence, convened to discuss the Draft Understanding. He avoided not only Konoye but the subject of the meeting as well, talking incessantly of Hitler-*san* and Stalin-*san* as if they were his closest friends. Piqued at first, he became spirited and expansive as he boasted of how he had told Steinhardt that Roosevelt was

---

* Later Konoye repeatedly said, "If only I had ridden that day with Matsuoka!" His secretary, Ushiba, believes pain from piles was probably a contributing factor. If so, it was not the first time this relatively minor ailment changed history. Napoleon suffered intensely from hemorrhoids at Waterloo.

"Konoye may not have succeeded in placating Matsuoka," Ushiba commented further, "but his failure to ride with Matsuoka as he had planned may have been a turning point of history. It was really a great pity inasmuch as Konoye had been very keen on personally explaining to Matsuoka, and even restrained other Cabinet ministers from going to meet him. This incident throws much light on Konoye's character: he lacked persistence; he easily cooled off."

"quite a gambler" and that the United States was keeping both the China Incident and the war going with her aid. "I told him the peace-loving President of the United States should co-operate with Japan, which is also peace-loving, and that he should inveigle Chiang to make peace with us." He also related that Ribbentrop had told him that Germany had signed the pact with Russia only because of "unavoidable circumstances" and that if it came to war, Germany would probably be able to defeat Stalin in three or four months.

But the business of the conference could not be avoided indefinitely. When the Draft Understanding was finally brought up, Matsuoka burst out stridently, "I cannot agree to this, whatever you Army and Navy people say! First of all, what about our treaty with Germany and Italy? In the last war the United States made use of Japan through the Ishii-Lansing agreement,* and when the war was over, the United States broke it. This is an old trick of theirs." Suddenly he announced that he felt very tired and needed "a month's rest" to think things over, and went home.

His arrogant manner had not been of a kind to bring reassurance, and as the meeting continued far into the night, both Tojo and General Muto recommended that the Draft Understanding be approved without further delay. The following day Konoye summoned his Foreign Minister. Matsuoka had calmed down, but about all he would say was, "I wish you would give me time to forget all about my European trip; then I'll consider the present case."

A week passed without any action from Matsuoka, and pressure began to build in the Army and Navy for his removal. Whether he was so offended that negotiations had been initiated without him that he was deliberately sabotaging them or was merely being properly cautious for fear that an amateur attempt at peace might lead to disaster, it was difficult to tell.

The reason Matsuoka himself gave was that the Draft Understanding was merely a plot of the Army, and Colonel Iwakuro was making a cat's-paw out of him. So he did nothing, while the Army and Navy fumed and the negotiators in Washington wondered what had gone wrong. It was hardest on the impetuous Iwakuro. Finally, on April 29, the Emperor's birthday, he could restrain

---

* In 1917 the United States consented to Japan's request that her "special interests" in China be recognized, but terminated the ambiguous agreement after the Armistice.

himself no longer and suggested telephoning Matsuoka. It was indiscreet, but indiscretion was Iwakuro's creed and his associates were persuaded by his enthusiasm. It was decided that he and Ikawa should make the call from Postmaster General Walker's secret headquarters in New York City. By the evening they were in Room 1812 at the Berkshire Hotel, and began toasting the Emperor in port. The colonel had a small tolerance for wine and after two glasses he was feeling light-headed. At eight o'clock (it was ten o'clock the next morning in Japan) he put in the call to Matsuoka's home in Sendagaya.

"Congratulations on your trip to Europe," Iwakuro began. "About the fish I sent you the other day, how did you find it? Please have it cooked as soon as possible. Otherwise it will go bad. Nomura and all the others are expecting to have your reply soon."

"I know, I know," said Matsuoka curtly. "Tell him not to be so active."

Iwakuro wished he could have slapped Matsuoka for answering so rudely. "Please find out how others think about it. If you keep the fish around too long, it will surely go bad. Please be careful. Otherwise people will hold you responsible for everything."

"I know," was the blunt answer. Iwakuro hung up, muttered something incomprehensible, and to Ikawa's consternation, abruptly passed out.

The following day the two men called on former President Herbert Hoover, who welcomed them warmly but observed that since the Republicans were not in power, they could be of little help in the negotiations. "If war comes, civilization will be set back five hundred years," he said and added somberly, "The negotiations should be completed before summer or they will fail."

In Tokyo, Matsuoka was still delaying the reply to Hull. He had informed Hitler of the Draft Understanding and was waiting for his comments.* To those who pressed for action, he repeated that before approving the Draft Understanding, Japan should ask

---

* Matsuoka also promised the German ambassador, General Eugen Ott, who expressed fears that the negotiations in Washington would negate the Tripartite Pact, that if the United States entered the war, Japan would definitely get in it. Notwithstanding, Hitler was suspicious of Matsuoka, and told Mussolini that Matsuoka was a Catholic who also sacrificed to pagan gods and "one must conclude that he was combining the hypocrisy of an American Bible missionary with the craftiness of a Japanese Asiatic."

"Then the War Will Be a Desperate One"

America to sign a neutrality treaty which would be in effect even if Japan and Britain went to war. Nomura was told to sound out Hull on such a treaty. Naturally, Hull rejected the proposal peremptorily. This irritated Matsuoka no end; he told the Emperor on May 8 that if the United States entered the war in Europe, Japan should back their Axis allies and attack Singapore. He predicted that the talks in Washington would come to nothing, and that if they did succeed it would only mean that America had been placated at the expense of Germany and Italy. "If that happens, I am afraid I cannot remain in the Cabinet."

When Prince Konoye heard this—from the Emperor himself, who expressed his "astonishment and grave concern"—he secretly met with his War and Navy ministers, General Tojo and Admiral Koshiro Oikawa, and they agreed to force the fractious Foreign Minister to act. A reply accepting the main conditions of the Draft Understanding was drawn up, and Matsuoka was instructed to send it without delay.

On May 12 Nomura brought this document to Hull's apartment. Hull read it with disappointment. It "offered little basis for an agreement, unless we were willing to sacrifice some of our most basic principles, which we were not." Still, it was a formal proposition and he decided "to go forward on the basis of the Japanese proposals and seek to argue Japan into modifying here, eliminating there, and inserting elsewhere, until we might reach an accord we both could sign with mutual good will."

The problem—already beset by language difficulties, stubbornness, rigidity and confusion—was further aggravated by American intercepts of Japanese messages. Diplomatic codes, supposedly unbreakable, had been cracked by American experts, and messages from the Japanese government to its diplomats overseas were being intercepted and deciphered under the cover name of Operation MAGIC. Consequently, Hull usually knew what was on Nomura's mind before he walked into a conference.* But since many of the

---

* About two weeks earlier Ambassador Hiroshi Oshima had cabled from Berlin that he had just been told by Dr. Heinrich Stahmer, a Foreign Ministry official in charge of Japanese-German affairs, that German intelligence was fairly certain the American government was reading Nomura's coded messages. "There are at least two circumstances to substantiate the suspicion," said Oshima. "One is that Germany is also reading our coded messages. And the other is that the Americans once before succeeded in

decoded messages were not considered worthy of Hull's attention — a naval officer made this decision on his own — and since messages were translated by men not fluent in the stylized and difficult language of Japanese diplomacy, Hull was occasionally misled.

The judge from Tennessee, moreover, was constantly annoyed at the perpetual, "frozen" smiles of the Japanese, and either ridiculed or made fun of their bowing and "hissing."* As a result, it was easy for his chief adviser, Dr. Hornbeck, to persuade him that the Japanese were not to be trusted and that any compromise with Japan would be a betrayal of American democratic principles.

Hornbeck, a highly ethical man like his superior, who had been brought up in China, was by nature antagonistic to the Japanese and looked on their expansion from a purely moralistic standpoint. Hornbeck's associate in the State Department, J. Pierrepont Moffat, described him as regarding "Japan as the sun around which her satellites, Germany and Italy, were revolving." A proponent for economic warfare since the fall of 1938, he stood for "a diplomatic 'war plan.'" Stubborn and sensitive, he was convinced that Japan was a "predatory" power run by arrogant militarists who were encouraged by world timidity to go from aggression to aggression. He had always felt they could only be blocked by a series of retaliations, ending, if need be, in economic sanctions. This program should be put into effect even if it ended in war; bowing to the militarists' demands would eventually end in war, anyway. Like so many intellectuals — and he was one of the most brilliant men in the foreign service — he was opinionated.** He was also dictatorial and could easily override more objective subordinates, such as the modest Joseph W. Ballantine, the department's leading Japan expert.

During these trying days Hull and Nomura often met at the Wardman Park Hotel in an effort to work out their differences, but

---

compromising our codes, in 1922, during the Washington Conference." But Kazuji Kameyama, chief of the Cable Section, assured Matsuoka that it was humanly impossible to break the diplomatic code, and it was assumed that any secret information America obtained had come through security leaks.

* Snakes and cats hiss by expelling breath. Japanese do just the opposite, *sucking* in at times of cogitation, uncertainty or embarrassment.

** "I am still convinced," Ushiba wrote in 1970, "that *on the U. S. side*, Hull's formalism and orthodox diplomacy and Hornbeck's stubbornness proved the undoing of Konoye's efforts (granted there was much more stubbornness on the Japanese side!)"

made little progress. Part of their trouble came from Tokyo, where Matsuoka was making provocative announcements both privately and publicly. On May 14 he told Ambassador Grew that Hitler had shown great "patience and generosity" in not declaring war on the United States, and that American attacks on German submarines would doubtless lead to war between Japan and America. The "manly, decent and reasonable" thing for the United States to do, he said, was "to declare war openly on Germany instead of engaging in acts of war under cover of neutrality." Grew with all his sympathies could not bear such an insult, and he rebutted Matsuoka's assertions point for point. Matsuoka realized he had gone too far and after the meeting wrote a conciliatory note:

> . . . I was wondering, to be frank, why you appeared so disturbed when I referred to the American attitude and actions. After Your Excellency's departure, it all suddenly dawned on me that I misused a word. . . . Of course, I didn't mean to say "indecent." No! I wanted to say "indiscretion."
> I write you the above in order to remove any misapprehension; I'd feel very sorry if I caused any.

Three days later Matsuoka wrote Grew again. In a long, disjointed letter marked "Entirely Private" he said he knew how to be "correct" as a foreign minister but often forgot that he was foreign minister. Furthermore, he hated the so-called correct attitudes of many diplomats which "hardly get us anywhere" and then admitted that he thought in terms of one, two and even three thousand years, and if that sounded like insanity he couldn't help it because he was made that way.

Indeed, more than one thought this last was the case. At a recent liaison conference Navy Minister Oikawa had remarked, "The Foreign Minister is insane, isn't he?" And President Roosevelt, after reading a MAGIC translation of instructions sent by Matsuoka to Nomura, thought they were "the product of a mind which is deeply disturbed and unable to think quietly or logically."

Prince Konoye, however, believed Matsuoka's provocative, inflammatory and sometimes erratic statements were purposely made to frighten opponents; perhaps that was why he kept aiming so many barbs at America. But if this had started as a tactic and he sincerely wanted peace, it ended in disaster. Because of his insults and delays, the talks in Washington had about reached an impasse. Matsuoka knew this was happening, yet he continued insulting and delaying and looking to Hitler for advice. He was deliberately wrecking the negotiations probably out of his egomaniacal conviction that he and he alone knew the real America and could resolve the controversy.

He remained belligerent while Nomura and Iwakuro talked peace, and Hull, understandably, concluded that he was being misled. On June 21 the Secretary of State at last answered the Japanese proposal: Japan would have to abandon the Tripartite Pact, and he rejected the Japanese plan to retain troops in certain areas of North China to help the Chinese combat the Communists.

Konoye and his cabinet were dismayed. It wasn't even as acceptable an offer as the Draft Understanding. Why had the Americans changed from their "original" proposal? wondered Konoye, still unaware that Hull had never regarded the Draft Understanding as a basis for negotiations.

What infuriated Matsuoka was an Oral Statement that accompanied Hull's answer to the effect that recent public statements by certain Japanese officials—and it was obvious he meant Matsuoka—seemed to be an unsurmountable roadblock to the negotiations. The Foreign Minister took this as a personal insult, and cause for breaking off the talks in Washington altogether.

This concern and confusion was eclipsed the next day, Sunday, June 22, when Hitler invaded Russia. The Japanese were taken by surprise, although Ambassador Oshima, after talks with Hitler and Ribbentrop, had cabled sixteen days earlier that war between Germany and Russia was imminent.

It also came as a blow to Stalin, despite 180 German violations of Soviet air space (including penetrations as deep as four hundred miles) in the previous two months. There were also unheeded warnings of an impending attack from official Washington and London—and Stalin's own secret agent in Tokyo, Richard Sorge, who had correctly predicted in the spring of 1939 that Germany would march into Poland on September 1. Sorge not only dispatched photocopies of telegrams from Ribbentrop informing his ambassador in Tokyo, General Eugen Ott, that the Wehrmacht would invade the Soviet Union in the second half of June, he also sent a last-minute message on June 14: "War begins June 22." In the first few hours the Luftwaffe wiped out 66 Soviet airfields and destroyed 1,200 planes while ground forces swept forward capturing almost 2,000 big guns, 3,000 tanks and 2,000 truckloads of ammunition.*

The news of the attack reached Tokyo a little before four o'clock on Sunday afternoon. Within minutes Matsuoka phoned the Lord Privy Seal, Marquis Koichi Kido, and asked for an audience with the Emperor. Kido was a small, neatly compact man of fifty-two, with a trimmed mustache, and had, like Konoye, been a protégé of Prince Saionji's. The liberal political philosophy and logical reasoning which characterized the last *genro* (he had died the previous year at the age of ninety-one) had always made a deep impression on him, particularly Saionji's repeated warnings that Japan's policy must be based on co-operation with Britain and America. Accordingly, Kido had actively opposed the seizure of Manchuria, the push into China and the Tripartite Pact. His grandfather by marriage, as it were, was Koin Kido, one of the four most illustrious leaders of the Meiji Restoration,** but the young man had earned every advancement by his own industry and ability. As Lord Keeper of the Privy Seal, Kido was the permanent confi-

---

* According to *A Short History of the U.S.S.R.:* "The country's poor preparedness was due to grave errors of judgement made by Stalin in evaluating the general strategic situation and in his estimates of the probable time the war would break out. . . . Hitler hoped that his surprise attack would knock out the Red Army, and to be sure, Stalin's errors of judgement, and his outright mistakes, went a long way to further his designs."

Early in 1969, however, the Soviet Communist party's most authoritative journal, *Kommunist*, declared that Stalin was an "outstanding military leader," and that Nikita Khrushchev's dramatic attack on Stalin at the 20th Party Congress in 1956 was completely unfounded. "Not a stone remains of the irresponsible statements about his military incompetence, of his direction of the war 'on a globe,' of his supposedly absolute intolerance of other views, and of other similar inventions grasped and spread by foreign falsifiers of history." This reappraisal was echoed a few days later by the Red Army newspaper *Krasnaya Zvezda* in a lengthy attack on "revisionists" in such countries as Czechoslovakia, Yugoslavia and France.

** In going over this portion of the manuscript for corrections, Marquis Kido wrote: "My grandfather is generally called Koin, but the proper pronunciation of the Japanese characters is Takayoshi." Takayoshi had no son to carry on the family name, and his nephew Takamasa (his younger sister's son) was legally made a Kido after he married Takayoshi's only daughter. She died and Takamasa married again; Koichi Kido was the eldest son of that union.

dential adviser to the Emperor on all matters ("I was to the Emperor what Harry Hopkins was to President Roosevelt") and Hirohito had grown to lean on his counsel. Konoye and Kido were probably the two most influential civilians in Japan, and though close friends, were almost exact opposites in character as well as appearance. Already highly respected as a hard-headed, practical man, the Privy Seal was direct and decisive, a pragmatist. He was an able administrator and every detail of his life was carefully planned, precisely executed. In golf, which he played with zealous regularity, he was such a model of precision with his modulated swing that his partners called him "Kido the Clock."

After arranging a five-thirty audience for Matsuoka, Kido informed the Emperor that the Foreign Minister's views probably differed from Konoye's. "I would like His Majesty to ask him if he has consulted with the Prime Minister regarding the question, and tell him that this question is extremely important," said Kido. "Therefore he should confer closely with the Prime Minister and tell him that the Emperor is basically in agreement with the Prime Minister. Please excuse my impertinence for daring to give His Majesty this advice."

When Matsuoka spoke to the Emperor, within the hour, it was evident he had not yet talked with Konoye. He was sure Germany would quickly defeat Russia,* and recommended an immediate attack on Siberia and a postponement of the push to the south. Astonished, since this policy meant expansion in two directions, the Emperor asked Matsuoka to consult with Konoye and indicated that the audience was over.

Matsuoka did see Konoye but listened to no advice, and continued to call for an attack on Russia in private as well as at liaison conferences. These were ordinarily held at the Prime Minister's official residence. They were informal gatherings of the Big Four of

* The U. S. military agreed. Secretary of the Navy Frank Knox prognosticated that "it would take anywhere from six weeks to two months for Hitler to clean up in Russia." Secretary of War Henry Stimson wrote in his diary; "I cannot help feeling that it offers to us and Great Britain a great chance, provided we use it promptly," and then told Roosevelt that in his opinion it would take Germany from one to three months to whip the Soviet Union. Ambassador Grew thought only good could come of the attack and wrote in his diary: "Let the Nazis and the Communists so weaken each other that the democracies will soon gain the upper hand or at least be released from their dire peril."

the Cabinet—the Prime Minister, Foreign Minister, War Minister and Navy Minister—with the Army and Navy Chiefs and Vice Chiefs of Staff. Other Cabinet ministers and experts occasionally attended to give counsel and information. The Prime Minister sat in an armchair near the center of a medium-sized conference room surrounded by the others. Three secretaries—the Chief Secretary of the Cabinet, the chief of the Military Affairs Bureau of the War Ministry and the chief of the Naval Affairs Bureau of the Navy Ministry—sat near the entrance.

The conferences were lively. There was no presiding officer, no strict protocol, and arguments were common. The meetings had been started in late 1937, to co-ordinate activities of the government and the military, discontinued for some time, then resumed in late 1940 when the situation became more critical.

Three days after Matsuoka's audience with the Emperor, he met direct opposition from the military, who were not eager for a simultaneous fight with the Soviet Union and America. Naval operations against both these countries, said Navy Minister Oikawa, would be too difficult. "To avoid this kind of situation, don't tell us to attack the U.S.S.R. and at the same time push south. The Navy doesn't want the Soviet Union provoked."

"When Germany wipes out the Soviet Union, we can't simply share in the spoils of victory unless we've done something," said Matsuoka and then uttered words which were strange coming from a foreign minister. "We must either shed our blood or embark on diplomacy. And it's better to shed blood." The following day he pressed his argument. What was more important, the north or the south? he asked.

Of equal import, replied Army Chief of Staff Sugiyama. "We're waiting to see how the situation develops." He did not reveal that if Moscow fell before the end of August, the Army would attack Siberia.

"It all depends on the situation," said Army Vice Chief of Staff Ko Tsukada, a bright, short-tempered man. "We can't go both ways simultaneously."

After the conference Colonel Kenryo Sato continued the debate with Tojo, who felt Matsuoka had made several good points. "We gain nothing in the north," said Sato. "At least we get oil and other resources in the south." He was as brilliant and impulsive as General

Ishihara and Colonel Iwakuro, and often served as the official spokesman for Army policy. He was already notorious throughout the country for having yelled "Shut up!" at a Diet member who kept interrupting his speech.

Wary as he was of Sato's quixotic behavior, Tojo had come to depend on advice from the "Shut up" colonel. Sato's logic made him wonder, "If we declare war on the Russians, would the United States back them up and declare war on us?"

"It's not impossible. America and the Soviet Union have different systems, but you never can tell in war."

The following day Tojo gave Matsuoka no support at all. But the Foreign Minister was undaunted. He argued that reports from Ambassador Oshima indicated that the war in Russia would soon be over and that England would capitulate before the end of the year. "If we start discussing the Soviet problem *after* the Germans beat the Soviets, we'll get nowhere diplomatically. If we hit the Soviets without delay, the United States won't enter the war." He was confident, he said, that he could hold off the United States for three or four months with his diplomacy. "But if we just wait around to see how things will turn out, as the Supreme Command suggests, we'll be encircled by Britain, the United States and Russia. We must first strike north, then south." He went on and on almost compulsively until he saw that his words were having no effect. Then, in an attempt to force the issue, he said, "I would like a decision to attack the Soviet Union."

"No," said Sugiyama, who spoke for all the military.

Matsuoka's strongest ally was in Berlin, but Hitler himself had yet to come out with a flat request to attack Russia. He did this three days later, in the form of a telegram from Ribbentrop to his ambassador in Tokyo. On the morning of June 30 General Ott transmitted this request to Matsuoka, who used it as a principal argument at the liaison conference that afternoon. Germany, he announced, was now formally asking Japan to come into the war. He became so fervent in his appeal for an attack on Russia that one listener likened it to "a vomit of fire." "My predictions have always come true," Matsuoka boasted. "Now I predict that if war starts in the south, America and Britain will join it!" He suggested postponing the drive south and was so persuasive that Oikawa turned to Sugiyama and said, "Well, how about postponing it for six months?"

It looked as if Matsuoka had abruptly turned things around by his oratory. A Navy man leaned over and whispered to Army Vice Chief of Staff Tsukada that perhaps they should consider the postponement, but Tsukada could not be swayed; with a few impassioned words of his own, he brought Oikawa and Sugiyama back to their original position. At this point Prince Konoye, who had been almost silent until then, said that he would have to go along with the Supreme Command. There was no more to say. The long debate was over and the decision was made to go south.

The final step was to get formal approval from the Emperor. This would come automatically at a ceremony held at the Imperial Palace, an imperial conference. At these meetings the Emperor traditionally did nothing but sit silent and listen to explanations of the policy in question. Afterward he would indicate his approval with a stamp of his seal. The members were comprised of those who attended liaison conferences, an expert or two, and the President of the Privy Council, a civilian who represented the Throne in a sense by occasionally asking questions the Emperor himself could not.

The conference to approve the move south was convened on July 2. The members sat stiffly on both sides of two long tables covered with brocade, but the minute the Emperor entered the room they shot to their feet. His skin, like that of his three brothers, was smooth as porcelain and of unique coloring. His army uniform did not make him look a bit martial. He stepped up to the dais and sat down before a gold screen, facing south, the direction to be honored according to court etiquette. He seemed detached, as if above worldly affairs.

Below, the members sat down at right angles to His Majesty and stared woodenly at each other, hands on knees. Then the ceremony began. All but the President of the Privy Council, Yoshimichi Hara, had rehearsed what they would say. First Prince Konoye rose, bowed to the Emperor and read a document entitled "Outline of National Policies in View of Present Developments." It was the plan to go south; the first step would be occupation of French Indochina. This, hopefully, would come without bloodshed by exerting diplomatic pressure on the Vichy government; but if persuasion failed, military force was to be used, even at the risk of provoking war with America and Britain.

Sugiyama bowed and said he agreed that Japan should push south. "However, if the German-Soviet war develops favorably for our empire, I believe we should also use force to settle this problem and so secure our northern borders."

Admiral Osami Nagano, Chief of the Navy General Staff, also felt it was necessary to go south despite the risks. When he finished, the President of the Privy Council began asking questions, some of them more embarrassing than expected at such a formalized meeting. What were the realistic chances of taking Indochina by diplomatic means? he wondered.

"The odds are that diplomatic measures won't succeed," replied Matsuoka. Still against going south, he had to argue the majority decision.

Hara was a small, mild-looking man but he was not at all intimidated by the stern faces of the generals and admirals. He emphasized that military action was "a serious thing." And wasn't sending troops into Indochina while attempting to ratify a treaty between Japan and France inconsistent with the Imperial Way of conducting diplomacy? "I do not think it wise for Japan to resort to direct, unilateral military action and thus be branded an aggressor."

"I will see to it that we won't seem to be involved in an act of betrayal in the eyes of the world," Matsuoka assured him.

Hara remained dubious. Why not go north? he suggested and began using some of Matsuoka's own arguments. Hitler's attack on Russia presented the chance of a lifetime. "The Soviet Union is spreading Communism all over the world and we will have to fight her sooner or later. . . . The people are really eager to fight her." What was supposed to be a formality threatened to turn into a debate. "I want to avoid war with the United States. I don't think they would retaliate if we attacked the Soviet Union." On the other hand, Hara feared a move into Indochina would bring war with the Anglo-Saxons.

Matsuoka had used the same words the day before. "There is that possibility," he agreed.

Sugiyama privately thought that Hara's questions were "sharp as a knife," but curtly pointed out that the occupation of Indochina was "absolutely necessary to crush the intrigues of Britain and America. Moreover, with Germany's military situation so favorable, I don't believe Japan's advance into French Indochina will provoke America to war." He warned, however, of counting out the Soviet Union prematurely. They should wait "from fifty to sixty days," to make certain that Germany would win. The finality of his statement shut off further discussion, and any hopes that Matsuoka might have had about resuming the debate vanished. A vote was taken and the policy document unanimously approved. Japan would go south.

Throughout the proceedings the Emperor had been sitting silent and impassive, as custom decreed, his mere presence making any decision legal and binding. The document was taken to the Cabinet secretariat, where a copy was made on official stationery. It was signed by Konoye and the Army and Navy Chiefs of Staff, brought to the Emperor and finally to the Privy Seal's office, where the imperial seal was affixed. It was national policy, and another step had been taken toward total war.

4.

Now Hull's counterproposal had to be dealt with. Matsuoka, predictably, was still in a rage over the Oral Statement, which criticized unnamed Japanese officials for inflammatory public remarks. This rather innocuous rebuke was, to Maysuoka, a personal insult as well as an unforgivable affront to Japan, and at a liaison conference on July 12 he said, with anger bordering on paranoia, "I've thought about it for the last ten days, and I believe America looks on Japan as a protectorate or a dependency! While I'm foreign minister, I can't accept it. I'll consider anything else, but I reject the Oral Statement. It is typically American to ride roughshod over the weak. The statement treats Japan as a weak and dependent country. Some Japanese are against me, and some even say the Prime Minister is against me." His words tumbled out, revealing as much resentment for his personal enemies as for Hull.

"Little wonder then that the United States thinks Japan is exhausted and therefore sends us such a statement. I propose right now that we reject the statement out of hand and break off negotiations with the United States!" He called Roosevelt "a real demagogue" and accused him of trying to lead America into war. As for himself, it had been his cherished hope since his youth to preserve peace between Japan and America. "I think there is no hope, but," he concluded irrationally, "let us try until the very end."

At last he had said something the military liked. Even if there seemed to be no hope, Tojo repeated, they should keep negotiating with America. "Can't we at least keep the United States from formally going to war by means of the Tripartite Pact? Naturally, the Oral Statement is an insult to our *kokutai* and we must reject it, as the Foreign Minister advises. But what if we sincerely tell the Americans what we Japanese hold to be right? Won't this move them?"

Navy Minister Oikawa was also for coming to some agreement with the Americans. According to reports, they weren't in any position to instigate a war in the Pacific. "Since we don't want a Pacific war either, isn't there room for negotiation?"

"Room?" Matsuoka retorted with some sarcasm. "They'll probably listen only if we tell them we won't use force in the south. What else would they accept?" He was in no mood for compromise. "They sent a message like this because they're convinced we submit easily."

It was obvious to Prince Konoye that Matsuoka was making this a personal issue and that it would be necessary to by-pass him. But the Foreign Minister's influence was still so great that the Prime Minister had to meet surreptitiously with key Cabinet members to draft their own conciliatory reply to Hull. This was presented to Matsuoka, but it took him several days just to read it—he claimed he was sick—and even after he had, he tried to delay matters. First, the Oral Statement should be rejected, then there should be a wait of several days before dispatching the answer.

Prime Minister Konoye agreed to reject the statement but insisted that both the rejection and the reply be sent simultaneously to Hull, to save time. Konoye gave these instructions to Matsuoka's associate Dr. Yoshie Saito, who promised to follow orders. He

"Then the War Will Be a Desperate One"

disobeyed—another act of *gekokujo*—and without consulting anyone, cabled a single message to Washington: the rejection of the Oral Statement. He held back the proposal for a few days, as Matsuoka had wanted, and Hull first saw it in an intercepted cable to Germany.

To the legal-minded Tojo such action was insupportable, and he told Konoye that Matsuoka should be dismissed at once. But the prince did not want open conflict with Matsuoka, who was still a public hero after his meetings with Hitler and Stalin. Konoye decided to get rid of him by subterfuge: he would ask the entire Cabinet to resign and then form a new one with a different foreign minister. He called an extraordinary session of the Cabinet at six-thirty on July 16, and when he made his proposal, no one objected; Matsuoka was home ill in bed.

This terminated the stormy career of the most controversial figure in Japanese diplomacy. The end had come through an act of insubordination committed for Matsuoka's sake by a faithful subordinate, but without his knowledge.

The following day the Emperor asked Konoye to form a new cabinet. He did so within twenty-four hours, which was possible only because there were so few changes. Matsuoka was replaced by an admiral who got along well with Americans, Teijiro Toyoda. One of his first acts was to cable his ambassador in Vichy that the Japanese Army would push into Indochina on July 24 no matter what the Vichy government decided to do. But on the day before the deadline, Vichy agreed to the peaceful entry of Japanese troops in southern Indochina. The ambassador in Vichy triumphantly wired Tokyo:

THE REASON WHY THE FRENCH SO READILY ACCEPTED THE JAPANESE DEMANDS WAS THAT THEY SAW HOW RESOLUTE WAS OUR DETERMINATION AND HOW SWIFT OUR WILL. IN SHORT, THEY HAD NO CHOICE BUT TO YIELD.

When Hull read this, courtesy of MAGIC, he was as indignant, and perhaps rightly so, as if Indochina had been taken by force. He pressed Roosevelt to retaliate by imposing a new embargo on Japan, despite a recent warning from the War Plans Division of the Navy that such action "would probably result in a fairly early attack by Japan on Malaya and the Netherlands East Indies, and possibly involve the United States in early war in the Pacific."

This time Roosevelt listened to those who, like Ickes, had long been urging him to act forcefully against all aggressors.* On the night of July 26 he ordered all Japanese assets in America frozen, and Britain and the Netherlands soon followed suit. In consequence, not only did all trade with the United States cease, but the fact that America had been Japan's major source of oil imports now left Japan in an untenable situation. To the *New York Times* it was "the most drastic blow short of war." To Japan's leaders it was much more. They had secured the bases in Indochina by negotiation with Vichy France, a country recognized if not approved by America, and international law was on their side; the freezing was the last step in the encirclement of the empire by the ABCD (American, British, Chinese, Dutch) powers, a denial to Japan of her rightful place as leader of Asia and a challenge to her very existence.

The frustration, near-hysteria and anger could be expected but not the confusion among the Supreme Command. Five days later Naval Chief of Staff Nagano, a cautious and sensible man, still had not recovered from an event that should have been foreseen. In an audience with the Emperor, he first said he wanted to avoid war and that this could be done by revoking the Tripartite Pact, which the Navy had always maintained was a stumbling block to peace with America. Then he warned that Japan's oil stock would only last for two years, and once war came, eighteen months, and concluded, "Under such circumstances, we had better take the initiative. We will win."

It was a curious performance. In one paragraph Nagano had put in a word for peace, cleared the Navy of responsibility for any diplomatic disaster, prophesied an oil famine, suggested a desperate attack and predicted victory.

---

* On the day after Hitler's invasion of Russia, Secretary of the Interior Harold Ickes wrote Roosevelt: "To embargo oil to Japan would be as popular a move in all parts of the country as you could make. There might develop from the embargoing of oil to Japan such a situation as would make it, not only possible but easy, to get into this war in an effective way. And if we should thus indirectly be brought in, we would avoid the criticism that we had gone in as an ally of communist Russia."

"Then the War Will Be a Desperate One"

The Emperor cut through the tangle with one question: "Will you win a great victory? Like the Battle of Tsushima?"

"I am sorry, but that will not be possible."

"Then," said the Emperor grimly, "the war will be a desperate one."

PART TWO

The Lowering Clouds

4

"Go Back to Blank Paper"

1.

Konoye's actions over the past few years had baffled those who sympathized with the tremendous problems he faced. Why had a liberal allowed the Army to gain ascendancy? Why had he subordinated himself to his own Foreign Minister, permitted him to endanger the negotiations in Washington? Ambassador Craigie was impressed by Konoye's numerous acts of statesmanship "only to be irritated just as often by his apparent lack of firmness in leadership and his failure at times of crisis to use his strong personal position to curb the extremists."*

* Ushiba, who was privy to Konoye's thoughts, comments: "A Churchill or a Kennedy might have succeeded in controlling the Army, but given the Japanese constitutional system, by which the Supreme Command was independent of the Prime Minister, and confronted with such a huge organization determined to control national destiny, it is doubtful if even Churchill could have succeeded. Konoye was no leader, was not a strong-man type, was not the kind of man whose outstanding feature is courage, resoluteness, dedication to a cause. He was, however, informed of what the Japanese Army was like, better perhaps than any other outsider, and concerned about taming it as much as anybody else. His philosophy was basically negative; that is, not to offend or provoke, and to defer the showdown as long as possible. If you stood in the Army's way, it would simply remove you and proceed to find another convenient blind or cover behind which it could do whatever it wanted."

In the opinion of Lieutenant General Teiichi Suzuki, director of the Cabinet Planning Board and an Army intellectual, Konoye wavered at critical moments not from weakness, but from intellectual doubts, and his objectivity rendered him almost incapable of making a clear-cut decision and taking action on it.

But both Suzuki and Craigie agreed on one thing—Konoye was another Hamlet. And like Hamlet he was finally spurred to decisive action—he would meet privately with President Roosevelt to settle once and for all the question of China.* On August 4 he summoned War Minister Tojo and Navy Minister Oikawa and told them of his decision. "If the President still does not see reason I shall, of course, be fully prepared to break off the talks and return home." Both Japan and America would have to make concessions, but he felt agreement could be reached if the high-level talks were "carried out with broad-mindedness." He promised that he would neither be "too anxious or hasty to come to terms, nor assume a supercilious manner or act submissively."

Tojo and Oikawa refused to commit themselves without consulting their colleagues. Within hours the admiral reported back that the Navy was in "complete accord and, moreover, anticipated the success of the conference." But Tojo found Army opinion divided. He wrote the Prime Minister that it was feared the summit meeting would weaken Japan's current policy, which was based on the Tripartite Pact, as well as cause repercussions at home. Nevertheless, the Army had no objections to the meeting so long as Konoye promised to lead the war against America if Roosevelt refused to appreciate Japan's position. He concluded the letter with the pessimistic observation that "the probability of failure of this meeting is eight to ten."

Konoye himself had no doubts, and over lunch told his close friend Shigeharu Matsumoto, editor in chief of the Domei News Agency, about the proposed meeting with Roosevelt. On the morning of August 6 the prince advised the Emperor of his intentions. "You had better see Roosevelt at once," said His Majesty, re-

* About this time Konoye called Admiral Isoroku Yamamoto, commander in chief of the Combined Fleet, to his private home and asked what chances there were in an attack on America. Yamamoto foresaw success for a year or so. "But after that I am not at all sure." This confirmed Konoye's own suspicions and his conviction that a meeting with Roosevelt was the only solution.

calling what Admiral Nagano had told him about the dwindling oil stockpile. The following morning a message was sent to Secretary of State Hull suggesting that Konoye and Roosevelt meet in Honolulu to discuss means of adjusting the differences between the two countries.

But Hull was dubious of Konoye's proposal. It had the same "hand-to-heart touch" used by Hitler on Chamberlain at Munich. Secretary of War Stimson was in accord and wrote in his diary: "The invitation to the President is merely a blind to try to keep us from taking definite action." After two days the Secretary of State saw Ambassador Nomura, who wanted a definite reply. But Hull, mixing accusations with moral observations, contended that it was now clear that those in Japan who favored peace "had lost control." The Japanese press "was being constantly stimulated to speak of encirclement of Japan by the United States." That very day, he continued, he had told correspondents "there is no occasion for any nation in the world that is law-abiding and peaceful to become encircled by anybody except itself." The frustrated Nomura finally asked if this was the reply to the suggested summit meeting and Hull reiterated everything he had just uttered, concluding that "it remained with the Japanese Government to decide whether it could find means of shaping its policies accordingly and then endeavor to evolve some satisfactory plan."

Since the Japanese military leaders felt they had bent a good deal to approve the meeting, its cool reception in Washington sharpened a growing suspicion. Did the Americans really want peace or were they playing for time? Each day twelve thousand tons of irreplaceable oil were being consumed and soon the armed forces would be as helpless as a whale thrown up on the beach.

Roosevelt was not on hand to discuss the situation. The cruiser *Augusta* was taking him to a rendezvous in Argentia Bay, Newfoundland, with Winston Churchill. On Sunday, August 10, the President attended church services on the deck of the British battleship *Prince of Wales,* in the shadows of its big guns. The lesson, appropriately, was from Joshua: "There shall not any man be able to stand before thee all the days of thy life: as I was with Moses, so will I be with thee: I will not fail thee, nor forsake thee."

After the service Roosevelt, in his wheelchair, was taken on a tour of the ship by Churchill. Belowdecks, Acting Secretary of State Sumner Welles was being shown two messages to Japan drafted by Churchill, to be sent simultaneously from Washington and London, warning of severe countermeasures if Japan continued her aggression in the southwest Pacific.

As Welles was leaving *Prince of Wales,* Churchill said he didn't think "there was much hope left unless the United States made such a clear-cut declaration of preventing Japan from expanding further to the south, in which event the prevention of war between Great Britain and Japan appeared to be hopeless."

The next day Roosevelt and Churchill conferred on *Augusta.* Roosevelt felt "very strongly that every effort should be made to prevent the outbreak of war with Japan." The problem was what line to take—tough, medium or soft? Tough, said Churchill; the proposals from Tokyo were no more than "smoothly worded offers by which Japan would take all she could for the moment and give nothing for the future."

Roosevelt suggested that he negotiate "about these unacceptable conditions" and win a delay of some thirty days while Britain secured its position in the Singapore area. The month gained would be valuable. "Leave that to me," he observed. "I think I can baby them along for three months."

Confident that he had swayed Roosevelt to take the "tough" line, Churchill telegraphed Foreign Secretary Anthony Eden:

. . . AT THE END OF THE NOTE WHICH THE PRESIDENT WILL HAND TO THE JAPANESE AMBASSADOR WHEN HE RETURNS FROM HIS CRUISE IN ABOUT A WEEK'S TIME HE WILL ADD THE FOLLOWING PASSAGE, WHICH IS TAKEN FROM MY DRAFT: "ANY FURTHER ENCROACHMENT BY JAPAN IN THE SOUTHWEST PACIFIC WOULD PRODUCE A SITUATION IN WHICH THE UNITED STATES GOVERNMENT WOULD BE COMPELLED TO TAKE COUNTERMEASURES, EVEN THOUGH THESE MIGHT LEAD TO WAR BETWEEN THE UNITED STATES AND JAPAN." HE WOULD ALSO ADD SOMETHING TO THE EFFECT THAT IT WAS OBVIOUS THAT THE SOVIET BEING A FRIENDLY POWER, UNITED STATES GOVERNMENT WOULD BE SIMILARLY INTERESTED IN ANY SIMILAR CONFLICT IN THE NORTHWEST PACIFIC.

"Go Back to Blank Paper"

Perhaps Churchill was right, but once at home Hull, who was himself convinced that nothing would stop the Japanese except force (recently, he had told Welles over the phone, "I just don't want us to take for granted a single word they say, but to appear to do so to whatever extent it may satisfy our purpose to delay further action by them"), convinced the President to reconsider and take a more moderate course. On August 17, though it was Sunday, he sent for Ambassador Nomura. Roosevelt was in high spirits and said that if Japan halted her expansion activities and decided "to embark upon a program of peace in the Pacific," the United States would be "prepared to reopen the unofficial preparatory discussions which were broken off in July, and every effort will then be made to select a time and place to exchange views." He was intrigued by the idea of a secret meeting and even suggested that it take place in Juneau, Alaska, "around the middle of October."

Nomura immediately cabled Tokyo: A REPLY SHOULD BE MADE BEFORE THIS OPPORTUNITY IS LOST.

The following afternoon, August 18, Ambassador Grew was summoned by Foreign Minister Teijiro Toyoda. The admiral ("a sympathetic and very human type," according to Grew) said he wanted to speak frankly, as a naval officer and not as a diplomat. Japan had gone into Indochina to solve the China affair and not because of pressure from Germany. The freezing of funds which followed had left "a big black spot on the long history of peaceful relations" between Japan and America, and future historians would be unable to understand if the negotiations broke down. The solution was a meeting between the two leaders of both countries in which the problems could be settled "in a calm and friendly atmosphere on an equal basis."

Grew, who had not been informed by the State Department of the proposed Konoye-Roosevelt meeting, was taken by the novel idea. Both leaders were gentlemen from distinguished families and they could reach an honorable settlement. Moreover, he would be in attendance and it could be the crowning moment of his own career.

With the heat so oppressive in the ministry, the admiral ordered iced drinks and cold wet towels, and suggested that they remove their coats. As they swabbed themselves with the towels, Grew said, "Admiral, you have often stood on the bridge of a battleship and have seen bad storms which lasted for several days, but ever since you took over the bridge of the Foreign Office you have undergone one long, continuous storm without any rest. You and I will have to pour some oil on those angry waves."

The meeting lasted for an hour and a half, and as soon as Grew returned to the embassy he sent an extraordinary message to Hull:

... THE AMBASSADOR [Grew] URGES ... WITH ALL THE FORCE AT HIS COMMAND, FOR THE SAKE OF AVOIDING THE OBVIOUSLY GROWING POSSIBILITY OF AN UTTERLY FUTILE WAR BETWEEN JAPAN AND THE UNITED STATES, THAT THIS JAPANESE PROPOSAL NOT BE TURNED ASIDE WITHOUT VERY PRAYERFUL CONSIDERATION. NOT ONLY IS THE PROPOSAL UNPRECEDENTED IN JAPANESE HISTORY, BUT IT IS AN INDICATION THAT JAPANESE INTRANSIGENCE IS NOT CRYSTALLIZED COMPLETELY OWING TO THE FACT THAT THE PROPOSAL HAS THE APPROVAL OF THE EMPEROR AND THE HIGHEST AUTHORITIES IN THE LAND. THE GOOD WHICH MAY FLOW FROM A MEETING BETWEEN PRINCE KONOYE AND PRESIDENT ROOSEVELT IS INCALCULABLE. THE OPPORTUNITY IS HERE PRESENTED, THE AMBASSADOR VENTURES TO BELIEVE, FOR AN ACT OF THE HIGHEST STATESMANSHIP, SUCH AS THE RECENT MEETING OF PRESIDENT ROOSEVELT WITH PRIME MINISTER CHURCHILL AT SEA, WITH THE POSSIBLE OVERCOMING THEREBY OF APPARENTLY INSURMOUNTABLE OBSTACLES TO PEACE HEREAFTER IN THE PACIFIC.

A few weeks before, Colonel Iwakuro and Ikawa, who had labored so diligently on the Draft Understanding, realized that their attempt at independent diplomacy had failed. On the last day of July they had left Washington, arriving home two weeks later. Iwakuro was struck by the warlike atmosphere in Tokyo on all levels. There was growing hatred of America and Britain and a general feeling that the ABCD encirclement was strangling the nation. In America the predominant mood, though anti-Axis, seemed one of peace. Antiwar groups were picketing the White House, and the isolationists' opposition to Roosevelt's aid to

China and Britain was widespread and vocal. A bill extending the service of draftees had passed with a margin of one vote, and in Army camps the word Ohio was given a cryptic meaning—Over the Hill In October.

Iwakuro made dozens of speeches to top-level military, political and industrial groups urging that the negotiations be continued; America's potential was far superior to Japan's and a conflict would end in disaster. But the staff officers were far more interested in talking about an advance to the south, and at naval headquarters one said, "Japan is blockaded by the ABCD line. We cannot afford to lose time. We have only one course now—to fight." Iwakuro remembered that several months before, the Navy had been almost solidly aligned for a peaceful settlement with America, and sadly concluded that "the die was cast."

Nevertheless, he refused to give up and went pleading from ministry to ministry. But his words had no more effect than "hitting a nail into rice bran." During the last week in August he attended a liaison conference, where he contrasted the alarming differences between American and Japanese war potential. In steel, he said, the ratio was 20 to 1; oil more than 100 to 1; coal 10 to 1; planes 5 to 1; shipping 2 to 1; labor force 5 to 1. The overall potential was 10 to 1. At such odds, Japan could not possibly win, despite *Yamato damashii*—the spirit of Japan. For once his listeners were impressed and Tojo ordered Iwakuro to make a written report of everything he had just said.

The following day Iwakuro arrived at the War Minister's office to discuss the report but was summarily told by Tojo that he was being transferred to a unit in Cambodia. "You need not submit the notes in writing I requested yesterday."

As Iwakuro was boarding the train for the first leg of the trip south, he told his friends, "So many of you have come to bid me farewell, but when I return to Tokyo—if I survive—I'm afraid I shall find myself alone in the ruins of Tokyo station."

Iwakuro's missionary zeal may have caused his banishment but he was not alone in his views, and they brought about a dramatic policy reversal. The military leaders had finally agreed, after long arguments, to avoid war with the United States even at the cost of major concessions. On the day of Iwakuro's departure—it was August 28—two messages were on their way to Franklin Roosevelt.

One was a letter from Konoye again requesting a meeting, and the other an official proposal to withdraw all Japanese troops from Indochina once the China Incident was settled or a "just peace" was established in East Asia. Japan further promised to make no military advances into neighboring countries and to take no military action against the Soviet Union as long as Russia remained "faithful to the Soviet-Japanese neutrality treaty" and did not "menace Japan or Manchukuo." Far more important, the Japanese consented to abide by Hull's basic four principles—which had by now arrived in an official U. S. missive.

. . . Regarding the principles and directives set forth in detail by the American Government and envisaged in the informal conversations as constituting a program for the Pacific area, the Japanese Government wishes to state that it considers that these principles and the practical application thereof, in the friendliest manner possible, are the prime requisites of a true peace and should be applied not only in the Pacific area but throughout the world. . . .

The proposal was a negation of policies championed for months—and, though limited, gave promise of more concessions to come. Roosevelt's first reaction to it was one of optimism and he made tentative plans to spend three days or so with Konoye. But Dr. Stanley Hornbeck didn't believe the offer was sincere and when Hull read MAGIC intercepts of a military build-up in Southeast Asia, it was not surprising that he, too, became suspicious of the Japanese. Nor was it any wonder that Roosevelt, who still "relished a meeting with Konoye," was easily persuaded that it should not be held "without first arriving at a satisfactory agreement." In other words, the Americans, who didn't believe what they were offered in the first place, would not bargain unless they were previously assured that their own conditions would be generally met.

In Tokyo, Grew and his staff were more than willing to take the new proposal at face value and were convinced that Konoye would agree "to the eventual withdrawal of Japanese forces from all of Indochina and from all of China with the face-saving expedient of being permitted to retain a limited number of troops in North China and Inner Mongolia temporarily." Accordingly, Grew pleaded that the Konoye-Roosevelt meeting be approved before time ran out. For months he had warned Washington that the Japanese Army was "capable of sudden and surprise action" and that traditionally in Japan "a national psychology of desperation develops into a determination to risk all."

This psychology of desperation overshadowed the session of the liaison conference which started at eleven o'clock on September 3, next door to the Palace in the Imperial Household Ministry.* As yet no official word had come from Roosevelt, and the members were filled with misgivings. Had it been a mistake to make such a conciliatory offer? Were the Americans simply playing for time?

"With each day we will get weaker and weaker, until finally we won't be able to stand on our feet," said Navy Chief of Staff Nagano. "Although I feel sure that we have a chance to win a war right now, I'm afraid this chance will vanish with the passage of time." There was no way to "checkmate the enemy's king"—industrial potential—and a decisive initial victory was essential. "Thus our only recourse is to forge ahead!"

These words brought the Army to the point of panic, and Chief of Staff Gen Sugiyama introduced a new element—a deadline. "We must try to achieve our diplomatic objectives by October 10," he said. "If this fails we must dash forward. Things cannot be allowed to drag out."

It was a perilous suggestion and might mean war. Yet the two who wanted peace the most, Prince Konoye and Foreign Minister Toyoda, raised no objections. Perhaps they secretly felt that the negotiations would be successfully concluded within the five weeks of grace, and the only substantial argument was over phraseology. After seven hours they all finally fixed the following policy: "For the self-defense and self-preservation of our empire, we will complete preparations for war, with the first ten days of October as a tentative deadline, determined, if necessary, to wage war against the United States, Great Britain and the Netherlands." Concurrently they would negotiate in a sincere attempt to attain mini-

---

* It was assumed that security leaks, such as those reported by Ambassador Oshima in Berlin, had come from Cabinet civilians, and to seal these off, all liaison conferences, after July 21, were held on the Palace grounds. MAGIC, of course, continued to keep U. S. officials informed of most political decisions.

mum objectives, but if it appeared that these were not met by October 10—war.

The operational plans for war had already been completed. Assaults by the Navy and Army would be launched simultaneously at Pearl Harbor, Hong Kong, Malaya and the Philippines.* The Army General Staff had learned about Pearl Harbor only a few days before. Several in the War Ministry also knew but, curiously, Tojo was not one of them.

The slim hope that this hastily conceived deadline would be reconsidered by the Cabinet before presentation to the Throne disappeared with the arrival, a few hours later, of a reply from Roosevelt to Japan's conciliatory proposal. It was in two parts: one was a polite refusal of Konoye's reiterated invitation to meet until they first came to agreement on the "fundamental and essential questions"; the other, an Oral Statement, was as vague and more disappointing. It was the kind of clever riposte so many diplomats seemed to delight in: it politely avoided promising anything of import while side-stepping the main issues. It noted "with satisfaction" Japan's willingness to abide by Hull's four principles but seemed to ask the question, "Do you really mean it?" and never mentioned Japan's offer to withdraw all troops from Indochina.

Since it seemed to be a deliberate rebuff (which it was not), as well as a belittling of concessions made by the Army at agonizing cost (which it was), the Cabinet approved the deadline policy without argument. On September 5 Konoye went to the Palace to request an imperial conference to make the policy official. First he stopped off at the office of the Privy Seal.

"How can you suddenly present such a proposal to the Emperor!" Marquis Kido exclaimed. It sounded to him like out-and-out preparations for war. "He won't even have time to consider it." Konoye's excuse was weak.

"Couldn't you make it vague?" Kido asked. "It's too dangerous to set the limit at mid-October."

Konoye shifted uncomfortably. "You must do something!" Kido persisted. Konoye muttered that the matter had been decided at the liaison conference, and what could he do now?

* Chapter 7 is devoted to the detailed development of plans for these attacks.

At four-thirty a chamberlain announced that the Emperor was ready to see the Prime Minister. His Majesty looked up from the proposed policy. "I notice you first speak of war and then of diplomacy. I must question the Chiefs of the General Staff about this tomorrow at the conference."

"The order in which the items are listed doesn't necessarily indicate importance," Konoye replied with embarrassment. He suggested that the Chiefs of Staff come at once and give a fuller explanation of the Supreme Command's position, and at six o'clock he returned with General Sugiyama and Admiral Nagano.

The Emperor asked if the operations in the south would succeed as planned and was given a detailed presentation of the operational plans for the Malay and Philippine campaigns. But these details didn't relieve his concern. "Is there a possibility that the operations will not proceed on schedule? You say five months, but isn't it possible it won't work out that way?"

"The Army and Navy have studied the whole matter a number of times," Sugiyama explained. "Therefore, I imagine we'll be able to carry out the operations as planned."

"Do you think the landing operations can be carried out so easily?"

"I do not believe it will be easy, but since both the Army and the Navy are constantly training, I feel confident we'll be able to do it successfully."

"In the landing maneuvers on Kyushu a considerable number of ships were 'sunk.' What would you do if the same thing happened in reality?"

Sugiyama was disconcerted. "That was because the convoy had started cruising before enemy planes were shot down. I don't believe that will happen."

"Are you sure it will work out as planned?" the Emperor persisted. "When you were War Minister you said Chiang Kai-shek would be defeated quickly, but you still haven't been able to do it."

"The interior of China is so vast," said the chagrined Sugiyama.

"I know, but the South Seas are much wider." The Emperor was agitated and showed it. "How can you possibly say you can end the war in five months?"

Sugiyama tried to answer. He said Japan's strength was gradually diminishing and that it was necessary to strengthen national prosperity while the empire still had its resiliency.

This was no answer and the Emperor interrupted him. "Can we absolutely win?"

"I couldn't say 'absolutely.' However, I will say that we can probably win; I don't dare say we can absolutely win. It won't help Japan to gain peace for half a year or a year if this were followed by a national crisis. I believe we should seek peace that will last twenty years or fifty years."

"Ah so, I understand!" the Emperor exclaimed in an unnaturally loud voice.

Sugiyama saw that he was still troubled. "We'd rather not fight at all. We think we should try our best to negotiate, and only when we're pushed to the edge shall we fight."

Nagano immediately came to his colleague's assistance. "It is, I think, like a critically ill patient awaiting a surgical operation." The decision to operate had to be made quickly. No operation meant the gradual decline of the patient. Operation, though an extreme measure, might save his life. But a quick decision was essential. "The Supreme Command hopes for successful negotiations, but if they fail, an operation is necessary." He quickly added that diplomacy was, of course, of "primary importance."

"Am I to understand that the Supreme Command now gives first preference to diplomacy?" Both Chiefs said yes and the Emperor seemed to be reassured.

But the next morning at nine-forty—it was September 6—he sent for Kido, just before the imperial conference was to start. Could Japan win a war against America? he asked. What about the negotiations in Washington?

Kido advised the Emperor to remain silent at first and leave the questions to Privy Council President Hara; he had already instructed Hara what these should be. But once the discussion was over, the Emperor should break precedence. He should cease to reign, that is, and momentarily rule: "Instruct the Chiefs of Staff to co-operate with the government in making the negotiations successful." Only through such a dramatic break in tradition could the disastrous deadline policy be reversed.

As members filed into the conference room, Konoye took aside General Teiichi Suzuki, who had been brought in as an expert on resources, and showed him the new policy. A glance convinced Suzuki that it should not be presented to the Emperor. Konoye was in accord but said that the Supreme Command, and Tojo in particular, insisted on speed, and if the imperial conference was put off even for twenty-four hours, the Cabinet would probably have to resign. "Whether we go to war or not will be decided later. This is merely a decision to prepare for battle while negotiating. Therefore I'm going to let this go through."

Promptly at ten o'clock the crucial meeting opened. "With your permission, I will take the chair so we may proceed," Konoye began, and reviewed the tense international situation. Everyone sat stiffly, hands on knees, as Navy Chief of Staff Nagano urged that every effort be made to negotiate. But if Japan's minimum demands were not met, the problem could only be solved by "aggressive military operations," despite America's "unassailable position, her vaster industrial power and her abundant resources."

The Army Chief of Staff reiterated the same hope for successful negotiations, and General Suzuki spoke about the grim state of national resources. Even with strict wartime control, the liquid-fuel stockpile would be exhausted in ten months. "If the negotiations in Washington succeed, fine; but if not and we wait too long, it would be disastrous." There were three alternatives: start war preparations at once; continue the negotiations; or just sit and starve. "The third is unthinkable. Therefore we must choose between the first two."

The practical Hara stood up. The time had passed for conventional diplomacy, he said, and praised Konoye for his resolution to meet Roosevelt and come to some agreement. He held aloft a draft of the new policy. "This draft seems to imply that war comes first and diplomacy second, but can't I interpret this to mean that we'll do our utmost in diplomacy and go to war only when there is no other recourse?"

"President Hara's interpretation and my intentions when I composed the draft are exactly the same," said Navy Minister Oikawa.

But the more the military explained, the more it bothered Hara. "This draft still gives me the impression that we will turn to belligerency rather than diplomacy. Or are you actually going to place emphasis on diplomacy? I should like to have the views of the government as well as of the Supreme Command."

In the embarrassing silence the Emperor stared at the conferees, then did the unheard-of. He said in his loud, high-pitched voice, "Why don't you answer?"

Not since the 2/26 Incident had he abandoned his role as passive emperor. His listeners were stunned at the sound of his voice and it was a long moment before a member of the Cabinet finally rose. It was Navy Minister Oikawa. "We will start war preparations but, of course, we'll also exert every effort to negotiate."

There was another pause as the others waited for one of the Chiefs of Staff to speak. But both Nagano and Sugiyama sat paralyzed.

"I am sorry the Supreme Command has nothing to say," the Emperor remarked. He took a piece of paper from his pocket and began reading a poem written by his grandfather, Emperor Meiji:

> *"All the seas, everywhere,*
>   *are brothers one to another*
> *Why then do the winds and waves of strife*
>   *rage so violently through the world?"*

The listeners sat awed by the Emperor's censure. There wasn't a sound or movement until the Emperor spoke again. "I make it a rule to read this poem from time to time to remind me of Emperor Meiji's love of peace. How do you feel about all this?"

Finally Nagano forced himself to stand up. "Representing the Supreme Command," he said humbly, head bowed, "I express our deep regret for not replying to His Majesty's request but—" He floundered in apology. "I think exactly the same as President Hara. I made two mentions on this point in the text. Since President Hara said he understood my intentions, I didn't feel there was any need to re-emphasize the point."

Sugiyama got to his feet. "It was exactly the same with me. I was about to rise from my seat to answer President Hara's question when Navy Minister Oikawa answered it for me." This made it unnecessary for the two Chiefs of Staff to speak. "However, I am overawed to hear His Majesty tell us directly that His Majesty regrets our silence. Allow me to assume that His Majesty feels we should make every effort to accomplish our goals by diplomatic means. I also gather His Majesty suspects that the Supreme Command may be giving first consideration to war, not to diplomacy." He assured the Emperor that this was not true.

2.

The decision to start war preparations at once while attempting to negotiate was much more than that. It meant, in fact, that hostilities would commence unless the negotiations were successfully concluded by October 10. The decision was made and approved with the Emperor's seal, but His Majesty's displeasure left a sense of doubt even among the military. He had put the accent on diplomacy, and Prime Minister Konoye realized that this gave him a last chance to achieve peace. The problem was not so much the Tojo group as the public. The controlled press had led the people to believe that the Anglo-Saxons were intent on reducing Japan to a third-rate nation, and out of all this came a rash of indignation meetings calling for action. The situation was so ominous that Ambassador Grew took to wearing a pistol, although it made him feel silly and "wild west."

The danger was real: two secret organizations, which had learned of the proposed Konoye-Roosevelt meeting, were plotting to murder the Prime Minister. One had decided to make a daring, gangland-style assault in Tokyo; the other, to emulate the bombing of Marshal Chang. The latter plan was devised by a lieutenant colonel named Masanobu Tsuji, already an idol of the most radical young officers. A chauvinist of the first water, he was determined to thwart a summit meeting that was destined to end in a disgraceful peace.

As his instrument of murder he chose a civilian who had already spent two terms in prison: once for something he had done —handing the Emperor a rightist petition demanding relief for the unemployed, and once for something he had not done—throwing a stick of dynamite into the Finance Minister's home. Yoshio Kodama, leader of the most active nationalist society, shared Tsuji's convictions and approved his plan. Konoye would have to go to the meeting by ship, and since there wasn't a good highway to the naval base at Yokosuka, would travel by train. As it passed over the Rokugo Bridge outside the capital, Kodama would set off an explosion.

Several hours after the imperial conference, Konoye called his mistress at the hairdresser's. There was a note of urgency in his voice as he told her to get ready at once; a car would call for her. A few minutes later she was driven to the home of Count Bunkichi Ito, son of Prince Hirobumi Ito, one of the four great men of the Meiji Restoration. There wasn't a servant in the house.

Two other cars arrived, one with Konoye and his private secretary, Tomohiko Ushiba; the other, diplomatic tags removed, carried Ambassador Grew and Embassy Counselor Eugene H. Dooman. Never before had either diplomat been invited to such a meeting. Traditionally, prime ministers had no social or official contact with foreign envoys except on state occasions.

Konoye introduced his mistress as "the daughter of the house"; she alone would serve them dinner and they could converse freely. For the next three hours Konoye and Grew talked "with the utmost frankness," with Ushiba and Dooman interpreting. Konoye assured Grew that both General Tojo and Admiral Oikawa wanted a peaceful settlement.

What about Hull's four principles? Grew asked.

Konoye said they were generally acceptable. "However, when it comes to applying them practically, various problems will arise, and to solve them I must have a meeting [with the President]." He admitted that he was to blame for the "regrettable state of relations" between America and Japan—he took the responsibility for the China Incident and the Tripartite Pact—and therefore was determined to take any personal risk to settle the differences between the two countries.

He and Roosevelt, face to face, could surely come to an agreement, but only such a meeting in the near future could accomplish this. Negotiations using the ordinary diplomatic channels would take a year. Konoye couldn't reveal, of course, that he had less than five weeks before the October 10 deadline. "A year from now," he said, "I'm not sure that anything can be done to solve our differences. But I can do it now. I promise that some agreement can be reached if I can only see him [Roosevelt]. I'll offer him a proposal which he can't afford to reject." After this cryptic remark he turned to Dooman, who was born in Osaka of missionary parents and who had already spent almost twenty-three years in Japan: "You know the conditions in this country. I want to tell you something you must not repeat to Mr. Grew. You should know so you can impress him with your belief in my sincerity. You realize that we cannot involve the Emperor in this controversy, but as soon as I have reached a settlement with the President I will communicate with His Majesty, who will immediately order the Army to cease hostile operations."

This was a bold plan, something never before attempted in Japan's history. Although impelled to tell Grew, Dooman promised to keep it a secret.

Konoye reiterated that Generals Tojo and Sugiyama had already given their consent to the proposal he could make to the United States, and the former had promised to let a full general accompany him to the summit meeting. "I will talk to the President with two generals and two admirals standing behind me." Admittedly, a certain group in the armed forces opposed peace negotiations, but with the full support of the responsible Chiefs of the Army and Navy, he was confident he could put down any opposition. He might be assassinated later, but if peace came, it would be worth it. "I do not care that much about my life."

Grew, deeply impressed by Konoye's obvious earnestness and willingness to abide by Hull's four principles, said that he was going back to the embassy and send immediately "the most important cable" of his diplomatic career.*

Though it was true that General Tojo had approved the summit meeting, he wasn't giving it his full support, so Konoye asked

---

* At one point in the message Grew either embellished Konoye's remarks or had not clearly understood the Prime Minister via Dooman's translation when he declared that the Japanese "conclusively and wholeheartedly agree with the four principles enunciated by the Secretary of State . . ." In his memoirs, Konoye recalled he had said: *"Gensokuteki ni wa kekko de aru ga . . ."*—"They are agreeable in principle." In a recent interview Ushiba confirmed the Konoye version and explained that several times during the meeting he had to correct Dooman's translations. Robert Butow translates the phrase "splendid as a matter of principle." Although "splendid" is listed in dictionaries as one translation for *kekko,* conversationally in this context it merely means "agreement without accent"—that is, "I'll go along with that."

The Grew interpretation later gave the Hornbeck group an excuse for labeling Konoye a liar.

Prince Higashikuni, uncle-in-law of the Emperor, to use his influence on the War Minister. The next morning Higashikuni summoned Tojo: "I hear the Emperor is very concerned over the Washington negotiations and is putting high hopes on the Konoye-Roosevelt meeting." As war minister, Tojo should respect His Majesty's feelings and take a more positive view of this meeting as well as of Japan's problems with America.

"I am sorry indeed for the inadequate explanation given to the Throne," said Tojo tightly. "In the future I will certainly see to it that the Army explains so His Majesty fully understands. I am quite aware of the Emperor's views on the Japan-U. S. negotiations and the Konoye-Roosevelt meeting." He promised to do his best as war minister to bring about the meeting, although he personally didn't think it had more than a 30 percent chance of success. "Nevertheless, if there is the slightest hope of success, I believe we should conduct the negotiations." He became more agitated and vowed that if the diplomatic settlement turned out to Japan's future disadvantage he would have to "remonstrate with His Majesty," and if the Emperor refused to heed this advice, he would be forced to resign. "That is the only way I can fulfill my loyalty to His Majesty."

Higashikuni let Tojo speak without interruption. Now he said reminiscently, "While I was in France, Pétain and Clemenceau told me, 'Germany was an eyesore to the United States in Europe and it did away with her in the Great War. In the next war it will try to get rid of another eyesore, this one in the Orient, Japan. America knows how inept Japan is diplomatically, so she'll make moves to abuse you inch by inch until you start a fight. But if you lose your temper and start a war you will surely be defeated, because America has great strength. So you must bear anything and not play into her hands.' The present situation is exactly as Pétain and Clemenceau predicted. At this time we must persevere so that we won't get into war with America. You're a member of the Konoye Cabinet. In the Army, an order must be obeyed. Now the Emperor and the Prime Minister want to bring about the negotiations. As war minister, you should either follow their line of policy or resign."

The desperation of the Japanese should have been obvious to

"Go Back to Blank Paper"

the Americans when Hull's cool reception of their offer to get out of Indochina and abide by his four principles was followed by two more Japanese proposals the very next day. One, submitted to Grew, promised to resort to no military action against any regions lying south of Japan and to withdraw troops from China once peace was achieved. In return America would rescind the freezing act and suspend her own military measures in the Far East and southwest Pacific.

This was an official offer, but the second was not. Without informing Tokyo, Nomura handed Hull a long statement drafted months earlier, during the days of Colonel Iwakuro; apparently the admiral thought the old formula would appeal to Hull. All it did was confuse him. With two proposals in hand, covering entirely different points, he quite rightly wondered just where Japan stood.

It took about a week to straighten out the tangle and answer the official proposal. Hull told Nomura it "narrowed down the spirit and scope of the proposed understandings," and handed over half a dozen pages of objections.

The delay and the apparent reluctance to come to a quick agreement convinced the militarists in Tokyo that Hull was playing for time. They turned on Konoye in public as well as in private. Widespread vocal criticism was climaxed by a physical attack on the Prime Minister on September 18. As he was leaving his quiet, rural refuge in Ogikubo, a suburb about forty-five minutes' drive from the center of Tokyo, four men, armed with daggers and swords, leaped up on the runningboards of his car. But the doors were locked and before the would-be assassins could break the glass they were seized by plain-clothes men.

Konoye was less concerned with violence than with the approaching deadline—he had less than three weeks to make a peaceful settlement and Roosevelt still declined to set a date for their meeting. Grew knew nothing about the deadline but sensed the urgency, four days after the assassination attempt, when he was summoned to the office of the Foreign Minister. Toyoda said he couldn't understand Hull's remark that the latest proposal narrowed the scope of the negotiations—on the contrary, it was widened. Toyoda was willing to go further, and set forth the peace terms Japan was now prepared to offer China: fusion of the Chiang

Kai-shek and Wang Ching-wei governments; no annexations; no indemnities; economic co-operation; and withdrawal of all Japanese troops except those needed in certain areas to help the Chinese fight the Reds.

Grew dispatched this new offer to Hull, and in view of the critical situation decided to make a special appeal of his own. Presuming on his long friendship with Roosevelt (they had served together on the staff of the Harvard *Crimson*), he wrote directly to the President:

I have not bothered you with personal letters for some time for the good reason that letters are now subject to long delays owing to the infrequent sailings of ships carrying our diplomatic pouches, and because developments in American-Japanese relations are moving so comparatively rapidly that my comments would generally be too much out-of-date to be helpful when they reach you. But I have tried and am constantly trying in my telegrams to the Secretary of State to paint an accurate picture of the moving scene from day to day. I hope that you see them regularly.

As you know from my telegrams, I am in close touch with Prince Konoye who in the face of bitter antagonism from extremist and pro-Axis elements in the country is courageously working for an improvement in Japan's relations with the United States. He bears the heavy responsibility for having allowed our relations to come to such a pass and he no doubt now sees the handwriting on the wall and realizes that Japan has nothing to hope for from the Tripartite Pact and must shift her orientation of policy if she is to avoid disaster; but whatever the incentive that has led to his present efforts, I am convinced that he now means business and will go as far as is possible, without incurring open rebellion in Japan, to reach a reasonable understanding with us. In spite of all the evidence of Japan's bad faith in times past in failing to live up to her commitments, I believe that there is a better chance of the present Government implementing whatever commitments it may now undertake than has been the case in recent years. It seems to me highly unlikely that this chance will come again or that any Japanese statesman other than Prince Konoye could succeed in controlling the military extremists in carrying through a policy which they, in their ignorance of international affairs and economic laws, resent and oppose. The alternative to reaching a settlement now would be the greatly increased probability of war,—*Facilis descensus Averno est*—and while we would undoubtedly win in the end, I question whether it is in our own interest to see an impoverished Japan reduced to the position of a third-rate Power. I therefore most earnestly hope that we can come to terms, even if we must take on trust, at least to some degree, the continued good faith and ability of the present Government fully to implement those terms. . . .

The letter had as little effect as earlier recommendations (in fact, it merely provoked a bland acknowledgment five weeks later) and Konoye felt so desperate at the finish of the September 25 liaison conference, where the Supreme Command demanded an irrevocable deadline of October 15, that he refused to eat the lunch prepared at Imperial Headquarters and instead invited the Cabinet to accompany him to his official residence. Here, he applied pressure on Tojo. Was the October 15 deadline a demand or a request on the part of the Supreme Command?

"It was a definitely set opinion but not a demand," replied the War Minister. It was just putting into effect what had been previously decided at the imperial conference of September 6. "And that decision cannot be easily changed now."

Against such resolve Konoye felt helpless and he told Marquis Kido that with the Army insisting on the deadline, all he could do was resign. Kido chastised him as if he were a child. Between Konoye and Kido, according to Ushiba, existed a unique informality. With the Privy Seal, Konoye showed a rare side of himself —he discarded all pretense. Now, since Konoye was responsible for the decision of September 6, it would be "irresponsible to step out by leaving things as they are." Be "prudent," Kido cautioned.

Konoye didn't answer. Despondent, his mood aggravated by another intense attack of piles, he left and told his private secretary he had to think things over in peace and tranquillity. And so, on September 27, he quit the capital for the nearby seaside resort of Kamakura.

3.

To the people in the State Department, nine thousand miles away, Japan's Prime Minister was an aggressor. Hull could not forget that Konoye had been prime minister when China was overrun and the Tripartite Pact consummated. And although Konoye expressed support for the four principles, did he mean it? For all these reasons any meeting with Roosevelt, without first working out the details, would be a fiasco.

Hull's apprehensions chilled Roosevelt's initial enthusiasm for the meeting, and on September 28 the President sent his Secretary of State a memo from Hyde Park:

> I wholly agree with your pencilled note—to recite the more liberal original attitude of the Japanese when they first sought the meeting, point out their much narrowed position now, earnestly ask if they cannot go back to their original attitude, start discussions again on agreement in principle, and reemphasize my hope for a meeting.

In Tokyo, however, Ambassador Grew had not yet given up hope, and he was so certain that those in Washington lacked insight into the problems faced by Konoye that the following day he sent another report to Hull. It was as much a warning as an appeal:

> ... THE AMBASSADOR [Grew] RECALLS HIS STATEMENTS IN THE PAST THAT IN JAPAN THE PENDULUM ALWAYS SWINGS BETWEEN MODERATE AND EXTREMIST POLICIES; THAT IT WAS NOT THEN POSSIBLE UNDER THE EXISTING CIRCUMSTANCES FOR ANY JAPANESE LEADER OR GROUP TO REVERSE THE PROGRAM OF EXPANSION AND EXPECT TO SURVIVE; THAT THE PERMANENT DIGGING IN BY JAPANESE IN CHINA AND THE PUSHING OF THE JAPANESE ADVANCE TO THE SOUTH COULD BE PREVENTED ONLY BY INSUPERABLE OBSTACLES. ...
> THE AMBASSADOR STRESSES THE IMPORTANCE OF UNDERSTANDING JAPANESE PSYCHOLOGY, FUNDAMENTALLY UNLIKE THAT OF ANY WESTERN NATION. JAPANESE REACTIONS TO ANY PARTICULAR SET OF CIRCUMSTANCES CANNOT BE MEASURED, NOR CAN JAPANESE ACTIONS BE PREDICTED BY ANY WESTERN MEASURING ROD. ...
> SHOULD THE UNITED STATES EXPECT OR AWAIT AGREEMENT BY THE JAPANESE GOVERNMENT, IN THE PRESENT PRELIMINARY CONVERSATIONS, TO CLEAR-CUT COMMITMENTS WHICH

WILL SATISFY THE UNITED STATES GOVERNMENT BOTH AS TO PRINCIPLE AND AS TO CONCRETE DETAIL, ALMOST CERTAINLY THE CONVERSATIONS WILL DRAG ALONG INDEFINITELY AND UNPRODUCTIVELY UNTIL THE KONOYE CABINET AND ITS SUPPORTING ELEMENTS DESIRING RAPPROCHEMENT WITH THE UNITED STATES WILL COME TO THE CONCLUSION THAT THE OUTLOOK FOR AN AGREEMENT IS HOPELESS AND THAT THE UNITED STATES GOVERNMENT IS ONLY PLAYING FOR TIME. . . . THIS WILL RESULT IN THE KONOYE GOVERNMENT'S BEING DISCREDITED AND IN A REVULSION OF ANTI-AMERICAN FEELING, AND THIS MAY AND PROBABLY WILL LEAD TO UNBRIDLED ACTS. . . .

He ended with the observation that unless America placed a "reasonable amount of confidence" in Konoye and his supporters to remold Japan, it was the end "to the hope that ultimate war may be avoided in the Pacific."

The next day Grew wrote in his diary that he had done his "level best to paint to our Government an accurate picture of the situation in Japan." He was upset by receipt from Hornbeck of a batch of recommendations he himself had earlier made to be firm with Japan.

I don't quite know just what was in Stanley Hornbeck's mind in sending me those excerpts, unless it was in the belief, and with the purpose of calling attention to that belief, that I am now advocating so-called "appeasement" in contradistinction to my former recommendations for a strong policy. In the first place, "appeasement," through association with Munich and umbrellas, has become an unfortunate, ill-used and misinterpreted term. It is not appeasement that I now advocate, but "constructive conciliation." That word "constructive" is important. It connotes building, and no one is going to be foolish enough to try to build any structure, if it is to be a permanent structure, on an insecure foundation. . . . What the eventual outcome will be, I do not know; nobody knows; but defeatism is not within my philosophy.

Hornbeck was right about Grew to a certain extent. Perhaps he *was* too trustful of the Japanese. Nor was he intellectual or even particularly keen. He did have three great assets: a sensitive wife with a rare sympathy for Japan; an adviser (Dooman) born in Japan with an equally rare understanding of that country's flaws and virtues; and finally, his own overriding sense of honor and duty. Moreover, his beliefs and convictions were shared by a canny British colleague, Ambassador Craigie. At four-twenty the next morning he telegraphed Foreign Secretary Anthony Eden:

> . . . I DO NOT QUESTION THE VIEW THAT JAPAN'S MOTIVES MAY BE MIXED, BUT IS THIS IN ITSELF A REASON FOR DOING NOTHING TO ENCOURAGE JAPAN ALONG THE NEW PATH ON WHICH THE PRESENT GOVERNMENT HAVE NOW ENTERED? EVEN ASSUMING JAPANESE POLICY TO BE ACTUATED SOLELY BY THE IDEA THAT IDENTICAL AMBITIONS CAN FOR THE MOMENT BEST BE SERVED BY A CHANGE OF TECHNIQUE (A VIEW TO WHICH I DO NOT ALTOGETHER SUBSCRIBE), THERE IS NO CHANCE OF JAPAN'S EXPANSIONIST AIMS BEING REALIZED IN THE IMMEDIATE POSTWAR FUTURE, ONCE GERMANY HAS BEEN DEFEATED. FOR THIS REASON AND BECAUSE TO KEEP JAPAN NEUTRAL WILL CONTRIBUTE TO THE DEFEAT OF GERMANY, I VENTURE THE OPINION THAT POST-MORTEM ON OUR HORIZON [This telegram was in code and a few words in the copy made available to the author were not decoded. HORIZON probably meant "part"] MAY LEGITIMATELY BE BOUNDED BY LIMITS OF WAR. . . .

Since Matsuoka's departure a radical change had occurred in the political situation and there was now a steady swing from the Axis.

> THE ALL-IMPORTANT QUESTION AT THE MOMENT IS THE DISCUSSION NOW PROCEEDING BETWEEN THE UNITED STATES AND THE JAPANESE GOVERNMENT. THE MAIN DIFFICULTY APPEARS TO BE THAT, WHILE THE JAPANESE WANT SPEED AND CANNOT YET AFFORD TO GO BEYOND GENERALIZATIONS, THE AMERICANS SEEM TO BE PLAYING FOR TIME AND TO DEMAND THE UTMOST PRECISION IN DEFINITION BEFORE AGREEING TO ANY CONTRACT FOR A STEP OF RAPPROCHEMENT . . . IF PERSISTED IN, IT BIDS FAIR TO WRECK THE BEST CHANCE OF BRINGING ABOUT A JUST SETTLEMENT OF FAR EASTERN ISSUES, WHICH HAS OCCURRED SINCE MY ARRIVAL IN JAPAN.

MY UNITED STATES COLLEAGUE AND I CONSIDER THAT PRINCE KONOYE IS TELEPHONE [probably "most"] SINCERE IN HIS DESIRE TO AVERT THE DANGERS TOWARDS WHICH HE NOW SEES THE TRIPARTITE PACT AND THE AXIS' CONNECTION (FOR WHICH HE NATURALLY ACCEPTS HIS SHARE OF RESPONSIBILITY) ARE RAPIDLY LEADING JAPAN . . . DESPITE THE EMPEROR'S STRONG BACKING, I DOUBT IF HE AND HIS GOVERNMENT BRITISH CONSULAR OFFICER [probably "can"] SURVIVE IF THE DISCUSSIONS PROVE ABORTIVE OR DRAG ON UNDULY.

He admitted that any agreement might make Chiang Kai-shek suspicious and discouraged, and that America's interest in the Far East was not wholly identical with Britain's.

. . . BUT THE RISKS MUST BE FACED EITHER REPAIRED [probably "in any case"], AND MY UNITED STATES COLLEAGUE AND I ARE FIRMLY OF THE OPINION THAT ON BALANCE THIS IS A CHANCE WHICH IT WOULD BE ILLEGIBLE [probably "inexcusable"] FOLLY TO LET SLIP. CAUTION MUST BE EXERCISED, BUT AN EXCESSIVE CYNICISM BRINGS STAGNATION . . .

It was not until October 2 that Hull finally gave some definite answers to the questions the Japanese had long been awaiting. He "welcomed" a summit meeting and found Konoye's acceptance of the four principles "gratifying," but the proposals themselves were unacceptable, particularly those on China—all Japanese troops had to be withdrawn without delay. Therefore the meeting would have to be postponed until there was "a meeting of minds on essential points."

"We have no desire whatever to cause any delay," he hastened to assure Nomura. It was a deception that must have been repugnant to such an honorable man; surely Hull had not forgotten the reiterated pleas of General George C. Marshall, the Army Chief of Staff, and Admiral Harold R. Stark, Chief of Naval Operations, for more time to reinforce the Pacific. Ironically, it was giving them less by accelerating Japan's necessity to make a decision for war. At eleven o'clock on October 5, the Army division and bureau chiefs met in Tojo's office and concluded: "There is no possibility to settle the matter by diplomatic negotiations. We must therefore petition the Emperor to hold an imperial conference and decide upon war."

Konoye returned from his holiday more discouraged than ever. His associates were just as disheartened. Marquis Kido alone had not given up hope for peace. "Judging the situation both at home and abroad, it is difficult to predict the outcome of a war between Japan and America," he told the prince. "We should, therefore, re-examine the situation. Instead of making an immediate decision to declare war on the United States, the government should make clear that its first consideration is to bring the China Incident to a successful conclusion. The people should be told flatly that we now face ten to fifteen years of *gashin-shotan*."*

It was a disagreeable solution, but realistic, and Konoye decided to pursue it. On the morning of October 12 he summoned the War, Navy and Foreign ministers and General Suzuki of the Cabinet Planning Board to his villa in Ogikubo. It was a fine Sunday, his fiftieth birthday.

Konoye's private home was a comfortable but far from ostentatious Japanese structure located on spacious grounds at the edge of the suburb. Just before the conference was to start, Chief Cabinet Secretary Kanji Tomita arrived with a note for Konoye from the chief of the Naval Affairs Bureau, Admiral Takasumi Oka: "The Navy does not want the Japanese-American negotiations stopped and wishes to avoid war if at all possible. But we cannot see our way to expressing this openly at the meeting."

Tojo somehow learned of the note and by the time he reached Ogikubo he had resolved to make Navy Minister Oikawa speak out plainly. It was cowardly of the Navy to *sekinin o nasuri-tsukeru* ("transfer their responsibility"). Tojo was so nettled that he was scarcely civil to Oikawa as they sat down at a table to begin the conference. Then he blurted out impetuously, "There is no point

---

* Literally, "sleep on kindling and lick gall." "This phrase is Chinese in origin," Marquis Kido explained in a personal letter. "In the dictionary it says: 'to suffer hardships and privations repeatedly in order to take revenge'; however, here it means to ask the people to endure a life of patience and austerity in order to accomplish our purposes. Not too long ago, after the Sino-Japanese War, when Japan was forced to return the Liaotung Peninsula by the Triple Intervention [of Germany, Russia and France], this phrase was first used in Japan to mean that we were to endure a life of patience and austerity until someday our national strength burgeoned and we would rise again."

in continuing the talks in Washington." His adamant stand forced the Navy to do what Oka had written they could not do: speak with candor. "We are now at the crossroads—war or peace," said Oikawa. "If we are to continue with diplomacy, we must give up war preparations and go in completely for talks—to negotiate for months and then suddenly change our tack won't do. . . . The Navy is willing to leave the decision entirely up to the Prime Minister . . ."

Whatever the choice, it had to be made at once, said Konoye. "It's risky either way. The question is, Which is riskier? If we have to make a decision here and now, I will be in favor of negotiations."

Tojo turned to Admiral Toyoda. "Mr. Foreign Minister, have you any confidence in negotiations?" he asked with more than a touch of sarcasm. "I'm afraid you can't persuade the Army General Staff, judging from what you've already said. I would like to hear if you have any confidence."

"Weighing both sides," Konoye replied in his stead, "I still choose negotiations."

"That's only from your own subjective point of view," said Tojo sharply. "You can't prevail on the Army General Staff." Oikawa said he concurred, but this only irked Tojo. He asked Konoye not to reach a hasty conclusion. "I want to hear the opinion of the Foreign Minister."

"That depends on the conditions," said Toyoda. "I think the thorniest issue today is the presence of troops in China, and if the Army won't concede a thing to the United States, then there's no point in continuing the talks. But if the Army can see its way clear to making some slight compromise, it may not be impossible."

"The stationing of troops is a matter of life and death to the Army!" Tojo burst out. "No concession in that direction!" Japan had already agreed in principle to the withdrawal of all troops from China, he continued. That, in itself, was a tremendous concession. Now it was obvious that America was demanding that Japan withdraw *all* troops *at once*. This was impossible. A million Japanese were still locked in battle in China. Japan could not withdraw completely until order was restored in China. The interior was a hotbed of Communists and bandits, and only the presence of Japanese troops in certain areas could guarantee law and order and the successful economic growth of that whole part of the continent. Total withdrawal before the aims of war had been accomplished "would not be in keeping with the dignity of the Army," and the entire General Staff "as well as the troops abroad" agreed with him.

"Don't you think now is the time to forget glory and reap the fruits?" Konoye remarked. Why not give in to America in form? That is, agree in principle to withdraw all troops, yet make an arrangement with China to retain some troops in unstable areas?

Unthinkable, said Tojo. If they made a pledge they would have to honor it scrupulously; and once they bowed to the American demand, the Chinese would show contempt. They were always most to be feared when contemptuous; withdrawal would lead to a complete loss of face and the rise of Communism. It would be like a run on the bank, and Korea as well as North China would be lost.

It was Tojo against the other four, but he stuck obstinately to his opinion. "The Army has no intention of changing the decision of the imperial conference which was held the other day [September 6]. If there is hope of success in negotiation before the deadline set by the Supreme Command, then the talks should continue. The Navy Minister said the decision for war or peace rests with the Prime Minister. I don't agree at all. The decision for war should be made jointly by the government and the Supreme Command. And I don't think there is any possible way to settle the problem by diplomacy at this stage."

"I'm not confident of victory in war," Konoye retorted. "I think there is no way to overcome the present difficulties except by diplomatic negotiations. As for war, I will leave that to a person who is confident of victory." He turned to Tojo. "If you keep insisting on war, I cannot hold myself responsible for that."

"Haven't we decided to go to war if diplomacy fails?" Tojo was exasperated. "Of course, you were present at that conference. I don't see why you can't assume responsibility for that."

"That decision was really *nai-nai*," said Konoye, meaning "only among ourselves"—that is, it was a secret decision and, with the Emperor's approval, could be reconsidered. Tojo took this literally to mean "of an unofficial nature"—an insult to the Emperor—and he was so visibly agitated that Konoye tried to elaborate. "Since I have greater confidence in negotiations, why should I hold myself responsible? That's all I meant. We must consider the decision for war as final only when there is no prospect of carrying on negotiations. And there is still a chance for success."

"Just suppose we do abandon war preparations," said Suzuki, envisaging another 2/26 Incident, "how can we control the Army?"

"If that is the case," said Tojo, "controlling the Army won't be difficult."

The argument continued through the afternoon, and finally ended in compromise: they would continue negotiations until October 15, or later if Imperial Headquarters approved it, but concede nothing on the stationing of troops in China to fight Communism.

Compromise or not, the meeting did have one good effect. Tojo had argued stubbornly, but on the way back to Tokyo he began to realize that the September 6 decision had been too hasty, since the Navy seemed to lack confidence. War under such circumstances could be a great mistake. Once back at the War Ministry, he summoned Kenryo Sato, who was now chief of the Military Affairs Section, and told him the Navy still seemed to be wavering.

"Mr. Minister," said Colonel Sato, "I will arrange a conference for you with the Navy Minister and the two Chiefs of Staff. Why don't you make it a private meeting over *sake* at a *machiai* [restaurant where geisha girls entertain]? You can say, 'Is the Navy confident or not about this war? The main role in such a war would be played by the Navy. If you men really don't believe in it, we must not fight this war. In that case, I promise never to say we're not fighting because the Navy lacks confidence. Instead I will take full responsibility and say, "I, the War Minister, will not fight." ' "

Tojo's face flushed and he began to sputter. "Do you mean to tell me that responsible men like the Navy Minister and the Chiefs of Staff would say at a *machiai* what they won't talk about at an imperial conference?" He refused to be party to such shameful subterfuge.

Out of the inconclusive meeting at Ogikubo came rumors of a Cabinet crisis and a possible declaration of war. Konoye was already regretting the compromise. With no further concessions on China, it would be impossible to conclude a settlement with America. He wondered what he could possibly do before time ran out, then decided to speak to Tojo informally. He phoned the War Minister early in the morning of October 14 and arranged to see him just before the ten o'clock Cabinet meeting.

"I can go along with you except for your stand on our troops in China," Konoye said and suggested they withdraw all troops at once "for formality's sake."

Tojo bristled; Konoye was already going back on his word. "If once we give in, the United States will assume a high-handed attitude and keep on acting that way. Your solution is really not a solution. War will crop up again in a few years. I respect you, Mr. Prime Minister, but your view is too pessimistic. You know our weak points too well . . . America has her weaknesses too."

"That's a matter of opinion." Konoye reminded him that on February 4, 1904, Emperor Meiji summoned Prince Ito and asked if Japan could defeat Russia. Ito replied that the enemy could be checked at the Korean border for a year. In the meantime America would be asked to mediate a peace. Relieved, Emperor Meiji had sanctioned a declaration of war. In the present case, however, there was no third party to mediate. Therefore, they must proceed with great caution, particularly since America had such tremendous superiority in material resources.

Tojo stiffened at the word "caution." "There are times when we must have the courage to do extraordinary things—like jumping, with eyes closed, off the veranda of the Kiyomizu Temple!"*

Konoye said that was possible only for a private individual. "People in responsible positions should not think that way."

Tojo looked at him with scorn and said, "All this is a matter of difference in our personalities, isn't it?" He thought, This man is too weak to be prime minister at such a critical time; he can't even keep a promise.

Tojo went into the Cabinet meeting determined to repudiate his own promise, and take such a strong stand that Konoye would be forced to resign. By the time the meeting started he had purposely worked himself into a state of excitement. Flicking a piece of paper, he said, "The Army will continue its preparations. I don't mean this will necessarily interfere with the negotiations, but I will not consider another day's delay!" He swung on Foreign Minister Toyoda and asked if he thought the talks with America would be successful.

* A Buddhist temple located on a hill at the edge of a ravine in Kyoto.

"The point of dispute," reiterated the admiral, "is the withdrawal of troops. The United States is not satisfied with Japan's reply. If we are to answer again on this matter, we must do so in a straightforward manner. . . . America is becoming more and more suspicious of our attitude, so we can't satisfy them unless we give them facts. They cannot understand Japan's way of carrying on peace talks while preparing for war."

"I make no concessions regarding withdrawal!" shouted Tojo as if he had lost his temper—and perhaps by now he had. "It means defeat of Japan by the United States—a stain on the history of the Japanese Empire! The way of diplomacy isn't always a matter of concession; sometimes it is oppression. If we concede, Manchuria and Korea will be lost." He repeated all his old arguments, but this time with a fervor that moved the listeners. Then he turned his wrath on the Navy, and Oikawa in particular, for failing to declare openly and frankly if they could beat America. Konoye and the Cabinet sat in silence, petrified by Tojo's "bomb speech."

Tojo's outburst did what he had hoped. Several hours after the meeting, General Suzuki came to his office to say that he was acting as Konoye's go-between: he could not continue as prime minister since the War Minister had publicly expressed such a forceful opinion.

Tojo refused to retract his statement and said Konoye could only continue in office if he was willing to go along. But others in the Army were alarmed at the thought of a Konoye resignation. General Muto conceded to Suzuki that although the Prime Minister was a coward, he alone could maintain the unity of the nation. "If he resigns, Japan cannot fight a war." Muto paced around and half jokingly said, "How about carrying out a big maneuver in Manchuria so the troops can let off steam?"

Later that afternoon Muto called on Konoye's cabinet secretary, Kanji Tomita, and said, "Somehow or other it seems that the reason the Prime Minister can't make up his mind is because the Navy can't make up its mind." The Army would have to reconsider the entire matter if it was sure the Navy really didn't want war. "But the Navy just says it will 'leave the decision entirely up to the Prime Minister.' Saying that isn't enough to control the inner circle of the Army. That can only be done if the Navy openly states, 'We don't wish war.' I wonder if you can arrange it so that the Navy says something along that line."

But the Navy still refused to make an official statement. "The most we can do," Admiral Oka told Tomita, "is ask the Prime Minister to deal with the matter at his own discretion."

All that day Suzuki, Tomita, Oka and Muto shuttled from office to office. Use of such go-betweens was common in critical times, since telephones might be tapped; moreover, ideas could be expressed through a middleman which would have been difficult to bring up face to face; and if things didn't go well, the go-between could simply be repudiated.

That night Suzuki returned to the War Ministry. He blamed the Navy for the impasse, then asked Tojo who should be the next prime minister. "I'd say it can be nobody but Prince Higashikuni," Tojo replied. "Even Konoye could not solve this problem, so we must call upon a member of the royal family." If the decision was for peace, the uncle-in-law of the Emperor was one of the few Japanese who could bring it about without a revolt within the Army. He could summon both Chiefs of Staff and tell them he'd decided against war. The Emperor could not do this—it was against custom and Constitution. But a prince of the royal family could, and his wishes would have to be followed by the military. Thus peace could come without civil disorder. Before they parted, Tojo said he didn't think he ought to meet again with Konoye or he might lose his temper.

Suzuki went directly to Konoye's villa in the suburbs and told him about Higashikuni as the War Minister's choice. Konoye was in accord. "Prince Higashikuni is a very good man. I know him well. He is against war. I will tell this to the Emperor when I see him tomorrow."

The next day was October 15, the deadline for peace, and Suzuki was busier than usual. In the morning he told Marquis Kido about the recommendation of Higashikuni for prime minister, but the Privy Seal showed no enthusiasm. The prince was "talented" but lacked political experience and training. More important, a member of the imperial family should not bear the responsibility in case war broke out.

At noon Suzuki heard from Konoye. He'd spoken to the Emperor, who, unlike Kido, considered Higashikuni a suitable candidate for prime minister. Konoye asked Suzuki to sound out the prince himself for his reaction.

"We in the Army are not all for war," Suzuki told Higashikuni. "I too believe you can control the situation." He added that Tojo himself felt Higashikuni alone could go directly to the Emperor and find out exactly what he wanted, and then control the Army, whatever the decision—war or peace.

"This is a very grave matter," said the prince. "I want some time to think it over. I'd like to talk with the War and Navy ministers before making up my mind."

That evening Konoye phoned Kido for advice. Should he talk to Prince Higashikuni informally? Too soon, said Kido. "But as long as the government takes the responsibility, I have no objection." Despite this lukewarm endorsement, Konoye secretly went at once to Higashikuni and said the negotiations could not succeed unless the Army agreed to withdraw all troops from China, and only a new cabinet led by the prince could resolve the matter and unite the Army and the Navy.

"This is too sudden and too difficult a question to decide on the spur of the moment," said the prince. "I'm against a prime minister from the royal family, but in case you organize a new cabinet and still can't come to an agreement with the Army, I might take office as a last resort, even at the risk of my life." He was far more enthusiastic about Konoye as prime minister and suggested that he form the new cabinet with a war minister who would be more open to peace than Tojo. He promised to use his considerable influence to bring this about. Konoye left the man he had come to proselyte, determined to succeed himself as prime minister.

His chief antagonist, Tojo, had also made a resolution. He was impatient for action; the deadline had come and none was being taken. Though torn by doubts, he made up his mind to force the issue by placing the question before the Emperor, and the following afternoon went to the man who could arrange an interview, Privy Seal Kido. "The time has come to act upon the decision of September 6," he demanded.

Kido said that decision had been made too abruptly, without sufficient deliberation. "It must be reconsidered."

There was reason in this reply, but Tojo brushed it off with a

"Yes, I know" and took a new tack. "How about a cabinet formed by a member of the royal family?"

Kido said it would not do to pick Higashikuni. "The royal family should join the government only in times of peace."

There was also reason in this reply, but it wasn't what Tojo wanted to hear. He paused to find a rejoinder, and finding none, reverted to the September 6 decision. It had to be carried out, he said stubbornly.

"If we do, what will happen to Japan?"

"What do you think?"

"I think," said Kido, "that Japan will become a third- or fourth-class nation."

It was a conversation that left Tojo dejected and Kido hopeful. He sensed Tojo's doubts and was satisfied that he could be dealt with once Konoye could be persuaded to "exert himself a little harder" in the quest for peace. By coincidence he was called to the phone; it was Konoye. "I am going to resign," he said abruptly.

What Kido had feared had come with unsettling suddenness, and now he faced a task made more difficult by the times. The new cabinet would be Japan's most critical, and the burden of choice was his own. Since the death of Prince Saionji in 1940, he, as privy seal, had taken over the last *genro*'s major task because the vacuum had to be filled and because he was one who never shirked responsibility, nor made a show of it. The very anonymity of his personality had left this assumption of power unchallenged.

The new cabinet would lead the nation to war or peace and it was up to him to see that it was peace. The man who would help make the choice was the one who had made it necessary. Just before dusk Prince Konoye appeared, worn by weeks of anxiety.

"The September 6 decision should be canceled; it is a cancer," said Kido. "It should then be reconsidered under someone who is familiar with the situation." The new prime minister could not be an outsider. He must be someone of stature who had participated in the arguments of the past few months. This limited the choice to two men—Admiral Oikawa and Tojo. Since Tojo had precipitated the present crisis, perhaps Oikawa, who had expressed some doubts about the outcome of a war, should be chosen. But Oikawa might not be acceptable to the young officers, who actually ran the Army; they might resist or even revolt.

The quiet, scholarly Oikawa would of course give a better impression on the international scene. "But if we appoint him," Kido told Konoye, "the Army wouldn't select a war minister." Therefore Tojo was the sole choice. He could control the fiery elements in the military in case the decision was peace; he was a man of character with no political ambitions. He was too direct to scheme and had shown, since his appointment as war minister, that he would do whatever His Majesty wished.

It was typical of Konoye that his immediate reaction was positive. Perhaps he was overreacting to his own antipathy to Tojo. They had reached the point where they could no longer meet face to face, yet Konoye began listing arguments (or were these rationalizations?) in his favor: not only could he control the Army but he had recently assumed a "rather humble" manner; he appeared to be reconciled to renewed negotiations with America. "Tojo told me the other day that since the Navy's attitude still wasn't clear, we should look into the matter thoroughly and reconsider the whole situation. So I don't think he will push for war on assuming the premiership. And he will be still more cautious if he gets words of counsel from the Throne."

Kido assured Konoye that the Emperor would surely ask Tojo to reconsider the decision. It was a scheme that no one but a pragmatist could have devised: to select a cabinet primarily because it could control the situation, and then force it to think in terms of peace by an extraordinary act of the Emperor.

Konoye left the Palace engrossed by the idea. But as he drove home with his son-in-law, he began to have doubts about Tojo, and did what few in the land would have dared—vocally blame the Emperor for the crisis. His Majesty had recently remarked, "How stupid the Army people are!" If he felt that way, why hadn't he expressed his views candidly, firmly? In normal times it was proper for an emperor to remain silent, but when the question of war or peace was at stake, he should unhesitatingly point the way.

Both Konoye and the Emperor were examples of what was most admirable in Japan, and what might lead to national disaster. Both were unselfish and without personal ambition, putting the welfare of the people ahead of everything else. Each showed he could step out of character and act decisively, but these times were too rare. This was the tragedy of Hirohito and Konoye—and Japan.

That day—October 16—a new patriotic song recently broadcast over radio station JOAK appeared in the *Japan Times & Advertiser*, the nation's leading English-language newspaper:

> *Siren, siren, air raid, air raid!*
> *What is that to us?*
> *Preparations are well done,*
> *Neighborhood associations are solid,*
> *Determination for defense is firm.*
> *Enemy planes are only mosquitoes or dragonflies.*
> *We will win, we must win.*
> *What of air raid?*
> *We know no defeat.*
> *Come to this land to be shot down.*

Eugene Dooman was still dressing the next morning when the phone rang. It was Ushiba, Konoye's secretary, asking if he could come over right away. Ushiba arrived "nervous and excited" while Dooman was at breakfast, and said he had been up all night helping Konoye make arrangements for a new prime minister. He had a letter from the prince to Ambassador Grew expressing "regret and disappointment" over his resignation. It had been drafted by Ushiba after a full explanation from Konoye of why Tojo had to be his successor. Only he would be able to revoke the decision for war—"to let the Navy do it would be too provocative."

. . . I feel certain, however, that the cabinet which is to succeed mine will exert its utmost in continuing to a successful conclusion the conversations which we have been carrying on up till today. It is my earnest hope, therefore, that you and your Government will not be too disappointed or discouraged either by the change of cabinet or by the mere appearance or impression of the new cabinet. I assure you that I will do all in my power in assisting the new cabinet to attain the high purpose which mine has endeavored to accomplish so hard without success. . . .

Shortly after one o'clock the *jushin*—the seven ex-premiers—met in the West Antechamber of the Palace to help select a prime minister. Kido was there, still determined to recommend Tojo; Konoye was not, since he was the outgoing premier.

Someone suggested that they choose a prince of the blood. Kido opposed this. If war came, "the imperial family might be faced with a storm of denunciation from the people." He suggested Tojo; he was "fully acquainted with the development of the situation" and could "effect real co-operation between the Army and the Navy." He also understood the need of re-examining the September 6 decision.

One Navy man, Admiral Okada—who as prime minister had so miraculously escaped assassination by the "2/26" rebels—disapproved someone like the War Minister. Hadn't the Army hierarchy Tojo represented proved it was tough and uncompromising? "To quote the Privy Seal: 'In the past the Army used to shoot rifles at us from the rear; I hope they don't start using cannon.'"

The man just quoted agreed that this was certainly a matter of concern; yet who but Tojo had the position, prestige and strength to control the young officers and rightists? Some Navy man?

"In my opinion, the Navy should absolutely not step in at this time," said Okada and recommended his liberal friend General Ugaki, who had favored a reduction of the armed forces back in the twenties.

Resistance to Tojo continued until three-thirty. Then Yoshimichi Hara, present in his capacity as President of the Privy Council, agreed to go along, provided Tojo would follow the policy laid down by the Emperor—that is, reconsider the September 6 decision. Koki Hirota—the civilian prime minister who had succumbed to Army pressure after the 2/26 Incident—asked if Tojo was also to retain his position as war minister.

"Yes," Kido replied.

"In that case, fine." That would give Tojo control of the Army radicals.

The other *jushin* gave their consent, but Hara spoke for all of them when he remarked, "I don't think the Privy Seal's choice is very satisfactory, but since it's the only specific one, we have nothing to do but give it a try."

Kido had got his way.

Tojo was packing. He was concerned about a possible reprimand from the Emperor for his part in the fall of Konoye and wondered where he would be assigned. At about three-thirty the Grand

Chamberlain phoned and asked him to report to the Palace at once. Tojo hastily stuffed into a briefcase some papers which might support his position.

He had gone to the Palace to be admonished, and was confounded to hear the Emperor say, "We order you to form a cabinet. Observe the provisions of the Constitution. We believe that the nation is facing an extremely grave situation. Bear in mind that the Army and Navy should, at this time, work in even closer cooperation. We will later summon the Navy Minister to tell him the same."

Tojo requested time to consider and went into the waiting room. He was joined a few minutes later by Admiral Oikawa, who had just been instructed by the Emperor to work "in closer cooperation" with the Army. Kido approached them. "I assume the Emperor has just talked to you both about Army-Navy cooperation," he said and explained what His Majesty could only imply. "With regard to the decision on our *kokutai* [national essence], it is the Emperor's wish that you make an exhaustive study of domestic and foreign conditions—without regard to the decision of the September 6 imperial conference. I convey this to you as an order of the Emperor."

It was unprecedented in Japanese history. No Emperor had ever before rescinded a decision of the imperial conference. Tojo was ordered to "go back to blank paper," that is, start with a clean slate and negotiate with America for peace.

Tojo could not fully comprehend what had occurred. He managed to tell Kido that he accepted the responsibility thrust on him by the Emperor. At the Yasukuni Shrine, where the souls of Japan's war dead were enshrined, he bowed his head in prayer. Appropriately a thousand dead warriors were just being enrolled in a mass ceremony. Tojo realized that he faced a completely new life. From now on he had to think as a civilian, not as a soldier. It was a disruptive turnabout, but he forced himself to examine the problems ahead: he must at once form a cabinet based solely on merit and experience and embracing all segments of Japanese life. His would not be a military but a national cabinet and he should, above all, scrupulously follow the wishes of the Emperor. He vowed to live by a new motto: "To Have the Emperor as the Mirror of my Judgment." He would take every decision to the Emperor. If His

Majesty's mirror was clean, Tojo would go ahead; if it was even slightly clouded, he would reconsider. What better criterion was there? The Emperor was born to be fair, belonged to no class and reflected the interests of the people exclusively.

He returned to find the War Ministry in ferment. Two excited generals intercepted him in the hall with their cabinet nominations. Tojo turned on his heel, muttered something about the military "meddling too much," and strode into his office to summon Naoki Hoshino, a close civilian associate from Manchuria. He was finally located at the Kabuki Theater, and when he arrived at the ministry, Tojo was sitting on the floor surrounded by papers. "I'd like you to be my secretary-general," said Tojo.

Together they began picking the new cabinet. "The Army should have no part in the selection," Tojo explained but suggested Hidehiko Ishiguro, a favorite of military men, as minister of education. Hoshino thought this might create troublesome opposition; why not keep the present minister, a professor?

"Good idea," said Tojo and crossed Ishiguro's name off his list. "Which do you think would be better as finance minister, Aoki or Kaya?"

"They're both fine men of character and experience," said Hoshino, but since the former was in Nanking and the latter in Tokyo, Tojo put a check opposite Okinori Kaya's name. "What do you think of Togo for foreign minister?"

Hoshino said he knew him well. They had worked together when buying the Chinese Eastern Railway from the Russians. "He's quite tenacious. I think he's a good man." Tojo made another check mark.

Hoshino began phoning those selected, asking for a quick decision. Seven accepted on the spot but four, including Kaya and Togo, had doubts and insisted on speaking to Tojo first. Kaya came at once. "There are many rumors of war between Japan and America," he said. "I hear the Army is advocating this. Are you for war or not?"

"I intend to bring a peaceful solution if possible. I have no desire for war."

"It's fine that you don't want to start war, but the Supreme Command is independent," Kaya retorted and reminded Tojo of Manchuria and China.

"I will never allow the Army to start war against the wishes of the Cabinet," said Tojo.

His candor impressed Kaya, but before accepting, he decided to phone Konoye despite the late hour. The prince advised him to accept the post and do what he could to work toward peace.

Shigenori Togo,* who came from a samurai family but was no relation of the famous admiral, arrived soon after Kaya. He was a heavyset, thoughtful man who talked deliberately in a heavy Kyushu accent that was harsh to Tokyo ears. To Grew he was grim and "ultra-reserved." An experienced career diplomat, he had an understanding of European ways and had scandalized his family by marrying a German. Unlike most diplomats, however, he was in the habit of saying what he meant with a bluntness that some construed as rudeness. He wanted to make sure he could negotiate in good faith. Why had Konoye failed in the negotiations with America?

Tojo was frank. Konoye had been dismissed because the Army had insisted on stationing troops in China. The Army would have to agree "to make genuine concessions" regarding the troops in China and other problems so a settlement could be reached "on a reasonable basis." Tojo added that he had no objection to reviewing any of the issues but insisted on an immediate answer so he could submit the list of ministers to the Emperor in the morning.

Togo accepted.

The next day the fifty-seven-year-old Tojo was promoted to full general, a rank commensurate with his new post. After the investiture ceremony of the Cabinet, he took the train for the Ise Shrine, the most sacred of all Shinto shrines, to pay homage, according to custom, to the Sun Goddess.

Publicly the selection of Tojo was greeted with enthusiasm. One newspaper, the *Yomiuri,* declared it should inspire the nation "to rise to the occasion and administer a great shock to the anti-Axis powers." But privately a few like Higashikuni were concerned. The prince wondered how Kido could possibly have recommended Tojo, since he was so "war-minded." And how could the Emperor have accepted him?

American opinion was divided as well. Otto Tolischus, the

---

* Pronounced approximately like Tohngo. In Japanese the sound of *g*, except when it is the first letter of a word, is somewhat similar to *ng*.

"Go Back to Blank Paper"

Tokyo correspondent of the *New York Times,* after discussing the matter with Embassy Counselor Dooman, wrote: "It would be premature to assume that the new Government will necessarily be dominated by the extremists whose belligerent pronouncements heralded the fall of Konoye. Tojo himself is a certain guarantee against this. . . . In some respects, the negotiations might even be facilitated by the change. . . . Now the United States knows that it is dealing with the Army directly."

But the one whose opinions would carry the most weight in the negotiations, Cordell Hull, characterized the new Prime Minister as a "typical Japanese officer, with a small-bore, straight-laced, one-track mind" who was "rather stupid." He had expected little good from Konoye; from Tojo he expected "even less."

5

The Fatal Note

1.

Even though the Russians didn't yet know the results of the imperial conference of July 2, one of their agents, Hotsumi Ozaki, had just heard a rumor of the decision to go south instead of attacking Siberia. For confirmation his chief, Richard Sorge, sent him to Manchuria, where he discovered that the Kwantung Army's secret order for three thousand railroad workers to help mount an attack on the Red Army had inexplicably been reduced to practically nothing. On October 4 Sorge radioed this information to Moscow, along with the latest diplomatic developments:

ACCORDING TO INFORMATION OBTAINED FROM VARIOUS JAPANESE OFFICIAL SOURCES, IF NO SATISFACTORY REPLY IS RECEIVED FROM THE U.S. TO JAPAN'S REQUEST FOR NEGOTIATIONS BY THE 15TH OR 16TH OF THIS MONTH, THERE WILL EITHER BE A GENERAL RESIGNATION OR A DRASTIC REORGANIZATION OF THE JAPANESE GOVERNMENT. IN EITHER EVENT . . . THERE WILL BE WAR WITH THE U. S. THIS MONTH OR NEXT MONTH. THE SOLE HOPE OF THE JAPANESE AUTHORITIES IS THAT AMBASSADOR GREW WILL PRESENT SOME SORT OF

ELEVENTH-HOUR PROPOSAL THROUGH WHICH NEGOTIATIONS CAN BE OPENED.

WITH RESPECT TO THE SOVIET UNION, TOP-RANKING ELEMENTS ARE GENERALLY AGREED THAT, IF GERMANY WINS, JAPAN CAN TAKE OVER HER GAINS IN THE FAR EAST IN THE FUTURE AND THAT THEREFORE IT IS UNNECESSARY FOR JAPAN TO FIGHT RUSSIA. THEY FEEL THAT IF GERMANY PROVES UNABLE TO DESTROY THE SOVIET GOVERNMENT AND FORCE IT OUT OF MOSCOW, JAPAN SHOULD BIDE HER TIME UNTIL NEXT SPRING. IN ANY EVENT, THE AMERICAN ISSUE AND THE QUESTION OF THE ADVANCE TO THE SOUTH ARE FAR MORE IMPORTANT THAN THE NORTHERN PROBLEM.

This remarkably accurate information, which helped influence the Red Army to transfer most of its troops from Manchuria to the western front, was the last sent by Sorge. A week later a member of his ring, Yotoku Miyagi, a thirty-eight-year-old artist with tuberculosis, was arrested by chance when a woman who had been picked up in a general anti-Communist drive by the *tokko* ("Thought" police) revealed that she had known him in America, where both had been members of the Communist party. Miyagi had become a Communist out of resentment for "the inhuman discrimination practiced against the Asiatic races" in the United States. He had in his possession a study of Japan's oil-stock level in Manchuria and other top-secret material, but refused to talk for a day. During a lunch break, in a unique try at suicide for a Japanese, Miyagi suddenly dived out a third-story window. A detective instinctively plunged after him. Both landed in a tree and Miyagi suffered a broken leg. After that he told everything he knew about Sorge's setup.

This resulted in Ozaki's arrest three days later. Both he and Miyagi were supposed to rendezvous with their chief that night, and when they failed to appear, Sorge suspected that they had been caught. As he gloomily drank cup after cup of *sake,* he became more certain than ever that his mission in Japan was over; recently he had drafted a message to Moscow requesting that he be sent to Russia or Germany "to embark on new activities."

As it happened, Sorge himself was safe for the moment. The Minister of the Interior was alarmed lest the resulting publicity reveal that Ozaki was "a close friend" of Konoye's (the connection was tenuous; he was merely an acquaintance and had gained access to the prince's celebrated discussion group, the Breakfast Club, through his classmate Ushiba), thus causing the government to fall. But since Konoye resigned the following day, this was no longer a consideration. Permission was granted to pick up Sorge.

Before dawn the next morning—the day Tojo was to be installed formally as prime minister—Sorge was arrested in bed and taken in pajamas and slippers to the Toriizaka police station. Ambassador Ott protested to the Foreign Ministry and demanded to see Sorge. When they met, Sorge seemed embarrassed. They talked of trivialities for a few moments, then Ott asked if Sorge had anything else on his mind. After a pause he said, "Mr. Ambassador, this is our final farewell. Give my regards to your wife and family."

At last Ott realized he had been betrayed by his friend. The two stared at each other silently, and once Sorge was taken away, the shaken Ott told the official in charge, "For the good of our two countries, investigate this case thoroughly. Get to the bottom of it."

At the liaison conference of October 23, Navy Chief of Staff Nagano observed somberly, "We were supposed to have reached a decision in October and yet here we are." The Navy was consuming four hundred tons of oil per hour. "The situation is urgent. We must have a decision at once, one way or the other."

The Army was in agreement. "There's already been a month's delay," Sugiyama said. "We can't waste four or five days in study. We must rush forward!"

Prime Minister Tojo's answer could have come from Konoye. "I can understand why the Supreme Command is urging haste, but the government prefers to study the matter carefully and responsibly, since we have new ministers of Navy, Finance and Foreign Affairs. We should make up our minds whether to accept the September 6 decision or look at it from a different point of view. Does the Supreme Command object?"

No, said Sugiyama and Nagano.

Tojo had met his first formal test with authority. Kido's instinct had been correct; Tojo had proved he could cope with a disgruntled military.

Subsequent liaison conferences during the next ten days were

The Fatal Note

devoted to the negotiations in Washington and the chances of success in case of war. The members agreed to maintain their stand on the Tripartite Pact and to honor Konoye's promise to adhere to Hull's four principles. The only discord was on the withdrawal of troops from China. Tojo, so adamant with Konoye, suggested that "as a diplomatic gesture" they should offer to withdraw all troops in about twenty-five years. Now it was Sugiyama who argued Tojo's former position. He adamantly refused time and again to make any concession. The Prime Minister found stronger support than he wanted from Foreign Minister Shigenori Togo, who said "it would be better to withdraw troops right away," and then that "everything would turn out for the better" if the American proposals were accepted, almost intact.

These suggestions were so disruptive—in fact, several thought Togo had lost his mind—that a motion was made for an adjournment until the next day. This was agreeable to Togo, who welcomed the chance "to get my mind in order."

It was Tojo who insisted that they continue. Every minute counted and a decision must be made, if they had to stay up all night. He urged them to study three courses: avoid war even at the expense of great hardship, or as Kido had put it, *gashin-shotan* —"to sleep on kindling and lick gall"; decide on war at once; or continue negotiations but be ready to go to war if necessary. Personally, he added, he was hoping that diplomacy would bring peace.

Sugiyama and Tsukada left the prolonged meeting, bewildered and distressed by Tojo's change in attitude; he was talking more like a civilian than a general. Tojo returned to his office and discussed the three alternatives with his favorite sounding board, Kenryo Sato, now a major general, who said an immediate declaration of war was folly. The Kido solution, *gashin-shotan*, would solve neither the China Incident nor the basic differences between America and Japan; nevertheless, this course would have to be taken if the Navy officially admitted lack of confidence. "If there is any real prospect of winning, I am of course for war. But if there's no chance of victory, it would be nonsense to start it."

Tojo needed little persuasion. He told Sato to induce Chief of Staff Sugiyama privately not to insist on immediate war at the crucial liaison conference the next morning. But Sugiyama answered with some sarcasm, "Tell the *War Minister* the only possible answer is war."

The conference was set for nine o'clock, but Tojo asked Sugiyama to see him earlier; he was hoping that a personal confrontation would lead to a compromise. At seven-thirty Sugiyama and his deputy, the outspoken Tsukada, arrived at the official residence.

"The Emperor," Tojo began, "is strongly opposed to abandoning diplomacy and starting a war in the south." He doubted that Sugiyama's views would change the Emperor's mind. "If you feel confident, please see him yourself. I have no objection."

The General Staff felt that the negotiations with America were at a dead end, Sugiyama replied, and as long as the United States remained stubborn there was neither opportunity nor need to continue the talks. There was but one solution—war! Then he berated Tojo, a military man, for siding with the civilians. Tojo made no reply; he was the Prime Minister, and secondarily War Minister.

The conference—it was the sixty-sixth since their inception in 1937—started on November 1 at the Palace in the Imperial Courtroom amidst an atmosphere of apprehension. With the fate of the nation in the balance, a prime minister was again at odds with the Army, which still held the voting majority. Tojo said he would like to discuss the three alternatives. What about the first —*gashin-shotan?*

One of his civilian supporters, Finance Minister Kaya, answered with two questions: "What if we go along as now, without war, and in three years the American fleet attacks us? Would the Navy have any prospect of winning then or not?"

"Who knows?" said Admiral Nagano.

"*Will* the U. S. fleet come and attack us or not?" pressed Kaya.

"I think the chances are fifty-fifty," said Nagano.

If it came, Kaya insisted, could the Navy win?

Nagano still refused to commit the Navy. "We can either avoid war now and go to war in three years; or go to war immediately and plan for it to continue for the next three years." It would be better, he said, to start war at once while Japan held the advantage.

Kaya reminded him that Nagano himself had admitted that victory was not certain if the war lasted for three years. "What's more, I firmly believe there is little chance of the United States'

The Fatal Note

attacking us and I must conclude it would not be a good idea for us to go to war at the present."

Another civilian, Foreign Minister Togo, supported him on both counts.

"Remember the old saying, 'Don't count on what won't happen,'" said Nagano. "The future is a question mark and anything can happen." Within three years America would be strong in Southeast Asia.

"All right, so when can we go to war and win it?" Kaya goaded him.

"At once," Nagano replied emphatically. "An opportune time for war will not come later!"

The conflict should be started at the beginning of December, said Sugiyama, but negotiations with America should be carried on to give Japan a military advantage. To Kaya, this was totally repugnant. "We have come to a great turning point in our 2,600-year history. The fate of our country hangs in the balance. It's simply outrageous for us to resort to diplomatic trickery!"

"We can't do such a thing!" Togo protested.

The Navy Vice Chief of Staff ignored their outbursts. "Speaking for the Navy, you can negotiate until November 20 [Tokyo time]."

The Army was not willing to wait that long—their deadline was November 13.

Togo was indignant. "I can't carry on diplomacy as foreign minister unless there is a chance of success. I simply cannot accept deadlines or conditions that will hinder hope of success. It's obvious you'll have to give up the idea of starting a war."

Prime Minister Tojo somehow remained calm, backing Togo and Kaya as often as he did the military. Gradually the Army began concentrating on Togo, and even tried to pressure him during the breaks. He was told, "If the Foreign Minister opposes war, all we have to do is replace him." After lunch, which was served at the conference table, Togo continued to berate the Army. "November 13 is too outrageous," he said. "The Navy puts it at November 20."

"Until November 13 at the latest!" said Tsukada. A delay would create confusion among operational units.

It was an admiral who objected to such rigid thinking. Navy

Minister Shigetaro Shimada didn't see why negotiations couldn't continue until November 29.

"Keep quiet, please!" exclaimed General Tsukada. "Your suggestion is out of order." He turned to Togo. "What deadline would you like?"

The discussion got out of hand. Tojo called a break. During the twenty-minute recess the Army conferred and concluded that negotiations *could* continue, if necessary, until November 30.

When the meeting reconvened, Prime Minister Tojo tried for one more concession. "Can't we make the deadline December 1?" he said. Psychologically it might give the diplomats much more time. "Can't you let negotiations go on just one more day?"

"Absolutely not," said Tsukada. "We absolutely cannot go beyond November 30."

"Tsukada-*san*," Admiral Shimada asked, "until exactly what time on November 30? Till midnight?" This would, in effect, put the deadline where Tojo wanted it—December 1.

"All right," Tsukada conceded, "until midnight."

With the deadline for negotiations tentatively agreed upon, the burden of convincing the Americans to come to agreement would rest on Foreign Minister Togo. He said he had drawn up two proposals to be sent to America. Proposal A was a somewhat watered-down version of their previous offers. In it the Army agreed to withdraw all troops from China, including those left as defense against Communism, by 1966. Proposal B was to be used in case Secretary of State Hull turned down the first, and constituted a *modus vivendi*, a temporary arrangement pending a final settlement, to be used as a last resort. It was designed to allay Hull's suspicions about the drive into Indochina and assure him that Japan was abandoning any idea of a military conquest of Southeast Asia.

In Proposal B, Japan promised not to make any more aggressive moves south, and once peace was restored with China or a general peace in the Pacific established, all troops would be pulled out of Indochina. In the meantime Japan would at once move all troops in south Indochina to the north of that country. In return, America was to sell Japan one million tons of aviation gasoline.

Proposal B was unacceptable. "Stationing troops in French Indochina keeps China under control, and also enables us to

The Fatal Note

get raw materials in the south on a fifty-fifty basis," said Sugiyama. "Moreover, it places us in a stronger position strategically toward the United States as well as in settling the China Incident. Coming to an agreement with the United States doesn't mean they will give us materials. We're against Proposal B." Such stubborn opposition forced Togo to come out in the open and say he really didn't think "A" would have much chance in Washington with such a short time left to negotiate. The only realistic hope of salvaging peace was to narrow the negotiations to the south. "You're putting me in a difficult position if you tell me to do something that can't be done."

A few—including Secretary-General Hoshino and Finance Minister Kaya—realized that he was right, but the Army remained adamant. "We absolutely cannot pull out our troops from southern Indochina!" Tsukada exclaimed and repeated Sugiyama's arguments. "Besides, withdrawal of these troops would place our supply routes for all materials from the south at the mercy of the Americans, who could cut them off whenever they wanted." It would merely delay the crisis for another six months and by then —because of the weather—Japan's chances to win a decision by arms would have come and gone. "Therefore, Proposal B is out. Just present Proposal A."

For hours the Army refused to accede to any suggestion of withdrawal from Indochina, while insisting that Hull be asked to unfreeze Japanese assets and cease his sabotage of a peaceful settlement of the China Incident.* It was a ridiculous proposition and Togo thought he could not possibly negotiate on such terms. In desperation he burst out, "We can't carry on diplomacy—but we still shouldn't start a war!"

---

* In addition to sending considerable supplies to China, America was now providing manpower. Claire Chennault, a former U. S. Army Air Corps colonel, and his Flying Tigers were openly training in Burma for air battle with the Japanese. On April 15, 1941, President Roosevelt had signed an unpublicized executive order authorizing Reserve officers and enlisted men to resign from the Army Air Corps, the Naval and Marine Air services so they could join Chennault's American Volunteer Group. Since the United States was not at war with Japan and could not deal openly with China, all arrangements had to be made with an unofficial agency to ensure secrecy. The Central Aircraft Manufacturing Company of China was set up and authorized to hire a hundred American pilots and several hundred ground crewmen to "operate, service and manufacture aircraft in China." The Japanese considered this a hostile, provocative act.

"That's why we should go ahead with Proposal A!" Tsukada shouted back.

"Yes," said Nagano, "we should just go ahead and negotiate with Proposal A."

Confronted as he was by combined Army-Navy opposition, Foreign Minister Togo still refused to back down on Indochina. How could he negotiate without any ammunition? The shouting reached such a peak that one of the secretaries—it was General Muto—proposed a ten-minute recess, then helped Tojo herd the three other Army men into an anteroom to reason with them. "If the negotiations fail on account of the Army's resistance to the Foreign Minister's proposal," Muto asked, "can the Army take the responsibility?" Tojo reminded them that the Emperor had called for "blank paper" and they should bow to his wishes. Finally Sugiyama reluctantly acquiesced, but only if Proposal A failed. He was still concerned about how the radicals in the Army might be kept from rebelling when they learned that Japan had made such a humiliating concession.

"I can handle that," said Tojo. The discussion simply could not go on and on. It was already after midnight.

The rest of the group was out in the imperial garden, recovering from the smoke and the heat of the argument. Admiral Nagano tapped Togo on the shoulder: "Can't the Foreign Ministry take over this task and straighten everything out by diplomacy? As far as the Navy is concerned you can settle the problem at your own discretion."

Togo was startled. A few minutes earlier this man had been an adversary. Encouraged by such unexpected support, he went back to the meeting more determined than ever. But once the discussion resumed, Nagano was back recommending war. It was another example of the Navy talking peace in private and war in public—to save face and get their share of military appropriations. "Of course, we may lose," he said, "but if we don't fight, we'd just have to bow to the United States. If we fight, there's a chance we can win. If we don't fight, wouldn't that be the same as losing the war?"

Nagano's words irked Tsukada, who found them cautious and vague. It seemed as if Nagano was set on going to war; why didn't he speak out, like Sugiyama? "All of us wonder if there isn't some way to achieve peace," he said urgently. "But no one is willing to say, 'Don't worry, I'll assume all responsibility even if the war is a long one.' However, we just can't maintain the status quo, so there is only one conclusion: we must go to war. I, Tsukada, believe we cannot avoid war. This is the moment. If we don't go to war now, we'll have to next year or the year after. This is the moment! The moral spirit of Japan, the Land of the Gods, will shine on our enterprise!" Japan's drive south would probably help Germany and Italy beat Russia and force China to surrender. The capture of Southeast Asia would be a mighty blow to America's resources. "We will build an iron wall, and inside it we will crush, one by one, our Asian enemies. We will also crush America and Britain!"

Tsukada's urgent call for battle was rebutted from an unlikely source—his own commander. Sugiyama said, "with extreme reluctance," that he would have to acquiesce to Togo's proposal to withdraw troops from southern Indochina. The abrupt shift came like an electric shock to all except Sugiyama's Army colleagues who had heard his concession in private. It was a considerable compromise, one that everyone knew would cause tremendous resentment throughout the ranks of the Army.

In return the military expected an end to civilian resistance and called for an immediate formal adoption of the deadline proposal. But Finance Minister Kaya refused to be rushed. "I cannot agree to a decision involving the destiny of Japan so suddenly," he said. He proposed they wait another day "to sleep on it," and the exhausted conferees filed into the garden at two o'clock in the morning.

As Kaya started home through the silent city he debated with himself. What if he persisted in opposing war? This would compel Tojo to dissolve the entire Cabinet, and the new one would undoubtedly bow to the militarists. On the other hand, there was still a possibility that the negotiations in Washington could be concluded successfully. Therefore, wouldn't it be wiser to go along with the proposal? Besides, if war did erupt, who was better equipped as finance minister to prevent inflation? His conclusions were logical but war with America was still unthinkable and he could not bring himself to phone Tojo and give his approval.

Togo was also debating with himself on the lonely trip home.

He had won his fight for Proposal B but he wasn't sure it would be enough to satisfy America. Perhaps more concessions could be wrung out of the Army if he resigned? After a few hours' sleep he called on an old friend, Koki Hirota, and asked for his opinion. The former prime minister thought he should stay in office and "work for the success of the negotiations." A new foreign minister would back the war party. It made sense.

Togo's next stop was Tojo's office. The Prime Minister had shown such reasonableness the day before that it encouraged Togo to ask for support in "persuading those concerned to make further concessions" if Hull reacted favorably to either "A" or "B."

Tojo did not disappoint him. He was more than willing to make further compromises if the Americans also came partway, and would soon tell an associate, "I'm praying to the gods that some way we'll come to an agreement with America." There was, he felt, a 50-50 chance that "B" would be accepted. Now only Kaya's resistance remained. All morning Tojo had pressed the Finance Minister by phone for a decision. Worn down by this persistency and unable to ignore the logic of his own arguments, Kaya drove to the Prime Minister's official residence, and about two o'clock informed General Tojo that he was reluctantly bowing to the majority opinion.

At last unanimity had been achieved. Now it was Foreign Minister Togo's well-nigh hopeless task to engineer peace before the deadline. The only chance for success in Washington, he decided, was to send assistance to Ambassador Nomura, who had already made several diplomatic blunders. Months before, the admiral himself had put in a request for Saburo Kurusu, an extremely able diplomat. He had signed the Tripartite Pact for Japan, but he also had strong ties with the United States. His wife was an American, Alice Jay, born of British parents on Washington Square, New York City.

Kurusu was hesitant but finally accepted the assignment. The difficulty was to get him to Washington as soon as possible and in utmost secrecy. If the war-minded staff officers or ultranationalists learned of the trip, his assassination was likely. A Pan American Clipper was scheduled to leave Hong Kong in forty-eight hours, but it would take several days to make arrangements to spirit Kurusu

The Fatal Note

there by naval plane. The problem was solved by Ambassador Grew, who phoned Maxwell Hamilton, chief of the Far Eastern Affairs Division in Washington. He persuaded Pan American to delay its flight for two days.

On the afternoon of November 4, Kurusu bade good-bye to Tojo, who said, "The American people are against war, and their supply of rubber and tin is dwindling," and added that he had thought the chances of Kurusu's success were 30 percent. In two days he had grown 20 percent more dubious. "Please do your best to reach an agreement."

Late that night Kurusu tiptoed into the bedroom and sat on his wife's bed. "Where are you going?" she asked. "Probably to the United States," he told her. She wrapped a steamer blanket around him and made him coffee. Since there was "every possibility" he might be assassinated she suggested that their twenty-two-year-old son, an Army aviation engineer, accompany him on the first leg of the journey from Tokyo Station to Yokosuka. The reporters would assume Kurusu was merely seeing his son off on an assignment. Kurusu agreed. As he left he said, "I may never return."

The next morning at ten-thirty, thirteen men filed solemnly into the conference room set up for the imperial conference. When the fourteenth man, the Emperor, appeared, the ceremony proceeded according to custom. There was a general feeling of anxiety as General Tojo explained that the September 6 decision had been reconsidered. "As a result of this, we have concluded that we must be prepared to go to war, with the time for military action tentatively set at December 1 [it sounded better than the actual date, midnight of November 30] while at the same time doing our best to solve the problem by diplomacy."

Foreign Minister Togo reviewed the diplomatic prospects. There was "little room left to maneuver diplomatically" and the chances of success were "we most deeply regret, dim."

General Suzuki reiterated the crucial problem of Japan's resources. "Briefly, we will have no easy task to fight a long war against Britain, America and the Netherlands, while still at war with China." However, the chances of victory in the first months were so bright that he felt war was the answer. It would be better than merely "waiting until the enemy applied the pressure."

Admiral Nagano called for secrecy of battle plans, since the fate of Japan depended on a decisive victory in the early moments of the war, and Sugiyama advised them to consider the importance of timing. "As far as operations, if the start of hostilities is delayed," he said, "the armament ratio between Japan and the United States will become increasingly unfavorable to us with the passage of time." He was fully confident of success in the early stages. "Nevertheless, we must face the fact that it will probably be a long-drawn-out war." Even so, he felt Japan could "establish a strategically impregnable position" and thus frustrate the enemy.

With all the brave talk, an air of growing despair hung over the room; and General Sugiyama himself called for a "stepping up" in diplomacy. In response to a question on the negotiations from Privy Council President Hara, Tojo said the Americans had answered with "flowery words." "The United States hasn't conceded a single point; all it does is make strong demands on Japan." The most serious point of argument was the stationing of troops in China, he said, and as he spoke about that frustrating war, became emotional. "We dispatched a million men at the cost of over one hundred thousand dead and wounded, bereavement of families, four years of hardship, and several tens of billions of yen." And if the troops were pulled out, China would rise up against Japan. "She would try to take over Manchuria, Korea and Formosa as well!"

Hara asked how America would react to Proposals A and B. Togo's answer was that Proposal A would not bring quick results. "I'm afraid we can't even settle things with Proposal B." There were only two weeks left to negotiate. "Therefore, I think chances of success are small. As foreign minister I will do my utmost but, I regret to say, I see little hope of success in the negotiations . . . about a ten percent chance of success."

"Forty percent!" said Tojo. He had apparently regained 10 percent of his optimism overnight.

Hara feared war was inevitable and warned of its racist implications. America, Britain and Germany all were Caucasian. "So I'm afraid that if Japan attacks America she will come to terms with Germany, leaving Japan all alone. We must face the possibility that hatred of the yellow race could shift the hatred now directed

The Fatal Note

against Germany to Japan, and as a result the German-British war would be turned against us."

Tojo also sounded a warning—the dangers of a prolonged war with a foe like the United States. "When I think about the increasing American strength in the southwest Pacific, the still-unfinished China Incident, and other things, I see no end to our troubles. We all can talk about *gashin-shotan* at home, but how many years and months will our people be able to endure it?" His answer implied the affirmative: despite his show of optimism for peace a few minutes earlier, he too agreed that they would have to go to war. "I am afraid we would become a third-class nation in two or three years if we just sat tight." Morally there were grounds for war, since Britain and America threatened Japan's very existence. "Also, if we govern occupied areas with justice, the hostile attitude toward us will probably soften. America will be outraged at first but then she'll come to understand [why we waged war]. Anyway, I will carefully avoid making this a racial war. Do you have anything more to say? If not, I take it the proposals have been approved in their original form." There were no further comments. This time, unlike the last conference, the Emperor remained silent.

2.

Grew understood how frustrated the Japanese leaders were and to what that frustration might lead. Several days before the historic imperial conference of November 5, he had written in his diary: "Japan is obviously preparing a program of war, to be carried out if her alternative program of peace should fail. Resort to the former may come with dramatic and dangerous suddenness." In this mood he sent Hull an ominous cable once more recommending a reconciliation:

. . . IF THESE EFFORTS FAIL, THE AMBASSADOR [Grew] FORESEES A PROBABLE SWING OF THE PENDULUM IN JAPAN ONCE MORE BACK TO THE FORMER JAPANESE POSITION OR EVEN FARTHER. THIS WOULD LEAD TO WHAT HE HAS DESCRIBED AS AN ALL-OUT, DO-OR-DIE ATTEMPT, ACTUALLY RISKING NA-

TIONAL HARA-KIRI, TO MAKE JAPAN IMPERVIOUS TO ECONOMIC EMBARGOES ABROAD RATHER THAN TO YIELD TO FOREIGN PRESSURE. IT IS REALIZED BY OBSERVERS WHO FEEL JAPANESE NATIONAL TEMPER AND PSYCHOLOGY FROM DAY TO DAY THAT, BEYOND PERADVENTURE, THIS CONTINGENCY NOT ONLY IS POSSIBLE BUT IS PROBABLE. . . .

This wasn't advocacy of appeasement or a compromise with principles.

. . . THE AMBASSADOR'S PURPOSE IS ONLY TO ENSURE AGAINST THE UNITED STATES BECOMING INVOLVED IN WAR WITH JAPAN BECAUSE OF ANY POSSIBLE MISCONCEPTION OF JAPAN'S CAPACITY TO RUSH HEADLONG INTO A SUICIDAL STRUGGLE WITH THE UNITED STATES. WHILE NATIONAL SANITY DICTATES AGAINST SUCH ACTION, JAPANESE SANITY CANNOT BE MEASURED BY AMERICAN STANDARDS OF LOGIC. . . . ACTION BY JAPAN WHICH MIGHT RENDER UNAVOIDABLE AN ARMED CONFLICT WITH THE UNITED STATES MAY COME WITH DANGEROUS AND DRAMATIC SUDDENNESS.

He prayed for understanding in Washington. "The trouble with you Anglo-Saxons," a Japanese friend had told him, "is that you regard and deal with the Japanese as grown-up people, whereas the Japanese are but children and should be treated as children."

Grew's message, however, was as usual ignored in the State Department. Stanley Hornbeck regarded the ambassador as old-fashioned and honorable but gullible. He was too influenced by Dooman, who had lived too long in the Orient to deal with the Japanese objectively; his pro-Japanese sympathy obviously colored every dispatch from Tokyo.

The MAGIC intercepts had convinced Hornbeck of Japanese duplicity. How could you trust a nation that played the two-faced game of talking peace while preparing for war? Moreover, he was so convinced that Japan was bluffing and would not dare fight America that he advised Hull to ignore Grew's latest warning.

Ironically, it was the two military Chiefs—General Marshall and Admiral Stark—who were making a joint appeal to Roosevelt

The Fatal Note

to do nothing that might force a crisis. The defeat of Germany, after all, was the major strategic objective. "If Japan be defeated and Germany remains undefeated, decision will still not have been reached," they said and warned the President that war with Japan could cripple the Allied struggle against "the most dangerous enemy," Germany. They wanted no ultimatum issued to the Japanese for three or four months, until the Philippines and Singapore were strengthened.

Roosevelt began searching for a way that would, as he told Stimson, "give us further time," but even as he looked, received information that the crisis could not be avoided. It came in an intercepted message from Foreign Minister Togo to Ambassador Nomura, a long cable containing Proposals A and B, along with secret instructions. The cable was decoded, translated and rushed to Hull. The opening sentence of the instructions gave the impression that the Japanese had given up on the negotiations:

WELL, THE RELATIONS BETWEEN JAPAN AND THE UNITED STATES HAVE REACHED THE EDGE, AND OUR PEOPLE ARE LOSING CONFIDENCE IN THE POSSIBILITY OF EVER ADJUSTING THEM.

Such pessimism was not in the original, for Togo had written:

STRENUOUS EFFORTS ARE BEING MADE DAY AND NIGHT TO ADJUST JAPANESE-AMERICAN RELATIONS, WHICH ARE ON THE VERGE OF RUPTURE.

The translation of the second paragraph was even more misleading:*

CONDITIONS BOTH WITHIN AND WITHOUT OUR EMPIRE ARE SO TENSE THAT NO LONGER IS PROCRASTINATION POSSIBLE, YET IN OUR SINCERITY TO MAINTAIN PACIFIC RELATIONSHIPS BETWEEN THE EMPIRE OF JAPAN AND THE UNITED STATES OF AMERICA, WE HAVE DECIDED AS A RESULT OF THESE DELIBERA-

---

* Many Japanese are convinced that this and other diplomatic messages were purposely mistranslated. No evidence could be found of this. It is far more likely that the inaccuracies came from ignorance of the stylized Japanese used by diplomats. It is also possible that the hastily trained translators wanted to make their copy more readable and interesting.

TIONS, TO GAMBLE ONCE MORE ON THE CONTINUANCE OF THE PARLEYS, BUT THIS IS OUR LAST EFFORT. . . .

The original was responsible in tone:

THE SITUATION BOTH WITHIN AND OUTSIDE THE COUNTRY IS EXTREMELY PRESSING AND WE CANNOT AFFORD ANY PROCRASTINATION. OUT OF THE SINCERE INTENTION TO MAINTAIN PEACEFUL RELATIONS WITH THE UNITED STATES, THE IMPERIAL GOVERNMENT CONTINUES THE NEGOTIATIONS AFTER THOROUGH DELIBERATIONS. THE PRESENT NEGOTIATIONS ARE OUR FINAL EFFORT. . . .

The translation then stated that unless these proposals succeeded, relations between the two nations would be ruptured.

. . . IN FACT, WE GAMBLED THE FATE OF OUR LAND ON THE THROW OF THIS DIE.

Togo's actual words were:

. . . AND THE SECURITY OF THE EMPIRE DEPENDS ON IT.

Where Hull read—

. . . THIS TIME WE ARE SHOWING THE LIMIT OF OUR FRIENDSHIP: THIS TIME WE ARE MAKING OUR LAST POSSIBLE BARGAIN, AND I HOPE THAT WE CAN THUS SETTLE ALL OUR TROUBLES WITH THE UNITED STATES PEACEABLY,

Togo had written:

. . . NOW THAT WE MAKE THE UTMOST CONCESSION IN THE SPIRIT OF COMPLETE FRIENDLINESS FOR THE SAKE OF PEACEFUL SOLUTION, WE HOPE EARNESTLY THAT THE UNITED STATES WILL, ON ENTERING THE FINAL STAGE OF THE NEGOTIATIONS, RECONSIDER THE MATTER AND APPROACH THIS CRISIS IN A PROPER SPIRIT WITH A VIEW TO PRESERVING JAPANESE-AMERICAN RELATIONS.

The Fatal Note

Hull got just as inaccurate a version of Togo's specific instructions regarding Proposal A, as the following excerpts show:

What Hull Read	*What Togo Wrote*
THIS PROPOSAL IS OUR REVISED ULTIMATUM.	THIS IS OUR PROPOSAL SETTING FORTH WHAT ARE VIRTUALLY OUR FINAL CONCESSIONS.
(NOTE: SHOULD THE AMERICAN AUTHORITIES QUESTION YOU IN REGARD TO "THE SUITABLE PERIOD [for retaining Japanese troops in China]," ANSWER VAGUELY THAT SUCH A PERIOD SHOULD ENCOMPASS 25 YEARS.)	(NOTE) IN CASE THE UNITED STATES INQUIRES INTO THE LENGTH OF THE NECESSARY DURATION, REPLY IS TO BE MADE TO THE EFFECT THAT THE APPROXIMATE GOAL IS 25 YEARS.
. . . IN VIEW OF THE FACT THAT THE UNITED STATES IS SO MUCH OPPOSED TO OUR STATIONING SOLDIERS IN UNDEFINED AREA OUR PURPOSE IS TO SHIFT THE REGIONS OF OCCUPATION AND OUR OFFICIALS, THUS ATTEMPTING TO DISPEL THEIR SUSPICIONS. . . .	IN VIEW OF THE STRONG AMERICAN OPPOSITION TO THE STATIONING FOR AN INDEFINITE PERIOD, IT IS PROPOSED TO DISMISS HER SUSPICION BY DEFINING THE AREA AND DURATION OF THE STATIONING . . .
. . . WE HAVE HITHERTO COUCHED OUR ANSWERS IN VAGUE TERMS. I WANT YOU IN AS INDECISIVE YET AS PLEASANT LANGUAGE AS POSSIBLE TO EUPHEMIZE AND TRY TO IMPART TO THEM TO THE EFFECT THAT UNLIMITED OCCUPATION DOES NOT MEAN PERPETUAL OCCUPATION . . .	. . . YOU ARE DIRECTED TO ABIDE, AT THIS MOMENT, BY THE ABSTRACT TERM "NECESSARY DURATION," AND TO MAKE EFFORTS TO IMPRESS THE UNITED STATES WITH THE FACT THAT THE TROOPS ARE NOT TO BE STATIONED EITHER PERMANENTLY OR FOR ANY DEFINITE PERIOD.

(4) AS A MATTER OF PRINCIPLE, WE ARE ANXIOUS TO AVOID HAVING THIS INSERTED IN THE DRAFT OF THE FORMAL PROPOSAL REACHED BETWEEN JAPAN AND THE UNITED STATES . . .

WITH REGARD TO THE FOUR PRINCIPLES [of Hull], EVERY EFFORT IS TO BE MADE TO AVOID INCLUDING THEM IN THE TERMS OF A FORMAL AGREEMENT BETWEEN JAPAN AND THE UNITED STATES . . .

To Hull, this last example alone was convincing-enough proof of Japan's deceitful intentions to underline his old suspicions. Actually, it was a colossal blunder. The translator had taken the "FOUR" of "FOUR PRINCIPLES" and made it point (4), concluding part of the instructions following "(1) NON-DISCRIMINATION AND TRADE," "(2) INTERPRETATION AND APPLICATION OF THE TRIPARTITE PACT" and "(3) WITHDRAWAL OF TROOPS." By making this excerpt appear to be one of the main divisions of the message and changing "WITH REGARD TO THE FOUR PRINCIPLES" into "(4) AS A MATTER OF PRINCIPLE" and arbitrarily inserting the word "ANXIOUS," the translator had misled Hull into believing that the Japanese were trying to avoid committing themselves to a formal agreement on *any* of the proposed points.

On the evening of November 7 Nomura arrived at Hull's apartment with Proposal A. Hull glanced through it rapidly; he already knew all about it—or thought he did—and was convinced that it contained no real concessions. His attitude was so obvious that Nomura asked for an appointment with the President. Every day was precious and the admiral was desperate. He was being pressed for a quick decision at the urging of the Japanese Chiefs of Staff; Hull was holding up the decision because the American Chiefs of Staff wanted time. This maneuvering at cross-purposes unfortunately was contributing to the deterioration of the negotiations.

When Nomura finally got to see the President three days later he pointed out the "considerable concessions" made by Japan and reiterated the need for haste. Roosevelt must also have been mindful of Marshall and Stark's plea for time in his reply that "nations must think one hundred years ahead, especially during the age through which the world is passing." A mere six months had been spent in the negotiations. It was necessary to be patient;

The Fatal Note

he didn't want a temporary agreement. Nomura cabled Togo that the United States "was not entirely unreceptive" to Proposal A. The wishful-thinking admiral was ready to grab at any straw of hope.

So was Bishop James Walsh. Just back from another trip to the Far East, he made one more attempt to bring Japan and America together in the form of a long memorandum delivered to Hull on November 15. In reading it, Hornbeck added a number of sarcastic notes for Hull which revealed his own strong bias.

Where the bishop explained that the Emperor's sanction of any policy was regarded by all Japanese as "the final seal that makes it the irrevocable policy of the nation," Hornbeck noted in pencil: "If a policy sanctioned by the Emperor is 'irrevocable,' then the alliance with the Axis is *irrevocable*." And to a long plea for understanding between the two countries, he put down: "Naive."

"It is perhaps worthwhile to recall," Walsh observed, "that the Chinese were well on the way to actual collaboration with Japan when the Manchurian Incident rudely arrested the movement and turned the Chinese radically in the other direction." Opposite this, Hornbeck penciled: "He speaks as though the *Chinese* had started the 'Manchurian Incident.'" And when Walsh noted that "There is no real peace anywhere in the Far East today," Hornbeck wrote down: "And for that *fact* who are responsible?—the Japanese (& the Germans)."

That very day Special Envoy Saburo Kurusu arrived in Washington after a tiring trip across the country, and two days later Ambassador Nomura brought him to Hull's office. One glance at the diminutive, bespectacled man with the neat mustache who had signed the Tripartite Pact was enough for the Secretary of State to conclude that he was not to be trusted. "Neither his appearance nor his attitude commanded confidence or respect," Hull wrote in his memoirs. "I felt from the start that he was deceitful. . . . His only recommendation in my eyes was that he spoke excellent English, having married his American secretary."

Convinced that Kurusu was privy to his government's trickery and would try "to lull us with talk until the moment Japan got ready to strike," Hull escorted the two Japanese the few hundred yards to the White House. Roosevelt put himself out to be affable: "As Bryan said, there is no last word between friends."

Kurusu replied that a way must be found to avoid war. The Pacific was "like a powder keg." Roosevelt agreed that a broad understanding should be reached.

As for the Tripartite Pact, Kurusu said he didn't see why America, "which has been a strong advocate of observance of international commitments, would request Japan to violate one." Japanese leaders had already assured the Americans that the pact would not automatically lead to war; that would require an independent decision. Moreover, an understanding between Japan and America "would naturally 'outshine' the Tripartite Pact, and American apprehension over the problem of application of the pact would consequently be dissipated." It was a step toward actual abrogation of the treaty, but Hull didn't believe a word Kurusu said; it was merely "some specious attempt to explain away" the pact.

Roosevelt remained friendly, and reaffirmed that there was "no difference of interest between our two countries and no occasion, therefore, for serious differences," and even offered to act as "introducer" between China and Japan.

3.

That same day Prime Minister Tojo made a speech in the Diet which was also broadcast to the nation. It dealt with the negotiations in Washington and he pointed out that their success would depend on three things: America must not interfere with Japan's solution of the China Incident; she must "refrain from presenting a direct military menace to our empire" and call off the economic blockade; and exert efforts to "prevent the extension of the European war" to East Asia.

There was thunderous applause, whereas excellent speeches ordinarily failed to get much of a response. In the diplomatic box of the U. S. embassy, the naval attaché leaned over and whispered to his companions. An *Asahi Shimbun* reporter noticed this and wrote:

> . . . The four staff members of the American embassy suddenly went into a huddle and conversed with each other, and then all vigorously

The Fatal Note

shook their heads, although no one knows what they meant by this. All others in the visitors' gallery looked at them with fixed attention.

What the naval attaché whispered was: "Well, he didn't declare war, anyway."

Among the leaders of Japan hope dwindled as each day passed with no definite word from Washington on Proposal A. America's attitude seemed to be stiffening on the major issues. All that remained was the last resort, and Togo cabled Nomura to present "B." On November 20 the admiral read it to Hull, who took it as an ultimatum and in his memoirs described the conditions as "of so preposterous a character that no American official could ever have dreamed of accepting them." But he hid his feelings to "avoid giving the Japanese any pretext to walk out of the conversations" and said he would give the proposal "sympathetic study."

His reaction was unfortunate and uncalled-for. Only one of Proposal B's five conditions—the one to stop giving aid to China—was unreasonable. This paragraph aroused him so much that he made it the most vital issue. In a fit of temper he burst out, "In the minds of the American people there is a partnership between Hitler and Japan aimed at enabling Hitler to take charge of one-half the world and Japan the other half." The Tripartite Pact strengthened the public in this belief, he added, and began to assail it vigorously.

Nomura turned to Kurusu helplessly. Little more than a week before, Hull had admitted that the pact was not a major problem. Yet three times in the past few days he had declared that as long as Japan clung to it, a peace settlement could not be taken seriously. Why was the pact being elevated again to importance? It was almost as if nothing had changed in Japanese-American relations since the days of Matsuoka.*

Hull's subordinates also had a similarly curious reaction to Proposal B. The man most sympathetic to Japan, Joseph Ballantine, feared its acceptance would mean "condonement by the United States of Japan's aggressions, assent by the United States to un-

---

* There were several possible reasons why Hull revived this dead issue: out of moral indignation; out of fear of denunciation from the American public, which generally equated Japan with Nazi Germany, if any agreement was reached with Japan; to prepare the public for a war with Japan by raising the specter of a Hitler-Tojo joint attack.

limited courses of conquest by Japan in the future . . . betrayal by the United States of China . . ." and "a most serious threat to American national security."

Such talk of aggression made little sense. The proposal adequately covered Southeast Asia and the southwest Pacific and offered peace in China. Japan could not have committed further aggression without breaking her own proposal, and if the Americans had wanted a definite pledge to stop military expansion they probably could have gotten it.

It was not really a question of Proposal B itself, but of State Department refusal to accept it at face value. What the Japanese Army considered a major concession and had accepted only after bitter arguments—withdrawal of troops from southern Indochina to the north—was scorned by Ballantine. It was a "meaningless" offer, since the Japanese could easily return the same troops to southern Indochina "within a day or two."

Roosevelt, on the other hand, must have been impressed by "B" because he responded with his own *modus vivendi*. He wrote it out in pencil and sent it on to Hull.

6 months

1. U. S. to resume economic relations—some oil and rice now —more later.
2. Japan to send no more troops to Indochina or Manchurian border or any place South—(Dutch, Brit. or Siam).
3. Japan to agree not to invoke tripartite pact even if U. S. gets into European war.
4. U. S. to introduce Japs to Chinese to talk things over but U. S. to take no part in their conversations.

Later on Pacific agreements.

This *modus vivendi* was further evidence that Roosevelt, unlike Hull, was a practitioner of *Realpolitik,* and brought about the first genuine relaxation of American rigidity, the first realistic hope for a peaceful settlement. Though it must have offended Hull's purist nature, he dutifully began putting it into diplomatic form. Despite personal reservations about Kurusu and suspicions

The Fatal Note

of his superiors back in Tokyo, he was still willing to negotiate.

Since the talk with Hull had revealed the great importance he still attached to the Tripartite Pact, Kurusu called the following day at the State Department with a draft letter declaring that Japan was not obligated by that agreement to collaborate or cooperate in any aggression by any third power.

... My Government would never project the people of Japan into war at the behest of any foreign power: it will accept warfare only as the ultimate, inescapable necessity for the maintenance of its security and the preservation of national life against inactive justice.

I hope that the above statement will assist you in removing entirely the popular suspicion which Your Excellency has repeatedly referred to. I have to add that, when a complete understanding is reached between us, Your Excellency may feel perfectly free to publish the present communication.

Neither the indirect negation of the Tripartite Pact nor the offer to publish it allayed Hull's suspicions, which were "confirmed" a day later in an intercept from Tokyo to Nomura extending the deadline of negotiations to November 29 (Washington time).

... THIS TIME WE MEAN IT, THAT THE DEADLINE ABSOLUTELY CANNOT BE CHANGED. AFTER THAT THINGS ARE AUTOMATICALLY GOING TO HAPPEN.

That evening—it was Saturday, November 22—Kurusu and Nomura called at Hull's apartment to urge a prompt reply to Proposal B. They were smiling and courteous. It was a "strain" for Hull to respond amiably, knowing what he did "of Japan's nefarious plans" from MAGIC. "There they sat, bowing agreeably, Nomura sometimes giggling, Kurusu often showing his teeth in a grin, while through their minds must have raced again and again the thought that, if we did not say Yes to Japan's demands, their government in a few days would launch new aggressions that sooner or later would inevitably bring war with the United States and death to thousands or millions of men."

Hull said, "It's a pity that Japan cannot do just a few peaceful things to help tide over the situation."

Nomura was just as ill at ease. He reiterated the need for haste and pressed for an item-by-item answer.

"There is no reason why any demand should be made on us," was the testy reply. "I am quite disappointed that despite all my efforts you are still trying to railroad through your demand for our reply." Hull could see no reason why Tokyo couldn't wait for a few days, but did promise to get an answer as soon as possible. This would be Monday at the earliest, since he had to consult several friendly governments with interests in the Far East. The answer Hull had in mind was his version of Roosevelt's hastily scribbled *modus vivendi.*

On Monday, November 24, Hull invited representatives of England, China, Australia and Holland to his office and passed around copies of the latest draft of the Roosevelt plan. Dr. Hu Shih, the Chinese ambassador, was troubled. Why should five thousand Japanese be allowed to remain in Indochina? Hull replied that in General Marshall's opinion, even twenty-five thousand troops wouldn't be a menace. "While my government does not recognize the right of Japan to keep a single soldier in Indochina," he explained, "we are striving to reach this proposed temporary agreement primarily because the heads of our Army and Navy often emphasize to me that time is the all-important question for them, and that they must be fully prepared to deal effectively with a possible outbreak by Japan."

The Dutch minister, Dr. Alexander Loudon, forthrightly declared that his country would support the *modus vivendi,* but the other three had to wait for instructions. Irked and impatient, Hull said, "Each of your governments has a more direct interest in the defense of that area of the world than this country. But your governments, through some preoccupation in other directions, do not seem to know anything about this matter under discussion. I am definitely disappointed at this unexpected development, at their lack of interest and lack of disposition to co-operate."

The next day Dr. Hu apologetically handed Hull a note from his Foreign Minister stating that Chiang Kai-shek had had a "rather strong reaction" to the *modus vivendi* and felt that America was "inclined to appease Japan at the expense of China."

Exasperated, Hull said America could of course kill the *modus vivendi,* but if so, she was "not to be charged with failure to send

The Fatal Note

our fleet into the area near Indochina and into Japanese waters, if by any chance Japan makes a military drive southward."

Although it was dark by the time Dr. Hu left, Hull called together his staff for further discussion. He himself was strongly in favor of sending the *modus vivendi* to the Japanese despite the slender chance of acceptance. If nothing else, it would underline "for all time to come that we were doing everything we could to avoid war, and a Japanese rejection would serve more fully to expose their predetermined plan for conquest of the Orient."

Later that night a cable for Roosevelt arrived from Churchill:

> . . . OF COURSE, IT IS FOR YOU TO HANDLE THIS BUSINESS AND WE CERTAINLY DO NOT WANT AN ADDITIONAL WAR. THERE IS ONLY ONE POINT THAT DISQUIETS US. WHAT ABOUT CHIANG KAI-SHEK? IS HE NOT HAVING A VERY THIN DIET? OUR ANXIETY IS ABOUT CHINA. IF THEY COLLAPSE, OUR JOINT DANGERS WOULD ENORMOUSLY INCREASE. . . .

Obviously Chiang Kai-shek had carried his complaints to London and this subtle rebuff wore out Hull's last patience. MAGIC had assured him that Proposal B was the last offer Japan would make and that the negotiations would definitely be terminated at the end of the month. That Tojo was prepared to make still further concessions in a sincere attempt for peace he did not know, nor would he have believed it if he had. Ever since midsummer he had been "well-satisfied that the Japanese were determined to continue with their course of expansion by force."

That was why Chiang's objection and Churchill's half-hearted endorsement, coupled with his own doubts and exhaustion from months of negotiating, caused him at this moment to shelve the *modus vivendi*. Instead he would offer the Japanese "a suggested program of collaboration along peaceful and mutually beneficial, progressive lines." His assistants began putting this new proposal into draft form.*

---

* At Sugamo Prison, after the war, Tojo told Kenryo Sato that if he had received the Roosevelt *modus vivendi,* the course of history would probably have changed. "I didn't tell you at the time, but I had already prepared a proposal with new compromises in it. I wanted somehow to carry out the Emperor's wishes and avoid war." Then he heaved a big sigh. "If we had only received that *modus vivendi!*"

Stimson was making an entry in his diary. He described a meeting that noon of the so-called War Cabinet at the White House:

... [Roosevelt] brought up the event that we were likely to be attacked perhaps next Monday [December 1], for the Japanese are notorious for making an attack without warning, and the question was ... what we should do. The question was how we should maneuver them into the position of firing the first shot without allowing too much danger to ourselves. It was a difficult proposition. Hull laid out his general broad propositions on which the thing should be rested—the freedom of the seas and the fact that Japan was in alliance with Hitler and was carrying out his policy of world aggression. The others brought out the fact that any such expedition to the south as the Japanese were likely to take would be an encirclement of our interests in the Philippines and cutting into our vital supply of rubber from Malaysia. I pointed out to the President that he had already taken the first steps towards an ultimatum in notifying Japan way back last summer that if she crossed the border into Thailand she was violating our safety and that therefore he had only to point out [to Japan] that to follow any such expedition was a violation of a warning we had already given.*

The following day, November 26, Secretary of the Treasury Henry Morgenthau, Jr., arrived at the White House just as Roose-

* This entry was later used by revisionist historians such as Charles Beard to bolster their claim that President Roosevelt purposely maneuvered Japan into an attack on American territory. A superficial reading of the controversial diary entry and subsequent remarks by Stimson seem to indicate that the anti-Roosevelt group is correct, but a study of the records of the discussions between the President and his advisers in the last days of November make it evident that they were expecting an onslaught on Singapore, Thailand or some other part of the Southeast Asian continent. They certainly did not appear to anticipate an initial attack on any American territory such as the Philippines or Guam, much less Hawaii. Thus, when Roosevelt said "we were likely to be attacked" he probably used "we" meaning the ABCD powers. It was a "difficult proposition" just because he did not expect a direct assault on the United States, and the problem was to make an attack on Singapore or Thailand seem to be a "first shot" against America. There were two ways to carry on this "maneuvering"—with a diplomatic warning to Japan or with a message to Congress so phrased that if Japan made a move south, even without directly menacing American territory, we would take it to be an assault on our vital interests—and, as it were, an assault on the United States.

In the absence of positive proof this assumption, and it can only be an assumption, seems much more logical and fair than the wishful reasoning of those who disapproved of almost everything Roosevelt did.

velt was starting his breakfast. The phone rang before the President could eat his kippered herring. It was Hull, who told of the Chinese protests to the *modus vivendi*. "I will quiet them down," Roosevelt said and went back to his breakfast. By now it was cold, so he pushed it aside, inspiring Morgenthau to jot down in his notes: "I don't think the President ought to see me or anybody else until he has finished his breakfast."

Hull was already on the phone with Stimson, telling him that he had "about made up his mind not to give . . . the proposition [the *modus vivendi*] . . . to the Japanese but to kick the whole thing over—to tell them that he has no other proposition at all."

This prompted Stimson to check with Roosevelt by phone to find out if the paper he had sent the night before about the new Japanese expedition from Shanghai into Indochina had been received. Roosevelt reacted so violently that Stimson commented in his diary that he "fairly blew up—jumped up into the air, so to speak"—and said no, he hadn't seen it and it "changed the whole situation because it was an evidence of bad faith on the part of the Japanese that while they were negotiating for an entire truce —and entire withdrawal [from China]—they should be sending this expedition down there to Indochina."

Not much later Hull appeared in person. He recommended that in view of the opposition of the Chinese they drop the *modus vivendi* and offer the Japanese a brand-new "comprehensive basic proposal for a general peaceful settlement."

Still angry at the news of the Japanese convoy, Roosevelt approved, and that afternoon Kurusu and Nomura were summoned to the State Department. At five o'clock Hull handed them two documents, "with the forlorn hope that even at this ultimate minute a little common sense might filter into the military minds of Tokyo."

Kurusu and Nomura expectantly began reading the first paper, an Oral Statement which set forth that the United States "most earnestly" desired to work for peace in the Pacific but that it believed Proposal B "would not be likely to contribute to the ultimate objectives of ensuring peace under law, order and justice in the Pacific area . . ." In place of Proposal B, Hull offered a new solution and it was embodied in the second paper, marked "Strictly Confidential, Tentative and Without Commitment." Kurusu read its ten conditions with dismay. It peremptorily called for Japan to "withdraw all military, naval, air and police forces from China and Indochina"; to support no other government or regime in China except Chiang Kai-shek's; and, in effect, to abrogate the Tripartite Pact.

It was far harsher than the American proposal made on June 21 and Hull had drawn it up without consulting General Marshall or Admiral Stark, who happened to be in the act of drafting still another memorandum to Roosevelt begging for more time to reinforce the Philippines. Hull's proposal again raised the dead issue of the Tripartite Pact, though Kurusu had already given written assurance it had little significance, and introduced a new proposal calling for "a multilateral nonaggression pact among the British Empire, China, Japan, the Netherlands, the Soviet Union and Thailand and the United States." Kurusu knew this would complicate an already complicated situation and cause more delay. When Nomura sat down, too stunned to talk, Kurusu asked if this was the American reply to Proposal B.

It was, said Hull, and pointed out the economic advantages to Japan if she accepted: an offer to unfreeze Japanese funds, make a trade agreement based upon reciprocal most-favored-nation treatment, stabilize the dollar-yen rate, reduce trade barriers and grant other considerable economic concessions.

Kurusu foresaw that in Tokyo this would be regarded as an insult, as a bribe, and began taking exception to the conditions. He didn't see how his government could possibly agree to the immediate and unconditional withdrawal of all troops from China and Indochina, and if the United States expected Japan "to take off its hat to Chiang Kai-shek and apologize to him," no agreement was possible. He requested that they informally discuss the proposal at greater length before sending it on to Tokyo.

"It's as far as we can go," said Hull. Public feeling was running so high that he "might almost be lynched" if he let oil go freely into Japan.

Kurusu observed with mordant humor that at times all "statesmen of firm conviction" failed to find public sympathy. Wise men alone could see far ahead and they sometimes became martyrs, but life was short and one could only do his duty. Dejected, he added that Hull's note just about meant the end, and asked if they were not interested in a *modus vivendi*.

The phrase had become an unpleasant one to Hull. We explored that, he said curtly.

Was it because the other powers wouldn't agree? Kurusu asked.

It was uncomfortably close to the truth. "I did my best in the way of exploration," said Hull.

4.

The first news of Hull's reply reached Tokyo late in the morning on November 27. It came in a message from the military attaché in Washington to Imperial Headquarters which began by announcing that the United States had replied in writing to Proposal B but that "there was no gleam of hope in negotiations." Staff officers huddled around the communications room, anxiously waiting while the rest of the message, containing the gist of Hull's proposal, was being decoded.

The message was sent at once to the Palace, where a liaison conference was in session. It arrived just as the meeting adjourned for lunch and Tojo read it aloud. There was dumfounded silence until someone said, "This is an ultimatum!" Even Togo, who had held forth slight hope of success, never expected this. "Overpowered" by despair, he said something in such a stutter that no one could understand him; the Hull note "stuck in the craw." His distress was intensified when he saw that several Army men were pleased, "as if to say, 'Didn't we tell you so?'"

But to one Navy man, Admiral Shimada, it was "a jarring blow." Hull's reply was "unyielding and unbending" and didn't so much as recognize the fact that Japan had made significant concessions.

The demands were equally outrageous to a peacemaker like Kaya. Hull obviously knew that Japan would have to refuse them. He was rejecting an immediate accommodation and seemed to be wanting endless discussions instead. It was just a stall for time. America had made up her mind to go to war—to attack Japan! That Japan had already offered to withdraw troops from southern Indochina at once wasn't enough; Hull wanted all troops withdrawn at once from Indochina and China. An impossibility.

What particularly infuriated every man in the room was the categoric demand to quit *all* of China. Manchuria had been won at the cost of considerable sweat and blood. Its loss would mean economic disaster. What right did the wealthy Americans have to make such a demand? What nation with any honor would submit?

Hull's proposal was the result of impatience and indignation, but the passage that most incensed the Japanese had been tragically misunderstood. To Hull, the word "China" did not include Manchuria and he had no intention of demanding that the Japanese pull out of that territory. Back in April he had assured Nomura that there was no need to discuss recognition of Manchukuo until a basic agreement had been reached, and he imagined that the issue was disposed of. To the Japanese, however, the Hull note had to be taken at face value. After all, the Americans had hardened their position on a number of issues since the days of the Draft Understanding.

The American reply should have been clear on this point; at the very least, the Japanese reaction would have been far less bitter. The exception of Manchuria would not have made the Hull note acceptable as it stood, but it might have enabled Togo to persuade the militarists that negotiations should be continued; it could very well have forced a postponement of the November 30 deadline.*

Thus it was that two great nations who shared a fear of a Communist-dominated Asia were set on a collision course. Who was to blame—the United States or Japan? The latter was almost solely responsible for bringing herself to the road of war with America through the seizure of Manchuria, the invasion of China, the atrocities committed against the Chinese people, and the drive to the

---

* All of the men at the liaison conference, from Tojo to Togo, believed that Hull's reference to "China" included Manchuria. In 1967 a number of Tojo's close associates were asked what might have happened *if* Hull had clarified that point. Kenryo Sato, learning the truth for the first time, slapped his forehead and said, "If we had only known!" Very excitedly he added, "If you had said you recognized Manchuria, we'd have accepted!" Suzuki, Kaya and Hoshino would not go that far. Kaya, now a leading politician, said, "If the note had excluded Manchukuo, the decision to wage war or not would have been rediscussed at great length. There'd have been heated arguments at liaison conferences over whether we should withdraw at once from North China in spite of the threat of Communism." At least, said Suzuki, Pearl Harbor would have been prevented. "There might have been a change of government."

The Fatal Note

south. But this course of aggression had been the inevitable result of the West's efforts to eliminate Japan as an economic rival after World War I, the Great Depression, her population explosion, and the necessity to find new resources and markets to continue as a first-rate power. Added to all this were the unique and undefined position of the Emperor, the explosive role of *gekokujo,* and the threat of Communism from both Russia and Mao Tse-tung which had developed into paranoiac fear.

Americans, too, suffered from paranoiac fear, theirs of the "yellow peril," and yet, oddly, they had no apprehensions about Japan as a military foe and reveled in stories of Nipponese ineptitude. According to one story going around Washington, the British had built warships for Japan so top-heavy that they would capsize in the first battle. The Japanese air force was also generally ridiculed, its pilots regarded as bespectacled bunglers, more to be laughed at than dreaded. Perhaps this sense of superiority subconsciously tempted some American leaders, including Roosevelt, to drive the Japanese to the limit of their forbearance.

How could a nation rich in resources and land, and free from fear of attack, understand the position of a tiny, crowded island empire with almost no natural resources, which was constantly in danger of attack from a ruthless neighbor, the Soviet Union? America herself had, moreover, contributed to the atmosphere of hate and distrust by excluding the Japanese from immigration and, in effect, flaunting a racial and color prejudice that justifiably infuriated the proud Nipponese. America should also have perceived and admitted the hypocrisy of taking such a moral stand on the four principles.* Her ally, Britain, certainly did not observe them in India or Burma, nor did she herself in Central America where "gunboat diplomacy" was still upholding the Monroe Doctrine. Her self-righteousness was also self-serving; what was morality at the top became self-interest at the bottom.

---

* Morality is an unstable commodity in international relations. The same America that took a no-compromise stand on behalf of the sanctity of agreements, maintenance of the status quo in the Orient, and the territorial integrity of China, reversed herself a few years later at Yalta by promising Russia territory in the Far East as an inducement to join the war in the Pacific. A rapprochement with Japan in 1941 would admittedly have meant American abandonment and betrayal of Nationalist China. Yet it might have led to a more stable non-Communist China in the long run.

Finally, America made a grave diplomatic blunder by allowing an issue not vital to her basic interests—the welfare of China—to become, at the last moment, the keystone of her foreign policy. Until that summer America had had two limited aims in the Far East: to drive a wedge between Japan and Hitler, and to thwart Japan's southward thrust. She could easily have attained both these objectives but instead made an issue out of no issue at all, the Tripartite Pact, and insisted on the liberation of China. For this last unattainable goal America's diplomats were forcing an early war that her own militarists were hoping to avoid—a war, paradoxically, she was in no position to wage. America could not throw the weight of her strength against Japan to liberate China, nor had she ever intended to do so. Her major enemy was Hitler. Instead of frankly informing Chiang Kai-shek of this, she had yielded to his urgings and pressed the policy that led to war in the Far East—and the virtual abandonment of China. More important, by equating Japan with Nazi Germany, her diplomats had maneuvered their nation into two completely different wars, one in Europe against Fascism, and one in the Orient that was linked with the aspirations of all Asians for freedom from the white man's bondage.

There were no heroes or villains on either side. Roosevelt, for all his shortcomings, was a man of broad vision and humanity; the Emperor was a man of honor and peace. Both were limited—one by the bulky machinery of a great democracy and the other by training, custom and the restrictions of his rule. Caught up in a medieval system, the Japanese militarists were driven primarily by dedication to their country.* They wanted power for it, not war profits for themselves; Tojo himself lived on a modest scale. Prince Konoye's weaknesses came largely from the vulnerable position of a premier in Japan, but by the end of his second cabinet he had transformed his natural tendency for indecisiveness into a show of purpose and courage which continued until his downfall. Even Matsuoka was no villain. Despite his vanity and eccentricities this man of ability sincerely thought he was working for the peace

---

* After his trial Tojo admitted that the independence of the Supreme Command had led to Japan's ruin. "We should have risen above the system we inherited, but we did not. It was the men who were to blame. . . . Especially myself."

of the world when he saddled Japan with the Tripartite Pact; and he wrecked the negotiations in Washington out of egotism, not malice.

Nor were Stimson and Hull villains, though the latter, with his all-or-nothing attitude, had committed one of the most fatal mistakes a diplomat could make—driven his opponents into a corner with no chance to save face and given them no option to capitulation but war.

The villain was the times. Japan and America would never have come to the brink of war except for the social and economic eruption of Europe after World War I and the rise of two great revolutionary ideologies—Communism and Fascism. These two sweeping forces, working sometimes in tandem and sometimes at odds, ultimately brought about the tragedy of November 26. America certainly would never have risked going to war solely for the sake of China. It was the fear that Japan in partnership with Hitler and Mussolini would conquer the world that drove America to risk all. And the ultimate tragedy was that Japan had joined up with Hitler mainly because she feared the Anglo-Saxon nations were isolating her; hers was a marriage in name only.

A war that need not have been fought was about to be fought because of mutual misunderstanding, language difficulties, and mistranslations as well as Japanese opportunism, *gekokujo,* irrationality, honor, pride and fear—and American racial prejudice, distrust, ignorance of the Orient, rigidity, self-righteousness, honor, national pride and fear.

Perhaps these were essentially the answers to Händel's question: "Why do the nations so furiously rage together?" In any case, America had made a grave mistake that would cost her dearly for decades to come. If Hull had sent a conciliatory answer to Proposal B, the Japanese (according to surviving Cabinet members) would have either come to some agreement with America or, at the least, been forced to spend several weeks in debate. And this hiatus would in turn have compelled postponement of their deadline for attack until the spring of 1942 because of weather conditions. By this time it would have been obvious that Moscow would stand, and the Japanese would have been eager to make almost any concessions to avoid going into a desperate war with an ally which now faced inevitable defeat. If no agreement had been reached, America would have gained precious time to strengthen the Philippines with more bombers and reinforcements. Nor would there have been such a debacle at Pearl Harbor. There is little likelihood that the implausible series of chances and coincidences that brought about the December 7 disaster could have been repeated.

6

Operation Z

1.

In early summer of 1939 when the Army was urging closer ties with Germany and Italy, Navy Minister Mitsumasa Yonai and his deputy had opposed any pact. The Army was sure that by conquering all Europe, Hitler would be in a position to help Japan settle the China Incident. But Admiral Yonai and his deputy were convinced that a war between England and Germany would be a prolonged affair. Eventually America would get into it, Germany would wind up the loser, and if Japan had a treaty with Hitler, she would find herself fighting the United States all alone.

The Navy Vice Minister was even more outspoken than his chief, publicly predicting that Japan would be defeated in any war with the United States. He was only five feet three inches tall (the exact height of the legendary Admiral Togo), but gave an impression of size with his broad shoulders and barrel chest. He was Admiral Yamamoto and his first name, Isoroku (meaning "fifty-six"), was the age of his schoolmaster father at the time he was born. He had enlisted in the Navy "so I could return Admiral Perry's visit," and subsequently lived in America—at Harvard as a student and in Washington as naval attaché. Consequently he had sounded the warning of her industrial strength so often and so persuasively that Yonai, fearing that Yamamoto might be assassinated by ultranationalists, sent him to sea in August 1939 as commander of Combined Fleet.

The basic strategical plans of Japan's admirals in the thirties had been to let her enemy, America, sortie from Pearl Harbor to make the initial attack: as the Americans proceeded they would be harassed by submarines while the Japanese fleet simply waited in their own territory. By the time the forces met in Japanese waters, the Americans would be so weakened by losses that they could be defeated in one great surface battle somewhere west of Iwo Jima and Saipan.

Once Yamamoto assumed command of the fleet, however, he extended the theoretical battle line to the Marshall Islands, which, together with the Carolines, had been turned over to Japan as mandates after World War I and constituted her possessions farthest east in the Pacific. Then in 1940, while witnessing the remarkable achievements of carrier-based planes in the spring fleet maneuvers, he turned to his chief of staff, Rear Admiral Shigeru Fukudome, as they paced the deck of the flagship *Nagato* and said, "I think an attack on Hawaii may be possible now that our air training has turned out so successfully." In one sudden crushing blow the American fleet at Pearl Harbor would be crippled, and before it could be rebuilt Japan would have seized Southeast Asia with all its resources.*

The idea for a surprise attack was based on the tactics of his

---

* It is intriguing to speculate on the inspiration for Yamamoto's plan for an attack on Pearl Harbor. In 1921 a book entitled *Sea Power in the Pacific* was published in the United States, written by Hector C. Bywater, naval correspondent for the London *Daily Telegraph*. Four years later, part of this book was expanded into a novel under the title *The Great Pacific War*. In it, Bywater described a Japanese surprise attack on the U. S. Asiatic Fleet in Pearl Harbor, with simultaneous assaults on Guam and the Philippines, and with landings on Luzon at Lingayen Gulf and Lamon Bay. The Navy General Staff in Tokyo, which had had *Sea Power in the Pacific* translated and distributed among top naval officers, also adopted *The Great Pacific War* for the curriculum at the Naval War College.

At the time *The Great Pacific War* was published, Yamamoto was serving as naval attaché in Washington. In September 1925 the New York *Times Book Review* featured the book on page one, under the headline IF WAR COMES IN THE PACIFIC. Undoubtedly Yamamoto, an obsessive student of naval affairs, had the book called to his attention.

hero, Admiral Togo, who had, without any declaration of war, assaulted the Second Russian Pacific Squadron at Port Arthur in 1904 with torpedo boats while its commander, an Admiral Stark, was at a party. The Russians never recovered from this loss—two battleships and a number of cruisers—and the following year almost their entire fleet was destroyed in the Battle of Tsushima during which, incidentally, young Ensign Yamamoto lost two fingers on his left hand.

(The concept of achieving decisive victory by one surprise blow lay deep in the Japanese character. Their favorite literary form was the *haiku,* a poem combining sensual imagery and intuitive evocation in a brief seventeen syllables; a rapier thrust that expressed, with discipline, the illumination sought in the Japanese form of Buddhism. Similarly, the outcome in judo, *sumo* [wrestling] and *kendo* [fencing with bamboo staves], after long preliminaries, was settled by a sudden stroke.)

Yamamoto was not the only one thinking seriously of an air attack on Pearl Harbor. In Tokyo, Commander Kazunari Miyo, the aviation operations officer of the Navy General Staff, was trying to convince his chiefs that the way to beat a powerful enemy like America was to force her into a decisive battle as soon as possible. This could be done by using giant six- to eight-engine aircraft in a number of bombing raids on the U. S. fleet at Pearl Harbor. The Americans would either have to flee to the mainland or come out and fight near the Marshalls on Japanese terms.

Although the idea was never seriously considered by Miyo's superiors, the discussion at naval headquarters might have been overheard. On January 27, 1941, Dr. Ricardo Rivera Schreiber, the Peruvian envoy in Tokyo, told a friend, First Secretary Edward S. Crocker of the American embassy, of a rumor that the Japanese intended to make a "surprise mass attack on Pearl Harbor" with all their strength. Crocker passed this on to Ambassador Grew, who cabled Washington. The message was routed to Naval Intelligence, which reported that "based on known data regarding the present disposition and employment of Japanese Naval and Army forces, no move against Pearl Harbor appears imminent or planned for the foreseeable future."

At that moment Yamamoto was already moving forward. On February 1 he wrote an unofficial letter to Rear Admiral Takijiro

Onishi, chief of staff of the Eleventh Air Fleet, outlining his plan and asking Onishi to carry out a secret study of its feasibility. Onishi turned to his friend and subordinate, Commander Minoru Genda, one of the Navy's most promising officers, whose influence extended far beyond his rank—in China his brilliant innovations in mass long-range fighter operations had won him fame. Now he was asked to study the Yamamoto plan. After ten days he presented his conclusions: the attack on Pearl Harbor would be difficult to mount, and risky, but contained "a reasonable chance of success."* Onishi forwarded this report to Yamamoto, along with his own deductions. The admiral was by then discussing the attack with his own operations officer, Captain Kameto Kuroshima, a brilliant eccentric who would absent-mindedly roam the flagship in kimono leaving a trail of cigarette ashes behind him. Orderlies referred to him as "the foggy staff officer." Kuroshima closeted himself in his cabin for several days and finally emerged in a cloud of garlic, incense and cigarette smoke with a detailed plan entitled Operation Kuroshima.**

Success rested on two precarious assumptions: that the Pacific Fleet (the United States Fleet had been so renamed on February 1) would be anchored at Pearl Harbor at the time of attack; and that a great carrier force could be moved halfway across the Pacific Ocean without being detected. Only a gambler would embark on such a venture and Yamamoto was certainly this. He was an expert at bridge and poker, as well as at *shogi* (Japanese chess). Once an American asked him how he had learned bridge so quickly. "If I can keep five thousand ideographs in my mind," he explained, "it is not hard to keep in mind fifty-two cards." He often told Commander Yasuji Watanabe, perhaps his favorite staff officer, that gambling—half calculation, half luck—played a major role in his thinking. As for the Hawaii attack, it was dan-

* The main source of this information is Minoru Genda, whose testimony was inconsistent. He was questioned on November 28, 1945, by Captain Payton Harrison, USNR, with Douglas Wada interpreting. Captain Harrison conducted several more interrogations, and Genda also made a deposition for the defense in the Tokyo trials. Each time the facts varied: the Pearl Harbor attack was conceived on February 1 in a conversation with Admiral Onishi; then, it was outlined in a letter from Yamamoto to Onishi, but he gave three different dates—January 27, February 1 and February 10.

** After the war, shortly before his death, Kuroshima told Miyo, "The Pearl Harbor attack was my idea."

gerous but the odds were too good not to take. "If we fail," he said fatalistically, "we'd better give up the war."

Two days after sending the letter to Onishi, Yamamoto outlined the plan to Captain Kanji Ogawa of Naval Intelligence, requesting that he collect as much data as possible about Hawaii. Although Ogawa already had a small group of spies in the islands—a timid German named Otto Kühn who needed money, a Buddhist priest and two Nisei—they merely provided unimportant bits of information. He decided to send in a naval intelligence expert who had already been selected and prepared for such a mission, even though an amputated finger made him readily identifiable. Takeo Yoshikawa was a twenty-nine-year-old ensign from Section 5, the American desk. He was slender, good-looking and appeared younger than his years.

Yoshikawa had attended the Naval Academy at Etajima, where he was a swimming champion (before graduating, every cadet was required to swim the ten miles of cold, jellyfish-ridden waters from the famed shrine at Miyajima to Etajima) and won fourth rank at *kendo*. He was a unique scholar. While his mates crammed for exams, he studied Zen Buddhism to attain spiritual discipline. Even so, he graduated on schedule and after a term as code officer on a cruiser, attended torpedo, gunnery and aviation schools. Heavy drinking, however, led to stomach trouble and temporary retirement from the service. He returned as a Reserve officer in Naval Intelligence. At first he served in the British section, then was transferred to the American section, where he sifted through a mountain of material that had accumulated, familiarized himself with ship movements and memorized various types of naval equipment.

In the spring of 1940 he was asked by his section chief, Captain Takeuchi, if he would volunteer to serve in Hawaii as a secret agent. He would get no espionage training, not even a single manual, and would in effect be on his own. Yoshikawa accepted and turned into a civilian, assuming the cover name of Tadashi Morimura. In preparation for his role as consular official, he let his hair grow and began to study international law and English at Nippon University. He passed the diplomatic exams and divided his time between the Foreign Ministry, where he did research on American politics and economy, and Section 5.

By the time Admiral Yamamoto made his request for additional Hawaiian intelligence it was spring of 1941, and Yoshikawa was ready. On March 20 he boarded the liner *Nitta-maru* at Yokohama. A week later he arrived in Honolulu, keyed up at the thought of pitting himself against the U. S. Navy. Consul General Nagao Kita greeted him cordially and the following night took him to the Shunchoro, a Japanese restaurant located on a hill overlooking Pearl Harbor. The proprietress, Namiko Fujiwara, came from Yoshikawa's own prefecture, Ehime. She told him she had five geishas, trained in Japan. The assignment would not be a dull one.

Yoshikawa got a salary of $150 a month, as well as $600 for six months' expenses. He began operations, improvising his own methods. First he made a grand tour of all the main islands, followed by two auto trips around Oahu, and then an air junket over Oahu wearing a loud aloha shirt like any other tourist and accompanied by a pretty geisha. After a second tour of the islands he was sure there were no naval ships except at Pearl Harbor and decided to concentrate on Oahu. Twice a week he took a six-hour drive around the island and visited the Pearl Harbor area every day. As a rule, he would simply gaze at it from the crest of a hill, but several times he got inside the gates. Once, armed with a lunch box, he followed a group of laborers and spent the day wandering around without being questioned; he tapped a big oil tank to see how much was inside and discovered that full tanks usually leaked and could easily be detected from outside the fence. Another time he persuaded a hostess at an officers club to hire him as a kitchen helper at a big party, but all he learned was how Americans wash dishes.

The large Japanese community was no help at all. Yoshikawa sounded out many individuals, usually over drinks at the consulate, but discovered that almost all considered themselves loyal Americans; to Yoshikawa it didn't make sense to be American while worshiping at Buddhist temples and Shinto shrines and contributing generously to the Imperial Army's relief fund. One old man did promise to set fire to a sugar-cane field in case of war and talked freely of all the guns he'd seen, but Yoshikawa discounted the man's reports when he began describing one on top of Diamond Head as "big as a temple bell."

Gossiping with American sailors was just as fruitless. They talked a lot without saying a thing. What information he got was by simple, unexciting methods. He sat on a tatami in the Shunchoro with the geishas—sometimes Shimeko, sometimes Marichiyo—and drew diagrams of the ships in the sprawling harbor below. On his regular drives he usually took a girl—a geisha or one of the maids at the consulate—because guards stopped him if he was alone.

Once he taxied up to Hickam Field, the big Army Air Corps bomber base near Pearl Harbor. At the gate he told the guard he was meeting an American officer and was waved on. As the cab slowly cruised around the base, Yoshikawa made mental notes of the number of hangars and planes, and the length of the two main runways. He also attended an air show at Wheeler Field, a fighter air base in the center of Oahu. He sat on the grass with other spectators watching P-40 fighter pilots do aerobatics; several swooped through an open hangar. He made no notes, but memorized the number of planes and pilots, hangars, barracks and soldiers. He never photographed anything, depending instead on his "camera eyes."

Once a week he submitted a report to Kita, who sent his chauffeur with the coded messages to the Mackay cable office in Honolulu. Within a month Yoshikawa was sure he was being "tailed" by the FBI in a black car with radio antenna. Kita warned him to be more careful but Yoshikawa stubbornly continued his routine; before long the two men found themselves quarreling almost every day.

2.

By April the Pearl Harbor plan had a new name—Operation Z, in honor of the famed Z signal given by Admiral Togo at Tsushima: ON THIS ONE BATTLE RESTS THE FATE OF OUR NATION. LET EVERY MAN DO HIS UTMOST. Now it was time to turn it over to those who would have to put it into effect—the First Air Fleet.

On April 10 Rear Admiral Ryunosuke Kusaka was made chief of staff of the First Air Fleet. He was sturdy and energetic, with a candid face. His father had been a business executive, but young

Kusaka's calling was the sea. After graduation from the Naval Academy in 1913 he spent most of his time in naval aviation, once crossing the Pacific in the *Graf Zeppelin* as an observer. He captained two carriers, *Hosho* and *Akagi,* and before coming to Tokyo, commanded the 24th Air Squadron in Palau.

After reporting to the Navy General Staff, the forty-eight-year-old admiral was brought to the office of a former classmate at the Naval War College, Admiral Shigeru Fukudome, the then chief of the Operations Bureau. "Take a look at this," Fukudome told his colleague and held out a sheaf of papers written in ink. A glance through the pages made it clear to Kusaka that the writing was Onishi's. "This is supposed to be an operational plan," he said, "but we can't use it in a real fight."

"This is merely a proposal. Nothing has been decided yet. In case of war, we need a practicable plan from you. Make it work."

Kusaka took a train south to Hiroshima, where he reported to his new chief, Vice Admiral Chuichi Nagumo, on board the flagship *Akagi.* Nagumo was short, slight. A torpedo expert, he knew little of aviation, and told Kusaka he would have to be responsible for Operation Z. Kusaka was no flier, either; he considered himself "an aviation broker." The details would have to be drawn up by men with intimate knowledge of flying, so he summoned the senior staff officer, Commander Tamotsu Oishi, and the aviation staff officer, Commander Minoru Genda. The latter, of course, knew all about Pearl Harbor, but kept it to himself when Kusaka told the two to draw up a complete, workable plan.

The more Kusaka studied the project the more he doubted its feasibilities: it was too risky, and defeat in such an initial battle would mean losing the war. As Operation Z developed, so did Kusaka's concern. He visited Admiral Onishi late in June and pointed out the flaws in the plan so persuasively that Onishi finally conceded it was too much of a gamble.

Kusaka suggested that they go to Yamamoto.

"You were the one who started this argument," said Onishi. "You tell him."

Kusaka returned to *Akagi,* got permission from his commander to see Yamamoto, and took a launch to *Nagato,* the flagship of the Combined Fleet. The plan was too speculative, he said, and summed up all his arguments.

Yamamoto took Kusaka's criticisms good-naturedly. "You just call it speculative because I play poker and mah-jong, but actually it isn't." These words ended the interview, but not Kusaka's anxiety. Downcast, he was walking toward the gangway when he felt a tap on his shoulder. It was Yamamoto. "I understand why you object, but the Pearl Harbor attack is a decision I made as commander in chief. Therefore I'd appreciate it if you will stop arguing and from now on make every effort to carry out my decision. If in the future you should have any objections from other people, I'll back you up."

Oishi worked out the overall plan and Genda studied the techniques of air attack—he had been thinking of a concentrated carrier strike since watching an American newsreel in 1940—while Kusaka himself devoted his energies to the aspect he felt was the most vulnerable: bringing the Striking Force within air range of Pearl Harbor without being discovered. It seemed an impossible task. Japanese ships were faster than American, but at the expense of armor and cruising range. The ships in the Striking Force, except the new carriers *Shokaku* and *Zuikaku,* simply did not have the fuel capacity to approach Pearl Harbor. How would he be able to refuel on the run?

There was also the element of surprise. What course would ensure it? He called in Lieutenant Commander Toshisaburo Sasabe, the staff navigation expert, and told him to study the nationalities and types of ships which had crossed the Pacific during the past ten years. Sasabe reported that no ships traveled at latitude 40 degrees north during November and December because of rough seas. The first thing that came to Kusaka's mind when he read Sasabe's report was the surprise attack made by Yoshitsune Minamoto in the twelfth century upon the enemy's supposedly impregnable castle; Minamoto had gained access by launching an assault from a completely unexpected quarter.* Kusaka could do the same thing by striking at Pearl Harbor from the north; the U. S. fleet usually held maneuvers southwest of

---

* This battle, fought on February 7, 1184, followed by a sea victory a year later, decided the struggle between the Minamoto and Taira clans for domination of Japan.

Hawaii, on the assumption that any attack would come from the Japanese base on the Marshall Islands. The one drawback—and it was a considerable one—was the problem of refueling his ships in the rough seas, but Kusaka dismissed it at once; he would overcome that problem by discipline and training.

The precise course to the launching site now had to be worked out. On the basis of information from Hawaii, Kusaka expected U. S. Navy flying boats to patrol an area five hundred miles out of Pearl Harbor while other PBY's covered five hundred miles south of Dutch Harbor in the Aleutians. The Striking Force, he concluded, would have to navigate undetected through this neglected part of the ocean by heading almost due east to a point approximately eight hundred miles north of Pearl Harbor. Here, the day before the attack, the ships would refuel for the last time and at dark steam south toward their target. At first light the planes would take off.

Ordinarily the training and operation of planes was the responsibility of each carrier's captain or squadron commander, but this attack had to be co-ordinated by a single flight commander. The man selected was the squadron leader on *Akagi,* Commander Mitsuo Fuchida, whose flying skill was exceeded by his ability to lead. A thirty-nine-year-old veteran of the China War, he had already logged 3,000 hours in the air. Not all of the carrier captains could accept Fuchida's commanding their planes, however, and it took Kusaka himself to bring them into line.

The primary target, according to Genda's plan, was Battleship Row, the two lines of battleships moored off Ford Island in the middle of Pearl Harbor. First, torpedo planes would swoop down and launch their cargo at the outside row, then the inside line would be attacked by high-level (horizontal) and dive bombers.

Kusaka didn't believe this second assault could succeed without an accurate bombsight—the Japanese knew of America's Norden bombsight but had been unable to acquire the plans—or a bomb capable of piercing a battleship's thick armor without detonating. The answer to the first problem was constant practice with the erratic Type 97 bombsight, a copy of a German model; for the second, Genda, Fuchida and the engineers finally hit upon a simple solution: reconstruct battleship shells into bombs, with their outer faces so reinforced that they would not explode on impact.

Not until the outbreak of hostilities in Europe had the Japanese Army General Staff thought in terms of a major war. Previously their operations had been limited to the Asian continent, but once England became one of the belligerents, they made preparations for action against her and possibly America. They dispatched one of their shrewdest officers, Major Kumao Imoto, to investigate the strategic feasibilities of Southeast Asia. He worked his way from Hong Kong to Hanoi, Saigon and on to Singapore. Upon his return he drafted invasion plans for both Hong Kong and Singapore.

The following year other officers went farther south to probe possible invasions of Java, Sumatra and the Philippines. But the plans that evolved were vague and no practical spy network was even established. A smattering of Japanese nationals and retired officers was willing to serve on a volunteer basis, and there was some help from natives. Many Filipinos still carried bitter memories of Emilio Aguinaldo's unsuccessful but heroic attempt to overthrow American rule around the turn of the century, and in British and Dutch territories the vast majority was in favor of an overthrow of white domination.

In December 1940—about the same time Yamamoto was seriously pondering the attack on Pearl Harbor—three divisions in China were ordered to start training for operations in the tropics. A special unit, the Formosan Army Research Department, was established to collect all data on tropical warfare in Southeast Asia within a period of six months. It was a small group, commanded by a Colonel Yoshihide Hayashi, but the driving force was provided by the controversial Colonel Masanobu Tsuji, who made a commonplace of eccentricity; once he had burned down a geisha house filled with fellow officers in a fit of moral indignation. With his roundish face, bald head and small, blinking eyes, he looked like the typical staff officer, but his brilliant maverick spirit inspired fanatic devotion in the younger staff officers. They revered him as Japan's "God of Operations," the hope of the Orient. Some of his superiors, however, had grave reservations. General Hitoshi Imamura, one of the most respected figures in the Army, saw the genius in Tsuji—but also the madman. A number of his peers, such as Colonel Takeo Imai, regarded him as a clever, fanatic idealist with a one-track mind who thought, like the legendary Kanji Ishihara, that he alone was right. Tsuji was, in fact, a protégé of Ishihara's. He, too, was determined to make Manchuria into a Buddhist paradise of five nationalities living in harmony, but he wanted to go much further; he dreamed of making Asia one great brotherhood, an Asia for the Asians.

Yoshio Kodama (who would be inveigled by Tsuji to plan to assassinate Prince Konoye by dynamite) first met him at the Nanking Army headquarters. He had a letter to Tsuji from Ishihara, and was told by Colonel Imai, "Oh, that crazy man lives in a filthy little room behind the stable." Kodama asked Tsuji why he lived alone in such squalor.

"These headquarters officers are all rotten," Tsuji answered with disgust. "They are only working for their medals. Every night they go to parties and play with geishas. Since the China Incident, all the military have gone bad. They hate me because I know all this and speak out." He did more than speak. He turned one fellow staff officer over to the *kempeitai* for "corruption," who then committed suicide.

On January 1, 1941, this colorful figure found himself in Formosa—exiled there, according to rumor, by Tojo, who had always opposed Ishihara—and involved in a seemingly useless project. Instead of feeling sorry for himself, he threw himself wholeheartedly into his personal assignment, the Malayan campaign. Within two months, through various sources, he learned that the island of Singapore, connected to the tip end of the Malay Peninsula by a 1,100-yard-long causeway, was a fortress impregnable from the sea but practically defenseless from an attack in the rear.

One of Tsuji's chief assistants was a fellow eccentric, Captain Shigeharu Asaeda, an agile, muscular six-footer of twenty-nine. He had always wanted to be an engineer, but since his father was poor, he had drifted into the Military Academy because it was free. After graduating from the War College, he fought in China so recklessly that Tsuji sought him out. The two took to each other at once, for both burned with the same idealism and spirit of adventure. When Asaeda was transferred to a desk job in the War Ministry he became so bored that he abandoned not only the Army but his wife and family as well. He disguised himself in civilian clothes, took a new name, wrote a letter informing his wife and parents that he was "going to commit suicide in the Inland Sea," and left Tokyo. He was actually off to join the Indonesian fight against Dutch colonialism.

On his way south he asked Tsuji for help. Though Tsuji promised to keep his friend's whereabouts a secret, within hours a disgruntled Asaeda was on his way back to Japan under guard. He expected to be court-martialed, but the Army, which did not want the public treated to a scandal, simply retired him from the service; perhaps his heroism in China tempered a harsher sentence. In any case, he again left his family and returned to Formosa to confront the man who had betrayed him. Such was the force of Tsuji's personality that Asaeda found himself volunteering as a secret agent. He was to assemble firsthand information on Burma, Malaya and Thailand. With fanatic intensity Asaeda immersed himself in round-the-clock studies of the language and geography of each country he was to infiltrate.

About the time Yoshikawa began operations in Hawaii, Asaeda set off for Thailand pretending to be an agricultural engineer. Judicious bribes enabled him to photograph key areas; and talks with hundreds of natives, some of high rank, convinced him that Thailand was the best springboard for operations against Burma, and could be taken over bloodlessly.

The Burman border was closely guarded by the British, but after several months he managed to slip through and collect the material Tsuji wanted. By the time he returned to Formosa he had discovered terrain and climate peculiarities that changed the accepted theories of tropical warfare.

In June, secret maneuvers were held on Japanese-controlled Hainan—a large island just off southern China in the Gulf of Tonkin—under the supervision of Hayashi and Tsuji. New concepts, based on information from Asaeda and research in Formosa, were tested. It had been regarded as suicidal to send transports jammed with men and horses through the suffocating heat of the tropics. Tsuji was certain it was solely a matter of training and discipline. His method of proof was uniquely his own. He packed thousands of fully equipped soldiers into the sweltering holds of ships, three to a tatami (a mat about six by three feet), and kept them there for a week in temperatures up to 120 degrees with little water. These wilted men, along with horses and heavy equipment, were successfully landed on open beaches under the worst (simulated) circumstances. A final mock landing was made under combat conditions by a battalion of infantry, a battery of artillery and a company of engineers.

Now all that was needed was accurate information about the terrain and tides of the invasion beaches. To get this, Tsuji sent his one-man spy ring, the ubiquitous Asaeda, into Malaya itself.

Though the Navy had always opposed a drive to the south on the grounds that it would lead to a clash with America, Admiral Nagano had submitted an official proposal in mid-June advocating an advance into southern Indochina whether it would take force or not. As it happened, no force was needed against the Vichy government, but the act led to the freezing of Japan's assets in the United States and made war against the West appear inevitable. At first Army Chief of Staff Sugiyama disapproved plans to prepare operations at once to seize Southeast Asia but on August 23 he succumbed to pressure.

There was similar resistance in the Navy high command to Operation Z, led by the chief of the Operations Section, Captain Sadatoshi Tomioka. Late that summer he debated the risks involved with Yamamoto's "foggy staff officer," Captain Kuroshima. Tomioka charged that the southern campaign was being shortchanged; too much was being thrown into Operation Z, which might be a totally wasted effort. What if the attack planes found Pearl Harbor empty? His blood was as hot as Kuroshima's and their differences almost led to a fistfight but they parted friends, with the latter beginning to doubt his own arguments.

Yamamoto had no doubts whatsoever and the opposition from Tokyo made him more steadfast. One day he remarked to his chess partner, Watanabe, "I will just have to resign." Watanabe grinned. But this was not a passing mood. The admiral had made up his mind to use the threat of resignation as a last resort.

Training for the air attack on Pearl Harbor continued at an accelerated pace on Kyushu, the southernmost of Japan's four major islands, famed for its active volcanoes, men of warlike spirit, and pornography. Except for those involved in the planning, no one, not even the captains of the carriers, knew what the target would be. The fighter pilots at Saeki Air Base only knew they were being prepared for some great air assault involving all the fighter planes of four carriers. The dive bombers were located some 150 miles down the coast at Tominaka Air Base. Here the men were specializing in night attacks and accuracy, using as targets towed rafts which made a heavy wake.

The other fliers were near the mouth of Kagoshima Bay in the south. They had to double as high-level and torpedo bombers. Torpedo practice was more exhilarating, for they had instructions to do what almost every pilot longed to do—buzz civilians and stunt around buildings. Each plane had a crew of three: pilot, observer (who also acted as bombardier) and radioman (who doubled as gunner). It would fly over a mountain some 5,000 feet high behind Kagoshima City, then zoom down, playing tag with the Yamagataya Department Store and the railroad station and dodging between telephone poles and smokestacks before suddenly dropping to an altitude of 25 feet when it reached the piers. Here the observer pulled a toggle which supposedly launched a torpedo at a breakwater (Battleship Row) about three hundred yards away. Then the plane made a sharp right turn to avoid slamming into Mount Sakurajima, an active volcano on a little island in the bay, and continued, skimming the water, scaring the wits out of every fishing-boat skipper who had the misfortune to be nearby. It was great fun and it was legal. But the people of Kagoshima made numerous complaints. Couldn't the Navy control its young hotheads who were practically tearing the roof off the Hirano restaurant just to impress the geishas?

Genda had picked Kagoshima City—home of the lusty hero, Saigo*—because it presented most of the problems the torpedo bombers would have to face at Pearl Harbor. They would have to fly over a number of smokestacks and buildings, just as at Kagoshima City, and then drop down at suddenly reduced speed to launch their torpedoes at Battleship Row from an extremely low altitude. The reason why Genda insisted that they practice at such a suicidal height was that the waters of Pearl Harbor were shallow, and if dropped from the usual height, a torpedo would plow straight

---

* Takamori Saigo, the prototype of the Japanese man of action, led the Satsuma Rebellion in 1877 against the Meiji government. Though one of Japan's great heroes, the people failed to respond to his call for revolt. His statue, standing in Kagoshima, is still a shrine of Japanese *seishin* (spirit).

into the bottom. But even a drop from 25 feet would not solve the problem and Genda was deviling the experts at Yokosuka Naval Base to come up with a shallow-running torpedo.

Several hundred miles to the northeast on the rugged, spectacularly beautiful coast of Shikoku Island, a detachment of Navy men was carrying out another phase of Operation Z that completely mystified the inhabitants of Mitsukue. Every morning a dozen spirited young ensigns sailed out into Mitsukue Bay in fishing boats towing canvas-covered cigar-shaped objects about eighty feet long. Late in the afternoon the boats, mysterious canvas-covered objects and all, would return and the ensigns congregate at the Iwamiya Inn for dinner.

The canvas-draped objects were two-man midget submarines which their pilots were slipping through the mouth of Mitsukue Bay in a mock torpedo attack on American warships, but even their instructors did not know this was supposed to be Pearl Harbor.

On September 2 all fleet commanders and their key staff officers, as well as important personnel from Combined Fleet, the Navy General Staff and the Naval Ministry (about forty in all), gathered at the Naval War College in Meguro, a suburb of Tokyo, to conduct final tabletop maneuvers in the presence of several Army observers who had just been advised of Pearl Harbor. There were two general problems to be solved: first, to work out final details for a successful surprise attack on Pearl Harbor; and, second, to make a detailed schedule, from the naval point of view, for occupying Malaya, Burma, the Dutch East Indies, the Philippines, the Solomons and the central Pacific islands, including ultimately Hawaii.

Umpires were selected from the Navy General Staff and Navy Ministry and the rest were divided into three teams. Yamamoto himself led the N-team (Nippon); Vice Admiral Nobutake Kondo of the Second Fleet led the E-team (England); and Vice Admiral Ibo Takahashi the A-team (America). On September 5—the day before the Emperor recited his grandfather's poem—the war games got under way. Yamamoto set his Striking Force on its way to Hawaii over the huge game board, but before the carriers reached launching position, Takahashi's "American" search planes from

Pearl Harbor had discovered them. With the surprise element gone, a third of Yamamoto's planes were shot down and two carriers sunk. Despite these "losses," Yamamoto's plan was not dropped lest he make good his threat to resign and because Hitler's attack on Russia had made the Japanese position in Manchuria more secure.

Within a week the Navy planners completed a staff study setting November 16 as X-Day (their D-Day). An officer handed over about a hundred mimeographed copies of the forty-page study to Yeoman Second Class Mitsuharu Noda, a staff clerk on *Nagato,* and simply told him to take them to the flagship anchored off Kure. Each copy was in a black manila folder; curious, Noda glanced through one. It opened with the words: "Japan is declaring war on the United States, Great Britain (and the Netherlands)." Fascinated, he read the details of an attack on Pearl Harbor, complete with charts and codes.

Noda and an assistant wrapped the studies into four bundles and clambered aboard a train at Tokyo station. They spent that night on a third-class sleeper to Kure, using the bundles as head and foot rests.

The study called for four carriers and this brought protests from every staff officer in Combined Fleet and the Striking Force. At least six carriers were needed. Kusaka alone, however, was willing to do more than register a formal request for another two ships. He flew to Tokyo to fight for his convictions. After a day of frustrating argument with the Navy General Staff, he sent a telegram direct to Yamamoto, without consulting anyone, complaining about the lack of support from Combined Fleet.

Kusaka's efforts were in vain and, moreover, his was the painful task of deciding which two carriers to leave behind. He selected the two smallest—*Soryu* and *Hiryu*. Their commander was an old friend, Tamon Yamaguchi, whose temper was only matched by his courage. Kusaka asked Genda to transmit the unwelcome information in person, but he showed such reluctance that the admiral summoned Yamaguchi to *Akagi*.

The volatile Yamaguchi, a Princeton man, seemed to accept the decision, and sought solace in *sake*. He downed half a dozen shots and then, before Kusaka could stop him, charged into Admiral Nagumo's private office with a bellow. Such behavior was not unique in the Japanese Navy on this level, and Nagumo tried to calm him by saying that although *Soryu* and *Hiryu* had to be left behind, their well-trained crews could be switched to *Shokaku* and *Zuikaku*. This still left Yamaguchi out of the battle and he shouted, "I insist on taking *Hiryu* and *Soryu!*" The burly Yamaguchi lunged at Nagumo from behind and hooked the little admiral in a headlock.

Kusaka appeared in the doorway. "What's going on?" He tugged at Yamaguchi's arm.

Nagumo, face red but composed, said, "I'm good at judo so I can handle a drunk like this. Don't worry." He struggled to get free. Yamaguchi squeezed tighter. Nagumo got redder. Finally Kusaka got a headlock on Yamaguchi, pried him loose, pushed him into the next room and said, "Do what you like in here."

Yamaguchi's anger dissipated. A cherubic smile appeared on his round face and he began prancing around the room singing "Tokyo Ondo," a popular song.

The wrestling match brought no repercussions—or results—but a few days later Yamamoto himself got the two carriers reinstated with a phone call to Tokyo.

Several weeks later Kusaka summoned all carrier captains and their chief aviation officers to *Akagi*. He told them about Pearl Harbor and ordered targets changed from moving to stationary. At Tominaka Air Base a large rock fifteen feet in diameter was painted white, replacing the towed raft as a target. Lieutenant Heijiro Abe, who commanded ten high-level bombers, made an outline in lime of a battleship on a beach at Kagoshima Bay and told his men to drop their dummy bombs on it. Only he knew it was the outline of the battleship *California*.

Thanks to all the weeks of arduous practice, the bombing results were remarkable, with scores as high as eighty percent. But they had been achieved at a price; chickens were refusing to lay eggs because of the almost constant roar of planes.

3.

On the evening of September 24 the Mackay cable office delivered a coded radiogram to Consul General Kita in Honolulu. It was a message from Captain Ogawa ordering future reports on Pearl Harbor to be keyed to five subareas:

> . . . AREA A: THE WATERS BETWEEN FORD ISLAND AND THE ARSENAL. AREA B: WATERS ADJACENT TO BUT SOUTH AND WEST OF FORD ISLAND. AREA C: EAST LOCH. AREA D: MIDDLE LOCH. AREA E: WEST LOCH AND THE CHANNEL.

Kita passed this on to Yoshikawa, who made several tours of all areas and four days later cabled back a list of warships at anchor. It included a battleship, heavy and light cruisers, destroyers and submarines—but no carriers.

Another Navy agent was at work in Mexico City, but his cover was in grave danger of being exposed. Commander Tsunezo Wachi had been posing for the past year as assistant naval attaché. He was the chief of "L," Japan's largest overseas espionage ring, and his primary mission was to intercept messages of the U. S. fleet in the Atlantic. He soon broke the simple American code and was sending accurate reports to Tokyo on all naval movements in the Atlantic.

As a sideline he was buying mercury—he had already picked up some two thousand 90-lb. bottles—through a Mexican general. Since mercury was on the embargo list, these bottles had to be secreted in big drums, the top half containing bronze scrap. Late in September, however, one bottle was broken while its drum was being loaded onto a Japanese ship, and the mercury spilled out. Wachi's espionage career would have ended but he had smuggled in a big bundle of $1,000 bills for just such an emergency. His contact, an influential Mexican banker, promised to suppress the story and gave him a list of officials to be paid off—$100,000 was written opposite the name of the President of Mexico.

Wachi paid willingly, for he was on the verge of a major espionage breakthrough. A cashiered American Army major was already on his payroll at $2,000 a month. The disgruntled major, using the code name of Sutton, had given Wachi detailed reports of all naval shipping through the Panama Canal which he knew were accurate from his own intercepts. Once war broke out, Wachi planned to send Sutton to Washington, where he still had a number of friends in high places, as well as access to the Army-Navy Club.

On October 22—five days after the Emperor had ordered Tojo to form a new cabinet—Colonel Tsuji himself went on an espionage mission. Captain Asaeda had brought him information about the beaches and tides of Malaya, but he wanted to take a look for himself and persuaded Captain Ikeda, commander of a reconnaissance squadron, to fly him over the peninsula. At dawn the two men took off from Saigon, the new headquarters of the invasion forces, in an unmarked, unarmed twin-engine plane with fuel for five hours. Tsuji was wearing an air force uniform in case they were forced down in British territory.

They traversed the Gulf of Siam and two hours later could see the eastern coastline of Malaya stretched out clearly in front of them. On the left was Kota Bharu, the northernmost town of British-held Malaya, and on the right, Pattani and Singora, two Thai coastal towns. They flew directly over Singora and its pitiful airstrip. There were rubber plantations on either side of the main road. One good battalion, Tsuji figured, could seize the airfield and use it as a base of operations. He excitedly took a picture.

Next they turned toward the west coast of Malaya. Rain had lowered the visibility, so Tsuji told Ikeda to drop to 6,500 feet. Suddenly they saw a large air base through the haze. Tsuji shouted that it was Alor Star, a British base, and Ikeda pulled up into the storm and headed south. They flew over two equally impressive British aerodromes, turned back north and saw clearly two more fields, just as large. Tsuji was stunned. A small Japanese base at Singora would be helpless in the face of air attacks from such modern installations. Alor Star itself, as well as Kota Bharu, would have to be seized at "any sacrifice" within hours after the first landings.

They landed at Saigon with ten minutes of fuel left. "I saw all I wanted to see," Tsuji told the pilot, "and now I know we will win."

Still in air force uniform, Tsuji reported his findings to the Army commander and his staff, and new operations were devised which called for simultaneous landings of the 5th Division (at Singora and Pattani) and part of the 18th (at Kota Bharu); the 5th Divi-

Operation Z

sion would seize the strategic bridge over the Perak River and occupy the Alor Star air base while the men of the 18th Division, after taking Kota Bharu and its field, would push south down the east coast.

Tsuji knew that it would be almost impossible to get the Army General Staff to accept such a radically different plan without loss of face, so he flew to Tokyo in order to present it in person. But even the remarkable Tsuji could not have succeeded without the help of an old friend, Colonel Takushiro Hattori, recently promoted to chief of the Operations Section of the Army General Staff. Hattori was not only stirred by Tsuji's daring flight but convinced his solution alone would work. Against considerable opposition, Hattori persuaded Army Chief of Staff Sugiyama to approve the Tsuji proposal.

In Hawaii, the regular diplomatic courier had just arrived with a package of $100 bills and instructions to deliver the money to a German on the payroll, Otto Kühn. An acquaintance of Himmler, who didn't like him, he had quit the Nazi party and come to Hawaii. Here he had lost his capital in a furniture venture and was now living off espionage and the profits from his wife's beauty salon. As yet he had done little for the Japanese except boast of his contacts.

Consul General Kita wrote "Kalama" on a sheet of paper, tore it in half through the word and sent one of the pieces to Kühn. Then he summoned Yoshikawa, gave him the other half, and asked him to take it "to a German-American who will carry on espionage when we all leave Hawaii."

Yoshikawa was reluctant—he knew nothing about any German and didn't want to act as a messenger boy—but Kita insisted. He went over to the safe and brought out the package, wrapped in newspapers, which contained $14,000 and a message. "Show your half of the paper to the German; if he has the other half, give him the money." Yoshikawa was also to get an answer to the message.

Not long before sunset on October 28 Yoshikawa, wearing green pants and an aloha shirt, strode out the front gate of the consulate and into a waiting taxicab. After climbing Diamond Head, it proceeded up the east coast for several minutes. About a mile from Kühn's house Yoshikawa dismissed the cab and sauntered down the road until he came to the right address, a large house with a spacious courtyard. Yoshikawa knocked at the kitchen door, but no one answered. He went inside, calling, "Hello . . . hello?" He waited for ten minutes; then, out of nowhere, a man appeared. He was in his early forties.

"Otto Kühn?"

The man nodded, but in case it was an FBI agent, Yoshikawa inconspicuously slid his half of the paper onto the edge of a table. The other turned pale and started to tremble but drew out a piece of paper. Still without saying a word, Yoshikawa matched the two pieces—"Kalama." He followed the equally silent Kühn out the back door to an open-air summer house, a Hawaiian-style gazebo. Here he handed over the bundle and told Kühn there was a message inside. Kühn fumbled with the package until he found unsigned instructions requesting a test with a shortwave transmitter. Using the call letter EXEX on frequency 11980, Kühn was to get in touch with station JHP at 0100 Pacific standard time on November 3 and at 0530 on November 5.

Yoshikawa asked for a reply and for the first time Kühn spoke. "I'll give the consul general an answer in two or three days," he said in a high, shaky, almost inaudible voice, then wrote down on a piece of paper that he could not make the test. He sealed the note in an envelope and handed it to Yoshikawa.

It was dusk by the time Yoshikawa reached the highway, half expecting some FBI man to jump out at him. He caught a taxi and, with relief, headed back for the consulate.

Two more secret agents were on their way to Oahu aboard the liner *Taiyo-maru*. One was Commander Toshihide Maejima, a submarine expert, disguised as a ship doctor. The other was the assistant purser, Takao Suzuki. Only the ship's captain and purser knew he was Suguru Suzuki, the youngest lieutenant commander in the Navy and an aviation expert. He was the son of a general and nephew of a famous admiral, the Grand Chamberlain Kantaro Suzuki, who had escaped assassination so narrowly during the 2/26 Incident. His primary mission was to determine the exact positions of the targets, what types of bombs should be used, a possible emergency landing site and—most important—whether the Lahaina

Operation Z

harbor on the island of Maui was still a base for U. S. naval ships. If so, a large number of planes would have to be diverted from the attack on Pearl Harbor. And he had been told to study sea and weather conditions on the trip to Honolulu. *Taiyo-maru* was going out of its way to track the exact course that Nagumo's Striking Force was scheduled to take.

The American passengers aboard were comfortable in spite of the heavy seas, but most of them, like Carl Sipple and his wife, felt ill at ease. The Sipples had left Japan with their two small children because of the growing international tension. Their uneasiness increased as day after day passed without an announcement of the ship's position. Considering how windy and cold it was and how low the sun stood above the horizon, they guessed they were far north of the usual shipping lane, and there was no trace of other vessels. Were they being taken to another port? The Sipples tried to send a radiogram to friends in Honolulu, but no messages could be dispatched. *Taiyo-maru* was on radio silence.

Before dawn of November 1 the ship finally approached Oahu. Sipple went up on deck to get a glimpse of Diamond Head and at first light saw a small white launch in the ship's wake. Fighter planes circled above, then swooped so low that the passengers could exchange waves with the pilots.

Suzuki was on the bridge, scanning the mouth of Pearl Harbor with binoculars. It was barely wide enough for one big ship to slip through. Just after six o'clock a launchload of U. S. Marines boarded and stonily stood guard at the bridge and engine room. Suzuki guessed they were there to prevent any attempt to sink the ship at the entrance of Pearl Harbor.

He accosted the group of port officials, including several U. S. Navy officers, who came aboard to pilot the ship into Honolulu, and offhandedly asked how deep the water was, and if there were any mines. The answers came readily. Over drinks at the ship's bar he also learned there was a steel net across the mouth of the harbor which opened and closed automatically, and that the whirling gadget on the mast of a nearby British warship was something called radar.

But the rest of his mission could not be carried out. Kita sent a staff member with a warning that it would be wiser if the two agents stayed aboard the ship. Suzuki industriously made up a list of ninety-seven questions. He was told the answers would be brought back before the ship left.

The questionnaire was turned over to Yoshikawa. "On what day of the week are the greatest number of ships in the harbor?" That was easy—Sunday. "Are there any large flying boats on patrol?" That too was easy—the big PBY's went out every morning and evening. "Where do the ships that leave the harbor go, and why?" He had no idea, but surmised from the ships' speed and the time they were gone that they traveled some five hundred miles for maneuvers. "Is there an antisubmarine net at the mouth of Pearl Harbor? If so, describe." He had only heard there was but decided to find out for himself. Wearing his sporty outfit of the usual green trousers and aloha shirt and carrying a bamboo fishing pole, he walked down the highway past Hickam Field, then crossed a barren area toward the mouth of Pearl Harbor, ready to pose as a Filipino if caught. He walked into a small woods next to some naval buildings and almost blundered into sailors hanging up wet laundry. He hid in the brush until sunset. He thought briefly of committing suicide if he was apprehended, but decided to just say, "I give up," and to hell with it.

At dusk he crept to the entrance of the harbor. He heard voices and froze until there was silence. Then he lowered himself gently into the water, and quietly fluttering his legs, swam fifty yards into the channel. He groped with his feet. Nothing. He dived for the net but was so excited that he had only enough breath to go down a few yards. Five more times he dived. Still nothing. He swam back to shore. These were his most anxious moments as an agent, and in the end he had nothing positive to report.

On *Taiyo-maru,* Suzuki spent hours observing and taking pictures of the Pearl Harbor entrance and the adjoining Hickam Field. During the next few days various consular employees carrying newspapers walked past the Marines guarding *Taiyo-maru.* Inside the newspapers was the information Suzuki wanted.

By November 5, the day of departure, he knew the thickness of both the concrete roofs of the hangars at Hickam Field and the armor of the battleships, and had pictures of Pearl Harbor taken from surrounding hills, as well as recent aerial photographs. He summarized all he could on a single sheet of paper and hid it. His mission was completed at three o'clock in the afternoon, when the final courier came aboard ship just prior to sailing time with a locked diplomatic pouch containing Yoshikawa's latest findings and the most accurate maps.

4.

Off Kyushu a large crate was brought aboard Nagumo's flagship, *Akagi,* and carried to Kusaka's office. Inside was a seven-foot square mock-up of Oahu. For the next few days Genda, the planner, and Fuchida, the leader, memorized every feature of the terrain.

The Combined Fleet moved from its regular base off Sakurajima, the beautiful little island two hours' sail south of Hiroshima, into Bungo Strait, where it posed as the U. S. Pacific Fleet. Nagumo's carriers moved to within two hundred miles of the "Americans" and launched dive bombers and their fighter escort, followed by high-level and torpedo bombers. The planes assembled without an intercom system, by means of signals chalked on slates and held up in the cockpits.

The ultimate technical problem—a suitable torpedo—had finally been solved by Captain Fumio Aiko, a torpedo expert at Yokosuka. He made wooden fins from aerial stabilizers and fitted them on torpedoes. After scores of tests in Kagoshima Bay, 80 percent of the torpedoes ran shallow enough for the Pearl Harbor waters. Now the problem was to manufacture the improvised fins in time for the attack.

All objections within the Navy to Operation Z ended on November 3 when Yamamoto and his key staff officers flew to Tokyo to see Nagano. At the end of the discussion the Chief of Staff sighed and said, "As for the Pearl Harbor attack, my judgment is not always good, because I'm old. So I will have to trust yours."

Two days later Yamamoto issued "Combined Fleet Top Secret Operation Order No. 1," a bulky 151-page document. It outlined naval strategy for the first phase of hostilities covering not only Pearl Harbor but more or less simultaneous assaults on Malaya, the Philippines, Guam, Wake, Hong Kong and the South Seas.

Yamamoto then assembled all squadron leaders to his flagship and told them about Pearl Harbor.* "This time," he said, "you must not think lightly of your enemy. America is not an ordinary foe and will never fall short as one."

On November 6 General Count Hisaichi Terauchi took command of Southern Army, which was made up of four armies. He was to seize all American, Dutch and British possessions in the "southern area" as soon as possible. After simultaneous attacks on Malaya and the Philippines, Lieutenant General Tomoyuki Yamashita (pronounced Ya-*mash*-ta) would take Malaya and Singapore with the 25th Army. Lieutenant General Masaharu Homma, an amateur playwright and leader of the pro-British-American minority in the Army, was to conquer the Philippines with the 14th Army. General Tsukada, who had represented the Army at so many stormy liaison conferences, was made Terauchi's chief of staff. Many officers at Army General Staff headquarters watched him leave Tokyo with foreboding. Now who could control the tempestuous younger officers?

Within twenty-four hours Yamamoto issued his second secret order setting the tentative date to start hostilities as December 8. Two factors had determined the choice: there would be a full moon, which would facilitate launching from the carriers, and it would be Sunday (December 7) in Hawaii. From Yoshikawa's reports it had been established that the Pacific Fleet usually entered Pearl Harbor on a Friday and left the following Monday.

On November 10 Admiral Nagumo put Yamamoto's plan into effect by issuing his first operational order. There was an understanding that if diplomatic negotiations with America were successfully concluded even at the very last moment, the attack on Pearl Harbor would be called off and the Striking Force returned to a rendezvous point at latitude 42 degrees north by longitude 170 degrees east, where it would stay in a state of readiness until further instructions.

The six carriers were stripped of personal belongings and unnecessary equipment and loaded with extra jerricans and drums of

---

* Lieutenant Commander Shigeru Itaya, who would command all the fighter squadrons, was the only fighter squadron leader present. The others had already been informed of Pearl Harbor by Genda. He told them it would have to be a one-way mission but when they vowed to kill the men who had made such a plan, he promised to get it changed.

oil. All ships were under tight security. Usually when a fleet left Japan it was stocked with tropical clothing and special food for southern climates. This time the sailors would need foul-weather clothing, antifreeze grease, special weatherproof gun tarpaulins and other equipment for the cold, and Kusaka hoped it could all be collected without arousing suspicions.

On November 16 the Pearl Harbor Carrier Striking Force (*Kido Butai*) gathered at the mouth of the Inland Sea. It was a formidable armada: six carriers; two fast battleships with 14-inch guns, *Hiei* and *Kirishima;* two heavy cruisers, *Tone* and *Chikuma;* a light cruiser; eight destroyers; and a train of three oilers and a supply ship. Two of the carriers, *Akagi* (Red Castle) and *Kaga* (Increased Joy), had been converted from a battle cruiser and a battleship and displaced more than 30,000 tons. *Hiryu* (Flying Dragon) and *Soryu* (Green Dragon) were only 18,000 tons, but of more modern design. *Shokaku* (Soaring Crane) and *Zuikaku* (Happy Crane) were the newest and largest, 826 feet long, almost exactly the same size as America's most formidable carrier, *Enterprise*. The six carriers held 360 planes: 81 fighters, 135 dive bombers, 104 high-level (horizontal) bombers and 40 torpedo bombers, which had only thirty torpedoes fitted with the new fins. The remaining hundred would not be ready for more than a week and *Kido Butai* would have to start without them.

Late the following afternoon Yamamoto visited *Akagi* to wish Nagumo and key personnel good luck. Fuchida thought the admiral looked grim as he warned of the strongest foe in their history, but later at a farewell party in the wardroom Yamamoto's confidence was infectious. He said, "I think this operation will be successful," and a rousing toast was drunk to the Emperor.

Soon after dark *Akagi* slowly steamed out of Saeki Bay flanked by two destroyers. Her lights were out and crystals had been temporarily removed from the communications equipment to ensure radio silence. But the ships left behind in the Inland Sea were ready to set up a large volume of radio communication to mislead enemy listeners.

On the quarterdeck of *Nagato*, hands behind his back, Yamamoto paced back and forth, stopping every so often to stare at the dim shape of the departing carrier. Confident as he was of Operation Z, he still dreaded war with America. "What a strange position

I find myself in now," he had recently written an Academy classmate, "having to make a decision diametrically opposed to my personal opinion, with no choice but to push full speed in pursuance of that decision. Is that, too, fate? And what a bad start we've made. . . ."

One by one, at irregular intervals, other ships in the Striking Force weighed anchor and headed on separate courses for a rendezvous some thousand miles north of Tokyo. It would have been too obvious to set sail directly en masse for Oahu. Instead *Kido Butai* would reassemble at Eterofu Island in the Kuriles which possessed a large deep bay, rough in summer but strangely calm in winter. The island was an ideal clandestine rallying point. Its single village comprised three dwellings, a small concrete pier, a post office and a wireless station. To be on the safe side, the gunboat *Kunajiri* was already impounding outgoing mail and telegrams, while patrol boats rounded up any fishermen in Hitokappu Bay.

Kaga was the last carrier still left in the Inland Sea. It was being loaded with the final modified torpedoes. Once the ship got under way the captain gathered the entire crew on deck to announce that they were heading for Hitokappu Bay and then Pearl Harbor—where Yoshikawa was watching a large battleship enter the harbor along with eight destroyers. Already at anchor were five heavy cruisers and one *Enterprise*-class carrier.

Taiyo-maru was docking in Yokohama. The vital information Suguru Suzuki needed was still locked in the diplomatic pouch. And now he had to turn it over to a Foreign Ministry representative. Empty-handed, he took the train to Tokyo, where Admiral Nagano ordered him to leave at once for Hitokappu Bay with the latest information from Hawaii. But the pouch had been lost in transit. The Foreign Ministry officials knew nothing about it, neither could they locate it, and Suzuki was forced to head north on the battleship *Hiei*, bringing only a single sheet of paper which contained his own summary of the missing information and a sketch of Pearl Harbor made from memory.

Urgent though his mission was, it took him four days to reach *Kido Butai*. He learned that the missing diplomatic pouch had finally been found in Tokyo, only to disappear again. The courier plane with the pouch aboard, sent out two days earlier, had not yet arrived and Suzuki had to brief Genda, Kusaka and other staff officers on the basis of his page of notes. He described Hickam and Wheeler fields in detail and said there were 350 Army planes on Oahu.* No one at the Japanese consulate had seen any ships at Lahaina and he had confirmed this on the voyage back to Japan over drinks from half a dozen returning Nisei.

On *Akagi,* ship captains and their executive officers were given the course. One of the captains wanted to know what to do if he ran into a Soviet merchant ship out of Vladivostok. "Sink it," was the answer. "Sink anything flying any flag."

In the late afternoon on November 25 more than five hundred flying officers from all the carriers jammed into *Akagi*'s aviation-crew quarters, which had been stripped of bunks and tables. Nagumo outlined the attack. It was the first time most of them had heard the words Pearl Harbor. As the admiral spoke, excitement mounted and when he ended with a "Good fight and good luck!" there was a deafening cheer.

When the noise died down, Genda and Fuchida detailed the attack on the Pearl Harbor mock-up. Each flier was given pictures of American warships and islands near Oahu which could be used for forced landings; friendly submarines would be at marked positions to pick them up.

It had grown so dark and the seas were so rough that many of the fliers could not get back to their own ships. That night, the eve of departure, there was a giant *sake* party aboard *Akagi.* But the commander in chief was in no mood for celebration. For a man of courage, Nagumo was a compulsive worrier and the past week he had been telling his chief of staff over and over, "I wonder if it will go well," and Kusaka would invariably reply, *"Daijobu"* —"Don't worry."

But Nagumo could not be reassured. Long after midnight he got out of bed and ordered his aide to rouse Lieutenant Commander Suguru Suzuki. Still in sleeping kimono, he apologized

* Most of his information was fairly correct except for this figure. There were 231 (Army) planes in all the Hawaiian islands.
The courier plane with the vital information arrived several hours after the Striking Force departed. Suzuki had remained behind and he ordered the pilot to give chase and drop the material on *Akagi.* But the plane ran into a local snowstorm and had to turn back.

for waking Suzuki, but something bothered him. "You're absolutely certain no one sighted the Pacific Fleet in Lahaina?"

"Yes, Admiral."

"Is there any possibility the Pacific Fleet might assemble in Lahaina?"

"None."

Nagumo seemed to relax. He nodded his thanks. Suzuki retired, grateful and moved that he had been able to calm his commander's fears.

The morning of the twenty-sixth dawned bright and clear with unusually high pressure for this time of year. The seas had calmed. It seemed a good omen; but just as the fleet was weighing anchor, one of the giant screws of *Akagi* got fouled in wire, and a sailor fell into the icy waters of Hitokappu Bay.

Half an hour late, the armada finally got under way, except for the man overboard who could not be found. There was a feeling of excitement and purpose on every ship and as they filed past Eterofu, fringed with its usual veil of mist, the heavy cruisers and battleships test-fired their guns by throwing live rounds into a hillside of the island. The sound of the guns and the splashes of snow bursting on the hill like huge white flowers stirred the men.

In Washington, Hull's uncompromising note was being typed out for Ambassadors Kurusu and Nomura.

7

"This War May Come Quicker Than Anyone Dreams"

1.

On the morning after Hull sent the note, Secretary of War Henry Stimson phoned him to ask whether he had dispatched the *modus vivendi* to Japan. The Secretary of State replied, "I have washed my hands of it and it is now in the hands of you and Knox—the Army and the Navy."

Stimson called Roosevelt and expressed concern about reports that a large Japanese expeditionary force was moving out of Shanghai for the south. Shouldn't a final alert be sent to Lieutenant General Douglas MacArthur, commander of the United States Army Forces in the Far East (USAFFE), in the Philippines advising him to be "on the *qui vive* for any attack"? The President thought it was a good idea, and at nine-thirty Stimson summoned to his office Brigadier General Leonard T. Gerow, chief of the General Staff Operations Division, as well as Secretary of the Navy Frank Knox and Admiral Harold ("Betty") Stark, the Chief of Naval Operations.

Once more the military urged that a crisis be postponed as long as possible. Stimson said that he also would be "glad to have time," and thought Stark was being "as usual, a little bit timid and cautious" when it came to a real crisis, but he "didn't want it at any cost of humility on the part of the United States or of reopening the thing which would show a weakness on our part."

The war warning they finally radioed to MacArthur read:

NEGOTIATIONS WITH THE JAPANESE APPEAR TO BE TERMINATED TO ALL PRACTICAL PURPOSES WITH ONLY THE BAREST POSSIBILITIES THAT THE JAPANESE GOVERNMENT MIGHT COME BACK AND OFFER TO CONTINUE PERIOD JAPANESE FUTURE ACTION UNPREDICTABLE BUT HOSTILE ACTION POSSIBLE AT ANY MOMENT PERIOD IF HOSTILITIES CANNOT, REPEAT CANNOT, BE AVOIDED THE UNITED STATES DESIRES THAT JAPAN COMMIT THE FIRST OVERT ACT PERIOD THIS POLICY SHOULD NOT, REPEAT NOT, BE CONSTRUED AS RESTRICTING YOU TO A COURSE OF ACTION THAT MIGHT JEOPARDIZE YOUR DEFENSE . . .

A similar message was sent to General Walter C. Short, commander of the Hawaiian Department of the Army, but it also ordered him to do nothing "to alarm civil population or disclose intent."* General Short took the entire warning to mean he should institute a sabotage alert. He informed Washington of this but apparently nobody there read his reply carefully. He was never told he had missed the import of the instructions.

Admiral Stark wrote his own message to the naval commanders in the Pacific—Admiral Thomas C. Hart in the Philippines and Admiral Husband E. Kimmel in Hawaii. It was clear and to the point:

THIS DISPATCH IS TO BE CONSIDERED A WAR WARNING X NEGOTIATIONS WITH JAPAN LOOKING TOWARD STABILIZATION OF CONDITIONS IN THE PACIFIC HAVE CEASED AND AN AGGRESSIVE MOVE BY JAPAN IS EXPECTED IN THE NEXT FEW DAYS X THE NUMBER AND EQUIPMENT OF JAPANESE TROOPS AND THE ORGANIZATION OF NAVAL TASK FORCES INDICATES AN AMPHIBIOUS EXPEDITION AGAINST EITHER THE PHILIPPINES THAI OR KRA PENINSULA OR POSSIBLY BORNEO X EXECUTE AN APPRO-

---

* The Army Pearl Harbor Board later sarcastically referred to this as the "Do or Don't Message."

PRIATE DEFENSIVE DEPLOYMENT PREPARATORY TO CARRYING OUT THE TASKS ASSIGNED IN WPL 46 [War Plan] x . . .

Despite these alerts, the negotiations continued in name. That same day Kurusu and Nomura called on the President. Roosevelt said he still hadn't given up hope for a peaceful settlement. But the recent occupation of Indochina, troop movements to the south and hostile talk from Japan all had had "the effect of a cold bath on the United States Government and people."

Just before midnight Kurusu phoned Tokyo, using a clumsy voice code that wouldn't have deceived a layman. The negotiations, for example, were "marriage proposal"; Roosevelt was "Miss Kimiko"; a critical turn was the "birth of a child." For seven minutes Kurusu talked to Kumaichi Yamamoto, chief of the American Bureau in the Foreign Ministry, as American intelligence recorded every word.* He asked how things were in Japan. "Does it seem as if a child might be born?"

"Yes," Yamamoto replied firmly, "the birth of the child seems imminent."

". . . In which direction . . ." Kurusu hesitated, realizing he was not using the code. "Is it to be a boy or a girl?"

Yamamoto laughed, then caught on. "Oh, it's to be a strong healthy boy. . . . The matrimonial question, that is, the matter pertaining to arranging a marriage—don't break them off."

"Not break them? You mean talks?" asked the befuddled Kurusu. "Oh, my," he said helplessly and added with a resigned laugh, "Well, I'll do what I can." He paused. "Please read carefully what Miss Kimiko had to say as contained in today's telegram. . . . They want to keep carrying on the matrimonial question. They do. In the meantime we're faced with the excitement of having a child born. On top of that Tokugawa [the Japanese Army] is really champing at the bit, isn't he? Tokugawa is, isn't he?" He laughed nervously. "That's why I doubt if anything can be done."

Yamamoto said he didn't think it was as bad as all that. "Well, we can't sell a mountain [Well, we can't yield]."

"Oh, sure, I know that. That isn't even a debatable question any more."

---

* The U. S. translation is the only source available. No Japanese record could be found, and both Yamamoto and Kurusu are dead.

"Well, then, although we can't yield, we'll give you some kind of a reply to that telegram."

"In any event," Kurusu went on, "Miss Kimiko is leaving town tomorrow, and will remain in the country until Wednesday."

"Will you please continue to do your best?"

"Oh, yes. I'll do my best. And Nomura's doing everything too." Yamamoto asked if the talks that day with Miss Kimiko contained anything of interest. "No, nothing of particular interest, except that it is quite clear now that southward—ah . . ."—Kurusu began to flounder again—"the south—the south matter is having considerable effect."

"I see. Well, then, good-bye."

"Good-bye," said the relieved Kurusu.

The next day MAGIC uncovered even more important information from an intercepted message to Consul General Kita sent from Tokyo nine days earlier:

. . . In case of emergency (danger of cutting off our diplomatic relations), and the cutting off of international communications, the following warning will be added in the middle of the daily Japanese-language shortwave news broadcast:

(1) In case of Japan-U. S. relations in danger: HIGASHI NO KAZE AME [east wind, rain]

(2) Japan-U.S.S.R. relations: KITA NO KAZE KUMORI [north wind, cloudy]

(3) Japan-British relations: NISHI NO KAZE HARE [west wind, clear]

This signal will be given in the middle and at the end as a weather forecast and each sentence will be repeated twice. When this is heard, please destroy all code papers, etc. This is as yet to be a completely secret arrangement.

This "winds" message created a turmoil in Washington. Alarmed intelligence officers made arrangements to monitor around the clock all future Japanese newscasts for the key phrases, unaware that a packet of untranslated intercepts could instantly have unmasked the attack on Pearl Harbor. Yoshikawa's espionage reports were piling up in the busy translators "Incoming" baskets—too low on the priority list for even a cursory examination.

That same morning—it was November 28—Stimson burst into Roosevelt's bedroom, finding the President still in bed but in conference, with more news of the southbound Japanese expedition. Stimson wanted to attack it with Philippine-based B-17's but Roosevelt would not be panicked, and when he met a few hours later with the War Council it was agreed that there should be no precipitous countermeasures. Japan would only be warned that "we should have to fight" once her troops reached a certain point. It was also decided to have the President send a personal message to the Emperor expressing a desire for peace and a warning that war was bound to come if Japan persisted in her aggression.

It was a good idea and the Emperor would have been receptive. He had just requested the *jushin* to re-examine the entire situation and report back to him. The former prime ministers—Prince Konoye was the eighth—had not been involved in the previous decisions and would have a more objective viewpoint. Marquis Kido, the Privy Seal, had wanted the meeting conducted in the presence of His Majesty, but Prime Minister Tojo refused on the grounds that the *jushin* had no legal function. A compromise was reached: after the meeting the senior statesmen would lunch with the Emperor and express their opinions.

The next morning at nine-thirty, November 29, they met in the Imperial Court Room with Tojo, four of his Cabinet ministers and Privy Council President Hara. It was more of an informal discussion than a conference; there was no presiding officer and no decision was to be made. Baron Reijiro Wakatsuki, long an opponent of militarism, wanted to know more about the deadline for negotiations. "Does this mean there is no room for further talk?"

Foreign Minister Togo said there was "no use going any further," and Tojo felt there was "no hope for diplomatic dealings." From now on diplomacy should solely be used "to facilitate operations."

"Are we to go to war upon abandoning negotiations?" insisted Wakatsuki.

"Until today we have tried our best to reach a diplomatic solution," Tojo said, "conducting ourselves with extreme prudence. But now we don't have to be ashamed of mobilizing military force as a dignified and just action."

This did not satisfy the baron. Like Kido, he thought that *gashin-shotan* (enduring hard times) would be better for Japan than war.

What if we resorted to *gashin-shotan* and still ended up in war?

asked General Suzuki. "Then we wouldn't have a chance in the world of winning it."

This prompted so many questions from Wakatsuki that Tojo impatiently interrupted. "Please trust what we say. We can occupy the sphere [Southeast Asia] and get enough oil. In three years we can gradually expand our sphere. As for aircraft oil, we can somehow manage; as for iron and steel, last year's production was four million seven hundred and sixty thousand tons. We can increase this after three years."

"I don't understand what I've heard so far," Admiral Keisuke Okada interjected, taking up the questioning. What about the European war, for example?

"We are going hand in hand with Italy and Germany, with whom we have a treaty," Tojo replied. This was a strategic necessity that would enable Japan to move west and join up with Hitler's forces. "We must crush England." India would be an objective on the way. "Then we'll carry out Near East joint operations in line with the German-Soviet war."

Okada didn't think this grandiose plan would work, nor would expansion to Southeast Asia bring any increase in production. "Shipping of materials back home will get tight. After three years, I couldn't even dream of production. What are you going to do about raw materials?"

These were realistic fears but Tojo's response was brusque. "The question of resources is precarious, but we can manage. All other things being equal, I think we can get along. Please trust us."

"Very doubtful," Okada remarked. "You can go on building up armament plants, but how are you going to get hold of raw materials? It is not an easy task. We'll soon run out of natural resources."

"We will go on a priority principle."

Okada turned his attack in a new direction and asked if the Navy was good enough to beat America.

Tojo, who had still to get a positive answer from the Navy, said that Japan, by taking strategic points one by one, was preparing for a long war and would emerge victorious.

"So far so good," Okada said wryly. "But there are many xyz's. With the U. S. building program as it is at present, don't you think there is some danger?"

"Everything is being taken into consideration," said the exasperated Tojo and lost his composure. "Suppose we don't fight. What would be the result? We just can't bow to England and the United States. We've lost one hundred and sixty thousand lives so far in the China Incident. Now more than two million people are suffering. No more suffering! If we go on like this for a few years, we'll lose our chance to fight. We're already losing valuable time for operations!"

But Okada was not to be cowed and became openly sarcastic. "We're trying to come to an amicable settlement with America so we can redeem the blood being shed every moment! We're building up the Greater East Asia Co-prosperity Sphere just for this purpose. We import great quantities of rice from these countries, yet they are still poverty-stricken! We want to take care of these people. Labor and shipping is short, and to make them happy we must make sacrifices. Buying materials there by Army scrip is simple injustice."

Tojo ignored the mockery. "That all depends on how we appeal to the people's feeling," he said. "We must make good use of native organizations. At first the people will find life difficult but very soon they will get on well."

It was past noon and the meeting was adjourned for lunch with the Emperor. Afterward everyone, including His Majesty and Kido, moved to the Imperial Chamber. The Emperor said, "We're going through very difficult times, aren't we?" It was a polite invitation to speak out.

"We don't have to worry about the spiritual strength of our people," said Baron Wakatsuki, "but we must carefully study whether or not we have the material resources to carry out a long war. This morning we listened to the government explanations, but I'm still concerned."

Tojo reminded the Emperor that what had been said was based on the unanimous views of the Cabinet and the Supreme Command.

"I've also been listening to the government explanations, and I too am not yet convinced," said Okada.

Neither was Prince Konoye. "I wonder if it is necessary to resort immediately to war even if the negotiations have broken down. I feel we might find a solution and still keep the status quo. In other words, to remain in the condition of *gashin-shotan*."

Nor was Admiral Mitsumasa Yonai. "I'm not able to express a concrete opinion, since I don't have the background. But if you'll forgive the slang, I'm afraid that by trying to avoid *jiri-hin* [slow poverty] we'll end up in *doka-hin* [instant poverty]."

Only two *jushin* generals, Nobuyuki Abe and Senjuro Hayashi, put their complete trust in the Tojo government. It appeared the session was over, but Wakatsuki wanted to bring up still another point. Tojo tried to stop him but the baron would not be silenced. "If our very existence is at stake, we should go to war even in the face of possible defeat and a scorching of our land, but to push a national policy for an ideal—for instance, the establishment of the Greater East Asia Co-prosperity Sphere or the stabilization of East Asia—and to spend our national strength shackled by such ideals, that is indeed dangerous. And I'd like you all to think it over."

Stubbornly, Tojo reiterated that the whole matter had been discussed for hours on end at liaison conferences. They had explored in detail whether Japan could get the necessary supplies for a long war, and when and how the war, once started, could be brought to an end. The first aspect depended on the outcome of the initial stage of the conflict, and the second might be resolved through the mediation of the Soviet Union or the Vatican.

In the face of almost universal disapproval Tojo had not wavered, and Kido—who had not uttered a word, but taken voluminous notes—realized the situation was "beyond control." The influence of the Throne had failed. War was inevitable and the rise or fall of Japan was in the hands of the gods.

It was already four o'clock but Tojo's day was by no means over. He immediately convened the 74th Liaison Conference, and it was agreed to warn Hitler and Mussolini that the Japanese-American negotiations were certain to be broken off and that there was imminent danger of war.

Foreign Minister Togo asked Navy Chief of Staff Nagano what the zero hour was. Finance Minister Kaya also had to know; once hostilities started, the stock market would drop precipitously. Only with the knowledge of the exact hour could he prevent a crash.

"Well, then," said the reluctant Nagano, "I'll tell you. The zero hour is . . ."—he lowered his voice—". . . December 8." This

"This War May Come Quicker Than Anyone Dreams"

was news even to General Tojo.* "There is still time, so you'd better come up with the kind of diplomacy that will help us win the war."

"I understand," said Togo. "But can't we tell our representatives [Kurusu and Nomura] that we've made up our minds? We've told the attachés [in Washington], haven't we?"

"We haven't told the naval attaché," Nagano answered.

Togo wondered why Nagano was acting so suspiciously. "We can't go on keeping our diplomats in the dark, can we?"

Nagano finally had to answer. "We're going to make a surprise attack," he said. His deputy, Vice Admiral Seiichi Ito, explained that the Navy wanted the negotiations with America left hanging until hostilities had begun so the initial attack would be a complete surprise.

Togo restrained himself. He was quite calm when he said that Japan would lose international good faith unless she made a proper notification of her intent. But his self-control gave way, and he began to stutter that the Navy plan was "entirely unpermissible, being in contravention of accepted procedure." It was unthinkable for Japan "to commit irresponsible acts which would be hurtful to the national honor and prestige."

Someone remarked, "This is one occasion when the entire population of Japan will have to be like Kuranosuke Oishi." Oishi was the leader of the forty-seven *ronin* who pretended to be a dissolute drunk.

Togo said he had a previous engagement, suggested the meeting adjourn and shot back his chair. As he was rising, Ito asked a favor for the Navy; if prior notification had to be given, couldn't it go to Ambassador Grew rather than to Hull?

Togo answered with a brusque "No!" and shouldered his way out of the room. He went directly to his office and composed cables to Berlin and Rome which were dispatched late that night. The one to Ambassador Hiroshi Oshima revealed that the negotiations had failed.

* He knew about the combined Army and Navy operations in the Philippines and Malaya, but it was not until the following day that he learned of Pearl Harbor, and even then he was given no operational details. None of the civilian members of the Cabinet or high court officials, like Kido, yet had an inkling of the main target—nor would they be told.

> ... IN THE FACE OF THIS, OUR EMPIRE FACES A GRAVE SITUATION AND MUST ACT WITH DETERMINATION. WILL YOUR EXCELLENCY, THEREFORE, IMMEDIATELY INTERVIEW CHANCELLOR HITLER AND FOREIGN MINISTER RIBBENTROP AND CONFIDENTIALLY COMMUNICATE TO THEM A SUMMARY OF THE DEVELOPMENTS. SAY TO THEM THAT LATELY ENGLAND AND THE UNITED STATES HAVE TAKEN A PROVOCATIVE ATTITUDE, BOTH OF THEM. SAY THAT THEY ARE PLANNING TO MOVE MILITARY FORCES INTO VARIOUS PLACES IN EAST ASIA AND THAT WE WILL INEVITABLY HAVE TO COUNTER BY ALSO MOVING TROOPS. SAY VERY SECRETLY TO THEM THAT THERE IS EXTREME DANGER THAT WAR MAY SUDDENLY BREAK OUT BETWEEN THE ANGLO-SAXON NATIONS AND JAPAN THROUGH SOME CLASH OF ARMS AND ADD THAT THE TIME OF THE BREAKING OUT OF THIS WAR MAY COME QUICKER THAN ANYONE DREAMS.

Curiously, Togo did not order Oshima to ask for a German declaration of war in case Japan and America fought. He did summon Ambassador Ott. If worst came to worst, would Germany come to Japan's assistance? Ott answered without hesitation: We will give you all possible help.

The message to Oshima was intercepted by MAGIC and passed on to Roosevelt. Equally alarming was a United Press dispatch in the *New York Times* from Tokyo that Sunday morning, November 30: Prime Minister Tojo had just made a provocative speech declaring that Chiang Kai-shek was "dancing to the tune of American and British Communism because the United States and Britain desire to fish in troubled waters" and stir up Asians one against the other. "This is the stock in trade of Britain and the United States and therefore we must purge this sort of action with a vengeance." Japan was determined to co-ordinate all Asians "so that a chorus of victory may go up in the camp of justice as speedily as possible," and nothing be allowed "to interfere with this sphere because this sphere was decreed by Providence."

It was a speech that Tojo had never made, nor even read, let alone approved. Someone else had written it and it had been read at a meeting commemorating the first anniversary of the Sino-Japanese Basic Treaty. Its belligerency had been exaggerated by poor translation. The expression "we must purge this sort of action with a vengeance," for example, should have read, "this sort of practice must be stopped."

There was also an item in the *Times* indicating that the President might curtail his Thanksgiving holiday at Warm Springs, Georgia; and late that night Kurusu again phoned Kumaichi Yamamoto in Tokyo. "The President is returning tomorrow!" he said. "He is hurrying home."*

"Is there any special significance to this?"

"The newspapers have made much of the Premier's speech, and it is having strong repercussions here."

"Is that so?" Yamamoto didn't know what Kurusu was talking about.

"Yes, it was a drastic statement he made. The newspapers carried large headlines over it; and the President seems to be returning because of it. There no doubt are other reasons, but this is the reason the newspapers are giving." Kurusu was disturbed and showed it. "Unless greater caution is exercised in speeches by the Premier and others, it puts us in a very difficult position . . ."

"We *are* being careful."

"We here are doing our best, but these reports are seized upon by the correspondents and the worst features enlarged upon. Please caution the Premier, the Foreign Minister, and others. Tell the Foreign Minister that we had expected to hear something different, some good word, but instead we get this [the "Tojo" speech]." Kurusu paused, then asked, "Are the Japanese-American negotiations to continue?"

"Yes."

Irritated, Kurusu said, "You were very urgent about them before, weren't you; but now you want them to stretch out." He did not know that the negotiations were now to be used solely to mask the Pearl Harbor raid but he was getting suspicious and just recently had mused to Masuo Kato of the Domei News Agency, "Am I being used as a smoke screen?" He began to scold Yamamoto. "Both the Premier and the Foreign Minister will need to change the tone of their speeches! Do you understand? Please, all, use more discretion."

---

* This dialogue is taken from the MAGIC translation, "a preliminary condensed version" of the eight-minute conversation.

The Emperor's official sanction was the last formal step before war. At five minutes after two on Monday, December 1, the imperial conference was opened in Room One East of the Palace in the usual formal style. Face stern and voice clipped, Prime Minister Tojo announced that Japan could not submit to American demands to quit China and nullify the Tripartite Pact, or her very existence would be in jeopardy. "Matters have reached the point where Japan must begin war with the United States, Great Britain and the Netherlands to preserve her empire."

After Tojo detailed the long, tedious history of the American-Japanese negotiations, Admiral Nagano rose and spiritedly declared that the officers and men of the Army and Navy were "burning with a desire to serve their Emperor and their country even at the cost of their lives." This was followed by dissertations on problems ranging from public morale, emergency precautions and food supplies to the nation's economy and finance.

The Emperor, on his dais, sat passive and silent. Occasionally he nodded and seemed to be in an excellent mood. Sugiyama was "awed and deeply moved by His Majesty's graceful humor," but Finance Minister Kaya thought it was obvious he did not want war.

Privy Council President Hara began to ask questions and the last were the most unsettling. "What will happen in case of air raids? . . . What will we do if a great fire should break out in Tokyo? Do you have a plan for this?"

General Teiichi Suzuki said that there would be simple shelters for those who remained in the city. The reply was unsatisfactory, but even Hara found this no reason to make any more concessions to America. "The United States is acting in a conceited, stubborn and disrespectful manner," he said. "If we gave in, we'd surrender in one stroke what we won in the Sino-Japanese and Russo-Japanese wars as well as the Manchurian Incident. We cannot do this."

Tojo himself summed up what they all felt. The Japanese Empire stood at the threshold of glory or collapse. "We tremble with awe in the presence of His Majesty. . . . If His Majesty decides on war, we will all do our best to repay our obligations to him by bringing the government and the military closer than ever together, resolving that a united nation will go on to victory, making every effort to achieve our national purposes and thereby putting at ease His Majesty's mind."

There was nothing else to do but bow to the Emperor, who then, silent, without expression, left the room. Those remaining signed the documents proposing war, which were delivered to the Emperor. For some time he pondered the matter until he felt assured that the decision to initiate hostilities was not being pushed through by a few aggressive military men. He told Kido that Hull's demands were too humiliating. He had already defied tradition and training by insisting on a return to "blank paper," and could do no more. He affixed his seal to the historic papers. The decision for war was formally sanctioned.*

In one week the simultaneous attacks would begin, and their success depended entirely on the element of surprise. But late that night a cable arrived from China with news that the secret was in jeopardy. It was from General Tsutomu Sakai, commander of the 23rd Army, which was poised near Canton to seize Hong Kong. A transport plane bound for Canton had crashed in Chinese-held territory, and one of its passengers was Major Tomozuki Sugisaka, a courier carrying the secret orders concerning the surprise attacks.

There was alarm at Army General Staff headquarters. The Navy was summoned to an emergency meeting. Had Major Sugisaka had time to destroy the secret documents before the crash? Had

---

* In January 1946 the Emperor broke his silence about these events in a rare display of confidence to his Grand Chamberlain, Hisanori Fujita: "Naturally, war should never be allowed. In this case, too, I tried to think of everything, some way to avoid it. I exhausted every means within my power. However, my utmost endeavor was to no avail, and we plunged into war at the end. It was truly regrettable. . . .

"The Emperor of a constitutional state is not permitted to express himself freely in speech and action and is not allowed to willfully interfere with a minister's authority invested in him by the Constitution.

"Consequently, when a certain decision is brought to me for approval, whether it concerns internal affairs, diplomacy or military matters, there is nothing I can do but give my approval as long as it has been reached by lawful procedure, even if I consider the decision extremely undesirable. . . .

"If I turned down a decision on my own accord, what would happen? The Emperor could not maintain his position of responsibility if a decision which had been reached by due process based on the Constitution could be either approved or rejected by the Emperor at his discretion. It would be the same thing as if the Emperor had destroyed the Constitution. Such an attitude is taboo for the Emperor of a constitutional state." ("I believe," Fujita observed, "that His Majesty was talking abstractly about the prewar imperial conferences and so forth.")

the papers burned in the crash itself? Or were they already being rushed to Chiang Kai-shek, who would undoubtedly pass them on to Roosevelt? Should Operation Z be canceled?

The next morning these apprehensions seemed to be confirmed: a reconnaissance plane had sighted the wreckage of a big Army transport in a Nationalist stronghold about fifty miles northeast of Canton. According to the pilot, "the scene of the crash was already surrounded by the Chinese who were swarming like ants."

Still in suspense, Nagano and Sugiyama drove to the Palace to inform the Emperor of the exact date of attack. They told him that December 8 would be December 7 in Hawaii, a day of rest with most of the warships at anchor. The moon would also be in the right phase for launching the attack, since it would shine "from midnight to about sunrise." Nagano respectfully requested the Emperor to give his sanction to issuance of orders fixing December 8 as X-Day. His Majesty, without hesitation, approved.*

At two o'clock that afternoon Sugiyama sent a cable of two words to General Terauchi, commander of Southern Army: HINODE YAMAGATA. This was code for "The date for commencing operations [HINODE] will be December 8 [YAMAGATA]."

Three and a half hours later Yamamoto sent a slightly longer cable in a new code to the Pearl Harbor Striking Force: NIITAKA-YAMA NOBORE [Climb Mount Niitaka**] 1208. This meant: "Attack as planned on December 8."

Kido Butai was cruising eastward at a modest 14 knots to conserve fuel, advancing in ring formation with three submarines ahead scouting for neutral merchant ships which, if found, were to be boarded and seized. A chance encounter with the U. S. Pacific Fleet, however, could not be handled so easily. This awkward possibility was discussed time and again, and once the irrepressible Yamaguchi half jokingly suggested, "Fire a salute, shout '*Sayonara!*' and go back home." The remark brought laughter, but Kusaka thought, What else could we do? We're not yet at war.

* After the Tokyo trial U. S. Chief Prosecutor Joseph Keenan met the Emperor, who reportedly told him he didn't know Pearl Harbor was going to be bombed. From available evidence, however, it is evident he did know and approve of Operation Z. It is also well documented that he issued explicit directives to give America due notice before the attack.

** Mount Niitaka on Formosa was, at 13,599 feet (1,211 feet higher than Mount Fuji), the highest peak in the Japanese Empire.

The "Climb Mount Niitaka" message gave Kusaka a welcome sense of commitment. He felt as if a tremendous burden had been lifted from his back. They would launch one overwhelming attack and disappear. It was like *mamono* (devil), a tactic in *kendo:* one surprise thrust, then fall back like the wind. Still, there was always the chance that as they neared Pearl Harbor some American patrol plane would spot *Kido Butai* before the launching. In that case Kusaka was prepared to change tactics—to attack in full strength even though surprise had been lost.

The weather was the calmest it had been in the past ten years and refueling was no problem. Nagumo ordered all ship captains to travel without lights—and to inform their entire crews of Operation Z. That night a spirit of intense, subdued excitement swept from ship to ship.*

Back home that evening, the headline of the *Japan Times & Advertiser* read:

JAPAN WILL RENEW EFFORTS TO REACH
U. S. UNDERSTANDING.

2.

Hours after *Kido Butai* had left the icy waters of Hitokappu Bay, Lieutenant Commander Wilfred J. Holmes, whose job it was to plot Japanese ship movements, reported to his superior in the Navy's Communications Intelligence Unit in Pearl Harbor that the six enemy carriers were "in home waters." After that, however, Holmes admitted he had lost track of them. Day after day there was "no information" about the carriers.

Lieutenant Commander Edward T. Layton, Admiral Kimmel's fleet intelligence officer, relayed this information to his chief on December 2. If it disturbed Kimmel he didn't show it; in fact, he jokingly asked, "Do you mean to say that they could be rounding Diamond Head this minute and you wouldn't know?"

* Commander Naohiro Sata, *Kaga*'s Chief Aviation Officer, however, was openly critical of the entire operation. He told a group of pilots, "Here we are heading out into the North Pacific where not even a bird flies." What Japan needed was oil and that was far to the south. "Therefore, it is the height of stupidity to attack Pearl Harbor."

"I hope they would be sighted by now, sir."

A few miles away, in Honolulu, Consul General Kita had just received a message from Tokyo:

IN VIEW OF THE PRESENT SITUATION, THE PRESENCE IN PORT OF WARSHIPS, AIRPLANE CARRIERS, AND CRUISERS IS OF UTMOST IMPORTANCE. HEREAFTER, TO THE UTMOST OF YOUR ABILITY, LET ME KNOW DAY BY DAY. WIRE ME IN EACH CASE WHETHER OR NOT THERE ARE ANY BARRAGE BALLOONS ABOVE PEARL HARBOR OR IF THERE ARE ANY INDICATIONS THAT THEY WILL BE SENT UP. ALSO ADVISE ME WHETHER OR NOT THE WARSHIPS ARE PROVIDED WITH ANTITORPEDO NETS.

This message, which would have meant a warning of attack on Pearl Harbor to anybody reading it, was intercepted in Hawaii and passed on to the cryptographers in Washington for decoding, but since it concerned Hawaii and had nothing to do with diplomacy, its low priority sent it to the bottom of somebody's basket. Another important intercept consigned to a similar fate back in September—the one dividing Pearl Harbor into five subareas—had finally been translated, but Brigadier General Sherman Miles, chief of Military Intelligence, regarded it as a naval message of no concern to the Army while Lieutenant Commander Alvin D. Kramer, chief of the Naval Intelligence Translation Branch, marked it with a single asterisk, for "Interesting," rather than two, for "Urgent." As far as Kramer was concerned, it was merely "an attempt on the part of the Japanese diplomatic service to simplify communications."

Bernard Baruch, Roosevelt's unofficial adviser and Churchill's close friend, was in his Washington hotel room talking with Raoul Desvernine, an attorney representing the Mitsui combine. The lawyer said that Special Envoy Saburo Kurusu wanted to get a message directly to the President without going through Hull. Would Baruch help? Baruch passed on the request to Major General Edwin ("Pa") Watson, one of Roosevelt's secretaries. Watson phoned back to say the President refused to meet Kurusu without Hull but saw no objection to Baruch's finding out what the message was.

The next day, December 3, Baruch met Desvernine and Kurusu at the Mayflower Hotel. The Japanese ambassador vowed that he, the people of Japan and the Emperor all wanted peace but that the military leaders "were sitting with a loaded gun in each hand . . . determined to shoot." War could be averted if he could talk to the President, without the "hostile and untrusting" Hull, and tell him he could thwart the Japanese military by appealing directly and personally to the Emperor, who would then ask Roosevelt to mediate a settlement between Japan and China. The important thing, said Kurusu, was to keep the conversations going and this could best be done if Roosevelt sent a personal representative such as Harry Hopkins to Japan.

Although Baruch didn't think the proposals were "anything into which anybody could put their teeth," he promised to relay the information to the White House.

Another emissary of peace—Dr. E. Stanley Jones, a prominent Methodist missionary—was trying to present a similar suggestion to the President. He phoned his secretary, Marvin McIntyre, with a request to see the President on a matter he could not put on paper: a plan (inspired by Hidenari Terasaki, an official at the Japanese embassy) to avert war by a personal cable from Roosevelt to the Emperor. McIntyre told him to be at the East Gate of the White House in twenty minutes. A guide would take him through a secret entrance to the President's office so he wouldn't have "to run a barrage of reporters."

Roosevelt told Jones he'd already been considering a letter to the Emperor. "But I've hesitated to do it, for I don't want to hurt the Japanese envoys here at Washington by going over their heads to the Emperor."

"That is the point on which I have come," said Jones. The idea had originated with Kurusu and Nomura themselves. "They asked me to ask you to send the cable. But they also said there could be no record, for if it were known that they had gone over the heads of the Japanese government to the Emperor, their own heads wouldn't be worth much."

"Well, that cleans my slate," said the President. "I can do it."

Jones cautioned him not to send it through the Foreign Ministry but directly to the Emperor, otherwise it would never reach him. "I don't know the mechanics of it, but this is what they told me."

"I'm thinking out loud," Roosevelt mused. "I can't go down to the cable office and say I want to send a cable from the President of the United States to the Emperor of Japan. But I could send it to Grew." He could take it directly to His Majesty. "And if I don't hear within twenty-four hours—I have learned how to do some things—I'll give it to the newspapers and force a reply."

As Jones was leaving he asked the President never to mention Mr. Terasaki, who had come up with the idea.

"His secret is safe," Roosevelt promised.

The message would probably have been sent that day if it hadn't been for Hull. Still suspicious, he argued that an appeal to the Emperor should be a last-minute resort; besides, His Majesty was a mere figurehead under the thumb of Tojo's Cabinet, and a message by-passing its members would not only be resented but would be regarded as a sign of weakness.

Hull's suspicions were borne out by an intercepted dispatch from Tokyo. It ordered the embassy on Massachusetts Avenue to burn all but three codes and to destroy one of the two "B" code machines. An Army intelligence officer, sent to reconnoiter the embassy, found employees burning papers in the backyard. Chief of Military Intelligence Sherman Miles and his Far Eastern Section chief, Colonel Rufus S. Bratton, concluded that "at the least a break in diplomatic relations and probably war" was imminent.

On the other side of the world General Tomoyuki Yamashita was reading the attack order to division and detachment commanders and staff officers. They listened attentively, aware that Japan's destiny was at stake. There were tears on almost every face.

Three landings would be made at dawn of December 8 on the east coast of the Malay Peninsula near the border. Two were in Thai territory, Pattani and Singora, and one in Malaya, Kota Bharu. Inspired by a dream, Colonel Tsuji intended to take over neutral Thailand with a modern version of the Trojan Horse. A thousand Japanese in Thai uniforms would come ashore near Singora and round up café and dance-hall girls as a cover. They would then commandeer twenty or thirty buses, get aboard with the girls, and drive merrily down to the Malay border. Waving Thai flags with one hand and Union Jacks with the other, they would shout in English, "Japanese soldier is frightful!" and "Hurrah for the

English!" In the boisterous confusion, Tsuji was sure the border guards would let his soldiers cross into Malaya.

At dawn the next morning, December 4, a convoy of twenty-six transport ships left the island of Hainan, off the southernmost coast of China, and bore south toward the Malay Peninsula. Colonel Tsuji stood on the bridge of the Army transport *Ryujo-maru* and watched a deep-red sun rise in the east as the moon, looking like a tray, vanished in the west. Tsuji visualized the faces of his mother, wife and children. Except for the reassuring throb of engines, there wasn't a sound on the ship. All was peaceful.

Early that afternoon a liaison conference was convened to discuss the delivery date of the final note to Hull. Vice Admiral Seiichi Ito had no objections if it was handed over at 12:30 P.M., December 7, Washington time. Both Tojo and Togo were concerned that the note be presented *before* the attack. Ito assured them on that score, and the time was approved.

There was to be no simple declaration of war, as Togo wanted, merely a notice terminating the negotiations; the draft he presented reflected the common bitterness and righteous indignation felt after receipt of the Hull note and declared that Japan had been patient in its attempt to conciliate. "On the other hand, the American Government, always holding fast to theories in disregard of realities, and refusing to yield an inch on its impractical principles, caused undue delay in the negotiations." It concluded that Japan regretfully was forced to announce "that in view of the attitude of the American Government it must be concluded that it is impossible to reach an agreement through further negotiations."

Someone expressed the unrealistic hope that room be left for further negotiations. But the others realized this was, in truth, a declaration of war and that time had run out.

That day the Japanese fleet code was changed as a last-minute precaution. It blinded American naval intelligence, which no longer had any idea where the six carriers were and would need some time to break the new code. *Kido Butai* was already more than a third of the way to Hawaii, leaving behind it no telltale path of refuse. All garbage was stored away, and empty oil cans were crushed and piled on the decks. By late morning the final major reservicing point was reached—42 degrees north and 170 degrees east—and all ships were refueled. Earlier this could be accomplished at a maximum speed of 9 knots, but by now everyone was so adept it was done at 12. With the Striking Force loaded to capacity, all supply ships turned back except for three, which would make the final refueling in forty-eight hours.

That afternoon came the first alarm, a cable in the new code from Yamamoto: a radio message had been intercepted which had probably originated from an enemy submarine in their vicinity. Kusaka queried all his ship captains but no one had intercepted any unexplained message. Undeterred, the Striking Force turned southeast, maintaining speed despite heavy fog. For the fliers belowdecks the waiting seemed interminable. They busied themselves with painting, drawing and *kendo,* and at least one began writing a book. Fighter pilot Yoshio Shiga had produced eight watercolors of a temple and invited the officers on *Kaga* to a private showing. He felt sheepish displaying "such unserious work at such a serious time," but was certain that he would not be alive to exhibit them later. It had been weeks since the last maneuvers and many fliers feared they would lose their touch. Pilots sat in their planes to keep the feel of the controls; bombardiers gazed intently through bombsights. Only gunners had actual practice; they shot at kites.

The next day, December 5, Vice Admiral Ito called on Togo at the Foreign Ministry and said the notification should be presented to Hull at 1 P.M., Washington time, a half-hour later than previously requested. Why the delay? Togo asked. I miscalculated, was the reply. Togo asked how much time there would be between notification and attack. Ito refused to give the exact moment of attack on the grounds of "operational secrecy," but assured the Foreign Minister that there would be sufficient time. As he was leaving, Ito reiterated his warning not to cable the notification too early.

It was raining in Oahu. A small Piper Cub dawdled over Pearl Harbor with Yoshikawa on his last "sightseeing" flight. He had received an urgent cable that morning from Tokyo requesting "a comprehensive report on the American fleet." After landing, he made a final tour of Pearl City, confirming what he had seen from the air, and then cabled Tokyo:

"This War May Come Quicker Than Anyone Dreams" 239

> . . . THE FOLLOWING SHIPS WERE IN PORT ON THE AFTERNOON OF THE 5TH: 8 BATTLESHIPS, 3 LIGHT CRUISERS, 16 DESTROYERS.

The message was intercepted by MAGIC but the Yamamoto luck held. Once again, it was placed in a "Hold" basket.

3.

Tokyo newspapers such as the *Asahi Shimbun* continued to accuse the West of preparing for war. On December 6 the headlines read:

> U. S. USELESSLY EXTENDING TALKS,
> HAS NO INTENTION OF COMPROMISE WITH JAPAN
>
> U. S. LEADERS DISCUSS POLICY FOR JAPAN
> BUT NO CHANGE SEEN IN THEIR DOGMATIC VIEWS
>
> THAILAND IN AGONY FOR NEUTRALITY
>
> SCANDALOUS ENCIRCLEMENT OF JAPAN,
> TRAMPLING ON JAPAN'S PEACEFUL INTENTIONS.
> FOUR NATIONS SIMULTANEOUSLY
> START MILITARY PREPARATIONS

Otto Tolischus cabled the *New York Times* his impressions of the approaching crisis. Most Japanese, he wrote, refused to believe they were facing war with four nations simultaneously,

> . . . but their instinctive hopes are daily contradicted by the evidence of their senses. They listen to alarming statements by the highest Government officials about the greatest crisis Japan has ever faced in her 2,600-year history. They are called to mass meetings to hear denunciations of the enemy, and they read a steady war clamor in the press. They see air shelters and water reservoirs being built everywhere in preparation for air raids. They are being drilled in air raid defense, especially in fighting fires, the greatest dread of Japanese cities. Finally, they see taxes and prices rising. They know that all these things are not done for fun, and that war, real war, which only a short time ago

seemed so far away, is rapidly stretching out its fiery arms toward Nippon, land of the gods.

The people do not want war, but neither do they want to give up the fruits of the war they have been fighting, which has cost them such a lot of blood and treasure. They have been told that this war is a war of self-defense, to obtain elbow-room for the Japanese people, crowded into a few small islands with few national resources, and to liberate one thousand million of Oriental peoples from exploitation by the white races. . . .

It would be a great mistake to assume that the Japanese are so war-weary that they would be reluctant to fight if war really came to their land, or that their war potential is as small or as straitened as the outward picture might suggest. As members of a divine family state, in which patriotism and religion merge, they not merely say, "My country, right or wrong!" but they are convinced with all the fervor of religious faith that their country is right, whatever mistakes in tactics individual statesmen may take.

In Manila, Admiral Thomas Hart, commander of the Asiatic Fleet, predicted hostilities might begin at any moment. His inadequate fleet—one heavy cruiser, one light cruiser, thirteen World War I four-stack destroyers and twenty-nine submarines—was as ready for battle as it ever could be; ammunition was in the racks and warheads were on the torpedoes.

Unidentified aircraft had been reported the past three nights over nearby Clark Field, the main bomber base, but General MacArthur refused to be panicked. That afternoon he and Hart conferred with a visitor from Singapore, Vice-Admiral Sir Tom Phillips, commander of the British Far Eastern Fleet. A Japanese convoy sighted off Indochina near the Gulf of Siam was subsequently lost in a fog. Was it heading for a direct attack on Malaya and Singapore or merely landing in Thailand?

MacArthur reassuringly remarked that by April he would have a trained army of 200,000 men, and a powerful air force of 256 bombers and 195 fighter planes.

"Doug, that is just dandy," Hart interposed. "But how defensible are we right now?" The answer was painfully obvious. While MacArthur had about 130,000 men in uniform, almost 100,000 of these were poorly equipped Philippine Army divisions with a few months' training in close-order drill. About the only thing they could do well was salute. His air force was also inadequate. There were 35 Flying Fortresses and 107 P-40's.

After the conference Phillips—nicknamed "Tom Thumb" because of his stature; he was an inch shorter than Napoleon—made one specific request of Hart. He wanted four destroyers to accompany his fleet, which included the battle cruiser *Repulse* and the battleship *Prince of Wales,* on a sortie from Singapore up the east coast of Malaya as a countermove to the advancing convoy. No sooner had Hart agreed to send four of his own overage destroyers than a messenger arrived with a dispatch for Phillips: Singapore-based planes had again spotted the Japanese armada off the Thai coast.

"Admiral," Hart said to Phillips, "when did you say you were flying back to Singapore?"

"I'm taking off tomorrow morning."

"If you want to be there when the war starts, I suggest you take off right now."

That afternoon the final draft of the notification to Hull, together with general instructions for the Japanese embassy in Washington, was turned over to Kazuji Kameyama, chief of the Foreign Ministry's Cable Section. He was told to cable the instructions so they would arrive about 8 A.M., December 6, Washington time. This would be followed an hour later by the first thirteen parts of the notification—in English to prevent mistranslation. For security purposes the final part, the fourteenth, which would break off diplomatic negotiations, should not arrive until 4 or 5 A.M. on December 7.

Communications to Washington were generally good and never took more than an hour. Allowing additional time for further messages of correction and unforeseen difficulties, Kameyama sent the instructions and the first thirteen parts to the Central Telegraph Office at 8:30 P.M. Forty minutes later the instructions were cabled to Washington, and an hour after that, the first thirteen parts were on their way.

Kameyama went home well satisfied that the messages would surely arrive long before the deadline. The next afternoon he would send the crucial fourteenth part, followed half an hour later by a final cable instructing Kurusu and Nomura to deliver all fourteen parts to Hull at 1 P.M. on December 7, Washington time.

Kido Butai, completely blacked out, was speeding southeast at 20 knots through gales and high seas. Several of the exhausted lookouts had already been swept overboard and the fog was so thick that it was often impossible to see the ship ahead. But in spite of this and constant changes in course, the warships were still maintaining good formation.

Never before had the Japanese military custom of using Tokyo, not local, time been much of a problem, since cruises had invariably been to north or south in approximately the same time zone. Now it was disconcerting to find light at night and darkness in the day. The clock had to be forgotten and meals served according to the sun.

Alarms were keeping Nagumo in a state of anxiety that day. First came a report from Tokyo that a Russian ship was in the area. Six fighter planes on the decks of *Kaga* were warmed up and their pilots given orders to stand by, but nothing was sighted and the planes never took off. After dark a general alarm sounded on the flagship when someone noticed a light soaring overhead. Men ran to their battle stations and antiaircraft batteries of several ships zeroed in on the mysterious light. It was an illuminated balloon sent up by *Kaga* itself to determine wind direction.

Before retiring, Kusaka tried to reassure his commander with another *"Daijobu."*

"I envy your optimism," said Nagumo with a sigh.

4.

In Washington it was still Saturday, December 6, and there was concern among officials over a detailed British Admiralty report that a Japanese fleet of thirty-five transports, eight cruisers and twenty destroyers was moving directly toward the Malay Peninsula.* At his daily top-level naval meeting, Secretary of

---

* Some attention was diverted by a bitter political controversy involving treason. Several anti-Roosevelt Army officers had stolen top-secret documents revealing America's war plans and turned them over to three isolationist newspapers—the Chicago *Tribune,* the New York *Daily News* and the Washington *Times-Herald*—which simultaneously published these secrets on December 4 in an effort to prove that Roosevelt was a warmonger.

the Navy Frank Knox asked, "Gentlemen, are they going to hit us?"

Rear Admiral Richmond Kelly Turner, regarded as Admiral Stark's spokesman, said, "No, Mr. Secretary. They are going to hit the British. They are not ready for us yet."

There was no dissenting voice.

The Navy's Cryptographic Section was getting ready to relax for the weekend. Most of the staff would leave at noon. One translator, Mrs. Dorothy Edgers, with time on her hands, began sifting through untranslated MAGIC intercepts of low priority—those involving Hawaii that had been piling up. She'd only been on the job a few weeks and was still fascinated by everything around her. One message from Tokyo to Consul General Kita in Honolulu, dated December 2, asked about ship movements, anti-torpedo nets and barrage balloons at Pearl Harbor. Intrigued, she picked up another, dated December 3, from Kita to Tokyo. She became excited as she read a lengthy report from Yoshikawa describing in detail how Otto Kühn would transmit information about the fleet in Pearl Harbor to Japanese ships lying off Oahu by putting lights in windows, burning garbage as a smoke signal or placing want ads on the radio.

Suspicions aroused, she passed on the messages to Chief Ship's Clerk H. L. Bryant, but he said she could never translate the long intercept by noon and to let it ride until Monday. Mrs. Edgers refused to be put off and worked overtime, finishing the translation at 3 P.M. Just then Lieutenant Commander Alvin Kramer, chief of the Translation Branch, checked in for duty but instead of sharing her excitement, he merely criticized her work and began editing it. Finally he put it aside, telling her to run along; they could finish editing the long message sometime the next week. When Mrs. Edgers protested, Kramer said, "We'll get back to this piece on Monday," and once more discovery of Operation Z was narrowly averted.*

At the Japanese embassy on Massachusetts Avenue the telegram of instructions (in Japanese) and the first thirteen parts of

---

* After the war Colonel Rufus Bratton of Army Intelligence declared, "If we had gotten that message [on December 6] . . . the whole picture might have been different."

the long message to Hull (in English) had both come in. Late in the afternoon the cipher staff quit work to attend a farewell party for an embassy official who was being transferred to South America. They had only completed about eight parts.

First Secretary Katsuzo Okumura was personally typing out the deciphered parts which were too secret for any office typist to handle. When he finished he went to the basement playroom to relax. Two correspondents were playing ping-pong and one, Masuo Kato, came over to query Okumura about the liner *Tatsutamaru*, which had left Yokohama five days earlier and was due to reach Los Angeles on the fourteenth.

"I'll bet you a dollar the liner never gets here," said Okumura enigmatically.

President Roosevelt—perhaps influenced by Dr. Jones or Baruch or both—had finally made up his mind to send a personal message to the Emperor. Drafted by the White House, it reminded the Emperor that almost a century previously another President of the United States, Millard Fillmore, had sent a personal message to the Emperor of Japan offering friendship. After years of peace, war threatened because of the Japanese occupation of southern Indochina, and the people of the Philippines, Malaya, Thailand and the Dutch Indies now feared they too would be taken over.

None of the peoples whom I have spoken of above can sit either indefinitely or permanently on a keg of dynamite.

There is absolutely no thought on the part of the United States of invading Indochina if every Japanese soldier or sailor were to be withdrawn therefrom.

I think that we can obtain the same assurance from the Governments of the East Indies, the Governments of Malaya and the Government of Thailand. I would even undertake to ask for the same assurance on the part of the Government of China. Thus a withdrawal of the Japanese forces from Indo-China would result in the assurance of peace throughout the whole of the South Pacific area.

I address myself to Your Majesty at this moment in the fervent hope that Your Majesty may, as I am doing, give thought in this definite emergency to ways of dispelling the dark clouds. I am confident that both of us, for the sake of the peoples not only of our own great countries but for the sake of humanity in neighboring territories, have a sacred duty to restore traditional amity and prevent further death and destruction in the world.

He signed the letter "Franklin D. Roosevelt" and sent it to Hull along with a handwritten note:

> Dear Cordell: Shoot this to Grew—I think can go in gray code —saves time—I don't mind if it gets picked up.
>
> F.D.R.

At about 7:40 P.M. the State Department announced to the press that the President was sending a personal message to the Emperor, and the message itself was dispatched.

Secretary of War Henry Stimson was still in town at Woodley, his estate above Rock Creek Valley. He had decided not to go to Long Island for the weekend, since, as he wrote in his diary, the "atmosphere indicated that something was going to happen."

The U. S. Navy cryptographers were more industrious than the cipher staff at the Japanese embassy and by 8:30 P.M. all thirteen parts of the Togo message were typed and ready for distribution. Realizing how important it was, Commander Kramer began phoning those who should get copies. "I have something important that I believe you should see at once," he told Navy Secretary Knox; he also called the Director of Naval Intelligence, the Director of the War Plans Division and the White House. One man on his list couldn't be reached—Admiral "Betty" Stark was not at his quarters on Observatory Circle.

A little after 9 P.M. Kramer left his office and was driven by his wife to the White House grounds. In the mailroom of the office building near the White House he handed over a locked letter pouch containing a copy of the message to the man on duty, Lieutenant Robert Lester Schulz.

Schulz brought the pouch to the President's study, where Roosevelt was sitting at his desk talking to Harry Hopkins. After Roosevelt read the thirteen parts he silently handed the papers to his adviser. When Hopkins finished reading, Roosevelt said, "This means war."

While Schulz waited they talked about the crisis. "Since war is undoubtedly going to come at the convenience of the Japanese," said Hopkins, "it's too bad we can't strike the first blow."

"No, we can't do that. We are a democracy and a peaceful people." Roosevelt raised his voice. "But we have a good record." He reached for the phone to call Stark, but when told he was at the National Theater, hung up and said, "I'll call Betty later; I don't want to cause public alarm by having him paged in a theater."

Stark was taking a rare night off. He was watching the perennial *Student Prince,* but it made so little impression on him that later he couldn't even remember where he'd been on the night of December 6. War was imminent but what puzzled him was where the Japanese would strike. The troop convoy heading into the Gulf of Siam suggested Singapore, but it could be the Philippines or the Panama Canal. In any case he didn't have to worry about Hawaii. The Joint Army-Navy Hawaiian Defense Plan for protection of Pearl Harbor against a surprise air attack was so good that he had sent it to all his district commanders as a model.

General Sherman Miles, chief of Military Intelligence, happened to be at a dinner party given by Captain Theodore S. Wilkinson, the Director of Naval Intelligence, and he too read the thirteen parts. But to Miles they had "little military significance" and he was not particularly apprehensive. He phoned Colonel Bratton, his Far Eastern expert, and told him there was "no reason for alerting or waking up" General Marshall, who was spending a quiet evening at his quarters in Fort Myers with his wife. Miles went off to bed so unconcerned he didn't plan to go to his office the next morning.

It was past midnight, the first minutes of December 7. Some high officials were still awake, wondering when the Japanese would jump—and where. Not one—Roosevelt, Hull, Stimson, Knox, Marshall or Stark—expected it could be Pearl Harbor.

In Oahu it was still early Saturday evening. Like Marshall and Stark, the Army and Navy commanders of Hawaii had no worry of an air attack on Pearl Harbor. General Walter Short was on the *lanai* of his home at Fort Shafter holding an emergency meeting with his intelligence and counterintelligence officers. They were discussing the transcript of a telephone conversation monitored by the FBI from a local Japanese dentist to a Tokyo paper. Its editor had a strange curiosity about Hawaii: planes, searchlights, weather, even the flowers. Had the dentist-correspondent's remark that the hibiscus and poinsettia were in bloom any significance? Was it some code?

For almost an hour the general's wife had been waiting impatiently outside in a car, and at last Short told his visitors that nothing could be done until morning and joined his wife. It was fifteen miles to the Schofield Barracks Officers Club, which was putting on a special benefit show that Saturday night. They would have to hurry.

Admiral Kimmel was trying to relax at a private dinner party at Honolulu's "House Without a Key," but he was a dynamic, dedicated man who was only content when working. At nine-thirty he excused himself after drinking his usual single cocktail. He wanted to get to bed. He was to play golf in the morning with General Short, which belied the gossip that they were not on speaking terms. It would be one of the rare Sundays the admiral didn't spend at his desk.

Both Kimmel and Short were of the opinion that constant alerts were unnecessary. Warnings from Washington had not specifically implied any air attack on Pearl Harbor even as a remote possibility. Kimmel was prepared for submarine attacks; Short was ready for saboteurs. Neither had been significantly concerned by reports that the Japanese consulate in Honolulu had been burning papers the past two days and the Joint Army-Navy Hawaiian Defense Plan—the one so admired by "Betty" Stark—was not in effect on the night of December 6. In fact, normal peacetime liberty had been granted to men and officers that evening.

Only routine and limited air patrols were planned for the next morning; and aircraft batteries in the Pearl Harbor area were lightly manned. Most of the men aboard the ninety-four ships moored in the harbor, except the watch crews, were getting ready for bed. It was just another lazy, uneventful tropical evening.

The FBI agents who had so assiduously been tracking the innocent dentist still had no suspicion that a minor official at the Japanese consul, Tadashi Morimura, was actually an Imperial Navy secret agent named Yoshikawa. That night he was working late at the consulate on his final report. He had already cabled Tokyo a few hours earlier that he did not believe the battleships had antitorpedo nets and there was no barrage-balloon equipment near Pearl Harbor.

> . . . IN ADDITION, IT IS DIFFICULT TO IMAGINE THAT THEY HAVE ACTUALLY ANY. HOWEVER, EVEN THOUGH THEY HAVE ACTUALLY MADE PREPARATIONS, BECAUSE THEY MUST CONTROL THE AIR OVER THE WATER AND LAND RUNWAYS OF THE AIRPORTS IN THE VICINITY OF PEARL HARBOR, HICKAM, FORD AND EWA, THERE ARE LIMITS TO THE BALLOON DEFENSE OF PEARL HARBOR. I IMAGINE THAT IN ALL PROBABILITY THERE IS CONSIDERABLE OPPORTUNITY LEFT TO TAKE ADVANTAGE OF A SURPRISE ATTACK AGAINST THESE PLACES. . . .

Now he was at his desk writing that the following ships had just been observed at anchor: nine battleships, three light cruisers, three submarine tenders and seventeen destroyers, as well as four light cruisers and two destroyers at docks. Then he added that the heavy cruiser and carriers had left port and that it appeared "no air reconnaissance is being conducted by the fleet arm."

He buzzed for the radio-room code clerk, gave him the message and went for a stroll around the spacious consulate grounds. In the distance he could see a bright haze over Pearl Harbor but could hear no patrol planes. He went off to bed.

Tatsuta-maru, the passenger ship en route to Los Angeles, should have been near Hawaii at that moment but it had already, to the puzzlement and concern of its passengers, swung around and was heading back home. First Secretary Okumura was going to win his dollar bet with correspondent Kato.

In Manila, it was late afternoon of December 7. It had been a hot, clear day. Here apprehension was greater than in either Washington or Hawaii, for the Philippines could be a battlefront any minute. Unidentified aircraft were again reported over Clark Field.

That night the 27th Bombardment Group was giving a mammoth welcome party at the Manila Hotel in honor of Major General Lewis H. Brereton, commander of MacArthur's recently established Far East Air Force. It was a gala affair long to be remembered as "the best entertainment this side of Minsky's." But the guest of honor's mind was on war and his sadly inadequate air force. During the party Admiral Hart's chief of staff told him, "It's only a question of days or perhaps hours until the shooting starts," and a moment later MacArthur's chief of staff said the War Department believed hostilities might begin at any time.

As a precaution Brereton phoned his own chief of staff and told him to put all airfields on combat alert. Fortunately heavy air reinforcements were on the way. One convoy, carrying fifty-two dive bombers and two regiments of artillery as well as ammunition, was due January 4. In addition, thirty Flying Fortresses would arrive in a few days and almost double his puny force. Twelve had already taken off from California and would land at Hickam Field, next door to Pearl Harbor, soon after dawn.

At Clark Field, fifty air miles to the northwest, sixteen Flying Fortresses were lined up ready for flight. The wide field, rimmed by a few trees and waist-high cogon grass, was honeycombed with revetments, foxholes and slit trenches. To the northeast, cone-shaped Mount Arayat, named after the final resting place of Noah's Ark, rose dramatically out of the plains, weird and unworldly in the moonlight.

In a nearby barracks Staff Sergeant Frank Trammell was trying to contact his wife Norma in San Bernardino, California, by ham radio. It was queer. The air was dead. All he could raise was a city he was forbidden to talk to—Singapore.

This 220-square-mile island was sixteen hundred miles to the southwest, about the same distance and direction as a flight from New York to New Orleans. It was the keystone of the Allied defense system in Asia and if it fell, not only Malaya but all of the rich Dutch East Indies with its oil, tin and rubber would be lost.

That night the probing fingers of searchlights lit the sky above Singapore. Great 15-inch guns protected its sea approaches. And in the sprawling naval base—a labor of twenty years at the cost of £60,000,000—were moored the two mighty warships so feared by Council President Hara—*Repulse* and *Prince of Wales*.

The code warning "Raffles" had just been signaled throughout the Malayan Command, and British, Australian and Indian soldiers were standing to arms, prepared and confident. Singapore was an impregnable fortress.

About 1,650 miles to the north-northeast was Great Britain's other fortress in Southeast Asia, Hong Kong. This island was just a few minutes' ride by ferry from the mainland of southern China. Its 11,319 defenders were on the alert.

By midnight the spacious harbor—except for its usual patchy regatta of ketches, proas, junks and sampans—was almost empty. The previous night, pages had ranged the bars and ballrooms of hotels telling all officers and men of the merchant marine to report to their ships. The announcement about the Japanese convoy in the Gulf of Siam signified one thing alone in Hong Kong: the balloon had gone up. But, like Singapore, Hong Kong was ready and confident.

From Washington to Hong Kong it was expected that Japan would probably strike in hours. But in many places "readiness" was merely a word. Few were actually prepared for the brutal reality of war. And not one was yet aware of the detailed, ingenious Japanese plan of attack which was about to be loosed from Pearl Harbor to Singapore.

It had been a bright, warm, pleasant Sunday in Tokyo, but to Otto Tolischus it was "ominously quiet" and everyone in Japan "seemed to be waiting for something." He spent most of the day at his typewriter working on an article about Ambassador Grew for the *New York Times Magazine.* The old cry against "foreign barbarians," he wrote, was being revived now that the Japanese had learned all they could from the Occident about warfare.

. . . As a result the long-predicted war between the white and yellow races in general, and war between Japan and the United States in particular, has become an imminent possibility, and whether it shall become a grim reality is now the great issue being decided in Tokyo and Washington.

Tolischus read over what he had written. It sounded a little strong, but he decided to let it stand and sent it by messenger to Grew for approval.

It was not the imminence of war but the possible discovery of the secret attacks which concerned Japan's leaders that Sunday. Just before noon a cable reported that the convoy heading for the Malay Peninsula across the Gulf of Siam had been sighted by a British flying boat. A few minutes later it was learned that an

Army fighter pilot had shot down the British plane. But had the flying boat had time to radio back the information?*

Roosevelt's personal bid for peace—his letter to the Emperor— reached Tokyo at noon; however, a recent general directive would automatically hold it up for ten hours. The previous day Lieutenant Colonel Morio Tomura of the Army General Staff had phoned his friend Tateki Shirao, the censor for the Ministry of Communications, instructing him to delay all foreign cables on an alternating schedule of ten hours one day, five hours the next. Sunday, December 7, happened to be the day scheduled for ten hours.

Ambassador Grew first heard of the message from the daily San Francisco news broadcast but didn't receive it until ten-thirty in the evening despite its TRIPLE PRIORITY stamp. He was justifiably annoyed. It was fifteen minutes past midnight when Grew, decoded message in hand, arrived at Togo's official residence. He told the Foreign Minister that he had a personal message from Roosevelt to the Emperor and read it aloud.

Togo promised "to study the document" and "present the matter to the Throne." As soon as Grew left, Togo phoned Imperial Household Minister Tsuneo Matsudaira and asked if the Emperor could be disturbed at such a late hour. He was told to call Kido, since a message from the President was political, not ceremonial. Togo phoned the Privy Seal at his home in Akasaka. Kido said that under these circumstances His Majesty could be roused "even in the dead of night," and promised to leave for the Palace at once.

Togo drove to the Prime Minister's official residence. Does the message contain any concessions? was Tojo's first question. The answer was no. "Well, then, nothing can be done, can it?" Tojo remarked, but had no objection to Togo taking the letter to the Emperor. Together the two worked out a reply, which amounted to a polite refusal, and Togo got up to leave. "It's a pity to run around disturbing people in the middle of the night," he joked.

"It's a good thing the telegram arrived late," said Tojo, and he

---

* They must also have been jolted by an article by a retired admiral in Saturday night's edition of the *Japan Times & Advertiser*. The author boasted that U. S. naval authorities were "apparently talking in delirium when they say it is improbable for Japan to extend its activities to Hawaii, and that such an attempt is bound to end in failure."

was probably being facetious. "If it had come a day or two earlier we would have had more of a to-do."

Togo found Kido waiting for him at the Palace. "There's no use, is there?" said the Privy Seal upon learning what was in the message. "What's Tojo's opinion?"

"The same as yours."

5.

About the time Grew received the Roosevelt telegram, Commander Kramer was at his office in the Navy Department reading the fourteenth part of the message to Hull breaking off negotiations. It was 8 A.M., December 7, in Washington.

The entire fourteen parts were assembled, put in folders, and once more Kramer began his delivery rounds. By 10:20 he was back in his own office. Another important message was on the desk. It was the telegram from Togo to Nomura marked URGENT—VERY IMPORTANT, ordering the admiral to submit the entire message to Hull at 1 P.M.

While it was being put in folders Kramer hastily made a timezone circle and discovered that 1 P.M. would be 7:30 A.M. in Hawaii. Having spent two years at Pearl Harbor, he knew this was the normal time for the piping of the crew to Sunday breakfast—a very quiet time indeed. Disturbed, he headed down the corridors of the sprawling Navy Building for Admiral Stark's office.

On Massachusetts Avenue the Japanese were in a state approaching disorder. The cipher staff had returned to work after the farewell party and numerous *sake* toasts to finish the thirteen parts before midnight, then waited impatiently hour after hour for the final part. Finally at dawn everyone but a duty officer went home. About an hour later a bundle of cables arrived. One was Part Fourteen, sent from Tokyo by both Mackay and RCA and marked VERY IMPORTANT in plain English.

The duty officer called his colleagues, but it was almost 10 A.M. before the cipher crew was back on the job, grumbling about lost sleep. In the meantime First Secretary Okumura was slowly, labo-

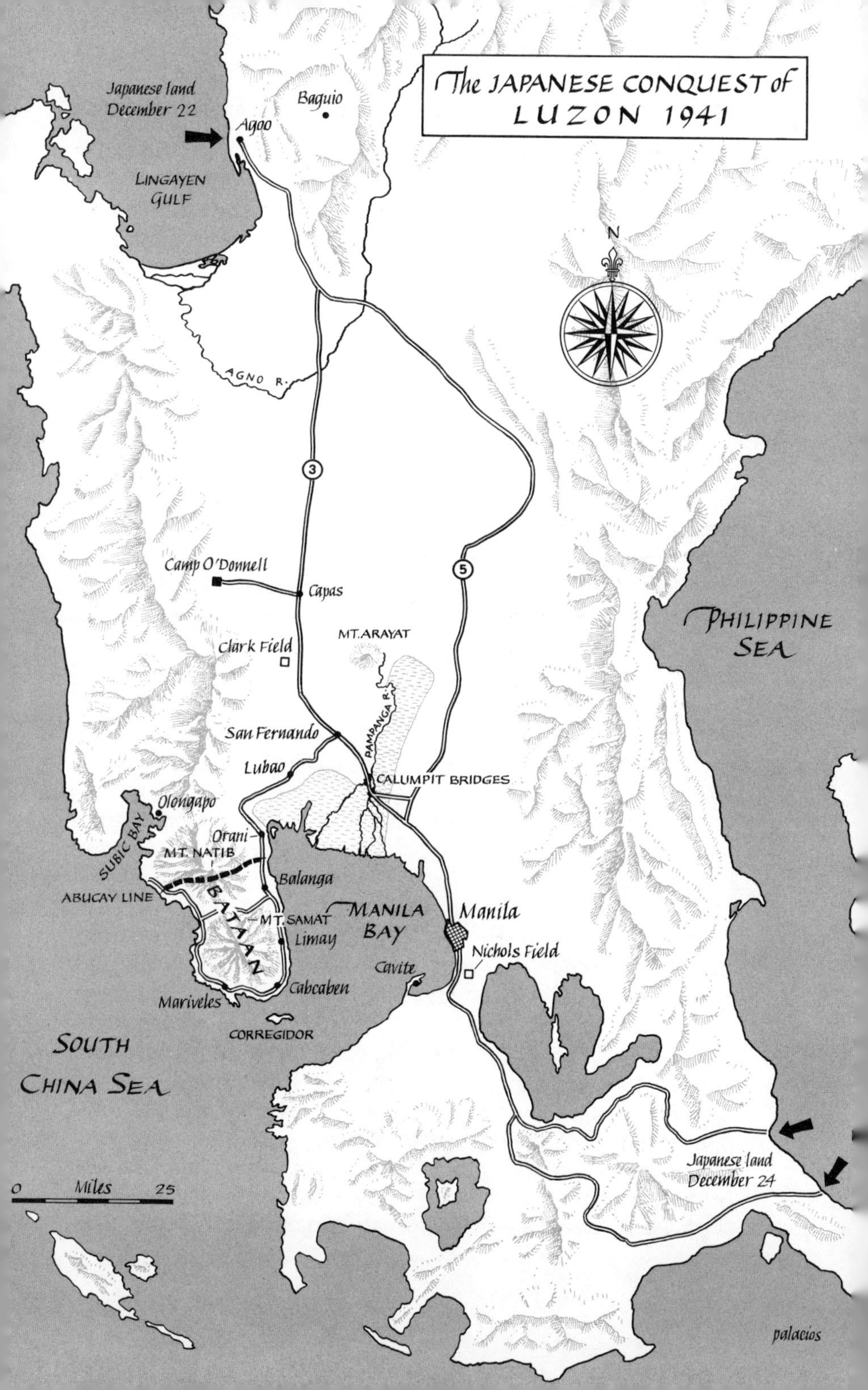
The JAPANESE CONQUEST of LUZON 1941
Japanese land December 22
Agoo
Baguio
LINGAYEN GULF
N
AGNO R.
3
5
Camp O'Donnell
Capas
Clark Field
MT. ARAYAT
PHILIPPINE SEA
San Fernando
PAMPANGA R.
Lubao
CALUMPIT BRIDGES
Olongapo
SUBIC BAY
Orani
MT. NATIB
Balanga
ABUCAY LINE
BATAAN
MT. SAMAT
MANILA BAY
Manila
Limay
Nichols Field
Cavite
Cabcaben
Mariveles
CORREGIDOR
SOUTH CHINA SEA
Japanese land December 24
0 Miles 25
palacios

riously tapping away at a typewriter in an attempt to get a clean copy of the message. But he was an amateur typist, and though he had been laboring for two hours, he was far from finished.

It wasn't until 10:30 that Nomura was reading the decoded instructions to hand the entire message to Hull at 1 P.M. He hadn't yet read the fourteenth part, which had arrived three and a half hours earlier but was yet to be deciphered. He hastily phoned Hull's office to set up the appointment. Sorry, was the reply, Secretary Hull had a luncheon engagement. "It is a matter of extreme importance," the admiral said urgently—and if not Hull, how about his undersecretary? After a pause he was told that Hull himself would be available.

A few minutes later Okumura finally finished his bumbling typing of the first thirteen parts, but the eleven pages of typescript were so full of erasures that he decided it would never do as an official Japanese document. He started to redo the whole thing, this time with the assistance of another amateur typist, a junior interpreter. Despite everything, Okumura felt sure that he could finish the entire document in time for the one o'clock appointment.

When Nomura was calling Hull, young Kramer stepped into Stark's office. The admiral, who had just returned from a leisurely walk around the grounds and greenhouses of his quarters, was engrossed in the fourteen-part message. While waiting in the outer office, Kramer pointed out to a colleague the possible significance of the one o'clock time with reference to Hawaii.

At last Stark finished the long message and then read the "one o'clock" note. "Why don't you pick up the telephone and call Admiral Kimmel?" an intelligence man suggested. Stark reached for the phone but decided his "war warning" of November 27 was enough to keep everyone on his toes. Besides, a raid on Pearl Harbor seemed most unlikely. He said he'd rather call the President and dialed the White House. The President's line was busy.

Even the fourteenth part had failed to alarm Colonel Bratton, but a glance at the "one o'clock" note sent him into "frenzied" action. Convinced that "the Japanese were going to attack some American installation," he literally ran to his chief's office. General Miles was at home. So was Marshall. Without going through channels, Bratton phoned Marshall's quarters just across the Potomac.

An orderly, Sergeant Aquirre, said the Chief of Staff had just left for his Sunday horseback ride.

Marshall had risen as usual at 6:30 A.M. but dawdled over breakfast with his wife, their first together in a week. They lived a restful, rather monastic life, since he had already collapsed twice from ill health. "I cannot allow myself to get angry, that would be fatal—it is too exhausting," he had recently told Mrs. Marshall. "My brain must be kept clear."

Unaware of the message which had meant "war" to the President the night before, he was heading at a lively gait toward the government experimental farm, the site of the future Pentagon Building. Ordinarily he rode for about an hour, but this time he took longer while Aquirre was searching for him in vain. By the time Marshall returned home to get the sergeant's message, it was 10:25. He phoned Bratton, but the latter was so circumspect in explaining the "most important message" that the Chief of Staff didn't realize its urgency. Marshall showered, sent for his limousine parked across the river at the Munitions Building and wasn't at his desk until a few minutes after 11 o'clock. He methodically read through the entire message, as unimpressed as Bratton. But, like Bratton, he was jolted by the implications of the "one o'clock" note. Using a yellow pad, he hastily jotted down a dispatch to his Pacific commanders:

The Japanese are presenting at 1 P.M. Eastern Standard Time today what amounts to an ultimatum. Also they are under orders to destroy their code machine immediately.

Just what significance the hour set may have we do not know, but be on the alert accordingly.

He phoned Stark. "What do you think about sending the information concerning the time of presentation to the Pacific commanders?"

"We've sent them so much already, I hesitate to send any more. A new one will be merely confusing."

Marshall hung up. Moments later the phone rang.

"George," Stark began in a concerned voice, "there might be some peculiar significance in the Japanese ambassador calling on

"This War May Come Quicker Than Anyone Dreams" 255

Hull at one P.M. I'll go along with you in sending that information to the Pacific." He offered the Navy's transmission facilities, which, he said, were very fast in emergencies.

"No, thanks, Betty, I feel I can get it through quickly enough."

"George, will you include instructions to your people to inform their naval opposites?"

Marshall said he would, and added a sentence to that effect on the yellow sheet. He marked it "First Priority—Secret," and ordered it rushed to the Message Center for transmission to the Panama Canal, the Philippines, Hawaii and San Francisco, in that order of priority. Concerned about time, he sent an officer several times to find out how long it would take to deliver the message. "It's already in the works. Will take maybe thirty to forty minutes to be delivered" was the reassuring answer from Colonel Edward French, chief of Traffic Operations. Marshall didn't consider using the direct scrambler telephone, since it could be easily tapped and the Japanese might deduce that their "unbreakable" code had been broken.

The message was enciphered and a few minutes after 12 noon in Washington, the commanders in San Francisco, the Panama Canal and the Philippines were warned. But Hawaii could not be raised because of atmospheric conditions. There was still, of course, the Navy's direct radio communications to Hawaii, but for some reason Colonel French eschewed the "very fast" facilities of the rival service for Western Union, which didn't have a direct line to Honolulu. The message wasn't even marked "Urgent."

The Combined Fleet, at anchor off the beautiful little islet Hashirajima, was on the alert, ready to sail from the Inland Sea to the aid of *Kido Butai* if necessary. Yamamoto had already issued his final order, an exact duplicate of Admiral Togo's message at Tsushima.

On *Nagato* there was a calm sense of watchful waiting. The earlier concern about the discovery of the Malay convoy was obviously groundless. As usual Yamamoto played Japanese chess with Commander Yasuji Watanabe. His mind was on the match and he won three of the five games. Afterward both men bathed and returned to the staff room. Then Yamamoto retired to his own cabin, where he composed a *waka,* a thirty-one-syllable poem:

> *It is my sole wish to serve the Emperor as His shield
> I will not spare my honor or my life.*

There were, in fact, two Japanese forces approaching Pearl Harbor. The second was a fleet of submarines. Eleven boats had taken the great-circle route and were converging on Oahu—four northeast of the island and seven in the channel between Oahu and Molokai. Nine others had come from the Marshalls and seven of these were lying just south of Oahu while the other two were nearing Maui to discover if the American fleet could possibly be at Lahaina.

Five other submarines, the Special Attack Unit, had surfaced under cover of darkness and had silently approached Pearl Harbor from the southwest. Each carried piggyback a midget two-man submarine seventy-nine feet long, which could travel at the remarkable speed of 20 knots submerged. The midgets were to steal into the channel, lie in wait off Battleship Row until the air attack started, then surface and launch their twin torpedoes at some capital ship. At first Yamamoto had canceled the raid on the grounds that it was suicidal. He finally relented when assured that every attempt would be made to recover the crews.

Just before 11 P.M., December 6, local time, the mother ships had stopped about eight miles off Pearl Harbor, and the tricky launching process began. Those on the decks of the submarines could see bright lights along the shore and even pick out neon signs on Waikiki Beach. Across the water came faint sounds of jazz. Minutes later four of the midgets were launched, but the fifth's gyrocompass would not work. It could not be repaired, but the two-man crew insisted on carrying out their mission. They climbed into their tiny boat. The mother ship dived, the securing clamps were cast off, and the midget started slowly for Pearl Harbor.

Kido Butai was racing full steam at 24 knots toward the launching point, two hundred miles north of Pearl Harbor. The men were at general quarters; the gun crews ready to fire at anything in sight. The pilots and crews had been routed from their bunks at 3:30 A.M., December 7, Hawaiian time. They had already written last letters and left in their lockers fingernail clippings and snips of hair for their families. They put on clean *mawashi* (loincloths) and "thousand-stitch" belts.* For breakfast they were served an extra treat, red rice and *tai,* a red snapper eaten at times of celebration.

The ships were rolling so badly that some waves swept onto the decks of the carriers. Because of this, the torpedo pilots were told they could not go in the first attack but must wait for the second, when it would be completely light. To no avail the pilots grumbled that after all their hard training they could take off in the predawn murk, no matter how rough the seas were.

Nagumo was still concerned about Lahaina, despite reassurance from a submarine on the spot and a message from Combined Fleet that the Pacific Fleet, except for the carriers, was at Pearl Harbor. He ordered search planes to make a last-minute reconnaissance. An hour before first light *Chikuma* and *Tone*—the two heavy cruisers leading the fleet, and only 150 miles from Pearl Harbor—each catapulted a pair of seaplanes into the light wind. Two of the planes started for Lahaina, two for Pearl Harbor. Their instructions were to get to their destinations half an hour before the attack and radio back reports on clouds, the speed and direction of the wind, and most important, where the Pacific Fleet really was.

Some 6,600 miles to the west, a large convoy was closing in on the Malay Peninsula in three sections. The main force, fourteen ships, headed for Singora. To its left, three ships approached Pattani. Farther to the left, another three transports were bound for Kota Bharu; they were the first to reach their destination, and at midnight, Tokyo time, they dropped anchor just off the city. There was a moon, but fortunately for the invaders it was covered by clouds. There was little pitch and roll, and everything augured well for an easy landing. Then, at 1:15 A.M., the transports' naval escort began bombarding the coast, the signal for the landing.

The war in the Pacific had started by mistake. It was only 5:45 A.M. in Hawaii. Originally Genda and Commander Miyo of the Navy General Staff had agreed to hit Pearl Harbor just before

---

* A bellyband worn as a good-luck charm. Mothers, wives or sisters would stand on street corners and ask passers-by to add their stitch to the belt until it had one thousand. This meant each belt contained a thousand prayers for good luck and a good fight.

dawn. But so many pilots complained of the hazard in taking off in pitch-dark that at the last moment Genda delayed the first strike by about two hours. Miyo had not learned of this until several days after *Kido Butai* left Hitokappu Bay and took it upon himself to remain silent because a change in schedule at that stage might not reach all commands. He accepted the entire responsibility for his decision and did not even tell Vice Admiral Ito that an attack might very well come in the Malay Peninsula ahead of time. "I was resigned to leave our fate to Heaven."

And so the Kota Bharu force began the war between East and West, between white and yellow, two hours and fifteen minutes before the first bombs were scheduled to drop on Hawaii. The question was: Would the British report the attack in time to alert Pearl Harbor?

At the first shot of war the carriers of *Kido Butai* had just slipped across the launching point and were not quite two hundred miles north of Pearl Harbor. The first faint light of day glimmered in the east. Pilots and flight crews strapped themselves into their planes; motors roared. In the sky were patches of clouds. Long heavy swells rolled the ships from 12 to 15 degrees. Maneuvers were usually canceled when swells exceeded 5 degrees, but today there could be no postponement.

Admiral Kusaka ordered the Z flag raised above *Akagi*. This was an exact copy of the one Togo had used at Tsushima, but in the intervening years it had become an ordinary tactical signal. Kusaka was sure that every man in the Striking Force would realize its symbolic significance, but several staff officers, including Genda, protested when they saw it go up. It would cause confusion. Reluctantly Kusaka revoked the command and ordered another flag raised that vaguely resembled Togo's signal.

The minute the sailors on *Kaga* saw the Z flag they excitedly hoisted their own. It was going to be another Tsushima! Then, inexplicably, *Akagi*'s flag fluttered down, and with it some of their enthusiasm.

On the decks of the six carriers, the planes of the first wave were lined up, with forty-three fighter planes in the van, followed by forty-nine high-level and fifty-one dive bombers, and forty torpedo planes in the rear—at the last moment it was decided to let them risk takeoff in the predawn gloom.

At the head of *Kaga*'s fighters was Lieutenant (s.g.) Yoshio Shiga, the amateur painter. He was champing, hoping to be the first to take off. He beckoned to one of his ground-crew men and told him to yank out the chocks at his own command—not to wait, as usual, for the flagman's signal.

On the bridge Chief Aviation Officer Naohiro Sata told the carrier captain, "Planes are ready," and the skipper turned *Kaga* into the wind. A triangular pennant with a white circle on a red background was run halfway up the mast of the command ship, *Akagi*. In this position, the aviation flag meant "Get ready for takeoff." Then it was hoisted to the top of the mast. Commander Sata was watching it from *Kaga;* when it was lowered he would give a hand signal to drop *Kaga*'s aviation flag.

Lieutenant Shiga was not watching his own carrier's flag. He had his eyes glued on *Akagi*'s. It dropped. He shouted, "Remove chocks!" and roared down the runway. *Kaga*'s captain was leaning out a window, expecting to see the usual courtesy salute, but Shiga was too intent on getting into the air before anyone else. His Type Zero* plunged off the deck, dropped precipitously to within 15 feet of the sea. He turned left and climbed, noticing with dismay that the first fighter pilot on *Akagi*, Lieutenant Commander Shigeru Itaya, had beaten him by a few seconds. He had not waited for his flagman either. Shiga took his time in the turn so that his squadron could catch up, then joined Itaya, who was commanding all the fighters. They streaked south in loose formation like a flock of swallows.

Behind them the high-level medium bombers were taking off. Squadron leader Heijiro Abe was in the first Mitsubishi to leave *Soryu*. Contrary to American practice, he was not the pilot but the navigator-bombardier. Concerned about the roll and pitch of the carrier, he looked back anxiously into the dimness as the others followed. To his relief all his planes were soon in a precise V formation behind the fighters. Next the Aichi Type 99 dive bombers got off the runway and joined up.

The takeoff of the Nakajima Type 97 torpedo bombers was

---

* The name came from the date of the plane's origin, 1940, the 2,600th year of Japanese recorded history.

the most hazardous, and putting them in the initial wave while it was still partially dark was a gamble. The first off *Hiryu* was squadron leader Hirata Matsumura. When he plunged from the deck it was like being sucked into a dark pit. He fought his way up to 500 feet and was immediately engulfed in dense clouds. He broke through into the open, then veered left. Once his men had collected, he met the *Soryu* torpedo planes, and together they tagged after the *Akagi* and *Kaga* planes at 13,000 feet. The entire launching had taken no more than fifteen minutes—a record—and a single aircraft, a Zero fighter, had crashed.

Up ahead, Shiga looked back upon a great straggling formation. Never before had he seen so many planes. Half an hour after the takeoff a huge, brilliant sun rose to the left. It was the first time Juzo Mori, a young torpedo pilot—son of a farmer—had ever seen a sunrise from the air. The planes ahead were etched in black silhouette against the red, and it was such a romantic, incongruous sight that he could not believe he was heading for Japan's most important battle. To Lieutenant Matsumura, the sunrise was a sacred sight; it marked the dawn of a new century.

In Pearl Harbor it was 6:30 A.M. The antitorpedo net across the entrance to Pearl Harbor was open for an approaching vessel, the target ship *Antares*. Outside the entrance to the harbor Lieutenant William Outerbridge, the young skipper of the destroyer *Ward,* had just been roused from his bunk, and wearing glasses and a Japanese kimono, was peering off the port bow at *Antares* in the murky light. It was towing a raft into Pearl Harbor. Outerbridge saw something else following. It looked like a submarine's conning tower. "Go to general quarters," he shouted. Just then *Antares* blinkered confirmation: "Small sub 1,500 yards off starboard quarter."

Ward closed to a hundred yards and fired Number 1 gun at point-blank range. It missed. Number 3 gun fired, hit the conning tower and the midget began to sink. While the crew was still cheering, Outerbridge shouted, "Drop depth charges!" The destroyer's whistle blasted four times and four charges rolled off the stern.

At 6:51 A.M. Outerbridge radioed the 14th Naval District: WE HAVE DROPPED DEPTH CHARGES ON SUB OPERATING IN DEFENSIVE AREA. Then, deciding this message wasn't strong enough, sent an-

"This War May Come Quicker Than Anyone Dreams" 261

other two minutes later: WE HAVE ATTACKED FIRED UPON AND DROPPED DEPTH CHARGES UPON SUBMARINE OPERATING IN DEFENSIVE SEA AREA.

Because of delay in decoding, the second message didn't reach Admiral Kimmel's chief of staff, Captain John B. Earle, until 7:12 A.M. A few minutes later Admiral Claude C. Bloch read it and said, "What do you know about it?"

Earle was dubious. "We get so many of these false sightings. We can't go off half-cocked."

Bloch saw his point. In the past few months there'd been a dozen such sub warnings—all false. "Ask this to be verified."

At almost this same moment another warning was being reported to the Army—and also discounted—from the Opana outpost at Kahuku Point on the northern tip of Oahu. Private George Elliott, Jr., of the 515th Signal Aircraft Warning Service, a recent transfer from the Air Corps, had seen a large blip on his radar unit at 7:06 A.M. He called over Private Joseph Lockard, who had much more experience. It was the largest group Lockard had ever seen on the oscilloscope and looked like two main pulses. He figured something had gone wrong with the machine, but after a check agreed with Elliott that it was really a large flight of planes.

By now Elliott had located the blip on the plotting board: 137 miles to the north, 3 degrees east. He was so excited that he suggested they call the Information Center at Fort Shafter. At first Lockard was reluctant but finally let his assistant make the call. The switchboard operator at the Information Center could find no one on duty except a pilot named Kermit Tyler. When told that the blips were getting bigger and that the planes were now only ninety miles from Oahu, Tyler said, "Don't worry about it," and hung up—the blips must represent the flight of Flying Fortresses coming in from the mainland or planes from a carrier.

In Washington it was 12:30 P.M. and Nomura was frantic. In thirty minutes he was to see Hull, and the fourteenth part of the note had just been deciphered and turned over to Okumura for typing. This harried man and his inept assistant were still punching away at the first thirteen parts. The confusion had been compounded when two "correction" messages were received: one amending a single word, and the other announcing that a sentence had been dropped in transmission. The first meant the retyping of one page, and the second, two pages.

As the minutes ticked away, Nomura returned to the doorway again and again, pleading with Okumura and his helper to hurry. The pressure created more mistakes. Already it was obvious that the envoys would be at least an hour late.

A Japanese floatplane from *Tone* was above Lahaina Roads and another from *Chikuma* was almost directly over Pearl Harbor. No one on the ground noticed either plane. Nor was any communications man listening when the plane over Lahaina radioed back to *Kido Butai* in simple code at exactly 7:35 A.M.:

ENEMY'S FLEET NOT AT LAHAINA 0305.

A moment later came another:

ENEMY'S FLEET IN PEARL HARBOR.

This was about "the most delightful message" Kusaka had ever received. Right on its heels came a third report: there were some clouds over Oahu, but the sky over Pearl Harbor was "absolutely clear."

Togo had just arrived at the Palace grounds. Stars shone brilliantly. It was going to be a fine day. The Foreign Minister was immediately ushered into the Emperor's presence. It was almost at the exact moment Nomura and Kurusu were supposed to see Hull. Togo read Roosevelt's message and the proposed draft of the Emperor's reply. The Emperor approved the reply, and his countenance, Togo thought, reflected "a noble feeling of brotherhood with all peoples."

The spacious plaza outside the Sakashita Gate was deserted, and as Togo drove away, the sole noise in the city was the crunching of gravel under the car tires. His mind was far away: in a few minutes one of the most momentous days in the history of the world would begin.

PART THREE

Banzai!

8

"I Shall Never Look Back"

1.

The first Zeros approached the northern tip of Oahu, Kahuku Point, at 7:48 A.M. Through clouds below him Lieutenant Yoshio Shiga, leader of the *Kaga* fighters, could barely make out a jut of land and a rim of white surf. A moment later he saw Fuchida's high-level command bomber and awaited a blue flare, the attack signal for the fighter planes, which were without radios. Those in the bombers were tuned in to a local Honolulu station. They heard the haunting strains of a Japanese song.

Banks of cumulus clouds clung to the peaks of the mountain ranges east and west of Pearl Harbor, but over the great naval base, lying in a valley between, the clouds were scattered. The sun shone brightly, its slanting rays giving the cane fields a deep-green hue. The waters of Pearl Harbor—originally named Wai Momi, "water of pearl"—glimmered a brilliant blue. Several civilian planes were lazily circling over the area, but of all the Oahu-based Army planes, not one was airborne. They were tightly bunched together, wing to wing, for security against saboteurs at Hickam, Bellows and Wheeler fields. So were the Marine planes at Ewa Field. The only American military planes in the air were seven Navy PBY's on patrol many miles to the southwest.

Antiaircraft defense was also off-guard. Three quarters of the 780 AA guns on the ships in Pearl Harbor were unmanned, and only four of the Army's 31 AA batteries were in position—and their ready ammunition had been returned to depots after practice, since it was "apt to disintegrate and get dusty."

Upon reaching Kahuku Point, Fuchida's plane—he was the observer—began circling around the west coast of Oahu to approach Pearl Harbor. At exactly 7:49 A.M. Fuchida radioed back to *Kido Butai* in Morse code: TO . . . TO . . . TO . . . This represented the first syllable of *Totsugeki!* (Charge!) and meant: "First wave attacking." As Fuchida neared the target, he was faced with a tactical decision. If in his judgment the Americans were completely surprised, the torpedo planes would streak directly for Battleship Row; if not, the fighters would first have to eliminate any interceptors. The sky ahead was empty and peaceful. Before long, Pearl Harbor—legendary abode of the shark goddess Kaahupahau—was spread out below like a huge relief map. It looked exactly as he had imagined. Still not a single fighter climbed up to challenge, neither was there one mushroom puff of AA fire. It was incredible.

At 7:53 A.M. he radioed to Nagumo TORA, TORA, TORA! The repeated code word, meaning "tiger," stood for "We have succeeded in surprise attack." He set off one blue flare to signal that surprise had been achieved. The nearest fighter squadron leader failed to waggle his wings in acknowledgment and Fuchida fired a second flare. Shiga, who was some distance to the rear, thought this was the two-flare signal indicating that surprise had *not* been achieved and that he was to head directly for Hickam Field to clear the skies there of enemy interceptors. He shot through Kola Kola Pass, signaling the others with his right hand to get into attack formation. The leader of the fifty-one dive bombers, Lieutenant Commander Kakuichi Takahashi, also misinterpreted the second flare and veered off to knock out the AA guns protecting Pearl Harbor.

But the torpedo bombers were heading straight for their targets. Lieutenant Commander Shigeharu Murata, had not been confused by the second flare, and radioed his forty bombers to proceed as planned. By the time he saw the mix-up, so many torpedo planes

"I Shall Never Look Back"

were in attack formation that he decided to go ahead with the strike on Battleship Row.

The torpedo planes from *Soryu* were cutting directly across the island through Kola Kola Pass behind Shiga's fighters, and Lieutenant Mori could make out slit trenches in the mountain slopes. They're ready for us! he thought with a start. As he emerged from the pass he swooped down at 130 knots, just clearing the barracks and hangars of Wheeler Field. Scanning the runway, he guessed there were two hundred fighters packed in neat rows. He was stunned. He hastily calculated that with at least five airfields on Oahu, there would be a thousand enemy fighters.* His machine-gunner began strafing the parked planes—probably the first shots fired that morning—and then Mori made for Pearl Harbor.

Royal Vitousek, a Honolulu lawyer, and his seventeen-year-old son Martin were circling the island in the family Aeronca when they saw two Japanese fighter planes—undoubtedly Shiga's—approaching. Vitousek dived under the raiders and headed for his home field to make a report. He prayed the Japanese would ignore his little plane. Shiga kept zigzagging toward Pearl Harbor. It reminded him of a Japanese box garden. The American ships looked bluish white, unlike the gloomy gray of Japanese warships. How beautiful, he thought, like peace itself. In seconds he was past Pearl Harbor and over his target, Hickam Field. There wasn't a single enemy fighter in the air or taking off. The attack *was* a surprise! He looked around. Where were the torpedo bombers? Now was the time to strike.

Just then a dive bomber roared down on Ford Island, loosed a bomb and zoomed up. A cloud of heavy black smoke billowed out of a hangar. It would obscure nearby Battleship Row by the time the torpedo bombers got there, and Shiga thought angrily, What is that crazy helldiver doing?** To the west he saw a lazy line of torpedo planes. Why were they coming in so slowly? Like children trotting to school. They approached the big battleships moored along the southeast side of Ford Island. This was Battleship Row, seven warships anchored together in two rows—five

---

* To Lieutenant Mori, "all planes looked like fighters." There were 231 Army planes of all types on Oahu, and 88 of these were under repair.

** The Japanese Navy pilots were so impressed by an American movie, *Hell Divers*, starring Clark Gable, that they had adopted the name.

on the inside, two on the outside. The line of planes dumped their torpedoes like "dragonflies dropping their eggs" and arced away. There was a pause. Then a jarring explosion. The battleship *Oklahoma* shuddered. In seconds two more torpedoes tore into her side and she took a list of about 30 degrees.

The next group of torpedo planes was Lieutenant Matsumura's, from *Hiryu*. His first view of Pearl Harbor was a forest of masts against the garish rising sun. They'd made it! "Look for carriers!" he called through the voice tube to his observer. He dropped to 150 feet over a field of waving sugar cane. Helldivers were plunging down on Ford Island through clouds of smoke. *"Bakayaro!"* he muttered. How could they make such a mistake and obscure the main targets! Half a dozen planes converged on a big ship that looked like a carrier on the northwest side of Ford Island. "Damn fools," he repeated. "Who can they be?" Before takeoff he had warned his men to leave this one alone. It was merely the thirty-three-year-old target ship *Utah*, her stripped decks covered with planks.

He circled out above the sea and turned back over Hickam at 500 feet so he could come in on Battleship Row. His path cut across a long line of torpedo planes from *Kaga* and *Akagi*—several were ablaze from enemy fire but continued on to ram their targets. He'd have done the same thing, he thought, as he skimmed through towering fountains of water. He went down to less than 100 feet and started a run on one of the ships in the outside row—it was *West Virginia*. Usually the pilot alone released the torpedo, but today, to make doubly sure, most navigator-bombardiers were also pushing their release buttons. *"Yoi* [Ready]," he called over the tube. Then: *"Te!"* (Fire!) As the torpedo was launched, he pulled the stick back sharply. "Is the torpedo running straight?" he called to the navigator. He was afraid it might dig into the mud.

Matsumura pushed in the throttle, but instead of making the standard left turn, climbed to the right. He kept looking back to keep his torpedo in view. In the oily water he saw American sailors; they seemed to be crawling in glue. He banked further and saw a column of water geyser from *West Virginia*.

This one moment was worth all the hard months of training. "Take a picture!" he shouted to the navigator, who thought he said "Fire!" and ordered the machine-gunner to open up. "Did you get the picture?" asked Matsumura. Without comment the navigator took a picture—of someone else's column of water.

Lieutenant Mori, who had swept directly across Oahu, was still looking for a target. He hedgehopped over Ford Island, but finding only a cruiser on the other side, made a semicircle and came back just above the waves toward *California* at the southern end of Battleship Row. At the last moment a breakwater loomed between him and the target. He climbed, circling over *Utah,* which looked as if it had been twisted in two, again went down to 15 feet and came at *California* from a different angle. His radioman-gunner took a picture of the torpedo explosion as Mori prepared to make his left circle to the assembly point. But his path was barred by a heavy pillar of smoke at the end of Ford Island and he was forced to bank right directly into the oncoming torpedo planes from *Akagi* and *Kaga;* he narrowly missed collision and his plane rocked from the turbulence. Bullets ripped through Mori's plane "like hornets." One set the navigator's cushion on fire, another grazed the hand of the machine-gunner, but none hit the fuel tanks.

The high-level bombers were going after the inner row of battleships and anything else that looked tempting. The battleships were obscured by smoke at first, but on the second pass the first five *Soryu* planes were able to unload their 1,760-lb. bombs on the badly listing *Oklahoma.* Squadron leader Heijiro Abe snapped a picture as his bomb smashed between two gun turrets, penetrated into an ammunition room and exploded. Great tongues of flame blasted out of half a dozen holes in the ship. A flood of tears obscured Abe's vision. He was ready to die.

2.

Vitousek landed his Aeronca a quarter of an hour after the encounter with the two Zeros and phoned Army and Air Corps duty officers that he had seen Japs over Oahu. Nobody would believe him or even send out an alert.

The first bombs had already hit Wheeler Field a few minutes earlier, shortly after 7:50 A.M. Second Lieutenant Robert Overstreet of the 696th Aviation Ordnance Company, asleep in the two-story wooden BOQ (bachelor officers quarters), was awakened by a deep rumble. He thought it was an earthquake until he heard a voice shouting, "Looks like Jap planes!" and someone else saying, "Hell, no, it's just a Navy maneuver."

Then Overstreet's door opened and a friend looked in, face white and lips trembling: "I think Japs are attacking!" Overstreet peered out the window and saw olive-drab planes overhead. One roared by so close that he could see the pilot and a rear gunner. On the fuselage and wing tips were flaming-red suns. He finished dressing on the run and outside the barracks came upon a group of fighter pilots.

"We've got to get down to the line and tag some of those bastards," Lieutenant Harry Brown shouted. But the closely grouped planes on the ramp were already on fire. "Let's go to Haleiwa," he said. This was an auxiliary sod field on the north coast, where a few P-40's and P-36's were kept. Brown and several other fighter pilots piled into his new Ford convertible and careened off. Lieutenants George Welch and Kenneth Taylor were right behind in another car.

As bombs continued to fall, Overstreet pushed his way through a crowd milling in confusion toward the permanent quarters area. Brigadier General Howard C. Davidson, the fighter commandant, and Colonel William Flood, the base commander, were standing in pajamas by their front doors, staring up in the sky, faces aghast.

"Where's our Navy?" Flood muttered. "Where're our fighters?"

"General, we'd better get out of here!" Overstreet shouted. "Those planes have tail gunners." At that moment Davidson noticed to his horror that his ten-year-old twin daughters were roaming the lawn, picking up empty Japanese cartridges as if it were an Easter egg hunt. Davidson and his wife rounded up their children; then he set off for the ramp to get some of his planes in the air. But those salvaged from the flames had no ammunition and the ordnance building, containing a million rounds of machine-gun ammunition, was ablaze. All at once the big hangar was racked by salvos that sounded like an endless string of giant firecrackers.

Fifteen miles to the south, at Hickam Field, two aircraft mechanics were walking toward the flight line. Jesse Gaines and Ted Conway had gotten up early to get a look at the B-17's due from the States. They'd never seen a Flying Fortress. At 7:55 a V formation of planes appeared in the west. As they began to peel off,

"I Shall Never Look Back"

Conway said, "We're going to have an air show." Then Gaines noticed something fall from the first plane and guessed it was a wheel. "Wheel, hell—they're Japs!" cried Conway.

As Gaines said, "You're crazy," a bomb exploded among the closely packed planes. The two started for the three-storied barracks, "Hickam Hotel." Gaines saw some gas drums and ducked behind them for protection. He felt something kick him in the rear. "Don't you know better than that?" a grizzled sergeant barked. "Those damn drums are full!" Gaines headed for the ramp. Looking up, he saw bombs wobble down, each one aimed directly at him. He scrambled in terror, first one way, then another.

Colonel James Mollison, chief of staff of the Hawaiian Air Force, was shaving when he heard the first bombs fall. He dashed to his office and phoned Colonel Walter C. Phillips, General Short's chief of staff, that the Japanese were attacking.

"Jimmy, you're out of your mind," said Phillips. "Are you drunk? Wake up!" Mollison held up the receiver so that Phillips could hear the explosions. Phillips was convinced, in fact dumfounded. "I'll tell you what," he shouted. "I will send you over a liaison officer immediately." Then the ceiling crashed all around Mollison.

Two miles to the north, in the center of Pearl Harbor, the first bomb was falling on the naval air station at Ford Island. From his seat in a parked PBY, Ordnanceman Third Class Donald Briggs decided a plane from the carrier *Enterprise* had spun in. Then the ground erupted all around him as a dozen more explosions followed in rapid succession.

In the first few minutes the Navy bases at Kaneohe and Ford Island, and the Army bases at Wheeler, Bellows and Hickam, as well as the lone Marine base, Ewa, were crippled. Not a single Navy fighter and only some thirty Army Air Corps fighters managed to get into the air.

A moment after the first bomb fell, the Pearl Harbor signal tower alerted Kimmel's headquarters by phone. Three minutes later Rear Admiral Patrick Bellinger broadcast from Ford Island:

AIR RAID, PEARL HARBOR—THIS IS NO DRILL.

At 8 A.M. Kimmel radioed Washington, Admiral Hart and all forces at sea: AIR RAID ON PEARL HARBOR. THIS IS NO DRILL. Even as these messages were going out, flames and billows of black smoke were rising from Pearl Harbor.

Not far from Battleship Row, Boatswain's Mate Graff of the oil tanker *Ramapo* scrambled down the ladder into the crew's quarters and yelled, "The Japs are bombing Pearl Harbor!" His shipmates looked at him as if he were joking as usual, and when he said, "No fooling," someone gave a Bronx cheer. "No crap. Get your asses up on deck!" Yeoman C. O. Lines clambered topside to the fantail just in time to hear a dull explosion and see a plane dive toward *California,* the first of the seven big vessels in Battleship Row.

Above her, in tandem formation, were *Maryland* and *Oklahoma.* A torpedo couldn't hit *Maryland* because she was berthed inboard, next to Ford Island. But the outboard ship, *Oklahoma,* was hit by four torpedoes within a minute. As she listed to port, Commander Jesse Kenworthy, senior officer aboard, ordered the ship abandoned over the starboard side. Inexorably the ship settled, its starboard propeller out of the water. Below, more than four hundred officers and men were trapped alive in the rapidly filling compartments. Next in Battleship Row came *Tennessee* and *West Virginia.* Like *Maryland, Tennessee* was inboard and protected from torpedo attack. On *West Virginia*'s battle conning tower, Captain Mervyn Bennion doubled up. A fragment, probably from an armor-piercing bomb that had just hit the nearby *Tennessee,* had torn into his stomach. Lieutenant Commander T. T. Beattie, the ship's navigator, loosened the skipper's collar and sent for a pharmacist's mate. Bennion knew he was dying, but his concern was how the ship was being fought. Fires swept toward the bridge.

Next in line came *Arizona* and the repair ship *Vestal.* The torpedo planes had missed *Arizona,* but a few minutes later high-level bombers found her with five bombs. One of these plunged through the forecastle into the fuel-storage areas, starting a fire. About sixteen hundred pounds of black powder, the most dangerous of all explosives, were stored here, against regulations. Suddenly the volatile stuff exploded, igniting hundreds of tons of smokeless powder in the forward magazines.

Arizona erupted like a volcano. Those on nearby ships saw her leap halfway out of the water and break in two. Within nine minutes the two fragments of the great 32,600-ton ship settled in the mud as sheets of flame and clouds of black smoke boiled above her

"I Shall Never Look Back"

wreckage. It didn't seem possible that a single one of the more than fifteen hundred men aboard could have survived. Ahead was the last ship in Battleship Row, *Nevada*. She was down several feet by the head from a torpedo in her port bow and a bomb in the quarterdeck.

All along Battleship Row, men were jumping overboard and trying to swim the short distance to Ford Island. But the surface was coated with a layer of oil, six inches deep in some places, and this finally burst into flames, killing most of those in the water.

On the other side of Ford Island, torpedo bombers were still assaulting one of the least important ships in the harbor—the ancient target ship *Utah*. At 8:12 A.M. she rolled over, keel sticking out of the water. Men on Ford Island could hear a faint knocking inside the hull.

Only one ship in the entire harbor was under way. This was the destroyer *Helm*, scurrying at 27 knots through the channel toward the mouth of the harbor and the relative safety of open water. The antitorpedo net, opened hours earlier for *Condor*, was still unaccountably agape, and the Japanese midget submarine with the faulty gyrocompass was trying to stab its way blindly into this opening and go after a battleship. The commander, Ensign Kazuo Sakamaki, surfaced to get his bearings. Ahead were columns of black smoke. "The air raid!" he called to his aide. "Wonderful! Look at that smoke. Enemy ships burning. We must do our best too, and we will."

At 8:15 he saw *Helm* knife out of the harbor, but he held his fire. His two torpedoes were marked for bigger game. He submerged and again aimed blindly at the harbor mouth. He hit a reef, backed away, tried again. This time he ran up so far on the reef that his conning tower stuck out of the water. An explosion shook the little boat violently. Something hit his head and he blacked out. When he came to, the tiny inner chamber was filled with acrid white smoke. He felt dizzy, sick. He reversed his engine. The boat refused to budge. On his stomach, he wormed his way up the narrow forward passage to begin the agonizing job of transferring 11-lb. ballast weights to the stern. At last he felt the submarine stir.

Helm continued to fire at the midget as it slid off the coral and vanished beneath the surface. SMALL JAP SUB TRYING TO PENE-TRATE CHANNEL, radioed the destroyer.

Inside the harbor, another midget was slowly rising to the surface just west of Ford Island. It was sighted at 8:30 and several ships opened fire. The midget launched her two torpedoes, one detonating against a dock, the other against the shore. Then the destroyer *Monaghan* rammed into the midget and dropped depth charges over the spot where it had disappeared.

Fighter pilot Shiga and his squadron of Zeros were lagging 8,000 feet above Hickam, waiting for enemy fighters to come up, but the only American plane in sight was a little yellow ship flying over the sea just east of the field. Shiga ignored it. Moments later he saw six huge four-engine planes coming in for a landing at Hickam.

They were the first of the dozen Flying Fortresses from California. At the sight of the high-flying Zeroes, Major Truman Landon, the squadron commander, thought, Here comes the U. S. Air Corps out to greet us. Then came the distant blinking of machine guns, and a voice shouted over the intercom, "Damn it, those are Japs!" Landon's planes scattered. One started north for Bellows while the rest hastily made for Hickam. Four of them landed safely, but one was shot in half by ground troops as it touched down.

Shiga and his men strafed Hickam in single file, raking a long line of parked planes, then hedgehopped for the sea to avoid AA fire. They turned and swept back. To Shiga's surprise, not one of the planes just strafed was burning. If they had been Japanese they would all be on fire. After three passes at Hickam, Shiga decided to hit Ford Island, but since it was covered with smoke, he led his men to the Marine field near Barbers Point, to the southwest. They left most of the parked fighters in flames.

The torpedo bombers were already droning away from Pearl Harbor. Lieutenant Mori had been driven off course by AA fire after hitting *California* and found himself over Honolulu. He banked away from this forbidden civilian area and headed for the assembly point. Just off the mouth of Pearl Harbor, his navigator said, "Mori-san, some strange-looking plane is on our tail." He turned and saw a little yellow biplane tagging along behind. "Scare it away," he told the radioman-gunner, who loosed a warning burst.

After Lieutenant Matsumura hit *West Virginia* he too flew south just in time to see *Helm* fire at Sakamaki's midget sub. He started for the destroyer, then remembered he had no torpedo. He saw a big passenger plane (it was one of the Flying Fortresses) and bore in so his machine-gunner could knock it down. It was too fast and Matsumura gave up the chase. He told the radioman-gunner to report the attack and got the sheepish answer, "I can't. I shot off our antenna."

One plane alone circled above Pearl Harbor. It was Fuchida assessing the damage. Battleship Row was a holocaust; every battleship still afloat was burning.

Now from the east a second wave of raiders—eighty dive bombers, fifty-four high-level bombers and thirty-six fighters—approached Oahu. At 8:55 A.M. Lieutenant Commander Shigekazu Shimazaki gave the signal for attack and the 170 planes shot over the mountains east of Honolulu and headed for Battleship Row and Drydock No. 1, where the eighth battleship, *Pennsylvania*, was berthed.

A principal target was *Nevada,* moving slowly past *Arizona,* which still belched huge tongues of flame. Gun crews shielded ammo from the intense heat with their own bodies. Already suffering from one torpedo hit, *Nevada* drew up to the toppled *Oklahoma*. Several men stood up on the sides of that ship and cheered as *Nevada* made for open water. But the attackers were finding the range, and six bombs hit within a few minutes. The bridge and forestructure of the battleship erupted in flames. *Nevada* turned to port, and with the help of two tugs, was beached not far from *Pennsylvania*'s drydock.

To the southeast the second group of six Flying Fortresses approached Waikiki Beach, and Captain Richard Carmichael, the squadron commander, began pointing out the sights to his co-pilot. He thought the planes ahead were part of some Navy maneuver until he saw flames and smoke at Hickam. Anxiously he called the tower for permission to land.

"Land from west to east," said Major Gordon Blake. "Use caution. The field is under attack."

As Carmichael lowered his wheels he became the target of violent AA fire from below. He broke off his approach and turned north to Wheeler. This field, too, was under heavy attack, and he had to make for Haleiwa. It was twelve hundred feet long, and by the time the mammoth B-17 skidded to a stop he had used every foot of it. All six of his planes landed safely: two at Haleiwa, one at Kahuku Golf Course and three at Hickam. When his first Flying Fortress touched down at Hickam, two sprucely dressed captains stepped out. "Get your ammo, load up and get ready to go!" shouted someone. The captains stammered that they were in no shape for battle. All their guns were packed in cosmolene and would take hours to clean.

At Wheeler the men were still groggy from the first attack when the second hit. Lieutenant Overstreet began arguing with a sergeant from the Base Ordnance Office about rifles and pistols.

"I doubt if I'm authorized to give you any without a hand receipt," said the reluctant sergeant above the din of exploding bombs.

"Hell, man, this is war!" Overstreet yelled. He got the guns.

At Ford Island all the Navy planes had been destroyed or were inoperable. With little else to do, six pilots hid behind palm trees to take pot shots at the invaders with their pistols.

The Army fighter pilots had some success; they shot down eleven Japanese. The two lieutenants from Wheeler—Kenneth Taylor and George Welch—accounted for seven of these.

The citizens of Honolulu were more reluctant than the military to believe that war had come to Hawaii. They ignored the noise; it was either maneuvers or practice firing of the giant coastal defense batteries at Fort DeRussy near Waikiki Beach. Edgar Rice Burroughs, author of the Tarzan stories, did not interrupt breakfast with his son at the Niumalu Hotel. Afterward they played tennis with two Navy wives, still unaware that the war had started a few miles away.

At his Waikiki apartment Robert Trumbull, city editor of the Honolulu *Advertiser,* was awakened by the telephone. His wife, Jean, answered it and came back half puzzled, half amused. A friend had called to say that from his vantage point on a hill it looked as if Pearl Harbor was being bombed "for real," and Trumbull as a newspaperman might know something about it.

"It's just another maneuver," said Trumbull. No sooner had he hung up than Ray Coll, his editor, called to say there was a reported raid on Pearl Harbor and to get down to the office at once. Incredulous, Trumbull hung up and phoned one of the best-informed reporters in town, who said, "What's the boss been drinking?"

Trumbull wasn't convinced until he heard Webley Edwards of station KGMB say, "The island is under attack! I repeat, the island is under attack! This is the real McCoy!" At his office Trumbull checked the flood of reports (all false) of sabotage by local Japanese: an arrow was cut out of a sugar-cane field pointing to Pearl Harbor; a high-powered radio transmitter was found in a gym owned by a Japanese.

Trumbull dialed the number to the residence of the governor of Hawaii. To his amazement Joseph Poindexter, the seventy-two-year-old governor, answered himself. He didn't know a thing about any attack, and in a skeptical but polite tone asked for details.

At 9:45 A.M. the skies above the smokebound harbor were all at once empty. The stench of burning oil was overwhelming. *Arizona, Oklahoma* and *California* were sunk at their berths. *West Virginia,* aboil with flames, was sinking. *Nevada* was aground. The other three battleships—*Maryland, Tennessee* and drydocked *Pennsylvania*—were all damaged.

In Honolulu the secret agent Takeo Yoshikawa had been eating breakfast when the windows started to rattle and several pictures dropped to the floor. He went into his backyard and looked up in the sky. There was a plane with Japanese markings. They did it! he told himself. This is just about perfect with so many ships in the harbor.

He clapped his hands and rushed to the back door of Consul General Kita's official residence. "Mr. Kita!" he called. "They've done it!" Kita came out and said, "I just heard 'East wind, rain' on the shortwave!"* This meant, of course, that Japanese-American

---

* Although both U. S. Army and naval intelligence were supposed to be monitoring Japanese shortwave newscasts around the clock for just such a "winds" message, this one was not intercepted. Neither was an RCA telegram that Kita had received from Tokyo at 3:20 that morning which, decoded, read: RELATIONS STRAINED BETWEEN JAPAN AND THE UNITED STATES AND BRITAIN.

The so-called "winds" code is still shrouded in mystery. Commander Laurence F. Safford, chief of the Communication Security Section, testified that he had received an intercepted "execute" of the "winds" code on December 4 or 5 in a Japanese weather broadcast indicating "War with the United States, war with Great Britain, peace with Russia." He showed the intercept to Kramer, who also believed it was a genuine execute but changed his mind when he testified because of evidence from MacArthur

diplomatic relations were in danger of rupture. "There's no mistake."

The two stood looking up at the dense black clouds rising over Pearl Harbor. Tears in their eyes, they clasped hands. Finally Kita said, "They've done it at last. Good job, Morimura."

Yoshikawa locked himself and a clerk in the code room and set about burning code books in a washtub. Within ten minutes there was a loud knocking. Someone shouted, "Open the door!" It was the FBI, alerted by the smoke.

The door caved in and half a dozen armed men burst in and began stamping on the burning code books. "Good-bye to the days of my youth—forever," whispered Yoshikawa. He walked out into the yard to watch the tiny planes above Pearl Harbor. The other members of the consulate were being rounded up and kept in the office, but nobody paid any attention to the secret agent. He returned to the office, found it locked, and suggested to an FBI man that he be incarcerated with the others.

"Who are you?"

"Morimura, an official."

"Get in," said the FBI man.

In Honolulu, few doubted any longer that it was war. Sixty-eight civilians lay dead. A single Japanese bomb had hit the city. The forty-nine other explosions were caused by spent AA shells improperly fused. Still, there was no panic. At the height of the attack Hawaiian girls in hula skirts appeared as usual at the Pan American dock, arms loaded with leis to bid aloha to departing Clipper passengers. They had to be told it was the end of traditional ceremony for a long, long time.

3.

Yamamoto and his staff aboard the flagship *Nagato,* anchored off Hashirajima, had all been awake since 2 A.M., an hour before

---

interrogations of Japanese who denied sending out any execute message. Their testimony must be discounted, however, since they also denied even setting up the "winds" code. Neither the original nor any copy of the "execute" teletype could be found in Navy files, and some critics of the Roosevelt Administration still maintain they were purposely destroyed to discredit the possibility that an execute was ever sent.

the scheduled attack. They sat around in silence, time and again getting up to examine a large chart. Chief Steward Omi passed around tea and cakes to relieve the tension. All at once a voice called excitedly over the voice tube, "We have succeeded in surprise attack!" It was the chief code officer in the message room and by a "skip" due to atmospheric conditions, he had just heard Fuchida signal, "TORA, TORA, TORA!"

The staff officers shook hands, bursting with elation and relief after their prolonged anxiety. Yamamoto tried to hide his emotions, but Watanabe could see that he, too, was excited. Omi brought out *sake* and *surume* (dried squid) to celebrate, and numerous toasts were tossed down. Every few minutes the voice tube would repeat triumphant reports from the attacking planes and frantic American messages: "All ships clear Pearl Harbor"; "This is no drill"; "This is the real McCoy."

Yamamoto gave orders to leave for Hawaii after dawn so that the Combined Fleet could support *Kido Butai* in case of a U. S. attack.

In Tokyo a relay of Fuchida's first signal, the tactical order to attack, was picked up at the message room of Navy General Staff headquarters. The code officer phoned the operations room and said, "The commander of *Akagi* is repeating 'TO' over and over." It wasn't in the code book and he had no idea what it meant. Commander Miyo spoke up and said he had originated that code long ago as squadron leader on *Kaga*. "They're doing fine," he said. "It means 'charge.'" It was the first good moment Miyo had had since hearing the report that the Malay invasion had jumped the schedule. A few minutes later the second message came in—this one in the code book: TORA, TORA, TORA.

The first planes found their way back to the carriers at 10 A.M. The weather worsened and a number of planes crashed on the pitching decks. As Matsumura's tail hook caught the landing wire on *Hiryu* he felt a surge of joy. He'd never expected to come back and there he was, alive!

Fuchida returned about an hour later and was greeted by an exultant Genda; then he went to the bridge and reported to Nagumo and Kusaka that at least two battleships had been sunk and four seriously damaged. He begged the admirals to launch another attack at once and this time concentrate on the oil tanks. American air power had been smashed, he assured them, and the second attack would just have antiaircraft fire to contend with.

Kusaka considered Fuchida's suggestion. His volatile friend Admiral Yamaguchi had already signaled that *Soryu* and *Hiryu* were prepared to launch another attack, and *Kaga*'s captain, at the urging of Commander Sata, also recommended a strike against installations and fuel tanks. The oil was an alluring target, but Kusaka believed a commander should not be obsessed by such temptations. The second attack would surely be no surprise; and no matter what Fuchida thought, the bulk of their planes would probably be shot down by AA fire. More important, the task force itself would be placed in jeopardy. *Kido Butai* was the heart of the Japanese Navy and should not be risked. From the beginning he had wanted to deliver a swift thrust and return like the wind.

"We should retire as planned," Kusaka advised Nagumo, who nodded.

A staff officer suggested that they try to locate and sink the American carriers. Opinion on the bridge was divided. "There will be no more attacks of any kind," said Kusaka. "We will withdraw."*

Secretary of the Navy Frank Knox was at his office in the Navy Department on Constitution Avenue. It was long past noon and he was getting hungry. He was about to order lunch when Admiral Stark burst in with Kimmel's "This is no drill" message.

"My God, this can't be true!" Knox exclaimed. "This must mean the Philippines."

Stark assured him grimly it did mean Pearl Harbor, and Knox picked up the phone with a direct connection to the White House. It was 1:47 P.M. Roosevelt was lunching at his desk in the Oval Office with Harry Hopkins. Knox read the dispatch.

"There must be some mistake," said Hopkins. He was sure "Japan would not attack in Honolulu" but Roosevelt thought the report was probably true and said, "It's just the kind of unexpected

---

* Some accounts state that Fuchida and Genda repeatedly pleaded with Nagumo to return. In an interview in 1966, Admiral Kusaka recalled that they merely suggested a second attack and that his words "We will withdraw" ended the discussion; thereafter no one expressed a forceful opinion.

"I Shall Never Look Back" 281

thing the Japanese would do." He talked at some length of his efforts to complete his administration without war, finally remarked somberly, "If this report is true, it takes the matter entirely out of my hands."

At 2:05 P.M. Roosevelt phoned Hull and in steady but clipped tones passed on the news. Hull told him that Ambassadors Nomura and Kurusu had just arrived and were in the Diplomatic Reception Room. Roosevelt advised him to receive them, but not to mention that he knew about Pearl Harbor. He should be formal, cool and "bow them out." Then the President called Secretary of War Henry Stimson, who was lunching at home, and excitedly asked if he had heard what had happened.

"Well," Stimson replied, "I have heard the telegrams which have been coming in about the Japanese advances in the Gulf of Siam."

"Oh, no, I don't mean that," said Roosevelt. "They have attacked Hawaii! They are now bombing Hawaii!"

Stimson replaced the receiver. Well, that was an excitement indeed, he told himself. His immediate feeling was one of "relief that the indecision was over and that a crisis had come in a way which would unite all our people."

At the State Department, Hull turned to Joseph Ballantine and said, "The President has an unconfirmed report that the Japanese have attacked Pearl Harbor. The Japanese ambassadors are waiting to see me. I know what they want. They are going to turn us down on our note of November 26. Perhaps they want to tell us that war has been declared. I am rather inclined not to see them." Finally he decided to take Roosevelt's advice and admit the envoys. Besides, there was "one chance out of a hundred" that the report wasn't true.

In the waiting room the anxious Nomura was still breathing heavily after the race from the embassy. He was already more than an hour late and knew the fourteen-part message contained several minor typographical errors. Okumura had wanted to retype the entire message but Nomura had impatiently snatched it away from him. He still hadn't had time to read it carefully.

At 2:20 P.M. Kurusu and Nomura were finally ushered into Hull's office. The Secretary of State greeted them coolly, refusing to shake hands. He didn't invite them to sit down.

"I was instructed to hand this reply to you at one P.M.," said the admiral apologetically, holding out the note.

Hull's face was stern. "Why should it be handed to me at one P.M.?"

"I do not know the reason," Nomura replied truthfully, puzzled that his friend should be so upset just because he and Kurusu were late.

Hull seized the note and pretended to glance through it. Ordinarily his speech was slow and gentle, but now the words tumbled out headlong as he assailed them bitterly, "I must say that in all my conversations with you during the last nine months I have never uttered one word of untruth. This is borne out absolutely by the record. In all my fifty years of public service I have never seen a document that was more crowded with infamous falsehoods and distortions—infamous falsehoods and distortions on a scale so huge that I never imagined until today that any government on this planet was capable of uttering them."

Nomura started to say something, but Hull raised his hand and dismissed them by a curt nod toward the door. Still bewildered, the admiral approached Hull, said farewell and held out his hand. This time the Secretary of State shook it, but as the two Japanese turned and walked out, heads down, Hull, reverting to his Tennessee vocabulary, was heard to mutter, "Scoundrels and pissants!"

At the embassy Okumura told them, "Our planes have bombed Pearl Harbor!" Military Attaché Isoda, eyes filled with tears, approached Nomura and sadly said it was regrettable that things "had come to such a pass" despite the admiral's efforts. "But, alas, this is Fate." Nomura was too deeply moved to be consoled, particularly by an Army man.

At the Navy Department, Admiral Stark had already sent a message to all commanders in the Pacific area and Panama: EXECUTE UNRESTRICTED AIR AND SUBMARINE WARFARE AGAINST JAPAN. A few doors away, Knox was on the phone with Pearl Harbor, talking to the commandant of the 14th Naval District, Admiral Claude C. Bloch, who described the damage he could see through his window. "*Oklahoma*'s badly hit. Also *Arizona*. But *Pennsylvania* and *Tennessee* are only superficially damaged, and we can raise *California* without too much trouble. Fortunately, there's no damage to the Navy Yard and oil reserves."

The Giants-Dodgers football fans at their radios were the first of the American public to learn of the attack. At 2:26 P.M. station WOR interrupted its broadcast of the game with the initial news flash. There was no announcement at the Polo Grounds itself, where Brooklyn had just scored the game's first touchdown, but there was a stir of curiosity when Colonel William J. Donovan was paged by Washington over the PA system. He headed the Office of the Coordination of Information, an intelligence organization.

Another announcement came just before the 3 o'clock broadcast of the New York Philharmonic concert. In Washington, Rear Admiral Chester W. Nimitz, chief of the Bureau of Navigation, was settling down to enjoy the Artur Rodzinski concert over CBS. When the broadcast was interrupted, he shot out of his chair and was on his way to the Navy Building.

A few blocks away Masuo Kato of Domei heard the news over a taxicab radio. "God damn Japan," said the driver. "We'll lick the hell out of those bastards now." In New York, radio station WQXR hastily switched its Gilbert and Sullivan program from *The Mikado* to *H.M.S. Pinafore* "in honor of the Royal Navy." And on the banks of the Potomac someone cut down one of the cherry trees donated years before by Japan. This sense of outrage was shared by a large group of Nisei living in the Manhattan area. Without delay the Tozai (East-West) Club of New York dispatched a telegram to Roosevelt:

WE THE AMERICAN CITIZENS OF JAPANESE DESCENT OF NEW YORK CITY AND VICINITY JOIN ALL AMERICANS IN CONDEMNING JAPAN'S AGGRESSIONS AGAINST OUR COUNTRY AND SUPPORT ALL MEASURES TAKEN FOR THE DEFENSE OF THE NATION.

A restive crowd had gathered outside the Japanese embassy on Massachusetts Avenue. Kurusu was summoned to the phone. It was Ferdinand Mayer, until recently an American diplomat; the two had become good friends in Berlin. Mayer said he would be glad to see Kurusu—without mentioning that he had called at the suggestion of Colonel Donovan, whose intelligence organization would soon become the Office of Strategic Services. America's first genuine espionage system.

His voice breaking, Kurusu thanked "Ferdinand" for phoning but said he "would hate to inconvenience" him, since there was a surly crowd outside the embassy. From the tone of his voice Mayer guessed Kurusu was "quite overwhelmed and in the deepest sort of despair."

Crushed as he was, Kurusu still had no feeling of bitterness toward Hull, who had despised him on sight—and shown it. That old man, he thought, had worked to the best of his ability to preserve peace. The trouble was that both America and Japan were like children. Diplomatically, neither was mature. Now the two children were playing foolish war games.

By evening the envoys were confined under guard in a luxury hotel by Assistant Secretary of State Adolf A. Berle, Jr. The admiral asked for a samurai sword but Berle rejected the request; Nomura's suicide might endanger Ambassador Grew.

That evening the Cabinet met in the Red Room on the second floor of the White House at eight-thirty. The members formed a semicircle facing Roosevelt, who sat behind his desk. This was the most serious meeting of a cabinet since the outbreak of the Civil War, the President solemnly announced. He enumerated the losses at Pearl Harbor, then slowly read a message he planned to make to Congress the following noon.

It was effective, Stimson thought, but didn't cover Japan's "lawless conduct in the past. Neither did it connect in any way with Germany." Hull, too, wanted Germany included, but Roosevelt said the message would be "more effective . . . and certain to be read if it was short." He could not be budged, even in the face of Hull's insistence that Congress and the nation would listen to "anything" the President had to say.

Stimson wanted to go further than Hull, and at the end of the meeting went up to Roosevelt and urged him to declare war against Germany before the indignation of the people subsided. The President refused but did promise to present the full matter to the people in two days.

Just before nine-thirty the leaders of Congress were ushered into the room: Vice President Henry Wallace and six senators, including Alben Barkley, Speaker of the House of Representatives Sam Rayburn and two congressmen. Roosevelt told them frankly what had happened in Hawaii. His listeners sat riveted in dead silence. When Roosevelt finished, Senator Tom Connally wondered why the fleet was "caught napping," but the others were still tongue-tied.

A little later in the evening Marine Captain James Roosevelt, the President's eldest son, came upon his father thumbing through his beloved stamp collection "with no expression on his face, very calm and quiet." He didn't look up, only said, "It's bad, it's pretty bad."

Mrs. Roosevelt found her husband more serene than she'd seen him for a long time and thought to herself that "it was steadying to know finally that the die was cast" and that the future "presented a clearer challenge than the long uncertainty of the past."

4.

Japan had started the war but had yet to declare it. At a hurriedly assembled Cabinet meeting an hour before dawn, Navy Minister Shigetaro Shimada calmly described the results of Pearl Harbor, cautioning his listeners to make allowances for the exaggerations of bomber pilots. Hastily an imperial rescript declaring war was composed, signed and sent on to the Privy Council.

The sun was rising as Privy Seal Kido, who had opposed the war, approached the Palace by car. Still staggered by Pearl Harbor, he closed his eyes, and bowing toward the sun, offered a prayer to the gods. He was profoundly grateful for the divine assistance that marked the beginning of Japan's desperate course. As a patriotic Japanese he fervently hoped for victory.

Several blocks away at the NHK (Japan Broadcasting Corporation) Building, announcer Morio Tateno checked the script of the first news program of the day. Curbing his agitation, he began to broadcast at exactly 7 A.M.: "We now present you urgent news. Here is the news. The Army and Navy divisions of Imperial Headquarters jointly announced at six o'clock this morning, December 8, that the Imperial Army and Navy forces have begun hostilities against the American and British forces in the Pacific at dawn today."

The news was blared through hundreds of loudspeakers in the streets. People stopped in their tracks, startled; then, as martial music blared out, many began clapping as if it were a ball game. The enthusiasm was general, but some of the older citizens started toward the Palace gates to pray for victory, not with jubilation but with solemnity.* In the plaza, newsvendors with "extras" trotted by, the bells around their waists jingling so loudly that they could be heard in Number Three East reception hall of the Imperial Palace.

In this spacious room the Privy Council was in session. The longest discussion was on a problem of little note: why the Netherlands was not included in the imperial rescript. There was another lengthy argument about use of the terms "America" and "England." One councillor protested that this would cause confusion and, moreover, would be impolite. Togo stubbornly refused to make the change; everyone in the world knew that America meant the United States of America.

Before noon the Emperor put his seal on the rescript and war was officially declared. He added one line expressing his personal regrets that the empire had been brought to war with Britain and America and toned down the closing phrase, "raising and enhancing thereby the glory of the Imperial Way within and outside our homeland," to "preserving thereby the glory of our empire."

Marquis Kido found the Emperor apparently undisturbed. Then His Majesty confessed that it had been a heartrending decision to declare war on the United States and Britain, and particularly

---

* Finance Minister Kaya feared that the news might cause a disastrous decline in the stock market and ordered his secretary, Hisatsune Sakomizu, to somehow control the situation. He advised two men of the problem: the president of the exchange and the head of the brokers' union, Aizawa by name. They decided that the opening prices could be raised if they bought heavily in Shinto, which, because of its name, had become something of a symbol in the market. When the stock exchange opened, Aizawa bought forty thousand shares. This pushed the price some 30 sen above the previous day's closing quotation. But almost immediately there was a general downward trend on the big board; the public was reacting to Tateno's announcement on the radio. Within an hour, however, an "extra" was distributed on the floor telling of great successes in the Pacific and on the Asian continent. In minutes the prices on the big board began climbing.

unbearable to make an enemy of such close friends as the British royal family. Kido made no reply. What could he say?

Prime Minister Tojo was already talking to the nation by radio, soberly, without any oratorical flourishes. The West, he said, was trying to dominate the world. "To annihilate this enemy and to establish a stable new order in East Asia, the nation must necessarily anticipate a long war. . . ." The fate of Japan and East Asia was at stake and the hundred million people of the empire must now pledge all energies—their lives—to the state.

There followed a recording of "Umi Yukaba," a martial song:

> *Across the sea, corpses in the water;*
> *Across the mountain, corpses in the field.*
> *I shall die only for the Emperor,*
> *I shall never look back.*

That afternoon as Prime Minister Tojo was leaving the official residence in riding clothes, his secretary, Colonel Susumu Nishiura, stopped him. "How can you go riding today? What would happen if you were injured?" Tojo went back inside without a word.

Japanese fears that the premature Malayan attack might compromise the Pearl Harbor strike were groundless. Surprisingly, London was not alerted. More surprising, word of Pearl Harbor itself did not reach Churchill until two and a half hours after the first bombs fell. And he had to learn it from a newscast. He was spending the weekend at his country residence, Chequers, with two American house guests—W. Averell Harriman, who was the U. S. Lend-Lease co-ordinator, and Ambassador John Winant. At 9 P.M. they all heard a BBC announcer go on and on about fighting everywhere but the Far East, before announcing matter-of-factly that the Japanese had attacked Hawaii.

The two Americans straightened in their chairs.

"It's quite true," said the butler, Sawyer. "We heard it ourselves outside. The Japanese have attacked the Americans."

After a moment's silence Churchill left for his office. Winant took for granted that he was going to declare war on Japan, as he had recently promised "within the moment." "Good God," Winant said, "you can't declare war on a radio announcement!"

"What shall I do?"

"I will call up the President and ask him what the facts are."

When the ambassador had Roosevelt on the line he said, "I have a friend who wants to talk to you. You will know who it is as soon as you hear his voice."

Churchill picked up the phone. "Mr. President, what's this about Japan?"

"It's quite true. They have attacked us at Pearl Harbor. We are all in the same boat."

"This actually simplifies things. God be with you." Churchill couldn't help feeling great elation, now that the United States was officially at his side. He recalled Sir Edward Grey's telling him more than thirty years earlier that America was like a gigantic boiler: "Once the fire is lighted under it, there is no limit to the power it can generate."

Saturated with emotion, he went to bed and slept soundly.

5.

During the plotting of the Malay campaign the perpetrators had counted on only an even chance that it could be launched in complete secrecy and drew up plans for the men making the initial landings to live off the land in case they were isolated by the British fleet. For a time the planners seriously considered having them plant seeds so they would survive a long siege, but this scheme was discarded as bad for morale.

The invasion of the Malay Peninsula that preceded Pearl Harbor evolved smoothly despite six-foot waves, and by the end of the day the Kota Bharu airport was in Japanese hands. But the other two landings to the north, across the border in Thailand, were impeded by faulty execution of orders. Major Shigeharu Asaeda was assigned to lead the way at Pattani. He had personally picked that beach on one of his secret missions as suitable for landing because its white sand at high tide indicated firm footing. The launches of the Pattani force churned toward the shore an hour before dawn. When the water was chest-high the troops, burdened by full field equipment, began leaping overboard. To his horror Asaeda found himself sinking in mud; the beautiful white sand did not extend into the water at low tide. Some of the men carrying machine guns were dragged down and drowned. It took the others almost three harrowing hours to slog the three hundred yards to solid ground, where they were raked by Thai fire.

At Singora the sand was solid and it looked as if Colonel Tsuji would make a reality of his imaginative scheme to crash the Malayan border in buses. Tsuji assumed that a major, who was posing as a clerk at the Singora consulate, had already persuaded the Thai Army and police not to interfere. But Major Osone was not on the beach waiting for the invaders. Tsuji went into town and finally managed to rouse the Japanese consulate by pounding at the gate. It was the portly consul himself who sleepily greeted them with a surprised "Ah so, the Japanese Army!" Behind him was the equally sleepy Major Osone. He had burned his secret code too soon and had been unable to decode the last-minute telegram with the exact time of the landing.

The exasperated Tsuji ordered the consul to drive him to the police station. In case persuasion failed, he had brought a large *furoshiki* containing 100,000 ticals of Thai money. They were not far from the station when a bullet smashed a headlight. "Don't shoot!" Tsuji's interpreter called out. "This is the Japanese Army. Join us and attack the British Army!" The answer was a volley of shots which seemed to be directed at the fat consul, whose gleaming white suit made him an inviting target. The Japanese returned the fire. It was the end of Tsuji's fanciful plan.

Off the tip end of the Malay Peninsula the citizens on the island of Singapore first learned of the war when bombs exploded at four o'clock in the morning. Half an hour earlier the fighter control operations room had received a report of unidentified aircraft 140 miles from Singapore, but no one at the Civil Air Raid Headquarters answered its repeated phone calls. Consequently, the lights of the city guided the invaders to their target; in fact, they stayed brightly lit during the entire raid. The custodian of the keys to the master switch could not be found.

Sixty-three people were killed and another 133 were injured, but there was still no sign of alarm in Singapore. The great majority was reassured by an order of the day issued by Air Chief

Marshal Sir Robert Brooke-Popham, commander in chief in the Far East.

We are ready. We have had plenty of warning and our preparations are made and tested. . . . We are confident. Our defences are strong and our weapons efficient. . . . What of the enemy? We see before us a Japan drained for years by the exhausting claims of her wanton onslaught on China. . . . Confidence, resolution, enterprise and devotion to the cause must and will inspire every one of us in the fighting services, while from the civilian population, Malay, Chinese, Indian or Burmese, we expect that patience, endurance and serenity which is the great virtue of the East and which will go far to assist the fighting men to gain final and complete victory.

Not everyone was assuaged by such rhetoric. Yates McDaniel, the American representative of the Associated Press, knew that the Brewster Buffalo fighter planes protecting Singapore were slow and cumbersome. He also knew there wasn't a single tank in Malaya; that almost every one of the great fixed guns of Singapore was pointing out to sea, useless in case of land attack down the peninsula; that the troops in Malaya had no jungle training; that the native groups had been excluded from any participation in the defense of their homes and that most of them hated the British more than they did the Japanese.

Late that morning McDaniel's good friend Vice-Admiral Sir Geoffrey Layton told him on the phone, "We're sending out two capital ships under 'Tom Thumb' Phillips." By his tone McDaniel guessed Layton strongly disapproved. "Would you like to go along?"

"How long will they be out?" McDaniel admired Phillips and had been struck by the strangely heroic figure of the little admiral standing on a box so he could look over the bridge.

"Five or six days." Layton explained that Phillips was determined to sail north, up the east coast of Malaya, and attack the invasion convoy which was still landing Japanese troops at two points.

McDaniel was tempted. It sounded like a good show, but since he was the only AP man in town, he had to refuse. He was concerned by Layton's obvious opposition to the plan. And he remembered the black cat of *Prince of Wales* sitting in President

Roosevelt's lap at the signing of the Atlantic Charter. It gave him a feeling of foreboding.

Just before sailing that afternoon, Phillips asked Air Vice-Marshal C. W. Pulford what air cover the fleet would get on its sortie. Pulford, a former Navy man, was eager to co-operate, but his airfields in northern Malaya were already reportedly knocked out. He promised to give Phillips air reconnaissance the next day, December 9, but didn't think he could spare any planes at all on December 10.

As Phillips boarded the 35,000-ton *Prince of Wales,* Captain L. H. Bell noticed his uneasiness. "I'm not sure," Phillips said, "that Pulford realizes the importance I attach to fighter cover over Singora on the tenth." He said he would ask him in a letter what he could do for certain.

The sun was setting as the fleet, under the code name of Force Z, steamed out of the sprawling Singapore base. *Prince of Wales* led, followed by *Repulse* and the destroyers. As they passed Changi Signal Station at the eastern end of the island, Phillips was handed a radiogram from Pulford: REGRET FIGHTER PROTECTION IMPOSSIBLE.

"Well," said Phillips, "we must get on with it." After the publicity about the two warships since their arrival in Singapore, it would have been unthinkable to retire. Force Z continued on its northern course.

In Manila, Major General Lewis Brereton, commander of MacArthur's Far East Air Force, requested permission to bomb Formosa, some six hundred miles north, with his Flying Fortresses. It was 7:30 A.M., five and a half hours after the first attack on Hawaii.

"I'll ask the general," replied Major General Richard K. Sutherland, MacArthur's chief of staff, and a moment later reported, "The general says no. Don't make the first overt act." Wasn't the bombing of Pearl Harbor an overt act? Brereton wanted to know. He was told there had been little reconnaissance on Formosa and such a raid would be pointless.

On western Formosa, Japanese naval officers of the Eleventh Air Fleet were equally frustrated. Fog had prevented them from taking off before dawn for strikes at Clark Field and its adjoining fighter bases. Now they feared that the Clark-based B-17's would suddenly appear overhead and smash their own planes lined up on the runways.

The only aircraft to leave Formosa were from an Army field and all they did was drop their bombs far north of Manila on unimportant targets. Reports of these nuisance raids reached Brereton's headquarters at Nielson Field, on the outskirts of Manila, at 9:25 A.M. Brereton phoned Sutherland again begging permission to bomb Formosa. Again he was turned down, and when MacArthur finally changed his mind after forty minutes it was so late that Brereton had to make new plans hastily.

His bombers were cruising aimlessly above Mount Arayat in order not to be caught on the ground, and for half an hour were not informed that it was a false alarm. They returned to Clark for refueling, followed by fighters flying cover.

Back at Nielson Field, new alarms were coming in to the Interceptor Command by phone and telegraph from towns all along the northwest coast of Luzon. Some spoke of twenty-seven planes that looked like fighters, others of fifty-four heavy bombers. The fog had lifted in Formosa, and 196 Japanese naval planes in several groups were nearing their targets on Luzon. The bulk was bound for Clark Field. Colonel Alexander H. Campbell, Brereton's aircraft warning officer, tried to make sense of the conflicting reports and concluded that one group was heading for Manila and several for Clark Field. At 11:45 A.M. he sent a teletype to Clark that failed to get through. Nor could anyone be raised on radio; apparently the operator was having lunch. Finally Campbell got a faint phone connection with Clark and was assured by a junior officer that he would immediately give the information to the base commander or operations officer.

By 12:10 P.M., all fighter pilots on Luzon were either in the air or on alert—except for those at Clark Field. The junior officer had not yet passed on Campbell's warning. Not a single fighter plane was flying cover over the parked Flying Fortresses.

At 12:25, twenty-seven new Mitsubishi high-level bombers roared over Tarlac, just twenty miles to the north. Their goal was Clark, where many of the ground crew were walking unconcernedly from the mess halls to the flight line. Ordnance men were loading bombs on the huge unpainted Flying Fortresses. Pilots of the eighteen P-40B fighters, under Lieutenant Joseph H. Moore, were lolling in their planes at the edge of the field near empty fuel-drum revetments.

At the 30th Squadron mess hall, mechanics and bomber crewmen were listening to a Don Bell broadcast over KMZH. "There is an unconfirmed report," said Bell, "that they're bombing Clark Field." This elicited laughter and catcalls. Indeed, there were those who refused to believe that Pearl Harbor had been attacked; it was probably some "eager beaver's" idea to put everyone on the alert.

The Japanese in the twenty-seven Mitsubishis could already see a mass of large American bombers glittering in the bright sun. Their target was ridiculously visible, parked out in the vast open plain with Mount Arayat rising up like a huge traffic marker fifteen miles east of the field. Just behind came twenty-seven more bombers, and hovering high above were thirty-five Zero fighters. It was 12:35 P.M. Ten hours after Pearl Harbor, every plane at Clark Field was a sitting duck.

At the edge of the field, New Mexico national guardsmen of the 200th Coast Artillery were eating lunch around their 37-mm. and 3-inch antiaircraft guns. At the cry "Here comes the Navy!" Sergeant Dwaine Davis of Carlsbad grabbed a movie camera bought with company funds and began taking pictures.

"Why are they dropping tinfoil?" someone asked.

"That's not tinfoil, and those are goddamn Japs!" Then there was a roar like the sound of rushing freight trains.

At the other end of the field a crew chief of the 20th Pursuit Squadron shouted, "Good God Almighty, yonder they come!" Lieutenant Joe Moore raced for his P-40B. Followed by six of his squadron, he taxied into position. He lifted into the air, swung wide and started a maximum power climb. Two others got off, but the last four planes were hit by bombs.

The air-raid siren shrieked, but the ground crews seemed transfixed by the great V formation overhead—until strings of bombs fishtailed toward them.

For the first time the national guardsmen at the AA guns fired live ammunition; much of their training had been with broomsticks and boxes or wooden models. Their bursts exploded far below the targets, but it was satisfying and somehow exhilarating to let loose at something in earnest.

All at once there was nothing to shoot at. The sudden silence came like a jolt. Corporal Durwood Brooks walked toward the flight line in a daze. The idea of war was new and terrifying. Bodies and limbs were scattered around. He saw a friend, a Polish boy of nineteen, in a slit trench. By some freak an explosive bullet had blown him up like a balloon; he looked almost transparent.

Men began emerging from the trenches like sleepwalkers, momentarily numb to the groans of the wounded. Buildings blazed and dark rolls of smoke churned from the oil dump across the field. But by a miracle only a few Flying Fortresses had been damaged.

Lieutenant Moore and his two companions were trying to give chase. They found to their amazement that the Zeros were faster and more maneuverable, climbing at an astounding rate. They had been assured there was no such thing as a good Japanese fighter plane, although exact data on these Zeros had been sent to the War Department by the brilliant and unorthodox Colonel Claire Chennault in the fall of 1940. The chief of the Flying Tigers had also elaborated in detail on ways whereby the heavier P-40 should be able to shoot down the faster Zero, but this information, which could have saved the lives of bewildered American pilots dying that moment, had been filed away. Chennault was too much of a maverick to be taken seriously by his superiors.

Almost unopposed, the Zeros began strafing the parked Flying Fortresses and P-40B's. They were joined by forty-four Zeros which had just raked a nearby fighter base and were after new blood. One by one the big Fortresses exploded as tracers ignited their gas tanks. Once again the attack was abruptly over. Black clouds of smoke drifted across the field. All of the fighter planes and thirty medium bombers and observation planes were on fire. All but three of the Flying Fortresses were destroyed. In one raid the Japanese naval fliers had crippled MacArthur's Far East Air Force. Every one of the Japanese bombers returned safely, as did all but seven fighters.

It was a second Pearl Harbor. In one day two of the three most powerful deterrents to quick Japanese success in Southeast Asia had been canceled: the Pacific Fleet and MacArthur's air force. The third was British Admiral "Tom Thumb" Phillips' powerful Force Z. According to the latest Japanese reconnaissance report, *Prince of Wales* and *Repulse* were still in Singapore harbor —too shallow for their conventional aerial torpedoes and well protected by antiaircraft.

If only the two big ships could be lured into the open sea.

At that moment they were steaming north toward the Japanese convoy.

At Pearl Harbor it was confirmed that 18 ships had been sunk or badly damaged; 188 planes destroyed and 159 damaged; 2,403 Americans killed. It was a disaster, but it could have been a catastrophe. Luckily, the carriers were at sea and the enemy had neglected to bomb the oil storage tanks at the Navy Yard and the submarine pens. Moreover, almost all of the sunk or damaged ships would eventually return to battle. The Japanese lost 29 planes and 5 midget submarines; 45 airmen had died, and 9 submariners. One, Ensign Sakamaki, was captured when his boat went aground on the other side of Oahu.

At dusk, smoke still spewed from the shattered fleet. Through a drizzling rain the stench of oil, fire and death was thick and nauseating. Rumor fed on rumor: eight Japanese transports were seen rounding Barbers Point . . . gliders and paratroopers had dropped at Kaneohe . . . other paratroopers were coming down in sugar-cane fields southwest of Ford Island, still others in Manoa Valley.

One official Navy report even claimed that paratroopers in blue coveralls with Rising Sun emblems were landing on the north shore. Fifth columnists, saboteurs and spies were reported everywhere—driving taxis, waiting on tables, tending gardens, selling groceries. They had ringed Oahu with sampans to direct the Japanese to their targets; they had driven milk trucks down airstrips, methodically knocking off the tails of American planes; they had poisoned reservoirs—in other words, there was no end to their mischief. Actually they had done nothing at all, but the man most responsible for guiding the raiders to their proper targets, Takeo Yoshikawa, was still hiding behind the identity of a minor consular official.*

---

* His true identity and mission were discovered only after the war.

It was unsafe to be abroad in the dark. Every moving object was a target for some edgy rifleman. At Wheeler someone heard a pilot mention poison gas, and the alarm was sounded. At Hickam a guard saw a dim form—it was a friend returning from the latrine—and fired several wild rounds, setting off a wild barrage of AA fire which created more casualties.

At Ford Island six planes from the carrier *Enterprise* were returning from a fruitless search for Nagumo's carriers. Despite a contrary radar report, they had searched to the southwest. This time Pearl Harbor was not caught napping and the planes were raked by antiaircraft fire. The score was almost perfect: of six planes, four were destroyed and one damaged.

Pearl City was blacked out, but the harbor glowed from burning ships. Flares dotted the overturned *Oklahoma*. Men with acetylene torches were trying to cut into the hull to rescue their suffocating comrades inside.

There were men trapped inside *West Virginia*, lying flat on her keel at the bottom of the harbor. A huge pocket of air was keeping some sixty survivors alive. They were vainly tapping on the sides of the ship to attract attention.

The reasons for the disaster would be debated bitterly for years. Stripped of politics and personalities, they were simple. The American military leaders had been assured that the Japanese could not mount an independent carrier striking force (after the fact they were still convinced that Nagumo had come from the Marshalls), and could not imagine that the Japanese would be "stupid enough" to attack Pearl Harbor. They were not alone in this. The Japanese Navy General Staff itself had branded Operation Z reckless.

In a deeper sense, every American would have to accept a share of the blame. The disaster was caused by a national unwillingness to face the facts of a world torn from its stable course after World War I by economic and social revolution, fostered by nationalism and racism, and the inevitable realignment of power in both hemispheres.

9

"The Formidable Years That Lie Before Us"

1.

On Monday morning Americans were still staggered by the worst military disaster in their history. There were no scenes of panic or even excitement, but strangers on the streets looked at one another with a new awareness. Personal problems were overshadowed by national catastrophe. The bitter wrangles between the interventionists and the "America Firsters" suddenly had no meaning.

The War Department feared a Japanese carrier attack on the locks of the Panama Canal or the aircraft factories on the California coast. Many eminent government officials were caught up in hysteria and one phoned the White House claiming that the West Coast was no longer defensible and demanded that battle lines be established in the Rocky Mountains.

Pearl Harbor had temporarily crippled American naval power in the Pacific, but it had another and more lasting effect. Telegrams and letters from the public flooded the White House pledging full aid and co-operation. Americans would never forget Pearl Harbor.

A little after noon on Monday, senators, congressmen and Supreme Court Justices filed into the House chamber. In the packed gallery was Mrs. Roosevelt. She was "deeply unhappy," recalling her anxieties about her husband and brother when World War I broke out. Now she had four sons of military age. Near her, at the President's request, was Mrs. Woodrow Wilson, the widow of another war President.

Just before one o'clock the Cabinet entered. Speaker Sam Rayburn rapped his gavel for silence and announced, "The President of the United States!" Roosevelt slowly walked in on the arm of his son James. The President opened a black loose-leaf notebook and began to read: "Yesterday, December 7, 1941—a date which will live in infamy—the United States of America was suddenly and deliberately attacked by naval and air forces of the Empire of Japan. . . ."

The speech, often interrupted by bursts of applause, continued for several minutes. In conclusion the President said, "I ask that the Congress declare that since the unprovoked and dastardly attack by Japan on Sunday, December 7, 1941, a state of war has existed between the United States and the Japanese Empire."

Roosevelt closed his notebook to a thunder of clapping, cheers and rebel yells. He raised his hand in acknowledgment, took his son's arm and left the dais. For the first time since he became President, Roosevelt had spoken for all Americans. People of every political conviction were welded into a single angry voice. Partisan politics, for the moment at least, were forgotten. America had declared total war.

2.

Shrouded by rain and clouds, *Prince of Wales* and *Repulse* were deep in the Gulf of Siam when they were sighted by the Japanese submarine *I-56* at 1:45 P.M. on December 9. The radioman on *I-56* tapped out the report, but the static was so bad that although he tried again and again, he couldn't make himself understood. Across the gulf, in Saigon, Rear Admiral Sadaichi Matsunaga of the Navy's 22nd Air Flotilla was sure that the two warships were at their home base. Two reconnaissance planes had just returned from Singapore with pictures of what looked like one of the big ships (it was actually a massive floating dock).

At 3 P.M. a message from *I-56* was at last heard in Saigon: two enemy men-of-war and four destroyers were heading north at 14 knots near Procondor Island. This seemed more logical than the reconnaissance report, and the admiral ordered planes to prepare for attack at sea. While torpedoes were hastily being loaded and unpinned, a large group of curious Army officers arrived. Somehow they had learned that the Navy had tracked down the two British ships. Each plane lifted off to enthusiastic cheers.

Thirty minutes later Vice Admiral Phillips aboard *Prince of Wales* signaled *Repulse* and the destroyer escort:

WE HAVE MADE A WIDE CIRCUIT TO AVOID AIR RECONNAISSANCE AND HOPE TO SURPRISE THE ENEMY SHORTLY AFTER SUNRISE TOMORROW, WEDNESDAY. WE MAY HAVE THE LUCK TO TRY OUR METAL AGAINST SOME JAPANESE CRUISERS OR SOME DESTROYERS IN THE GULF OF SIAM. WE ARE SURE TO GET SOME USEFUL PRACTICE WITH HIGH-ANGLE ARMAMENT, BUT WHATEVER WE MEET I WANT TO FINISH QUICKLY AND GET WELL CLEAR TO THE EASTWARD BEFORE THE JAPANESE CAN MASS TOO FORMIDABLE A SCALE OF AIR ATTACK AGAINST US. SO, SHOOT TO SINK.

For the next few hours every ship in Force Z was alive with quiet anticipation until it was announced at about 9 P.M. that they had been discovered by three enemy aircraft and would be returning to Singapore. There was open disappointment and sarcasm.

The three planes which had forced "Tom Thumb" Phillips to turn back were Allied and they either did not see the British fleet or neglected to report it. The admiral was reading a message from his chief of staff in Singapore: ENEMY REPORTED LANDING AT KUANTAN—a point on the east coast of Malaya midway between Singapore and Kota Bharu. Almost an hour after midnight Force Z changed course for Kuantan, where not a single invader was landing. Another Japanese submarine, *I-58,* sighted the British fleet at 2:10 A.M., December 10, and after maneuvering around, fired six torpedoes at *Repulse.* All missed. No one aboard the battle cruiser was aware of the narrow escape.

Soon after dawn Phillips came upon a suspicious-looking tug and four barges about a hundred miles off Kuantan. *Prince of Wales* and *Repulse*—escorted by only three destroyers, since one,

Tenedos, was already on its way home to refuel—headed toward the tug at 9 A.M.

By this time three Japanese groups, totaling ninety-six high-level and torpedo bombers, and ten search planes sent out from Saigon before dawn had about given up hope of locating the British. The search planes were in fact on their way home when, through the clouds, one of them sighted two battleships and three destroyers seventy miles southeast of Kuantan. Fifteen minutes later, at 10:30 A.M., radio contact was finally made with the twenty-seven torpedo planes of Kanoya Air Group. Its three squadrons altered course. Lieutenant Haruki Iki, leader of the 3rd Squadron, forgot exhaustion and hunger. His nine-plane squadron held the title of "Champions of the Navy" and he was eager to prove himself in action. In moments he saw, from 10,000 feet, what looked like a British observation plane dodging behind a cloud. The enemy fleet had to be near.

Genzan Air Group got the same message. Lieutenant Sadao Takai, leader of the 2nd Squadron, radioed his men and they all banked north-northwest, followed by the 1st Squadron. Clouds began to pile up but occasionally Takai could see patches of sea. His hands trembled. He had a strange impulse to urinate. He remembered what his commander had told him at takeoff: "Calm down and put your strength in your stomach."

On the 26,500-ton *Repulse,* CBS correspondent Cecil Brown was taking pictures of a gun crew playing cards. As the ship zigzagged, he snapped *Prince of Wales* half a mile ahead. At 11:07 A.M. he heard the loudspeaker announce: "Enemy aircraft approaching. Action stations!" Suddenly a file of nine planes loomed to the south. Rooted to the flag deck in fascination, he watched a cloud of fluttering bombs grow larger and larger. There was a dull thud and the ship shuddered. "Fire on the boat deck!" blared the loudspeaker. "Fire below!"

The two squadrons of Genzan Air Group approached and Lieutenant Takai heard his commander order "Assault formation," then, "Go in!" The 1st Squadron swept ahead of Takai in a gradual dive. Takai followed. Where were the enemy fighters? Antiaircraft fire engulfed the 1st Squadron but none was near Takai. Through binoculars he studied a large ship giving off a narrow plume of white smoke. It looked exactly like the battleship

Kongo and his blood ran cold. He called the observer over the voice tube, who answered shakily, "It looks like our *Kongo* to me, too."

Takai was down to 1,500 feet before he was certain it was not *Kongo*. He turned into the clouds to confuse the enemy and when he darted into the open again he was less than two miles from his target.

A bugle blew on *Repulse*. "Stand by for barrage!" roared the loudspeaker. Every gun blasted as Takai's nine torpedo planes swooped in. "Look at those yellow bastards come," Brown heard someone mutter. Torpedoes slapped into the sea one by one and swam toward the battle cruiser as if they had eyes, but *Repulse*, despite her twenty-five years, dodged each one with elephantine grace. "Plucky blokes, these Japs," someone else said. "That was as beautiful an attack as ever I expect to see."

On the bridge Captain William Tennant had just noticed "Not under control" balls hoisted above *Prince of Wales*. He asked the flagship what damage she had suffered but got no answer. She was listing 13 degrees to port and weaving uncertainly at 15 knots. Both port shafts had been knocked out in the first attack and her steering gear wouldn't respond.

Tennant signaled Admiral Phillips, "We have dodged nineteen torpedoes thus far, thanks to Providence," adding that all damage from one bomb hit was under control. No answer. Tennant took it on himself to radio Singapore: ENEMY AIRCRAFT BOMBING. The message was received at 12:04 P.M., and in eleven minutes six clumsy Brewster Buffalo fighters plodded off to the rescue.

Tennant again signaled Phillips. Again no answer. He reduced *Repulse*'s speed to 20 knots and moved toward the flagship to offer any assistance. Just then another ominous line of torpedo planes appeared on the horizon.

It was a squadron from the third section, Mihoro Air Group, led by Lieutenant (s.g.) Katsusaku Takahashi. Like Takai, he thought the ships ahead were Japanese—until they fired at him. He dived at the admiral's flag on *Prince of Wales*, but since the ship was turning away, he swung toward *Repulse*, a mile or so to the north. As he lowered to less than 200 feet, followed by his squadron, he estimated the speed of *Repulse* by its wake. He adjusted a simple aiming device in front of him. How could he possibly miss such a long target?

His plane was 2,500 feet from *Repulse*. "Ready," he said. The navigator-bombardier gripped the release. "Fire!" The navigator pulled up. The plane skimmed so low over the battle cruiser that Takahashi could see sailors in white scrambling from his machine-gunners' spray. Once Takahashi began a climbing turn he asked, "Did it drop?"

"No, sir."

"I'll come in again." Takahashi banked to the right and came in from the other side of *Repulse,* but once more the torpedo failed to drop. Doggedly Takahashi circled around for a third try. This time he began jerking up on his own release a mile from the target. As the plane swept over *Repulse,* he and the navigator were still struggling with their releases but to no avail. Their disappointment was bitter. However, the squadron had scored at least one hit. *Repulse* was listing to port.

Lieutenant Iki's nine planes drew near. Iki dropped below the clouds to 1,300 feet. Pompom bursts blossomed on both sides. His instinct was to pull up but he had to get in much closer. He skimmed 125 feet above the water into a wall of fire from *Repulse*. Eighteen hundred feet from the ship he yanked his release. He had her broadside!

Flak peppered his wings as he banked sharply to the left. Momentarily parallel with the ship, he could distinguish sailors in raincoats lying flat on the deck. The plane behind him, piloted by Chief Petty Officer Toshimitsu Momoi, became a ball of fire. The next, First Class Petty Officer Yoshikazu Taue's, exploded and the wreckage pinwheeled clumsily into the sea. At the bow of the battle cruiser, there were two rapid explosions. As Iki climbed to wait for his six remaining planes, he watched another torpedo drive home.

Repulse veered crazily. One torpedo had smashed into the starboard, two into the port. The fourth, Iki's, did the most immediate damage; it hit near the gun room, jamming the rudder. The battle cruiser was doomed and Captain Tennant coolly announced over the loudspeaker, "Prepare to abandon ship." He congratulated the men for fighting the ship so well and added, "God be with you." The list increased to 70 degrees. "Well, gentlemen, you had better get out of it now," he told his staff, but he himself remained rooted to the bridge. Several officers laid hands on him. He struggled but was bodily carried off.

The men formed orderly lines to abandon ship. One young sailor tried to push ahead until a second lieutenant calmly remarked, "Now, now, we are all going the same way too." As the ship took on more and more water, her bow lifted and those still in the superstructure felt giddy from the sway. A man dived from the defense control tower into the sea 170 feet below, but the next one smashed into the deck and a third hurtled into the funnel. At the stern a group of marines jumped off—and were sucked into the churning propellers.

At 12:33 P.M. the battle cruiser rolled over, then with ponderous majesty slid stern first, her bow sticking up "like a church steeple," underplates a gruesome red. From 5,000 feet, Iki looked down incredulous at the bow pointing straight at him. *Repulse* plunged out of sight. It was not possible. Planes couldn't sink a battleship so easily. *"Banzai, banzai!"* he shouted and threw up his hands. The bomber, with no hands on the controls, dipped.

The crew was also shouting in frenzy. They drank a *sake* toast. Below, Iki could make out hundreds of dots in the water. Two destroyers were picking up the survivors. It never occurred to Iki to strafe them. The British had fought gallantly, in the tradition of *bushido*. He had yet to learn that an enemy spared today may kill you tomorrow.

Mortally wounded by five torpedoes, *Prince of Wales* was barely under way as nine high-level bombers approached. At 12:44 P.M. bombs careened down. Only one struck home but it staggered the 35,000-ton battleship and she began to founder. Her beams were almost awash. Captain Leach ordered all hands to abandon ship, while he and Admiral Phillips stood together on the bridge and waved to their departing men. "Good-bye," Leach called to them. "Thank you. Good luck. God bless you." At 1:19 the battleship—nicknamed *"H.M.S. Unsinkable"*—keeled heavily over to port like a stricken hippopotamus and within a minute sank from sight, taking with her the little admiral and Captain Leach.

The six lumbering Buffalos from Singapore arrived to find a sky empty of Japanese planes. Flight Lieutenant T. A. Vigors peered down in shock at masses of men struggling in the water. They waved and held up their thumbs.

Takahashi, who had failed to release his torpedo, was halfway home. Upon hearing that *Prince of Wales* and *Repulse* were doomed he felt a strange sympathy—the British Navy was like a big brother. He fought the impulse, but tears blurred his goggles. Lieutenant Iki thought with sadness of Momoi and Taue. He knew his own torpedo had hit *Repulse* first but reported that the initial two hits had been made by his two dead comrades. It was the least thing, the last thing he could do for them. As Iki's squadron landed, exuberant mechanics crowded around each plane. The crews were dragged out, tossed into the air. After he escaped the friendly pummeling, one of Iki's pilots told him, "As we dived for the attack, I didn't want to launch my torpedo. It was such a beautiful ship, such a beautiful ship."

At naval headquarters in Tokyo, the senior officers found it difficult to accept that battleships in the open sea could have been sunk by planes. It meant the end of their concept of naval warfare. The airmen were exultant. What they had been preaching for the past decade was proved. The third and final deterrent to victory in Southeast Asia had been eliminated at the cost of four planes.

The next dawn Iki flew over the graves of *Repulse* and *Prince of Wales*. As he skimmed over the sunken ships he dropped bunches of flowers.

3.

About the time Force Z turned back toward Singapore, Adolf Hitler finally arrived in Berlin from the eastern front. He was doubly concerned—by a mammoth Soviet counteroffensive in front of Moscow and the news from the Pacific. In a flash Pearl Harbor had freed his chief adversary from worry over attack from the east; Stalin could now transfer almost all his strength in Asia against Germany. For months the Führer had been urging Japan to fight Russia and avoid war with America; at the same time Tokyo pressed Ambassador Hiroshi Oshima to get written assurances that Hitler would attack America if war started, while withholding any promise to assault Russia in return.

Foreign Minister Joachim von Ribbentrop told Hitler that General Oshima was demanding an immediate declaration of war against America but reminded him that according to the terms of the Tripartite Pact, Germany was bound to assist Japan only in case she was directly attacked.

"If we don't stand on the side of Japan, the pact is politically dead," Hitler said. "But that is not the main reason. The chief reason is that the United States already is shooting at our ships. They have been a forceful factor in this war and through their actions have already created a situation of war."

Ribbentrop must have been confounded. This was a startling reversal of Hitler's own insistence on keeping America out of the European war at all costs, and for months the Führer had shown remarkable restraint in view of the U. S. Navy's provocative actions against U-boats in the Atlantic. Now all at once Hitler seemed to welcome a clean break. Perhaps it was a result of his frustration over the reversals in Russia and his wish to ride the crest of Japanese victories, or perhaps his almost psychotic hatred of Roosevelt had taken over. Whatever the reason, it would be folly, a major psychological blunder, and would only solve another of Roosevelt's domestic problems. The President would not have to declare war on Germany and risk opposition from a substantial segment of America. National unity, so unexpectedly won at Pearl Harbor, would remain intact.

Hitler began to indulge in a frenzy of wishful thinking. How could a country like America—"half Judaized, half Negrified" and "built on the dollar"—hope to hold together? Besides, Pearl Harbor couldn't have come at a more opportune moment. Russia was counterattacking and "everybody in Germany was oppressed by the certainty that sooner or later the United States would enter the conflict."

Later in the day, after ordering Hans Thomsen, the chargé d'affaires in Washington, to burn his codes and confidential papers, Ribbentrop received an estimate from Thomsen that "within twenty-four hours the United States will declare war on Germany or at least break off diplomatic relations."

Ribbentrop knew Hitler was set on getting in his own declaration first "for the sake of prestige," and warned Thomsen to have no dealings with the State Department. "We wish to avoid under all circumstances that the Government there beats us to such a step."

On December 11 Hitler convoked the Reichstag. "We will always strike first!" he thundered. "We will always deal the first blow!" Roosevelt was as "mad" as Woodrow Wilson. "First he incited war, then falsifies the causes, then odiously wraps himself in a cloak of Christian hypocrisy and slowly but surely leads mankind to war, not without calling God to witness the honesty of his attack. . . .

"I think you have all found it a relief now that, at last, one nation has been the first to take the step of protesting against this historically unique and shameless ill treatment of truth and of right. . . . The fact that the Japanese government, which has been negotiating for years with this man, has at last become tired of being mocked by him in such an unworthy way, fills us all, the German people, and I think, all other decent people in the world, with deep satisfaction. . . .

"I have therefore arranged for passports to be handed to the American chargé d'affaires today, and the following—" His words were drowned in a bedlam of cheers.

"The Reich Government therefore breaks off all diplomatic relations with the United States and declares that under these circumstances, brought about by President Roosevelt, Germany too considers herself to be at war with the United States, as from today." Later that day Germany, Italy and Japan signed another tripartite pact asserting their "unshakable determination not to lay down arms until the joint war against the United States and England reaches a successful conclusion," and pledging under no circumstances to conclude a separate peace.

Three days later, at the presentation to Oshima of the Grand Cross of the Order of Merit, Hitler said, "You gave the right declaration of war." It was certainly proper to negotiate as long as possible, but "if one sees that the antagonist is interested only in putting one off, in shaming and humiliating one, and is not willing to come to an agreement, then one should strike—indeed, as hard as possible—and not waste time declaring war." Japan had shown "angelical patience toward that ruffian Roosevelt," he said and quoted a German proverb: "The most amicable man can't live in peace if his quarrelsome neighbor wants to fight."

Oshima spread out a map to brief Hitler on the war situation throughout the Pacific. "After the capture of Singapore, Japan must turn toward India," he said and suggested that Germany synchronize operations with Japan. "When Japan attacks India from the east, it will be most advantageous if German troops threaten India from the west." Hitler refused to commit himself but did promise to drive over the Caucasus as far as Iraq and Iran. He wanted their oil.

The day Hitler declared war on America, reports reached Manila of a tremendous Allied victory in Lingayen Gulf the previous night. The 21st Division of the Philippine Army had repelled a major Japanese landing. Most of the invasion vessels had been sunk and the beaches were strewn with Japanese bodies.

Life photographer Carl Mydans couldn't find one casualty along Lingayen Gulf. Except for Filipino soldiers lolling beside their weapons, the beaches were empty. An amused American major explained that a single unidentified boat at the mouth of the Agno River had touched off a furious barrage of every gun in the area, from 155-mm. guns to pistols. (Their target, a Japanese motorboat on reconnaissance, escaped unharmed to report that the main landing, to come eleven days hence, should be made at the northern end of the gulf, some thirty miles away, where there were almost no beach defenses.)

Major LeGrande A. Diller, MacArthur's press chief, released a statement on how the enemy landing had been thwarted. While other reporters were wiring their papers and magazines, Mydans buttonholed Diller. "Pic," he said, "I've just been to Lingayen and there's no battle there."

Diller jabbed a finger at his communiqué. "It says so here."

The story of "the Battle of Lingayen Gulf" brought a welcome surge of pride and relief to Americans. The *New York Times* banner headline that Sunday read: JAPANESE FORCES WIPED OUT IN WESTERN LUZON. Lingayen Gulf had been retaken from the Japanese in sensational fashion. United Press went further: there had been a fierce three-day fight at Lingayen Beach; 154 enemy boats were sunk without, miracle of miracles, a single enemy reaching shore alive.

The morning after the Lingayen Gulf communiqué, another

announced a second triumph in the Philippines: Captain Colin P. Kelly, Jr., had "successfully attacked the battleship *Haruna,* putting that ship out of commission." The crew of Kelly's Flying Fortress had sighted a large warship just off the north coast of Luzon and the bombardier, Corporal Meyer Levin, released three 600-lb. bombs. Two missed but one appeared to go down the smokestack and when dark clouds of smoke erupted, the crew of the B-17 was certain the ship had been mortally damaged.

On the way back to Clark Field, Kelly's plane was pounced by a Zero—its pilot was Saburo Sakai, already an ace. The Fortress burst into flames and Kelly ordered his men to bail out. The ship exploded with Kelly aboard and plummeted into a dirt road at the foot of Mount Arayat. Kelly had sacrificed his life so his crew could live, and America had her first super hero of World War II. Kelly's gallantry deserved the posthumous D.S.C. he was awarded, but he had not sunk *Haruna,* which was fifteen hundred miles away in the Gulf of Siam. There had not been a battleship near the Philippines. Nothing in the area had been sunk or, for that matter, badly damaged, but the facts became even more distorted with each telling. The most popular version, the one many Americans still retain, was that Kelly won the Medal of Honor (which he did not) by diving his plane into *Haruna*'s smokestack to become the first suicide pilot of the war.

At the same time the public was being lulled into overconfidence by dispatches from Clark Lee, the Associated Press correspondent in Manila, which derided the ability of the Japanese fighting man and the quality of his equipment. A competent newsman, Lee was merely repeating what he had been told by American military men: "The Japanese Army is an ill-uniformed, untrained mass of young boys between fifteen and eighteen years old, equipped with small-caliber guns and driven forward by desperate determination to advance or die." Their .25-caliber rifle and machine-gun bullets could not even kill a man. "They're no damned good on the ground," he quoted one cavalry colonel. "We licked the pants off them three times and were beaten only by their tanks and planes. When our tanks and planes go into action we'll chase them back to the sea. These Charlies—we call them Charlies—can't shoot. Somebody gets hit about every 5,000 shots."

MacArthur himself knew this was ridiculous. In 1905 he had studied voluminous reports of the Russo-Japanese War by American military observers, including General John J. Pershing: "Intelligence, patriotism, abstemiousness, obedience to, and inborn respect for, legally constituted authority go far toward achieving victory. When to these we add physical strength, a love of nature and of manly sports, modern organization, armament, equipment, and careful military training we have an army that will give a good account of itself. All of these were found in the Japanese army."

One observer noted that Japanese casualties were "curiously active in spite of their wounds, men shot through the head, neck, body, arms and legs being observed walking around or hopping around, as the case might be, cheerful and lively and indifferent to their wounds. They showed extraordinary vitality, with a noticeably less amount of nervous shock from wounds than I have observed in American soldiers whom I have seen similarly wounded in the Spanish war and the Philippine insurrection."

The initial phase of the Japanese master plan was working as neatly in the field as it had in tabletop maneuvers. The confusion in Malaya was short-lived and General Yamashita was driving steadily down the peninsula toward Singapore. Far to the north, at Hong Kong, the last Indian, Scotch and Canadian troops on the mainland of China were evacuated across the narrow bay to the island itself. The arrival of these defeated soldiers caused a near-panic, for it emphasized how desperate the British military position was in reality.

Out in the Pacific, the American island of Guam had fallen after a brief struggle in which seventeen American and Guamanians and one Japanese were killed. But at Wake Island, two thousand miles from Honolulu, American resistance was savage. Rear Admiral Sadamichi Kajioka's Wake Island Invasion Force—a light cruiser, six destroyers, two transports and a landing party of 560 infantry-trained sailors—was thrown back on the morning of December 11 by the small garrison under Marine Major James Devereux. Kajioka regrouped, got surface reinforcements from *Kido Butai* returning to Japan, and made a second assault early on the morning of December 23 with 830 men.

On the beach Devereux had 250 Marines, 100 civilian volunteers and no more than a few rounds of ammunition. The defenders fought desperately to the last bullet, but at eight-thirty Devereux was forced to walk out of his battered command post with a white rag on a swab handle and surrender to a Japanese officer who offered Devereux a cigarette and said he had attended the San Francisco Fair in 1939. That afternoon Admiral Kajioka, wearing spotless whites, medals and dress sword, came ashore to take formal possession of the two and a half square miles of coral rubble. It was renamed Bird Island.

Japan welcomed home the heroes of Pearl Harbor with celebrations and flowery congratulatory speeches but Yamamoto sounded a note of caution, warning his men to beware of smugness: "There are many more battles ahead."

Vice Admiral Nagumo was ordered to Tokyo along with the commanders of the two waves, Mitsuo Fuchida and Shigekazu Shimazaki, to report to the Throne. The Imperial Household had submitted a series of questions the Emperor would ask, and Kusaka had written down word for word the answers so Nagumo would not slip into the earthy phrases of his native Aizu. All went well at the audience until the Emperor began asking impromptu questions. While his two junior officers sweated in embarrassment, blunt little Nagumo reverted to colloquial terms, referring to American admirals as *aitsu* (that guy) and *koitsu* (this guy). The replies so fascinated the Emperor that the fifteen-minute audience stretched on for another half-hour. He asked Fuchida if any hospital ships had been hit or civilian or training planes knocked down. Instead of answering through an imperial aide, Fuchida became so flustered that he replied directly that no noncombatants had been attacked. It was a miserable moment for Fuchida—a worse ordeal, he thought, than the raid itself.

Roosevelt, Churchill and Stalin were united against Hitler, but at the moment the first two were desperately in need of help on the other side of the world. In Moscow, Foreign Secretary Anthony Eden put the question politely to Stalin in mid-December: would he join his allies and declare war on Japan? Stalin explained that he had been forced to withdraw troops from the Far East to hold back Hitler and didn't think he could replace them in less than four months. He couldn't declare war on Japan or provoke her until these forces were back to strength. Perhaps before then Japan would herself solve the problem by attacking Russia: he was inclined to hope that would happen, since it would be difficult to get much popular support for another war thousands of miles to the east.

Curiously, he was convinced that Japanese air successes would not have been possible without the Germans, who—according to one secret report—had contributed fifteen hundred aircraft and hundreds of pilots.

"Certainly the Japanese have shown more skill in the air than we expected," Eden remarked politely.

"We have had experience fighting the Japanese in the air and we have also carefully observed them in China for a very long time, and I have come to the conclusion that this is not really a Japanese war. I think some of the Japanese pilots were trained in Germany, and others are German."

"How do you think the airplanes got there?"

"Probably through South America."

Eden apologized for not sending ten squadrons to the Russian front; they would have to go to Singapore.

"I fully understand and have no objection," Stalin said.

"It is a great disappointment to us."

"I fully realize the position and that the situation has changed. We, too, have had our difficult periods."

"I very much appreciate the spirit of your answer," Eden said, "and if the wheel goes round again we shall be very glad to help."

On his part, Stalin was sorry he could not help in the Far East. "We can do nothing now, but in the spring we shall be ready, and will then help."

Eden made another effort to get a more definite commitment and used the deteriorating situation in Malaya as the excuse.

"If the Soviet Union were to declare war on Japan," Stalin replied, "we should have to wage a real war by land, on sea and in the air. It would not be like the declarations of war on Japan by Belgium and Poland. Consequently we have to make a careful estimate of the forces involved. At present we are not ready. . . . We would prefer that Japan should attack us, and I think it very probable that she will do so—not just yet, but later. If the Germans are hard pressed it is likely that they will urge the Japanese to attack us, in which case the attack may be expected about the middle of next year."

This did not satisfy Eden. "I fear that the Japanese may meanwhile adopt a policy of dealing with their opponents one by one, and may try to finish with us before attacking the Soviet Union."

"Great Britain is not fighting Japan alone. She has allies in China, the Dutch East Indies and the United States of America."

"The main attack at the moment is on Malaya, where our allies cannot help us much," said Eden. The next six months were going to be most difficult. "We have got to stick it out, and we shall do so. But it is a very uncomfortable situation." Even so, the Libyan campaign would not be called off just to increase the strength in Malaya. "The Far East must hold until we can afford to send reinforcements."

"I think that is quite sound. The weakest link of the Axis is Italy, and if this link is broken the whole Axis will collapse." Stalin couldn't help adding that if the British had attacked Italy in 1939, "they would not be masters of the situation in the Mediterranean."

Dinner that evening went on until dawn and several officers —notably the colorful Commissar for Defense, Marshal Semën Timoshenko—became intoxicated. Stalin turned to Eden in embarrassment. "Do your generals ever get drunk?"

"They don't often get the chance," was the diplomatic answer.

Churchill was aboard *Duke of York*, a day's sail from Chesapeake Bay, when he received a cable from Eden announcing that the talks with Stalin had "ended on a friendly note." He was bound for "Arcadia," code name of the first wartime conference between Britain and America and named after the region in Greece so famed for its pastoral innocence and contentment that it has become a universal symbol. The conference, designed to bring about the best means of fighting the Axis, was to belie its name from the beginning.

Churchill and his Chiefs of Staff expected to dominate "Arcadia," and by the time they arrived in Washington on the evening of December 22, they had formulated a detailed program: Germany was the prime enemy and her defeat was the key to victory. Italy and Japan would then speedily collapse. "In our considered opinion, therefore, it should be a cardinal principal of A-B [American-British] strategy that only the minimum of force necessary for the safeguarding of vital interests in other theatres should be diverted from operations against Germany."

But at the first meeting the following afternoon it was immediately apparent that the Americans had not come merely to listen and approve. They made it clear that only a frontal attack on Germany would bring victory and that the British concept of maneuver was nothing but a pecking away at the edges. It was an understandable conflict between a nation whose limited forces had already been strained by more than two years of war and one new to battle with almost unlimited resources and manpower. To the Americans, war was something like an athletic contest and little was thought of what would happen when peace came. The more sophisticated British regarded battle as flexible, a continuation of policy that could take surprising turns. Even the best friend the United States had among the British military leaders, Sir John Dill, privately felt that America had not—"repeat not—the slightest conception of what the war means, and their armed forces are more unready for war than it is possible to imagine."

4.

On the day Churchill arrived in Washington a large invasion force of eighty-five transports approached the Philippines. The submarine *Stingray* had sighted the convoy in time to alert General MacArthur, who expected the Japanese to land at the southern end of Lingayen Gulf where the bulk of his artillery was emplaced. The Japanese knew all about this concentration from "the Battle of Lingayen Gulf" and were about to land the 14th Army miles up the coast.

The Army commander, General Masaharu Homma, the amateur playwright, had long opposed the road to war. He had spent eight years with the British, including service in France in 1918 with the British Expeditionary Force and had deep respect for and some understanding of the West. Following the fall of Nanking, he had publicly declared that "unless peace is achieved immediately it will be disastrous," and then confided to General Muto that Tojo would make a poor minister of war.

Few of his men knew where they were. They had been secretly loaded five days earlier at Formosa and the Pescadores, and even those officers who knew their destination had the vaguest of instructions. The first of Homma's 43,110 men began going overside at two o'clock in the morning on December 22. The high seas almost swamped the first boats, and it took two and a half hours to load two battalions of infantry and a battalion of mountain artillery. Forty-seven minutes later the first boat ground onto a beach near the town of Agoo, but many of the landing craft which followed were overturned by the roaring breakers. On the beach the soldiers met no resistance.

By midmorning the entire first wave had landed and the beachhead was consolidated with spirited opposition from a lone Filipino battalion. Late that afternoon all the infantry and half the tanks were ashore and moving south down Route 3, the paved highway running along the coast to Manila.

In the capital MacArthur anxiously awaited news from Lingayen Gulf. He radioed Marshall a suggestion that carriers bring pursuit planes within range of the Philippines: CAN I EXPECT ANYTHING ALONG THAT LINE? Marshall replied that according to the Navy, this was impossible and MacArthur would have to rely on the planes already ferried as far as Brisbane in Australia.

At dawn General Brereton's remaining bombers—four Fortresses—attacked the Japanese convoy in Lingayen Gulf. They dropped 100-lb. bombs and then turned south for Australia. Homma was steadily pushing toward Manila and early in the afternoon attacked the unit blockading the main road. With scarcely ten weeks' training, few of these Filipino soldiers knew how to operate their antiquated Enfield rifles. They broke and fled, leaving the supporting artillery unprotected. Major General Jonathan M. ("Skinny") Wainwright, commander of all forces in northern Luzon, phoned MacArthur for permission to withdraw behind the Agno River.

With no air force or navy, MacArthur had to abandon his dream of holding the enemy at the beaches and was obliged to fall back on a plan drawn up by his predecessors. This was known as War Plan Orange-3 and provided for withdrawal of Fil-American forces to the Bataan Peninsula if enemy landings could not be contained. Here, within sight of Manila, the defenders would hold out for as long as six months until the Navy could bring in reinforcements. MacArthur had long since shelved this operation as defeatist. All he could do now was call in his staff and say, "Put WPO-3 into effect."

The situation was worse than MacArthur had feared. The next morning he discovered that his forces were caught in a giant pincers. Twenty-four Japanese transports had landed during the night at Lamon Bay, sixty air miles southeast of Manila, and almost ten thousand men of the 16th Division were advancing on Manila in three columns. At ten o'clock MacArthur ordered his South Luzon Force, two divisions, to retreat to Bataan. The battle in the south was over before it started and MacArthur was forced to give instructions to transfer his headquarters to Corregidor Island at dark.

Nearby in the Marsman Building, Admiral Hart told Rear Admiral Francis W. Rockwell, commandant of the 16th Naval District, that he was moving his headquarters south to Borneo so he could be with the operating fleet. Rockwell would assume command of all naval remnants. Their conversation was drowned out by the roar of planes and thunder of bombs exploding in the Walled City. They could see flames all over the port area. Dust from pulverized cement and stone mixed with black billows of smoke engulfed the entire Pasig River section.

At Malacañan Palace, President Manuel Quezon was exhorting his executive secretary, Jorge Vargas, and José Laurel to make a sacrifice without parallel for the good of the people: "You two will remain here and deal with the Japanese." He and Vice President Sergio Osmeña would join MacArthur on Corregidor.

All four of them must pledge never to reveal his order to Vargas and Laurel. But people will call me a collaborator, protested Laurel. He broke down and begged for permission to accompany Quezon to Corregidor. It was Laurel's duty, insisted Quezon, who was dying of tuberculosis. "Someone has to protect the people from the Japanese."

Outside, the streets swarmed with Army trucks and squat Pambusco buses overflowing with soldiers and supplies. Every vehicle was going north—toward Bataan, on the other side of the bay. As darkness came on, the steamer *Don Esteban,* with MacArthur and most of his staff aboard, plowed across the inlet toward Corregidor, less than thirty miles away. It was balmy and the moon was shining. In the distance, flames leaped up from Cavite Navy Yard's oil dump. Almost all of the men of USAFFE headquarters were in short sleeves. It was a strange Christmas Eve for Americans.

Seven hundred miles to the north another island bastion was about to fall. The Japanese held most of Hong Kong's mountainous thirty-two square miles. The British forces were split in two and their final lines were crumpling. There was little ammunition left and only enough water for another day or so. Though the resistance on the mainland had been disappointing, the stand on the island was stubborn, primarily because of the determination of the 1,759 men of the Hong Kong Volunteer Defence Corps. Dubbed "playboy soldiers" by the Regulars, this mixture of local British, Eurasian, Chinese and Portuguese civilian recruits had fought as well as any of the other troops and better than most.

By Christmas morning those defenders were overrun who were cut off at the narrow Stanley Peninsula on the southern end of the island, and uncontrolled groups of Japanese began butchering the wounded and raping Chinese and British nurses. The main force at Victoria, the capital of Hong Kong, was also close to being overwhelmed. At nine o'clock two prisoners of the Japanese—a retired British major and a civilian—were released with a message for Major-General C. M. Maltby, military commander of the colony: it would be useless to continue the fight and the Japanese had promised to hold fire for three hours while the British made up their minds.

Maltby held off until three-fifteen before reluctantly ordering his commanders to surrender. It was a humiliating end to British rule in China—and even with surrender the atrocities continued throughout Christmas night.

It was also a dark Christmas in the Philippines. That morning MacArthur reviewed the gloomy situation at his new headquarters on Corregidor, a small tadpole-shaped island three miles south of Bataan Peninsula in the mouth of Manila Bay. Whoever held it controlled the bay, for it stuck in its throat like a bone. The coastal-gun, mortar and antiaircraft batteries were formidable, and the labyrinthine tunnel system in the solid rock under Malinta Hill provided bombproof shelter for a hospital, headquarters, shops and storehouses.

The flow of American traffic was moving toward Bataan from every direction. Route 3 out of Manila was clogged with trucks, 155's on their carriages, naval guns on trucks, buses, cars, *calesas* and oxcarts. A couple of well-placed bombs on the two bridges at Calumpit, thirty miles north of Manila, over the wide, unfordable Pampanga River, would have cut off all forces from the south.

Ten miles above the bridges the line of vehicles turned left at San Fernando toward the peninsula. Here they met the van of Wainwright's main body flowing in from the north. The result was a monumental traffic jam and the road from San Fernando leading into Bataan was so narrow that traffic had backed up into town before noon.

The peninsula itself was bedlam. As thousands of frightened civilian refugees fleeing ahead of Homma's army streamed into Bataan on foot, in oxcarts and ramshackle cars, fragments of units arrived to find few road signs or markers and wandered about in confusion. The trenches and fortifications specified by WPO-3 existed on paper alone. The villagers should have been evacuated but someone had apparently forgotten to give the order; they stared in wonder as an endless parade of trucks, cars and guns rumbled past, coating their bamboo houses with thick layers of dust.

WPO-3 called for a six-month food supply, but there was not enough for a month. More provisions were on the way by water, rail and highway, but for how many more hours would the roads to Bataan be kept open? The one hope was that Wainwright's men could delay the enemy drive from the north another two weeks. This would give the troops on Bataan time to dig defenses while the South Luzon Force retreated up through Manila and into Bataan. At best it was a slim chance. Then came an official report that the Japanese had penetrated the Agno River line, the last formidable natural fortification between them and Bataan. It seemed unlikely that the poorly trained and exhausted defenders could hold back the Japanese long enough. Could they resist even until New Year's Day?

On Christmas Day a flying boat brought an admiral to Hawaii from the mainland. It was Chester Nimitz, the man chosen to relieve Admiral Kimmel and command all naval forces in the Pacific. His hair was turning white but he was trim-looking and his blue eyes were piercing. He had hoped for a sea command.

In a few hours Nimitz found what he had feared—too much pessimism. Morale was at "rock bottom" and he noticed that the shock of Pearl Harbor had turned several senior officers' hair white. He summoned the staff he had inherited, some of whom were taking sedatives on surgeon's orders. "There will be no changes," he said. "I have complete confidence in you men. We've taken a terrific wallop but I have no doubts as to the ultimate outcome."

In his Academy classbook he was described as a man "of cheerful and confident tomorrows," and true to form his calm serenity was infectious. But he knew the complete rehabilitation of spirit would take time. The Pacific Fleet would not be ready to strike back in force for several months.

The last survivors of those trapped inside the sunken battleship *West Virginia* finally lay lifeless on the lower shelf of storeroom A-111. On a bulkhead was a calendar with X's marked from December 7 through 23.

5.

"This is a strange Christmas Eve," Winston Churchill said emotionally. He was standing next to Roosevelt on the south portico of the White House addressing a crowd of thirty thousand gathered on the south lawn for the traditional lighting of the municipal Christmas tree. "Almost the whole world is locked in deadly struggle, and with the most terrible weapons which science can devise, the nations advance upon each other. . . . Here, in the midst of war, raging and roaring over all the lands and seas, creeping nearer to our hearths and homes, here, amid all the tumult, we have tonight the peace of the spirit in each cottage home and in every generous heart. . . . Let the children have their night of fun and laughter. Let the gifts of Father Christmas delight their play. Let us grown-ups share to the full in their unstinted pleasures before we turn again to the stern task and the formidable years that lie before us, resolved that, by our sacrifices and daring, these same children shall not be robbed of their inheritance or denied their right to live in a free and decent world."

He told his personal physician, Lord Moran, that he'd had palpitations during the ceremony and wanted his pulse taken. "It has all been very moving," he lisped excitedly. "This is a new war, with Russia victorious, Japan in, and America in up to the neck."

On Christmas morning Roosevelt took his guest to church, remarking, "It is good for Winston to sing hymns with the Methodies." He sang one he had never heard of before—"O Little Town of Bethlehem." After the service he spent hours preparing a speech for Congress. What mood would he find his listeners in the next morning? Some were not at all friendly to the British.

They were captivated from the moment he said, "I feel greatly honored that you should have invited me to enter the United States Senate Chamber and address the representatives of both branches of Congress. I cannot help reflecting that if my father had been American and my mother British, instead of the other way round, I might have got here on my own." A loud shout erupted when, speaking of the Japanese, he cried, "What sort of people do they think we are?" He continued, his voice rising above the din, to speak movingly and effectively of the task that lay ahead. "It is not given to us to peer into the mysteries of the future. Still, I avow my hope and faith, sure and inviolate, that in the days to come the British and American peoples will for their own safety and for the good of all walk together side by side in majesty, in justice, and in peace."

There was a spontaneous and unreserved burst of applause.

The American military leaders, however, were in no such mood. They had just been informed that their impulsive President had had himself wheeled into Churchill's room the previous night for an impromptu meeting—and agreed to consider giving the British the reinforcements promised to MacArthur if the line of supply to the Philippines was cut. The outraged American Chiefs appealed to Stimson, who became so "extremely angry" that he immediately phoned Hopkins to say the President would have to get a new Secretary of War if he kept on making such quixotic personal decisions. Roosevelt hastened to deny that "any such proposition had actually been made," and swore he had never considered siphoning off any supplies from MacArthur.

The first plenary session of "Arcadia" met that afternoon in an edgy, uneasy atmosphere, and it was Roosevelt himself who jolted the British by saying he was not satisfied that available resources were being put to their best use. Had the Chiefs of Staff discussed the possibility of a unified command in the Far East? He was echoing the suggestion of General Marshall, who the day before had told the British and American Chiefs of Staff that "there must be one man in command of the entire theater—air, ground, and ships."

Churchill violently disagreed. Unity of command was fine if there was one continuous front, as in World War I, but in the Far East some Allied units were a thousand miles apart. "The situation out there is that certain particular strategic points have to be held, and the commander in each locality is quite clear as to what he should do," he contended. "The difficult question is the application of resources arriving in the area. This is a matter which can only be settled by the Governments concerned."

Lord Beaverbrook, the Minister of Supply, passed a note to Hopkins:

> You should work on Churchill. He is being advised. He is open minded and needs discussion.

Encouraged by this, Hopkins privately told Churchill, "Don't be in a hurry to turn down the proposal the President is going to make to you before you know who is the man we have in mind." It was General Archibald Wavell.

The next evening the British Chiefs of Staff called on Churchill to say they were ready to accept a unified command in principle. They suggested that an American officer be chosen to head the ABDA (American, British, Dutch, Australian) command. Churchill imagined his Chiefs would be as delighted as he to hear that the Americans were willing to accept Wavell. But they interpreted this suggestion as a Roosevelt trick—the Far East was crumbling and Wavell would be blamed for the defeat.* Let some American take the post.

---

* Informed of his appointment, Wavell wryly said, "I have heard of men having to hold the baby, but this is twins."

Their attitude did not set well with Churchill. He could not believe Roosevelt was "attempting to shift disaster onto our shoulders," nor did he want to surrender responsibility for Singapore to the Americans. Think what the Australians would make of that! Prime Minister John Curtin had recently stated in an article: "Australia looks to America, free from any pangs as to traditional links or kinship with the United Kingdom."

As he argued, his indignation grew. The Chiefs' suspicions were insulting to the President—whose offer had been a friendly, generous gesture—and he would not stand for it. Argument ended, but not resentment. The British Chiefs felt they were becoming minor partners under the polite but forceful domination of their juniors.

Ironically, out of this squall came one of the most significant developments of the war—reaffirmation of a previous decision, the creation of a unified command system, a Combined Chiefs of Staff with headquarters in Washington, the new capital of Western democracy. This remarkable achievement, fathered by Marshall and fostered by Roosevelt, was made possible by the openmindedness of Winston Churchill. He saw beyond the objections and suspicions of his own Chiefs, to solidify Anglo-Saxon unity and achieve what he had come for: confirmation that Hitler was the main enemy and realization that the war in the Pacific would have to be, for the time being, a holding action.

On New Year's morning Roosevelt turned his mind from the military to global politics. He was wheeled into Churchill's room with a draft of a joint declaration by twenty-six nations fighting the Axis powers "to defend life, liberty, independence and religious freedom, and to preserve human rights and justice in their own lands as well as other lands" by waging common war against "savage and brutal forces seeking to subjugate the world." According to Hopkins, Churchill burst out of the shower stark naked. ("I never received the President without at least a bath towel wrapped around me," said Churchill.) Roosevelt apologetically made as if to leave but Churchill said, "The Prime Minister of Great Britain has nothing to conceal from the President of the United States."

The two men agreed on the draft, which was the genesis of the United Nations, and later in the day both signed it in the President's study, along with Soviet Ambassador Maxim Litvinov and Chinese Foreign Minister T. V. Soong.

"Arcadia" lasted for another two weeks. Much had been accomplished, but some of the British left disgruntled. "The Americans have got their way and the war will be run from Washington," Lord Moran wrote in his diary, "but they will not be wise to push us so unceremoniously in the future. Our people are very unhappy about the decision, and the most they will agree to is to try it out for a month."

Churchill himself went home in great good humor, exulting over the final joint production estimates reached at the conference: 45,000 tanks and 43,000 planes in 1942, and 75,000 tanks and 100,000 planes the following year. "He is drunk with the figures," commented Moran.

The decisions at "Arcadia" were picked up by a Japanese secret agent almost as soon as they were made. "Sutton," the cashiered American major, pumped this information from friends at the Army-Navy Club on Farragut Square and passed it along to Commander Wachi, the spy master in Mexico City. Sutton revealed that America's initial intentions to wage all-out war against Japan had been drastically altered and that the Allies would concentrate on defeating Hitler while holding Japan as best they could. He even had details of the final plan to defeat Japan by co-ordinated attacks of submarine packs and fleets of huge bombers; the latter would hit Kyushu from bases in China while the submarines cut all sea lanes to the homeland.

It was a major coup, as significant as any of Sorge's. Wachi sent it to Japan through two channels: a local German agent who dispatched reports to Berlin almost every night in code; and by ordinary airmail (the message was written in invisible ink bought from another German agent for $2,000) to the Japanese naval attaché in neutral Buenos Aires.

The information industriously gleaned by Major Sutton reached Tokyo from both sources, but naval headquarters was so intoxicated by recent victories that the report was merely glanced at, and forgotten.

10

"For a Wasted Hope and Sure Defeat"

1.

New Year's, the favorite Japanese holiday, was celebrated as usual in Tokyo. Debts were paid up; an endless parade thronged into the Meiji Shrine to throw coins at a donation chest on the stroke of midnight and, for good luck, buy red *daruma* dolls with weighted bottoms. The gaiety was not dampened by the war; on the contrary, it fostered a mood of expectancy. When would the next triumph come?

General Muto, chief of the Military Affairs Bureau, called on Shigenori Togo at the Foreign Ministry and after several cups of *toso* (New Year's wine) said, "The people are enjoying the victories too much. It won't do." It was going to be an arduous war. "Your policy, therefore, should be to end it as soon as possible." The first step was to replace Tojo as prime minister, said Muto, and left to tell the same things to a former premier who had long opposed military aggression, Admiral Okada.

The Japanese in the Philippines celebrated the day by converging on Manila from two directions. General Homma was just seventeen miles from the capital with little in front to stop him. The troops in the south had been slowed up some forty miles away because dynamiters had destroyed so many highway and railroad bridges, but they too faced almost no opposition. Homma halted his columns, ordering his men to clean themselves and tighten their formations. Unkempt troops, he knew, did not parade with pride and were more likely to loot and rape.

Stores were boarded up in the city. Near the dock area Carl Mydans of *Life* magazine watched looters rifle warehouses of everything from automobiles to unexposed movie film. When he returned to the Bayview Hotel his wife, Shelley, handed him a cable from *Life*. It requested: ANOTHER FIRST-PERSON EYEWITNESS STORY BUT THIS WEEK WE PREFER AMERICANS ON THE OFFENSIVE.

She showed her answer: BITTERLY REGRET YOUR REQUEST UNAVAILABLE HERE.

Smoke seemed to permeate Manila. The Pandacan oil fields as well as all Army and Navy installations were ablaze. At five forty-five Major General Koichi Abe led three battalions of his 48th Division into Manila from the north. They were greeted with silence by lines of sullen Filipinos. The cheers came from a handful of Japanese freed from internment.

From their hotel room the Mydanses watched three companies of Japanese soldiers and sailors form ragged lines on the lawn in front of High Commissioner Francis B. Sayre's residence across the boulevard. The American flag was lowered from a pole and three small cannon boomed as it fluttered to the ground. A sailor stamped on it and fastened in its place the emblem of the Rising Sun. As the new flag rose, the band spiritedly played the Japanese national anthem, "Kimigayo."

> *The Emperor's reign will last*
> *For a thousand and then eight thousand generations*
> *Until pebbles become mighty rocks*
> *Covered with moss.*

Across Manila Bay, General MacArthur's troops still streamed into Bataan for the final battle, but Homma and most of his staff concluded that this mass migration to the peninsula was merely a disorganized flight. He was confident, as were his superiors in Saigon and Tokyo, that Manila was the key to total victory. The Philippine campaign was over even if MacArthur did hold out on Corregidor and the tip end of Bataan for several weeks.

"For a Wasted Hope and Sure Defeat"   325

From Saigon, General Hisaichi Terauchi sent word to transfer the 48th Division to the Java invasion force. The successes in the Philippines and Malaya had exceeded all expectations and Terauchi could invade Java a month ahead of schedule.

Despite his easy victory, Homma was disturbed. Mopping-up operations would be difficult and the loss of the 48th, his best division, would place an unwarranted burden on the remaining troops. He asked to keep the division another month but was refused.

The 48th was on the front line in Bataan. Its replacement was the 65th "Summer" Brigade from Formosa, an occupation force of seventy-five hundred, comprised mostly of older men almost totally unprepared and unequipped for front-line duty. The unexpected assignment dismayed its commander, Lieutenant General Akira Nara, who had spent many years in the United States, where he attended Amherst College as a classmate of President Coolidge's son and graduated from the Fort Benning Infantry School.

On the night of January 5 Nara—a stocky, middle-aged man—led his troops toward the front on foot. Behind him, stretching halfway back to Lingayen Gulf, straggled his weary men, already delayed for days by American engineers who had left 184 destroyed bridges behind them.

The tropical evening was beautiful, the air fragrant with the exotic scent of frangipani. Bushes clustered with fireflies reminded Nara of Christmas trees, but those who trudged behind were too miserable to savor the beauties of the tropics.

They approached a Bataan crammed with some 15,000 Americans and 65,000 Filipino troops. Ten thousand of the latter were professional soldiers, the elite Philippine Division; the rest was a conglomerate ill-equipped group almost totally untrained. With this force and barely enough unbalanced field rations for 100,000 men for thirty days, MacArthur was supposed to hold out for six months. His greatest asset was the terrain. The peninsula, fifteen miles wide and twice as long, was almost completely occupied by the ancient remnants of two great extinct volcanoes, one in the north, one in the south. In between was thick jungle. There were but two roads. One was a semibelt highway coursing down the flat, swampy east coast, around the tip and two thirds of the way back up the other side of the peninsula. The other was a cobblestone road cutting across the midrift of Bataan through the valley between the two volcanoes.

MacArthur intended to make his first stand at a line about ten miles down the peninsula, running from Manila Bay across the northern volcano, whose mouth, after thousands of years, had been eroded into four jagged peaks. The eastern and highest peak was the precipitous Mount Natib.

By the morning of January 9 MacArthur's men were in position, and morale was high though they were already on half rations. They were tired of retreat and wanted to stand and fight. MacArthur split his battle line in two, assigning the left (the western half) to Wainwright, whose men were in no shape for immediate combat after their chaotic flight from Lingayen Gulf. It was obvious that the Japanese would first attack on the right side, down the east coastal highway. This sector was turned over to Major General George Parker, commander of the twenty-five thousand men who had escaped from the south with relative ease.

His right flank, the east coast, was flat and swampy, with fish ponds and rice paddies extending inland for about two miles. Then came gradually rising cane fields and little bamboo groves for another five miles. At this point Mount Natib began to rise dramatically. Since no military force on earth could possibly march across the complex of crags, ravines and cliffs, all matted with dense jungle growth, Parker's left flank ended abruptly at the foot of the rugged mountain.

This was the Abucay line, named after a cluster of nipa shacks for sugar-cane workers. The Filipinos were anxious to show MacArthur they deserved his faith and to prove that the rout on the humiliating retreat had been no fair test. Their American instructors were not as sanguine. But there was one advantage to the Abucay line—retreat would be difficult. It was fight or die.

A few miles to the north, General Nara's overaged and underarmed troops had just moved into position, relieving the cocky veterans of the 48th Division. At the War College, Nara had warned his pupils never to attack without accurate maps. Here he had a road map and several large-scale maps. Nor did he have a plan of attack; his instructions from 14th Army had merely been to "pursue the enemy in column down the highway," with the help of two artillery regiments and the 9th Infantry Regiment of the 16th Division.

He had been assured that there were no more than twenty-five thousand disorganized enemy troops on Bataan and that they would retreat pell-mell to the little town of Mariveles on the tip end of the peninsula at the first rattle of gunfire. Here they would make a brief stand before trying to escape to the island of Corregidor. All the same, Nara asked for time to make a survey. He was ordered to attack immediately. He hastily drew up a plan. It was perforce simple, with only a day for organization. He instructed his own 141st Infantry, under Colonel Takeo Imai, to attack straight down the coastal highway while the 9th Infantry, commanded by an old and trusted friend, Colonel Susumu Takechi, headed down the peninsula toward the slopes of Mount Natib. He would cross the supposedly impassable mountain and cut back to the coastal highway, thus encircling the enemy.

That afternoon, after an hour-long artillery barrage, Imai started down the highway while Takechi struck off into the tangled jungle. Imai had scarcely gone a hundred yards before the road ahead erupted with a series of thunderous roars. It was Parker's artillery. The Americans were not going to cut and run at the first volley.

The Filipinos weren't either. They fell upon the Japanese dispersed by the artillery bombardment and in the next forty-eight hours cut Imai's regiment to a third. Accordingly, Nara was forced to replace the remnants with a reserve unit. His troubles were just beginning. Not a word had come from Takechi; he should already have crossed Mount Natib and circled behind the enemy. Darkness came and he still had not appeared. The jungle had swallowed him up. Nara did not report this to Homma, neither did he record it in his war diary or brigade report; it was the least he could do for a classmate at the Academy. It meant the end of Nara's bold plan. Now he turned his efforts to rebuilding his lines. He shuttled Imai's exhausted troops to the west to fill in the hole vacated by Takechi and sent out orders to begin probing for a weak spot in the Abucay line.

That same day, January 13, Quezon sent a radiogram to Roosevelt through MacArthur complaining that the President had failed to keep his pledge to send aid to the Philippines. He urged him to direct the full force of American strength against the Japanese at once. His indignation carried over in an accompanying note to MacArthur:

> . . . Has it already been decided in Washington that the Philippine front is of no importance as far as the final result of the war is concerned and that, therefore, no help can be expected here in the immediate future, or at least before the power of resistance is exhausted? If so, I want to know, because I have my own responsibility to my countrymen. . . .
>
> I want to decide in my own mind whether there is justification for allowing all these men to be killed when for the final outcome of the war the shedding of their blood may be wholly unnecessary. It seems that Washington does not fully realize our situation nor the feelings which the apparent neglect of our safety and welfare have engendered in the hearts of the people here. . . .

MacArthur did not have to be persuaded. He hoped the message would stir up Marshall. To his own men on Bataan, however, he sent inspiring words he could not have fully believed:

> Help is on the way from the United States. Thousands of troops and hundreds of planes are being dispatched. . . . No further retreat is possible. We have more troops in Bataan than the Japanese have thrown against us; our supplies are ample; a determined defense will defeat the enemy's attack. . . .
>
> I call upon every soldier in Bataan to fight in his assigned position, resisting every attack. This is the only road to salvation. If we fight, we will win; if we retreat, we will be destroyed.

Most of the Americans on Bataan didn't believe it either. The Filipinos alone found inspiration in MacArthur's words, which made them more determined than ever to prove themselves worthy to fight under the Stars and Stripes. On the morning of January 16 the 51st Philippine Army Division launched a determined counterattack. In fact, they were so eager that one regiment far outran units on its flanks.

It was the opportunity Colonel Imai had been looking for. The Filipinos had formed a salient more dangerous to themselves than to him and he promptly struck at the eastern end of the bulge. At that moment, too, Colonel Takechi's lost regiment burst out of the

"For a Wasted Hope and Sure Defeat"

jungled slopes directly into the other side of the bulge. Assaulted from both sides, the Filipino salient crumpled and by noon collapsed. It left a two-mile hole in the Abucay line.

It was late afternoon by the time Takechi—face lined with fatigue and hunger, uniform in tatters—reported to Nara how he had become hopelessly lost on Mount Natib. The general was sympathetic and ordered him to go into reserve. Takechi saluted crisply, and without pausing for supplies or rest, led his troops off—not north into reserve but back to the south. He thought Nara was punishing him for getting lost; he was going to lead his men back over Mount Natib this time or die in the attempt.

The other side of Bataan, from Mount Natib to the South China Sea, was so inaccessible that as yet Homma had been unable to mount any appreciable offensive. But late the following afternoon five thousand Japanese moved opposite Wainwright's positions. Their commander, Major General Naoki Kimura, discovered that the American defense line extended only halfway up the western slope of Mount Silanganan, a peak two miles west of Mount Natib. He decided to do what Takechi had failed to do on the other side. Led by Lieutenant Colonel Hiroshi Nakanishi, seven hundred infantrymen secretly circled Wainwright's right flank and turned sharply west. By dawn of January 21 they reached the South China Sea, cutting off all of Wainwright's front-line troops.

To the east, the Abucay line was at the point of collapse. Troops sent in to boost the punctured front had become bogged down in the dense vegetation and rugged crevasses and never reached their positions. Along the front itself the troops were exhausted from constant fighting during the day and harassing attacks at night from infiltrators who terrorized the defenders with firecrackers and taunts over loudspeakers.

After a quick tour of Bataan, General Sutherland advised his chief to withdraw immediately to another defense line behind the cobblestone road bisecting Bataan. MacArthur ordered a general retreat, starting at darkness the following evening. At seven o'clock on January 24, trucks and men began pouring back from the Abucay line. By midnight the trail to the rear was jammed with battered buses full of gaunt-faced Filipinos in blue denims and coconut helmets, command cars packed with fatigued officers in filthy uniforms, and marching troops. There were no military police to regulate the flow to the rear, and units became separated in the nightmare chaos. Officers could do nothing but keep men and vehicles moving south and pray that no shells would fall.

Just before dawn the handful of troops holding the front lines began leapfrogging to the rear. They looked like walking dead. Unwashed and unshaven for nine days, their gaunt faces were blank. The withdrawal continued all through the next day, harried by Japanese planes which freely strafed and bombed the trails and the coastal road. Retreat turned into rout when the indomitable Colonel Takechi and his starved men burst out of nowhere. They had done the impossible, crossed Mount Natib.

By January 26 the new Fil-American line, connected by an ingenious network of communication and supply trails hacked out of the jungle, was almost completely manned. It lay in the valley between the two dead volcanoes, just behind the cobblestone road, and extended uninterruptedly from Manila Bay to the South China Sea. It was divided into two sectors, with Wainwright again commanding the western half and Parker the eastern. The troops rested in foxholes and dugouts, thanking God they had survived the arduous retreat from Abucay. In his position Lieutenant Henry G. Lee, of the Philippine Division, was composing a poem about the withdrawal. Bataan, he wrote, had been

> *. . . saved for another day*
> *Saved for hunger and wounds and heat*
> *For slow exhaustion and grim retreat*
> *For a wasted hope and sure defeat. . . .*

Like the Americans, the Japanese were in no condition to continue the battle. Nara's "Summer" Brigade was riddled with more than two thousand casualties. The survivors were exhausted and still stupefied by their first taste of battle.

The resumed fighting brought on even more confusion than at Abucay. Here the jungle was so dense that one Japanese force of a thousand men slipped through Wainwright's lines without being detected for three days. It took almost three weeks of desperate, deadly hand-to-hand combat to wipe them out. The Japanese also tried to outflank Wainwright by sea, landing in barges on the rugged west coast far behind the front. They planned to drive south to Mariveles and cut off supplies from Corregidor. Five separate landings were attempted over the next two weeks, and it wasn't until February 8 that the last pocket of infiltrators was eliminated. That same day Homma held an important conference at his command post in the sugar center of San Fernando. It was muggy, above 95 degrees. The general was tormented. He had already lost seven thousand men in combat on Bataan, and another ten thousand had been sticken with malaria, beriberi and dysentery. He had twice asked for reinforcements and been rejected twice.

There were only three Japanese infantry battalions strung across Bataan, and Lieutenant General Masami Maeda, Homma's chief of staff, warned that if MacArthur discovered this he could break through. The senior operations officer, Colonel Motoo Nakayama, still insisted the attack should be prosecuted vigorously. "The main effort, however, should be made along the east coast, not the west."

Maeda wanted Bataan merely blockaded while the rest of the archipelago was occupied. "By that time the men of General Matsukuasa [MacArthur] will be starved and ready to surrender."

Maeda was right, but to Homma it was unthinkable not to press for a quicker victory. Tokyo would never permit such face-losing strategy. He said a new and much more powerful offense had to be launched. To do this he would have to bear the unbearable—swallow his pride and once more ask for heavy reinforcements. Tears coursed down his face. As the staff started to file out he was handed a telegram from Tokyo. Tojo was displeased; there were victories everywhere except in the Philippines. A look of agony came over Homma's face and he slumped heavily onto the table. The unconscious commander was carried to the next room.

On Corregidor, Quezon in his wheelchair listened in mounting fury as Roosevelt told a radio audience how thousands of aircraft would soon be on their way to the battlefront—Europe. Quezon pointed to smoke rising from the mainland. "For thirty years I have worked and hoped for my people. Now they burn and die for a flag that could not protect them. *Por Dios y todos los santos!* I cannot stand this constant reference to England, to Europe. Where are the planes this *sinvergüenza* [scoundrel] is boasting of? How

American to writhe in anguish at the fate of a distant cousin while a daughter is being raped in the back room!"

He summoned MacArthur and said, "Perhaps my presence on Corregidor is not of value. Why don't I go to Manila and become a prisoner of war?" MacArthur thought such a surrender would be misinterpreted abroad. "I don't care what outsiders think," Quezon snapped, but agreed to think it over.

That night a young Filipino second lieutenant crawled up a rocky beach on Corregidor with a bag of ping-pong balls tied around him as a life preserver. He had swum from Bataan to warn Quezon of the increasing hostility between Filipinos and Americans at the front. "We feel we should have the same rations as the Americans," Antonio Aquino told the President. He was the elder son of Benigno Aquino, the sugar-cane king and speaker of the Philippine Assembly. "We eat only salmon and sardines. One can per day for thirty men, twice a day."

Quezon was enraged. He summoned his cabinet and said he would ask Roosevelt to let him issue a manifesto requesting the United States to grant at once absolute independence to the Philippines. Then he would demobilize the Philippine Army and declare the Philippines neutral. Consequently both America and Japan would have to withdraw their armies.

Vice President Sergio Osmeña tried to point out the consequences of such an action in Washington, but Quezon continued to rage. He was stilled by hacking coughs. To calm him, Osmeña reluctantly approved sending the message to Roosevelt. As usual, it would have to go through MacArthur. He not only let it pass but—rankled by the suspicion that Washington, and Marshall in particular, had let him down—supported it with his own grim assessment of the situation.* "There is no denying that we are nearly done," he wrote; Quezon's plan "might offer the best possible solution of

---

* MacArthur's staff was fiercely loyal and even more outspoken in their criticism of those back home. Like their chief, they believed that the man primarily responsible for their abandonment was George Marshall, who had presumably never forgiven MacArthur for not promoting him to general when MacArthur was Chief of Staff. Those close to Marshall insist he was too objective to let personal differences ever sway his military judgment. He knew and loved the Philippines (as a young lieutenant he had put up No Trespassing signs on the three little islands near Corregidor), but he had long been convinced that a massive U. S. commitment in the Pacific would be playing into Hitler's hands.

"For a Wasted Hope and Sure Defeat"

what is about to be a disastrous debacle." MacArthur was risking his military career but felt it was worth the gamble. Perhaps Quezon's desperate proposal would shock Washington into action.

It dismayed Marshall, as did the fact that MacArthur "went more than halfway toward supporting Quezon's position." Roosevelt's reaction was unequivocable. "We can't do this at all," he tersely told Marshall and Stimson. Until that moment the Chief of Staff had entertained some doubts about Roosevelt's leadership. The President's firm decision convinced him that he was, after all, "a great man."

Roosevelt had enough insight not to expect Quezon and MacArthur to agree with the policy determined by "Arcadia" that Hitler should be defeated first. He must somehow persuade them that everything possible was being sent to the southwest Pacific. By the middle of March seventy-nine thousand troops would have left for the Pacific front, almost four times the number heading for Europe. Most of the available planes were also bound for the Orient.*

It was vital that Quezon understand that there were two fronts—almost 200,000 tons of American shipping had already been sunk off the North Atlantic coast and Rommel was threatening to push the British back to Alexandria. Roosevelt had to find the right words to get all these facts to Quezon without a hint of threat or accusation.

He succeeded in masterful fashion: while rejecting Quezon's proposal as unacceptable to America, he gave his word that no matter what Quezon did, the United States would never abandon the Philippines.

SO LONG AS THE FLAG OF THE U. S. FLIES ON FILIPINO SOIL . . . IT WILL BE DEFENDED BY OUR OWN MEN TO THE DEATH. WHATEVER HAPPENS TO PRESENT AMERICAN GARRISON WE SHALL NOT RELAX OUR EFFORTS UNTIL THE FORCES WHICH ARE NOW MARSHALLING OUTSIDE THE PHILIPPINES RETURN

---

* It seems evident that Roosevelt wanted to do everything possible for MacArthur. On December 30, 1941, he wrote this memorandum to Secretary of the Navy Knox: "I wish that War Plans would explore every possible means of relieving the Philippines. I realize great risks are involved but the objective is important."

TO THE PHILIPPINES AND DRIVE OUT THE LAST REMNANT OF THE INVADERS FROM YOUR SOIL.

These words overwhelmed Quezon. He swore to himself and God that as long as he lived he would stand by America regardless of the consequences to his people or himself.

Roosevelt's reply to MacArthur was more direct:

. . . THE DUTY AND THE NECESSITY OF RESISTING JAPANESE AGGRESSION TO THE LAST TRANSCENDS IN IMPORTANCE ANY OTHER OBLIGATION NOW FACING US IN THE PHILIPPINES. . . . I PARTICULARLY REQUEST THAT YOU PROCEED RAPIDLY TO THE ORGANIZATION OF YOUR FORCES AND YOUR DEFENSES SO AS TO MAKE YOUR RESISTANCE AS EFFECTIVE AS CIRCUMSTANCES WILL PERMIT AND AS PROLONGED AS HUMANLY POSSIBLE.

This meant that the Philippines had been irrevocably written off, and MacArthur's own value was reduced to a symbol of resistance. He replied that he would fight to destruction on Bataan and then Corregidor, making them names for Americans to remember forever.

I HAVE NOT THE SLIGHTEST INTENTION IN THE WORLD OF SURRENDERING OR CAPITULATING THE FILIPINO ELEMENT OF MY COMMAND. . . . THERE HAS NEVER BEEN THE SLIGHTEST WAVERING AMONG THE TROOPS.

While this was an exaggeration, it was truer than it had been a few weeks earlier. Riddled as they were by dysentery and malaria, their uniforms in tatters, the half-starved men of Bataan were full of fight and confidence. The Japanese had been held, and Filipino recruits who had fled in panic from Lingayen Gulf had become tough and dependable.

2.

On the Malay Peninsula the Japanese rolled relentlessly toward the keystone of the British Empire in Asia, Singapore Island. On

"For a Wasted Hope and Sure Defeat"

January 7 General Wavell, chosen at "Arcadia" to command the entire area, flew from his headquarters in Bandung on Java to Singapore on a brief inspection tour. The previous night fifteen Japanese tanks had burst through the front lines of the 11th Indian Division to cross the strategic Slim River bridge, less than 250 air miles from Singapore itself. There wasn't a single Allied tank in all Malaya to stop them; British experts had decreed that armor was unsuited for jungle warfare.

Wavell drove north to find III Corps disorganized and the 11th Indian Division completely shattered. He ordered a general withdrawal of almost 150 miles to Johore Province, where Major-General Gordon Bennett and his Australians would make the final attempt to stop the invaders.

Wavell returned to Singapore to inspect the defenses on the north side of the great fortress island. He found nothing, not even detailed plans for resistance against land attack. To his consternation, he also learned that almost all of the island's great guns facing the sea could not be turned around to fire at the advancing Japanese.

Churchill was dumfounded by Wavell's report that Singapore, far from being impregnable, was almost naked. He blamed himself for putting his faith in Fortress Singapore and hastily penned this note for his Chiefs of Staff:

I must admit to being staggered by Wavell's telegram of the 16th. . . . It never occurred to me for a moment . . . that the gorge of the fortress of Singapore, with its splendid moat half a mile to a mile wide, was not entirely fortified against an attack from the northward. What is the use of having an island for a fortress if it is not to be made into a citadel? . . . How is it that not one of you pointed this out to me at any time when these matters have been under discussion? More especially this should have been done because . . . I have repeatedly shown that I relied upon this defence of Singapore Island against a formal siege, and never relied upon the Kra Isthmus plan. . . .

Not only must the defence of Singapore Island be maintained by every means, but the whole island must be fought for until every single unit and every single strong point has been separately destroyed.

Finally, the city of Singapore must be converted into a citadel and defended to the death. No surrender can be contemplated.

From the first the enemy had kept the British off balance in Malaya. Outnumbered more than 2 to 1, the Japanese never stopped to consolidate a gain, to regroup or wait for supplies; they surged down the main roads on thousands of bicycles and in hundreds of abandoned British cars and trucks. Whenever they came to a destroyed bridge, the cyclists waded across the river holding aloft their bikes or crossed on log bridges supported on the shoulders of engineers.*

The accelerating Japanese success was unforeseen on both sides. A captured British Engineer officer told Colonel Tsuji he had expected the defenses in northern Malaya to hold out for at least three months. "As the Japanese Army had not beaten the weak Chinese Army after four years' fighting in China we did not consider it a very formidable enemy."

Tsuji himself was often up front giving advice and pushing the troops forward. At one roadblock halfway down the peninsula he impatiently devised a frontal attack on the spot and phoned back to Army headquarters for reinforcements and cannon. The answer was no—make a flank attack. This tactic was successful, but at midnight Tsuji stormed into headquarters and wakened everyone with a shower of insults. "What are you doing sleeping while a battle is going on!" he roared and broke into the bedroom of Lieutenant General Sosaku Suzuki, Yamashita's chief of staff. The gentlemanly Suzuki greeted Tsuji with his usual courtesy. This only infuriated Tsuji more. "What do you mean wearing *nemaki* [nightwear] when I'm reporting from the front line!"

Cowed by such righteous indignation, as other generals before him, Suzuki drowsily changed into his dress uniform and buckled on a sword. "I am the chief operational staff officer responsible for the operations of the entire army," Tsuji raved on. "I submitted my idea based on actual front-line conditions and your rejection of my request means you no longer have confidence in me!" He shouted and swore and repeated the same accusations over and over until dawn. Finally he stamped out, wrote his resignation and handed it to Yamashita.

* At first tires blown out by the intense heat slowed the advance, but the Japanese soon learned to ride down the paved highways on the rims. The resulting clatter sounded like tanks and at night the defenders, particularly the Indians who were terrified of any kind of armor, would shout "Tanks!" and break for the rear.

He was so petulant that he refused to eat and sequestered himself in his bedroom. A week later he emerged. His actions were ignored by Yamashita and Suzuki, and he returned to his duties as if nothing had happened—as arrogant, inexorable and brilliant as ever.

Yamashita himself was under emotional stress. The son of a simple country doctor, he had not chosen the Army as a career. "My father suggested the idea," he said, "because I was big and healthy, and my mother did not seriously object because she believed, bless her soul, that I would never pass the highly competitive entrance examination." He was a heavyset man with bull neck and large head. His face was expressionless and he appeared insensitive, but inside he seethed with resentment. He felt his promotion to lieutenant general had been delayed for years because back in 1929 he had supported General Ugaki's plan to reduce the Army by several divisions, and his suspicions of superiors in both Saigon and Tokyo were beginning to verge on paranoia: General Terauchi was purposely holding back air support, and Tojo planned to have him assassinated once Singapore fell. Yamashita wrote in his diary: "It's a crime that there is no one in high places in Japan who can be relied upon," and "That damn Terauchi lives in luxury in Saigon, sleeps in a comfortable bed, eats good food and plays *shogi*."

His feelings of persecution reached a climax on January 23 when Terauchi's chief of staff arrived from Saigon with a packet of notes on how to capture the island of Singapore. Yamashita tore up the suggestions and confided to his diary: "If there are two ways of doing something, trust Southern Army to pick the wrong one."

In the meantime his troops methodically kept breaking through the static British lines of defense. It was clear that even Bennett's Australians could not hold them back and a general retreat from Malaya began. By midnight of January 31 almost all British troops had crossed the seventy-foot-wide causeway that connected the peninsula with the island of Singapore. Just after dawn a skirl of bagpipes could be heard, and to the tune of "A Hundred Pipers" the battered remnants of the Argyll Battalion, a mere ninety men, marched briskly onto the bridge. Bringing up the rear was their commander, the last man off Malaya.

Demolition squads laid final charges on the causeway and at eight o'clock there was a dull roar. When the smoke drifted away, onlookers could see water rushing through a wide gap. They figured their fortress was safely cut off from the Japanese; but the water in the gap was scarcely four feet deep at low tide.

Singapore, ten times the size of Manhattan, extended twenty-six miles from east to west, fourteen miles from north to south. Most of its population was crowded in the city in the south. Except for scattered towns and settlements, the rest of the island was covered with rubber plantations and jungle growth. The commander in chief was Lieutenant-General A. E. Percival, a tall, thin man with two protruding, rabbitlike teeth. He was a man of quiet charm and ability, but some felt he lacked the forcefulness to inspire the assorted units under him.

There were two ways to defend the island: hold at the beaches or fight the enemy inland with massed reserves. Even with a coastline of more than seventy miles, Percival decided to make his stand on the beaches. The situation seemed to favor him. His intelligence unit estimated he would have to face 60,000 Japanese troops, and he had 85,000 men. Of course, 15,000 of these were noncombatants and many of the others were untrained and poorly armed, but the enemy would suffer heavy casualties in the attempt to storm across Johore Strait.

In fact, he would only have to do battle with 30,000 Japanese. Their intelligence was as far off as Percival's. Tsuji, who had been given the responsibility of planning the invasion, was told there were merely 30,000 defenders. He sat up all that night drawing a plan that would throw the British off balance. The main attack would be made to the right of the causeway and at night by the 5th and 18th divisions. However, the Konoye Division would make a demonstration attack the previous day on the other side of the causeway to deceive the British. To ensure secrecy, all inhabitants within a dozen miles of the strait were to be evacuated while the two attack divisions moved stealthily into position, with orders not to build any cooking fires.

The following morning Yamashita assembled forty division commanders and senior officers in a rubber plantation and with flushed face read out the attack orders. *Kikumasamune* (ceremonial wine) was poured into each man's canteen cap and a traditional toast was drunk: "It is a good place to die; surely we shall conquer."

Yamashita set up headquarters in the Green Palace, built by the Sultan of Johore on a hill overlooking the causeway. It was a striking building of red brick and green tile surmounted by a five-story observation tower. The command post was set up at the top of the tower in a room with large windows, which gave Yamashita a panoramic view of the north coast of Singapore. It was the most vulnerable spot he could have chosen, but he reasoned that the British would never imagine he was foolhardy enough to use it. Moreover, he was certain it ran against British policy to bombard such a fine building.

During the following days, trains and three thousand trucks moved up big guns, ammunition and supplies. Hundreds of folding boats and landing craft were transported under cover of darkness and hidden in the bushes a mile or so from the shoreline.

On the evening of February 7 the demonstration by the Konoye Division began. With considerable commotion twenty motor launches landed four hundred men and two mountain guns on a small island in the strait overlooking Seletar Naval Base and Changi Fortress. The next morning at first light, artillery began pounding the fortress. As expected, the British rushed reinforcements above the causeway. After dark the 5th and 18th divisions hoisted their boats to their shoulders and carried them more than a mile to the strait. As they neared the shore a concentrated artillery barrage of 440 guns opened up. The first targets were the huge tanks at the naval base to prevent the British from dumping oil into the strait and igniting it. Next, the guns were trained on the pillboxes, trenches and wire entanglements below the causeway where the landings would take place.

At ten-thirty the first wave, almost four thousand men, boarded three hundred collapsible boats, landing craft and pontoons. The bombardment drowned out the sound of the motors as the little armada neared the northwest coast of Singapore. It was defended by twenty-five hundred Australians.

From the glassed-in tower Yamashita and his staff could see little of what was happening. It looked as if all of Singapore Island was engulfed in fire and explosions. Ten minutes later blue flares rocketed up from the island. The 5th Division had landed on schedule.

The first invaders had hit the beach at the end of Lim Chu Kang Road to be racked with heavy fire from Australians of the 24th Machine-Gun Battalion. Other landing craft beached on a nearby mangrove swamp area which was lightly defended. The outnumbered Australians fought hard all night but were unable to hold back the Japanese, and in the early-morning hours scores of tanks landed and strong infantry-tank teams moved inshore. By dawn there were fifteen thousand infantrymen and several artillery units on the island.

From the Green Palace tower Yamashita watched his men stream past rubber trees toward Tengah Airfield. Advance elements were already within ten air miles of the city of Singapore. By the end of the day Yamashita left the tower with his staff to cross Johore Strait in a raft made of three boats.

On Java, General Wavell decided to make a personal inspection of the embattled island. The Japanese controlled the air, but the following day the ABDA commander managed to break through. From the corridors at Percival's headquarters, staff officers could hear angry voices. Wavell was criticizing Percival for allowing the Japanese to establish a bridgehead so easily, and he got so exasperated with Bennett that he told the Australian commander to "get the hell out" and take his "bloody Aussies" with him.

Wavell ordered an immediate counterattack. Its utter failure did not inhibit him from issuing an order of the day that could have come from Churchill himself:

It is certain that our troops on Singapore Island greatly outnumber any Japanese that have crossed the Straits. We must defeat them. Our whole fighting reputation is at stake and the honour of the British Empire. The Americans have held out on the Bataan Peninsula against far greater odds, the Russians are turning back the picked strength of the Germans, the Chinese with almost complete lack of modern equipment have held the Japanese for 4½ years. It will be disgraceful if we yield our boasted fortress of Singapore to inferior enemy forces.

There must be no thought of sparing troops or the civil population and no mercy must be shown to weakness in any shape or form. Commanders and senior officers must lead their troops and if necessary die with them.

"For a Wasted Hope and Sure Defeat" 341

There must be no question or thought of surrender. Every unit must fight it out to the end and in close contact with the enemy. . . . I look to you and your men to fight to the end to prove that the fighting spirit that won our Empire still exists to enable us to defend it.

This done, he flew back to Java. In the dark he fell off a dock and broke two small bones in his back. From the hospital he signaled Churchill:

BATTLE FOR SINGAPORE IS NOT GOING WELL . . . MORALE OF SOME TROOPS IS NOT GOOD, AND NONE IS AS HIGH AS I SHOULD LIKE TO SEE. . . . EVERYTHING POSSIBLE IS BEING DONE TO PRODUCE MORE OFFENSIVE SPIRIT AND OPTIMISTIC OUTLOOK, BUT I CANNOT PRETEND THAT THESE EFFORTS HAVE BEEN ENTIRELY SUCCESSFUL UP TO DATE. I HAVE GIVEN THE MOST CATEGORICAL ORDERS THAT THERE IS TO BE NO THOUGHT OF SURRENDER AND THAT ALL TROOPS ARE TO CONTINUE FIGHTING TO THE END.

By sunrise the Japanese had taken almost half the island, including strategic Bukit Timah (Mountain of Tin), the highest point on the island. Advance units were approaching the racetrack at the edge of Singapore City. Nevertheless, Tsuji was dismayed by the increasingly stiff resistance, particularly from effective British artillery fire. The enemy seemed to have an endless supply of shells, while Japanese ammunition was already dangerously low. Moreover, it was now obvious that intelligence had grossly underestimated British strength at thirty thousand troops; there must be at least twice that many.

And so it was with covert desperation that Yamashita sent Percival a demand for surrender. Late that morning a reconnaissance plane dropped a tube marked by red and white streamers on the outskirts of the city. It contained a message signed by Yamashita but composed by Lieutenant Colonel Ichiji Sugita. The words were inspired by the surrender of the forty-seven *ronin*.

In the spirit of chivalry we have the honour of advising your surrender. Your army, founded on the traditional spirit of Great Britain, is defending Singapore, which is completely isolated, and raising the fame of Great Britain by the utmost exertions and heroic feelings. . . . From now on resistance is futile and merely increases the danger to the million civilian inhabitants without good reason, exposing them to infliction of pain by fire and sword. But the development of the general war situation has already sealed the fate of Singapore, and the continuation of futile resistance would only serve to inflict direct harm and injuries to thousands of non-combatants living in the city, throwing them into further miseries and horrors of war. Furthermore we do not feel you will increase the fame of the British Army by further resistance.

Percival did not send Yamashita a reply. He had been told to "fight to the end." As yet there was no panic in Singapore despite bombs and shells. Civilians were standing in line outside the cinema in the Cathay skyscraper to see *The Philadelphia Story,* and the Raffles Hotel was crowded with staff officers with nothing to do but drink and carp. Someone scrawled in chalk on a wall: ENGLAND FOR THE ENGLISH, AUSTRALIA FOR THE AUSTRALIANS, BUT MALAY FOR ANY SON OF A BITCH WHO WANTS IT.

Stragglers streamed down the main roads toward the city. An intelligence officer, David James, stopped a formation of Indians and asked their commander why they were going in the wrong direction. He said an Australian officer had advised them "to beat it because the Nips were coming over the hill." You're supposed to find the Japanese, not run a foot race with them, said James. "Quite so, but you don't remain where you are not wanted, do you?" answered the commander and led off his men at a jog.

Even several Australian units which had fought well in Malaya pushed aside MP's attempting to block their way to the city. "Chum, to hell with Malaya and Singapore," said one. "Navy let us down, air force let us down. If the 'bungs' [natives] won't fight for their bloody country, why pick on me?"

Sensing complete collapse, Percival formed a tight defense arc in front of the city, but by Friday the thirteenth it was apparent to every one of his commanders that Singapore was doomed. Wavell was asked to approve an immediate surrender, but his stiff answer from Bandung ordered the defenders to "continue to inflict maximum damage on enemy for as long as possible by house-to-house fighting if necessary." Percival replied that the Japanese controlled most of the reservoirs and there was little water left. Wavell replied:

> YOUR GALLANT STAND IS SERVING A PURPOSE AND MUST BE CONTINUED TO THE LIMIT OF ENDURANCE.

Ironically, Japanese concern over Singapore was growing on all levels. "I hope it won't turn out to be another Bataan," Admiral Matome Ugaki, Yamamoto's chief of staff, wrote in his diary. On the island itself Captain Asaeda prophesied that if the British held out for another week, "they'll beat us." Each field gun had a hundred rounds at most, and the big guns fewer than that. There was pressure on Yamashita to call off the attack and even to withdraw to the peninsula. He ordered the assault continued.

On the morning of February 15 Percival called a conference of area commanders and told them that there was almost no gasoline or field-gun and Bofors ammunition. In twenty-four hours there wouldn't be a drop of water. He said he would ask the Japanese to cease fire at four o'clock. Before the day was out, he got permission for what he had already planned to do. Wavell told him he was free to surrender once it was evident that he could do no more.

> . . . WHATEVER HAPPENS I THANK YOU AND ALL TROOPS FOR YOUR GALLANT EFFORTS OF LAST FEW DAYS.

From the heights at Bukit Timah, Yamashita watched a Union Jack still fluttering atop Fort Canning in the city of Singapore. It would take a week of hard fighting to take that hill alone, and many more days to break through the final defense lines. The field phone rang. A front-line commander reported that the British were sending out a flag of truce.

Colonel Ichiji Sugita, his neck encased in a plastic cast after a motorcycle crash, drove forward to meet the British parliamentaries. "We will have a truce if the British Army agrees to surrender," he said in Japanese. "Do you wish to surrender?"

The British interpreter, Captain Cyril H. D. Wild, said, "We do." He was tall, blue-eyed, the son of the Bishop of Newcastle.

Sugita told him to return with Percival and his staff. They met again at four forty-five and proceeded in two cars toward the Ford factory near the village of Bukit Timah. Next to Percival sat Sugita. He turned painfully to the general and said in halting English, "We fought for more than two months. Now we come to the end. I compliment you on the British stand." Percival politely mumbled a few amenities. His thin face was red, his eyes bloodshot.

The surrender party dismounted in front of the factory. They seemed arrogant to the Japanese, although it was Percival himself who carried the white flag. Inside the big rambling building they were surrounded by clamoring reporters, photographers and newsreel men. Five minutes later, at seven o'clock, Yamashita appeared, and the commotion increased as more than forty men crowded into one small room. The surrender had come so unexpectedly that Yamashita had not glanced at the surrender terms, which Sugita had typed out in English days earlier. "The Japanese Army will consider nothing but surrender," said Yamashita. He knew the British outnumbered him by far and his greatest concern was to prevent Percival from finding this out.

"I fear that we shall not be able to submit our final reply before ten-thirty P.M.," Percival replied. He had no intention of continuing the battle. He merely wanted to work out specific details before signing any surrender.

But Yamashita was sure the Englishman was stalling. Terms had to be settled before the enemy realized that the Japanese were numerically inferior. Street fighting in the city would be disastrous.* "Reply to us only whether our terms are acceptable or not," he said tersely. "Things must be settled swiftly. We are prepared to resume firing." Through a window came the glare of fires in Singapore.

Sugita saw that misunderstanding was threatening the surrender and took over from Yamashita's incompetent interpreter. He did little better. The disjointed argument continued, aggravated by Wild's poor command of Japanese and Percival's reluctance to submit on the spot.

* After the war Yamashita said, "I felt that if we had to fight in the city we would be beaten." He described his strategy at Singapore as "a bluff, a bluff that worked."

Yamashita lost his patience. "Unless you do surrender," he burst out, "we will have to carry out our night attack as scheduled."

"Cannot the Japanese Army remain in its present position?" the stunned Percival asked. "We can resume negotiations again tomorrow at five-thirty A.M."

"*Nani!*" Yamashita pretended indignation to hide his concern. "I want the hostilities to cease tonight and I want to remind you there can be no arguments."

It was not the gentlemanly surrender Percival wanted. "We shall discontinue firing by eight-thirty P.M.," he mumbled. "Had we better remain in our present positions tonight?"

Yamashita told him to do so. Firing would cease at eight-thirty and a thousand men could keep arms to maintain order in the city. Percival's vague manner made Yamashita suspicious. "You have agreed to the terms but you have not yet made yourself clear as to whether you agree to surrender or not." Percival could not speak. It was the worst military disaster in British history, the bitterest moment of his life. He cleared his throat but all he could do was nod.

In exasperation Yamashita told Sugita he wanted the British to give a simple answer. The interpreter, however, got involved in another lengthy discourse with Wild. Yamashita restlessly kept looking at his watch and finally shook a finger at Sugita. "There's no need for all this talk. It is a simple question and I want a simple answer." He turned to Percival and shouted, "We want to hear 'Yes' or 'No' from you! Surrender or fight!"

"Yes, I agree," said Percival faintly. He paused. "I have a request to make. Will the Imperial Army protect the women and children and British civilians?"

"We shall see to it. Please sign this truce agreement."

At seven-fifty Percival signed. Forty minutes later, as agreed, the roar of battle ceased abruptly. Singapore, the City of the Lion, the most famous fortress in the world, was Japanese. In seventy days Yamashita, at the cost of 9,824 battle casualties, had rolled 650 miles down the Malay Peninsula and across Singapore. The British had slightly fewer casualties, but surrendered more than 130,000 troops.

It was the greatest land victory in Japanese history. They had again proved dramatically to all their Asian brothers that the white man could be defeated. In Japan a jubilant government announced it was distributing two bottles of beer and a packet of red beans to every family, as well as three *go* of *sake*. Each child under thirteen got a box of caramel drops, cakes and assorted candies.

The *Asahi Shimbun* headlined its story of the battle: GENERAL SITUATION OF PACIFIC WAR DECIDED. "To seize Singapore Island in as little time as three days could only have been done by our Imperial Army," declared Colonel Hideo Ohira, chief of the Press Division. "Japan is the sun that shines for world peace. Those who bathe in the sun will grow and those who resist it shall have no alternative but ruin. Both the United States and Britain should contemplate the 3,000 years of scorching Japanese history. I solemnly declare that with the fall of Singapore the general situation of war has been determined. The ultimate victory will be ours."

Prime Minister Tojo told the Diet that Burma and the Philippines would be granted independence but that it would be necessary to retain Hong Kong and Malaya as vital bases in defense of Greater East Asia. "The objective in the Greater East Asia war," he said, "is founded on the exalted ideals of the founding of the empire and it will enable all the nations and peoples of Greater East Asia to enjoy life and to establish a new order of coexistence and co-prosperity on the basis of justice with Japan as the nucleus."

3.

Java had been almost isolated for a month. To the west, Sumatra was under attack by paratroopers and men from a recently landed convoy. To the east, another invasion convoy had just anchored off the exotic island of Bali.

At his headquarters in Bandung, high in the mountains of central Java, ABDA Commander Archibald Wavell was certain Java itself would be the next target. He was right. Two powerful invasion forces, each protected by strong cruiser and destroyer units, were already bound for that strategic island. The commander of the Netherlands Naval Forces—a short, rotund, balding vice admiral named C. E. L. Helfrich—was still of the opinion that the Japanese could be defeated at sea. He rejected the assumption of U. S. Admiral Hart, commander of the ABDA Navy, that the defense of the Dutch East Indies was a lost cause. The Dutch fleet had already sunk more Japanese tonnage than the combined American air, surface and underwater forces.

In fact, it was Admiral Helfrich's prodding that inspired the Americans to make their first surface attack since Pearl Harbor. On January 24 a quartet of four-stack destroyers dating from World War I slipped into Makassar Strait, between Borneo and Celebes, and sent three enemy transports to the bottom. It was a daring raid, brilliantly executed, and it forcefully proved Helfrich's point. He now pressed his belief that the place to stop the Japanese was at sea, not on the beaches of Java.

American reluctance to engage in surface combat was as puzzling to the Japanese as it was to Helfrich. Below the Philippines they had met almost no resistance and now held all of Borneo and the Celebes islands, and had secured strong footholds on New Guinea. Once Java was conquered, Southeast Asia's treasures of oil, tin and tungsten would be in their hands.

Wavell's evaluation of the threat to Java, where he was, was markedly different from his assessment of the problems faced by the defenders of Singapore. On February 22 he signaled Churchill:

I AM AFRAID THAT THE DEFENCE OF A.B.D.A. AREA HAS BEEN BROKEN DOWN AND THAT DEFENCE OF JAVA CANNOT NOW LAST LONG. . . . ANYTHING PUT INTO JAVA NOW CAN DO LITTLE TO PROLONG STRUGGLE: IT IS MORE QUESTION OF WHAT YOU WILL CHOOSE TO SAVE. . . . I SEE LITTLE FURTHER USEFULNESS FOR THIS H.Q. . . . LAST ABOUT MYSELF. I AM, AS EVER, ENTIRELY WILLING TO DO MY BEST WHERE YOU THINK BEST TO SEND ME. I HAVE FAILED YOU AND PRESIDENT HERE, WHERE A BETTER MAN MIGHT PERHAPS HAVE SUCCEEDED . . . I HATE THE IDEA OF LEAVING THESE STOUT-HEARTED DUTCHMEN, AND WILL REMAIN HERE AND FIGHT IT OUT WITH THEM AS LONG AS POSSIBLE IF YOU CONSIDER THIS WOULD HELP AT ALL.

GOOD WISHES. I AM AFRAID YOU ARE HAVING VERY DIFFICULT PERIOD, BUT I KNOW YOUR COURAGE WILL SHINE THROUGH IT.

The Allied air defense could no longer offer effective resistance. There were few British planes left after the disaster in Malaya; the Dutch were reduced to a handful of dilapidated aircraft; and of the 111 planes which America had rushed to Java, 23 heavy bombers and a few fighters remained.

Three days later Wavell turned over the final defense of the East Indies to the Dutch governor general and left Java. Helfrich's fleet was the only force that stood between Java and the two approaching Japanese invasion convoys. He no longer hoped to stop them but was determined to kill as many Japanese soldiers at sea as possible.

By dawn—it was February 26—the Western Assault Convoy of fifty-six transports was 250 miles from the western end of Java. It was escorted by one carrier, three light cruisers, two flotillas of destroyers and covered by four heavy cruisers. The Eastern Assault Convoy of forty transports was less than 200 miles from its goal, eastern Java. It was escorted by a light cruiser and seven destroyers. Near at hand were two heavy cruisers, a light cruiser and seven destroyers. Overall commander of these eighteen ships was Rear Admiral Takeo Takagi, able but cautious.

Just before noon the eastern convoy was sighted by two Allied planes. Helfrich, who had taken over command of the ABDA Navy from Hart, radioed Rear Admiral Karel W. F. M. Doorman, a countryman, to leave port at dark with the main force of fifteen ships and attack. A few hours later Helfrich learned about the convoy coming from the west. He ordered a smaller force—the light cruiser *Hobart*, two old cruisers and two equally aged destroyers —to meet this new threat as best it could.

At six-thirty Doorman sailed out of Surabaya. The shadowy column nosed north into the Java Sea through the violet light of early dusk. Though an inspiring sight, it was a patchwork fleet sharing no common doctrine or technique, with each of the four national groups a distinct and separate task force. It reminded a young lieutenant on the American heavy cruiser *Houston* of eleven all-stars playing Notre Dame without a single practice session.

All through the night Doorman's force swept along the coast but found nothing and turned back at daylight. It had no sooner nosed into Surabaya harbor around two-thirty in the afternoon

JAPANESE ATTEMPTS TO RETAKE GUADALCANAL 1942

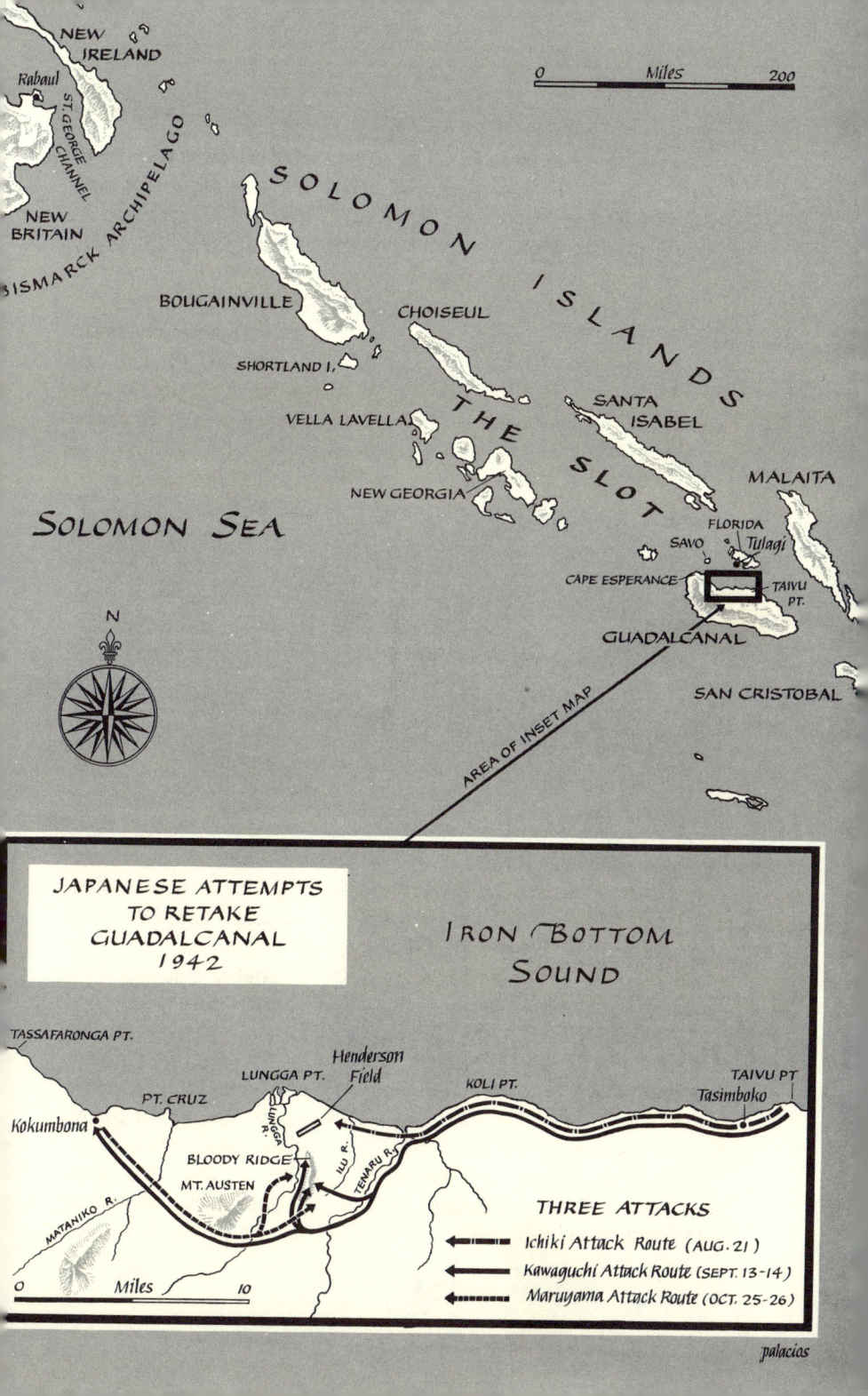

THREE ATTACKS
- Ichiki Attack Route (AUG. 21)
- Kawaguchi Attack Route (SEPT. 13-14)
- Maruyama Attack Route (OCT. 25-26)

palacios

than Doorman received a new order to engage an enemy force some ninety miles to the north.

Since the fleet had no common code of tactical signals, Doorman's first order was relayed by radio, signal flags and flashing light in plain English: FOLLOW ME, THE ENEMY IS 90 MILES AWAY.

There was rising excitement as the fleet turned and headed out to sea again. The three British destroyers, screening abreast, led the way followed by the light cruiser *De Ruyter*. Behind in column came the famed British heavy cruiser *Exeter;* *Houston,* host of President Roosevelt on four cruises; the Australian light cruiser *Perth;* and bringing up the rear, the Dutch light cruiser *Java.* To the left was a second column—two Dutch destroyers trailed by four antique American destroyers. But the fleet was blind. Doorman had no search planes to catapult from his cruisers; they had been left ashore the night before.

Admiral Takagi, however, knew Doorman's position. Three float planes had already sighted the ABDA column. He ordered the thirty-eight vessels of the eastern ship convoy to turn away and placed his own ships in battle position. Doorman had an extra light cruiser but Takagi had almost twice as many destroyers and this gave him a numerical advantage—eighteen warships to fifteen.

It was a clear, bright day and the Japanese imagined they could smell the fragrance of nearby Java. Sailors, wearing white fatigues and steel helmets, crowded into shrines and tied *hachimaki* tightly around their foreheads. Officers in trim white dress uniforms and baseball caps strained to see the enemy. Japan had not engaged in a major naval battle since Tsushima.

At four o'clock the cruiser *Jintsu* sighted mastheads seventeen miles to the southeast. Then lookouts on the two big cruisers, *Nachi* and *Haguro,* made out the lofty masts of *De Ruyter*. As it came closer, its towering, odd-shaped superstructure took on the alarming shape of some prehistoric monster.

Aboard *Nachi,* Takagi and his chief of staff, Captain Ko Nagasawa, were not sure they should become involved in a running sea battle. Their primary mission was to protect the transports, but Takagi gave orders to close in. At 28,000 yards Nagasawa asked for permission to fire. Takagi nodded, and at four-fifteen the eight-inch guns of *Nachi* and *Haguro* roared. A minute later the two Allied cruisers opened fire but it was an unequal duel with twelve big guns against Takagi's twenty.

The Japanese were approaching so fast that it soon became obvious they would pass across the head of the Allied column, "crossing the T." By this classic maneuver Takagi would bring his broadsides to bear on Doorman's cruisers, which could only retaliate with their forward guns. But the Dutch admiral perceived the trap and swung his cruisers 20 degrees to the left, away from the Japanese.

Takagi also turned, putting the two fleets almost parallel, heading west, with Doorman hemmed in between the Japanese and Java. Ten minutes later Nagasawa informed Takagi it was time to move in for the attack. "Proceed," said the admiral, who was a submarine expert. At 16,000 yards the Japanese destroyers loosed their torpedoes. Newly designed, they had the astounding range of 30,000 yards and their oxygen propulsion system left no telltale trail of bubbles.

Doorman had no idea they were coming until he saw columns of water spout high in the air. The new torpedoes had been set wrong and were exploding prematurely in mid-run. Their sudden appearance caused mounting panic; they must have come from a wolf pack of submarines.

The spouts also alarmed Nagasawa. He decided they must be enemy mines detonated from nearby Bawean Island. He warned Takagi it would be suicide to proceed farther, and orders to move to within 6,000 yards were canceled. Doorman had been given a respite. It was short-lived. At five o'clock, shells from *Haguro* crashed through an antiaircraft mount on *Exeter* and exploded in the boiler. The big cruiser, speed halved, lurched and turned hard left so *Houston* just behind wouldn't pile into its stern.

De Ruyter saw the melee behind and also turned left just as another school of torpedoes sliced toward the Allies. At five-fifteen the Dutch destroyer *Kortenaer* exploded and broke in two like a jackknife. Doorman signaled ALL SHIPS FOLLOW ME and turned southeast. He lost one more destroyer, *Electra,* but the wounded *Exeter* escaped in the smoke and confusion.

Now Doorman had only *Houston*'s six 8-inch guns to match Takagi's twenty. Behind dark clouds of smoke Doorman formed a new line, but within moments two big shells plowed into *Hous-*

ton. This time luck was with the Allies; both shells were duds. Doorman swung his line in an evasive counterclockwise circle, but *Nachi* and *Haguro* drew nearer. So did a destroyer flotilla.

Doorman called for smoke from the four American destroyers. Their commander, T. H. Binford, obliged and then on his own launched a torpedo attack on *Nachi* and *Haguro* from 10,000 yards. The cruisers managed to elude the torpedoes, but the daring of the attack forced Takagi to retire northward. He decided to wait until dark, the time the Japanese traditionally preferred to attack.

Though severely hurt, Doorman had no intention of withdrawing. Instead he began probing blindly for the Japanese transports. At nine o'clock his flagship reached shoal water and swung right to parallel the Java coast. The other cruisers followed, as did two British destroyers, *Encounter* and *Jupiter*. Twenty-five minutes later there was an explosion at the end of the line and *Jupiter* was enveloped in flames. She had most likely hit a drifting Dutch mine.

The other ships plunged uneasily into the dark. Nothing happened until nine-fifty. Then a parachute flare floated down, lighting up the column. The stalker was being stalked by one of Takagi's search planes. In rapid succession half a dozen more ghostly flares straddled the Allied line.

Takagi moved in, and just before eleven o'clock a lookout on *Nachi* sighted the enemy column through the special night glasses fixed on the bridge. Someone on *De Ruyter* finally saw the two Japanese cruisers on the port beam and mistakenly reported they were heading in the opposite direction. The Dutch cruiser fired. So did *Perth, Houston* and *Java*. The sky was bright with bursting star shells.

All at once the firing stopped. In the sudden blackness the Allies were unaware that *Haguro* and *Nachi* were silently closing in from behind. Nagasawa waited until he was within 10,000 yards of the enemy before he turned to Takagi and said it was time to launch torpedoes. The admiral approved and around eleven-twenty *Nachi* unleashed eight torpedoes and *Haguro* four. For several minutes the torpedoes slithered toward the oblivious Allied column, which held its course. Then *De Ruyter* erupted with a terrifying abruptness inexplicable to those aboard. As flames spread across her decks, rockets shot up from the stricken ship. Fire had touched off her pyrotechnic locker.

Four minutes later there was another deafening explosion, this time just behind *Houston*. It was *Java*. Burning furiously, her bow reared high into the air. Hundreds of crewmen dropped off like ants as the ship slid backwards into the dark sea. Then *De Ruyter* too vanished, hissing furiously as water enveloped her flames. With her went Doorman and 366 shipmates. One of his last orders was to leave any survivors "to the mercy of the enemy," and the new senior officer of the fleet, the captain of *Perth*, ordered *Houston* to follow as he speeded away to the southeast.

The Battle of the Java Sea, the greatest surface engagement since the Battle of Jutland in 1916, was over. Even in the daylight Takagi had been able to severely damage the Allied fleet, and in the darkness Doorman had had no chance at all against the specialized training of the Japanese. They had hardly been hit, but Doorman lost three destroyers, two light cruisers and his life.

Ten Allied ships survived the battle, and by first light they had managed to make their way back to either Batavia (soon to be renamed Djakarta) or Surabaya. The four American destroyers received permission to escape to Australia, and at five o'clock slipped out of Surabaya harbor past the moored *Exeter*. In the gloom they dashed safely through the narrow Bali Strait.

That same night *Perth* and *Houston* left Batavia to try to escape through Sunda Strait, which was scarcely fourteen miles wide. They plunged full steam into a Japanese armada: the four heavy cruisers, three light cruisers, about ten destroyers and the aircraft carrier *Ryujo* protecting the fifty-six transports of the Western Assault Convoy, which were dropping anchor at the western tip of Java in Bantam Bay.

Perth fought back valiantly on all quarters, but just before midnight a shell smashed into the ordinary-seamen's mess from the starboard side near the water line. Then a torpedo ripped into the same side near the forward boiler room. As the ship rapidly began to lose life, torpedoes and shells struck home in quick succession and she finally rolled over and sank.

Now it was *Houston*'s turn. She had already been damaged by a torpedo, and the big guns of the cruiser *Mikuma* were finding their target. Fifteen minutes after midnight a salvo ripped into the American cruiser's after engine room, scalding everyone to death. Steam geysered through jagged holes in the deck and the ship slowed. As the bugle sounded Abandon Ship a 5-inch shell exploded on the bridge, killing the captain.

Houston lay dead in the water, her guns sticking out at eccentric angles. Slowly she rolled to one side and paused. The Stars and Stripes waved—defiantly, it seemed—from the mainmast. Finally, at twelve forty-five, the ship shuddered and dived out of sight.

Of *Houston*'s 1,000 men, and *Perth*'s crew of 680, fewer than half were still alive, and many of those would perish in the oily waters. The Japanese had also been hurt, but not by *Houston* or *Perth*. Eight torpedoes aimed by *Mikuma* at *Houston* had missed and continued on toward the transports massed in Bantam Bay. Four were sent to the bottom, including *Ryujo-maru,* headquarters ship of General Hitoshi Imamura, commander of the 16th Army. Imamura and hundreds of soldiers leaped into the warm waters. The general and his aide grabbed pieces of wood, for neither wore a life jacket. Ashore the aide found his chief, face black from oil, seated on a pile of bamboo. "Congratulations," he said, "on the successful landing."*

The landings at Bantam Bay and on the north coast brought the final disintegration of Allied command on Java. In Bandung a British admiral told Helfrich, "I have instructions from the Admiralty to withdraw His Majesty's ships from Java when resistance will serve no further useful purpose. This time, in my judgment, has come."

"Do you realize you're still under my orders?" Helfrich retorted.

"I do, of course. But in this vital matter I cannot do other than my duty as I see it."

The American senior officer, Rear Admiral W. A. Glassford, sympathized with his British colleague but assured Helfrich he

---

* Commander Shukichi Toshikawa of the 5th Destroyer Flotilla was sent to apologize to Imamura for torpedoing the four transports and dumping the general into the bay. But Imamura's chief of staff advised Toshikawa to keep quiet; Imamura imagined a *Houston* torpedo had sunk him. "Let her have the credit," the chief of staff told Toshikawa. To this day official records on both sides have been crediting *Houston* with the hit.

still remained under his command. "Any order you give me will be obeyed at once."

But there were no meaningful orders to give. Helfrich sighed heavily. "You will order your ships to Australia," he said and thanked the American effusively for his help. As for the British admiral, he could give his ships any orders he wished.

The last British ships—*Exeter* and two destroyer escorts—were already heading northwest in hopes of escaping through Sunda Strait at dark. But Takagi sighted them at nine thirty-five in the morning, and with the help of dive bombers from the *Ryujo,* sank all three.

A little after midnight the last American plane took off from the dying island of Java with thirty-five passengers, and at dawn a flying boat lifted ponderously off a lake near Bandung for Ceylon. In it was Admiral Helfrich. He felt like a raw ensign.

Almost completely unopposed, Japanese land forces converged on Batavia and Bandung from two sides. The Dutch commander of the scattered and disorganized Allied forces knew that guerrilla warfare was impossible because the natives were too hostile to their Dutch masters. On March 8 he ordered everyone to lay down arms. The last message to the outside world came from a dispatcher at Bandung's commercial station. "We are shutting down," he said. "Good-bye till better times. Long live the Queen!"

Like Singapore, Java was gone. Despite the devastating defeat and bitter arguments and recriminations, the Americans, British, Dutch and Australians had achieved momentary unity in a gallant but hopeless battle at sea. Now there was only one remaining pocket of resistance inside the Japanese Empire—Bataan and Corregidor.

11

"To Show Them Mercy Is to Prolong the War"

1.

Bataan was quiet. The defenders set out patrols, and tried to strengthen the line across the peninsula. Food had become an obsession. Front-line troops got a third of a ration a day. The efforts to bring supplies to Corregidor and Bataan through the Japanese sea blockade had failed. There was so little fodder for the remaining cavalry horses and mules that General Wainwright, with tears in his eyes, ordered them all, including his own prize jumper, Joseph Conrad, to be destroyed.

By mid-February the sickness rate rose alarmingly. Bataan was one of the most malaria-infested areas in the world and the supply of quinine was almost gone. Weakened by hunger and dysentery, over five hundred men were hospitalized for malaria in the first week of March and doctors feared an epidemic. There was still talk of the "mile-long" convoy filled with supplies and reinforcements, but Filipinos as well as Americans repeated with relish the verse just written by correspondent Frank Hewlett, a frequent front-line visitor:

> *We're the battling bastards of Bataan:*
> *No mama, no papa, no Uncle Sam,*
> *No aunts, no uncles, no cousins, no nieces,*

*No pills, no planes or artillery pieces,
And nobody gives a damn.*

On March 10 Wainwright was summoned to Corregidor, where Sutherland informed him that MacArthur was leaving the next evening by torpedo boat for Mindanao, the southernmost island of the Philippines. A Flying Fortress would take him from there to Australia. Sutherland told Wainwright he would command all troops of Luzon as head of the newly established Luzon force. "If it's agreeable to you, General Jones will get another star and take over your I Corps."

MacArthur came out of a small gray house at the eastern end of Malinta Tunnel and said to Wainwright, "I want you to make it known throughout all elements of your command that I'm leaving over my repeated protests." He had considered disobeying direct orders from Washington so he could lead his troops to the end, but his advisers had persuaded him that he could do more in Australia for his beleaguered troops.

"Of course, I will, Douglas," said Wainwright.

"If I get to Australia, you know I'll come back as soon as I can with as much as I can."

"You'll get through."

"And back." MacArthur gave Wainwright a box of cigars and two large jars of shaving cream. "Good-bye, Jonathan." They shook hands. "If you're still on Bataan when I get back, I'll make you a lieutenant general."

The next evening, March 11, at about eight o'clock, *PT-41*, commanded by a colorful bearded lieutenant, John Bulkeley, pulled away from "The Rock" with General MacArthur, his wife, his four-year-old son, Arthur, General Sutherland and several other officers. MacArthur removed his familiar field marshal's cap, raising it in farewell to the small group on the pier.

For thirty-five hectic hours Bulkeley navigated *PT-41* through the enemy-controlled waters, and a little after dawn on March 13, made a landfall on the north coast of Mindanao near the Del Monte pineapple factory. MacArthur's face was pale, his eyes dark-circled as he stepped off the boat. He told Bulkeley he was recommending him and his crew for the Silver Star. "You've taken me out of the jaws of death and I won't forget it."

Waiting for MacArthur on an airstrip hacked out of long lines of pineapples was a worn-out B-17 flown from Australia. The general was infuriated that a single dilapidated plane had been sent and refused to let anyone get aboard. It wasn't until the evening of March 16 that three new Flying Fortresses touched down. MacArthur and his party took off soon after ten o'clock with each passenger, regardless of rank, allowed thirty-five pounds for luggage.*

The next morning MacArthur landed at Batchelor Field, thirty-five miles south of Darwin. "It was close," he told those anxiously awaiting him on the runway. "But that's the way it is in war. You win or lose, live or die—and the difference is just an eyelash."

Then came another eyelash escape. Two fighters appeared out of the blue just as MacArthur's plane took off. The MacArthur luck held and three hours later he landed softly at Alice Springs in the middle of Australia. Reporters clustered around for a statement and he scribbled a few lines on the back of a used envelope:

The President of the United States ordered me to break through the Japanese lines and proceed from Corregidor to Australia for the purpose, as I understand it, of organizing the American offensive against Japan, a primary object of which is the relief of the Philippines.

I came through and I shall return.

Tojo's chagrin at the stalemate in Bataan was aggravated by MacArthur's daring escape. He was no longer certain of Homma's ability to achieve quick success without help. The Prime Minister was reluctant to speak directly to Army Chief of Staff Sugiyama; instead he delegated his secretary, Colonel Susumu Nishiura, to convey his concern about Bataan.

Nishiura took the problem to the Chief of Operations, Colonel Takushiro Hattori, a long-time friend—as boys they had attended the same military school. Study convinced Hattori that what ap-

---

* Someone overheard an enlisted man remark that the mattress he'd put aboard the MacArthur plane was heavy and started a rumor that it was filled with gold pesos. The following day a few men were willing to swear that they had seen chests of drawers as well as a large refrigerator loaded. This fiction was built into a whispering campaign against MacArthur that still persists. Of a score of people interviewed, one alone maintained that he helped load the refrigerator and mattress full of pesos. The others declared categorically that the MacArthurs took the prescribed thirty-five pounds of luggage.

peared to be the strongest feature in the Bataan defense system was the weakest. This was Mount Samat, a rugged hill rising 1,920 feet just behind the center of the American front lines. Once in Japanese hands, Wainwright's entire line would fold. First should come a concentrated air and artillery bombardment on a two-and-a-half-mile sector in front of Mount Samat, followed by a full-scale infantry drive through the hole.

Hattori had no trouble in persuading General Sugiyama to approve the plan. Now, he thought, it would have to be presented to 14th Army so subtly that they would think it was their own idea and wouldn't lose face. He need not have worried. One glance at the proposal satisfied Homma that this was the solution of the problem that had been harassing him.

Wainwright was established in new headquarters on Corregidor. The War Department had promoted him to lieutenant general and made him commander in chief of all forces in the Philippines. MacArthur had not been consulted, perhaps because Washington knew he would never approve; he wanted to control the islands from Australia. Privately MacArthur did not feel Wainwright was qualified to assume overall command, and he reacted sharply when the new commander cabled Washington that his troops would be "starved into submission," unless he got food by April 15. MacArthur curtly radioed Marshall:

IT IS OF COURSE POSSIBLE THAT WITH MY DEPARTURE THE VIGOR OF APPLICATION OF CONSERVATION MAY HAVE BEEN RELAXED.

The Filipinos on Bataan still regarded MacArthur as the greatest man alive, and his pledge to return was a personal guarantee that their country would be freed. But an increasing number of Americans on Bataan felt he had abandoned them and passed around a parody of "The Battle Hymn of the Republic."

> *Dugout Doug's not timid, he's just cautious, not afraid,*
> *He's protecting carefully the stars that Franklin made.*
> *Four-star generals are rare as good food on Bataan.*
> *And his troops go starving on.*

April 2 was the eve of Good Friday. More significant, it was also the eve of the birthday of Japan's first emperor, the legendary Jinmu. By nightfall 50,000 Japanese, including 15,000 fresh troops from the homeland, were massed for the all-out attack. Behind them 150 guns, howitzers and mortars—many sent from Hong Kong—were ready to lay down the heaviest barrage of the campaign.

"Our four groups have been brought into line, and on a front of twenty-five kilometers ten flags are lined up," Homma wrote in his operational diary that evening. "Artillery is plentiful. . . . There is no reason why this attack should not succeed." It should take, he estimated, about a month.

Across the line waited 78,000 starving Americans and Filipinos, but only 27,000 were listed as "combat effective" and three fourths of these were weak from malaria. Dawn was clear. At ten o'clock the firing started. The Filipinos had never experienced anything so devastating. Shells seemed to explode on top of each other. It reminded American veterans of the heaviest German barrages in World War I.

Bombers of the 22nd Air Brigade approached unmolested in perfect formation and dropped tons of explosives on the two and a half miles in front of Mount Samat. Bamboo groves burst into flame. The phenomenon was treated lightly at first; men lit cigarettes on the burning trees. Then brush, dry as tinder, ignited and the heat became intolerable. Americans and Filipinos alike leaped from their foxholes and scrambled back to the second line of defense. Here foliage had been blasted away, leaving the ground almost barren, and the defenders thought they were safe. But a wind sprang up and flames leaped over the cleared area to the lush jungle growth beyond. The men were trapped in a circle of fire; hundreds were cremated. Those who escaped fled to the rear like frenzied animals, spreading panic.

Masked by smoke and flame, the Japanese infantry and tank attack began rolling south almost unimpeded at three o'clock in the afternoon. Within an hour they had ripped open a three-mile gap. General George Parker, commander of II Philippine Corps which defended the eastern half of Bataan, didn't learn this until dusk. He ordered his reserve, six hundred men, to plug up the hole. It was too late. By the end of the next day General Akira Nara swept west of Mount Samat while fresh troops from Shanghai circled around the other side of the craggy hill.

April 5 dawned hot. It was Easter Sunday. While many Americans and Filipinos, entrenched on by-passed Mount Samat, worshiped at sunrise services, shells began screeching overhead. Once the barrage lifted, Japanese troops started up the little mountain, and after lunch planted the Rising Sun on its summit. As Hattori had predicted, its seizure threatened the collapse of the entire defense system across Bataan. In desperation Parker ordered a counterattack, which failed, and by the following noon the entire left half of his corps had disintegrated. There was nothing to keep Nara from sweeping all the way to the end of the peninsula.

The lines still held on the right. East of Mount Samat, Brigadier General Clifford Bluemel, a peppery man who had terrorized his junior officers before Pearl Harbor, tried to counterattack with the 31st Division, but the collapse on his left forced him to pull back. Without orders he began forming a new defense line along the little San Vicente River. He confronted the demoralized stragglers with his Garand rifle. By threat and insult he herded them into new positions.

From the heights of Mount Samat, Colonel Hattori watched the plan he had conceived in Tokyo develop beyond his hopes. Close by, to the west, he could see Nara's troops stream relentlessly past scattered American units. To the east the assault by the Shanghai troops was beginning on Bluemel's hastily improvised line. By nightfall this alone stood between Homma and a complete rout—and it could not hold for long. On his inspection tour at daylight Bluemel confronted a truck column rumbling toward the rear. "The San Vicente line has broken!" shouted a GI from the first vehicle.

This time even Bluemel could not stop the stampede. It was appalling to see American soldiers running again and again from a fight. A mass of Filipinos surged toward him. Brandishing his rifle, he ordered them to form a line on either side of the trail. A shell burst along the road, then another and another. The men pushed past him, scattering in terror to the south. The irate general tried to grab and hold on to several, but they wrenched themselves loose.

2.

Major General Edward P. King, Jr., who had taken over command of the Luzon Force after Wainwright's promotion, was a modest man, courteous to all ranks, an intellectual with the air of a professor. An artilleryman of wide experience, he was an extremely able soldier, reasonable and realistic, who gave out orders in a quiet, undramatic way. On April 7, a few hours after Bluemel's line broke, he received a phone call from Corregidor. Wainwright said that since the troops on the western half of the peninsula were intact, why shouldn't they turn right and attack toward Manila Bay, cutting Homma's line in two?

It was true that the entire left half of the line was still in position, but King was sure they were in no physical condition to attack. Nevertheless, he reluctantly agreed to give it a try. The recently promoted Major General Albert M. Jones, commander of I Philippine Corps, was not so easily persuaded. The outspoken General Jones thought any attack was senseless and told Wainwright so directly in a three-way telephone conversation with King. With some exasperation Wainwright said he would leave the decision to King and hung up. King ordered Jones to pull back his men in four phases, then sent his chief of staff, Brigadier General Arnold J. Funk, to Corregidor to impress upon Wainwright the fact that surrender might come at any minute.

The gaunt Wainwright knew what the men on Bataan were going through but he was under constant pressure from MacArthur, down in Australia, to hold out. Recently MacArthur had radioed that he was "utterly opposed under any circumstances or conditions to the ultimate capitulation of this command," and that Wainwright should "prepare and execute an attack upon the enemy" once food supplies were exhausted.

Wainwright could not accept Funk's talk of capitulation. "General," he said in his slow drawl, "you will go back and tell General King he will *not* surrender. Tell him he will attack. Those are my orders."

"General, you know, of course, what the situation is over there." Funk's eyes brimmed with tears. "You know what the outcome will be."

"I do."

The next afternoon Colonel Takeo Imai planted a large flag on top of Mount Limay, one of the peaks of the southern volcano. He could see Japanese steadily pouring down the eastern half of Bataan. After dark he returned to the summit. Flashes of light came from the southern tip of Bataan where the enemy was blowing up equipment and munitions. Beyond he could make out the dark polliwog outline of Corregidor. Every so often angry spits of fire erupted from its heights; giant cannon were trying to stop the advance by interdicting the eastern road.

Fleeing before the Japanese columns, Americans and Filipinos poured out of the jungles into the toe of the peninsula. They came by trail, across rugged mountains, by the coast road. There was no order anywhere. Terror alone kept the exhausted men moving.

At the end of Bataan in the town of Mariveles a few boats were evacuating the last refugees to Corregidor while the remaining vessels were towed out into the bay and sunk. Mobs of disorganized soldiers bitterly watched the privileged few pull away from the docks: *they were going to join those draft dodgers on Corregidor where life was soft—with plenty of drinking water, canned food and romantic nurses; they would sit safely in Malinta Tunnel until the mile-long convoy arrived to relieve them; they would be the heroes while those left to rot on Bataan would be disgraced for throwing in the towel.*

Suddenly the ground began to shake violently. It was an earthquake, but some of the dazed men thought it was the end of the world.

At his office in Malinta Tunnel the distraught Wainwright phoned King at eleven-thirty in the evening on April 8 and told him to launch an attack northward with Jones's I Corps. King passed on the order to Jones, who characteristically replied, "Any attack is ridiculous, out of the question."

Forget the attack, said King. He knew Jones was right and that any more fighting at all would mean needless casualties. At mid-

"To Show Them Mercy Is to Prolong the War"

night King summoned his chief of staff and operations officer. There was no debate; the situation was hopeless. Wainwright was hamstrung by MacArthur's explicit order to attack until the end, and King decided to take the burden on his own shoulders. He knew full well he would have to disobey orders and that if he ever got back to the States, he would be court-martialed. But the lives of his 78,000 soldiers were more important than his honor. "I have decided to surrender Bataan," he said. "I have not communicated with General Wainwright because I do not want him to assume any part of the responsibility."

Just before two o'clock in the morning his phone rang. It was Jones. Before either could say a word there was a deafening roar. The roof of King's command post blew off and rubble showered down. The sky lit up fantastically. Then came other explosions, and roaring flames lit the sky.

"For crying out loud, Ned," Jones shouted. "What's going on?"

"The ammunition dump is blowing up," King replied calmly above the din.

"Hell, I can feel the ground shaking all the way up here. It must be an earthquake."

"I hate to tell you this, Honus, but I'm surrendering at six A.M." He told Jones to put white flags all along his line and destroy his artillery and machine guns.

"I don't see what else you can do," said Jones.

It wasn't until four hours later that the night duty officer in Malinta Tunnel informed Wainwright of King's surrender. "Tell him not to do it!" the general shouted. It was too late. "They can't do it! They can't do it!" he muttered. Finally he regained control of himself. He radioed MacArthur:

AT 6 O'CLOCK THIS MORNING GENERAL KING . . . WITHOUT MY KNOWLEDGE OR APPROVAL SENT A FLAG OF TRUCE TO THE JAPANESE COMMANDER. THE MINUTE I HEARD OF IT I DISAPPROVED OF HIS ACTION AND DIRECTED THAT THERE WOULD BE NO SURRENDER. I WAS INFORMED IT WAS TOO LATE TO MAKE ANY CHANGE, THAT THE ACTION HAD ALREADY BEEN TAKEN. . . .

At nine o'clock the stocky King, wearing his last clean uniform, headed up front in a jeep with his two aides, Majors Achille

Tisdelle and Wade Cothran. As Japanese guides escorted them to the Experimental Farm Station at Lamao, it occurred to King that Lee had surrendered to Grant at Appomatox on that same day, April 9. He remembered what Lee had said just before the ceremony: "Then there is nothing left to do but to go and see General Grant, and I would rather die a thousand deaths."

A shiny black Cadillac drove up with Colonel Motoo Nakayama. Through an interpreter, Homma's senior operations officer asked King if he was General Wainwright.

"No, I am General King, commander of all forces on Bataan."

Puzzled, Nakayama told him to get Wainwright; the Japanese could not accept surrender without him. King said he could not communicate with Wainwright. "My forces are no longer fighting units. I want to stop further bloodshed."

"Surrender must be unconditional."

"Will our troops be well treated?"

"We are not barbarians. Will you surrender unconditionally?"

King nodded. He said he had left his saber in Manila, and instead placed his pistol on the table.

Americans and Filipino soldiers huddled in disconsolate groups. There were tears of humiliation, but many wept from the relief of knowing their ordeal was over. They waited uneasily for the conquerors.

The first ones Air Corps Captain Mark Wohlfeld saw were packing a mountain gun. They had big smiles on their faces and spoke in gentle tones. These couldn't be such bad chaps after all, he thought with relief. Wohlfeld was from a dive-bomber group but had been fighting as an infantryman since January. Next came the Japanese infantry. Grim-faced, they immediately began stripping the prisoners of blankets, watches, jewelry, razor blades, mess equipment, food and even toothbrushes. One also found twenty rounds of .45-caliber pistol ammunition on Wohlfeld and, with shouts, began beating him on the head with his rifle barrel. Someone behind Wohlfeld muttered, "For Christ's sake, don't fall down!" Then the guard glimpsed a gold ring on Lieutenant Colonel Jack Sewell's finger and yanked at it. "It's my wedding ring," Sewell protested and withdrew his hand. The Japanese snapped the bayonet off his rifle and was going for the colonel when Wohlfeld came between. He tried to spit on the ring to loosen it but his throat was too dry. So was the colonel's. Wohlfeld smeared blood from his head on the finger. The ring came off.

Another Japanese enlisted man stole a ring just as his commanding officer passed by. The officer noticed that the ring bore the University of Notre Dame insignia. He hit the looter in the face and returned the ring to its owner. "When did you graduate?"
"1935."
A faraway look came over the Japanese officer's face when he said, "I graduated from Southern California in '35."

Wainwright's intolerable burden was somewhat lightened by a message from Roosevelt:

AM KEENLY AWARE OF THE TREMENDOUS DIFFICULTIES UNDER WHICH YOU ARE WAGING YOUR GREAT BATTLE. THE PHYSICAL EXHAUSTION OF YOUR TROOPS OBVIOUSLY PRECLUDES THE POSSIBILITY OF A MAJOR COUNTERATTACK UNLESS OUR EFFORTS TO RUSH FOOD TO YOU SHOULD QUICKLY PROVE SUCCESSFUL. BECAUSE OF THE STATE [over] WHICH YOUR FORCES HAVE NO CONTROL I AM MODIFYING MY ORDERS TO YOU. . . . MY PURPOSE IS TO LEAVE TO YOUR BEST JUDGMENT ANY DECISIONS AFFECTING THE FUTURE OF THE BATAAN GARRISON. . . . I FEEL IT PROPER AND NECESSARY THAT YOU SHOULD BE ASSURED OF COMPLETE FREEDOM OF ACTION AND OF MY FULL CONFIDENCE IN THE WISDOM OF WHATEVER DECISION YOU MAY BE FORCED TO MAKE.

And in Australia, MacArthur was reading a prepared statement to reporters: "The Bataan Force went out as it would have wished, fighting to the end its flickering, forlorn hope. No army has done so much with so little, and nothing became it more than its last hour of trial and agony. To the weeping mothers of its dead, I can only say that the sacrifice and halo of Jesus of Nazareth has descended upon their sons, and that God will take them unto Himself."

3.

Estimating that he would capture twenty-five thousand prisoners, Homma had turned over the logistics planning to his transportation officer, Major General Yoshikata Kawane. Kawane had divided the operation into two phases, and ten days before the final attack, presented the plan to Homma for approval. Colonel Toshimitsu Takatsu would be responsible for the first phase—bringing all the prisoners to Balanga, halfway up the peninsula. The distance for those who were at Mariveles, at the southern tip, would be nineteen miles—an easy day's march to any Japanese soldier—so there would be no need for transportation; nor would there be any need to issue food that day, since the prisoners could use their own rations. Kawane would personally supervise the second phase: the trip from Balanga to the prison camp. No more than two hundred trucks could be spared for the operation, but these would surely be sufficient to shuttle the prisoners the thirty-three miles from Balanga to the rail center of San Fernando. Freight trains would take the men north for thirty miles to Capas, a village just above Clark Field. From there they would be marched eight miles to their new home, Camp O'Donnell.

Kawane explained to Homma that the prisoners would eat the same rations as Japanese troops, and field hospitals were being established at Balanga and San Fernando; there would also be medical units, aid stations and "resting places" set up every few miles along the route.

Homma approved the plan. Tragically, it was based on fallacies. Wainwright's men were already starving and weak with malaria. And there would be seventy-six thousand prisoners, not twenty-five thousand.

At Mariveles, groups of three hundred were started up the road. Some had no guards; others had as many as four. The ditches along the zigzag route leading north were littered with abandoned equipment: burned trucks, self-propelled mounts and rifles. The prisoners trudged by King's former headquarters, where a side road led to Hospital No. 2. There a rumor had just spread through

"To Show Them Mercy Is to Prolong the War"

the sprawling open-air wards that the Japanese were freeing all Filipinos. The chief of surgery went from ward to ward trying to convince the wounded Filipinos it was a hoax. But Japanese hospital guards, apparently eager to rid themselves of responsibility, encouraged the patients to join the line of prisoners. Infected by mass hysteria, five thousand of them scrambled along the dusty trail; amputees, using tree limbs for crutches, hobbled off, their dressings unraveling. Within a mile the hysteria dissipated but by then the ditches were lined with dead and dying.

The marchers from Mariveles continued straight up the coast of Bataan. On the left was towering Mount Bataan, its peaks shrouded by clouds as usual. On the right were the blue-green waters of Manila Bay. Ordinarily it was a scene of lush tropical beauty—banana trees, nipa palms with long leaves, coconut trees gracefully bent. Today there was no beauty. The foliage was covered with a heavy coat of chalk from months of heavy American traffic, and the road itself was hardly visible through the choking dust clouds churned up by the Japanese howitzers, tanks, ammunition and supply vehicles and trailers loaded with strange-looking boats. They were streaming south in preparation for the assault on Corregidor. Infantrymen in trucks jeered at the marchers, and a few knocked off their hats and helmets with long bamboo poles. Occasionally a Japanese would stop the sport, apologize to the captives. Once a Japanese officer rushed up to an American tank commander and embraced him. They had been classmates at UCLA.

There was no consistency to the actions of the Japanese. One truckload of troops would toss down canteens to the prisoners, while the next swung "liberated" golf clubs at their heads. One thing, however, was becoming clear to the marchers: the situation grew worse as they moved up the peninsula.

The brutalities of that first day were spontaneous but they would not remain so. Colonel Tsuji had arrived in Manila several days earlier from Singapore, where five thousand Chinese had been murdered largely at his instigation for "supporting" British colonialism. He had already—unknown to Homma—convinced several admiring officers on the general's staff that this was a racial war and that all prisoners in the Philippines should be executed: Americans because they were white colonialists and Filipinos because they had betrayed their fellow Asians.

A division staff officer phoned Colonel Imai, conqueror of Mount Limay, and told him, "Kill all prisoners and those offering to surrender."

"How can I possibly obey such an order?" asked Imai. He demanded a copy in writing.

The staff officer informed him that it was an order "from Imperial Headquarters" and had to be obeyed.* Imai said he would not comply unless he received a written order, and hung up. He refused to carry out the decree and, incensed at this violation of the samurai code, ordered his staff to set all the prisoners free with directions on the best way to escape from Bataan.

His staff stared at him. Imai yelled at them to execute his command and not stand around "like so many wooden-headed dolls." More than a thousand prisoners were released. As Imai watched them go into the jungle he argued with himself that no Japanese general would have issued such an inhuman order. But if it was true, he would have to pretend that the prisoners had escaped on their own.

A similar order to kill prisoners was relayed verbally to Major General Torao Ikuta, commander of a recently arrived garrison unit, by a staff officer of a neighboring division. Like Imai, Ikuta and his chief of staff, Lieutenant Colonel Nobuhiko Jimbo, doubted that the order came from Imperial Headquarters. The staff officer said that his own division was already executing prisoners and advised Ikuta to do the same. The general refused to act without a written order.

Even in repose the marchers from Mariveles suffered all through the sultry night. They were so jammed together in enclosures that it was difficult to turn over. Captain Mark Wohlfeld finally got to sleep despite the drone of mosquitoes in his ears. He was wakened by spasmodic kicks from the soldier behind him and muttered to him to lie still. The usual stench grew worse and Wohlfeld opened his eyes inquisitively. His face was lying on filthy rags. He jumped up, and in the bright tropical moonlight examined the rags. They were the trousers of the man behind him and were

* Homma remained ignorant of this order to his death. His chief of staff learned about it only after the war.

dripping with feces and blood. "That rotten son of a bitch!" Wohlfeld shouted. He crammed the trousers in the soldier's face. "Get up!" When the man didn't move, Wohlfeld dragged him to a narrow aisle. He was dead.

Suddenly Wohlfeld felt himself flung head over heels by Japanese guards. This was repeated several times, and whenever he fell among the prisoners they would curse and throw him back to the Japanese. Finally Wohlfeld landed on his feet, and waving his arms in abject surrender, pointed to the dead American. He pantomimed for permission to carry him back to the "sick-rows." He didn't have the strength to pick up the emaciated corpse. When neither the guards nor his fellow prisoners offered to help, he grasped the dead soldier under the arms and hauled him off.

He was allowed to rinse himself in a creek. He crawled back to his place and told his neighbors exactly what had happened and how terrible he felt about having abused a fellow American soldier who had shit himself to death. He didn't know how he would be able to live with himself and said he would remember the incident ever after with remorse. He warned them to be quiet lest they get another visit from the Japanese MP's.

4.

According to General Kawane's calculations, it would take the prisoners a single day to march to Balanga, but some of them were on the road for three days. With each mile the guards became more confused and irritated, and consequently more brutal. The sun was blistering and there was little shade for the marchers on the long stretches between towns. Thick dust from the road clung to their sweating bodies, stung their eyes and turned their damp beards to a dirty white. Near Balanga the jungle still smoldered from the cataclysmic Good Friday bombardment. The rolling hills, stripped of trees and foliage, were a bleak desert of blackened stumps. As the long lines of prisoners filed into the outskirts of town they instinctively broke for the cool-looking waters of the Talisay River. Perhaps half made it; the rest were callously driven back to the road.

By daylight of April 11, Balanga was swollen with milling

captives and shouting guards, constantly fed by two streams of humanity, one from Mariveles, one—Jones's men—from the west. It was already obvious that the estimated total would be drastically exceeded. An attempt was made to feed the prisoners their first meal but the unmanageable numbers led to aggravating inequities. Some were given rice, salt and water; many got nothing.

From Balanga on, Kawane had planned to transport all the prisoners in trucks to San Fernando, but it was evident that more than half would have to continue marching; for the first time in history, numbers of American generals were walking toward a prison camp.

General Jones led his column past a burned-out village, its charred ruins still giving off a faint, acrid odor. To the left was the torn battlefield of the Abucay line, and beyond towered Mount Natib. It was past midnight by the time the Jones party reached Orani, eight miles above Balanga. They were shoved into a rice paddy enclosed by barbed wire. The foul odor was overpowering; feces crawling with maggots covered the area. It was, thought Jones, another Andersonville.

With dark came another nightmare. The air was oppressive; vicious mosquitoes swarmed in. It took an hour to get permission to visit the latrine pits, which were open morasses of excrement. Anyone who slipped in had to be pulled out by a comrade willing to take the risk, and those who lost consciousness after falling in were doomed to drown in the sea of feces. In the morning Mark Wohlfeld noticed several bodies floating in one pit. He gestured to a guard that he was willing to drag out the bodies, and several other Americans offered to help. The guard shouted for two companions, who seized Wohlfeld as if to toss him in the latrine. Instead they flung him to the ground. They kicked him and beat him with truncheons. Wohlfeld struggled to his feet as quickly as possible, and covered with filth from rolling near the latrine, staggered back to his place.

In an adjoining field a Japanese officer shouted a command; his men clapped hands three times—to simulate the flapping of a rooster's wings at dawn—and prayed out loud to the Sun Goddess. The prisoners were fed *lugao,* a rice mush that tasted like paste. No one left a particle. It was sixteen miles to the next station, Lubao, but it seemed twice that under the tropical sun. Again good treatment was a matter of luck. One set of guards would permit their charges to rest at proper intervals under shade trees and drink from the numerous roadside artesian wells. The next set would kick over cans of water placed on the highway by civilians, and "rest" their groups by forcing them to squat for an hour in the blazing sun.

Corpses, swollen to monstrous size by the heat, lined the ditches. Crows tore open the cadavers with their beaks; buzzing hordes of fat greenbottle flies clustered at every open wound. Scores of the bodies were beheaded. After counting twenty-seven, Lieutenant Colonel Allen Stowell told himself, "You've got to cut this out," and began marching with eyes fixed straight ahead.

Lieutenant Tony Aquino, the young Filipino who had swum to Corregidor to see President Quezon, had been walking without rest or water. He had lost more than fifty pounds since he came to Bataan, but his legs were swollen. In front of him an American staggered and crumpled to the road. A guard kept kicking him in the ribs. The American tried painfully to rise and extended a pleading hand to the Japanese. The guard deliberately placed the tip of his bayonet on the prisoner's neck and drove it home. He yanked it free and plunged it again into the American's body as Aquino and the others watched helplessly.

Farther back the pugnacious General Bluemel marched next to Brigadier General Luther Stevens. A Japanese soldier in a passing truck swung viciously at Stevens' head with a bamboo pole. Bluemel grabbed his staggering colleague and the two stumbled toward the ditch. A guard pointed a revolver at Bluemel, motioning him to move off, but he ignored the order. He helped the dazed Stevens to his feet, but his legs gave way and Bluemel had to drag him to the middle of a rice paddy. Another guard thought they were escaping and charged at them with fixed bayonet. He saw Stevens' bloody head just in time; he prodded Bluemel back to the highway. Stevens crawled behind some undergrowth and watched motionless as the column disappeared. But for Bluemel's courage he would probably be dead. His respite didn't last long, however; he was discovered and taken prisoner by another Japanese unit.

At a resting place a few miles to the north, Corporal Roy Castleberry watched two civilians dig a hole and lay a delirious American captain in it. The captain suddenly began a desperate struggle to escape his grave. A guard ordered the Filipinos to hit the American with their shovels. They refused until the Japanese raised his rifle menacingly. Faces twisted in agony, they beat the captain back into the hole and buried him alive. Horrified, Castleberry saw a hand feebly, hopelessly, claw in the air above the grave.

As the prisoners finally left Bataan and turned east toward Lubao, they faced a brutal stretch of completely unshaded road. Thirst had become intolerable for some and they risked their lives to sneak into adjoining fields for the meager moisture in sugar cane. Those unwilling to take the chance scrambled for the chewed cane dropped by their bolder comrades. Most of them were so dehydrated that they could not urinate, and those who did winced in agony as if hot irons had been shoved up their penises. Even so, it brought unspeakable relief.

At Lubao, a sprawling city of thirty thousand, the streets were lined with weeping people. They tried to throw the prisoners boiled eggs, fried chicken wrapped in banana leaves or pieces of *panocha* (hard brown sugar), but the surlier guards kept the crowds back with swinging rifle butts. Every so often an old woman swathed from crown to ankle would pull some staggering prisoner from the line and stand over him with her long skirts.

At the far edge of town the Japanese began herding the vanguard of marchers into a large corrugated-tin building, a rice mill, until several thousand men were packed inside. There was a single water spigot. The remaining prisoners were grouped outside the mill. They too had only one faucet. At the rice mill brutality was routine. Prisoners were slashed with sabers for minor insubordinations and beaten to death for no apparent reason.

The final lap to San Fernando, the rail center, was the second shortest, only nine miles, but the cruelest. The asphalt road, churned by tanks and trucks, was molten from the sun's rays, and to barefoot marchers whose soles were already raw it was like walking over hot coals. The last mile seemed endless to the dehydrated, starving men. At the outskirts of town they passed between parked lines of trucks, which formed a gantlet, and soldiers in the trucks swung their rifle butts at the Filipinos and Americans floundering through. In the town itself hordes of civilians from all over Luzon were looking for loved ones. The crowd moaned and wept as the skeleton army dragged by.

Here at last part of Kawane's plan was carried out with some measure of efficiency: the prisoners got rice balls, water and medical treatment. They were imprisoned in makeshift places—a pottery shed, the Blue Moon dance hall, empty lots, old factories, school buildings and yards, and the large circular cockfight arena near the railroad station.

Lieutenant Aquino's group was locked up in a decrepit vinegar factory. He dropped exhausted on a straw mat. Fourteen hours later he was wakened and escorted to a Japanese barracks where he found his father with a Japanese colonel. Father and son embraced.

"Mr. Aquino is a good friend of Japan," said the colonel, a *kempei* commander, in a British accent, and told young Aquino he could go home. But the lieutenant could not desert his men. He requested more food and medicine for all the prisoners.

"Your father was right," the colonel remarked. "He said you would refuse. Please accept my apologies for the way you all have been treated."

Once alone with his son, Benigno Aquino revealed that President Quezon had ordered Laurel and himself to pretend to collaborate with the Japanese; the first step would be to press for the early release of all Filipinos from prison camp.

"Hurry, Papa, we are dying like flies."

The men were herded into boxcars, similar to the French 40 and 8 of World War I. Over one hundred were jammed into each small car. Those with dysentery were unable to control themselves; others vomited on their comrades. The stench became almost unbearable as the trains slowly headed north on the three-hour trip to Capas. Some of the men died in the crush but were held erect by the pressing mob. There was momentary relief at the few stops; each time friendly guards opened the locked doors. The fresh air was like elixir. Filipinos were always on hand to pass out bottles of water, tomatoes, bananas, rice, eggs, coffee, sugar cane. Americans with a low opinion of Filipinos began to appreciate their courage and humanity.

At Capas the trains were unloaded. There was still an eight-mile march over a shadeless, dusty road to Camp O'Donnell, but anything was better than the cramped boxcars. At last the prisoners came to a maze of tumble-down buildings spread out on a vast plain. Guards herded them through a gate flanked by towers spiked with machine guns and up a hill to a building flying the Japanese flag. They sat in the sun for an hour before an officer, the commandant of the camp, strode out the door. He faced the prisoners and announced in a belligerent voice, through an interpreter, that the United States was his greatest enemy and that the Japanese were going to whip the Americans if it took a hundred years.

"Captain, he say you are not prisoners of war," the interpreter told Captain Ed Dyess's group. "You will be treated like captives. He say you do not act like soldiers. You got no discipline. You do not stand to attention while he talk. Captain, he say you will have trouble from him."

Two days after the first group plodded into Camp O'Donnell, the Manila Sunday *Tribune* published pictures of the march, along with a Japanese-inspired story:

The task of making observations upon the tragic aspect of marching war prisoners from the Bataan front, where they surrendered on April 9, to San Fernando, Pampanga, previous to their entrainment to their permanent concentration camp is a sad one; hence, our effort to avoid details about the whole episode.

So the public would not get the wrong impression from such an enigmatic remark, however, we make it plain that the Imperial Japanese Forces, whose business is clearly to prosecute the present war to its successful termination, are going well out of their way to feed and help 50,000 men who once were their enemies beyond most reasonable men's expectations.

If, in spite of the humane treatment the Japanese are giving these prisoners, the latter are too weak to reach their destinations, we have only the high command of the American forces to blame for surrendering when many of their men had already been terribly weakened by lack of food and by diseases.

Homma was so absorbed with mounting the assault on Corregidor that it was two months before he learned that more Fil-

Americans had died on the march than on the battlefields of Bataan. Only 54,000 men reached Camp O'Donnell, but many escaped and no one will ever know the exact death toll. Between 7,000 and 10,000 died on the march from malaria, starvation, beatings or execution. Of these, approximately 2,330 were Americans.

Most of the survivors were certain that the march was a cruel plan of the Japanese high command. But the cruelty was not systematic. The prisoners lucky enough to ride in trucks from Balanga to San Fernando suffered little, and a number of those who marched were adequately fed and encountered not a single brutality. Yet comrades a mile behind were starved, beaten and murdered.

Brutality to the Japanese soldier was a way of life. He took the slaps and beatings of his officers as a normal kind of reprimand, and in turn slapped and beat those under him. When prisoners failed to understand his orders or were too weak to follow them, he often, out of impulse or frustration at their apparent disobedience, resorted to violence and even murder. To the Japanese soldier, moreover, there was no such thing as surrender. He fought to the death. If taken prisoner while wounded or unconscious, he was forever disgraced. He was dead to his own family and his name was removed from the village or ward register. His soldier's manual read: "Bear in mind the fact that to be captured means not only disgracing the Army but your parents and family will never be able to hold up their heads again. Always save the last round for yourself."

Such training and background were responsible for much of the brutality but additional murders resulted directly from the unauthorized, oral order emanating from Colonel Tsuji. General Ikuta and Colonel Imai undoubtedly were not alone in refusing to follow this order; but others had obeyed it in full or in part, since they had been conditioned from childhood to carry out a command swiftly, without question. The average Japanese found it easier to follow than take the initiative and, in the Army particularly, was a slave to conformity in every aspect of life—he accepted without question, for example, that at inspections his penis had to be on the left side.

Nor was Colonel Tsuji the only one calling for vengeance against the whites and their dark-skinned collaborators. On April 24 the *Japan Times & Advertiser* printed an article which publicly echoed Tsuji's demands that no mercy be shown to prisoners of war.

> . . . They [the Allies] surrender after sacrificing all the lives they can, except their own, for a cause which they know well is futile; they surrender merely to save their own skins . . .
>
> They have shown themselves to be utterly selfish throughout all the campaigns, and they cannot be treated as ordinary prisoners of war. They have broken the commandments of God, and their defeat is their punishment.
>
> To show them mercy is to prolong the war. Their motto has been, "Absolute unscrupulousness." They have not cared what means they employed in their operations. An eye for an eye, a tooth for a tooth. The Japanese Forces are crusaders in a holy war. Hesitation is uncalled for, and the wrongdoers must be wiped out.

The atrocities unleashed by such fanaticism inevitably became a focal point of hate and revenge to the Allies.

12

"But Not in Shame"

1.

The succession of brilliant and unexpectedly easy victories in the Pacific had brought dissension rather than unity to the Japanese Supreme Command. The original war plan called for the seizure of raw materials in Southeast Asia; the conquered territory would be fortified into a strategic web of bases for long-range naval operations. The Army still felt the only sensible course was to make the web so strong that America would be forced eventually to make some sort of peace. But the Navy had experienced such exhilarating triumphs that it was no longer willing to accept such a limited, defensive role. Why not operations against Australia, Hawaii and India? These would generate great naval battles, and as in the Battle of the Java Sea, the enemy would be destroyed. So far less than 25,000 tons of shipping had been lost in conquering all of Southeast Asia, and the biggest warship sunk had been a destroyer.

The Navy began pressing upon the Army a series of plans reaching far beyond the original goals. One was to destroy the British fleet in the Indian Ocean and join up with the Germans. There was a more ambitious plan, aimed at America—cut the supply line between the United States and Australia. If the American fleet dared sortie to break this blockade, the result would be the long-dreamed-of Decisive Battle for the supremacy of the Pacific.

The Navy envisaged invasion of Australia itself with five Army divisions. This daring operation was drawn up by Captain Sadatoshi Tomioka of the Navy General Staff. At a joint operational meeting his opposite number in the Army, Colonel Takushiro Hattori, ridiculed the idea. Australia was twice the area of occupied China and its conquest would require not only the main body of the Combined Fleet but a dozen infantry divisions as well. The shipping for the Army alone would run to 1,500,000 tons. Tomioka suggested that they use the Kwantung Army in Manchuria, which was on garrison duty along the Soviet border. Hattori was against using so many troops on what would essentially be a diversionary effort; every man in uniform would be needed in the protracted struggle with the West. Seeing that Tomioka remained unshaken, Hattori picked up a cup. "The tea in this cup represents our total strength," he said and spilled it on the floor, "you see it goes just so far. If your plan is approved I will resign."

On March 7 a liaison conference brought their differences into the open. Echoing Hattori, General Moritake Tanabe argued that the Army's main objective was to build "a political and military structure capable of withstanding a long war." Neutralization forays in certain areas were practical, but only as long as they were on a modest scale. From now on the enemy should be forced into fighting far from his own bases on Japanese terms. Before Pearl Harbor they had all agreed on this strategic concept. Why improvise now? It would lead to catastrophe.

The Navy insisted that it was vital to keep the enemy on the defensive—anything else would invite disaster. Admiral Takasumi Oka wanted to destroy enemy sea power and wipe out any key bases that might be used for a counterattack "by the positive employment of forces in the Australian and Hawaiian areas."

The unresolved debate carried over into heated meetings at the Army and Navy Club which at times came close to physical violence. It was two weeks before a compromise could be reached: the Australian invasion was scrapped but the Army agreed to less enterprising projects such as an amphibious assault on Port Moresby, a town four hundred miles north of Australia, on the east coast of New Guinea, the second largest island in the world.

Hattori and Tomioka met informally and came to further accord. The latter agreed to abandon the plan to meet Hitler in the Indian Ocean, while Hattori approved the conquest of three island groups off the northeast coast of Australia—Samoa, Fiji and New Caledonia. This would cut the supply line between Australia and America at minimum cost.

On March 13 Tojo and the two Chiefs of Staff went to the Palace to submit a joint report to the Emperor on the new war policy: "It will not only be most difficult to defeat the United States and Britain in a short period, but the war cannot be brought to an end through surrender. It is essential to further expand the political and military advantages achieved through glorious victories since the opening of hostilities, by utilizing the present war situation to establish a political and strategic structure capable of withstanding a protracted war. We must take every possible step, within the limits of our national capabilities, to force the United States and Britain to remain on the defensive. Any definite measure of vital significance to be effected in this connection will be given thorough study and will be presented to His Majesty for approval each time."

The hard-won compromise was accepted by everyone but the most influential man in the Navy. Spurred by his gambler's instinct, Admiral Yamamoto was set upon launching another audacious attack on American territory—an invasion of Midway, an atoll comprising two small islands, less than thirteen hundred miles northwest of Pearl Harbor. This alone would protect the homeland from a direct surprise attack by the Pacific Fleet.

Yamamoto's plan found few adherents in the Navy General Staff, and he sent his favorite chess partner, Commander Yasuji Watanabe, to Tokyo to win support. But Captain Tomioka and Commander Kazunari Miyo, the aviation operations officer, were not impressed by his advocacy. How could Midway be held, let alone supplied, assuming it was taken? Moreover, it offered few rewards. On the other hand, seizure of the three island groups near Australia would surely lure the U. S. fleet to the Decisive Battle in an area where Japan could get support from the neighboring Solomon Islands.

The argument was settled not by reason but by threat. Watanabe took Yamamoto's case to their superior, Admiral Shigeru Fukudome. Miyo persisted in his arguments, and Watanabe went off to telephone Yamamoto. He brought back an ultimatum: it was either the Midway operation or Yamamoto's resignation. Navy Chief of Staff Nagano ruled: "In that case, we might as well let him try his plan."

This was April 5. Eleven days later a directive was issued to invade Midway and the Aleutians. Tomioka and Miyo were "mortified," but had no choice but to end all resistance. No specific date, however, was set by Tokyo, despite Yamamoto's insistent requests. The Navy General Staff saw no need for haste. It took an American named Doolittle to spur them into action.

2.

Shortly after Pearl Harbor, President Roosevelt had remarked that he would like to bomb the enemy mainland as soon as possible to avenge in small part the "sneak" attack. The distance involved made it seem like wishful thinking until it occurred to the operations officer on Admiral King's staff that long-range Army bombers might be launched from a carrier's deck. The idea intrigued King and the Army Air Corps, and by the beginning of March, twenty-four crews were at Eglin Field, Florida, learning how to lift off a modified twin-engine B-25 bomber from a 500-foot runway. Their commander was a remarkable combination—an aeronautical scientist and a daring pilot with several speed records to his credit. Lieutenant Colonel James H. Doolittle was the first man to fly across the United States in twelve hours; the first to do the impossible, the outside loop; and the first to land a plane blind.

On April 1 the sixteen crews finally selected for the mission boarded the carrier *Hornet* at Alameda Air Station in California while the other eight crews looked on with envy. The next day after breakfast Doolittle collected the men in an empty mess hall and began, "For the benefit of those who have not already been told or have been guessing, we are going to bomb Japan." Thirteen planes would drop their four bombs apiece on Tokyo; three single planes would hit Nagoya, Osaka and Kobe. "The Navy will get us in as close as possible and launch us off the deck." They would not return to the carrier but would overfly Japan and make for small fields in China. Did anyone want to back out? No one did.

Just before noon, accompanied by one heavy and one light cruiser, four destroyers and an oiler, *Hornet* with the sixteen B-25's lashed to her decks, passed under the Golden Gate Bridge. The departure of the bombers on their secret mission was witnessed by thousands of onlookers.

On April 8 Admiral William Halsey—"Bull" to reporters, but Bill to his intimates—steamed out of Pearl Harbor on the carrier *Enterprise* with two heavy cruisers, four destroyers and an oiler. He was to rendezvous with *Hornet* and her escort and accompany them to the launching point.

The Japanese knew nothing of the double sortie until two days later when Combined Fleet radio intelligence men intercepted messages between the two forces and Pearl Harbor. They deduced that if the Americans continued to proceed westward, Tokyo would be bombed. Because of the limited range of a carrier plane, the American ships would have to approach within four hundred miles before reaching the launching point. Since a surveillance net extended seven hundred miles offshore, there would be ample time to attack the enemy before the planes could take off. The assessment was accurate except for one thing—these were no ordinary carrier planes and they were scheduled to take off five hundred miles from the target.

On April 13 the two American units merged into one formidable group, Task Force 16, and steamed directly for Tokyo. The crews' confidence in the secrecy of their mission was shaken three days later when they heard a propaganda broadcast from Radio Tokyo: "Reuters, British news agency, has announced that three American bombers have dropped bombs on Tokyo. This is a most laughable story. They know it is absolutely impossible for enemy bombers to get within five hundred miles of Tokyo. Instead of worrying about such foolish things, the Japanese people are enjoying the fine spring sunshine and the fragrance of cherry blossoms."

The following day the fliers reported to the flight deck for a special ceremony. Captain Marc A. Mitscher handed over to Doolittle five Japanese medals awarded to Americans. The recipients had all asked that they be attached to a bomb and returned to Japan. While the medals were fixed to a bomb, fliers chalked on derisive slogans like *"I don't want to set the world on fire, just Tokyo,"* and *"You'll get a BANG out of this!"*

Doolittle ended the horseplay by announcing that they would take off the next day. Task Force 16 would arrive at the launching point a day ahead of time. This was their last briefing. Doolittle would leave first, timed to reach Tokyo at dusk. "The rest of you will take off two or three hours later and can use my fires as a homing beacon."

There was one last-minute question that no one had put before: what to do in case of a crash-landing in Japan. That was up to each pilot. Doolittle didn't intend to be taken prisoner. "I'm going to bail my crew out and then dive it, full throttle, into any target I can find where the crash will do the most good. I'm forty-six years old and have lived a full life."

The next morning at three o'clock, while they were still more than seven hundred miles from Tokyo, the secrecy of the mission—and therefore its success—was directly threatened. The radar of *Enterprise* detected two enemy ships off the port bow some twelve miles away. Several minutes later a light flickered on the horizon. Task Force 16 changed course and General Quarters was sounded on every ship. For half an hour the men waited uneasily. Then the All Clear sounded and the fleet resumed its westerly course as if nothing had happened.

The weather was foul and the ships pitched and rolled. Just before dawn three search bombers left *Enterprise* to probe two hundred miles ahead. One of the pilots sighted a small patrol boat through the murky gray overcast; he turned back and dropped a bean-bag on the carrier's deck. In it was a scrawled message:

> Enemy surface ship—latitude 36–04N, Long. 153–10E, bearing 276° true—42 miles. Believed seen by enemy.

As a precaution Halsey swung all his ships to port. Within an hour, lookouts on *Hornet* herself sighted a small patrol vessel—it was No. 23 *Nitto-maru*—which began sending a message in the clear that three enemy aircraft carriers had been sighted seven hundred miles from Tokyo. Then another patrol boat was sighted little more than six miles away. Halsey ordered them both sunk and flashed a message to *Hornet:*

LAUNCH PLANES X TO COL. DOOLITTLE AND GALLANT COMMAND GOOD LUCK AND GOD BLESS YOU.

On the bridge of *Hornet,* Doolittle pumped Mitscher's hand and scurried down the ladder to his cabin, shouting, "Okay, fellas, this is it! Let's go!" The klaxon screeched. The bullhorn boomed: "Army pilots, man your planes!"

No one realized as keenly as the pilots how seriously this abrupt change jeopardized their chances for success—and survival. Everything had been planned precisely to the last gallon of gas, and now 150 miles had been added to their flight. Moreover, the surprise element was gone and they would have to bomb in daylight. All the same, they were eager to go and one refused an offer of $150 from a relief crewman to take his place.

As Commander John Ford, the noted movie director, and his crew took pictures, a mechanical donkey began pulling the twin-ruddered bombers into position. The first plane, Doolittle's, had 467 feet of runway. Ten extra 5-gallon cans of gasoline were loaded into each plane; the main tanks were topped.

Doolittle gave his engines full throttle and they roared so that some of the pilots feared he'd burn them up. The wheel blocks were yanked away and the plane lunged ahead, the left tire following a white line running down the port side of the deck. The port wing of the B-25 hung over the side of the carrier as the bomber clumsily wobbled forward, flaps down, into the teeth of the gale sweeping down the deck.

The other pilots watched tensely, wondering if the stiff wind would be enough to help lift Doolittle in time. If he didn't make it, they surely wouldn't. The B-25 gained speed. To some pilots Doolittle's acceleration seemed agonizingly slow, but just as the bow of the carrier was lifted high by the heavy sea, he pulled up the bomber with yards of deck to spare. It was 7:20 A.M.

There were spontaneous cheers as the Doolittle plane circled, passed low over *Hornet* and took a direct course for Tokyo. The remaining bombers began rolling heavily down the deck one at a time, each "sweated" into the air by the onlookers. All went well until the last plane slowly taxied toward the starting line. Suddenly one of the deck crew—Seaman Robert W. Wall—lost his footing and was blown like a tumbleweed by the preceding plane's blast into the spinning left propeller. It mangled his left arm but knocked him free.

Feeling the jar, the pilot glanced back to see Wall sprawled on the deck. Rattled, he put his flap control lever back in retract instead of neutral. The plane struggled off the end of the deck and abruptly dropped out of sight under the bow. The deck crews were certain it was going to plunge into the sea; then, to their relief, they saw it skimming just above the waves. Ponderously it lifted, turned and followed the other planes. It was 8:20 A.M.

Naval headquarters in Tokyo were aware that an aerial attack was imminent, but the position given by *Nitto-maru* made them equally certain it would not come for another day. All available planes—90 fighters and 116 bombers—were alerted and Vice Admiral Nobutake Kondo was ordered to leave Yokosuka Naval Base at once and intercept the Americans with six heavy cruisers and ten destroyers.

At 9:45 A.M. a patrol plane reported it had come across a two-engine bomber flying westward some six hundred miles from land. But no one believed the report; the Americans didn't have twin-engine planes on carriers. The bombing attack could not possibly come until the next morning at the earliest, when the enemy carriers would be within three hundred miles of the coast.

By coincidence, just as the last planes were leaving *Hornet* an air-raid drill began in Tokyo. It was a tame affair, without as much as the shriek of a siren, and civilians ignored orders of officious air wardens to seek shelter. Instead they watched fire-fighting brigades show off their equipment. By noon it was all over. Most of the barrage balloons had been hauled down and three fighter planes circled lazily above the city. It was a warm, pleasant Saturday and the streets were again busy with shoppers and pleasure seekers.

A few minutes later Doolittle reached the coast of Japan eighty miles off course to the north. He banked left. In the plane behind, Navigator Carl Wildner began looking for fighter interceptors but all he saw were trainers rolling and looping. As the B-25 skimmed over the countryside he noticed people going about unconcerned. He passed over a military camp low enough to make out a group of officers, their swords flashing in the sunlight.

The most important officer in Japan was in a plane trying to land through the line of oncoming American bombers. That morning

Prime Minister Tojo had learned that an enemy task force was somewhere off the coast but had been assured it would be safe to take an inspection trip by air to Mito Aviation School. As his American-made passenger plane approached the landing field, a two-engine craft came up on the right. Tojo's secretary, Colonel Nishiura, thought it was a "queer-looking plane." It came so close that the pilot's face was visible, and it occurred to Nishiura—it's American! It flashed by without firing a shot.

At exactly 12:30 P.M. Doolittle was over his target. Using a twenty-cent "Mark Twain" bombing device, which was more accurate for a low-altitude attack than the overrated Norden bombsight, Fred Braemer released the first bomb. There was no effective opposition from fighters or antiaircraft as plane after plane swept over the city dumping their explosives. One of the pilots, Captain Edward York, discovered that he didn't have enough gas to get sufficiently deep into China and turned northwest for Vladivostok, though it meant probable internment. "I'll bet we're the first B-25 crew of five to bomb Tokyo and cross Japan at noon on a Saturday," joked the co-pilot to ease the tension.

Except for those near the impact areas, the citizens of Tokyo assumed the American attack was just a realistic climax to the air-raid drill. Nor did the truth come from radio station JOAK, which had abruptly gone off the air with the first explosions. Children in schoolyards and people in the crowded streets waved at the passing planes, mistaking their circular red, white and blue markings—similar to those used by the Allies in World War I—for the Rising Sun. Not a plane was shot down.

Planes passed over the Imperial Palace but nothing was dropped. The crews had cut cards to see who would go after the Emperor's residence, but Doolittle had issued explicit orders to avoid the Palace grounds as well as hospitals and schools.

At the Army and Navy Club, Captain Tomioka was having lunch with Colonel Hattori. Their discussion of the Midway invasion, which both continued to oppose, was interrupted by the crump of bombs. "Wonderful!" Tomioka exclaimed, guessing that they came from enemy carrier planes. If the American fleet moved in closer, the Navy could have its Decisive Battle in homeland waters.

This possibility never occurred to the man most eager about Midway. Instead Admiral Yamamoto was so stricken by shame at the attack on the capital that he left the pursuit of the Americans to Matome Ugaki, his chief of staff, retired to his room and refused to come out. Chief Steward Heijiro Omi had never seen him so pale or depressed.

Admiral Ugaki was unable to locate the enemy fleet and that evening wrote in his diary: "We must improve countermeasures against future enemy attacks by checking the types and numbers of planes. At any rate, today the victory belonged to the enemy." He wondered if the American task force had reversed course and run or was preparing another air assault on Tokyo.

Halsey had long since turned back toward Pearl Harbor; there were no more bombers to launch. Captain York's plane arrived safely in Vladivostok, where the crew of five was interned by the Russians. The other fifteen bombers came down in Japanese-occupied China. Three men were killed in crash-landings or bail-outs; eight were captured and brought to Tokyo for trial.* The rest, including Doolittle, were alive and heading by various routes for Chiang Kai-shek's lines.

The feat lifted the morale of Americans still shaken by the fall of Bataan. It seemed to be a pledge that America would soon go over to the attack, and Allies on every battlefield and in every prison camp found fresh hope. Newspapers in the United States headlined the story with exuberance. DOOLITTLE DID IT, crowed the Los Angeles *Times*. Roosevelt added to the public's delight over the surprise raid by announcing, with his flare for the dramatic, that the bombers had taken off from Shangri-La.

The foray caused no outward panic in Japan, but was a psychological shock to a nation brought up to believe for centuries that somehow the homeland would always be safe from assault. The newspapers belittled it as a "complete failure," yet pictured Doolittle's men as demons who "carried out an inhuman, insatiable, indiscriminate bombing attack on the sly," and demonstrated

* The captured fliers gave their interrogators such confusing accounts (some said they came from the Aleutians, some from a special carrier no one had ever heard of, some from a mysterious island in the Pacific on no map) that Ugaki issued an order to somehow "solve the riddle of the enemy attack." The prisoners were, according to Ugaki's diary, "forced to tell the truth," and finally revealed most of the facts of the attack, but by that time Halsey was halfway to Pearl Harbor.

"their fiendish behavior" by ruthlessly strafing civilians and noncombatants. As testimony of the effective Japanese air defense of Tokyo, a wing and a landing-gear tubing of a B-25 (secretly brought over from China) were exhibited at the Yasukuni Shrine Provisional Festival; a parachute was effectively draped over a ginkgo tree in full bloom.

The raid itself *was* a failure as far as physical damage was concerned, but the fact that it had happened forced the Supreme Command to overreact. Four fighter groups were reassigned to protect Japan from assaults that were not even being planned by the enemy. The China Expeditionary Army was ordered to cease other operations and rout out enemy air bases in the Chekiang area.

More important, it finally brought an end to opposition within the Navy to the Midway campaign. Yamamoto came out of his one-day retirement to renew demands that the invasion be executed promptly. Unless Midway—which had probably been the base of the air attack—was captured shortly, air and sea patrols in front of the homeland would have to be strengthened at the expense of battle area. Those who had been hoping to sabotage the project by a series of delaying actions capitulated, and on April 20 at a joint Army-Navy meeting, the Navy General Staff proposed that the plan to cut the Australian life line by seizing Samoa, Fiji and New Caledonia be postponed so the Midway invasion could proceed as soon as possible. The Army still considered it a risky venture, but with Nagano openly supporting Yamamoto, reluctantly approved the operation. It was no time to create antagonistic feelings between the two services. Besides, the Navy would go ahead with the invasion no matter what the Army said.

3.

General Homma's guns began to churn Corregidor into a no man's land. Though morale was fairly high among the defenders, there was little hope that the island could be held long. A favorite song was "I'm Waiting for Ships That Never Come In," and some of the men sarcastically wondered if the V's for Victory chalked on so many helmets stood for Victim.

On April 29 Japanese artillery fire and bombing reached a crescendo. It was the Emperor's birthday. Two ammunition dumps exploded, solid rock cliffs were disintegrated and uncontrollable grass fires swept the little island, covering it with thick clouds of smoke and dust. The next day, and the next, there was no respite. The bombardment concentrated on the big mortars of Batteries Geary and Way which covered the approach from Bataan. By the morning of May 2 Battery Geary was still intact, but not for long. At noon an explosion rocked Corregidor like an earthquake. Battery Geary erupted. The barrels of its eight 10-ton mortars were tossed into the air like match sticks, one landing 150 yards away on the pockmarked golf course.

Corregidor now had little except its beach-defense troops to hold off the landings. Of the 4,000 in number at the fall of Bataan, there were little more than 3,000 effectives left because of extensive bombardment casualties. Of these, about 1,300 were well-trained fighters from the 4th Marine Regiment. The rest was a conglomerate force of Filipino fliers and artillerymen and American refugees from Bataan.

Life outside Malinta Tunnel was dangerous, but at least there was fresh air and light. The 10,000 people who lived safely in the rambling underground system suffered from an intolerable tension nicknamed "tunnelitis." The dust made breathing difficult, and the smell of death from the hospital pervaded every lateral. When the blowers were off during bombings, the air became fetid, the heat almost unbearable. Huge black flies, roaches and other insects overran the place. Tempers grew short: arguments sprang up over trifles.

On May 3 General Wainwright was told that the water supply was dangerously low and radioed MacArthur:

SITUATION HERE IS FAST BECOMING DESPERATE.

The following day sixteen thousand shells burst on the island. The terrified beach defenders crouched in their shallow foxholes, filled with an overpowering hatred for the "tunnel rats." But those inside were not comforted by the protection Malinta offered. The almost continuous drumfire of explosions drove many to the point of hysteria. In his little whitewashed office Wainwright wrote Marshall an estimate of the situation:

> IN MY OPINION THE ENEMY IS CAPABLE OF MAKING ASSAULT ON CORREGIDOR AT ANY TIME.
> SUCCESS OR FAILURE OF SUCH ASSAULT WILL DEPEND ENTIRELY ON THE STEADFASTNESS OF BEACH DEFENSE TROOPS. CONSIDERING THE PRESENT LEVEL OF MORALE, I ESTIMATE THAT WE HAVE SOMETHING LESS THAN AN EVEN CHANCE TO BEAT OFF AN ASSAULT. I HAVE GIVEN YOU, IN ACCORDANCE WITH YOUR REQUEST, A VERY FRANK AND HONEST OPINION ON THE SITUATION AS I SEE IT.

Homma was again behind schedule. Corregidor should have fallen two weeks earlier but the invasion had been delayed by a malaria epidemic in the infested river valleys of southern Bataan which was finally brought under control by quinine tablets flown in from Japan.

On the evening of May 4 Homma stood above the little harbor of Lamao and anxiously watched landing craft carrying two thousand men and several tanks disappear in the dusk toward Corregidor. The odds were chilling; the assault troops faced at least seven times their number on the fortress island. They were to land in two waves on the north beach of Corregidor's polliwog tail and push west toward Malinta Hill, where they would wait for reinforcements the following night. But in the darkness the erratic tides and currents pushed the small invasion fleet a mile off its course, and as the first boats approached shore they met devastating fire from two 75-mm. guns, saved for just such an emergency. Boat after boat was blown out of the water. The barrage became so intense that many of the invaders leaped from their boats too soon and were dragged under water by almost a hundred pounds of equipment. Less than one third of the entire assault force survived. They were led by their commander, Colonel Gempachi Sato, toward the east mouth of Malinta Tunnel.

At midnight a Marine messenger raced into the tunnel. Six hundred Japs had landed! For three hours Wainwright remained in suspense. Then came news that a Marine AA gun pit, one mile from the tunnel, had been seized. The next message, moments later, was a radiogram from Roosevelt. He praised the defenders as "living symbols of our war aims and the guarantee of victory."

Just before dawn, five hundred untrained sailors—the last reserves—left the mouth of the tunnel and crawled up toward the fighting. Together with the Marines of Headquarters and Service Company, they launched an attack that completely surprised the Japanese, who were waiting for plane and tank support, and forced them to fall back on both flanks. But at ten o'clock the Americans could hear the ominous rumble of tanks.

Once Wainwright learned that armor was moving against men with no antitank defenses, a nightmare flashed through his mind—a tank nosing into the tunnel and spraying lead at the wounded and nurses.

"We can't hold out much longer," he told his staff. At ten-fifteen he ordered Brigadier General Lewis C. Beebe to broadcast a previously prepared surrender message. In a choked voice Wainwright said, "Tell the Nips that we'll cease firing at noon."

To limit his own surrender to the four little islands in Manila Bay, he radioed Major General William F. Sharp, commander of all troops in the southern islands, releasing to him the rest of the Philippines.

Guns were spiked, codes burned and radio equipment smashed. Wainwright wrote out his last message to Roosevelt.

WITH BROKEN HEART AND HEAD BOWED IN SADNESS BUT NOT IN SHAME I REPORT TO YOUR EXCELLENCY THAT TODAY I MUST ARRANGE TERMS FOR THE SURRENDER OF THE FORTIFIED ISLANDS OF MANILA BAY. . . . THERE IS A LIMIT OF HUMAN ENDURANCE AND THAT LIMIT HAS LONG SINCE BEEN PASSED. WITHOUT PROSPECT OF RELIEF I FEEL IT IS MY DUTY TO MY COUNTRY AND TO MY GALLANT TROOPS TO END THIS USELESS EFFUSION OF BLOOD AND HUMAN SACRIFICE.
IF YOU AGREE, MR. PRESIDENT, PLEASE SAY TO THE NATION THAT MY TROOPS AND I HAVE ACCOMPLISHED ALL THAT IS HUMANLY POSSIBLE AND THAT WE HAVE UPHELD THE BEST TRADITIONS OF THE UNITED STATES AND ITS ARMY.
MAY GOD BLESS AND PRESERVE YOU AND GUIDE YOU AND THE NATION IN THE EFFORT TO ULTIMATE VICTORY.

WITH PROFOUND REGRET AND WITH CONTINUED PRIDE IN MY GALLANT TROOPS I GO TO MEET THE JAPANESE COMMANDER. GOODBYE, MR. PRESIDENT.

All American guns ceased firing. Wainwright waited for two hours, then drove east in a Chevrolet with five others to Denver Hill. They continued on foot past the dead and dying and were met near the top of the hill by a Japanese group. An arrogant lieutenant said surrender must include all American and Filipino troops in the archipelago.

"I do not choose to discuss surrender terms with you," said Wainwright. "Take me to your senior officer."

Colonel Motoo Nakayama, who had accepted King's surrender, stepped forward. Wainwright told him he would surrender the four islands in Manila Bay. Nakayama replied angrily that he had explicit orders from Homma to bring Wainwright to Bataan for the capitulation ceremony only if he agreed to relinquish all his troops.

As yet General Homma had no idea that Corregidor wanted to give up. A report had come in that thirty-one boats had been sunk the night before, and the reinforcement wave would have to be canceled, since there were just twenty-one landing craft left. He knew he faced disgrace. Suddenly a staff officer burst in with the news that a white flag was fluttering over Corregidor. Homma was so relieved that he radioed Nakayama to disregard former orders and bring Wainwright to Bataan at once.

At four o'clock in the afternoon Wainwright, leaning heavily on his cane, thin body bent, once more stepped on Bataan soil at Cabcaben. Two cars brought the party to a small house, painted blue, surrounded by a luxuriant growth of mangrove. The Americans waited on the open porch; to the south out in Manila Bay they could see Corregidor still erupting with shell bursts—the battle had apparently not ended as far as the Japanese were concerned. The general and his companions were given cold water and lined up for pictures by Japanese newsmen.

Finally, at five o'clock, a Cadillac drew up and the barrel-chested General Homma, looking crisp and vigorous in his olive-drab uniform, stepped out. He welcomed the Americans. "You must be very tired and weary."

Wainwright thanked him and they all sat on the porch around a long table. Wainwright handed over a signed note surrendering Corregidor and Forts Hughes, Drum and Frank, the four islands in Manila Bay. Homma had some command of English but wanted his staff to understand the proceedings and asked an interpreter to read it aloud. His face was stony; he said he could only accept the surrender of all troops in the Philippines.

"The troops in the Visayan Islands and Mindanao are no longer under my command," Wainwright explained. "They are commanded by General Sharp, who in turn is under General MacArthur's high command."

Homma flushed. Did Wainwright take him for a fool? He ordered his interpreter to tell Wainwright the Japanese had intercepted messages from Washington confirming Wainwright's position as commander in chief of all Philippine forces.

But Wainwright insisted that he had no authority over Sharp. Losing all patience, Homma banged the table with both fists. He faced his new chief of staff. "What should we do, Wachi?" Major General Takaji Wachi said he was sure Wainwright was lying. "In that case, we cannot negotiate," said Homma curtly. "Let us continue the battle." He turned back to Wainwright and informed him in a controlled voice that he could only negotiate with his equal, the commander in chief of all forces in the Philippines. "Since you are not in supreme command, I see no further necessity for my presence here." He started to rise.

One of Wainwright's companions called out in alarm, "Wait!" There was a quick conference among the Americans. Pale, Wainwright turned to Homma and forced himself to say, "In face of the fact that further bloodshed in the Philippines is unnecessary and futile, I will assume command of the entire American forces in the Philippines at the risk of serious reprimand by my government following the war."

But Homma was too offended to accept the abrupt turnabout. He doubted Wainwright's sincerity. Stiffly he told the American commander to go back to Corregidor and think the matter over. "If you see fit to surrender, then do so to the commanding officer of the regiment on Corregidor. He in turn will bring you to me in Manila. I call this meeting over. Good day." He nodded and walked to his Cadillac.

"But Not in Shame" 393

The distraught Wainwright had chewed the cigarette in his mouth to shreds. "What do you want us to do now?" he asked Nakayama.

"We will take you and your party back to Corregidor, and you can do what you damn please."

The entire emotional exchange had taken place through interpreters whose translations had been vague. No one knew exactly what had been said except a completely bilingual newsman named Kazumaro Uno who had been raised in Utah. He sympathized with the plight of the Americans and explained to Nakayama that Wainwright was quite ready to surrender all the Philippines.

Somewhat mollified, Nakayama said he would accompany Wainwright to Corregidor and added, "First thing tomorrow morning you will go to General Homma with a new surrender and a promise to contact the other American forces in the Philippines."

Wainwright saw many campfires all over Corregidor and guessed that the Japanese had already landed reinforcements. He was led around Malinta Hill and introduced to the island commander, Colonel Sato. The tunnel had been cleared except for those in the hospital. Now Sato was preparing to attack the main part of the island, Topside. Immediate unconditional surrender to Sato was the only way Wainwright could save his men from slaughter, and in the feeble light he signed a document accepting all of Homma's original demands. He felt drained of energy.

It was midnight. Wainwright was escorted to the west entrance of Malinta Tunnel, past solemn groups of Americans and Filipinos. Some of the men reached out to touch his hand or pat his shoulder. "It's all right, General," said one. "You did your best."

His eyes filled with tears.

Wainwright's humiliation was just beginning. The following morning he summoned his operations officer, Colonel Jesse T. Traywick, Jr. The Japanese would fly the colonel to Mindanao so he could personally deliver a letter to General Sharp explaining the situation.

... You will therefore be guided accordingly, and *will* repeat *will* surrender all troops under your command both in the Visayan Islands and Mindanao to the proper Japanese officer. This decision on my part, you will realize, was forced upon me by means beyond my control. . . .

Traywick was empowered to place Sharp under arrest if he failed to follow instructions implicitly. Wainwright broke down. "Jesse," he said, "I'm depending on you to carry out these orders."

Wainwright and five of his officers were taken by assault boat to Bataan late that afternoon. At Lamao they were kept waiting for two hours but did receive their first food in two days, rice and bony fish. At dusk they started the tedious trip to Manila by car. Around eleven o'clock the party arrived at radio station KZRH and was met by Lieutenant Hisamichi Kano of the Propaganda Corps, who had been educated in New York and New Jersey. He greeted Wainwright affably and offered the Americans some fruit.

Wainwright had difficulty reading the prepared speech, which was a combination of his letter to Sharp and Japanese interpolations, until Kano reworded it into more colloquial English. Shortly before midnight Wainwright, so gaunt that he looked almost like a skeleton, sat down at a small round bamboo table and began speaking into a microphone in a voice husky with suppressed emotion. He addressed Sharp directly, ordering him to surrender all forces. "You will repeat the complete text of this letter and such other instructions as Colonel Traywick will give you by radio to General MacArthur. However, let me emphasize that there must be on your part no thought of disregarding these instructions. Failure to fully and honestly carry them out can have only the most disastrous results." He almost choked as he warned that the Japanese would continue operations unless the orders were carried out scrupulously and accurately. "If and when such faithfulness of execution is recognized, the commander in chief of the Japanese forces in the Philippine Islands will order that all firing be ceased." He coughed and paused. "Taking all circumstances into consideration, and—"

There was another longer pause. Wainwright seemed unable to continue. The Filipino announcer, Marcela Victor Young, broke in and signed off. It was 12:20 A.M., May 8.

Kano led the emotionally drained Wainwright and his companions to his office. He poured them drinks from a bottle of Scotch while the Americans tried to comfort their stricken commander.

The speech was heard by Americans and Filipinos all through the islands. Was it really Wainwright talking? If so, did he have a pistol at his head? General Sharp didn't know what to do. That morning he'd received a message from Wainwright relinquishing his command and now he was taking it back. He requested instructions from MacArthur. MacArthur in turn radioed Washington that he placed "no credence in the alleged broadcast by Wainwright." His reply to Sharp went out at 4:45 A.M.:

> ORDERS EMANATING FROM GENERAL WAINWRIGHT HAVE NO VALIDITY. IF POSSIBLE SEPARATE YOUR FORCE INTO SMALL ELEMENTS AND INITIATE GUERRILLA OPERATIONS. YOU, OF COURSE, HAVE FULL AUTHORITY TO MAKE ANY DECISION THAT IMMEDIATE EMERGENCY MAY DEMAND. KEEP IN COMMUNICATION WITH ME AS MUCH AS POSSIBLE. YOU ARE A GALLANT AND RESOURCEFUL COMMANDER AND I AM PROUD OF WHAT YOU HAVE DONE.*

This message neither reassured Sharp nor clarified the situation. But it did leave the decision up to him, and he decided to wait for Wainwright's emissary. Two days later, upon Traywick's arrival after a harrowing trip, Sharp read Wainwright's letter and concluded there was no alternative. He immediately ordered the commanders of the various islands to "cease all operations against the Japanese Army at once" to save further bloodshed, then radioed MacArthur:

. . . DIRE NECESSITY ALONE HAS PROMPTED THIS ACTION.

In Washington, General Marshall was reading a message from MacArthur:

> I HAVE JUST RECEIVED WORD FROM MAJOR GENERAL SHARP

---

* When Marshall subsequently attempted to get Wainwright a Medal of Honor, MacArthur refused to approve on the grounds that his actions did not warrant this great distinction and it would be an injustice to others who had done far more. It was not until after the war that Wainwright at last received the decoration from President Truman. Bitterness toward MacArthur over this and similar matters still exists among the surviving group of officers close to Wainwright, nicknamed the Wainwright Travelers.

THAT GENERAL WAINWRIGHT IN TWO BROADCASTS ON THE NIGHT OF THE 7/8 ANNOUNCED HE WAS REASSUMING COMMAND OF ALL FORCES IN THE PHILIPPINES AND DIRECTED THEIR SURRENDER GIVING IN DETAIL THE METHOD OF ACCOMPLISHMENT. I BELIEVE WAINWRIGHT HAS TEMPORARILY BECOME UNBALANCED AND HIS CONDITION RENDERS HIM SUSCEPTIBLE OF ENEMY USE.

But it was too late to prevent the surrender of all the Philippines.

Their conqueror was in no triumphant mood. He was in disfavor with the Army General Staff; it had taken him too long to achieve victory. Moreover, General Count Hisaichi Terauchi, commander of Southern Army, was displeased with Homma's lenient treatment of Filipino civilians. Homma had forbidden pillage and rape and ordered his troops not to regard the Filipinos as enemies but to respect their customs, traditions and religion. His defense was that he had been scrupulously following the Emperor's instructions to bring enlightenment to Southeast Asia.

But what exercised Terauchi most was Homma's suppression of a propaganda pamphlet describing the exploitation of the Islands by the Americans. Homma told Terauchi to his face that the Americans had never exploited the Philippines and that it was wrong to make such false statements. "They administered a very benevolent supervision over the Philippines. Japan should establish an even better and more enlightened supervision."

Homma's insistent tolerance left Terauchi more resolved than ever to send an adverse report to Tokyo from his headquarters in Saigon. It also provoked a small but influential group of his own subordinates, those under the influence of Colonel Tsuji, into secret retaliation. In Homma's name, they sent out orders countermanding his liberal policy.

Homma had no knowledge of this until two days after Wainwright's surrender. Major General Kiyotake Kawaguchi, commander of Japanese forces in the Visayans, burst into Homma's office, his ten-inch Kaiser mustache bristling. He accused Homma of having authorized the execution of Chief Justice José Abad Santos and wanted to know the reason why. Santos had been captured on Negros Island with his son and brought to Kawaguchi's headquarters on Cebu in April, on the evening Bataan fell. Santos was willing to work with the Japanese, and Kawaguchi had radioed Manila a recommendation that he be given a position in the Laurel "Quisling" government. The answer was unexpected: HIS GUILT IS OBVIOUS. DISPOSE OF HIM IMMEDIATELY.

This was an outrageous betrayal of *bushido* and the Emperor, and Kawaguchi had thrown a staff officer from Manila named Inuzuka out of his office for insisting on the execution of Santos' son as well. Then he wrote a letter to an old friend, Major General Yoshihide Hayashi, Military Administrator of 14th Army, reiterating why the two Santos should be spared. Two weeks later Kawaguchi received another dispatch from Manila. It ordered him to deliver the two Santos to the Davao garrison commander on Mindanao for immediate execution. The indignant Kawaguchi responded by crumpling up the message.

But it was followed by the persistent Inuzuka, who had come to make sure that the executions took place. Kawaguchi summoned the two prisoners and told them he had done his utmost to save their lives but was now forced to execute the elder Santos in the name of the 14th Army. "I promise to protect your son, so don't worry," he told the father.

Santos said he had never been anti-Japanese. "I appreciate your kindness toward me and my son and wish glory for your country." He stilled his son's pleas for mercy; they could only embarrass the general. "When you see Mother, give her my love. I will soon die. Be a man of honor and work for the Philippines." Santos was taken to a nearby coconut plantation. He declined to be blindfolded and crossed himself just before the shots of the firing squad rang out.

Homma was dumfounded to learn of Santos' execution from Kawaguchi. He, too, had had high regard for Chief Justice Santos and appreciated his friendship for Japan. He remembered approving Kawaguchi's original request for clemency and had ordered Hayashi to take care of the matter. Mortified, he told Kawaguchi, "I regret very much what has happened."

The following day Kawaguchi confronted Hayashi. "What a *keshikaran* [shameful] thing you did!" he burst out. "I trusted you as my classmate."

Hayashi was defensive; Homma had already admonished him. "But," he excused himself, "Imperial Headquarters was so insistent about the execution of Santos."

"Whom do you mean by 'Imperial Headquarters'?"

"It was Tsuji."

Homma's reprimand had little effect on those staff officers determined to carry out Tsuji's policy of revenge. Several weeks later when General Manuel Roxas, former Speaker of the House of Representatives, was captured on Mindanao, a message came from Manila ordering the local commander, General Torao Ikuta, to execute Roxas "secretly and immediately." It was authorized in the name of Homma and stamped by Hayashi and three staff officers.

On Bataan, Ikuta had refused to shoot prisoners without a written order, but even though he had one this time, he found himself incapable to act, and turned over the responsibility to his chief of staff, Colonel Nobuhiko Jimbo, a balding man with glasses and a Tojo mustache. As a Catholic, Jimbo was tormented while he drove Roxas and another high-ranking captive, a governor, toward the execution grounds. Throughout the hour-long trip past hemp fields and coconut groves, the governor begged for his life. He was an administrator, not a soldier; he had always co-operated with the Japanese and should be treated differently from General Roxas. His voice became so hysterical that Roxas patted his shoulder and said, "Look at the *sampaguita*." He pointed at clusters of delicate white blossoms, the national flower of the Philippines. "Aren't they beautiful?"

No samurai could have acted more nobly and Jimbo decided to try to save Roxas no matter what the consequences. He left his two charges under guard in a small town and returned to Davao; somehow he had to persuade General Ikuta to ignore the execution order.

Jimbo's arguments were all that Ikuta needed. The two men decided to use Roxas to help restore law and order, but for a while he would have to be kept hidden. What they did could not be kept secret for long. An officer arrived from Manila; Jimbo was to be court-martialed for his "high-handed" actions.

Jimbo flew up to Manila to confront Homma himself, but since the general was out of his office, he had to speak instead to his chief of staff. General Wachi couldn't believe such an order had gone out, particularly after Homma's violent reaction to the execution of Santos.

Jimbo showed him the original document. Although Wachi was not able to cancel any order stamped with Homma's name, he wrote out another, temporarily suspending the execution. He told Jimbo to wait and pushed his way into Hayashi's office, where the general and four staff officers were in conference. Jimbo could hear Wachi's angry voice: "Did you men issue the order to execute General Roxas?" Hayashi and the others denied it; it would be violation of a specific order by General Homma. How could Wachi ask such a question?

"Colonel Jimbo, come in!" Wachi hollered.

The staff officers glared at Jimbo as he pulled out the execution order—but were forced to confess that they had stamped it "without giving it too much thought." There was an awkward pause. Hayashi wheeled on Jimbo and shouted, "You have done a terrible thing to us!"

Later that night Wachi came to Jimbo's room at the Manila Hotel. Homma was pleased with Jimbo's initiative and had already issued an order countermanding the Roxas execution. Moreover, he would report the matter, including Jimbo's part in it, to the Emperor.*

So Roxas was saved, but the episode emphasized the subversion in Homma's own command. It also further undermined a career already in jeopardy. As a commander in the field Homma had not been as aggressive as Tokyo wanted, and in peace he was far too lenient toward the Philippine people. Even after Terauchi's admonition he continued to treat the Filipinos as potential friends rather than a conquered enemy. Against advice from his staff he ordered the release of all Filipino soldiers in the prison camps.

---

* Roxas survived the war to become the first President of the Republic. When he learned in August 1946 that the man who had saved his life was still a prisoner in North China awaiting trial as a war criminal, he wrote a personal letter to Chiang Kai-shek requesting amnesty for Jimbo. He was released and returned to Japan the following year and is now living in Tokyo. As Vice President of the Order of the Knights of Rizal [Dr. José Rizal], Tokyo Chapter, he is authorized to use the title Sir Nobuhiko.

He was relieved of his command, ordered to Japan and forced to retire in semidisgrace without making the traditional report of a returning commander to the Emperor.*

* After the war Homma was tried, convicted and executed as a war criminal by the man he defeated, MacArthur. Homma's chief defense council, John H. Skeen, Jr., called it "a highly irregular trial, conducted in an atmosphere that left no doubt as to what the ultimate outcome would be." The others on the defense staff signed a letter to Homma stating that he had been unjustly convicted. Associate Justice Frank Murphy of the U. S. Supreme Court protested the verdict. "This nation's very honor, as well as its hope for the future, is at stake," he wrote. "Either we conduct such a trial as this in the noble spirit and atmosphere of our Constitution or we abandon all pretense to justice, let the ages slip away and descend to the level of revengeful blood purges. . . . A nation must not perish, because in the natural frenzy of the aftermath of war, it abandoned the central theme of the dignity of the human personality and due process of law."

While Homma was awaiting sentence he wrote his wife, Fujiko: "In the twenty years of our married life we've had many differences of opinion and even violent quarrels. Those quarrels have now become sweet memories. . . . Now as I am about to part from you, I particularly see your good qualities, and I have completely forgotten any defects. I have no worry about leaving the children in your hands because I know you will raise them to be right and strong. . . . Twenty years feel short but they are long. I am content that we have lived a happy life together. If there is what is called the other world, we'll be married again. I'll go first and wait for you there but you mustn't hurry. Live as long as you can for the children and do those things for me I haven't been able to do. You will see our grandchildren and even great-grandchildren and tell me all about them when we meet again in the other world. Thank you very much for everything."

The last words from Homma came in a letter to his children just before the execution: "There are six men here who have been sentenced for life. It will be better to be shot to death—like dying an honorable death on the battlefield—than spending a disgraceful life in such a cage the rest of one's life. Don't lose courage, children! Don't give in to temptation! Walk straight on the road of justice. The spirit of your father will long watch over you. Your father will be pleased if you will make your way in the right direction rather than bring flowers to his grave. Do not miss the right course. This is my very last letter."

The Tide Turns

1.

By the end of April Captain Kameto Kuroshima, the "foggy staff officer," had transformed Yamamoto's basic idea into an intricate war plan that involved almost two hundred ships maneuvering in close co-operation over a battlefield stretching two thousand miles from the Aleutians to Midway, which was 2,300 miles east of Japan. On the face of it, the objective was to capture Midway and the western Aleutians. These islands would then become key points in a new outer perimeter stretching all the way from Kiska in the north, through Midway and Wake to Port Moresby in the south, just three hundred miles from Australia. Patrol planes based on these three islands could detect any enemy task force attempting to pierce the empire's inner defense. In fact, however, the seizure of Midway was of secondary importance to Yamamoto; it was merely bait in the trap designed to lure the remnants of Nimitz' fleet out of Pearl Harbor so it could be destroyed. That would mean the end, or at least postponement, of American efforts to dislodge the Japanese from their recent conquests in Southeast Asia.

The commanders who would have to fight the battle—including Admiral Nagumo's chief of staff, Ryunosuke Kusaka—were summoned to the recently completed 63,000-ton battleship *Yamato,* the new flagship of the Combined Fleet which bore the ancient name for "Japan," to be briefed by Yamamoto personally. In the past five months Nagumo's Striking Force had devastated Pearl Harbor, battered Darwin harbor, sunk two British heavy cruisers off Colombo, and the carrier *Hermes* and other ships off Trincomalee, on Ceylon, without a single surface loss. Nevertheless, Kusaka had serious reservations. Another major operation, he said, would be foolhardy. *Kido Butai* had steamed fifty thousand miles since Pearl Harbor and the ships needed reconditioning. The crews, too, needed a rest; exhaustion was so prevalent that some men were actually seeing ghosts. Yamamoto overrode the objections. He ordered preparations accelerated.

At the same time another important plan was set in motion. This was Operation Mo, the invasion of Port Moresby on the Coral Sea. Its fall would lead to easy conquest of the rest of New Guinea and place Australia itself in peril. As a preliminary, a force seized Tulagi, a small island some twenty miles north of Guadalcanal in the Solomon Islands, and began constructing a seaplane base. The next day, May 4, the Port Moresby Invasion Force left Rabaul, since January the staging area for operations in the South Pacific at the upper tip of New Britain in the Bismarck Archipelago. There were fourteen transports escorted by a light cruiser and six destroyers, and covered by the light carrier *Shoho,* four heavy cruisers and a destroyer.

Most of this was known to Admiral Nimitz; his cryptanalysts had broken the Japanese fleet code. He had already dispatched Task Force 17—two carriers, six heavy cruisers, two light cruisers and eleven destroyers—under Rear Admiral Frank Jack Fletcher to intercept the Japanese.

Fletcher had reached the Coral Sea off northeastern Australia by the time he learned of the Tulagi landing. He immediately launched an air attack of ninety-nine planes on Tulagi from his flagship, the carrier *Yorktown.* To counteract this unexpected threat Vice Admiral Takeo Takagi, victor of the Battle of the Java Sea, was sent south from Bougainville with two heavy carriers, *Zuikaku* and *Shokaku,* two heavy cruisers and six destroyers.

The two opposing forces drew closer, and it was Takagi who made the first contact. On the morning of May 7 one of his search

The Tide Turns

pilots who spotted the oiler *Neosho* and a destroyer became overly excited and he reported them as an enemy carrier and cruiser. Two waves of high-level bombers and thirty-six dive bombers sank the destroyer and left the oiler helplessly adrift. While Takagi was concentrating his force on these minor targets, ninety-three planes from *Yorktown* and *Lexington* found the light carrier *Shoho* and began an aggressive bomb and torpedo attack. About 160 miles away comrades on the mother ships strained to hear this action on their radios, but the static made it difficult. Suddenly the voice of Lieutenant Commander Robert Dixon, leader of a scout bomber squadron, came in strong and clear: "Scratch one flattop! Dixon to carrier. Scratch one flattop!" At last, after five months, a Japanese ship larger than a destroyer had been sunk.

In Rabaul the overall commander of Operation Mo, Vice Admiral Shigeyoshi Inoue, radioed the transports to turn back and wait until the seas were cleared of Americans. That afternoon visibility decreased and squalls limited aerial observation. By midnight the two enemy fleets had lost contact.

Takagi, aboard a heavy cruiser, signaled Rear Admiral Tadaichi Hara, commander of the two carriers: CAN YOU LAUNCH A NIGHT AIR ATTACK? Hara signaled back from *Zuikaku* that he was prepared to send twenty-seven planes. They took off just before dusk but found nothing. On the way back, however, they were set upon by a group of Fletcher's fighters. Nine Japanese were shot down; the others dispersed and tried to make their way home in the dark. One cluster of six eventually found a carrier and let down to join the other planes in the landing pattern. As the first Japanese skimmed the deck, landing hook extended, he was blasted over the side with a hail of gunfire. The carrier was *Yorktown*.

After the fiasco, Takagi decided to retire temporarily to the north. Several hours later he doubled back toward the American carriers at 26 knots, and just before dawn on May 8, he dispatched twenty-seven search planes. The first carrier battle in history was imminent. Fletcher had radar but his carriers had operated together less than a week. Takagi had no radar but his two carriers had been working as a division for more than six months. Fletcher had 122 planes, Takagi one less. They were well matched, with Takagi having the slight advantage of cover from an overcast.

But the first break went to Fletcher. At eight-fifteen one of his search pilots sighted the Japanese Striking Force. He circled, counting the ships, and radioed:

TWO CARRIERS, FOUR HEAVY CRUISERS, MANY DESTROYERS, STEERING 120 DEGREES, 20 KNOTS. THEIR POSITION 175 MILES, ROUGHLY NORTHEAST.

Fletcher ordered both carriers to launch air strikes, and around eleven o'clock thirty-nine planes from *Yorktown* came upon *Shokaku,* screened by heavy cruisers and destroyers. *Zuikaku,* just ten miles away, was hidden by a dense squall. *Shokaku* avoided torpedoes, but dive bombers made two direct hits which started fires. Another wave, twenty-four planes from *Lexington,* found the carriers. *Shokaku* escaped with one more bomb hit. Her fires were brought under control and she headed for home.

Simultaneously the Japanese also found the Americans. Seventy planes converged on Fletcher's two carriers. One bomb pierced the flight deck of *Yorktown,* but fires were skillfully brought under control. *Lexington* was not so lucky; two torpedoes ripped into her port side, while small bombs struck the main deck forward and the smokestack structure.

The air attacks had been costly to both sides and by noon the battle was over. It was the first naval engagement in which opposing ships never saw each other or exchanged gunfire. It appeared as if Fletcher had emerged the victor. He had sunk a light carrier, a destroyer and three small vessels while losing one destroyer and an oiler. Then two explosions rocked the wounded *Lexington* and set off uncontrollable fires. Shortly after five o'clock Rear Admiral Aubrey Fitch, commander of the Carrier Group, leaned over the flag bridge and called down to *Lexington*'s skipper, Captain Frederick C. Sherman, "Well, Ted, let's get the men off."

They lined up their shoes on the flight deck and calmly began going over the sides, as unconcerned as if it were a drill. One group went below to the ship's service store; they filled their helmets with ice cream and ate it while waiting in line on the flight deck. As the last man, Captain Sherman, started down the life line, he told himself, Wouldn't I look silly if I left this ship and the fires went out? But he clambered down the line, and once the survivors were clear, four torpedoes from the destroyer *Phelps* drove into the carrier's starboard side. She shuddered and steam rose in billowing clouds.

"There she goes," said an officer watching from a nearby cruiser. "She didn't turn over. She is going down with her head up. Dear old *Lex*. A lady to the last."

With the sinking of *Lexington* the battle became a tactical victory for Takagi, but the more important strategic triumph still was Fletcher's. Admiral Inoue was forced to postpone the Port Moresby operation. Fletcher had accomplished his mission, and for the first time since Pearl Harbor a Japanese invasion had been thwarted.

Takagi, however, was reluctant to give up. He was getting set to engage the Americans in a night battle when he learned that his own destroyers were almost out of fuel. Grudgingly he turned back for Rabaul. Far to the north, at his homeland anchorage Yamamoto was still resolved to pursue the Americans. Through Rabaul he ordered Takagi to attack in spite of the fuel shortage. Takagi obediently reversed course, but it was too late. Fletcher had vanished.

Both sides claimed victory. The *New York Times* of May 9 announced:

JAPANESE REPULSED IN GREAT PACIFIC BATTLE,
WITH 17 TO 22 OF THEIR SHIPS SUNK OR CRIPPLED:
ENEMY IN FLIGHT, PURSUED BY ALLIED WARSHIPS

The *Japan Times & Advertiser* proclaimed that the enemy was panic-stricken. The source was a correspondent in Buenos Aires who wrote: "The effect of the terrible setback in the Coral Sea is indeed beyond description. A state of mania is prevalent in the American munitions fields."

Hitler was exultant. "After this new defeat the United States warships will hardly dare to face the Japanese fleet again, since any United States warship which accepts action with the Japanese naval forces is as good as lost."

2.

Japanese newspaper accounts accurately reflected the jubilation at Imperial Headquarters—both *Lexington* and *Yorktown* had been sunk, a crushing blow to American power in the Pacific. The "triumph" stilled the objections of those who regarded the Midway operation as too hazardous. Coral Sea had been won by the 5th Air Squadron, the least experienced in the fleet. What chance would the Americans have against the veterans of the 1st and 2nd Air Squadrons? *Zuikaku* and *Shokaku* arrived home a few days later. The "inferior" American pilots had inflicted more damage than first reported. Both would have to be scratched from the Midway invasion. *Zuikaku* had lost too many planes and pilots, and it would take a month to repair *Shokaku*.

But nothing could undermine the supreme optimism that swept through Combined Fleet, and even Kusaka, recently so pessimistic, was sure *Kido Butai* could "beat the hell out of the Yankees." The result was a relaxation of security measures. In contrast to preparations for Pearl Harbor, there was little attempt to disguise the flow of messages that marked the final stages, and staff officers openly discussed Operation Midway in restaurants and teahouses.

On the evening of May 25 Yamamoto invited several hundred officers, including Nagumo and Kusaka, to a party on *Yamato,* which lay off Hashirajima in the Inland Sea. Too late Yamamoto's steward, Heijiro Omi, discovered that the cook had made a grievous mistake. The *tai,* a fish cooked from head to tail, had been broiled in *miso* (salted bean paste) instead of salt; and the saying "to put *miso* on food" was a metaphor meaning "to make a mess of things." Omi scolded the chef and in turn was scolded by the admiral's flag secretary, but Yamamoto himself ignored the blunder and endless *kampai* (toasts) were drunk in heated *sake* to the Emperor and victory.

The following day at the final briefing Kusaka asked a question which, surprisingly, had not been posed before: "If we sight the American fleet, should we attack it or take Midway first?" Admiral Matome Ugaki, who had prepared for the battle by getting a haircut and a new set of false teeth, turned to Nagumo and said it would be his decision. "You are in the front line and can assess the situation better than we can."

Kusaka refused to accept the responsibility; only Combined Fleet could make the proper decision, since the operation was so complicated and involved so many units. Besides, *Akagi* had a short mast and was not equipped to intercept enemy messages, whereas Yamamoto's flagship had a very high mast and the latest facilities. Ugaki said this was immaterial; radio silence would have to be maintained, since the whole plan depended on surprise.

On *Akagi* there was such a feeling of confidence that many fliers had brought aboard personal belongings and a plentiful supply of beer and *sake*. One man, Lieutenant Heijiro Abe, did not share their faith. At the last moment he advised Commander Minoru Genda to call off the operation. Abe, who had dropped a bomb on *Oklahoma,* had just received a letter from a friend in China wishing him luck on the attack of "M." Everyone seemed to know about Midway, said Abe, and he predicted that they would be "beaten in a bag." But Genda said it was too late to cancel the operation; other units were already on the move.

At six o'clock in the morning on May 27, Nagumo's Carrier Striking Force—a light cruiser, eleven destroyers, two battleships (including *Haruna,* supposedly sunk by Colin Kelly) and four carriers—filed slowly through the Inland Sea toward Bungo Strait as the sailors on the other ships of the Combined Fleet cheered them on. The following day the force scheduled to invade the Aleutians left its port at the northern tip of Kyushu; on June 3, the day before the raid on Midway, planes from two light carriers would bomb Dutch Harbor to divert Nimitz' attention to the north. Far to the south, on Saipan in the Marianas, a dozen transports filled with the five thousand men who would take Midway set off, accompanied by a light cruiser, a tanker and a covering force of four heavy cruisers.

Early on the morning of May 29, the rest of the Combined Fleet moved out of the Inland Sea—first Vice Admiral Nobutake Kondo's Midway Invasion Force, then the Main Force of thirty-four ships led by Yamamoto's flagship, *Yamato*. In all, eleven battleships, eight carriers, twenty-three cruisers, sixty-five destroyers and almost ninety auxiliary ships plowed eastward in the most ambitious naval operation ever conceived by man. More oil would be used in this single operation than the peacetime Navy consumed in a year.

As before, Japanese success depended on secrecy, but as at the Coral Sea, Nimitz knew a massive attack was being mounted thanks to his Combat Intelligence Unit, some 120 men, including the sunken *California*'s entire band (musicians were eminently suited for such work), under Lieutenant Commander Joseph John Rochefort. They were on duty practically around the clock in a windowless basement in the Navy Yard, protected by vault-like doors, steel-barred gates and constant guards—and they were reading 90 percent of the code messages sent out by Combined Fleet. The scattered information about Midway was, in a sense, a gift from the Japanese Navy. On May 1 it had scheduled one of the periodic revisions of its main code which always blacked out information until Rochefort's men broke it. But the old code was still in effect because of the rush of work. Besides, Japanese naval intelligence experts were positive their codes could not be broken.

On May 20 the bits and pieces about the invasion fell into place with the interception of a lengthy order issued by Yamamoto. Fifteen percent of the message was missing, but the magnitude of the operation was evident. All that was left in doubt was the target, which was referred to simply as "AF." Rochefort felt reasonably sure it was Midway, but Washington experts were just as positive it stood for Oahu.

Nimitz agreed with Rochefort, and flew to Midway to determine what additional equipment and how many more men were needed to stem a large-scale amphibious attack. Every plane he could spare was dispatched to Midway. Nimitz also enlarged the tiny island's garrison to two thousand, set up three submarine patrol arcs and ordered installation of additional antiaircraft batteries. To confirm the location of "AF," Nimitz had Midway transmit a fake message in the clear complaining of the breakdown of its distillation plant. The Japanese took the bait and two days later radioed Tokyo that "AF" was low on fresh water.

With this corroboration Nimitz decided to meet the Japanese head-on. They would be lying in wait for him, but Nimitz knew he had to meet the challenge of Yamamoto's armada, even though he had only eight cruisers, seventeen destroyers and two carriers. The third, *Yorktown*, had not yet reached Pearl Harbor after the damage it had absorbed at Coral Sea. Repairs would take about ninety days.

Nimitz called in his two commanders, Fletcher and Rear Admiral Raymond A. Spruance—a last-minute substitute for Halsey, who was suffering from a skin disease. He ordered them "to inflict maximum damage on enemy by employing strong attrition attacks." They were to strike again and again from the air and "be governed by the principle of calculated risk, which you shall interpret to mean the avoidance of exposure of your force to attack by superior enemy forces without good prospect of inflicting, as a result of such exposure, greater damage on the enemy."

The day after Nagumo's four carriers had left the Inland Sea, Spruance sailed out of Pearl Harbor on the carrier *Enterprise*, with *Hornet*, six cruisers and eleven destroyers making up the rest of Task Force 16. Two days later Fletcher followed, with two cruisers and six destroyers, on *Yorktown*. Thanks to the almost superhuman efforts of fourteen hundred workmen, the estimated three months' repair of the damaged carrier had been accomplished in two days.

That same day Yamamoto, trailing Nagumo by six hundred miles, received three distressing messages. First, he learned that aerial reconnaissance of Pearl Harbor would be impossible; by chance an American seaplane tender had anchored at the exact point where the reconnaissance planes from Kwajalein Atoll in the Marshalls were to have been refueled by submarines. Second, the seven submarines which were to form a picket line between Oahu and Midway and intercept American carriers heading toward *Kido Butai* could not, for some reason, get into position in time.* Finally, and most disturbing, from a submarine patrolling the waters around Midway came a report that the island seemed to be on a strict alert with intensive air patrols; many construc-

---

* Rear Admiral (Captain at the time) Keizo Komura, skipper of the cruiser *Chikuma* at Midway, revealed in 1967 that a typographical error in the orders had sent the submarines to the wrong positions. Combined Fleet attempted to conceal the blunder, but Komura learned of it soon after the battle from an officer on Yamamoto's staff.

tion cranes were visible, indicating a probable expansion of defenses. Yamamoto was going to relay this information to the man who most needed it—Nagumo—but his operations officer, Captain Kuroshima, insisted on continued radio silence.

Unaided by radar, the Striking Force steamed ahead shrouded in a thick mist. The following day, June 2, was worse. Nagumo and Kusaka peered anxiously from the bridge of *Akagi* at a blanket of heavy fog. It kept them hidden from enemy observation, but made navigation at close quarters hazardous. Kusaka still fretted about the dual tactical mission: to attack Midway on June 4 in preparation for the landing two days later, and to find and destroy Nimitz' fleet. How could they do both? The second mission required freedom of movement and secrecy, but if they bombed Midway, both mobility and secrecy were gone. It was "like a hunter chasing two hares at once."

In Nagumo's presence he put the question to the staff. Captain Tamotsu Oishi gave the most succinct answer: "The Combined Fleet operation order gives first priority to the destruction of enemy forces. Co-operation with the landing operation is secondary. But if we do not neutralize the Midway-based air forces as planned, our landing operations two days later will be strongly opposed and the entire invasion schedule will be upset."

Where is the enemy fleet? Nagumo wondered. Nobody knows, Oishi confessed. "Even if they are already aware of our movements and have sortied to meet us, they can't be far out from base at this moment and certainly can't be near us." Therefore the Midway attack should take place as scheduled. The others agreed.

That day the new edition of the fleet code finally went into effect and the cryptanalysts in the Pearl Harbor basement were temporarily in the dark. But it made no difference. Nimitz already knew enough. The next morning Midway received the first visual report that an invasion was imminent. Ensign Jack Reid, on patrol in a Catalina out of Midway, came upon what looked like a cluster of "miniature ships in a backyard pool" about thirty miles ahead. "Do you see what I see?" he asked co-pilot Hardeman. Hardeman took the glasses. "You're damn right I do."

MAIN BODY, Reid flashed to his base on Midway.

It was, however, the invasion transports, and they in turn

sighted the Catalina and alerted Yamamoto. *Akagi* intercepted the message, but Nagumo was unconcerned. The Striking Force was still undetected. His complacency was not shared by those on the bridge of *Yamato*. Never had Yamamoto or his staff imagined that the transports would be discovered before the first air assault on Midway.

By nightfall the Japanese were rapidly converging on Midway from the northwest and by dawn would be at the launching point, two hundred miles from the target. Fletcher and Spruance had positioned themselves three hundred miles east-northeast of the island. Fletcher, who was in overall command of the two task forces, guessed correctly that Reid had only seen transports, but it did indicate that carriers were not far behind. At 7:50 P.M. he headed southwest, with the conviction that tomorrow could be "the most important day in the history of the U. S. Navy." By daybreak he would be north of Midway, in perfect position to attack the enemy striking force. It was a remarkable deduction; the American carriers would be about a hundred miles from *Kido Butai*.

By visual signal Spruance informed his men they would probably encounter a superior force, four or five carriers, and that success in the battle would be "of great value to our country." Somehow, by that mysterious grapevine prevalent on every American ship, word spread that the Japanese code had been broken and that a trap was being set. There was a feeling of excitement in the wardrooms and mess halls.

3.

At 2:45 A.M. on June 4, *Akagi*'s loudspeakers blared and aircrews tumbled out of bunks. All over the ship there was a spirit of celebration, almost gaiety, as if the battle had already been won. Mitsuo Fuchida had led the attack on Pearl Harbor and was supposed to do the same at Midway. He was in sick bay, stricken by appendicitis the first night at sea. In a nearby cot was his friend Minoru Genda. He had a bad cold and his eyes looked feverish. Still in pajamas, Genda shuffled up to the bridge and apologized to Nagumo for being so late. He assured his chief that he was fit enough to direct and take personal charge of the attack. The admiral affectionately put an arm around his shoulder, and everyone on the bridge was buoyed to see him. Belowdecks the aircrews were eating the traditional breakfast served for decades to Japanese setting off to battle: rice, soybean soup, dry chestnuts and *sake*.

The four carriers were now 240 miles northwest of Midway, steaming full into the wind. Genda ordered preparations for the first wave against the tiny atoll. At 4:30 A.M. Kusaka gave the word to commence launching. Suddenly Fuchida appeared. He could not stay below and had staggered out of sick bay to watch his substitute, First Lieutenant Joichi Tomonaga on *Hiryu*, lead the raiders. The air officer waved his green lantern and the first Zero fighter skimmed down the illuminated flight deck and flung itself into the black sky. A chorus of spontaneous cheers was swept off the deck by the wind. Eight Zeros followed, then eighteen dive bombers.

Within fifteen minutes all four carriers had cleared their decks of planes; 108 were in the air, but the people below could only make out a long chain of red and blue lights strung toward Midway. At the same time Genda ordered seven reconnaissance planes to fan out to the east and southeast in search of American carriers. Five hurtled off, but one from the heavy cruiser *Tone* was delayed by catapult trouble. Kusaka thought a stronger reconnaissance should be made but said nothing. It was Genda's show (on practically any subject Nagumo accepted Genda's recommendations without question. Indeed, cynics referred to the Striking Force as "Genda's fleet") and it was not at all likely that the enemy carriers were anywhere in the area. They shouldn't arrive from Pearl Harbor for forty-eight hours, but just in case they appeared unexpectedly, Kusaka ordered thirty-six planes armed with torpedoes brought up to the flight decks of *Akagi* and *Kaga*.

Not only was the American fleet closer than the Japanese thought but their own carriers were about to be discovered. At 5:25 A.M. a Catalina search plane from Midway, piloted by Lieutenant Howard Ady, burst out of the clouds near *Kido Butai* and he stared in awe at a mass of ships. It was "like watching a curtain rising on the Biggest Show on Earth." ENEMY CARRIERS, Ady

The Tide Turns

radioed. He slipped the clumsy PBY behind the clouds, and circled. He came up on Nagumo's ships from the rear and identified two carriers and several battleships.

Ady's reports indicated that he had found the Japanese Striking Force, but Admiral Fletcher decided to wait for more explicit information. He radioed Spruance:

> PROCEED SOUTHWESTERLY AND ATTACK ENEMY CARRIERS WHEN DEFINITELY LOCATED. I WILL FOLLOW AS SOON AS PLANES RECOVERED.

On Midway, radar picked up the first wave of oncoming Japanese around 5:50. Air-raid sirens shrieked as planes took off pell-mell. While six Navy Avenger torpedo planes and four Army Marauders, also armed with torpedoes, headed north toward the enemy carriers, twenty-five Marine fighter pilots in obsolete Brewster Buffalos and Grumman Wildcats climbed northwest. Within minutes they encountered the raiders. They flung themselves into battle, but they were outnumbered and outclassed by the Zeros. Fifteen Marines were shot down and the Japanese swept unopposed to their target. Dive bombers plummeted through heavy antiaircraft fire and blasted buildings, oil tanks and the seaplane hangar. John Ford, who had filmed the takeoff of the Doolittle fliers, was high up in a powerhouse with his movie camera. There came a blast, and shrapnel tore into his shoulder. He picked himself up, put the camera to his eye and continued to follow the action.

For twenty minutes the Japanese had their own way and when the last had turned out to sea, Midway's two islands appeared to be a mass of smoke and flames. But Lieutenant Tomonaga stayed long enough to see that he had failed to destroy American capabilities. Enemy planes (they were dive bombers) were still taking off from the airstrip and heading out toward *Kido Butai*. He radioed at 7 A.M.: THERE IS NEED FOR A SECOND ATTACK.

For more than an hour there had been a state of consternation on Nagumo's flagship, *Akagi*. Ady's Catalina had been sighted and an air raid from Midway was expected. The heavy clouds began to clear, uncovering *Kido Butai*. At 7:10 a destroyer out front hoisted a flag signal: "Enemy planes in sight."

The four Marauders and six Avengers from Midway came boring in with their torpedoes. Zero fighters screening the carriers dived and spun three into the ocean. Antiaircraft fire from destroyers, cruisers and the battleship *Kirishima* picked off two more. But three of the attackers penetrated far enough to launch torpedoes at *Akagi*. The flagship swerved and the torpedoes churned harmlessly by. This raid, together with Tomonaga's request for another strike, prompted Nagumo to order a second attack on Midway, whose planes were a greater present threat to his carriers than the possibility of meeting the American fleet.

The decision had, in truth, been made by Nagumo's chief of staff. As at Pearl Harbor, Kusaka was the de facto commander; he never failed to consult Nagumo before taking action, but as yet none of his decisions had been countermanded. The latest one meant that the torpedo planes on *Akagi* and her sister ship, *Kaga*, had to be rearmed with bombs, and there was chaotic activity as these planes were lowered from the flight decks to their hangars. In the midst of this hubbub a message came in at 7:28 from one of *Tone*'s search planes that "ten ships, apparently enemy" were 240 miles north of Midway. There was agitation on *Akagi*'s bridge —this put the American fleet two hundred miles to the east!

For the first time since Pearl Harbor, luck had deserted the Japanese in battle. If the plane from *Tone* that had been delayed for thirty minutes on its catapult had gone off on schedule, it would have discovered the Americans before the Japanese torpedo planes were lowered for rearming, and they could now be winging toward *Enterprise, Hornet* and *Yorktown*. As it was, crucial time was lost while crews again went through the arduous task of refitting the planes with torpedoes.

At 7:47 A.M. Kusaka asked the *Tone* plane pilot to ascertain the ship types, but before the answer came, sixteen enemy planes appeared in the distance. These were the Marine dive bombers which, by-passing Tomonaga's planes, had left Midway minutes after the air-raid alarm and headed for the carriers. Now their commander, Major Lofton Henderson, ordered a glide-bombing attack, since his inexperienced pilots knew little about dive bombing. They bore down on *Hiryu*. Kusaka saw the light carrier enveloped in a smoke screen and towering waterspouts. Zeros managed to cut down half the Marines but the rest kept resolutely

The Tide Turns

on course, released their bombs and returned to Midway. *Hiryu* emerged unscathed.

Then, at 8:09, came good news. The *Tone* search plane reported that the enemy ships were "five cruisers and five destroyers." However, there was no time for congratulations; 20,000 feet overhead fifteen Flying Fortresses were dropping bombs. Having left Midway before dawn to attack the transports, they had found carriers instead. The B-17 crews watched their bombs fall among the swerving carriers and radioed erroneously that they had scored four hits; there were none.

Kusaka was impressed by the variety of attacks: with torpedo planes, in a glide-bombing approach, with dive bombers and high-level bombers. The Americans were like Hiru-Daikokuten, the legendary demon with three heads and six arms. In ten minutes he learned of another—and more dangerous—threat. The *Tone* plane radioed:

ENEMY FORCE ACCOMPANIED BY WHAT APPEARS
TO BE AIRCRAFT CARRIER BRINGING UP THE REAR.

Kusaka believed the report; his staff did not. If there was a carrier in the area, why hadn't it already launched an attack? Besides, the three ineffectual raids from Midway had proved that the enemy was not to be feared.

At 8:30 A.M., just as the first of Tomonaga's planes began returning from Midway, the *Tone* plane sent still another report: two enemy ships, probably cruisers. It was obvious that the American force was so big that it had to include at least one carrier. Kusaka wanted to attack but was in a quandary. The fighter planes which would escort the carrier strike were circling overhead to intercept any attackers and were running low on fuel. And what about Tomonaga's planes? If they weren't recovered, scores of the Navy's best pilots would be lost and future operations jeopardized.

He turned to Nagumo and suggested that they delay the strike, then asked Genda for his opinion. Genda was anxiously watching the clusters of Tomonaga's planes hovering over their carriers, many nursing the last gallons of fuel in their tanks. Almost every pilot was a personal friend. "I believe all our aircraft should first land and refuel," he said.

The planes on the decks of *Akagi* and *Kaga* were again lowered, this time to clear the way for the fighters and the exhausted Midway raiders. It was 9:18 A.M. by the time the last plane was recovered. Then *Kido Butai* raised speed to 30 knots and turned sharply from southeast to north-northeast to head in the general direction of the American fleet.

Crews worked feverishly on all four carriers to prepare thirty-six dive bombers, fifty-four torpedo bombers and their fighter escort for the assault. The Decisive Battle for the Pacific they had dreamed of for years was at hand.

4.

Fletcher had ordered Task Force 16 to attack the enemy carriers as soon as they were definitely located. Spruance had planned to hold off his strike until *Enterprise* and *Hornet* were as close as a hundred miles from the target, but the report of the raid on Midway inspired his chief of staff, Captain Miles Browning, to urge an earlier attack—it might catch the Japanese in the act of refueling their planes.

Spruance was a studious, brainy commander who was aggressive only when he thought it worth the risk. He was the antithesis of the man he had relieved—the ebullient, explosive Halsey—and avoided any publicity ("A shy young thing with a rather sober, earnest face and the innocent disposition of an ingenue"—according to his class book at Annapolis—who would "never hurt anything or anybody except in Line of Duty"). Even on *Enterprise* he was an enigma, a quiet, solitary man who paced the deck interminably for exercise and spent hours alone in his cabin studying charts.

The extra distance added a hazard he ordinarily would not have accepted, but the possibility of catching the Japanese off-guard outweighed the risk. His first important decision was to heed Browning. His second, just as important, was to order every operational plane, except patrol craft, to join in the attack. Sixty-seven dive bombers, twenty fighters and twenty-nine torpedo planes began leaving his two carriers at 7:02 A.M. They would have barely enough fuel to return home. It was no time for caution.

Fletcher, some fifteen miles behind Spruance, didn't start launching from his single carrier for an hour and a half, and it was 9:06 A.M. by the time seventeen dive bombers, six fighters and twelve torpedo planes had left the flight deck of *Yorktown*.

Twelve minutes later Nagumo made his abrupt turn to the north-northeast. While consciously avoiding another Midway-based air strike, he had inadvertently turned away from the 151 American carrier planes trying to find him.

Minutes after the turn, *Hornet*'s dive bombers and fighters reached the point where they were to intercept the Japanese carriers. The leader, Commander Stanhope Ring, saw clouds to his right (Nagumo was behind them) and veered southeast toward Midway—away from *Kido Butai*.

But three groups of lumbering torpedo planes—one from each of the American carriers—were almost directly on target. The first were fifteen unescorted Douglas Devastators from *Hornet*. Their leader, Lieutenant Commander John Waldron, had not followed the dive bombers on to Midway; he had a hunch the Japanese would turn to the east. Waldron was seamy-faced, square-jawed, part Sioux Indian. The night before he had written to his wife: "If I do not come back—well, you and the little girls can know that this squadron struck for the highest objective in naval warfare—'To Sink the Enemy.'" At the end of a message to his men he wrote: "If there is only one plane left to make a final run in, I want that man to go in and get a hit."

He banked east and for several minutes could see nothing. Then in the distance, eight miles away, he made out four carriers in boxlike formation. Twenty-five or thirty Zeros began diving at the Devastators, their cannon exploding. Waldron ignored them. He waggled his wings and slanted down at a carrier full speed, his men trailing behind. A plane tumbled like a bird shot by a hunter.

"Was that a Zero?" asked Waldron above the racket of machine-gun fire from the rear seat. His gunner-radioman, Horace Dobbs, didn't hear. It was a Devastator. Another one plunged down. Still Waldron bore in. As the attackers neared the carrier they were confronted by a wall of harmless-looking black puffs and strings of bright tracers. Another Devastator splashed into the sea. Waldron's left gas tank erupted in flames. Ensign George "Tex" Gay, who was flying at the tail of the formation, saw him stand up and try to get out of the cockpit as the burning plane skimmed the water. All at once a wave caught the undercarriage. It was the end of Waldron and Dobbs.

Still another torpedo plane pinwheeled into the sea—and another—and another. That left Gay and two others. Two explosions. Only Gay was left. He remembered Waldron's instructions for the last plane "to go in and get a hit."

"They got me." It was his radioman, Bob Huntington. Gay turned and saw Huntington's head limp. A bullet dug into Gay's right arm. He had the carrier straight ahead. It turned to starboard and he also swung right. He released a white-nosed torpedo and executed a flipover, skimming ten feet above the carrier's bow. As he started a turning climb he was riddled by Zeros. His Devastator pancaked into the sea. He pulled at the canopy. It was stuck. He tugged. No good. The plane was rapidly filling with water. He gave a yank. The canopy opened and he squirmed out. As he surfaced he thought he heard an explosion—his "pickle" must have got the hit! But like the torpedoes from all the other planes, this one had missed and was settling harmlessly far beyond the carrier.

Within minutes, torpedo planes from *Enterprise* and *Yorktown* also found Nagumo. Fourteen Douglas Devastators from the first carrier attacked without fighter escort. Ten were shot down; four managed to launch their missiles. Then the twelve torpedo planes from *Yorktown* appeared. Their six escorting fighters were swamped by Japanese interceptors, but five torpedoes were released.

One American headed straight for *Akagi*'s bridge. Kusaka ducked as the Devastator roared a few feet over his head and plunged into the sea. Kusaka was shaken by the realization that the American was as determined as any samurai. He silently prayed for him.

In all, nine torpedoes were launched but not a single one found its mark. All that was left of the American air strike was the dive bombers and it looked as if they would not even find the Japa-

The Tide Turns

nese; already those from *Hornet* had gone on to Midway, and the seventeen from *Yorktown,* under Lieutenant Commander Maxwell Leslie, were miles southeast of the target.

The other thirty-seven dive bombers—they were led by Lieutenant Commander Clarence W. McClusky and came from *Enterprise*—had taken off more than an hour before Leslie. McClusky, like others before him, had missed Nagumo's Striking Force and gone on toward Midway, but finding nothing, turned back north.

At 9:55 A.M. he sighted the white wake of a Japanese destroyer scudding northeast. He hoped it was joining up with the carriers and followed. He heard Captain Browning shout excitedly over the radio telephone, "Attack! Attack!"

"Wilco," McClusky replied, "as soon as I find the bastards." He kept on course for another twenty minutes, found nothing. His fuel was dangerously low but he decided to continue on for another minute. It was 10:20 A.M.

At last all the Japanese torpedo planes were back on the flight decks, along with their refueled fighter escorts. The four carriers turned into the wind in preparation for launching. In a quarter of an hour every plane would be in the air.

At that moment McClusky's thirty-seven Douglas Dauntless dive bombers appeared from the southwest. In addition to his own squadron, McClusky commanded those of Lieutenants Wilmer Earl Gallaher and Richard H. Best. Two carriers were turning into the wind to launch and he ordered Best to attack what looked like the smaller one—it was *Akagi.*

"Earl," he told Gallaher, "you follow me down." They nosed over toward *Kaga.*

Gallaher aimed at a huge Rising Sun, about fifty feet across, painted in blood-red on the flight deck. Ever since the day he saw *Arizona* lie smashed and smoldering in Pearl Harbor he had vowed to go after an enemy carrier. At about 1,800 feet he released his bomb, then pulled up into a steep climb and kicked the Dauntless around. He kept watching his bomb—something he had warned his pilots never to do—tumble closer and closer to the target. It exploded on the after part of the flight deck, and he thought exultantly, *Arizona,* I remember you!

The crew of *Kaga* looked up startled as Dauntlesses began plunging out of the sun. Bombs fell into the sea on both sides. *Kaga* could not be hit; she was charmed. Then in rapid succession four bombs slammed into the after, forward and middle sections of the flight deck. *Kaga* erupted with fires.

On the flagship, Kusaka was so transfixed by *Kaga*'s fate that he didn't notice dive bombers streaking for his own ship. He heard an eerie whistle and looked up. Three bombs, dropping so close and straight that they seemed to be connected by a wire, were coming at him. All three hit the line of planes preparing to take off, and erupted in a single shattering explosion. The ship trembled as in an earthquake. The amidship elevator was twisted grotesquely. Planes upended rakishly and burst into flames. Their bombs and torpedoes began to explode one by one, driving away fire-control parties. The blaze spread to fuel and munition reserves carelessly stacked on deck. These too exploded. Huge chunks were torn out of the flight deck. The bridge shook like a tree house in a hurricane.

Akagi was helpless. Flames licked the glass windows of the bridge. Above the din, Kusaka shouted to Nagumo, "We must move to another ship!" Nagumo refused. Kusaka said the ship could no longer steer and had no communications.

Nagumo kept saying, "We are all right," over and over again.

Thousands of gallons of burning fuel cascaded into the lower decks, and torpedoes stored in the hangars began detonating. Blasts of fire shot out through the sides of the ship like a huge blowtorch. Nagumo still refused to leave his position at the compass. Captain Taijiro Aoki, skipper of the carrier, shouted that he alone would be responsible for the ship. "You and your staff can do nothing, so please transfer to another ship!"

Nagumo ignored him. Kusaka began reprimanding his superior; he was commander of the entire Striking Force, not the captain of a single ship. Finally Nagumo nodded but it seemed to be too late. The bridge was almost surrounded by fire. "Break the window!" Kusaka hollered to the youthful flag secretary. Glass shattered. Two ropes were lowered forty-five feet to the deck. Kusaka pushed Nagumo out first and the little admiral clambered down nimbly. The heavyset Kusaka went next, but he could not control his descent. The rope burned through his hands as he dropped to the deck. He landed in a heap, stunned. He had no left shoe. His hands were raw and both ankles were badly sprained but he felt no pain. He looked for a path through the flames. Machine-gun bullets, ignited by the heat, ricocheted off the carrier's island. Far away he heard staff officers calling to hurry and he hobbled over the hot deck through flames toward the voices.

Moments after McClusky discovered *Kido Butai,* so did Leslie, the commander of the seventeen dive bombers from *Yorktown.* He had noticed smoke smudges on the horizon and banked northwest. Through clouds he caught a glimpse of *Hiryu* and *Soryu.* He patted his head in signal and pushed over in a steep dive on the latter.

Within half an hour *Soryu* was engulfed in flames. At 10:45 A.M. her skipper, Captain Ryusaku Yanagimoto ordered Abandon Ship but refused to leave himself. A Navy wrestling champion, Chief Petty Officer Abe, climbed up to the bridge. "I have come on behalf of all your men to take you to safety," he said. The captain turned away. Sword in hand, he began singing "Kimigayo," the national anthem.

In minutes, fifty-four American planes had fatally damaged three carriers. Only *Hiryu* was left. The last chance for victory depended on Rear Admiral Tamon Yamaguchi, the Princeton man who not long before had wrestled with Nagumo. At 10:40 A.M. six fighters and eighteen dive bombers had left *Hiryu* to search out an enemy carrier. They would not have found it by themselves. Their guides were Leslie's dive bombers, who unwittingly led them all the way to Fletcher's flagship. *Yorktown* fighters ripped into the attacking Japanese, but half a dozen managed to break free and drop their bombs. Three of these tore into the carrier, which still showed scars from the Battle of the Coral Sea. Two boilers were knocked out, bringing the burning ship to a standstill at 12:30 P.M. Within an hour, however, damage-control parties had subdued the flames and got the carrier under way. By that time another wave from *Hiryu* was forty miles away. Ten Nakajima torpedo planes came at *Yorktown.* While their six-fighter escort tied up the carrier's interceptors, the Nakajimas slipped under the fighter defense, and despite heavy antiaircraft fire sent two torpedoes into *Yorktown.* The damage was severe and the ship listed so badly by 3 P.M. that Captain Elliott Buckmaster ordered Abandon Ship.

This left only two American carriers, both commanded by Spruance. At 3:30 he ordered dive bombers to make their second strike. Under Lieutenant Gallaher—McClusky had been wounded —twenty-four unescorted dive bombers headed for *Hiryu*. Spruance radioed Fletcher, who had transferred to the cruiser *Astoria,* for further instructions. The answer was: "None." From now on the battle was in Spruance's hands.

5.

Aboard *Yamato,* Yamamoto was still four hundred miles to the west when he received word at 10:30 A.M. that *Akagi* was on fire. He didn't appear troubled by the news. Twenty minutes later the radio room sent up a full report from Nagumo:

FIRES RAGING ABOARD KAGA, SORYU AND AKAGI RESULTING FROM ATTACKS BY ENEMY CARRIERS AND LAND-BASED PLANES. WE PLAN TO HAVE HIRYU ENGAGE ENEMY CARRIERS. WE ARE TEMPORARILY WITHDRAWING TO THE NORTH TO ASSEMBLE OUR FORCES.

Yamamoto still seemed unperturbed. As if nothing had happened, he started a game of chess with Watanabe. Further information elicited a noncommittal "Ah so." Finally, ninety minutes after getting the first report, he ordered the invasion transports to retire, and the two light carriers which had launched a diversionary bomb attack on Dutch Harbor the previous day to head toward Midway and assist Nagumo. His own powerful Main Force was to continue steaming east full speed while Vice Admiral Kondo, who was covering the transports, brought his powerful fleet, including the carrier *Zuiho,* up from the south. From three directions formidable new forces were converging on Midway. The Decisive Battle was still to be fought.

The surviving crews returning to *Hiryu* from the second attack on *Yorktown* reported that they had destroyed two carriers, and Yamaguchi ordered a third strike. But before the first plane could

The Tide Turns

be rolled into position, a lookout shouted, "Enemy dive bombers!" To the southwest a string of planes struck out of the sinking sun like a snake. It was terrifying. The crew looked up helplessly as Gallaher's twenty-four dive bombers swooped in. Four bombs smashed around the bridge. Fires spread rapidly from plane to plane until the flight deck was a holocaust.

"Look at that bastard burn!" Gallaher muttered over his radio.

Nagumo and Kusaka were aboard a new flagship, the light cruiser *Nagara*. With all four carriers on fire and out of action, Kusaka still wanted to attack. He couldn't put any weight on his injured ankles and ordered a sailor to carry him piggyback up to the bridge. He urged Nagumo to mount a night attack with destroyers, cruisers and battleships.

This was Nagumo's element—a surface fight. "Now it will be my battle," he said. The remnants of the once powerful *Kido Butai* began to stalk the Americans.

Spruance guessed the Japanese intentions, and cautious though he was, was tempted to accept the challenge, then remembered Nimitz' "calculated risk" instructions. This time the risk was too great. The Japanese commander was probably hoping for a showdown, and his crews were trained night fighters. Spruance turned back east.

The sea northwest of Midway was a flaming graveyard. *Soryu* tilted. On nearby destroyers her agonized survivors watched the ungainly carrier disappear at 7:13 P.M. with a furious hissing as water enveloped the flames. With her went 718 trapped or dead men and one who had lashed himself to the bridge, Captain Yanagimoto. A muffled underwater explosion shook the surrounding ships. Forty miles to the south *Kaga,* a mass of flames, was racked by two explosions. In minutes the battered carrier and eight hundred of her crew were swallowed up by the sea.

For several hours Nagumo searched the dark sea but could not locate the enemy. It was obvious there would be no night battle. He summoned his staff and ordered a general withdrawal to the northwest. Captain Oishi, who had helped plan the Pearl Harbor attack, was in a state bordering hysteria. He searched out Kusaka in the officers' infirmary. "We started the war and we are responsible for this disaster," he said. "We should all commit hara-kiri!"

He added that the entire staff agreed with him and he wanted Kusaka to tell Nagumo.

"*Bakayaro!*" said Kusaka. "Assemble all the other idiots in the staff room." He was carried down the passageway in his white hospital gown to confront the staff. "You men cheer when the battle is successful. When it isn't, you threaten hara-kiri. You're acting like hysterical women." They faced a long war and he forbade "such nonsense."

Kusaka had himself transferred to Nagumo's cabin. "Are you too planning suicide?" he asked and began lecturing the little admiral on his duty to Emperor and nation. Nagumo admitted that he could see his point but questioned its application to "the commander of a fleet." Kusaka reacted so vehemently at this that Nagumo relented and assured him he would do nothing rash, adding characteristically, "*Daijobu*"—"Don't worry."

On *Yamato,* Yamamoto's staff was desperately looking for some way to inflict serious damage on the enemy and compensate for the loss of four carriers. Spruance had not risen to the bait and the most impractical schemes were considered. Captain Kuroshima, for example, suggested that they shell Midway with all battleships.

Chief of Staff Ugaki coldly remarked that this was "stupidity." The battleships would be sunk by air and submarine attacks before they could move in close enough to use their guns. Furthermore, another air strike should be postponed until the Aleutian force joined them. "But even if that proves impossible and we must accept defeat, we will not have lost the war. There are still eight carriers in the Combined Fleet. We should not lose heart. In battle as in chess, it is the fool who lets himself be led into a reckless move out of desperation."

"How can we apologize to the Emperor for this defeat?" asked one staff officer.

Yamamoto had been listening quietly. "I am the only one who must apologize to His Majesty," he said and instructed Watanabe to send orders to Kondo and Nagumo to withdraw. Choked with emotion, Watanabe sat down to write out the distasteful orders and managed to compose them without using the word "withdraw."

The remnants of *Kido Butai* began to turn back, but the fires on both *Hiryu* and *Akagi* were raging out of control. *Akagi*'s captain

The Tide Turns

requested permission to scuttle her. The idea was unthinkable to most of Yamamoto's staff. Ugaki called them "old women," but Kuroshima argued that the Americans would seize the ship and "exhibit it in San Francisco as a museum." There were tears in Yamamoto's eyes. Years before, he had skippered the carrier. He said evenly, "Have destroyers torpedo *Akagi*."

The pragmatic Ugaki went off and wrote in his diary: "Emotion must not be mixed with reason." He was more concerned with the fact that the enemy had somehow been forewarned about the Midway operation. Perhaps an American submarine had discovered Nagumo en route or a Russian ship had sighted the Aleutian force. Either that or the fleet code itself had been broken.

Hiryu's skipper, Captain Tomeo Kaku, didn't have to radio Combined Fleet for permission to scuttle. Admiral Yamaguchi, who had commanded the two light carriers from *Hiryu*, took on the responsibility and ordered the destroyer *Kazagumo* to sink the flaming wreck. At 2:30 A.M. on June 5, Yamaguchi summoned the crew topside and told the eight hundred survivors that he alone was responsible for the loss of both *Hiryu* and *Soryu*. "I shall remain on board to the end. I command all of you to leave the ship and continue your loyal service to His Majesty." They all faced the Imperial Palace. The admiral led them in three cheers for the Emperor.

Yamaguchi gave his senior staff officer, Commander Seiroku Ito, his last message. It was to Nagumo, his wrestling antagonist, and typically, called for "a stronger Japanese Navy—and revenge." The staff drank a silent toast in water. Yamaguchi handed Ito his black deck cap and asked him to give it to Mrs. Yamaguchi. Then he turned to Captain Kaku, who would share his fate, and said, "There is such a beautiful moon tonight. Shall we watch it as we sink?"

Even Admiral Kondo's fleet was not to escape intact. Two heavy cruisers, *Mogami* and *Mikuma*, victims of a night collision, lagged so far behind the retiring forces that Spruance's planes were able to catch up with them early on June 6. *Mikuma* was sunk but *Mogami*, though hit six times, limped safely off.

The only real success won by the Japanese came too late to influence the battle. That same day Lieutenant Commander Yahachi

Tanabe sighted the crippled *Yorktown* from the bridge of *I-168*. The submarine slipped under the ring of covering destroyers and launched two torpedoes into the carrier and one into the destroyer *Hammann*. The destroyer went down in four minutes, but *Yorktown*, veteran of the first two carrier battles in history, died hard. She sank the following day just after dawn with all battle flags flying.

It was small compensation for the loss of four carriers and the flower of the Japanese naval air force. One of the greatest sea battles of all time was at last over and America had gained control of the Pacific. The outcome had been determined by Japanese overconfidence, a code broken by a few men in a basement, and the resolution of men like Waldron, McClusky and Gallaher. In every battle luck plays a part. At Midway it went against the Japanese; the half-hour delay of the *Tone* search plane led to catastrophe. In war there is a time for caution and a time for boldness. Yamamoto conceived the Midway operation too recklessly and his commander fought it too carefully. On the other hand, Spruance was bold at the right time—by launching his strike early and with all available planes—and prudent when he should be—by refusing to accept Nagumo's challenge for a night encounter. Spruance, however, would not have had his chance but for the wisdom of a man more than a thousand miles from the battle area; Chester Nimitz had made all the right decisions before a shot was fired.

"The Navy has made a great mistake," General Moritake Tanabe whispered to Tojo at a party for members of the German and Italian embassies.

"At Midway?" asked the tight-lipped Tojo.

"Yes, they have lost four carriers."

Tojo couldn't resist remarking that the Navy had gone into the operation against the advice of the Army, then said, "The news must not leak out. Keep it a complete secret."

The following day Tojo reported to the Emperor but said not a word about Midway.* Later at a restricted session of Imperial

---

* The Emperor was usually apprised of the performance of his fighting forces; in fact, there was a "hot line" to his military aide which was open at all hours in case important news was received by Army Headquarters in the middle of the night. It is safe to say that the Emperor's information about

Headquarters, the Prime Minister recommended that attention be diverted from the naval debacle by publicizing the Aleutian operation. The force which had steamed toward Midway to help Admiral Nagumo had been ordered to return north; on June 7 the small but strategic islands of Attu and Kiska were occupied without a casualty.

In America, Midway was already a household word and the battle was celebrated as the turning point of the war in the Pacific. Nimitz himself, though some criticized his considered words as premature, said in his communiqué of June 6:

> Pearl Harbor has now been partially avenged. Vengeance will not be complete until Japanese sea power is reduced to impotence. We have made substantial progress in that direction. Perhaps we will be forgiven if we claim that we are about midway to that objective.

On June 7 the Chicago *Tribune* jeopardized the secret that had made victory possible—the breaking of the Japanese fleet code. The strength of the Japanese forces at Midway, it revealed, was well known in American naval circles several days before the battle began. The Navy, upon learning of "the gathering of the powerful Japanese units soon after they put forth from their bases," had guessed that "Dutch Harbor and Midway Island might be targets."

The dispatch carried no byline, but it had been sent from the Pacific by war correspondent Stanley Johnston. It went on to describe the composition of the Japanese forces in detail, and named the four carriers of the Striking Force and the four light cruisers supporting the Invasion Force. The Navy feared that the release of such accurate information would alert the Japanese to the fact that their code had been broken.

The fear was groundless; the Japanese Navy, convinced their fleet code was unbreakable, attributed the rout at Midway to overconfidence. Kusaka held himself responsible for the debacle. He should not have allowed Genda to send out so few search planes.

Japanese fortunes of war was as accurate as Roosevelt's or Churchill's about their own, and much better than Hitler's on the German battles. The announcement about the defeat at Midway was probably withheld from His Majesty at this time because of shock and in anticipation of confirmed details.

On June 9, still in winter uniform, he was rolled up in a bamboo mat, lowered in a cutter and taken alongside *Yamato*. He was picked up like a parcel and set on the deck. He gave Yamamoto and his staff a personal report of the battle, adding a request that the Navy, which occasionally issued false communiqués, tell the people the whole truth, since this was a war involving every citizen.

Once they were alone, Kusaka told Yamamoto that *Kido Butai* would take all the blame for the defeat. "If you want someone to commit hara-kiri as a token of responsibility, let me do it." But he said that he really hoped instead to be Nagumo's chief of staff with a new carrier force that could avenge Midway. "I would like you to give it consideration."

"I understand," Yamamoto answered huskily. Kusaka was excused and Yamamoto took to his bed with severe stomach pains. The chief surgeon diagnosed it as "roundworm" but Steward Omi was sure it had been caused by the disastrous events of June 4.

In Japan, Tojo's orders to conceal the defeat were carried out. Survivors of the sunken ships were isolated, and the truth about Midway was withheld from leading officials as well as the public. Imperial Headquarters announced on June 10 that Japan had at last "secured supreme power in the Pacific" and that the war had been "indeed determined in one battle." To celebrate the victory the enthusiastic people of Tokyo staged a flag procession and a lantern parade.

In Tennessee, Ensign Kazuo Sakamaki, the only survivor of the midget submarine attack on Pearl Harbor and for some time the sole Japanese prisoner of war, saw no reason to celebrate. He believed what he read about Midway in American newspapers. On his long journey to Tennessee he had seen countless factories and endless fields and he knew that tiny Japan had yet to feel the full might of the United States. Midway was just the beginning of the end of Japan's hope of conquest.

PART FOUR

Isle of Death

14

Operation Shoestring

1.

Gen Nishino was a slight man of thirty-seven, about five feet tall. He looked frail and sensitive—and was—but had already survived arduous months in China reporting that disjointed war for his newspaper, the *Mainichi*. Several months after Pearl Harbor he was ordered to cover the campaign in the south. His greatest concern was not for his life but for the $25,000 worth of yen he would be carrying for expenses. His city editor wished him bon voyage, gave him an amulet for good luck and said, "Don't get killed."

Nishino, who headed a team of eight newsmen, set sail for Davao, the main port of southern Mindanao, but it was not until June 7, a week after their arrival, that he learned his group was going to ship out with the 17th Army for New Caledonia (this was part of the operation to cut off Australia). However, the Nishino party never got there. Three days later they were caught up in the excitement that swept the Japanese Empire when the victory at Midway was announced. They joined officers in the dining room of their hotel for an impromptu celebration. Even a severe earthquake failed to dampen the enthusiasm. One young officer joked that San Francisco was the center of the quake and all America had collapsed.

Nishino couldn't shake a nagging doubt after reading newspaper accounts of the battle; they were suspiciously vague. He left the party and went up to his room, where there was a shortwave radio. He turned the dial slowly until he heard a Strauss waltz; then a woman's voice announced that this was Radio San Francisco and that America had won a tremendous naval victory. It seemed like the usual propaganda until the newscaster confidently listed details of the various units involved at Midway and named the four Japanese carriers that had been sunk.

Nishino couldn't escape the feeling that this was the truth. Yamamoto had been crushed. Down below he could hear the jubilant clink of beer bottles above the din and felt a wave of pity for the young officers so innocently celebrating a spurious triumph. He thought of telling them what he had heard but knew it would be a mistake. They wouldn't believe him and he'd be arrested by the *kempeitai*.

His suspicions were finally confirmed two months later when the 17th Army and the *Mainichi* group set off—not for New Caledonia but for an island in the Solomons that didn't appear on their maps. Its name was Gadarukanaru.

In English it was called Guadalcanal and American interest in this remote island evolved from a bitter debate between the Army and the Navy over which should have the dominant role in the Pacific. In March two separate commands had been set up by the Joint Chiefs of Staff. From Melbourne, Douglas MacArthur commanded the Southwest Pacific Area, comprising the Philippines, the South China Sea, the Gulf of Siam, most of the Netherlands East Indies, Australia *and* the Solomons. The Pacific Ocean Areas —the rest of the Pacific, including the Marshalls, the Carolines and the Marianas—were under the control of Admiral Nimitz in Pearl Harbor. Out of this divided command, from the very first, came almost as much diffused effort and conflict as those existing in Tokyo.

MacArthur warned time and again that the Japanese were converging most of their power in *his* area and that there would be a disaster unless he got more men and matériel than Nimitz. Then came Midway and MacArthur saw it as an opportunity for quick victories. He radioed Washington an optimistic plan: he would

Operation Shoestring

overrun New Ireland and New Britain in a few weeks, "forcing the enemy back to his base at Truk." Besides his own three infantry divisions MacArthur would need "one division trained and completely equipped for amphibious operations and a task force including two carriers."

General Marshall, Army Chief of Staff, was impressed enough to write Fleet Admiral Ernest J. King, his opposite number, an urgent request to lend MacArthur several Marine units and two or three carriers. But before this letter could be delivered, Marshall received one from King curtly disposing of the MacArthur plan. The Navy was already considering operations against the same objectives and they would be "primarily of a naval and amphibious character supported and followed by forces operating from Australia." In other words, the Navy would do the job with MacArthur's assistance.

This, of course, was completely insupportable to MacArthur. He and he alone should lead the assault, since it lay within his domain. The Navy agreed that one man should be in charge, but not a general; a landlubber might place their precious carriers in jeopardy in the dangerous waters around the Solomons.

Marshall backed MacArthur and the argument stretched on until King reached the end of his patience. He warned Marshall that he was going to start an offensive "even if no support of Army forces in the Southwest Pacific is available." The Army Chief of Staff's first impulse was to answer in kind, but he decided to hold off a reply until he regained his composure.

Not so MacArthur. He lost his temper and radioed Washington:

IT IS QUITE EVIDENT IN REVIEWING THE WHOLE SITUATION THAT NAVY CONTEMPLATES ASSUMING GENERAL COMMAND CONTROL OF ALL OPERATIONS IN THE PACIFIC THEATER, THE ROLE OF THE ARMY BEING SUBSIDIARY AND CONSISTING LARGELY OF PLACING ITS FORCES AT THE DISPOSAL AND UNDER THE COMMAND OF NAVY OR MARINE OFFICERS. . . .

It was, he charged, all part of a master plan for "the complete absorption of the national defense function by the Navy" which he had "accidentally" uncovered when he was Chief of Staff.

> ... BY USING ARMY TROOPS TO GARRISON THE ISLANDS OF THE PACIFIC UNDER NAVY COMMAND, THE NAVY RETAINS MARINE FORCES ALWAYS AVAILABLE, GIVING THEM INHERENTLY AN ARMY OF THEIR OWN AND SERVING AS THE REAL BASES OF THEIR PLANS BY VIRTUE OF HAVING THE MOST READILY AVAILABLE UNITS FOR OFFENSIVE ACTION.

While Marshall agreed in spirit with MacArthur, he realized that the best solution was a fair compromise. He asked King to meet him and work out the problem amicably. They sat down face to face, and it was a measure of King's own maturity that the gruff and bleak admiral was equally willing to make concessions. In many respects Marshall found it easier to deal with King than with MacArthur, who was "supersensitive about everything" and "thought everybody had ulterior motives about everything."*

During the next few days the men hammered out a general plan for the ultimate objective—seizure of the New Britain–New Guinea area—by dividing the offensive into three separate parts. Task One, under Nimitz, was the assault about August 1 on the Japanese seaplane base at Tulagi, the tiny Solomon island twenty miles north of Guadalcanal, while MacArthur would be responsible for Tasks Two and Three, the seizure of the rest of the Solomons, the northwest coast of New Guinea, and the key base of Rabaul on New Britain.

The recent fall of Tobruk to Rommel had already brought a sense of impending disaster to Washington. Then on July 2—the same day the operation in the Pacific was approved by the Joint Chiefs of Staff—two alarming bulletins arrived: Sevastopol, in the Crimea, had collapsed, and in North Africa the British Eighth Army had been forced to retreat to the gates of Alexandria. What if the German forces in Russia broke through to the Caucasus and linked up with Rommel? Then it would only be a question of time before an even more ominous link-up with the Japanese. Added to all that was the rising toll of Allied merchant shipping losses in the At-

---

* The quotes came from a postwar interview between Marshall and his official biographer, Forrest Pogue. "With Chennault in China and MacArthur in the Southwest Pacific," Marshall reminisced wryly, "I sure had a combination of temperament."

lantic. In June alone, more than 627,000 tons had been sunk and the rate was rising.

It was, thought Marshall, "a very black hour."

The Pacific theater alone gave the Allies grounds for optimism. Hopes centered on the plan to seize Tulagi, which the Japanese had occupied in May. As yet the island of Guadalcanal was of incidental interest to the planners, and the officer Nimitz had placed in charge of Task One, Vice Admiral Robert L. Ghormley, first heard of the possibility of attacking it on July 7 when he was in Melbourne conferring with MacArthur. The information came in a radiogram from Nimitz revealing that the Japanese were building a small airfield on Guadalcanal and suggesting that it be taken simultaneously with Tulagi.

Both MacArthur and Ghormley agreed in principle, but both expressed their objections to the immediate launching of Task One; there was a single amphibious division, not enough shipping and a dangerous scarcity of planes. Moreover, the carriers of the Amphibious Force would have to remain too long in the Guadalcanal-Tulagi area far beyond the range of Allied land-based air protection and at the mercy of Japanese land-based aircraft. The Joint Chiefs ignored their separate recommendations and ordered the invasion to take place as scheduled; only by taking such prompt action could the Americans capitalize on the victory at Midway and seize the initiative in the Pacific. The operation was given a symbolic name, Watchtower.

Guadalcanal was Japan's southernmost outpost, significant merely as a base for any naval action in the Solomon area. It was a quiet, peaceful island 10 degrees below the equator, ninety-two miles long and thirty-three miles wide, about twice the size of Long Island. From the air it looked like a tropical paradise of lush green mountains, forested shores and colorful coral reefs. In reality it was paradise lost, a study in dramatic contrasts—peaks, barren hills and dense dark-green jungles, white cockatoos and ferocious white ants, myna birds and malarial mosquitoes; bone-chilling torrential rains and insufferably hot, dusty plains. It was an island of bananas, limes, papayas—and crocodiles, giant lizards, fungus infections, poisonous spiders, leeches and scorpions. "If I were a king," author Jack London once said, "the worst punishment I could inflict on my enemies would be to banish them to the Solomons."

A series of blue-green, jagged, quiescent volcanoes towering as high as 8,000 feet ran down the island like a backbone, and the only possible place for military operations was the narrow strip of rolling hills and plains running along the north coast. And even this area was forbidding, cut by many rivers and by ridges with stretches of razor-sharp grass.

In late 1567 a young Spaniard, Don Alvaro de Mendaña, set sail from Peru to find King Solomon's gold mines and after eleven weeks came upon a verdant group of islands. He named them the Solomons but they contained so little gold and were so inaccessible that there were few visitors in the centuries to follow.

The natives—woolly-headed, coal-black Melanesians—paid little attention to those who did come. They preferred to carry on their own bloody wars and headhunting to wiping out the pale-skinned intruders. They listened politely to missionaries, and it wasn't until 1896 that the first important confrontation between East and West occurred. In that year the Albatros Expedition, sponsored by the Geographical Society of Vienna, landed on Guadalcanal and marched across the plains and foothills to mile-high Mount Tatuve. The eighteen Austrians planned to scale it and ignored the natives' warnings that everyone on the island would die if any man "conquered" the mountain of their Great Spirit. The Austrian leader, the eminent geologist Heinrich Foullon von Norbeeck, replied that they had come a long way to climb Tatuve and were going to do it. The next morning while the Austrians breakfasted, a great number of natives quietly surrounded them but felt such pity for those who were about to die that they let them finish their meal before they attacked. The Austrians, however, fought so desperately that they drove off the natives, at a cost of six dead, including their intrepid leader. Thus ended the first battle of Guadalcanal.

At the time of Pearl Harbor the Solomons were an Australian mandate. Its capital on Tulagi consisted of a small hotel, a wireless station, a street of shops and a few neat bungalows for officials. Neighboring Guadalcanal couldn't claim that much civilization—all it had were several Catholic missions, a few coconut plantations and a Burns Philp trading station. A single trail led along the north coast through the plantations, but inland there were only native footpaths and it was the rare white man who dared follow them.

One of these was District Officer Martin Clemens, a former Cambridge athlete of renown, dedicated to keeping peace among the natives, who sometimes reverted to savage customs. Soon after the Japanese invasion he and four other men were stationed at various places on Guadalcanal as coastwatchers for the Royal Australian Navy. They were to radio reports on Japanese troopship and plane movements to the Directorate of Naval Intelligence in Australia. Like most of the other coastwatchers in the Solomons and Bismarcks, they were planters or civil servants who had lived for years in the area, and it was these intrepid men who had alerted Washington of the enemy build-up on the island. They continued to keep close watch on the enemy: there were 2,230 Japanese on the island, mostly laborers and engineers, and they had almost finished a primitive airfield for the Navy on the north coast.

The overconfidence of the Japanese Navy that had led to Midway was not diminished by the defeat; the Navy high command did not expect a counteroffensive in the Pacific for months. Its false sense of security was not shared by Lieutenant Commander Haruki Itoh of the Naval Intelligence Center in Tokyo. Late in July his unit picked up two new Allied call signs in the southwest Pacific. Since both stations operated on the commander-in-chief circuit (4205 kc series) and both communicated directly with Pearl Harbor, Itoh deduced that either could be headquarters for a new enemy task force. On August 1 radio direction finders located one station in Nouméa, New Caledonia, and the other near Melbourne. The first, guessed Itoh, was the headquarters for Admiral Ghormley and the second the base of a British or Australian force. Consequently, he and his staff concluded that the Allies were about to start an offensive on the Solomons or New Guinea. An urgent warning was radioed to Truk and Rabaul, but it was ignored in both places.

2.

Though Ghormley was in nominal command of Operation Watchtower, he could not exercise tactical control from Nouméa, so he left this to Vice Admiral Frank Jack Fletcher, veteran of

Coral Sea and Midway. Fletcher, as well as those who would have to carry out the assault, was not enthusiastic about Watchtower because of the meager forces available and the necessarily hasty preparations. It was nicknamed "Operation Shoestring."

On July 26 Fletcher summoned all unit commanders of the Expeditionary Force to a rendezvous in the South Pacific four hundred miles south of Fiji. The meeting on Fletcher's flagship, *Saratoga,* opened on a note of comedy. A garbage chute inadvertently dumped milk over an admiral climbing aboard. At the conference in the wardroom, Major General Alexander A. ("Archie") Vandegrift, the red-cheeked commander of the seventeen thousand Marines who would take Tulagi and Guadalcanal, found Fletcher lacking in "knowledge of or interest in the forthcoming operation." Fletcher, who looked "nervous and tired," openly discussed his doubt about the successful outcome of Watchtower. He was even more disheartened when he learned that it would take five days to disembark Vandegrift's troops on Guadalcanal. Fletcher was the one flag officer present who had experienced the devastation of Japanese air attacks (he had lost *Lexington* at Coral Sea and *Yorktown* at Midway) and he blanched at the idea of exposing his three flattops (there was but one other heavy carrier in the Pacific) to such peril. "Gentlemen," he said, "in view of the risks of exposure to land-based air, I cannot keep the carriers in the area for more than forty-eight hours after the [initial] landing."

Vandegrift controlled his temper; five days of air cover was cutting it dangerously thin. Rear Admiral Richmond Kelly Turner, commander of the Amphibious Force, whose tongue was as sharp and whose nature was as crusty as King's, concurred. But Fletcher's sole concern was the possible end of American carriers in the Pacific. They would leave on D-day plus 3—and that was final.

Vandegrift was furious as he left the ship and his mood was not improved by a botched landing rehearsal in the Fijis. It was, he thought dejectedly, a complete bust, and he could only console himself that "a poor rehearsal traditionally meant a good show."

At dusk on August 6 Admiral Turner's Amphibious Force approached the Solomons from the south. Four transports and four destroyer-transports were bound for little Tulagi while fifteen transports and cargo transports headed for Guadalcanal. They were escorted by eight cruisers (three of them Australian) and a destroyer screen. One hundred miles to the south lurked the Air Support Force: three carriers, a battleship, five heavy cruisers, sixteen destroyers and three oilers. At dawn the carriers would launch their fighters and bombers.

The invasion fleet—a total of eighty-two ships—probed north at 12 knots through a light haze. On the transports, engineers checked engines on landing craft as boatswain's mates tested falls and davits. The air was sticky and it took little movement to bring on streams of sweat. The order Darken Ships went out. In the sleeping quarters men lolled on bunks fully clad, playing cards, reading, or writing letters home. The mess halls were jammed with Marines listening to the roar of jukeboxes and watching buddies jitterbug alone or with partners. On *American Legion* the man who would lead the first unit ashore at Guadalcanal, Colonel Le Roy P. Hunt, was entertaining his officers with a one-man show. A bemedaled veteran of World War I—wounded and gassed—he clogged away to his own vocal accompaniment of "I Want a Girl Just Like the Girl That Married Dear Old Dad."

General Vandegrift was at the rail of Turner's flagship, *McCawley*, a transport known as the "Wacky Mac," trying to see through the darkness. He was in good spirits despite the "bleak" prospects. The invasion could be what Wellington called Waterloo —a "near-run thing." They were going in with little and without knowing how strong the enemy was. He pushed away from the rail and groped his way back to his stifling little cabin to finish a letter home:

Tomorrow morning at dawn we land in the first major offensive of this war. Our plans have been made and God grant that our judgment has been sound. . . . Whatever happens you'll know that I did my best. Let us hope that best will be enough.

By midnight the men who would have to make the first American landing of the war were in their bunks—sleeping or trying to sleep. Two hours later lookouts sighted a black pyramid in the distance. It was Savo, a small volcanic island lying north just off the western end of Guadalcanal. The haze had lifted and the ships of the Amphibious Force, still undetected, slipped into calm waters. At two-forty a message was relayed to the flagship that Cape Esperance, at the tip of Guadalcanal, was thirteen miles away. The transport groups separated, those bound for Tulagi continuing north beyond Savo and the rest making a sharp right turn into the channel between Savo and Cape Esperance. The still waters gave the men on watch "the creeps." The land breeze, usually welcome after weeks at sea, was rank with the stench of swamp and jungle.

At three o'clock reveille sounded on *McCawley*. Vandegrift ate breakfast, and as the eastern horizon grew bright, returned to the deck. There was no sign of the enemy. Was it some trap? The transports edged toward their destinations: Beach Blue on Tulagi, and Beach Red, located near the center of the north coast of Guadalcanal, just three miles from the almost completed airfield.

Around six-fifteen three cruisers and four destroyers belched fire in unison. Standing on the bridge of *American Legion,* correspondent Richard Tregaskis watched "the red pencil-lines of shells arching through the sky" toward Guadalcanal. Two minutes later, through the din, he could distinguish another roar, more distant. A cruiser and two destroyers were flinging shells at Tulagi.

There was still no movement along either Beach Red or Blue. The Japanese apparently had been caught completely off-guard. Within thirty minutes all transports were in position. Dive bombers and fighters from the three carriers appeared overhead and began strafing the beaches and bombing target areas. They were met with desultory antiaircraft fire.

"Land the landing force!" intoned the loudspeakers.

On the transports Marines lined up at debarkation stations. Men who had been raucous were mute. A few joked and several uttered the usual "Well, this is it." The 36-foot personnel landing craft were let down by hand. Booms gently lowered the 45- and 56-foot cargo craft while Marines in green dungarees—rifles slung over backs, canteens bulging from hips, heavy packs filled with everything from head nets to fend off mosquitoes to personal mementos—clambered down debarkation nets that slammed into the ships' sides with each gentle roll.

At Tulagi, Marines scrambled ashore but saw no one. It was as if the island were uninhabited. At eight-fifteen their commander signaled: LANDING SUCCESSFUL NO OPPOSITION. An hour later the first boat grounded off Beach Red on Guadalcanal and the men dropped into the warm shallow water. Everyone expected a withering blast, but as they crossed the bare beaches and plunged into the jungle, not a shot was fired at them.

From *McCawley,* Vandegrift was scanning 1,500-foot Mount Austen, which reared up behind the airfield. A plantation manager had called it "a hill only a couple of miles from the coast" but it looked like Mount Hood and was much farther inland. Was all the information so inaccurate? His men were held up only by the humid heat and a rain forest. Dripping with perspiration, often with no scouts ahead or flankers on either side, they blundered forward. Fortunately they met no enemy. The bombardment had driven almost all the Japanese back into the hills.

Their superiors in Rabaul had heard about the invasion before the first shell fell. The radio operator at Tulagi signaled: LARGE FORCE OF SHIPS, UNKNOWN NUMBER OR TYPES, ENTERING THE SOUND. WHAT CAN THEY BE? It was obviously a hit-and-run raid, but Rear Admiral Sadayoshi Yamada, commander of the 25th Air Flotilla, sent out long-range search planes to investigate. Before they could report, another message came in from Tulagi—the last: ENEMY FORCES OVERWHELMING. WE WILL DEFEND OUR POSTS TO THE DEATH, PRAYING FOR ETERNAL VICTORY.

Yamada summoned his squadron leaders and informed them that the scheduled attack on New Guinea was canceled; instead they were to hit the Guadalcanal area at once with every medium bomber, dive bomber and fighter that could get into the air. Tadashi Nakajima, commander of the fighters, protested. Guadalcanal was almost six hundred miles to the southeast and he would lose at least half his planes. The most experienced pilots alone could survive a mission of that range. The two men argued vehemently until Nakajima agreed to send eighteen planes.

He told his men they were going to fly the longest fighter operation in history. "Stick to your orders, and above all, don't fly recklessly or waste your fuel." The pilots waited in their Zeros until the twin-engine bombers—twenty-seven in all—roared down the runways. Nakajima signaled his men and guided his own tiny fighter down a narrow strip covered with a layer of dust and ash from the active volcano rising in the background. Some days its violent eruptions threw rocks high into the air threatening the planes on the field, but today all that issued from the cone was a streamer of smoke.

The bombers swept low over Bougainville on their way to Guadalcanal. A planter named Mason counted them and radioed Australia on the "X" frequency for emergency traffic: TWENTY-SEVEN BOMBERS HEADED SOUTHEAST. It was picked up by a number of stations, including Port Moresby, which relayed it to Townsville, Australia, and from there to the powerful transoceanic station at Pearl Harbor. Within minutes every American ship off Guadalcanal and Tulagi was ready.

As the bombers neared their targets, the fighters caught up with them. Saburo Sakai, who had already shot down fifty-six planes, including Colin Kelly's Flying Fortress, saw an awesome sight spread out before him—at least seventy enemy ships clustered off the beaches. The bombers swung around for their runs. All at once half a dozen enemy fighters appeared high above in the sun. They were new to Sakai, chubbier than any other American fighter he'd seen: they must be the Grumman Wildcats, a type reportedly in the area.

The carrier-based Wildcats swept toward the bombers which were dumping their loads on ships near Savo Island. Sakai watched in frustration as the bombs fell around the ships throwing up harmless geysers of water. How stupid to expect to hit moving ships from four miles up! Why hadn't they been armed with torpedoes?

The Grummans made one pass through the bomber formation before they were driven off by the Zeros. Sakai was puzzled by the American pilots' lack of aggressiveness—then he noticed a single Wildcat successfully holding off three Zeros. He gaped. Every time a Zero got the Wildcat in his sights, the American would flip his stubby plane away wildly and get behind the Zero—never had Sakai seen such flying. He loosed a burst at the Grumman; it rolled, came around in a tight turn and climbed straight up at Sakai. He snap-rolled but the American clung on. It took a series of tight loops before Sakai could get the Wildcat in his sights again. He sprayed between five and six hundred rounds into the plane.

The Wildcat did not come apart or catch fire. How could it stay

Operation Shoestring

in the air? Where had the Americans got such planes and pilots? He opened his cockpit window and stared at his opponent, a big man with a fair complexion. He challenged his adversary with a gesture of "Come on if you dare!" but the pilot must have been seriously wounded, for he did not attack despite his advantageous position. Sakai felt admiration for the dauntless foe and reluctantly turned his 20-mm. cannon on the Grumman. The plane exploded, and far below Sakai could see the pilot drifting toward land in his parachute.

The bombers had done no damage, and the transports headed back to the beaches to unload. But within an hour a second wave of bombers forced the transports to scatter again. In two strikes the Japanese had succeeded merely in delaying the landing operation for several hours. The same number of bombs could have blown up most of the supplies stacked on the beaches and jeopardized the troops on shore.

In Rabaul the import of the landing was not recognized by Lieutenant General Harukichi Hyakutake, commander of the 17th Army. New Guinea was still the main target and his attention was focused on a plan to cross the Owen Stanley Range and take Port Moresby. Not a single soldier could be spared for what was merely a diversion. Vice Admiral Gunichi Mikawa completely disagreed with him. He commanded the recently organized Eighth Fleet and had just arrived in Rabaul with a double mission: to spearhead a new drive south and to protect the Solomons from any Allied counterattack. The first reports of the landings had indicated beyond doubt that it was a major invasion, but he knew it was useless to argue with the Army. If anything was to be done immediately, it was up to the Navy alone. He managed to assemble 410 sailors, some rifles and a few machine guns and dispatched them at once to Guadalcanal in the transport *Meiyo-maru*. Then he radioed the Navy General Staff in Tokyo for permission to launch a surface attack the following night on the American transports.

It sounded too audacious to Navy Chief of Staff Nagano—Mikawa would have to break through a formidable ring of warships that far outgunned him—and he passed on the decision to Combined Fleet. Yamamoto knew that Mikawa was not at all reckless and radioed him direct: WISH YOUR FLEET SUCCESS.

Mikawa was advised to command the battle from Rabaul, but

being a true samurai, the gentle, soft-spoken admiral boarded the heavy crusier *Chokai* that afternoon. Ordering his other seven ships —four heavy cruisers, two light cruisers and a destroyer—to follow in column, he headed south through the St. George Channel.

The area was poorly charted and the few maps available were unreliable. It would be humiliating to run aground, and for hours the admiral pored over charts with his staff navigator. Finally he decided to lurk above Bougainville out of range of any American carrier planes until late the next afternoon. Then he would lead his little fleet into that dangerous channel through the Solomons (the Americans would nickname it "The Slot"), trusting to luck that no Allied search plane would sight him in the fading light. It was dangerous, but if he didn't take the chance he would never reach Guadalcanal in time. All depended on surprise.

But he had been discovered. A U. S. submarine, the *S-38,* lying in ambush at the mouth of the St. George Channel, was almost run down by Mikawa's column. Swaying in the wash, *S-38* was too close to fire her torpedoes. Her captain, Lieutenant Commander H. G. Munson, a veteran of the frustrating Java campaign, radioed:

TWO DESTROYERS AND THREE LARGER SHIPS OF UNKNOWN TYPE HEADING ONE FOUR ZERO TRUE AT HIGH SPEED EIGHT MILES WEST OF CAPE ST. GEORGE.

3.

By dusk on D-day, eleven thousand Marines had landed on Guadalcanal without a casualty. The beaches were piled high with supplies and ammunition. The next afternoon a battalion advanced to the airfield against practically no opposition. The Marines found an almost completed 3,600-foot airstrip; it was abandoned. The entire garrison—leaving meals on tables—had fled inland without trying to destroy any installations or supplies or blow up the runway. They left behind stacks of rifles, machine guns, trucks, steam rollers, cement mixers, ammunition, gasoline, oil and two radar scopes as well as large quantities of rice, tea, beer and *sake*. Nearby were two large electric-power generators, machine shops, an elaborate air-compressor factory for torpedoes, and an ice plant, which soon had a fresh sign: TOJO ICE PLANT, UNDER NEW MANAGEMENT.

Mikawa's ships had reached Bougainville at dawn. The admiral sent out four search planes and scattered his fleet to deceive any Allied scout. At ten-twenty an Australian bomber, a Hudson, began circling over his flagship. *Chokai* reversed course as if heading back to Rabaul, but when another Hudson appeared, Mikawa decided to brazen it out. The column re-formed and headed down toward the narrow passage through the Solomons. Before long one of his own search planes reported sighting eighteen transports, six cruisers, nineteen destroyers and a battleship near Savo Island. The enemy seemed to be split in two forces—the main one guarding the Guadalcanal transports, the other Tulagi. The Americans had twenty-six warships to his eight, but perhaps he could destroy one of the forces before it could join up with the other. What concerned Mikawa most was the carrier force. Where was it?

Admiral Turner was still unaware that an enemy fleet was heading toward his Amphibious Force. The report from the submarine was too inconclusive and the Australian search pilot had decided that his information wasn't important enough to break radio silence. Turner was preoccupied most of the day with two bombing raids that caused more confusion than damage; the destroyer *Jarvis* was hit by a torpedo, and the transport *George F. Elliott* set afire.

By late afternoon—just as the Marines were taking over the airfield on Guadalcanal—Mikawa's column at last entered the almost unbelievably blue waters of the Solomons passage and started southeast directly for Guadalcanal. It should reach the enemy about midnight and the battle plan had to be simple, since the eight ships had never before maneuvered as a unit or sailed in formation. At four-forty, orders were sent by blinker from *Chokai* to the other ships: "We will proceed from south of Savo Island and torpedo the enemy main force in front of the Guadalcanal anchorage, after which we will turn toward the Tulagi forward area to shell and torpedo the enemy. We will then withdraw north of Savo." The recognition signal would be white sleeves streamed on both sides of the bridge.

As Mikawa neared Guadalcanal the dangers of being discovered increased and there was little room in the narrow waters to evade bombers. Every minute of daylight seemed interminable.

Just before dusk a lookout on *Chokai* shouted, "Mast ahead on the starboard!" Sirens shrilled and bells clanged as the men scrambled to their battle stations and trained guns to starboard. It was a friendly ship, the seaplane tender *Akitsushima* heading for the bulky island sticking out of the water to the right, New Georgia.

Admiral Turner was not blind to the significance of The Slot. Any sailor could see it was the highway between Rabaul and Guadalcanal. He had ordered a Catalina to patrol the upper area where Mikawa had been steaming since dawn, but unknown to Turner, the PBY never took off. As darkness fell on the Amphibious Force, a messenger from the flag coding room handed the admiral a copy of a dispatch from Fletcher to Admiral Ghormley in Nouméa:

FIGHTER PLANE STRENGTH REDUCED FROM NINETY-NINE TO SEVENTY-EIGHT X IN VIEW OF THE LARGE NUMBER OF ENEMY TORPEDO PLANES AND BOMBERS IN THIS AREA I RECOMMEND THE IMMEDIATE WITHDRAWAL OF MY CARRIERS X REQUEST TANKERS SENT FORWARD IMMEDIATELY AS FUEL RUNNING LOW.

Turner was incensed. He was being left "bare arse" without carrier support and would have to pull out at dawn; he couldn't risk another air strike without carrier-plane protection. He ordered General Vandegrift and Rear Admiral V. A. C. Crutchley, commander of the cruiser-destroyer covering force, to report immediately to his flagship, *McCawley,* anchored off Guadalcanal. Crutchley was a British officer, winner of the Victoria Cross at Jutland, a hearty man with a full red beard. He had already deployed his ships in three protective groups around the transports and freighters. The Southern Force—three cruisers and two destroyers—was stationed between Savo and Cape Esperance. The Northern Force, with the same number of ships, barricaded the line between Savo and Tulagi while the Eastern Force—two light cruisers and two destroyers—stood off to the east.

There was no battle plan, and the good-natured Crutchley had simply ordered the Northern force to operate independently and conform in general to the movements of the Southern Force, which

Operation Shoestring

Crutchley himself would command. When Crutchley received Turner's urgent summons, he signaled the captain of the cruiser *Chicago* to take temporary command of the Southern Force and steered down the darkened coast of Guadalcanal in his flagship, *Australia,* in search of *McCawley;* it would be quicker to reach her in a cruiser than in a small boat.

Nobody in the covering force suspected that a surface attack was imminent and ships remained in a second condition of readiness. No one thought to inform the commander of the Northern Force, Captain Frederick L. Riefkohl on the heavy cruiser *Vincennes,* that he was now senior officer of both forces guarding The Slot. Nor did Captain Howard D. Bode of *Chicago* bother to take his proper position as temporary commander of the Southern Force ahead of *Australia*'s sister ship, *Canberra.*

Australia poked around in the gloom for almost two hours before finding *McCawley.* Turner and Crutchley discussed a message from the Australian search pilot who had discovered Mikawa that morning. It had finally come after eight hours' delay—and was misleading: it said that the Japanese force consisted of three cruisers, three destroyers and two seaplane tenders or gunboats. The key words to both admirals were "seaplane tenders" and they concluded this meant an air attack in the morning. Certainly no one would launch any kind of night surface attack with three cruisers. Besides, there had been no report from the PBY that Turner had ordered sent out that morning.

Aboard a small boat General Vandegrift was still hunting for *McCawley* through the mass of blacked-out ships and it wasn't until after eleven that he finally joined the conference. The night was hot, overcast, oppressive. Vandegrift thought the two admirals "looked ready to pass out," and he himself was worn by his exertions on Guadalcanal.

While they drank coffee Turner showed his subordinates Fletcher's message. Vandegrift was as angry as Turner about Fletcher; he was "running away twelve hours earlier than he had already threatened." Turner believed he should withdraw his transports soon after dawn and asked Vandegrift's opinion.

"We are in fair shape on Guadalcanal," said the general, but he doubted that many supplies had been unloaded at Tulagi. He would like to check in person.

"I thought you would want that," Turner remarked, peering over his glasses. "I have a minesweeper standing by to take you over there."

Crutchley offered to take Vandegrift to the minesweeper on his way back to his flagship. The general declined but Crutchley insisted. "Your mission is much more urgent than mine."

It was not quite midnight when the two boarded Crutchley's barge. To the left a heavy rain squall had sprung up near Savo, forming a curtain between the Northern and Southern Forces. To the right they could see a red glare—the transport *George F. Elliott* was still burning. As Vandegrift disembarked, Crutchley shook his hand. He knew what the withdrawal of transports meant to the Marines, but said, "Vandegrift, I don't know if I can blame Turner for what he's doing."

Mikawa's column was coming on Savo at 26 knots, trailed by phosphorescent wakes. The flagship *Chokai* led the way, followed at 1,300-yard intervals by the four other heavy cruisers and the two light cruisers, with the lone destroyer bringing up the rear. Decks were cleared for action; topside flammables were jettisoned, and depth charges and unnecessary gear stowed below. Every captain passed on to his men Mikawa's final message, similar to one by his hero, Lord Nelson: "Let us go forward to certain victory in the traditional night attack of the Imperial Navy. May each one of us calmly do his utmost."

Above all, Mikawa feared the enemy carrier force. He knew it was nearby from numerous high-frequency radio messages such as RED 6 TO RED BASE and GREEN 2 TO GREEN BASE. But there was still a good chance of escaping back through the Solomons passage in the daylight hours.

Directly ahead in the darkness, Crutchley's cruiser groups lumbered off Savo on their monotonous patrols, those on watch exhausted from forty-eight hours on constant alert. All the cruiser captains were asleep.

Mikawa saw the volcano of Savo rise out of the sea. No one on the bridge spoke. One, two, three minutes slowly passed. Unlike the Americans the Japanese had no radar, only eyes sharpened by night training. The starboard lookout on *Chokai* saw a dim form. "Ship approaching, thirty degrees starboard!" he called out. It was the U. S. destroyer *Blue*. She and the destroyer *Ralph Talbot*, which was six miles to the northeast, were pickets, the American early-warning system. But their sonar and radar, strangely, gave no indication that a Japanese column was bearing down on them.

"Prepare for action," said Mikawa, and to keep out of sight, ordered, "Left rudder. Slow to twenty-two knots."

The black line of ships silently turned, starboard guns ready to blast *Blue,* but all she did was reverse course and sail off at a leisurely 12 knots toward *Ralph Talbot,* which had also reversed course. The two sentries passed and drew away, leaving an open gate for the oncoming raiders.

Mikawa knifed forward and was in the center of the Amphibious Force, thanks to an unbroken series of Allied mishaps: he had been sighted three times, but to no avail. The B-17's patrolling The Slot had missed him entirely, and the extra search order by Turner had not been carried out. Finally, the two picket destroyers had almost been run down by the column, yet had not been alerted by lookouts or radar or sonar operators; either the blips were not seen or they were presumed to be friendly and ignored. In addition, a floatplane—one of three sent out after dark by Mikawa—had been sighted before midnight and reported by *Ralph Talbot.* It, too, had been assumed to be friendly. As at Pearl Harbor, no one could believe an attack was imminent.

Chokai swung below Savo, unobserved. A lookout saw a cruiser on the port bow. A minute passed. Nothing happened. It was a false alarm. Port lookouts barely discerned what looked like a destroyer moving very deliberately to the west. It was the destroyer *Jarvis,* torpedoed in the daylight air attack, and steaming back to Australia for repairs. Mikawa's incredible luck held. *Jarvis,* too, failed to notice the Japanese column, which was finally swallowed up by a heavy curtain of rain.

Chokai signaled with hooded blinkers visible only to those in the column: "Prepare to fire torpedoes." A port lookout made out a ship almost ten miles away in the glare of the burning *Elliott.* "Cruiser, seven degrees port!" At 1:36 A.M. a starboard lookout called out, "Three cruisers, nine degrees starboard, moving right!" It was the heart of Crutchley's Southern Force, the heavy cruisers *Canberra* and *Chicago* and the destroyer *Patterson.*

"Commence firing," Mikawa said quietly and the order was relayed to the torpedo crews. "All ships attack" was the next command. Schools of long-range torpedoes that could carry a thousand pounds of explosives eleven miles at 49 knots churned toward *Canberra* and *Chicago*.

The two big cruisers were heading slowly to the northwest, guarded by two destroyers, *Bagley* to starboard and *Patterson* to port. Finally, at 1:43 A.M., someone on *Patterson* made out several ships in the distance and the alarm was sounded by radio: WARNING—WARNING—STRANGE SHIPS ENTERING HARBOR!

The warning was unnecessary. Overhead, parachute flares exploded in the darkness behind the Allied ships, making them as distinct as silhouettes in a shooting gallery. The flares had been dropped by Mikawa's three "friendly" floatplanes.

On the bridge of *Canberra* a lookout called an officer's attention to a vague form ahead in the pounding rain. A ship, a strange ship. It began spitting fire. As the two Australians intuitively flinched, a pair of torpedoes plowed into *Canberra*'s bow. From above, shells hurtled into the cruiser, killing the captain and the gunnery officer. Her main guns useless, the big ship listed, dead in the water. Fire coursed through the companionways, fed by linoleum on the decks. The paint on the bulkheads burst into flame; the upholstered furniture in the wardrooms went up like tinder. Men frantically tried to jettison gasoline and ammunition, but it was too late. Explosions wracked the ship.

The destroyers on either side of *Canberra* fought back blindly, but *Patterson* was promptly pinpointed by searchlights and knocked out of action. *Bagley* rushed at the enemy, got into position to launch torpedoes—there were no firing primers.

With *Canberra* an inferno, Mikawa's fleet turned on *Chicago*. The temporary commander of the Southern Force, Captain Bode, wakened out of a sound sleep, got to the bridge just before a torpedo crunched into the bow. Despite a 16-foot hole and a shell hit, *Chicago* still looked for a target. Sighting something to the west—it was the sole Japanese destroyer—she gave chase. Bode was inadvertently steaming away from the main battle. Worse, he had yet to warn the Northern Force of what was happening.

On *McCawley*, Admiral Turner knew of the battle only from the flash of guns followed by the freight-car rumble of shells. What struck him was that the fate of the Marines on Guadalcanal and Tulagi and the sailors in the helpless transports was at stake.

These thin-skinned ships had pulled anchor and were milling around in the darkness.

Admiral Crutchley was far from the action on *Australia*. He ordered seven destroyers to join his flagship at a set rendezvous—if they were not engaged with the Japanese. In the turmoil the order was misunderstood and four destroyers pulled out of the battle.

Mikawa had disposed of the Southern Force in about six minutes without taking a hit. He continued his counterclockwise swing around Savo to find new targets. Three heavy cruisers followed the flagship *Chokai*, but the next in line, *Furutaka*, was so far behind that it mistakenly swung to starboard and the next two ships followed, splitting Mikawa's force in two. The mistake put Mikawa in an enviable tactical position: he had four cruisers west of the Northern Force and three on the other side. The five American ships, three heavy cruisers and two destroyers, were about to be flanked on both sides—simultaneously, and without warning from Captain Bode.

At 1:48 A.M., lookouts on the heavy cruiser *Astoria* saw torpedoes approach—they came from *Chokai* and they all passed by. Wakened by the general alarm, Captain William Greenman rushed to the bridge and wanted to know who the devil had sounded the alarm and why the ship's main battery was blasting away. He was sure whatever they were shooting at was friendly. "Let's not get excited and act too hastily," he said. "Cease firing." He changed his mind quickly enough when he saw splashes falling around the cruiser *Vincennes*. "Commence firing!" he shouted and ordered a slight turn to port. "Our ships or not, we've got to stop them!"

Salvo after salvo from *Chokai* crashed into *Astoria*, knocking out all power and killing everyone in turret No. 2. The cruiser coasted to a stop, her decks aflame—and every fire main was ruptured.

Nearby the heavy cruiser *Quincy* was also on fire from a hit on a scout plane and its store of fuel. The cruiser made a perfect target and was caught in a devastating crossfire. "We're going down between them," Captain S. N. Moore phoned his gunners. "Give them hell!" Shells tore into *Quincy,* and Moore finally ordered the signalman to beach the doomed ship on Savo, four miles to port. A shell exploded on the bridge, flinging bodies like dolls, killing almost everyone. Moore lay near the wheel, mortally wounded. He tried to get up but fell back with a moan. The ship heeled rapidly to port and began sinking by the bow.

The commander of the Northern Force, Captain Riefkohl of *Vincennes,* still didn't know a battle was going on. He had heard *Ralph Talbot*'s report of a plane overhead just before midnight, but assumed like so many others that it was friendly and went to bed. The roar of guns, he surmised, had been set off by some small Japanese ship trying to steal past the Southern Force. From his bridge Riefkohl felt two underwater explosions and saw gun flashes and made another bad guess: the Southern Force was shooting at enemy planes.

He was annoyed—but not perturbed—when searchlights illuminated the three cruisers of the Northern Force at 1:50 A.M. He radioed the Southern Force to shut them off. As if in reply, spouts shot up five hundred yards away. Captain Riefkohl at last realized he was in a fight. *Vincennes'* 8-in. guns bellowed and one salvo hit *Kinugasa,* but the scout planes on *Vincennes'* stern burst into flame and she, like *Quincy,* became an easy target. Riefkohl ordered a zigzag course to avoid the deadly assault, but two, perhaps three torpedoes exploded in a port fire room. Steam pressure dropped steadily. Another torpedo hit the No. 1 fire room. *Vincennes* wallowed in the water. Shell after shell ripped along the decks. Fires broke out in the movie locker and searchlight platform. Riefkohl was wondering if he should abandon ship. Then the Japanese searchlights blacked out. The firing ceased as abruptly as it had started. It was 2:15 A.M.

Mikawa signaled: "All ships withdraw." On every side he could see flaming wreckage. It reminded him of the water lantern festival at Lake Hakone. He was tempted to turn back and attack the transports, but his own ship had been hit three times and his fleet was scattered. It would take more than an hour to get back into battle formation; by the time he sank the transports it would be dawn and he would have to make the long run back to Rabaul in broad daylight at the mercy of American carrier-based planes. He remembered what Admiral Nagano had told him before he left Japan: "The Japanese Navy is different from the American Navy. If you lose one ship it will take years to replace." He also remembered how contemptuously the 17th Army in Rabaul had talked of

Operation Shoestring

the U. S. Army; how easy it was to beat them in battle. Why then should he risk his precious fleet just to sink Army transports? He gave the order to make for Rabaul.

Mikawa's concern about the carrier planes was logical, but he need not have worried. Fletcher had already turned his back on the Solomons and within an hour would get Ghormley's permission to retire completely from the area.

Mikawa had inflicted on the U. S. Navy its most humiliating defeat at sea. Shortly after she started up The Slot, the battered *Quincy* went down, and a quarter of an hour later *Vincennes* took her final plunge. Then *Astoria* and *Canberra*—burning furiously in the cold, driving rain—sank beneath the waters of what would be known as Ironbottom Sound.

At dawn the waters around Savo were heavy with oil, wreckage and half-dead men clinging to bits of flotsam. It was more crushing than the debacle at the Java Sea. The Japanese, who had not lost a ship, had destroyed four modern heavy cruisers, killed 1,023 men and wounded another 709. And though Mikawa had not attacked the transports, he left such terror in his wake that every Allied ship —warships as well as transports, cargo vessels and minesweepers— fled the area toward Nouméa; the abandoned Marines of Guadalcanal and Tulagi were short of ammunition and had enough food for little more than a month.

What happened at Savo was bitterly debated and recollected with rancor and shame by the men of the U. S. Navy. No one was punished as a result of an official investigation, but Captain Riefkohl emerged a broken man who went about like the Ancient Mariner telling his story over and over of how *Vincennes* had kept Mikawa from destroying the transports by putting a shell into *Chokai*'s chart room. Captain Bode committed suicide.

15

Green Hell

1.

In Tokyo the victory at Savo overshadowed the significance of the American seizure of Guadalcanal. All the same, it was an annoyance to the Navy and with reluctance they informally asked Army General Staff operations officers if they would mind clearing the island. The Army asked how many troops would be needed for the operation. Not too many, said the Navy. The American invasion was little more than a nuisance involving a mere 2,000 Marines; the enemy could not possibly mount a major counterattack up through the Solomons for a year.

The Army operations officers agreed to recommend the plan to Tojo, and before the end of the week the Army General Staff radioed General Hyakutake in Rabaul to mop up Guadalcanal with 6,000 men—a Special Naval Landing Force of 500 men; the Kawaguchi Detachment of 3,500, and the Ichiki Detachment, the 2,000 men who had been scheduled to seize Midway and were now back on Guam.

Kiyotake Kawaguchi—the mustached general who had tried in vain to save Chief Justice Santos—was on Koror, one of the Palau island group some six hundred miles east of Mindanao, and from the moment he read his change of orders sending him to the Solomons, he instinctively guessed the import of the American invasion. He showed Nishino, the *Mainichi* reporter, a map of the Solomons and pointed to a tiny speck. "This is our new destination—Gadarukanaru. I know you think this might be small-scale warfare. It's true there will be nothing heroic in it, but I'd say it will be extremely serious business." Kawaguchi somberly predicted that the island would be the focal point in the struggle for the Pacific. "If you decide to continue on with us, you must put your life in my hands. Both of us will probably be killed." Nishino said he would go and they shook hands.

Two nights later, on August 15, Kawaguchi instructed his squad leaders to distribute three months' pay to the troops. They were embarking on "a very important mission" and many would die. "Have the men send most of the money home and spend the rest on eating and drinking so they can enjoy their last night here."

Soon after dawn the 3,500 men of the Kawaguchi Detachment, still feeling the effects of their all-night celebration, began boarding two 10,000-ton transports. The decks of *Sado-maru* were hot from the tropical sun and burned Nishino's feet through his sneakers. He watched the soldiers file into the spacious hold and pack themselves into the bunks. Electric fans brought blasts of warm air, so Nishino returned topside. The decks were steaming from a recent squall.

As the ship weighed anchor, a large black dog paddled from the shore and scrambled up the last loading platform. He darted frantically around until he found his master, a young lieutenant named Ueno. "All right, I was wrong," the lieutenant said apologetically to the dog; he had given him away the night before.

For three days the transports plowed southeast toward Rabaul at 16 knots. The soldiers jogged around the decks singing military songs, lounged, did setting-up exercises. Their spirits were high despite the enervating heat. At supper they were issued warm beer, which put them in an exuberant mood: They had no fear of the Americans, they boasted; all they had to do was attack them at night. Their training manual said: "Westerners—being very haughty, effeminate and cowardly—intensely dislike fighting in the rain or mist or in the dark. They cannot conceive night to be a proper time for battle—though it is excellent for dancing. In these weaknesses lie our great opportunity." They reminisced about their easy conquest of Borneo. "After we got through firing there wasn't a blade of grass," said one youngster. "I'm not going to let any grass grow on Dakarunaru."

"It isn't Dakarunaru, it's Gadarukanaru," a sergeant corrected him. "Remember the name, will you?"

Six destroyers—they carried the first echelon of the Ichiki Detachment—made a landfall off Taivu Point on the north shore, only twenty-five miles east of the Guadalcanal airstrip. Boats were lowered and just before midnight—it was August 18—Colonel Kiyono Ichiki and 915 men came ashore. Like the Marines, they met not a single round of fire.

WE HAVE SUCCEEDED IN INVASION, Ichiki radioed Rabaul. His orders were to wait until the second half of his detachment arrived a week later and then retake the airstrip which the Japanese had almost completed in July. But he was so confident that he left 125 men to guard the beach and struck off up the coast.

His presence on Guadalcanal was known to the Marine commander but only from inconclusive evidence—the wake of the destroyers. However, combined with reports of enemy landings west of the airstrip (this was the 500-man Special Naval Landing Force, which never became significantly involved in the fighting), it was sufficient to convince General Vandegrift that a major counterattack was imminent. He sent out probing patrols to the west, east and southeast. He also asked a native sergeant major named Vouza (he was a scout for Martin Clemens of the Australian Coastwatching Service) to take a patrol south, then circle back north to the coast.

It took the bandy-legged Vouza and his men little more than a day to reach the sea. On August 20 they discovered the Ichiki Detachment. (It was within ten miles of the airstrip and Ichiki's latest message to Rabaul had indicated his optimism: NO ENEMY AT ALL. LIKE MARCHING THROUGH A NO MAN'S LAND.) Vouza tried to creep in closer for more information but was captured and brought to Ichiki. When he was stripped a tiny American flag, a souvenir, fell out of his loincloth. Vouza refused to answer questions. He was tied to a tree; his face was beaten almost to a pulp by rifle butts. He stubbornly shook his head. He was bayoneted twice through the chest. Still he said nothing. A soldier thrust a bayonet through his throat.

But Vouza was not dead, and at dusk when Ichiki and his 790 men moved on along the beach, he began chewing through his ropes. Finally he freed himself and with determination managed to crawl back to the Marine lines. He gasped out that "maybe two hundred and fifty, maybe five hundred" Japanese were approaching their perimeter. He fainted but came to long enough to say, "I did not tell them."

Ichiki was forming his troops in a coconut grove on the east bank of a sluggish stream between him and the airstrip, little more than a mile away. This was the Ilu River (mistaken for the Tenaru by the Marines), which formed a natural defense line, and Ichiki was certain there were Marines on the other side. At the mouth of the Ilu he found a narrow 45-yard-wide sand bar which penned up its green, stagnant water and formed a bridge almost to the other side.

He was sure he had achieved surprise but the Americans were well dug in across the river waiting for him, alerted by Vouza and a Marine patrol which had captured enemy maps. At about one-thirty in the morning Ichiki gave the order to attack. Mortars arched their rounds toward the Americans and machine guns raked the jungle beyond the river. Then several hundred Japanese burst out of the grove and headed for the sand bar with fixed bayonets and cries of "Banzai!" On the run they fired from the hip and lobbed grenades.

A volley of rifle fire met them head-on, followed by a whiplash of machine-gun fire. The first Japanese, officers brandishing sabers, were cut down. Canister shots from a 37-mm. gun toppled scores of men. A few made it across the Ilu but the fusillade forced the survivors to flee back to the coconut grove.

Vandegrift was already mounting a counterattack from the south with his reserve battalion, commanded by Lieutenant Colonel Leonard Cresswell. By dawn Cresswell was across the river and leading his men down the east bank. At two o'clock in the afternoon he approached the coconut grove. Ichiki was cut off.

But the Japanese would not surrender. Wounded men would cry out, and Americans who went forward to help were blown up by grenades or picked off by sharpshooters. The Marines were encountering a new kind of war, one without quarter. Vandegrift decided, therefore, to send in a platoon of light tanks.

Late that afternoon five tanks clanked over piles of Japanese bodies on the sand bar and made for the grove, blasting canister shots from their 37-mm. guns. They butted into palm trees, knocking down snipers, and ran down cornered Japanese until the treads of the tanks looked like "meat grinders." First Lieutenant Sakakibara and an enlisted man barely escaped being crushed by scrambling into the sea and hiding with their noses just above the water level.

By dusk there was only a handful of Japanese left in the grove. They clustered around the wounded Ichiki, who clutched the regimental flag. "Burn the colors," he ordered. The colorbearer poured gasoline on the flag, which was soaked with Ichiki's blood, and set a match to it just as a tank found the little group. Before Ichiki could be mowed down with the others he drew his sword and committed hara-kiri.

Pieces of bodies, blown to bits by Marine howitzers or shredded by canister, littered the grove. The trail of tanks could be followed by tread tracks over mangled bodies. There was not a sign of life in the grove. Almost 800 Japanese had been killed, at the cost of 35 dead and 75 wounded Americans. When it was dark the sole Japanese survivors, Lieutenant Sakakibara and his companion, crept out of the sea and headed back along the coast to their 125 comrades who had been left to guard the supplies.

For the first time both Army and Navy leaders in Tokyo began to take the American presence in Guadalcanal seriously. The Army plan to retake the island now also had Admiral Yamamoto's full support. He saw Guadalcanal as another opportunity for Combined Fleet to lure the Americans into the decisive sea battle.

Four slow transports, already bound for Guadalcanal with the rest of the Ichiki Detachment and five hundred sailors trained as infantrymen, were instructed to turn back and rendezvous with the Guadalcanal Supporting Forces, which had hastily been assembled by Yamamoto and was sailing south toward the Solomons. In the lead were six submarines, followed closely by the overall commander, Vice Admiral Kondo, and a group of six cruisers and a seaplane carrier. Behind steamed the newly formed *Kido Butai,* still led by Nagumo, but with only two big carriers, *Zuikaku* and *Shokaku,* and an escort of two battleships and three heavy cruisers. Accompanying them was the Diversionary Group—the light carrier *Ryujo,* a heavy cruiser, and two destroyers—which was to be sent out at the psychological moment as bait for the American carriers.

It was not long before the Americans learned of the formidable surface force advancing toward them from the north and they were forced to meet this new threat head-on. Admiral Ghormley sent out Admiral Fletcher to do battle with Task Force 61—three large carriers (*Enterprise, Saratoga* and *Wasp*), seven cruisers and eighteen destroyers. By dawn on August 23 Fletcher was less than 150 miles east of Guadalcanal, in perfect position to block the Japanese charge. Several hours later an American patrol plane sighted the four Japanese transports and their immediate escort— a light cruiser and five destroyers under the command of an obstinate rear admiral, Raizo Tanaka—and radioed back that troopships were heading for Guadalcanal. Tanaka was as wily as he was aggressive. He kept bearing south until 1 P.M., then put the transports out of range of aerial attack by reversing course. Five hours later Kondo's large force, which was forty miles to the east and still undiscovered, did the same.

Tanaka's move misled Fletcher into assuming that there wouldn't be a major engagement for several days and he sent the *Wasp* group south to refuel. It was an unfortunate decision that deprived him of one third of his power on the eve of battle.

Just before dawn on August 24, the Diversionary Group swung back south to tempt Task Force 61. Then the rest of the Japanese armada also reversed course, lurking out of sight and waiting for Fletcher to take the bait. At 9:05 A.M. an American patrol plane discovered the little carrier and her three escorts 280 miles northwest of Task Force 61. Fletcher hesitated even after it was reported two and a half hours later that the Diversionary Group was less than 250 miles away. But at 1:30 P.M. his skepticism vanished when his radar blips showed planes heading for Guadalcanal.

They were fifteen fighters and six bombers from *Ryujo* bound for the airfield on Guadalcanal. Recently completed (named Henderson Field after Major Lofton Henderson, who was killed at Midway), it was the base for two Marine squadrons—nineteen

Wildcat fighters and a dozen Dauntless dive bombers—and fourteen P-400's from an Army fighter squadron.

Fletcher moved fast, and within fifteen minutes thirty dive bombers and eight torpedo bombers were launched from *Saratoga*. In two hours the Dauntlesses found *Ryujo* and began diving at her from 14,000 feet. In the midst of the attack, six Douglas Devastators swept in and released their torpedoes from 200 feet. At least four bombs and one torpedo smashed into the little carrier. She listed 20 degrees to starboard and came to a dead stop.

Ryujo was doomed but she had accomplished her main purpose; she had diverted Fletcher's attack and allowed *Kido Butai* to locate *Saratoga* and *Enterprise*. Fifty-one Wildcats tried to screen the two carriers, but twenty-five Aichi dive bombers broke through. At exactly 5:14 P.M. a bomb penetrated through five decks of *Enterprise* and exploded in the chief petty officers' quarters. Two more bombs with instantaneous fuses ripped up the flight deck. By the time the raging fires were brought under control, seventy-six men had died and *Enterprise* was forced to retire toward Pearl Harbor for major repairs.

With a single carrier left, Fletcher did not relish a night battle and wisely decided to turn south. Nagumo chased him until 8:30 P.M., then gave up. The Battle of the Eastern Solomons was over. Like Coral Sea, it appeared to be inconclusive. A small Japanese carrier had been sunk, while Fletcher had been deprived of the services of *Enterprise* for at least two months. More important, however, Fletcher lost seventeen planes to Nagumo's seventy, and the Japanese could not afford the loss of so many experienced crews. As at Coral Sea, the Japanese imagined they had inflicted heavy losses on the Americans. Returning pilots reported they had sunk or heavily damaged three carriers, a battleship, five heavy cruisers and four destroyers. And one of these carriers was allegedly *Hornet* (she wasn't in the battle); Doolittle's sneak attack on Tokyo had been avenged.

The Guadalcanal Supporting Forces retired but Tanaka continued doggedly down the Solomons passage, even though the transports could not possibly reach Guadalcanal until daylight. The risk was great but he tried to minimize it by sending five of his destroyers ahead to shell the planes at Henderson Field. All through the night they ranged along the north coast bombarding the airfield, then left to join the transports coming from the north.

The next morning at 9:35 eight Marine dive bombers from Henderson, led by Lieutenant Colonel R. C. Mangrum and out on a quest for enemy carriers, accidentally discovered the transports and their escort. They plummeted down on the light cruiser *Jintsu,* Tanaka's flagship, and *Kinryu-maru. Jintsu* was able to limp away, but the burning transport had to be abandoned. As the destroyer *Mutsuki* began picking up survivors she was attacked by eight Flying Fortresses based on Espíritu Santo Island, in the New Hebrides. The captain, Commander Kiyono Hatano, had little regard for American high-level bombers and continued his rescue operations. This time the B-17's had a stationary target, and three bombs ripped into *Mutsuki*. "Even the B-17's can make a hit once in a while," gasped Hatano as he swam to safety.

Tanaka stubbornly kept moving toward Guadalcanal and would have attempted to land the fifteen hundred reinforcements in the daylight. All that stopped him was a message from Rabaul ordering him to return at once to Shortland, the little island off Bougainville that had become the springboard for what the Americans called the "Tokyo Express"—the runs down to Guadalcanal.

The memory of these losses was still vivid in Tanaka's mind when, on the morning of August 29, he met with the officer who would lead the second assault on Henderson Field. General Kawaguchi and his 3,500-man detachment had just arrived in Shortland by way of Rabaul and he wanted to get to Guadalcanal as soon as possible—on barges. Tanaka was glad to provide transportation but insisted on using destroyers. One reason Ichiki had been wiped out, Kawaguchi countered, was because he hadn't been able to take sufficient equipment and food on destroyers. The next day they resumed the argument, but Tanaka's reasoning, based on personal experience, eventually won Kawaguchi over. Late that afternoon the general summoned his commanders to the mess of his transport and told them they were transferring to destroyers for the run to Guadalcanal. Colonel Akinosuke Oka, a regimental commander, thought this would be too dangerous. "I think it would be better to go by motorboat, weaving our way secretly from island to island."

In the stifling heat the two men debated at length the merits of

"Rat Express" (destroyers) and "Ant Freight" (motorboats). Kawaguchi finally ended the argument by compromise. "I will lead the main unit directly to Taivu Point by destroyers. Colonel Oka will lead Headquarters and First Battalion by motorboat to the northwest end of Guadalcanal." Kawaguchi made two red marks on a large map, one at Taivu Point (the same place selected by Ichiki), where he would disembark with 2,400 men, and the other at Kokumbona, about ten miles west of the airfield, where Oka and the remaining 1,100 troops would land. From these two points he and Oka would simultaneously head inland to get behind Henderson in position for a joint attack.

The general stepped onto an empty cider box. "Gentlemen," he said, "I think our faith is our strength. Men who fight bravely, never doubting victory, will be the victors in the long run. Before we get to the battlefield we must sail three hundred miles and may very well encounter enemy attacks en route." Advance elements had been attacked but safely landed by destroyers at Taivu Point during the previous two nights. "But we have trained ourselves, haven't we? I swear to all of you that we will smash the enemy. On to Guadalcanal!"

"To Guadalcanal!"

"We solemnly swear to fight to the end," shouted an officer and raised his glass in a toast.

Correspondent Nishino followed Kawaguchi topside. Enlisted men and junior officers were diving into the blue-green water and swimming back to the ship.

"They need constant training, Nishino-*san*," Kawaguchi remarked. A young, fully clad lieutenant leaned on the rail, a cigarette dangling from his lips. "Hey, Lieutenant," Kawaguchi called to him. "Why aren't you in there with the others?"

The lieutenant quickly dropped his cigarette into the water and sprang to attention. While he was mumbling an excuse, Kawaguchi summarily pushed him over the rail. "There are some lazy ones," he observed. "In war when you're thrown into the sea, even a hammer has to swim."

That midnight the detachment transferred to destroyers and motorboats. Kawaguchi, with Nishino, climbed aboard the destroyer *Umikaze*. When they were alone in the general's cabin, Kawaguchi revealed that the Americans were well dug in and had almost endless supplies. "When we come to think of such things it seems extremely difficult for a small unit like ours to retake the airfield. Wouldn't you think the destruction of the Ichiki Detachment would be a lesson to us? But Imperial Headquarters belittles the enemy on Guadalcanal and declares that once we land successfully, the Marines will surrender." He stopped as if alarmed by his own words. "It's not a problem for us to discuss here."

Nishino was wakened by a chilly breeze. At eight twenty-five a bugle, the signal for departure, sounded and the eight slender destroyers, two abreast, began gliding southeast at 26 knots. It was the last day of August. Deep in the hold the roar of the revolving screws, coupled with the suffocating heat, drove Nishino to the open deck. He was almost blown off his feet by the brisk wind. It was cloudy, a good time to start the hazardous trip down the channel. The lashing spray forced him back to the hold just in time to hear a ship's officer tell a group of soldiers that they should reach Guadalcanal several hours before midnight. A petty officer began checking the soldiers' lifebelts. "Don't worry about air attacks," he said cheerfully.

All through the nerve-wracking day sailors urged the soldiers to avenge comrades who had been trapped on Guadalcanal by the invasion. The soldiers promised to "wipe out every last Yankee." After dinner the sailors returned to the hold with beer, cider, tobacco and candy. "We are responsible for the sea!" bellowed one tipsy sailor. "You're responsible for the island. Okay? So good luck!" He began pumping hands with every soldier within reach.

A soldier gave a sailor half of his wrinkled pack of Kinshi cigarettes and said, "Let's celebrate with a smoke if we ever meet again alive." Another pair exchanged fingernail clippings. "Please send them to my son if I die," said the soldier. "The boy is only two years old." "This is my mother's name and address," said the sailor.

The eight ships, rolling violently, drove ahead full speed through the blackness. Their wakes were like an endless display of fireworks; the water was filled with millions of noctilucae—luminescent creatures. A dark shadow of land materialized half a mile away. It was Taivu Point. Launches, cutters and rowboats were lowered and the soldiers piled in silently. The ships' guns leveled on the coconut trees that lined the beach. All Nishino could hear as he dropped into a boat was the muted hubbub of debarkation.

His boat ground into the sand and he clambered awkwardly over the side. The surf, brilliant with noctilucae, pushed him ashore. He waited for the crack of fire from the silent line of coconut and palm trees. There was only the sound of his comrades and the crunch of surf.

He staggered up to dry sand and looked at his watch. It was one minute past nine, Tokyo time; here it was an hour later. His body glistened from the waist down with the tiny phosphorescent animals, and the long beach itself, alive with crowds of luminescent men, was a shiny belt. He stood entranced in a world of fantasy.

"How beautiful," said a voice next to him.

Nishino moved toward the jungle until he was halted by another voice: "What unit are you from?" He saw a silhouette. It was a Japanese soldier in tattered uniform. Several other figures appeared from the jungle like ghosts. They were survivors of the first Ichiki echelon.

"Glad to see you," said the gaunt soldier. "But shake those damn worms off you. The enemy can see them from the air." His voice trembled as he anxiously pointed to the ground. "It's suicide to leave footprints in the sand," he said. "We're always being attacked by U. S. planes." The Ichiki men expertly wiped out footprints with palm leaves as they backed off to the edge of the jungle. They bowed and were gone.

Kawaguchi saluted the destroyers, then led the way into the jungle. It was so dark that each man had to hang on to the shoulder of the one ahead. They came to a narrow river bridged by a fallen tree. Nishino couldn't see the river but could tell it was deep by the rush of water. As he crept across the slippery tree he almost panicked. What if he fell? His 70-lb. pack would drag him under. Compulsively he began cataloguing everything on his back: a movie camera, two still cameras, film equipment, clothing, food and five books—a selection of Chinese poems, a geography of the Solomons, two volumes of French poetry, and an English copy of *The Good Earth*.

By the time he finished the list he was on the other side. He stepped off into something that felt like spongy cushions. Huge rain drops began to penetrate the umbrella of the jungle, then the drops turned into a shower. The trail became blocked with thick tangles of vines studded with long sharp thorns and huge trees with knobby roots. Kawaguchi stopped, and the men curled up on the ground and tried to sleep in the beating rain. Nishino began shivering. Mosquitoes swarmed over his face; their bites stabbed him like inoculating needles.

In the darkness they were roused, and they continued to grope through the jungle, circling back toward the coast. By dawn they reached Tasimboko, a deserted village near the beach, three miles west of Taivu Point. Here they ate their first meal on Guadalcanal. It had been prepared by the Navy and packed in each man's *hango* —a covered metal mess kit about the size and shape of a binocular case. Inside was an unexpected treat: white rice, dried fish (heads and all), fish paste and cooked beef. In thanks each soldier raised his *hango* to his forehead and bowed.

Their breakfast was interrupted by the frantic barking of the large black dog which had swum after Ueno. "Enemy plane!" the lieutenant shouted and dropped to the ground. The drone of engines could be heard faintly in the distance. In moments a dozen planes swept across so low that the leaves rustled, and continued toward Taivu Point.

All during the morning P-400's, Wildcats and dive bombers from Henderson searched along the coast but each time the big dog's warning barks came in time. Then the Americans began to attack the area blindly. Nishino scrambled behind a log, chased by a line of tracers that reminded him of the stitches of a sewing machine. He heard the whistle of falling bombs. Explosions shook the earth and he was showered with branches and dirt. A dozen men were killed.

That night Nishino went to sleep in one of the abandoned huts of the village but was wakened by a voice shouting, "Guard Company, rally!" A figure looked into the hut. "Newsmen, report to headquarters." Nishino and his five men ran toward the beach through the dark jungle. In his eagerness Nishino slammed into tree after tree before he came to Kawaguchi's command post behind a sand dune overlooking the sea. Over the rumble of surf came the sound of motors.

"Prepare to fire!"

Peering over the edge of the dune, he saw the outline of landing craft not a hundred feet away. Nishino didn't have a helmet and he was afraid he'd die before he could file his first story.

"Fire!"

Bullets ricocheted off the sides of the landing craft. There was no answering volley. A voice cried out in Japanese, "My arm! I've been hit!"

"Cease firing!" shouted an officer behind the dunes. "They're friends."

"*Oi!*" called a voice from the beach. It was one of the men from part of the second echelon of the Ichiki Detachment; they were to join Kawaguchi in the attack on Henderson. Two men were killed and eight wounded. Worse, the fusillade had alerted the Americans and within minutes the jungle was illuminated by flares. Planes began strafing and bombing the village and the beach. A young soldier near Nishino cried out in pain, "I'm wounded! My shoulder." He writhed and grimaced. Nishino held a towel to the wound. "Please don't make fun of me," said the youngster. "We're going to suffer real pain in battle, aren't we?"

Although the Americans had discovered Kawaguchi's position, he refused to move; he was waiting for a report that Oka had landed on the other side of Henderson Field. Why had he allowed himself to be talked into letting Oka go by Ant Freight? Day after day while Vandegrift's planes strafed and bombed the village Kawaguchi waited in vain. One day Nishino counted seventy-one raids. The entire area was a desolation of bomb craters and smoldering tree trunks. The men were afraid to build fires and subsisted on fruit and raw rice.

At three o'clock on September 4 a report finally came from Colonel Oka: he was "approaching" Guadalcanal in his motorboats. Kawaguchi ordered First Lieutenant Nakayama to take three men and circle behind the airfield; they were to locate Oka and tell him the details of the joint attack, since it was too dangerous to send the information by radio. It was a hazardous mission, said the general, and success in the battle depended on perfect timing. He presented Nakayama with the only personal item of food he had brought from Palau—a can of sardines.

Kawaguchi gave the scouts a two-day start, and just before sunset on September 6 led the way along the beach. He left 300 men and a few artillery pieces behind to guard the supplies but still was far above strength with 3,100 troops; 1,000 were from the second Ichiki group. At Koli Point, ten miles east of Henderson, they would turn south and strike off into the jungle to circle behind the field.

Ships were skirting the shore so closely that Kawaguchi could hear the sound of winches. Across the water came faint voices—speaking English. Orders were passed down the line to crouch in place. Nishino peered out and in the light of the moon saw what looked like a cruiser, five destroyers and five transports. As the cruiser began moving along the coast toward Henderson, followed by the transports and destroyers, Nishino made out the silhouettes of sailors on the decks. It was the first time he had ever seen the enemy.

Kawaguchi guessed the ships had just transported Marines up the beach for a surprise attack on the village he had evacuated. He hoped the guard detail could hold off the enemy but he couldn't afford to send a single man back to help them.

It was not a landing force, but a convoy from Nouméa—two transports and escort—on its way with more supplies for Vandegrift. The following night there *was* a Marine amphibious landing near Tasimboko. The Marines beached just above the village. The Kawaguchi rear guard put up a token defense, killing two Americans, before disappearing into the jungle. The Marines sailed back with captured documents and Kawaguchi's dress uniforms. "The bastard must have been planning to shine in Sydney society," one Marine remarked.

Oka himself had just landed thirty miles on the other side of Henderson, after delays caused by aerial attacks and storms. During the harrowing, week-long trip down the Solomons passage he had lost 650 men, and the 450 survivors, with no food and little ammunition, were in no shape to fight.

Kawaguchi assumed that the Oka group had arrived intact and on September 8 gathered his officers near Koli Point for a final battle briefing. Nishino stood next to the general in the drizzling rain, taking notes. They would continue along the beach to the Tenaru River and follow it upstream for almost two miles. Here the artillery and most of the Ichiki men would make a crossing and head directly west until they were about a mile and a half east of the airfield. The main body would continue south for several miles, then arc around until it was behind Henderson. In the meantime Oka's 1,100 men would get into position west of the airfield.

A few minutes before nine in the evening on September 13 the artillery group to the east would start a barrage to make the enemy think the attack was coming from that direction, while the Navy laid down a bombardment from the sea. At exactly nine o'clock Kawaguchi and Oka would attack simultaneously from the south and west.

"We will take the enemy airfield by surprise," said Kawaguchi. Handlebar mustache dripping water, he looked up from his notes at the officers who stood stiffly in silence. "As you know, gentlemen, the Americans have been strongly reinforced with men and supplies. Perhaps they are stronger than we are. Above all, their air force cannot be underestimated. Our troops must also overcome difficult terrain problems before we even reach the enemy lines. We are obviously facing an unprecedented battle. And so, gentlemen, you and I cannot hope to see each other again after the fight. This is the time for us to dedicate our lives to the Emperor."

"*Hai!*" The officers shouted the resounding "Yes!" in unison.

The rains slackened. There came a cry of "*Hikoki!*" (Planes!). The men were about to scatter when they heard a derisive cackle and saw a parrot fly off clumsily. For the past few days parrots had been mimicking the men by screeching, "*Oi, Jotohei!*" (Hey, Private First Class!). They had added a third Japanese word to their growing vocabulary.

Kawaguchi laughed with the rest of the officers and brought out a small bottle of whiskey. "Now, gentlemen, before we resume the march, shall we drink to success?" He poured a few drops in the cap of each officer's canteen. He turned to Nishino. "You, too."

In the distance were the dull thuds of explosions. Nishino thought it was American artillery. He had been hearing it day and night. But it came from Japanese bombers and was aimed at Henderson Field; and the night explosions were bombardments from Japanese warships.

"To the detachment's good luck in battle forever," said Kawaguchi. "*Kampai!*"

As the officers started back to their units and a detail began burning important papers, the general pointed out the enemy's positions to Nishino on a mimeographed map. "No matter what the War College says, it's extremely difficult to take an enemy position by night assault." He lowered his voice. "There were a few cases in the Russo-Japanese War but they were only small-scale actions. If we succeed here on Guadalcanal, it will be a wonder in the military history of the world."

They turned inland into jungle that seemed impenetrable, hacking their way through stout vines, traversing dark rain forests, clambering up and down precipitous ravines and rugged ridges. They traveled by night, stumbling over roots and falling into holes. Someone discovered phosphorescent moss and this was rubbed on the back of the man ahead. They sloshed through swamps dank with the stench of rotting vegetation and so treacherous that it took hours to go a few hundred yards. Added to this physical hardship was the growing fear that the Americans would suddenly ambush them.

Nishino's assistants had long since thrown away their cameras and supplies, but he himself refused to give up anything and scrambled at the heels of the long-legged Kawaguchi, conscientiously noting down everything the general said or did.

Dysentery from drinking river water was sweeping the ranks and already more than half the men had malaria. They subsisted on small quantities of dried fish, crackers and hard candy; they still had plenty of rice but dared not keep a fire going for more than a few minutes. On September 10 they reached the Tenaru River and the artillery peeled off, along with most of the Ichiki men, and headed directly toward Henderson while Kawaguchi and the main group kept plodding south to get behind the airfield.

For a week Lieutenant Nakayama and his three men—Corporal Abe, Lance Corporal Inenaga and Private First Class Morita—had been pushing ahead of Kawaguchi trying to make contact with Colonel Oka. They were half starved, exhausted. Their uniforms were ripped, their bodies slashed with deep cuts. They had fought off an attack by a native and his pack of ferocious dogs with saber and bayonets, and waded miles down a mountain stream only to find it so deep near the bottom that they had to turn around and struggle all the way back.

On the day Kawaguchi's force separated, they heard the distant rumble of engines. They were approaching the airfield. They turned west and at every clearing expected to come upon Oka. But they met no one and by dark were at the end of their endurance. Nakayama opened their last provision, Kawaguchi's can of sardines. The fish seemed to melt in their mouths. They sucked juice from vines and lay down to sleep. The next morning they were stopped by a wide dark-blue river. (It was the winding Lungga, which, a mile downstream, went past Henderson Field.) They waded toward the sea close to the bank and in the afternoon came to a small barren hill. Nakayama climbed it. On the other side, Americans squatted around a fire. It was the heart of the Marines' western perimeter. The crackle of frying and the smell of meat was almost unbearable.

The four scouts circled the Americans and came to another clearing blasted out of the jungle by bombs. There were a dozen foxholes—all empty except for discarded ammunition boxes and cans of rations. What kind of soldiers were these Americans? The scouts ate ravenously. It was as though they had "a new life." One of the men broke wind.

"It seems you're at last feeling human," said Nakayama.

"Yankee, smell my fart," was the cocky reply.

They crossed the river and kept moving due west into a patch of jungle, finally emerging from the dense growth into another clearing. The sun was painfully dazzling.

"*Oi!*"

Startled, they turned. A Japanese sailor, bare from the waist up, rifle in hand, stared at them. They embraced the sailor and began pummeling him. The sailor thanked them for coming. His eyes seemed abnormally large and bright. "You are friends in need," he said. His unit had been stationed at the airfield, and since the invasion had eaten nothing except berries which tasted delicious but turned putrid in the mouth. Every day at least one man died without complaint, "only licking his palms" for a last taste of salt. The sailor began weeping and dropped on his knees. "Please, soldiers, avenge us."

For two more days the scouts struggled west through the jungle and finally reached the Mataniko River, seven miles from Henderson. It was the morning of September 13, the date of the general attack. Would they ever find Oka? They turned north and followed the river downstream. At two-fifty Nakayama saw soldiers ahead fording the river. They were small. Japanese. It was the Oka group.

Nakayama found enough strength to relay the battle plan to Oka

Green Hell

before collapsing at the colonel's feet. Almost inaudibly he said he was ready to die in battle.

"Let us die together," said Oka. He looked at his watch. In six hours the attack was scheduled to start. For the first time since landing he broke radio silence and informed Kawaguchi that he was moving east.

Kawaguchi had reached his jumping-off point the previous night, a hill three miles south of Henderson. Under deep jungle cover the men were making a final check of their equipment. The general had called in his company and platoon leaders. He told them it was essential to break through the American lines that night and retake the airfield. "You must put the enemy to rout and crush them by daybreak. The time has come for you to give your lives for the Emperor." In Rabaul he had been informed there were 5,000 Americans guarding Henderson, but if all went well his 2,100 men, Oka's 1,100 and the artillery-Ichiki group of more than 1,000 would be victorious.

2.

Earlier that morning General Vandegrift had surveyed the wreckage of Henderson Field caused by the naval bombardment the night before, and told his operations officer, "We're going to defend this airfield until we no longer can. If that happens, we'll take what's left to the hills and fight guerrilla warfare." He now had more than nineteen thousand troops but still felt outnumbered. According to reports, sizable Japanese detachments had landed on both sides of Henderson and were preparing to close in. For two weeks enemy warships had been shelling the Marine positions at night almost at will and his men were becoming increasingly intimidated by these fearsome raids—the Tokyo Express. His little air force was fighting off bomber attacks almost daily, but losses were heavy and he didn't know when replacement crews and planes would arrive.

Vandegrift was certain of one thing: there would be no help from the Navy for some time. Recently Rear Admiral Turner had flown in with a message from Ghormley: a shortage of ships, planes and supplies prevented the Navy from giving further support to the Guadalcanal operation.

The Marines all along the perimeter were instructed to dig in, wire up tight and get some sleep. An attack could come at any time.

At dusk Kawaguchi's 2,100 men stealthily started down the hill toward the airfield. They came to a grassy plain and crossed it in the ghostly light of the new moon. They stopped and readied for the attack. Nishino felt someone grasp his hand. It was a private named Hayashi who had become a close friend since their departure from Palau. He had enlisted three months after graduating from college and was engaged to be married, but had left Japan so unexpectedly that he had not even said good-bye to his fiancee. "Perhaps I'll be killed tonight," he said. "I often used to think of going back home and marrying my girl but now I don't have such dreams. This is my address. When I'm dead, will you write to my . . . mother?"

Nishino squeezed his hand reassuringly, hoping that Hayashi, in turn, would write his wife if he was killed. Quietly the men stacked their knapsacks. Those who had fresh underwear changed; they wanted to be clean when they died. Officers crisscrossed each other's backs with strips of white cloth so their men would be able to follow them in the dark. Lieutenant Kurakake went them one better. In Borneo he had bought a large bottle of Guerlain for his wife. He doused himself with the perfume and said, "Follow your noses."

Kawaguchi had just learned that a winding ridge, running from north to south, lay between him and Henderson. It was a natural barricade, but since there was not enough time to circle it, he gave orders to storm the tip end from the front and sides.

Kawaguchi moved out with Nishino close behind, notebook in hand. He carried an Eastman 8-mm. movie camera and two still cameras, strung across his chest like a Mexican bandit's bandoleer. Someone slipped. There was a light metallic clink. A rifle shot cracked.

Again silence. A twig snapped, followed by two more reports. How could the enemy have discovered them so soon? An officer stumbled across a wire. He whispered to keep quiet and probed on the ground until he found something—a small black object that resembled a microphone. It had to be some kind of listening device. Young Private Hayashi found three more like it and brought them to Kawaguchi. "*Kakka-dono* [Your Excellency, sir]," he said, saluted and stood at rigid attention.

Kawaguchi was amused. He explained to Hayashi that in addressing officers up to a colonel's rank, it was proper to use "*-dono*." "You should simply address me as Your Excellency Kawaguchi."

"But I thought it would be impolite if I didn't add 'sir'!"

Cautiously they moved forward through the dense undergrowth until they reached the southern tip of the ridge. Here they were forced to split into two sections. One of Nishino's shoelaces, rotten from the jungle march, snapped and when he stooped to tie it, someone bumped into him.

"*Yama* [Mountain]," he whispered.

"*Kawa* [River]," came the countersign.

There was a shout from a bush just ahead. A grenade exploded and in the flash Nishino saw an American. A smaller figure lurched with a bayonet and the Marine fell. Again there was eerie silence, then another grenade explosion, a shriek of pain. Nishino noticed the scent of Guerlain and moved toward it.

"Japs!" some American shouted. Silence. "Japs! Front five!"

A few minutes before nine o'clock the quiet was shattered by a series of blunt explosions. It was the artillery unit Kawaguchi had left to make the diversionary attack. Almost immediately these guns were joined by a distant rumble and then the jarring crash of heavy shells. Japanese warships were once more bombarding Henderson.

At nine o'clock shouts of "*Totsugeki!*" (Charge!) echoed along the line. Led by dark figures wearing the unearthly white crosses, Kawaguchi's 2,100 men closed in on the tip of the ridge.

The Marines dug in on the serpentine ridge were under the command of Colonel Merritt ("Red Mike") Edson. They were outnumbered about 3 to 2. The Raider Battalion held the center and right flank, while the left flank was manned by the Parachutists under Harry Torgerson, a burly, pugnacious captain who had had most of his trousers blown off in a dynamite attack on a Tulagi cave.

Red signal flares shot up, followed by a barrage of Japanese mortar fire. The sky seemed full of fireworks. Parachute flares burst overhead, momentarily blinding the Marines. The Parachutists on the left heard a rhythmic slapping of gun butts coming from the foot of the ridge and a chant repeated over and over: "U. S. Marines be dead tomorrow!" Figures filtered through the darkness below, swarmed up the ridge.

One forward company, Captain Justin Duryea's, was almost cut off. He ordered smoke pots. The flash of explosions reflected against the billowing smoke and someone yelled "Gas!" In the confusion the companies on the advanced slopes began to pull out of their exposed positions. The withdrawal endangered one flank of Major William J. McKennon's company, but he knew the ridge had to be held at all costs or it would be the end of Henderson. He moved his men back slowly, spreading them out to right and left.

Torgerson was all over the left flank rallying his troops with encouragement and insults. He shouted at the men by name and dared them to attack. A few lagged back, were kicked into place, and the entire line started forward.

The Japanese rushed to meet them, supported by desultory light-machine-gun fire. But three of McKennon's machine guns opened up, bowling over the Japanese "like tenpins." A second wave surged forward and was hurled back. It was, thought McKennon, like a rainstorm beating down, subsiding and resuming a moment later with equal fury.

On the crest of the ridge Colonel Edson was talking to one of his captains on the phone. A voice broke in: "Our situation here, Colonel Edson, is excellent. Thank you, sir." It was obviously no Marine. The Enemy had tapped the line somewhere and this meant the Raider company on the right was cut off and had to be pulled back. The line out front was dead, so Torgerson sent a noncom forward; his bull voice could be heard above the din of battle: "Red Mike says it's okay to pull back!"

The entire end of the ridge seemed engulfed by Japanese, and Edson hugged the ground, telephone in hand, until he saw Marines scrambling to the rear. He grabbed two as they went by and yelled, "The only thing the Japs have that you don't is guts!" He picked up his phone and called in artillery. "Closer, closer," he said as he watched fountains of dirt march steadily toward him.

The attack was broken, but within half an hour there was another. It was preceded by smoke bombs and shouts in English of "Gas attack! Marine, you die!" In the smoke and confusion Edson was no longer able to maintain contact with his commanders. He ordered his outnumbered men back to the northern end of the ridge, a half mile from Henderson Field.

The Japanese stumbled over bodies of their own men in a blind rush forward—slowed but not stopped by machine-gun fire and an almost continuous barrage of grenades and mortar shells. In the vanguard on one side of the ridge were the remnants of a battalion led by a captain named Kokusho. Their headlong charge was interrupted by the discovery of a pile of Marine field rations. They wolfed down ham, sausage and beef. Kokusho lit an American cigarette, took a few deep puffs, and ordered his men to move out again against a battery of antiaircraft guns up ahead. "I'm not going to let any of you get in front of me, understand?" He cocked his helmet back, raised his sword and shouted *"Totsugeki!"*

They were caught in a cross fire, but Kokusho reached one of the guns followed by a handful of his own troops and a group of artillery men armed with bamboo spears. Kokusho was wounded in the face, and his uniform was splattered with blood. He gave a cry of *"Banzai!"* and started for the next gun position. He was staggered by a bullet but he leaped onto a gun platform. As he triumphantly raised his sword, a grenade exploded in his face. From the ground he mumbled *"Totsugeki! Totsugeki!"* and died, sword still in hand.

All along the ridge devastating fire from the Americans was stopping the most fanatical charges. Round after round from 105-mm. howitzers, some fired as close as 1,600 yards, tore into the attackers. At two-thirty in the morning Edson picked up his phone. "We can hold," he told Vandegrift.

Dawn revealed the ridge as a slaughterhouse. From now on it would be known as Bloody Ridge. Six hundred Japanese were sprawled in the grotesque positions of death. There were forty dead Marines. The dazed defenders congratulated one another on being alive and exchanged stories of the enemy: the wounded who called for help—and exploded hidden grenades when an American approached; prisoners who kept pleading "Knife!" and pointing to their bellies.

Survivors were still making suicidal forays. Vandegrift was in front of his command post reading a message. He looked up at the cry of *"Banzai!"* to see three Japanese charging headlong at him; one of them, an officer, was flourishing a sword. Shots cut down all three at Vandegrift's feet.

The Japanese slowly withdrew toward Mount Austen, to reorganize, dragging hundreds of wounded with them. A rough count was taken—only eight hundred effectives remained. Nothing had worked according to plan. They had run into a rugged natural barricade, and the Marine defense had been unexpectedly strong. Moreover, a vital element had been missing; Colonel Oka never joined in the battle.

The colonel's position remained a mystery until that afternoon, when firing was heard from the northwest. Oka was at last attacking! But the crackle of fire died down almost immediately. Obviously he had met more than he could handle and would be of no help. A second assault was doomed before it started. Nevertheless, Kawaguchi was resolved to make a suicidal effort to redeem his failure—at least he would die in battle. At dusk he again led his men toward Henderson Field. After a two-hour march the ridge loomed once more before them. This time they started circling around it.

Kawaguchi gave the order to charge, and eight hundred men loped forward in the dark. Marine artillery had zeroed in on the area, and the Japanese were engulfed in a hell of explosions. It was far worse than the night before. Machine-gun bullets ripped through the brush. The ground shook incessantly like a never-ending earthquake. Trees toppled over; red-hot pieces of shrapnel whistled through the air. Kawaguchi could not turn back. He pressed on toward the airfield, but there was no escape anywhere. Fire followed their advance and eventually pinned them down. All night they hugged the ground. At dawn there were a few pitiful bursts from the last Japanese machine guns, the crump of mortar explosions in return, then silence.

"Okasan!" pleaded a soldier, calling for his mother. Another youngster wanted water and clutched at Nishino's leg with one arm; the other was a gushing stump. Nishino shook his canteen. Empty. He put the damp spout to the soldier's dry lips. He gulped, smiled wanly and died.

The sun was blinding and Nishino found it difficult to keep his eyes open. They burned and everything looked milky. What had been jungle was a barren wasteland. A few tree trunks stood like ruined Grecian columns. Nishino saw Yoshino, his liaison man, stagger to his feet and called to him in a croaking voice, "Hit the dirt, you fool!" Yoshino dropped beside him as a mortar round exploded yards away. Nishino covered his eyes and ears. He shivered from a malaria chill. Shells continued to plow into the ground probing for them. He felt his body slowly rise in the air and fall—again and again—as in a slow-motion movie. Overcome by an irresistible drowsiness, he let his head come to rest on the leaves. His body seemed to be sinking into something unknown and he wondered if he was going to sleep or if he was dying. Faces came to his mind: first his city editor, Honda; then his wife, looking very sad. There followed a procession of friends and, strangely, Verlaine and François Villon. He heard distant thunder like the crash of a tidal wave, and his body was again slowly lifted from the ground. He felt his breast pocket; a seashell rosary was still there, and the amulet Honda had given him for luck at the time when he told him not to get killed. He could see a little better. Less than a half a mile away was the end of a runway; they had almost made it to the airfield. As if in a dream, he started to creep back.

3.

The Battle of Bloody Ridge had ended but Vandegrift's men, wracked by dysentery, fungus infections and malaria, scarcely resembled victors. The real crisis in the Pacific, however, was one the Marines on Guadalcanal were not even conscious of. Operation Shoestring had opened with three heavy carriers. Then *Enterprise* was so badly damaged in the Battle of the Eastern Solomons that she had to return to Pearl Harbor for extensive repairs. A week later the submarine *I-26* put a torpedo into *Saratoga*. Only twelve men were injured—Admiral Fletcher was one of them—but it would be months before the big ship could return to duty.

This left *Wasp*—and *Hornet,* which had arrived too late for the Battle of the Eastern Solomons. And the day after Bloody Ridge two Japanese submarines, *I-15* and *I-19,* penetrated the destroyer rings around these two flattops and moved into position to fire torpedoes. It was a clear, pleasant day with a brisk 20-knot trade wind. *Wasp* had just slowed down in order to launch twenty-six planes and take aboard eleven others which had been out on patrol. Startled lookouts saw torpedoes—a spread from *I-19*—approaching "hot, straight and normal," and gave the alarm. The skipper, Captain Forrest Sherman, ordered a turn to the right, but two torpedoes plunged into the starboard side of the carrier. Explosions shuddered through *Wasp,* and she began to list heavily.

Five miles away, torpedoes from *I-15* were churning toward *Hornet.* They all missed her but just before three o'clock one struck the battleship *North Carolina,* blasting a hole eighteen by thirty-two feet below the water line. Two minutes later another ripped open the destroyer *O'Brien.* The fires on *Wasp* were already out of control. A monumental explosion rocked the carrier. At three-twenty Sherman was forced to abandon ship. The Navy had one battleship and one carrier to back up the Marines on Guadalcanal.

On the hillside overlooking Bloody Ridge, Kawaguchi, uniform in tatters, faced the battlefield, bowed his head and clasped his hands together in prayer for the dead. Now his task was to get his men back safely to the coast. He decided it was shorter to keep heading west and follow the path of the scouts he had sent to search out Oka.* By the second day hundreds of walking wounded had collapsed, and exhausted litter carriers had to abandon scores of others on the trail. There was no order at all. They traveled in groups of fifteen or twenty, each at its own pace. Nishino's left arm was useless and he was weak from malaria. Weighted down by his heavy money belt of 50,000 yen, he followed the ragged column along the slopes of Mount Austen, through endless jungles. There was nothing to eat but grass, moss and an occasional betel nut. He passed scores of bodies in blood-soaked uniforms. Most had outstretched arms as if reaching for something.

By the sixth day the noncoms had to lash the younger soldiers with switches to keep them moving. Nishino could hardly put one foot in front of the other. Just before noon he emerged from the dark jungle into a palm grove. Ahead was an endless expanse of

* More than half of the Ichiki men returned on their own to the coast in the other direction, the way they had come.

green sea. They had come out at Point Cruz, seven miles west of the airfield.

"*Oi!* The sea!" a soldier shouted and led the way into the surf, clothes and all. They gulped down salt water. Nishino called out a warning but one private shouted back, "I don't mind if I die!" Nishino tried a mouthful of water but had to spit it out. He picked several little stones and licked the salt; it tasted almost sweet. He gathered another handful of pebbles and went back to the grove.

All afternoon they lazed around, drinking coconut milk, eating the white meat and discussing the battle. "We say we have Japanese *seishin,* but those Yankees have their own, don't they! On the night of the thirteenth when we attacked the gun position, an American jumped at me but I bayoneted him. He screamed, but just before he died he set off a red signal flare. In a moment mortar shells came in all around us. My comrades all died. Only I escaped."

There was silence. "That's Yankee spirit," murmured another man.

"That's it."

"They love their country too. We're not the only ones."

Guadalcanal already had a new name—Starvation Island. *Ga,* the first syllable of Gadarukanaru, means among other things "hunger." Even during the indescribable ordeal of the march to the sea, one sentence always brought sardonic laughter: "The sky may fall but never Gadarukanaru"—the line supposedly uttered by the Navy commander of the island just before the Americans landed.

On September 18, four days after the Bloody Ridge battle, the Marines were reinforced with 4,200 men of the 7th Marine Regiment. They landed along with trucks, heavy engineer equipment, ammunition and supplies, and for the first time since he had been left stranded by the Navy, Vandegrift felt in control of the situation. He had a total of 23,000 men and an aggressive if dwindling air force that was more than holding its own.

But this confidence was not shared by his superiors. The next day Hanson Baldwin, the military correspondent for the *New York Times,* informed him that Washington was extremely alarmed by the situation on Guadalcanal, and Ghormley's headquarters in Nouméa even more so.

The aggravated Vandegrift said he "could neither understand nor condone such an attitude." It was obvious that the seizure of Guadalcanal "had caught Japan away off guard," and intercepted messages "pointed in certain cases to mass confusion at top command levels."

"Are you going to hold this beachhead?" Baldwin asked. "Are you going to stay here?"

"Hell, yes. Why not?"

Kawaguchi decided to send the reporters back to Rabaul. Nishino wanted to stay, but the general told the *Mainichi* group they had to leave. "After you've gone we shall fight resolutely and I hope to welcome you again on this island, gentlemen."

Nishino grasped his hand. It was bony, hot from fever.

At Shortland Island, Nishino transferred from a destroyer to the transport *Daifuku,* where he ran into an old acquaintance, Major General Yumio Nasu, commander of an "infantry group" of the 2nd Division.* The general failed to recognize him until he introduced himself.

"Ah so, Nishino, you seem to be terribly ill," he said. "Gadarukanaru?" He moved his chair nearer. His division was bound for Guadalcanal and he wanted firsthand information. Nishino hesitated, but Nasu said, "I'd like to hear what an amateur thinks about things."

Nishino told about the fate of the Kawaguchi Detachment, of incessant air raids, of the Marines' use of electric warning devices, their endless food supplies, their inexhaustible ammunition and their surprising *seishin.*

"It's very serious," the general muttered. "What should be done?"

"Under such circumstances, I would say that if we keep sending in forces piecemeal, they will be swallowed up one by one. It's the worst thing to do, don't you agree, sir?" Nasu's interest encouraged him to be candid. "If I talked like this to anyone else, I'd probably be sent off to jail." Japanese soldiers were being asked

---

* Before Pearl Harbor, a Japanese army division had two infantry brigades, each with two infantry regiments. After Pearl Harbor, a division had one infantry group consisting of three infantry regiments.

Green Hell

to give their lives without proper equipment and supplies. "The last hope of our soldiers before they die is to see planes marked with the Rising Sun. They tell me they have the spirit to fight without food, but they can do very little on spirit alone."

"I agree," said Nasu. "It's a great pity we don't have enough planes and ships to do what you want."

Nasu was the vanguard of a new offensive to take Henderson Field. In Rabaul, General Hyakutake had decided to go to Guadalcanal and take personal command of the campaign. He was going to bring with him the 17th Army artillery—field pieces, 100-mm. guns and huge 150-mm. howitzers.

A series of joint Army-Navy meetings convened in 17th Army headquarters to co-ordinate the operation. One of the observers was Lieutenant Colonel Tsuji, "God of Operations." He had persuaded his superiors in Tokyo to send him south to find out what was really going on at Guadalcanal.

Tsuji listened without comment as General Hyakutake and the Navy argued endlessly over the means of transporting the 2nd Division to Guadalcanal. The Navy insisted that they be sent by the usual "Rat Express" or "Ant Freight." The general said the risk was too great; the 2nd Division had to be taken as a body in one large convoy under powerful naval escort. Impossible, said the Navy. They couldn't afford to provide more than "rat and ant" transportation: "How can we shake a sleeve we don't have?"

The Navy's refusal to commit important surface units to the operation enraged Hyakutake and he delivered a reckless threat. "If the Navy lacks the strength to escort the Second Division properly to Guadalcanal, we will go in transports without any escort. And Seventeenth Army Headquarters will lead the way!"

Tsuji knew that if Hyakutake was forced to abide by his rash plan, it meant almost certain destruction of all the transports, and he abandoned his role as observer. He met privately with Hyakutake and offered to fly up to Truk, where he could present the general's arguments direct to Admiral Yamamoto.

Tsuji found Yamamoto on the battleship *Yamato* in the great Truk harbor. The admiral was on the floor of his cabin engrossed in writing bold Japanese characters with a brush—perhaps it was a poem for some admirer or a slogan for a schoolboy. His short, powerful body seemed to be bursting from his uniform.

Yamamoto listened in silence, occasionally nodding his head, as Tsuji dramatized the sacrifices made by the detachments which had previously been sent to Guadalcanal: "Our supply has been cut off for more than a month. Officers and men have to dig grass roots, scrape moss and pick buds from the trees and drink sea water to survive." They were all thinner than Gandhi. The new invasion force must be transported intact, and with supplies, to the island or it too would fail. "I beg you provide it with a strong escort. If the Navy finds it impossible to do this, then Army Commander Hyakutake is determined to lead the convoy himself and is prepared to be wiped out in his attempt to retake the island."

Yamamoto began to speak slowly. He admitted that the mistakes of the Navy had aggravated the hardships of the soldiers on Guadalcanal. "Very well," he said deliberately, "I, Yamamoto, will be personally responsible. If necessary, if we have to bring *Yamato* alongside the island, I promise to escort the transports the way the Army wants. There is only one thing—to save my face, don't let Hyakutake-*san* sail on a transport. Please have him go on a destroyer so he can land safely. His command capabilities are needed on the island."

Tears streaked Yamamoto's impassive face. Tsuji, also in tears, impulsively wished he could die under Yamamoto's command as a Navy staff officer.

There were many officers in the Japanese Army who would not have accepted—as Yamamoto so readily did—the realities of Guadalcanal. Nishino had just arrived in Rabaul by transport from Shortland, intent on making a report in person to 17th Army headquarters. He was taken to the office of the adjutant, a lieutenant colonel named Fukunaga, who asked, "How's the island?"

Nishino disliked him on sight. He was haughty and his well-fed body looked greasy—so unlike the skeletons on Guadalcanal. "Our friends on Gadarukanaru are now surviving on fighting spirit alone. But it won't last much longer. Let me beg you, sir, to supply them with as much food as possible—"

"Are you criticizing the Army?" he accused.

"This is not criticism." Nishino explained that he only wanted to tell the truth about Guadalcanal. He began to feel dizzy and put his hands on the adjutant's desk to steady himself.

"This is the tropics," said the colonel. "Why are you so pale?" It too came out like an accusation.

"I've been in the jungle. There's no sunlight there."

"You just lack *seishin!*"

"My *seishin* saved me from the hell of Gadarukanaru. If you go there, you'll see." It was useless to talk to such a fool. He turned to leave.

"Eat tomatoes, that'll do you good!" Nishino was almost at the door when he heard, "Hey, you!" Fukunaga's voice was ominous. "Just remember, we'll never let you return to Japan. It would be like sending a spy back home."

16

"I Deserve Ten Thousand Deaths"

1.

Before Colonel Tsuji left *Yamato,* Admiral Yamamoto put his verbal promise on paper: the Combined Fleet would escort the 2nd Division transports to Tassafaronga Point, and Henderson Field would be shelled by battleships on the eve of the landing. Yamamoto went further. He saw in Guadalcanal yet another opportunity to force the Decisive Battle that obsessed Japan's military leaders. Once Hyakutake launched his general attack on the airfield and began to make progress, Combined Fleet would compel the U. S. Navy to wage a major engagement. It would be the end of American naval power in the Solomons and the beginning of the end of their authority in the Pacific.

Tsuji returned to Rabaul to work out final plans for the attack on Henderson with General Hyakutake's senior staff officer. Colonel Haruo Konuma—his father ran a small silk-weaving plant—had followed the classic military route: cadet school, Military Academy and War College. Chief of the Strategy and Tactics Section of the General Staff at the time of the American occupation of Guadalcanal (even he had not heard of the island), he was not involved in the operation until September. To dislodge the enemy, he concluded, it would take a full division, heavy guns, tanks and substantial quantities of ammunition and supplies. But these could not be transported to Guadalcanal without wholesale support by the Army air force. The Navy fliers were trained to screen warships rather than transports.

Operations Chief Takushiro Hattori saw the merit of his argument but vetoed it; he was afraid that the Soviet Union might attack the Kwantung Army if so many planes were withdrawn from Manchuria. Although his plan was rejected, his services were not. He was selected to go to Rabaul as Hyakutake's operations officer. Konuma refused at first. He not only doubted the feasibility of retaking Guadalcanal—Ichiki and Kawaguchi had already failed miserably—but had no confidence that the Navy would supply strong enough escorts for convoys.

It took more than the persuasion of his department chief to change his mind. Colonel Tsuji, his close friend and classmate at the War College, offered his services as unofficial adviser, and his reputation for overcoming all obstacles was such that Konuma, albeit reluctantly, took the post.

The first problem he faced in Rabaul did not originate with the Navy but with the Army. Hyakutake's chief of staff, General Akisaburo Futami, was a sick man, which may in part have accounted for his conviction that Guadalcanal was a lost cause. At every meeting—even at the conferences with the Navy—he would repeat over and over again, "We must not try to retake Guadalcanal; we have no chance of winning there!"

By-passing Hyakutake, Konuma radioed the Army General Staff direct, demanding a replacement. Before the day was over, Futami was relieved but there continued to be command problems. Since Kawaguchi had failed, the younger staff officers wanted him taken off Guadalcanal and returned to Tokyo lest his critical attitude toward Imperial Headquarters infect newcomers. But Konuma remembered him as an able and bright officer and arranged to have him brought up to Rabaul for interrogation. Kawaguchi arrived in a torn, filthy uniform. His report of the tribulations of his detachment was irrefutable and Konuma advised Hyakutake to let him command one of the units in the coming attack. Who else knew the conditions and terrain so intimately?

Recently arrived reinforcements and supplies allowed Vandegrift to set up a complete perimeter defense, studded with foxholes and machine-gun emplacements, and following hills and ridges wherever possible. There was enough barbed wire to surround the entire front with two bands of double-apron fencing.

With more than nineteen thousand men Vandegrift at last felt ready to inaugurate a limited offensive of his own against the concentration of Japanese to the west. On September 23 he sent one battalion southwest; upon reaching the slopes of Mount Austen, it began looping back toward the sea along the east bank of the Mataniko River closely tagged by another battalion. Surprisingly, they met no resistance. As these two forces approached the mouth of the river, they were joined by a third battalion which had come the easy way, along the coast.

The following day, September 27, the Marines tried to push across the river but were unexpectedly pinned down by enemy fire. A message back to Colonel Edson, commander of the joint forces, got so badly scrambled in the heat of action that "Red Mike" took it to mean that his troops had successfully crossed the Mataniko. Consequently he ordered another battalion to make an amphibious landing at Point Cruz and trap the retreating enemy. This battalion landed without opposition and advanced 350 yards inland before the enemy attacked from both flanks. Badly mauled, the Marines fought their way back to the beach and were evacuated under heavy fire to a destroyer. Sixty Americans died.

There were no more than five thousand Japanese scattered on both sides of Henderson and most of them were starving. Probably not more than half that number was capable of bearing arms, but these men were prepared to fight to the death. Their first aggressive reaction at the Mataniko convinced Vandegrift that he was facing a much stronger force. The Navy, which had abandoned the Marines after the Savo debacle, did not agree. Admiral Turner wrote Vandegrift that it was time to press the enemy. "I believe you are in a position to take some chances and go after them hard," he said.

Stung, Vandegrift radioed back that reconnaissance "would tend to show that we may expect an attack in force from additional troops to be landed some time around the first of October when the moon is favorable to such landing and operations." Accordingly, he added, a major Marine push would be dangerous. He was irked that Turner couldn't realize that the Japanese were merely slacking off while they mounted a new offensive.

Two days later Admiral Nimitz flew in and patiently listened to Vandegrift's argument that the principal mission of the Marines was to hold Henderson Field. The admiral was sympathetic but noncommittal. That evening over a drink he said, "You know, Vandegrift, when this war is over we are going to write a new set of *Navy Regulations*. So just keep it in the back of your mind because I will want to know some of the things that ought to be changed."

"I know one right now. Leave out all reference that he who runs his ship aground will face a fate worse than death. Out here too many commanders have been far too leery about risking their ships."

Nimitz smiled, but something about his manner gave Vandegrift the feeling that he understood the problems on Guadalcanal and would send out more air, ground and sea reinforcements. Heartened by Nimitz' visit, Vandegrift decided to launch another limited attack to keep the enemy off balance. This time he ordered a full regiment to move down the coast from the east to the mouth of the Mataniko, and sent three battalions through the jungle about a mile inland to cross the river secretly upstream and catch the Japanese in a pincers.

The regiment reached the east bank of the river and began making obvious preparations for crossing. Men moved about noisily, and amphibious tractors rumbled around just behind the lines. This diversion allowed the three battalions to cross the Mataniko on the morning of October 9 without being discovered. They then wheeled sharply to the right toward the sea, entrapping the Japanese along the west bank. Tons of artillery and mortar shells were dumped onto the Japanese positions. Those who tried to escape over the ridges were caught in the open and cut down by automatic-weapon fire. The Marines reported that more than seven hundred Japanese (almost one third of their entire effective force on the island) lay dead along the Mataniko. The Marines lost sixty-five.

Yamamoto kept his word, and that midnight the transports carrying the 2nd Division, as well as 17th Army Headquarters, safely reached Tassafaronga Point. General Hyakutake—accompanied by Kawaguchi, Konuma and Tsuji—waded ashore. With them was

Major General Tadashi Sumiyoshi, commander of 17th Army artillery units.

As bags of rice and other supplies were brought to the shore, ragged figures emerged from the brush and timidly approached. They looked like walking skeletons; their hair was long and dirty and their torn, begrimed clothing no longer resembled uniforms. One man told Tsuji they were survivors of the Ichiki and Kawaguchi detachments and they had come to help unload the supplies.

Kawaguchi led Hyakutake and his party down the beach toward the new headquarters of the 17th Army. It was dawn, October 10, by the time they reached their destination near a small river five miles west of the Mataniko. At breakfast Hyakutake received a report that most of the rice unloaded the night before had been stolen by the volunteer coolies. "It is my fault for having brought such loyal soldiers to such a miserable lot," said Hyakutake. "May they fill their stomachs with our food and be remade into good soldiers."

All along the coast near Hyakutake's headquarters the last survivors of the Battle of Bloody Ridge were stumbling out of the jungle. Their ribs protruded. Their black hair had turned a dirty brown and could be pulled out in patches. Their eyebrows and eyelashes were dropping off and their teeth were loose. For almost three weeks no one had had a bowel movement and their bodies were so starved for salt that the sea water tasted sweet. The water brought on a painful urge to evacuate but they were too weak. They had to help each other with fingers. The relief was indescribable.

The dismay that Hyakutake felt at the sight of such suffering was compounded when he learned the details of the devastating defeat at the Mataniko. He radioed Rabaul: SITUATION ON GUADALCANAL IS FAR MORE SERIOUS THAN ESTIMATED, and asked for more reinforcements and supplies at once.

Furthermore, the Marine victory made it necessary for Konuma and Tsuji to draw up another battle plan, to start in about ten days. Instead of attacking straight down the coast across the Mataniko, they would make a surprise night attack on Henderson from the rear. While the 2nd Division pushed through the jungle behind Mount Austen, General Sumiyoshi would keep the Americans occupied by shelling their positions from the west bank of the

Mataniko and then, several hours before H-hour, launch an infantry attack of regiment size as a diversion—and draw the Americans to the Mataniko. At H-hour Lieutenant General Masao Maruyama, commander of the 2nd Division, would launch a simultaneous two-pronged attack from the south. The main body—commanded by General Yumio Nasu, who had first learned about Guadalcanal on Shortland from Nishino—would turn left and come up the corridor between Bloody Ridge and the Lungga River while the right flank, under Kawaguchi, advanced to the east of the ridge over almost the same ground he earlier fought. Kawaguchi felt apprehensive about the plan but he was in too precarious a position to argue that this particular terrain was too rugged for an attack, particularly since it was logical to make a flanking attack where the enemy least expected it.

Success depended on the prompt arrival of artillery and ammunition, as well as on the completion of a semicircular trail which led behind Mount Austen and then northward along the Lungga River to a point just below the airfield. Fortunately it had been started a month earlier and was almost finished. It ran fifteen miles through jungle so thick that men could not walk upright for more than a few paces. The Army Engineers had only hand tools with which to cut down large trees and hack through tough vines as thick as a man's arm. The felled trees were placed along either side of the trail; bushes and roots were cut away. Log roads spanned marshes, and camouflage netting hid stretches across grass plains. Ravines as wide as a hundred feet were bridged with thick vines, with smaller vines serving as handrails up steep inclines.

It was already nicknamed "the Maruyama Trail" after the resolute commander of the 2nd Division. Maruyama was a mild-looking man, imperturbable under fire. He had no illusions about the difficulties of his mission but realized its significance. Before they set out for Guadalcanal he told his troops: "This is the Decisive Battle between Japan and the United States, a battle in which the rise or fall of the Japanese Empire will be decided. If we do not succeed in the occupation of these islands, no one should expect to return to Japan alive."

The first answer to Hyakutake's urgent call for reinforcements was a modest force of two small seaplane carriers and six destroyers. They came down Solomons passage at full speed on October 11, bringing four big howitzers, two field guns, an antiaircraft gun, ammunition, assorted supplies and 728 troops.

They were sighted by a B-17, and at dusk an American task group of two heavy and two light cruisers and five destroyers, commanded by a veteran of World War I, Rear Admiral Norman Scott, speeded at 29 knots from its hiding place less than a hundred miles below Guadalcanal, to catch the enemy convoy before it reached the island. Unlike previous American units, Scott's was ready and eager for night battle; for weeks the crews had been kept at their stations from sunset to dawn. What Scott didn't know was that lurking behind the convoy was a special bombardment force—the three heavy cruisers and two destroyers of Rear Admiral Aritomo Goto.

The sky was slightly overcast and the sliver of a new moon gave off almost no light. There was a gentle breeze as Scott approached Cape Esperance from the southwest just before ten-thirty, cruisers in column, one destroyer on either side. Scott planned to turn right at the cape in order to contact the enemy and be in position to hit the transports when they tried to unload on the north coast of Guadalcanal. He signaled his ships to form a single column and prepare for battle.

About forty miles to the northwest Goto was approaching Savo with his three cruisers in column—the first was his flagship, *Aoba*—flanked by the two destroyers. The transport group was ahead, just off Cape Esperance, and starting down the coast toward Tassafaronga Point to land its valuable cargo.

Around eleven o'clock the eight ships were discovered by one of Admiral Scott's planes but reported only as "one large, two small vessels." Friend or foe? Scott wondered. And, if enemy, where were the rest of the transports? He set out to look for them and turned left to pass six miles west of Savo. The light cruiser *Helena* had already picked up the Japanese column with its new SG search radar, but her commander, Captain Gilbert C. Hoover, wanted to make sure before passing on the information to Scott. The flagship *San Francisco* was not yet equipped with SG, and Scott had no idea that Goto was bearing down on him. Upon reaching the north end of the little volcanic island at eleven-thirty, he ordered the entire column to reverse course. Two minutes later the nine ships started heading back to the southwest at 20 knots, patrolling the passage between Savo and Cape Esperance. After ten more minutes Captain Hoover at last signaled Scott that there was definitely an enemy six miles to the northwest and coming fast.

Then the light cruiser *Boise* reported "five bogies." Scott was confused; "bogey" usually meant an unidentified plane. At last *San Francisco*'s less efficient radar found Goto's flagship just 5,000 yards away. Before Scott could determine whether it was friend or foe, Captain Hoover got a message from a lookout: "Ships visible to the naked eye." By voice radio Hoover asked permission to open fire. Scott laconically answered "Roger," meaning "Message received," but fortunately Hoover took it for its code meaning, "Commence firing." And so, shortly before midnight, *Helena* opened up on Goto.

With no radar at all, Goto was taken completely by surprise. As other ships joined in the bombardment, he assumed that the transport convoy was firing on him because it had mistaken him for the Americans in the dark. He ordered the column to turn right and almost immediately was knocked to *Aoba*'s deck, mortally wounded, by one of the shells exploding the length of the cruiser.

Like Goto, Scott imagined friend was attacking friend and ordered Cease Firing a minute after the first shots. It took him another four minutes to learn the truth, but once Scott was sure it was the enemy out front, he bore in tenaciously to give the Japanese their first real challenge in a night battle. The action was furious and bold, with both sides loosing salvo after salvo on the other and refusing to back off. By the time all firing had ceased, about twenty minutes after midnight, the waters between Cape Esperance and Savo were ablaze with flaming ships. *Aoba,* though hit forty times, escaped up The Slot with the dying Goto, but the cruiser *Furutaka* and the destroyer *Fubuki* were sinking.

The American task group was also hurt. *Boise* was an inferno and the magazines threatened to go up at any moment. Then sea water cascaded in through a shell hole, flooding the magazines. Only one of Scott's ships was in desperate shape, the destroyer *Duncan;* its fires could not be controlled. For the first time the Japanese had been beaten at their own game—night battle—and the Americans were elated. The humiliating Battle of Savo had been avenged. Victory it was, but as at Savo, where Admiral Mikawa had allowed the American transports to land, the Battle of Cape Esperance had diverted the winners from the Japanese convoy. During the fierce melee, the transports were putting ashore the artillery, ammunition and reinforcements that General Hyakutake needed so desperately.

The seesaw battle of supply, however, went to the Americans the next day, October 13: 2,852 GI's of the Americal Division, along with sixteen British Bren-gun carriers, twelve 37-mm. guns, ammunition, trucks and a mountain of provisions were unloaded at Lungga Point in spite of two bombing raids. Now Vandegrift had 23,088 men to defend his perimeter, and judged by Japanese standards, he was unbelievably rich in all kinds of supplies.

Still, there was no time for complacency. At noon two dozen Japanese planes bombed Henderson from an altitude of 30,000 feet with devastating accuracy, and before Seabees could clear away the worst of the rubble, another fifteen bombers droned over to rip up the airstrips. Combat Engineers swarmed back to work and finished filling in the holes. There was an unearthly shriek followed by an explosion on the main runway. General Sumiyoshi had already moved up the first of his 150-mm. howitzers to the Mataniko River and he continued to pound the field so unerringly that the Marines nicknamed the long-range gun "Pistol Pete."

Nor was this the end of Japanese harassment for the day. At dusk two battleships, *Kongo* and *Haruna,* plowed toward Guadalcanal, along with six destroyers. The big warships hoped to blast Henderson out of existence with their mighty 36-cm. guns.* Together they carried over nine hundred shells. Some were Type 3 incendiaries, but most were the brand-new Type Zero armor-piercing bombardment shells.

Just before midnight the raiders, still undetected by the Americans, approached Guadalcanal at 18 knots, guided by oil drums set afire by Japanese infantrymen. *Kongo* led, with *Haruna* a thousand yards behind, all sixteen of their big guns trained to the south. Shortly after one o'clock, October 14, they began spewing out incendiary shells. In moments Captain Tomiji Koyanagi, skipper of

---

* The diameter of their barrels was slightly over 14 inches.

Kongo, could see a lake of fire to starboard. It was Henderson! He gave orders to load up with the new armor-piercing shells. The cannonade became even more deafening, and on Guadalcanal spouts of flame shot up from exploded fuel and ammunition depots. The Marines burrowed into their foxholes or crouched helplessly in shelters as the earth shook. It was the most terrifying experience in their lives and Vandegrift himself was shaken. Finally, after half an hour, the firing stopped. "I don't know how you feel," said his operations officer, "but I think I prefer a good bombing or artillery shelling."

Vandegrift nodded. "I think I do—" His words were cut off by a violent explosion. The concussion bowled over everyone in the shelter. *Kongo* and *Haruna* had resumed the bombardment on the return trip up the coast.

So far, not a plane or ship had gone out to challenge the Japanese, but now four torpedo boats from Tulagi rushed at them, launching torpedoes and spraying the area with machine-gun fire. It was a gallant gesture, but they were driven off by destroyers and their torpedoes skipped past the battleships.

For an hour and a half the bombardment continued. With ammunition almost exhausted—814 armor-piercing shells and 104 incendiaries had been flung at Guadalcanal—the Japanese were ordered to cease fire. *Kongo* and *Haruna* turned north, slipping between Savo and Tulagi at 29 knots.

Henderson Field had been blasted almost beyond recognition. Bits of clothing and equipment dangled from phone wires. Forty-one men lay dead, many others were wounded. Vandegrift's tiny Cactus Air Force ("Cactus" was the code name for Guadalcanal) was a shambles. There was almost no aviation gas; only thirty-five fighters and seven dive bombers were operable. Army fliers eyed the ravaged field and wondered if they could get in the air with their P-400's and Airacobras. "We don't know whether we'll be able to hold the field or not," a Marine colonel told them. "There's a Japanese task force of destroyers, cruisers and troop transports headed our way. We have enough gasoline left for one mission against them." He told them to load up with bombs and go after the enemy. "After the gas is gone we'll have to let the ground troops take over. Then your officers and men will attach yourselves to some infantry outfit. Good luck and good-bye."

Gone were the high hopes of yesterday; a feeling of doom settled over the island. The night bombardment had done more than physical damage; Marines would never forget the primal terror that came when the very earth writhed and exploded in the dark.

The report that another Japanese convoy was heading for the island was true. Six big new high-speed transports loaded with four thousand men, fourteen tanks and a dozen 15-cm. howitzers and assorted supplies were coming down The Slot protected by destroyers and fighter planes.

The Cactus Air Force managed to get eleven planes off the ground, but the best they could do was slightly damage one destroyer. By midnight the transports were unloading off Tassafaronga Point as two heavy cruisers, *Chokai* and *Kinugasa,* ranged up and down the coast lobbing in 8-inch shells. Their captains had been so sure they would be sunk that all men had been told to prepare to swim for shore and join the soldiers as infantrymen. But like the battleships, *Kongo* and *Haruna,* they escaped without damage up The Slot after firing 752 shells.

Three empty transports also managed to withdraw; however, the other three were still unloading at dawn when the remnants of Vandegrift's planes, after a frantic scramble for fuel, took to the air. All three ships were set afire and had to be run aground. Most of the tank fuel went up in flames, detonating countless rounds of ammunition, but the troops aboard did make it to shore along with the tanks and howitzers. Now Hyakutake had more than fifteen thousand able-bodied men and adequate artillery. He was as ready as he ever would be for his offensive.

Vandegrift suspected that most of the supplies had been landed and radioed Nimitz, Ghormley and Turner that at least fifteen thousand Japanese and a considerable amount of equipment and supplies were now on the island.

... OUR FORCE EXCEEDS THAT NUMBER BUT MORE THAN HALF OF IT IS IN NO CONDITION TO UNDERTAKE A PROTRACTED LAND CAMPAIGN DUE TO INCESSANT HOSTILE OPERATIONS ... THE SITUATION DEMANDS TWO URGENT AND IMMEDIATE STEPS: TAKE AND MAINTAIN CONTROL OF SEA AREAS ADJACENT TO CACTUS TO PREVENT FURTHER ENEMY LAND-

INGS AND ENEMY BOMBARDMENT SUCH AS THIS FORCE HAS TAKEN FOR THE LAST THREE NIGHTS; REINFORCEMENT OF GROUND FORCES BY AT LEAST ONE DIVISION IN ORDER THAT EXTENSIVE OPERATIONS MAY BE INITIATED TO DESTROY HOSTILE FORCE NOW ON CACTUS.

Nimitz' inspection of Guadalcanal and Nouméa had convinced him that Ghormley had to be replaced with a more aggressive commander, a man who would see opportunities rather than difficulties. On October 18 he radioed Halsey:

YOU WILL TAKE COMMAND OF THE SOUTH PACIFIC AREA AND SOUTH PACIFIC FORCES IMMEDIATELY.

Halsey got the message moments after his flying boat touched down on the waters of Nouméa harbor. He read it twice in wonder and then exclaimed, "Jesus Christ and General Jackson! This is the hottest potato they ever handed me!" He went from astonishment to apprehension. He knew only enough about the situation in the South Pacific to realize it was desperate; and he regretted having to relieve his old friend Bob Ghormley, who had played on the same football team at the Academy.

Halsey ordered Vandegrift to fly down to Nouméa. The Marine general reported that his men were "practically worn out" by more than two months of lean diet, disease, bombings, bombardments and *banzai* attacks, and had to have air and ground reinforcements.

The stocky Halsey, gray eyebrows bristling, thoughtfully drummed his fingers on the desk. "Are we going to evacuate or hold?" he asked.

"Yes, I can hold. But I have to have more active support than I have been getting."

Admiral Turner protested. The Navy was doing all it could to send in more supplies, but there were no warships to protect transports, neither was there a base at Guadalcanal where they could find shelter. Moreover, enemy submarines were getting more numerous and increasingly aggressive.

Halsey knew Turner was right, but Guadalcanal *had* to be held. "All right," he told Vandegrift, "go on back. I'll promise you everything I've got."

2.

On Guadalcanal 5,600 men of Maruyama's 2nd Division—not including artillery, engineer and medical troops—had begun their march toward Mount Austen. They planned to be in position to attack on the night of October 21. Just before they left, Hyakutake's senior staff officer, Colonel Konuma, took Tsuji aside and said he had hoped to direct operations in person but had to remain at 17th Army headquarters to act as chief of staff. "Would you go in my place?" he asked. There was nothing Tsuji wanted better. Besides, he would have "jumped into fire" for a friend like Konuma.

Starting off with a compass and a single inaccurate map, General Maruyama led his force down the trail. The first day was an easy walk through coconut groves and over barren ridges, and that night the men settled down as if it were a camping trip. But at midnight a torrent of rain beat down on the sleeping men. They tried to protect themselves with huge umbrella-like leaves. Shivering, soaking wet, miserable, they huddled together for warmth.

The next day the long line was swallowed up by a dark, dense, hilly forest. The white-haired Maruyama led the way, pushing himself forward with his white cane. Beside him General Nasu, a *hachimaki* tied around his forehead, was wracked by malaria, but he continued stolidly without complaint. At a break he called to Tsuji, "I have something good but there's only a spoonful left." The general reached for a round cigarette tin which was attached to his waist by a string, much in the same way his ancestors had carried pillboxes. Tsuji found about a spoonful of sugar at the bottom of the can and poured half into his palm. He gave the rest to his aide. Nothing had ever tasted so sweet.

The Maruyama Trail narrowed, forcing the men to walk single file. The winding column crossed hill after hill, rivers, streams, inching forward slowly, painfully, like a great worm. Each man carried, in addition to his pack, some part of a field gun, a shell or other equipment. Since it was too dangerous to cook, all—from Maruyama to the lowliest private—lived on half rations of rice. They scaled steep cliffs with ropes, hauling up light field pieces and machine guns by sheer muscle. But by the third day the task was too much except for the hardiest, and gun after gun had to be abandoned at the side of the trail.

Since it was obvious that they could never keep their schedule, Maruyama radioed 17th Army headquarters that the attack would have to be postponed one day. On October 22 Maruyama still had not reached his line of departure and he made another postponement of twenty-four hours. By afternoon his men had circled around Mount Austen. Here the 2nd Division split in two, with Nasu and Division Headquarters continuing on the trail directly toward Henderson Field. Kawaguchi, who would command the right flank, turned off to the southeast with three infantry battalions and three machine-gun and trench-mortar battalions.

As Kawaguchi left the main body, he encountered Tsuji. The colonel had no use for Kawaguchi. First, he was a loser and a complainer; second, he was one of the so-called "liberal" officers who, like Homma, had tried to save captured Filipino leaders from their just fate—death. But the general was not aware of his enmity. "I'm glad to find you here," he began and went on to discuss his misgivings about the Tsuji-Konuma plan of attack. It could not possibly work: although Nasu would be attacking over fairly good terrain on the left flank, his own advance on the right would be over much the same ground where his detachment had suffered such a disaster in September. The area around the ridge was just too rough for a frontal type of assault.

"Have you seen the Navy's aerial photographs?" he asked. In his opinion these recent pictures indicated that the Americans had greatly strengthened and enlarged their perimeter defense. "They show clearly that I have no chance of success with a frontal assault. I would like to lead the right column in a circle *behind* the enemy's eastern flank." This was a point southeast of Henderson, with nothing but rolling open hills, fields and sparse woods to traverse. He knew that section well from personal observation. Nasu could advance as planned, and the two forces would catch the Americans in a real pincers.

"I don't need to see the pictures," Tsuji replied. "I'm familiar with the terrain and I agree fully with your proposal." Kawaguchi wanted to take his suggestion to Maruyama, but Tsuji assured him that wouldn't be necessary. "I will explain personally to His Excellency Maruyama. I wish you great success." He extended his hand. "Well, the battle is really getting interesting, isn't it?" he said and laughed. As Kawaguchi was soon to find out, the Machiavellian colonel never told Maruyama about the conversation.

On the morning of October 23, Maruyama was not yet in position and made a third postponement, issuing final orders to launch the general attack the following day at midnight. He added his personal exhortation for every officer and man "to fight desperately and fulfill his duty in repayment of His Majesty's favor."

Kawaguchi didn't get the message until midafternoon, when he was still at least a day and a half's march from his new line of departure. In the emergency he cable-phoned Maruyama that he couldn't get into position in time. Maruyama curtly replied that there could be no further delays, and it suddenly dawned on Kawaguchi that the division commander knew nothing about his verbal agreement with Tsuji of the day before. Controlling himself, Kawaguchi said, "In that case, I will carry out the night assault with my advance unit, the Third Isshiki Battalion."

Maruyama began shouting that Kawaguchi would follow orders to the letter. With that he slammed down the receiver, so angry that his hair seemed to bristle—the stories about Kawaguchi were apparently true. He got Kawaguchi on the phone again. "Major General Kawaguchi," he said stiffly, "report immediately to Division headquarters." He was to turn over command of the right flank to Colonel Toshinari Shoji.

It was Tsuji himself who phoned 17th Army headquarters with the information. "Kawaguchi refused to advance," he told Konuma, "and the division commander relieved him of his command." He gave no details.

On the coast General Sumiyoshi was ready for his diversionary attack. All his heavy artillery and ammunition had been manhandled into position several miles west of the Mataniko River. Early that evening, the twenty-third, he opened his attack, a day ahead of time. He had not received notice of the third postponement.*

---

* After the war Maruyama and Hyakutake blamed each other for failing to notify Sumiyoshi in time. The latter said it had been Maruyama's responsibility to keep Sumiyoshi informed of the final postponement. The former claimed that Hyakutake had overestimated the progress of the march and had directly ordered the Sumiyoshi attack on the twenty-third.

After a heavy bombardment he sent nine tanks across a sandbar in the van of his infantry. They were met by a counterbombardment so effective that only one tank managed to reach the other side of the river. It ran into the sea, however, wallowing about in the surf until it stalled and was blasted to pieces by a 75-mm. tank destroyer. Six hundred Japanese infantrymen lost their lives.

It was a useless gesture. The diversion had failed and by now the Americans were alerted. The next afternoon they discovered that the enemy was behind Henderson in force: first a column was detected crossing the foothills of Mount Austen, then someone noticed a Japanese officer studying Bloody Ridge through field glasses, and finally a Marine from the Scout-Sniper Detachment reported seeing "many rice fires" rising out of the jungle two miles south of the ridge.

Tsuji and Konuma had guessed correctly that Vandegrift never expected a major attack from this direction. But unlike the Kawaguchi Detachment, which had arrived behind Henderson undiscovered, Maruyama's presence was now known. Marine Colonel Lewis "Chesty" Puller, a short man with a pouter-pigeon chest who had survived a hundred combats in the "banana wars" of Haiti and Nicaragua, walked along the lines south of the airfield personally checking the positions. He ordered his men to dig in deeper and to set up more sandbags. Shell fragments and other pieces of metal were hung on barbed wire to give audible warning of any surprise assault at night, while men using bayonets as scythes cut fields of fire in the seven-foot-tall grass out front. Lookouts were posted on top of a barren knoll. Puller's Marines were ready.

Maruyama wasn't—but thought he was. Nasu was in position on the left, but Kawaguchi's replacement, Colonel Shoji, had encountered such precipitous ravines and dense jungles after leaving the Maruyama Trail that he had not yet been able to get his main body to the original line of departure.

An hour before midnight huge drops of rain fell slowly, heavily, like blobs of oil. They plummeted faster—and faster, becoming an almost solid sheet of water. Maruyama, his staff and Tsuji scrambled up a disintegrating hill to a small flat ledge. The staff sat in a tight circle, huddling together around Maruyama to keep him warm. A few minutes after midnight they heard small-arms fire from the right. It grew in intensity. Had Shoji broken through or been thrown back?

A report finally came in by phone from Matsumoto, a division operations officer on liaison duty with Shoji. "The right flank attacked the airfield," he cried. "The night attack is a success!"

"*Banzai!*" Maruyama shouted impulsively.

Now they could hear firing on the left—the ping of rifles and the low chuckle of machine guns. It was Nasu. Then a roar of mortar and heavy-artillery fire. The Americans! The response was so immediate and so intense that Tsuji feared something had gone wrong. The others—including Maruyama—were infected by his anxiety and sat rigid.

The phone rang again. "I was mistaken about the success of the right flank," said Matsumoto. "They haven't reached the airfield yet. They crossed a large open field and thought it was the airfield. It was a mistake." Shoji's meager vanguard, forced to attack prematurely at midnight, was already pinned down.

The bombardment on the left continued, louder than ever. An hour passed without a report from Nasu. Tsuji was struck with "an omen of doom" and his bones "felt cold."

Nasu's first charge had been forced back by a furious mélange of Marine small-arms, automatic-weapon and artillery fire. Critically ill from malaria, Nasu remained near the front, more afraid of dying from the disease than of the explosions around him. His troops—the 29th Regiment—regrouped, but a second charge in a new direction was stemmed by Puller's men. Again and again Nasu's men tried to penetrate the American defenses, hastily shored up by GI's of the Americal Division, but each attack grew weaker.

In the rear Kawaguchi sloshed disconsolately through the jungle in search of Maruyama's headquarters. To the right he heard the rumble of battle. He slumped against a tree as rain streamed over his head. His career was over. What did life have to offer now? Curling up in the hollow of some tree roots, he dozed off, wondering almost disinterestedly if the rain would wash him away.

By dawn Nasu had lost half of his troops. Practically the entire 29th Regiment, the best in the 2nd Division, had been wiped out. Its commanding officer and the regimental flag were missing.

"*Soka* [That's it]," muttered Maruyama when he heard the report. His staff advised him to withdraw, but he would not listen.

He phoned Nasu and said Division was giving him its last reserves for an all-out attack the following night.

It would have been normal for a commander who was called upon to launch a major attack after a crushing defeat to ask for more time to prepare. "Let me carry out the attack *tonight*," Nasu replied in a feverish voice. He gave no reasons and was so insistent that Maruyama acceded; Nasu would know what was best.

Nasu called for another shot to control his temperature, which was already over 40 degrees Celsius (104 degrees Fahrenheit), and prayed that he would live to lead the assault.

The first message to Admiral Yamamoto from his liaison officer on Guadalcanal was *"Banzai."* It was code for "We have seized airfield." Yamamoto radioed Vice Admiral Kondo to head south with his armada, which included Nagumo's *Kido Butai,* and force the Americans into a battle. Another, much smaller naval group— eight destroyers and the light cruiser *Yura*—was already on its way to back up Maruyama's assault on the airfield with a daylight naval bombardment.

A second message from Guadalcanal about the continued fighting at the airfield failed to deter Yamamoto and his staff, but a third, at 6:23 A.M., announcing that the Americans held Henderson, made Yamamoto hesitate. With the airfield still a threat he ordered Kondo to mark time, so his formidable aggregation of vessels milled around three hundred miles northeast of Guadalcanal.

But the *Yura* force, oblivious of what had taken place, continued down the channel. By the time its commander learned that the airfield had not fallen, planes from Henderson swept down on his ships. A bomb plunged into *Yura*'s central boiler room, killing all occupants. The cruiser sluggishly started back north, but other bombs turned her into a helpless hulk. The skipper, Captain Shiro Sato, gave the order to abandon ship, then tied himself to the bridge with a rope.

Yamamoto was right in thinking that the Americans would come out to challenge any carrier force moving south. In Nouméa, Halsey had already ordered the commander of Task Force 16, Rear Admiral Thomas Kinkaid, to bring his ships—two carriers, *Enter-*

prise and *Hornet,* nine cruisers and twenty-four destroyers—to a point off the Santa Cruz Islands, about four hundred miles east of Guadalcanal. Kinkaid was to stop any carrier force heading toward the island.

On the afternoon of October 25, American patrol planes discovered two large enemy groups 360 miles from Task Force 16. From his flagship, the *Enterprise* (back in action after around-the-clock repairs in Pearl Harbor), Kinkaid sent out a search and then a strike, but *Kido Butai* had seen one of the enemy patrol planes, a PBY. Nominally Admiral Nagumo was under Kondo but in reality he acted independently, and without asking Kondo's permission, he ordered a turn north, away from a confrontation.

Yamamoto, however, had already decided that there was to be a fight no matter what the outcome of the battle for Henderson Field, and Nagumo's hasty withdrawal brought to a head a disagreement over the use of *Kido Butai.* For weeks Yamamoto had pressed Nagumo, without ever making it a direct order, to take his carriers south and engage the American carriers. But his chief of staff, Kusaka, persuaded Nagumo each time that this would be a foolhardy venture; it would lead to another Midway.

Late that afternoon Yamamoto decided to force Nagumo into action. He dispatched a message, deliberately insulting in tone, "urging" Nagumo to attack "with vigor." Nagumo summoned Kusaka to his little battle room under the bridge. Kusaka could see that his chief was upset. Nagumo said he could not ignore Yamamoto's latest message, and he wanted Kusaka's support this time.

"I admit I've objected to your suggestions, but you are the commander and must make the final decisions," Kusaka replied. "It's your battle. If you really want to head south, I'll go along with your verdict." However, he reminded Nagumo, they had not yet located the enemy fleet and warned him that they themselves would undoubtedly be discovered by B-17's operating from Espíritu Santo. "But now that your mind is made up, I want you to know that we shall not be destroyed without first destroying the enemy."

Kusaka returned to the bridge in the gathering darkness and ordered the carrier striking force—three flattops, a heavy cruiser and eight destroyers—as well as the Vanguard Group of two bat-

"I Deserve Ten Thousand Deaths"

tleships, four cruisers and seven destroyers, to turn south toward the enemy at 20 knots.

The two enemy carrier forces were closer to each other than either realized. Admiral Kinkaid (described in the *Annapolis Yearbook* of 1908 as a "black-eyed, rosy-cheeked, noisy Irishman who loves a roughhouse") was coming up toward *Kido Butai* on an aggressive zigzag course.

On Guadalcanal, General Nasu had hastily moved into position for attack. On the left was his own reserve regiment, the 16th, and the remnants of the 29th; on the right were the reserves sent by Maruyama. After nightfall the feeble Nasu led the first charge, using his sword as a cane. He managed to hobble across the line of barbed wire before a volley of rifle fire flashed in the dark. A bullet tore into Nasu's chest. All along the line automatic-weapons fire raked the attackers. Within minutes almost every commander down to the company level was dead or wounded. Their men continued to drive forward. Whenever they were stopped, they reformed and charged again. The GI's and Marines refused to give ground. In the lulls the two sides shouted at each other. "Blood for the Emperor!" yelled a Japanese in English. "Blood for Eleanor!" retorted a Marine. The shouting turned to insults. "Tojo eat shit!" taunted a GI of the Americal Division. There was a moment's pause, then from the other side: "Babe Ruth eat shit!"

The fighting continued until midnight. The assault was crushed and the survivors filtered back over the bodies of their comrades. In two days Nasu's attacks had left more than three thousand Japanese dead or dying in the uprooted jungle. It was as if a fire storm had swept over the area. The wounded Nasu was carried on a litter back to Division headquarters. As he held out a feeble hand to Maruyama and opened his mouth to speak, he died.

3.

Early in the morning on October 26, Nagumo and Kusaka stood anxiously on the bridge of the carrier *Shokaku*. Kusaka's prediction that they would be discovered was borne out at two-thirty; a communications officer reported that a plane, probably a

B-17, was nearby. For twenty minutes Nagumo stood silent, his face "like stone," staring up at the black sky. His vigil was ended by a sudden explosion, and then another. Two huge columns of water geysered near the flagship.*

Nagumo turned to his chief of staff. "What you said before was true. Reverse course, full speed."

Hiding his indignation, Kusaka told the helmsman to head north at 24 knots. He also ordered twenty-four search planes to fan out to the south; he would not be caught as he was at Midway.

The Japanese fleet had been found and it was up to Halsey in Nouméa to determine what to do about it. Obviously a strong enemy force was coming down toward Guadalcanal and it was equally obvious that it was stronger, at least in carriers, than Kinkaid's task force. Just before dawn Halsey made the decision that most Americans in the Pacific were hoping for. He radioed all combat commands: ATTACK REPEAT ATTACK. The United States Navy was at last going on the offensive.

Kinkaid headed toward *Kido Butai* and had no sooner sent out search planes than he himself was discovered by one of the aircraft long since dispatched by Kusaka: ONE CARRIER AND 15 OTHER SHIPS BEARING NORTHWEST. For weeks Kusaka had avoided battle, but with the enemy 250 miles away he unhesitatingly ordered an attack wave to take off at once.

At seven o'clock eighteen torpedo bombers, twenty-two dive bombers and twenty-seven fighters began lifting off *Kido Butai*'s three carriers—*Shokaku, Zuikaku* and little *Zuiho*—and before the last planes left the decks, Kusaka ordered a second wave to follow as soon as possible. Never before had he fussed during a battle, but today he was so conscious of the mistakes of Midway that he kept shouting impatiently from the bridge for *Shokaku*'s deck officers to move faster. Through his glasses he could see that things were going even slower on *Zuikaku*. He stamped a foot angrily and told the flagman to signal: "What's the delay?"

He ranged around the bridge until the last of the dozen torpedo bombers, twenty dive bombers and sixteen fighters of the second wave were airborne. From his window he shouted to hose down

---

* The attack came not from a B-17, but from two lumbering PBY's carrying torpedoes and bombs.

the decks and prepare for enemy attack. Not a single fighter was left to protect the two big carriers and *Zuiho,* but Kusaka, now that he was committed to battle, was so agitated that he did not care. "Bring spears, enemy," he muttered to himself. "Anything!"

The first American strike group left almost half an hour after the initial Japanese wave, and by eight-fifteen there were seventy-three dive bombers, torpedo bombers and fighters winging toward *Kido Butai.* The Japanese and American strike forces passed within sight of each other. For some time neither side broke formation and kept driving on to its own destination, but a dozen Japanese fighters could resist the temptation no longer and swung back. They caught up with a group of nineteen *Enterprise* planes and knocked down three Wildcats and three torpedo bombers at a cost of three of their own planes.

The first Japanese dive bombers were less than fifty miles away when Kinkaid received radar verification. He controlled all fighters from his flagship, *Enterprise,* but until this moment his experience had been confined to battleships and cruisers, and he hesitated momentarily before sending up the Wildcats to intercept. Before they could gain altitude, the Japanese had begun their attack on *Hornet—Enterprise* was ten miles away, hidden by a local rain squall. At nine-ten the Aichis nosed over, plummeting down on the carrier. One bomb hit near the flight deck, two barely missed but battered the hull. The squadron commander purposely dived at the stack. His plane caromed off and plunged into the flight deck, where its two bombs exploded.

Nakajimas were already sweeping in low. Two torpedoes ripped into the engineering space, exploded and shook the entire ship. *Hornet* staggered, came to a stop. As she lay helpless in the water, another group of Aichis began boring in, recklessly raking the smoking ship from stem to stern with half a dozen more bombs. Within ten minutes the Japanese were heading back for home, and *Hornet,* listing 8 degrees, was covered with flames.

Hornet's own Dauntless dive bombers were getting some measure of revenge on *Chikuma,* a cruiser running interference for Nagumo's carriers. A bomb plunged into the bridge. Captain Keizo Komura, standing starboard of the compass, was knocked backwards by the blast. Almost everyone else on the bridge was dead. Komura staggered to his feet, his head roaring; his eardrums were broken. Through the voice tube he ordered the ship to change course. Another bomb hit the bridge. "Jettison torpedoes!" he shouted and someone made a hand signal. Seconds after the last one was released, a bomb exploded in the empty torpedo room.

Another group of Dauntlesses sighted *Shokaku*. Ignoring heavy flak, they dived on Nagumo's flagship in single file. Kusaka felt the ship shudder as the first 1,000-lb. bomb struck. There were more explosions—he lost count. The flight deck was in flames. Was this another Midway? He called the engine room by voice tube and was told there was no damage there. "We can go thirty-two knots, sir." But communications were out and Kusaka decided to transfer the flag to a destroyer. He ordered the helmsman to reverse course and head out of danger. She was followed by *Zuikaku*, a 50-foot hole in her flight deck; she had been put out of action by audacious attacks from two passing American search-plane pilots—Lieutenant Stockton Strong and Ensign Charles Irvine.

Several hundred miles away, forty-three Japanese dive bombers and torpedo bombers were heading for Kinkaid. The dive bombers came first and were picked up by radar at a distance of fifty-five miles. But again Kinkaid hesitated to send up fighters from *Enterprise* to intercept them. Completely unopposed, the Aichis started to dive, and it looked as if America's last carrier in the Pacific would go the way of *Hornet*. Then antiaircraft gunners from *Enterprise* and her screen opened up. The fire was concentrated and accurate—particularly from the battleship *South Dakota* and the cruiser *San Juan*—and only two bombs hit the carrier; a third exploded so close to the hull that a main turbine bearing was damaged. Within minutes, however, fires were contained, machinery adjusted and holes patched, and by the time the Japanese torpedo planes appeared, the big flattop was able to dodge everything fired at her.

More Japanese raiders were less than a hundred miles away and fast approaching—a strike force from *Junyo,* the single carrier in Kondo's Advance Force. It was made up of seventeen dive bombers and escorted by a dozen fighters under Lieutenant (s.g.) Yoshio Shiga, the amateur artist who had distinguished himself at Pearl Harbor. The sun was almost directly overhead, and below he could see whitecaps on the blue sea. At eleven-twenty he spotted a large carrier, pushing forward "with a bone in its teeth." It looked alive but the decks seemed to be empty. Then two fighters took off. (There were other Wildcats hidden in the squall clouds above.)

Until that moment Shiga had been repeating to himself, "Leave some for us," but now his anticipation turned into anxiety. Had the first Japanese wave been knocked down without scoring any hits? The bombers were already forming up for the attack. The fighters were ordered to escort them in their dive, one with one. However, there were more Aichis than fighters, so Shiga signaled that he would protect the first two—a job no fighter pilot relished. Just before leaving *Junyo,* Shiga had cautioned his inexperienced young pilots to stay with the bombers and not be drawn off into duels with enemy fighters. "Don't separate. That's an order." But as he got into position behind Lieutenant Masao Yamaguchi, leader of the bombers, he noticed several of his Zeros lured out of line by the Wildcats in the clouds. It was to late to call them off and Shiga followed Yamaguchi, who was diving directly at *Enterprise* through bursts of ack-ack. At 9,000 feet Yamaguchi lowered his flaps to check speed. Shiga's Zero had no flaps, and to keep from passing Yamaguchi, he had to pull the stick to his stomach and go into a tight loop. He was pressed against the back rest and almost blacked out before coming out of the loop. He glanced around to see if there were any enemy fighters near and to make sure he wasn't blocking the next dive bomber.

Flak blossomed on all sides and he went into a second tight loop, and a third, continually losing altitude. He looked around but couldn't find Yamaguchi. His escort duties were over and he searched for enemy interceptors. Two stubby fighter planes were just ahead. They must be Grumman Wildcats! He had heard awesome stories of their fire power and indestructibility. As he approached they split apart and he banked after the leading one. Strangely, it took no evasive action, and just as he was about to shoot, the other Wildcat came in fast on his tail. This was why so many of his comrades had been shot down lately! He tried to isolate one of the Americans time and again, but the other always darted in on the attack.

Enterprise successfully dodged all of Yamaguchi's bombs, but *South Dakota* and *San Juan,* which had helped save the carrier earlier, came in so close to throw up flak that both were hit. One bomb exploded on the battleship's No. 1 turret and another pierced the cruiser, exploding near the ship's bottom.

A second wave of fifteen planes from *Junyo* found *Hornet* in tow behind the cruiser *Northampton*, and six Nakajimas swept across the water toward the crippled carrier. The cruiser captain ordered the towline cut so that his ship could evade torpedoes. This left *Hornet* almost dead in the water, and without fighter cover. The declining efficiency of Japanese pilot replacements was evident: five torpedoes missed the almost stationary target. But the sixth ripped into the starboard side; there was a sickly green flash followed by a hissing, then a dull rumble. The deck on the port side "seemed to crack open" and fuel oil erupted, flinging sailors down the slanted deck. The after engine room began flooding as the starboard list increased to 14 degrees. The word went out to prepare to abandon ship. Six high-level bombers, also Nakajimas, came over in a perfect V formation. One bomb hit the flight deck just as the Americans began scrambling down lines to the water.

By now Shiga and his fighter pilots had returned to *Junyo* with a report that the carrier seemed "very much alive" when they left her. He recommended another strike. An operations officer asked if he could return in the dark.

"It's not a question of returning," said Shiga. He had expected to die at Pearl Harbor and felt he was living on borrowed time. "It has to be done. If possible, send out a homing signal." Some carrier captains didn't like to reveal their positions this way. "If you don't send it out, I'll come back anyway. Then watch out!" It was half joke, half threat.

Only one officer among the dive bombers had survived the first attack, a plump, baby-faced youngster, Shunko Kato. This had been his first mission and when Shiga awakened him and said they were going to attack again, Kato's face drained of color. "This is a battle to avenge your squadron leader," said Shiga. "That's war."

Kato sat up in his bunk. "Let's go."

Shiga summoned the five fighter pilots he felt could make it back in the dark, and the five men who would pilot the dive bombers. "This is the last attack," he said. "You helldivers do everything Yamaguchi taught you. Get in as close as you can to

"I Deserve Ten Thousand Deaths" 509

the target before releasing your bombs." He turned on his own pilots. "Don't you fighter planes ever separate from me again. If you do, I'll shoot you down."

With Shiga in the lead, the eleven planes took off. In the setting sun he thought he saw something way down. Several minutes later, he discerned ships through the cloud patches, one a carrier. It was the wrong ship, *Hornet,* and was already dead in the water. Kato and his dive bombers hurtled down. This time Shiga managed to stay with Kato until he saw his bomb plunge into the hangar deck. Shiga banked and swept back over the carrier. To his puzzlement there were few figures on the flight deck. It was a dead ship.

His problem now was to return to *Junyo.* He gathered his planes like a mother hen and headed back under darkening skies. Would there be a homing signal? He located the proper cycle on his radio. At first he heard nothing, then came a welcome series of beeps. *Junyo* was transmitting!

Dinner that night for Shiga and his men was grim. There were empty chairs all around the tables, with plates of food standing uneaten. There was no boasting or elation over the triumphs of the day.

The reports of the fliers were so impressive that Kondo's entire Advance Force, as well as Vanguard Group, was sent out to engage the enemy in a night battle. The two intact carriers, *Zuikaku* and *Junyo,* were to follow in case another strike could be launched. The Vanguard Group came upon *Hornet,* her entire length ablaze. She was still afloat despite nine torpedoes from her screening destroyers, which fled at the sight of the enemy. The Japanese, in turn, sent four torpedoes of their own into the abandoned hulk, and finally, at one thirty-five, October 27, the ship that had launched the first planes to bomb Tokyo, plunged out of sight. The rest of the American fleet could not be found. The Battle of the Santa Cruz Islands was over.

An hour before dawn Nagumo and his staff transferred from the destroyer to *Zuikaku.* From reports of pilots and crews Nagumo and Kusaka estimated that at least two cruisers, one destroyer, one battleship and three carriers had been sunk. Midway had been avenged and the Japanese Navy at last ruled the seas around Guadalcanal.

Yamamoto's evaluation was even more favorable. His chief of

staff, Admiral Ugaki, radioed Tokyo that four flattops and three battleships had been sunk. He could not sleep and strolled in the moonlight along the decks of *Yamato,* reveling in the fact that the great victory had come on America's Navy Day. He retired to his cabin and wrote three *haiku* poems:

> *After the battle I forget the heat*
> *while contemplating*
> *the sixteen-day moon.*
>
> *Contemplating the moon,*
> *I mourn*
> *the enemy's sacrifice.*
>
> *Beneath the moon*
> *stretches a sea at whose bottom*
> *lie many ships.*

The Japanese had won a decided tactical victory without losing a ship, but the Americans had gained valuable time and thwarted the enemy's ambitious combined operations to retake Henderson Field. In addition, sixty-nine Japanese planes had failed to return to their carriers, and another twenty-three were lost in emergency landings. It would take months to replace these planes and crews.

But in Tokyo the victory was considered so momentous that the Emperor wrote an imperial rescript praising Yamamoto for the "brave fight" put up by the Combined Fleet. In it His Majesty did predict that the situation in the Solomons would "become more and more difficult." As he presented the rescript to Navy Chief of Staff Nagano, he said, "I add my personal wish to the latter part of the rescript, that is, regarding the struggle for Guadalcanal. It is a place where a bitter fight is being waged between forces of Japan and the United States and is, moreover, an important base for the Imperial Navy. I hope that the island will be recovered by our forces as soon as possible."

By now, however, Yamamoto and Ugaki had privately concluded that it would be next to impossible to retake Guadalcanal. Three times the Army had failed. With the Americans strengthening their garrison almost daily, how could a fourth attempt possibly succeed?

"I Deserve Ten Thousand Deaths"

On Guadalcanal, Hyakutake's chief of staff, Colonel Konuma, had been forced almost to the same conclusion. He was hoping that the Americans would not learn that Maruyama's division had been virtually annihilated; if they did, they might launch an attack of their own that would no doubt wipe out the entire Japanese force on the island.

Colonel Tsuji was on his way back over the Maruyama Trail with a firsthand report of the condition of the 2nd Division. En route he found battalion commander Minamoto lying at the side of the trail, the lower half of his body soaked in blood. "Hold on," Tsuji told him. "We'll have someone come back for you."

"I haven't eaten since day before yesterday," said Minamoto in a weak voice.

From his *hango,* Tsuji put two chopstickfuls of rice in the wounded officer's mouth. Minamoto pointed feebly to a group of his men lying nearby. They opened their mouths like baby sparrows as Tsuji went to feed each one of them.

It took Tsuji five days to reach the coast and 17th Army headquarters. He ordered rice sent to the front and dispatched a radiogram to Army Chief of Staff Sugiyama in Tokyo:

I MUST BEAR THE WHOLE RESPONSIBILITY FOR THE FAILURE OF THE 2ND DIVISION WHICH COURAGEOUSLY FOUGHT FOR DAYS AND LOST MORE THAN HALF THEIR MEN IN DESPERATE ATTACKS. THEY FAILED BECAUSE I UNDERESTIMATED THE ENEMY'S FIGHTING POWER AND INSISTED ON MY OWN OPERATIONS PLAN WHICH WAS ERRONEOUS.

He said he deserved "a sentence of ten thousand deaths" and requested permission to stay on Guadalcanal with the 17th Army. The answer came on November 3:

YOUR APPLICATION FOR TRANSFER TO 17TH ARMY IS NOT APPROVED. RETURN HERE TO REPORT ON BATTLE SITUATION.

Late that afternoon Colonel Ichiji Sugita (who had interpreted for General Yamashita at the surrender of Singapore) turned up at 17th Army headquarters exhausted, his uniform scarcely recognizable. He had been supervising the diversionary action of General Sumiyoshi's troops on the Mataniko River. His face was pale, his eyes strangely bright as he reported that the Americans had broken through the 4th Regiment, the infantry unit holding the bulk of the line on the east bank of the river. "The regimental commander is going to make a last attack with the remaining hundred and fifty men and the regimental flag. I am going with them!"

"Don't be so rash, Sugita," said Tsuji. "There will be no attack. Put the regimental colors in the center and have the men dig in around them. The enemy will never charge; besides, in the jungle out there, artillery and bombing isn't too effective. It's merely a question of holding out another day or two." Reinforcements were already landing. Sugita, leaning on a piece of bamboo, hobbled back toward the Mataniko River.

The reinforcements comprised the advance guard of the 38th Division. With them was another good friend of Tsuji's, Colonel Takushiro Hattori. The newcomer from Tokyo, looking spruce in a brand-new uniform, exuded his usual confidence. As long as this man is alive, Tsuji thought, we don't have to worry. The two shook hands fervently.

The following day General Kawaguchi left the island in disgrace, "feeling as if my intestines were cut." He nursed more hatred for his countryman Tsuji than for the enemy.

17

The End

1.

On the night of November 9, the commander of the 38th Division, Lieutenant General Tadayoshi Sano and his Headquarters detachment arrived at Tassafaronga Point to join the advance guard units. They had come safely down the Solomons passage in five destroyers, but the main body of the division and other reinforcements for General Hyakutake—some 12,000 men and 10,000 tons of supplies—were still at Shortland Island. It was decided to send them all in one convoy—eleven transports and cargo ships escorted by a dozen destroyers. They would be preceded by a Raiding Group—a force of two battleships, one light cruiser and fourteen destroyers—whose mission it was to neutralize Henderson Field by bombardment, after which the convoy could safely make the run to Guadalcanal.

The Raiding Group, under the command of Vice Admiral Hiroaki Abe, started down toward Guadalcanal on the morning of November 12, and by late afternoon was one hundred miles north of Savo Island. The Americans had known of its presence for hours and surmised it was coming either to shell Henderson or to attack an American transport convoy that was anchored off Guadalcanal with 6,000 troops, ammunition, 105-mm. and 115-mm. howitzers, and rations. By dusk the last of these troops had been disembarked, and the transports and cargo ships, with two thirds of the supplies still in their holds, started hastily withdrawing to the south.

They were escorted to the open sea by Task Group 67.4, commanded by Rear Admiral Daniel J. Callaghan, a deeply religious, close-mouthed man. Once the transports were safely on their way to Nouméa, Callaghan turned back and headed along the north coast of Guadalcanal toward Savo. His mission was to stop Abe and he had to do it with two heavy cruisers, three light cruisers and eight destroyers. He would be outgunned by the oncoming Japanese but his was the sole American naval force in the area.

He had recently taken over command from Norman Scott, a classmate at the Academy, and he did what Scott had done at the Battle of Cape Esperance—put his ships in a single line with four destroyers in the lead and four bringing up the rear. It was easier for a column to navigate in such dangerous waters. He rode in the heavy cruiser *San Francisco*, despite its ineffective search radar—perhaps for sentimental reasons, since he had been her skipper and had such a close relationship to the crew that they still called him "Uncle Dan"—though not to his face.

The last thing Admiral Abe expected was any night action. There were no American battleships in the area, and cruisers wouldn't dare attempt to stop him. His two battleships, with *Hiei* in the lead, slipped past the tip of Santa Isabel Island and continued south toward Savo with six destroyers and a light cruiser screening, and with destroyers on either flank to fend off any torpedo boats.

Their course led them into a heavy rainstorm northwest of Savo, but Abe did not reduce speed; the squall would hide them from air, surface and submarine attacks. The storm did not let up, however, and when Abe learned that the weather over Guadalcanal was just as bad, he ordered all ships to make a simultaneous 180-degree turn and reduce speed to 12 knots. Half an hour later the rain stopped, and though Abe had just received a report of Callaghan's presence somewhere in Ironbottom Sound, he ordered another countermarch toward Savo.

It was well past midnight by the time the cone of the little island reared up. The mountains of Guadalcanal beyond were a dim mass.

Ground observers on the island radioed they could see no enemy ships off Lungga Point and Abe decided to make his bombardment run. He ordered the thin-skinned Type 3 shells loaded in all main batteries of the two battleships.

It was not until 1:24 A.M., November 13—a Friday—that the Americans discovered Abe. The TBS (Talk Between Ships) on *San Francisco*'s bridge began squawking: "Contacts bearing 312 and 310, distant 27,000 and 32,000 yards." It was *Helena*. She had picked up Abe's horseshoe screen and the two battleships. Callaghan turned his columns north to try to cross the T.

The range between the two forces closed fast. Five minutes passed, then ten, as Callaghan anxiously kept calling over TBS for further information. Radar was not serving him well, for at 1:41 lookouts on his leading destroyer saw two Japanese destroyers unexpectedly materialize out of the darkness. The destroyer *Cushing* swung hard left to avoid collision, and caused a violent chain reaction down the column.

The cruiser *Atlanta* swerved sharply and Callaghan, on the ship behind, demanded, "What are you doing?"

"Avoiding our own destroyers," replied the cruiser's captain.

There was almost as much confusion on Abe's bridge. On sighting the enemy he had ordered the *Hiei* and *Kirishima* gunners to replace the incendiary shells with armor-piercing rounds. In a stampede, every available man on *Hiei* rushed to stack the Type 3 shells on the deck. There was chaos in the dark and each minute seemed interminable. One enemy round landing in the lines of incendiary shells would make a torch of the big ship.

Four more minutes passed. At 1:49 *Hiei*'s searchlight stabbed through the darkness and found the bridge of *Atlanta*, some 5,000 yards ahead. The American ships reacted quickly and a dozen water spouts rose in front of *Hiei*. Her own 14-inch guns blasted. A salvo of one-ton shells crashed down on *Atlanta*. The bridge disintegrated. Admiral Scott and all but one of his staff were dead.

Only then did Callaghan order, "Odd ships commence fire to starboard, even ships to port." But his column had become intermingled with the enemy and each ship began firing at anything in sight. A spread of torpedoes from one of Abe's destroyers slammed into *Atlanta*, almost lifting her from the water. She settled but was helpless, out of the battle.

Hopelessly entangled, the two forces went at each other at close quarters in the most tempestuous melee of the war.

"Cease firing own ships!" Callaghan ordered, and as the shelling momentarily ceased, *Kirishima* commenced pumping her huge shells at the *San Francisco*. At least four other Japanese ships converged on the American flagship.

"We want the big ones!" Callaghan called to all his ships. "Get the big ones first!"

A shell exploded on *San Francisco*'s bridge killing everyone except the captain, who was mortally wounded, and Lieutenant Commander Bruce McCandless. He was appalled by the sight—bodies, limbs, gear littered the deck. A siren moaned as water poured down from the deck above. McCandless conned the wounded ship through the reckless traffic, toward Guadalcanal.

At 2 A.M. Abe's flagship, battered by fifty topside hits, turned to port, and accompanied by *Kirishima*, steamed north. The battle had lasted for less than half an hour, but Ironbottom Sound was ablaze with burning wrecks. Only one American ship escaped injury, and *Atlanta* and two destroyers were going down. One Japanese destroyer had been sunk and another was drifting, and *Hiei* was so slowed that it seemed likely she would be unable to get out of range of American planes before dawn.

Callaghan's headlong plunge into the enemy had saved Henderson Field from a devastating pounding—at the cost of hundreds of lives, including Admiral Scott's and his own.

The rising sun revealed seven crippled ships off Guadalcanal —five American and two Japanese. Some were burning hopelessly, some were abandoned, and one—*Portland*—was so bent that it kept circling. Nor was the ordeal over. As the five surviving American ships left the scene of battle and made for the New Hebrides, just before 11 A.M., the captain of *I-26* sighted one of them, *San Francisco*, and loosed a spread of torpedoes. They skimmed harmlessly by the damaged cruiser, but one crunched into the port side of *Juneau*. From *San Francisco*, McCandless saw the ship blow up "with all the fury of an erupting volcano." A huge brown cloud boiled up, followed by a thunderclap. When the cloud lifted the cruiser was gone. It was awesome.

Captain Gilbert Hoover on *Helena*, who as senior officer was in command of the little American flotilla, feared that other ships would probably be sunk if he stopped to pick up survivors. And so the four intact vessels raced off without leaving lifeboats or rafts, and some seven hundred men—almost the entire crew of *Juneau*, including the five Sullivan brothers—perished.*

The slow-moving *Hiei* could not escape either. Since dawn she had successfully been fighting off planes until a bomb disabled her steering mechanism and she began to circle helplessly. In the next few hours the big ship was battered by Flying Fortresses and torpedo planes from Henderson Field. Two torpedoes finally left *Hiei* dead in the water. Her crew was transferred to destroyers and moments later she plunged out of sight, stern first.

The loss of a battleship was a serious blow to Yamamoto, but he did not waver in his determination to get the convoy of eleven transports safely to Guadalcanal. And that meant Henderson Field had to be temporarily put out of action. That night there was another run of the fearsome "Tokyo Express"; cruisers and destroyers scudded down The Slot full speed and bombarded the airfield for thirty-seven minutes. It was a terrifying experience for the Marines, but only eighteen planes were destroyed and the runways were operational by the next morning.

The eleven transports, escorted by a dozen destroyers, under the command of the redoubtable Rear Admiral Raizo Tanaka, were already halfway to Guadalcanal, and they continued down the narrows even after two dive bombers from *Enterprise* discovered them at 8:30 A.M. Three hours later, thirty-seven Marine and Navy planes from Henderson swept in and severely damaged two transports. Still, Tanaka refused to withdraw; Hyakutake had to have the reinforcements and supplies. With destroyers belching out a black smoke screen, convoy and escort continued south on a zigzag course. All through the day the attacks continued and the Henderson fliers were joined by Flying Fortresses from Espíritu Santo and by bombers and fighters from *Enterprise*. Tanaka transferred troops from sinking transports to destroyers which then returned to Shortland, but kept his other ships moving ahead. Before the sun set, six transports had been sunk and one disabled. The last four transports, accompanied by the remaining

* The U. S. Navy thereafter never assigned more than one member of a family to a single ship.

four destroyers, drew closer to Guadalcanal in the growing darkness.

Yamamoto ordered Admiral Kondo to lead an attack personally down the Solomons passage with the battleship *Kirishima*, two heavy cruisers, two light cruisers and a destroyer squadron. Such a force under such a commander should be able to blast Henderson Field into oblivion.

This time, however, the Japanese would be opposed by battleships. Task Force 64—two battleships and four destroyers—had been detached from Kinkaid's carriers and rushed ahead to save Henderson. Halsey would have done this earlier had he not been reluctant to leave *Enterprise* (the last operational carrier in the Pacific) unprotected during daylight hours.

Task Force 64 had been hiding all day about a hundred miles southwest of Guadalcanal. Early that evening its commander, Rear Admiral Willis A. ("Ching") Lee, brought it up the west coast of the island. The four destroyers, followed by the battleships *Washington* and *South Dakota*, continued north, past Cape Esperance and Savo. At 10:52 P.M. the column turned to starboard. *Washington*'s radar picked up a ship coming down The Slot. It was Kondo's lead vessel, the light cruiser *Sendai*.

Lee waited for twenty-four minutes before ordering his captains to fire. *Sendai* hurriedly retired, but other Japanese ships moved forward in a resolute attack. By 11:35 all four American destroyers—two of them sinking—were out of action, and *South Dakota*, crippled by power failure, had become the target for *Kirishima* and the two heavy cruisers. The Japanese were so absorbed that they failed to notice *Washington* 8,000 yards off. She rapidly flung seventy-five 16-inch shells at *Kirishima*. Nine smashed home, as did numerous 5-inch shells. The great battlewagon's top structure was aflame and she kept turning in a circle, out of control. The captain slowed the ship in an attempt to steer with the engines, but it was useless.

At 12:25 A.M. Kondo, aboard the heavy cruiser *Atago*, ordered a withdrawal. Lee had prevented him from attacking Henderson and had given him a tactical beating as well. Imagining he had won the battle, Kondo retired to the north under cover of smoke, leaving *Kirishima* and a disabled destroyer behind. *Kirishima*'s captain was finally forced to scuttle his ship. He transferred his crew to a destroyer which returned for that purpose, and ordered the Kingston valves opened. The battleship sank northwest of Savo.

Standing off a few miles to the north, Tanaka witnessed the action with concern. He had already sent three of his destroyers to help Kondo, and now decided to make a run for Tassafaronga Point with his last destroyer and the four transports. There was not enough time to unload the troops before dawn by landing craft and he radioed Rabaul for permission to run the transports aground. Rabaul turned down the request but Kondo told him to go ahead. So much time had elapsed that gray light was already showing in the east as the four big transports plowed into a beach near Tassafaronga Point.

Almost simultaneously eight Marine dive bombers from Henderson, led by Major Joe Sailer, swept in, evaded eight float Zeros and hit the transports with three bombs. They were followed by more Marine Dauntlesses and a succession of Navy torpedo planes. By early afternoon the carnage was so grisly that some American aviators vomited at the sight of the bloody waters covered with fragments of bodies.

Of the 12,000 troops and 10,000 tons of supplies that had left Shortland, only 4,000 shocked men and 5 tons of supplies were safely beached. The three-day naval battle for Guadalcanal was at last over, and it had ended in catastrophe for the Japanese Navy, with 77,609 tons of shipping sunk—two battleships, one heavy cruiser and three destroyers, plus eleven ships of Tanaka's convoy. Hyakutake's hopes for a final great offensive were crushed.

General Vandegrift, who had been the victim of Navy timidity since his landing, for the first time expressed unqualified approval of that branch of the service in an ecstatic message to Halsey:

WE BELIEVE THE ENEMY HAS SUFFERED A CRUSHING DEFEAT—WE THANK LEE FOR HIS STURDY EFFORT OF LAST NIGHT—WE THANK KINKAID FOR HIS INTERVENTION YESTERDAY—OUR OWN AIRCRAFT HAS BEEN GRAND IN ITS RELENTLESS POUNDING OF THE FOE—THOSE EFFORTS WE APPRECIATE BUT OUR GREATEST HOMAGE GOES TO SCOTT, CALLAGHAN AND THEIR MEN WHO WITH MAGNIFICENT COURAGE AGAINST SEEMINGLY HOPELESS ODDS DROVE BACK THE FIRST HOSTILE STROKE AND MADE SUC-

CESS POSSIBLE—TO THEM THE MEN OF CACTUS LIFT THEIR BATTERED HELMETS IN DEEPEST ADMIRATION.

Roosevelt was just as jubilant. Within a few days the Allies had scored four notable victories: the successful landings in North Africa, Montgomery's triumph over Rommel at El Alamein, the gallant Russian stand at Stalingrad—and now Guadalcanal. "For the past two weeks we have had a great deal of good news," he told the New York *Herald Tribune* Forum, "and it would seem that the turning point in this war has at last been reached."

In Tokyo the Army General Staff was still resolved to retake Guadalcanal and made a drastic realignment of forces. Hereafter Hyakutake's entire 17th Army would concentrate on the Solomons while the 18th Army took over its duties in eastern New Guinea, and both operations would be under the command of Lieutenant General Hitoshi Imamura. One of the most respected men in the military service, Imamura had succeeded in taking Java with dispatch as well as quickly establishing order throughout the Netherlands East Indies with a minimum of force. His liberal methods, however, had brought on his head so much criticism from powerful forces in the General Staff itself that for a time his career was in danger.

Imamura began his occupation by releasing Achmed Sukarno from his prison cell. Sukarno, the most influential revolutionary leader in the Indies, was brought to Imamura's official residence, an elegant structure recently occupied by the Dutch governor. "I know that you're not the kind of man who would just obey my orders," said Imamura. "Therefore I won't give you any. I won't even tell you what to do. All I can promise is that I can make the Indonesians a happier people under our occupation if they learn our language. Anything further will have to be done by the Japanese government. I cannot promise independence."

In addition to promoting the Japanese language, Sukarno helped set up a committee of fifteen Indonesians and five Japanese to listen to local grievances. Complaints of Imamura's liberalism reached his immediate superior in Saigon, General Terauchi. He passed them on to Tokyo, and Generals Akira Muto and Kyoji Tominaga of the War Ministry were sent to Batavia to in-

The End

vestigate. Imamura was aggressive in defense of his policy. "I am merely carrying out the Emperor's instructions," he said. "If you find that my administration is not successful, relieve me. But first see the results." They were impressed by what they saw. In their report they advised Prime Minister Tojo and Chief of Staff Sugiyama to give Imamura a free hand.

Now Imamura was to command an Army Group, comprising the 17th and 18th Armies, but his assignment was the most difficult facing any Japanese officer. In Tokyo he went to the Imperial Palace to receive his orders from the Emperor. As the general was bowing himself out, His Majesty said, "Imamura! I understand that my soldiers are suffering terribly on Guadalcanal. Go as soon as you can and save them. Even one day is important." Imamura saw tears glisten on his imperturbable face.

At Army General Staff headquarters, Imamura was told that he and Admiral Yamamoto would work together to intensify air attacks in the Solomons and to reinforce the troops on Guadalcanal. Then the two would mount a joint offensive to retake Henderson Field and Tulagi.

Imamura arrived in Rabaul, New Britain, on November 22. He radioed Hyakutake, who was still on Guadalcanal, that he was sending two fresh divisions within a month; he asked for a complete factual report "without hiding anything."

Hyakutake had just lost a thousand men on the Mataniko front. He radioed Imamura that his troops had been living on grass roots and water for a month.

... AN AVERAGE OF 100 MEN STARVE TO DEATH DAILY. THIS AVERAGE WILL ONLY INCREASE. BY THE TIME WE GET TWO DIVISION REINFORCEMENTS, DOUBTFUL HOW MANY TROOPS HERE WILL BE ALIVE.

The General Staff had not prepared Imamura for this but he was committed to their ambitious plans by his personal vow to the Emperor to retake Guadalcanal. For the moment all the general could do was send a message of sympathy to the men of Guadalcanal calling their bravery "enough to make even the gods weep," and asking them to "set His Majesty's heart at ease" by helping him retake the island.

It was the Army General Staff alone that remained irrevocably committed to the continuation of the Guadalcanal campaign. Their demands for more men, supplies and particularly another 370,000 tons of shipping had finally forced the War Ministry to reassess the situation. The chief aim, at present, said the War Ministry, was to increase the national power and war potential, and the requisition of additional ships would decrease the number of civilian ships, thereby decreasing national power. This would be worse than the loss of Guadalcanal.

The General Staff said it was ridiculous to set up Imamura's new command without giving him ships to transport his troops —he would be "a man without a head."

"Today there is the impression that Japan is on the verge of rise or fall," Colonel Sako Tanemura, who had witnessed most of these arguments, wrote in his unofficial "Imperial Headquarters [Army] Diary" on November 18. It was like the lull before a great storm. "Does the General Staff have good prospects of success? If not, what should it do to get out of the difficulty? The Supreme Command must reflect carefully to cope with this touchy situation. Advance or withdraw! It is very delicate. No one is confident of victory . . . but the fake pride of Imperial Headquarters is forcing us to wage the Decisive Battle on Guadalcanal. If we should be defeated on Guadalcanal, it is certain we will lose the Pacific war itself."

While debate over shipping dragged on, the Navy devised a makeshift operation to resupply Guadalcanal. Large metal drums partially filled with medical supplies or basic victuals with just enough air space for buoyancy were to be strung together with rope and hung from a destroyer's gunwales. Upon arrival at Guadalcanal the string of drums would be cut loose as the destroyer made a sharp turn. A motorboat or a swimmer would pick up the buoyed end of the rope and bring it ashore, where soldiers would haul in the long line of drums.

First test of the new system came on the night of November 29. Admiral Tanaka, on the flagship *Naganami,* led a column of eight destroyers down the Solomons passage at 24 knots. Six of the ships were necklaced with from 200 to 240 drums apiece. The first and last destroyers acted as escort. Just before eleven o'clock the convoy passed west of Savo and swung left toward Tassafa-

The End

ronga. As it approached the point, the six supply destroyers broke off and prepared to loose their drums. There wasn't a breath of wind, and the sea was like black glass.

One of the destroyers discovered ships, bearing 100 degrees, and signaled Tanaka: "Seven enemy destroyers sighted." The admiral gave orders to cease unloading and take battle stations.

Coming toward them was an eleven-ship formation—five cruisers in column with three destroyers on either flank—commanded by Rear Admiral Carleton H. Wright. His flagship, *Minneapolis*, had already made radar contact but the admiral hesitated to send his van destroyers into the attack. Ten minutes later the destroyer *Fletcher*'s radar showed the Japanese on the port bow 7,000 yards away. Her skipper, Commander William M. Cole, asked Wright for permission to fire torpedoes; the admiral again hesitated—he thought the distance was too great—and it took Cole four minutes to convince him it wasn't. At eleven-twenty Cole finally launched ten torpedoes. A moment later Admiral Wright ordered his cruisers to commence firing. "Roger! And I do mean Roger!" Wright said over voice radio. His cruisers opened up with their 5-, 6- and 8-inch guns, and shells began to rain on Tanaka's lead ship, *Takanami*. She was almost ripped to pieces, but the crew continued working their guns until the ship exploded.

The cheering on *Minneapolis* was cut short as the cruiser was jarred twice by Japanese torpedoes. A third ripped into the port bow of *New Orleans;* two magazines exploded, ripping off the forward part of the ship. Almost simultaneously *Pensacola* was staggered by a hit below the mainmast on the port side, which flooded her after engine room.

While *Northampton* was avoiding the three damaged cruisers, *Oyashio* sent two torpedoes into her. The explosions were so cataclysmic that men on the bridge of nearby *Honolulu* broke uncontrollably into tears. *Northampton* listed sharply to port, afterpart in flames, and had to stop to check flooding. But she was beyond help and sank stern first.

Tanaka had already withdrawn. In the half-hour battle he had whipped the much heavier American force. At the cost of a single destroyer and without radar, he had sunk one cruiser and badly damaged three others. But his mission had failed; not a drum was delivered to the starving men of Guadalcanal.

Two nights later Tanaka made a second attempt. This time seven drum-laden destroyers survived an ineffectual Allied air raid, and reached Tassafaronga Point intact. The drums, 1,500 in all, were cut loose, but little more than 300 could be hauled to the beach. Tanaka tried again several days later; air and torpedo-boat attacks, however, were so effective that the entire convoy had to turn back.

On Guadalcanal, starvation and malaria had become the real enemy of Hyakutake's men. Formal battle would have dissipated Japanese resistance in a matter of days and Colonel Konuma had to devise new tactics to cope with the combined Marine-GI attacks. Japanese soldiers dug individual foxholes and were ordered to stay in them even if the Americans overran their positions. Each foxhole would become a little fortress and Konuma gambled that the Americans would not accept the losses to overcome such a guerrilla-type defense.

Those who were too weak from disease and hunger to fight crowded the beaches. The air was putrid from the smell of rotting corpses. Large bluebottle flies feasted on the wounded and sick who were unable to drive them off. The men devised a mortality chart:

He who can rise to his feet . . . . . .30 days left to live
He who can sit up . . . . 20 days left to live
He who must urinate while lying down . . 3 days left to live
He who cannot speak . . . . 2 days left to live
He who cannot blink his eyes . . . . . dead at dawn

2.

Colonel Tsuji, who had confessed he deserved "a sentence of ten thousand deaths" for his mistakes on Guadalcanal, was back in Tokyo with a new recommendation for saving the island. He convinced the General Staff that Lieutenant Colonel Kumao Imoto of the Operations Section should be sent, as Tsuji had, to supervise the new offensive on Guadalcanal.

Tsuji's influence was as effective as ever, and early in December Imoto left Tokyo. Imoto had accepted the assignment, but privately he disagreed with his superiors; in his opinion Guadalcanal should be evacuated. He stopped at Truk to report to Combined Fleet, where Admiral Ugaki, one of his instructors at the War College, told him, "This is a most difficult situation. Let's not worry about who should take the initiative in solving the problem. Our sole concern should be to decide what ought to be done at the present moment."

It was an abstruse way—understandable only to one used to Navy subtlety—of advising Imoto that withdrawal from Guadalcanal was the only alternative. "I understand what you mean," said Imoto. He flew on to Rabaul with the conviction that Admiral Yamamoto shared his chief of staff's conclusions—and he was right.

At Imamura's headquarters Imoto encountered vehement criticism of General Staff policy. "The people in Tokyo are insane!" one of Imamura's officers blurted out during the map games held to work out the details of the Guadalcanal offensive. "Do you honestly think there is the slightest chance of success in another attack?"

Nevertheless, Imoto forced the games through to their conclusion. He had to demonstrate the futility of further attacks before revealing his own reservations. The games proved what they all feared: hardly a transport reached the island.

In the corridors of Army headquarters in Tokyo, where the War Ministry and the Army General Staff shared the same building on Ichigaya Heights, there was already talk of withdrawal from Guadalcanal. The first general officer to suggest this course of action openly was Major General Kenryo Sato, Tojo's adviser and chief of the Military Affairs Bureau of the War Ministry. Perturbed by the General Staff's insistence on another 620,000 tons of shipping, he told Tojo they should "give up the idea of retaking Guadalcanal."

"Do you mean withdrawal?" Tojo asked sharply.

"We have no choice. Even now it may be too late. If we go on like this, we have no chance of winning the war." The position on Guadalcanal, moreover, was untenable. The enemy completely controlled the air and sea. "If we continue to hang on, it will end up as a battle of attrition of our transports."

Tojo heard Sato out but remained troubled by the Emperor's order to retake Guadalcanal; also, he was reluctant to interfere with military authority. He still believed, in spite of nagging doubts, that the General Staff should remain independent of the government. "Besides, even if we wanted," he finally said, "we couldn't give the General Staff all the ships they demand. If we did, our steel-production quota of over four million tons would be cut by more than half and we would be unable to continue the war." He was torn by old loyalties. His face became pinched. He asked Sato if a reduction in the number of ships would oblige the General Staff to decide on withdrawal.

"Not immediately," Sato replied. But he brightened at the thought of intrigue. He suggested that they make no mention of withdrawing for the time being, but give the Army only their share of shipping. Tojo nodded grimly.

At the next Cabinet meeting Tojo pushed through a plan to give the Army and Navy a total of but 290,000 tons, with the promise that more would follow, if possible. This resolution brought the continuing argument between the War Ministry and the Army General Staff to a crisis. Sato spoke for Tojo and his reasoning was sound; what infuriated the General Staff most was his implication that the operation on Guadalcanal would have to be "suspended."

Under pressure from the General Staff, Tojo convened a special meeting of his cabinet on the evening of December 5 to reconsider the demands for more shipping. It was agreed to give both services another 95,000 tons. The increase was so small that Sato's assistants warned him to explain the matter to the General Staff in person. But it was already past ten o'clock and Sato said that he would wait until morning. As he entered his quarters the phone was ringing. Lieutenant General Moritake Tanabe, the Vice Chief of Staff, asked Sato to come to his official residence at once and explain the Cabinet's decision.

At the door of Tanabe's house Sato heard angry shouts from inside. He recognized the voice of the Army's Chief of Operations, the impulsive and hot-tempered Lieutenant General Shinichi Tanaka. Inside, Sato was confronted by seven or eight members of the General Staff.

"*Bakayaro!*" Tanaka shouted. He had been drinking.

When Sato turned to leave, Tanaka reached for his sword. Several of his colleagues seized him but he broke away, rushed at

Sato and hit him in the face. Sato punched back. The two generals swung at each other as several General Staff officers shouted encouragement to Tanaka, made savage by the "power of *sake*." Sato broke loose and pushed his way out of the hostile room. It was the first fight he had ever walked away from.

With Sato gone, the impetuous Tanaka still could not be restrained. It was well past midnight when, belligerent with charges and demands, he burst into the home of Tojo's deputy in the ministry. Heitaro Kimura, a quiet man, apologized to Tanaka for the "insufficiency of my efforts" and finally persuaded him to go home. Even when he was sobered up the next morning, Tanaka continued his attacks. This time his victim was General Teiichi Suzuki of the Cabinet Planning Board. This intemperate display hardened Tojo's position. He told Sato to inform the General Staff that "come what may" the Army was to get only what the Cabinet had decreed.

It was clear to the General Staff that Tojo's ultimatum meant eventual suspension of the battle for Guadalcanal. The division chiefs held an emergency meeting and then, uninvited, drove in a body to the Prime Minister's official residence. In the anteroom Sugiyama took aside Colonel Tanemura, the diarist, and whispered, "If there is another quarrel, bring *him* [Tanaka] out at once."

Tanaka was ushered into a Japanese-style room where Sato and two others were sitting on the floor. Sato and Tanaka stared at each other as if ready to resume their fight. The atmosphere grew increasingly embarrassing. Finally, just before midnight, Tojo entered in kimono and lowered himself to the tatami. Tanaka begged him to reconsider the demand of the General Staff. Calmly, without a trace of emotion, Tojo refused. For half an hour the two argued, their voices rising. Tanaka lost all control. "What are you doing about the war?" he shouted. "We'll lose it this way. *Kono bakayaro* [you damn fool]!"

Tojo stiffened. "What abusive language you use!" he said. The room was hushed. Tanemura entered from the anteroom and took Tanaka's arm. "The Chief's orders," he said.

Tanaka, after being officially reprimanded for insulting a superior officer, was dismissed from his position, but as so often was the case in Japan, his crude and violent advocacy won the Army a temporary victory. The following evening Tojo bowed to the General Staff's request for more shipping.

3.

Six hundred miles due west of Henderson Field lay the eastern tip of the second largest island in the world. Ungainly New Guinea, shaped very much like a plucked turkey, sprawled laterally for fifteen hundred miles. It was rugged, savage country, hardly worth fighting for except for its peculiar strategic position as a stepping stone—first by the Japanese to Australia and now by the Allies to New Britain and its vital port, Rabaul.

Thirty thousand American and Australian troops under Lieutenant General Robert Eichelberger had fought their way from Port Moresby—on the south coast of the Papua peninsula, which pointed like a stubby finger at Guadalcanal—to take Buna Village on the opposite side of the promontory.

"Bob, I want you to take Buna or not come back alive," MacArthur had told Eichelberger. "And that goes for your chief of staff too."

It was a victory achieved at high cost in lives and suffering. The troops had been forced to cross the formidable Owen Stanley Range while fighting battles as fierce as those on Guadalcanal under just as miserable conditions. Though Buna had fallen, the ordeal was far from over. As on Guadalcanal, the Japanese refused to admit they were defeated and were making Australians and Americans pay for every yard of territory.

Attention at Imperial Headquarters, however, remained focused on Guadalcanal, where disaster was even more imminent. It was becoming more and more difficult to get supplies through. The drum supply system had proved impractical. Only limited amounts of medicine and food could be brought in by submarines stripped of torpedoes, guns and shells, or dropped from planes.

The Navy was ready to abandon Guadalcanal; and Yamamoto had let it be known in high circles that he favored such action immediately. But the Army General Staff still stood firm—in public. In private, however, informal conversations were going on among its members about how to withdraw without losing face.

After all, they *had* promised the Emperor victory on Guadalcanal.

The urgency of the situation was emphasized by a radiogram from General Hyakutake on December 23:

NO FOOD AVAILABLE AND WE CAN NO LONGER SEND OUT SCOUTS. WE CAN DO NOTHING TO WITHSTAND THE ENEMY'S OFFENSIVE. 17TH ARMY NOW REQUESTS PERMISSION TO BREAK INTO THE ENEMY'S POSITIONS AND DIE AN HONORABLE DEATH RATHER THAN DIE OF HUNGER IN OUR OWN DUGOUTS.

On Christmas Day the Army and Navy leaders held a formal emergency meeting at the Imperial Palace to resolve the problem. It was no longer a question of whether withdrawal was necessary, but which service would have the courage to recommend it officially and thereby risk accepting the blame for defeat. Chief of Staff Nagano, his assistant Ito, Admiral Fukudome and Captain Tomioka represented the Navy; Chief of Staff Sugiyama and Colonel Tsuji represented the Army.

Admiral Fukudome, Nagano's Chief of Operations, urged withdrawal but he himself hesitated. "What do you think of joint tactical map games before we decide?" he suggested.

Tsuji erupted. More than anyone else in the room he realized what each day's delay meant to the starving men on Guadalcanal. Waving his arms, he exclaimed that it was the Navy's duty to study general trends *before* an emergency arose. "You are all very well posted on the battle situation and yet you can't even reach a decision. You had better all resign! I've often been on destroyers and undergone heavy air raids. The naval commanders I met there all told me, 'The big shots at the Tokyo Hotel [Navy General Staff] and the *Yamato* Hotel [Combined Fleet] should come out here and see what we have to take and then they might understand!'"

Tomioka agreed with Tsuji on withdrawal but was so aroused by the insult to the Navy that he shot to his feet. "What are you trying to say? That destroyer commanders are all faint of heart? Take that back!"

"Have you ever been to the fighting front?" Tsuji said accusingly. "Do you understand what's going on out there today?"

Tomioka, who had pleaded again and again for sea duty,

plunged toward Tsuji. Fukudome intercepted him and said, "I am sorry, Tsuji-*kun*. What you say is true."

It may have been true, but Nagano still insisted on map games. They demonstrated again what everyone knew—that less than one fourth of any reinforcements and supplies would arrive intact. The argument went on, with each service continuing to blame the other for the situation on the island. The Army wanted to know how it could win without ammunition and food. "You landed the Army without arms and food and then cut off the supply. It's like sending someone on a roof and taking away the ladder."

The Navy sarcastically wanted to know how long this business of reinforcements would go on. The Army replied in kind that it could win if it were given *half* of what the enemy had. "Up till now we've only received one percent."

There was no way out of such a bitter debate—until Colonel Joichiro Sanada arrived on December 29 from Rabaul with a report which was supported by almost every Army and Navy officer he had interviewed in the Solomons, including Imoto and Imamura's operations officer: all troops should be withdrawn from Guadalcanal as soon as possible. The island could be retaken "only by a miracle," and future military operations "must not, out of eagerness to regain Gadarukanaru, be jeopardized by following previous plans and by continuing a campaign in which neither the high command [17th Army] nor the front-line commanders have any confidence."

Sanada's report settled the matter for both the Army and the Navy. Sugiyama seemed "rather relieved" and Nagano, without further argument, agreed to remove Hyakutake's troops from the island by destroyers by the end of January if possible.

The two Chiefs of Staff reviewed the problem for the Emperor at an imperial conference on the last day of the year, then formally recommended the evacuation of both Guadalcanal and Buna in New Guinea. The Emperor turned to Nagano and observed in his expressionless manner that the United States seemed to have won by air power, then asked an embarrassing question: Why was it that it took the Americans just a few days to build an air base and the Japanese more than a month or so? "Isn't there room for improvement?"

"I am very sorry indeed," Nagano acknowledged humbly; the

The End

enemy used machines while the Japanese had to rely on manpower.

But it was apparent that His Majesty was not pleased with the answer. For two hours he continued to probe the defeat, to the discomfort of the two Chiefs. Finally he raised his already high-pitched voice: "Well, now the Army and Navy should do their best as they have just explained." He approved withdrawal from Guadalcanal and Buna.*

Aboard *Yamato* that night Admiral Ugaki made the final entry in his diary for 1942:

. . . How splendid the first stage of our operations was! But how unsuccessfully we have fought since the defeat at Midway!

Our strategy, aimed at invasion of Hawaii, Fiji, Samoa, and New Caledonia as well as domination over India and the destruction of the British Eastern Squadron, has dissipated like a dream. In addition, the occupation of Port Moresby and Guadalcanal has been frustrated. A welter of emotions are awakened in my breast as I look back upon the past. In war things often do not turn out as we wish. Nevertheless, I cannot stem my feeling of mortification. The desperate struggles of our officers and men are too numerous to mention.

I express my heartfelt thanks to them and at the same time offer my condolences to those who died a glorious death at the front.

Even in defeat the Japanese had left an indelible impression on the victors of Guadalcanal and New Guinea. Lieutenant General George C. Kenney, chief of the Allied Air Forces in the southwest

---

* Contrary to widespread belief, the Emperor took a lively, personal interest in military operations. On January 9, 1943, His Majesty told Sugiyama, "The fall of Buna is regrettable, but the officers and men fought well. I hear the enemy has ten tanks or so; don't we have any tanks in that area? And what is the situation in Lae? . . . I am very pleased with the improvement made by antiaircraft units throughout Burma." When Sugiyama reported to the Throne several weeks later on the failure of transporting reinforcements to Lae, the Emperor said, after offering the Army Chief of Staff a chair—an indication of favor, "Why didn't you change your mind at the last minute and land on Madang [a port northeast of Lae]? We must admit we suffered a setback, but if we take it to heart I believe it will be a good lesson for future operations. Make every effort so I don't have to worry in the future. Increase air support, build roads where our troops can pass safely, and gain firm footholds step by step. Give enough thought to your plans so that Lae and Salamaua don't become another Guadalcanal."

Pacific, reported to General H. H. ("Hap") Arnold, head of the U. S. Army Air Forces, that those back home, including the War Department, had no conception of the problems in the southwest Pacific.

. . . The Jap is still being underrated. There is no question of our being able to defeat him, but the time, effort, blood and money required to do the job may run to proportions beyond all conception, particularly, if the devil is allowed to develop the resources he is now holding.

Let us look at Buna. There are hundreds of Bunas ahead for us. The Jap there has been in a hopeless position for two months. He has been outnumbered heavily throughout the show. His garrison has been whittled down to a handful by bombing and strafing. He has had no air support, and his own Navy has not been able to get past our air blockade to help him. He has seen lots of Japs sunk off shore a few miles away. He has been short on rations and has had to conserve his ammunition, as his replenishment from submarines and small boats working down from Lae at night, and, once, by parachute from airplanes, has been precarious, to say the least. The Emperor told them to hold, and, believe me, they have held! As to their morale—they still yell out to our troops, "What's the matter, Yanks? Are you yellow? Why don't you come in and fight?" A few snipers, asked to surrender after being surrounded, called back, "If you bastards think you are good enough, come and get us!"

. . . I'm afraid that a lot of people who think this Jap is a "pushover" as soon as Germany falls, are due for a rude awakening. We will have to call on all our patriotism, stamina, guts, and maybe some crusading spirit or religious fervor thrown in, to beat him. No amateur team will take this boy out. We have got to turn professional. Another thing: there are no quiet sectors in which troops get started off gradually, as in the last war. There are no breathers on this schedule. You take on Notre Dame, every time you play!

4.

On the afternoon of January 13, 1943, ten destroyers carrying a thousand men and supplies left Shortland. In one was Colonel Imoto. He had helped Imamura's staff and several naval officers hastily draw up a plan of evacuation, Operation KE. His present assignment was to transmit the order to Hyakutake and assist him as a member of his staff.

The first thing Imoto saw as he disembarked near Cape Esperance was a dead body; the beach that led to 17th Army headquarters was a trail of corpses. It was midnight when he finally reached Hyakutake's camp—a complex of tents and jerry-built shelters near Tassafaronga Point.

He blundered around in a chilling rain until he found Colonel Haruo Konuma and several staff officers in a leaky tent. They were lying on beds made from coconut leaves and covered with mosquito netting. All, that is, but Major Mitsuo Suginoo, who was shaving by candlelight. He and Imoto had served in the same regiment and he greeted his friend with enthusiasm. "I'm preparing to die tomorrow," he said half in jest.

"That's an admirable attitude," Imoto replied in the same spirit.

Konuma led Imoto to the next tent to meet the new chief of staff—Futami's replacement—Major General Shuichi Miyazaki. Imoto sat down stiffly facing the general and said, "I have brought General Imamura's order for the Seventeenth Army to withdraw from Guadalcanal."

"How could we go home after losing so many men?" Konuma broke in. He had ordered the men to die in their foxholes.

Miyazaki was equally outraged. "In a situation like this, to consider such an operation would be unthinkable even in a dream! We don't mean to disobey the order but we cannot execute it. Therefore we must attack and die, and give everyone an example of Japanese Army tradition."

Imoto's arguments had no effect on the two emotional officers. Konuma doubted that any withdrawal was feasible; the men out front were too entangled with the enemy, and if any of them did manage to get on ships they would end by drowning. "It's impossible, so leave us alone!"

As a last resort Imoto drew out the order from Imamura. "Don't you realize that this is an order of withdrawal from the commander of the Army Group based on the Emperor's order!" They had no right to oppose it.

Miyazaki finally got control of himself. "You are correct," he said. "This is not our decision. The Army commander must make it."

Imoto was brought to General Hyakutake at dawn. His tent was snuggled at the roots of a huge tree. He was sitting Japanese style on a blanket before a table—a biscuit box—meditating. He opened his eyes. Imoto explained why he was there. Hyakutake stared wordlessly at him for a minute and closed his eyes again. Finally he said quietly, "This is a most difficult order to receive. I cannot make up my mind right now. Give me a little time."

The morning lull was broken by a rumble of explosions; the Americans were resuming their daily bombardment. It was almost noon before Imoto was summoned to Hyakutake's tent.

"I will obey the order," the general stated with dignity, "but it is very difficult and I can't say if the operation will succeed. At least I will do my best."

Konuma knew the men in the front lines felt even more strongly about retreat than those at headquarters and would find it unbearable to leave dead comrades behind. He volunteered to go up front. The commanders of the 2nd and 38th divisions accepted the orders but it would be necessary to tell their men it was simply a strategic withdrawal, not that they were being taken off the island.

On the night of January 23 the troops up front began stealing from their foxholes and back through the next line of defense toward Cape Esperance, where they would be evacuated in three sections over a period of one week. Incredibly, the Americans—fifty thousand strong now—did not pursue. The following night the leapfrogging continued. Again there was no pursuit. Finally the rear guard itself started pulling back a little at a time. Still the Americans failed to press forward and within a week Japanese scouts alone, keeping up a deceptive volume of fire, maintained contact with the foe. By the end of January the remnants of the 38th Division had reached Cape Esperance. The following night, February 1, nineteen destroyers would stand less than a thousand yards offshore and flash blue signals to Hyakutake's men hiding in the coconut groves with their landing craft.

By dusk on February 1 the Americans still imagined they faced an enemy in force. They did know a fleet of destroyers was coming full speed down The Slot but assumed it was another troop convoy which had to be stopped. At six-twenty, when the Japanese were halfway to Guadalcanal, twenty-four bombers covered by seventeen Wildcats converged on the destroyers. They were driven off by thirty Japanese fighters after damaging but one ship.

At Cape Esperance the landing craft were brought out of cover and the men lined up to get aboard. Colonel Imoto admired the beautiful evening and wished he could enjoy it in peaceful times. In his pocket he had a letter from Hyakutake addressed to General Imamura. Several PT boats careened in toward the beach, but their pilots saw nothing in the dark and swung off. The minutes passed slowly. It was after ten o'clock. Had the first evacuation been postponed? From the blackness in the direction of Savo Island blue signal lights flashed.

While four destroyers patrolled cautiously, the other fourteen crept silently to within 750 yards of the shore. They stopped their engines but didn't drop anchor. The commander of the little fleet, Tomiji Koyanagi—promoted to rear admiral after his shelling of Henderson from *Kongo*—paced the bridge of his flagship, anxiously watching landing craft emerge from the gloom. One bombing attack, even if it failed, could cause havoc.

A destroyer's gun thundered nearby and there followed a blaze of light. A PT boat had been set afire. Had they been discovered? Other PT boats began boring in. Two were sunk, the rest driven off. But where were the planes from Henderson? By this time the destroyers were loaded; it had taken little more than half an hour to get 5,424 men aboard. Emaciated, eyes sullen, they stared without expression, overcome by the bitterness of defeat and the humiliation of leaving behind comrades who had not been given proper burial rites.

The destroyers pulled out into the night, still unopposed by the Cactus Air Force, leaving the Americans with the belief that their enemy had again been reinforced. Army Major General Alexander M. Patch, who had relieved Vandegrift early in December, feared that a new Japanese offensive was being mounted, and his three divisions continued their unwarranted respect for the thin shell of Hyakutake's rear guard.

In the afternoon on February 4 the second rescue column, nineteen destroyers, came down the Solomons passage to evacuate 4,977 men. A single ship was damaged. Admiral Koyanagi attributed success largely to "heavenly assistance," but feared the third and last rescue mission would meet with disaster. At nine-thirty in the morning on February 7, eighteen destroyers left

Shortland. Koyanagi was so apprehensive that he ordered ten of them to provide cover. Once again a destroyer was damaged en route and had to be towed off by another, leaving but six for transportation. Four headed for Guadalcanal and the others for nearby Russell Island.

The last troops, including Hyakutake and his headquarters, were waiting on the beach along with several hundred sick and wounded who had managed to make their way to the evacuation area. Pfc. Tadashi Suzuki, one of the few survivors of the Ichiki Detachment, was unable to climb a rope ladder and had to be boosted aboard a destroyer by two sailors. On the deck he felt safe, as if he were on Japanese soil. But he couldn't forget the hundreds of sick comrades he had left lying along the beaches, too feeble to be saved and equipped only with grenades to blow themselves up at the last moment. Rice balls mixed with green peas were passed out. Although Suzuki couldn't taste the food, he gulped it down, vowing to send his sons and grandsons into the Navy; sailors were well fed until they died.

Not a single American plane attacked the convoy on the long trip back to Shortland; 2,639 more men had been evacuated.* In all, more than 13,000 were saved. It was cold comfort: 25,000 others, dead or within hours of death, had been left behind (1,592 Americans died—1,042 Marines and 550 GI's). Many thousands of tons of shipping had been lost in repeated efforts to supply the island. Moreover, although the Imperial Navy had fought well and gallantly, sinking about as many warships as were sunk, the vessels Japan lost were irreplaceable.

In a Manila hospital a skeletal little man approached the cot of General Kawaguchi, who was slowly recovering from malaria and

---

* According to Lieutenant Commander Haruki Itoh (the signal officer who had warned his superiors in vain of the American invasion of the Solomons), it was no miracle but the result of a fake message he sent out from Rabaul at 4 A.M., February 8. Pretending it came from a Catalina patrol boat and using American call signs, he radioed: HENDERSON, HENDERSON, URGENT SIGNAL, THIS IS NUMBER 1 SCOUT PLANE CALLING. When Henderson acknowledged the message, Itoh "reported" that he had sighted a Japanese task force of two carriers, two battleships, ten destroyers. A little later Itoh's men heard the fake message being relayed to Nouméa and Pearl Harbor and concluded that they had lured American planes away from the returning destroyers. U. S. naval historians, however, discount the story, pointing out that nothing in their records substantiate such a claim.

malnutrition. At first the general did not recognize Nishino, the correspondent. They grasped hands and stared at each other. The general confided that on his arrival in Rabaul from Guadalcanal he had been treated as an incompetent and a coward; his career was over—all because of Tsuji.

"I know how you feel better than anyone else," said Nishino. "But the day is bound to come when the truth about Guadalcanal will be known and people realize you were right."

Bitterly the general blamed Tsuji for the defeat on Guadalcanal. "We lost the battle. And Japan lost the war." Tears spilled onto the pillow.

Nishino gripped the general's feeble hand. "You must think of yourself and get well." He gave him a box of *sushi,* a concoction of rice, raw fish and other delicacies.

To be polite Kawaguchi took a mouthful. A smile came over his face. *"Wa!"* he exclaimed. *"Umai!"* (Delicious!).

940.53
TOL
TOLAND, J.
THE RISING SUN

Vol.1
Copy B

Goshen Public Library

1. Books may be kep two weeks and may be rene
once for the same period, except 7 day books and m
zines.

2. A fine is charged for each day a book is not re
according to the above rule. No book will be is
any person incurring such a fine until it has bee

3. All injuries to books beyond reasonable wear a
losses shall be made good to the satisfaction of
Librarian.

4. Each borrower is held responsible for